Diodoros of Sicily: *Bibliotheke Historike*

Volume 1

Books 14–15: The Greek World in the Fourth Century BC from the End of the Peloponnesian War to the Death of Artaxerxes II (Mnemon)

Diodoros of Sicily (*c*.90–*c*.30 BC) spent thirty years producing an encyclopedic compendium of world history from its mythical beginnings to his own day. His is the only surviving, connected account of Greek affairs from 480/79 to 302/1. The books translated in this volume cover the years from the end of the Peloponnesian War to the aftermath of the Battle of Mantineia in 362/1. These were crucial years in the struggle for supremacy in Greece amongst the Greek states, Sparta, Athens and Thebes, before they were overtaken by the unexpected rise of Macedon. Diodoros also provides the only extant account of the career of Dionysios I of Syracuse and the Cypriot war between Persia and Evagoras of Salamis. The translation is supported by extensive notes and the Introduction examines Diodoros' moral and educational purpose in writing, the plan of his work, the sources he used and his qualities as an historian.

Phillip Harding is Emeritus Professor of Classics and Ancient History at the University of British Columbia, where he taught for thirty-six years. His publications include: *From the End of the Peloponnesian War to the Battle of Ipsus* (Cambridge, 1985), *Androtion and the* Atthis (1994), *Didymos: On Demosthenes* (2006), *The Story of Athens* (2008) and *Athens Transformed, 404–262 BC* (2015).

Diodoros of Sicily
BIBLIOTHEKE HISTORIKE
Volume 1
Books 14–15

The Greek World in the Fourth Century BC
from the End of the Peloponnesian War to the Death
of Artaxerxes II (Mnemon)

Translation with Introduction and Notes by

PHILLIP HARDING
University of British Columbia

CAMBRIDGE UNIVERSITY PRESS

CAMBRIDGE
UNIVERSITY PRESS

University Printing House, Cambridge CB2 8BS, United Kingdom

One Liberty Plaza, 20th Floor, New York, NY 10006, USA

477 Williamstown Road, Port Melbourne, VIC 3207, Australia

314–321, 3rd Floor, Plot 3, Splendor Forum, Jasola District Centre,
New Delhi – 110025, India

103 Penang Road, #05-06/07, Visioncrest Commercial, Singapore 238467

Cambridge University Press is part of the University of Cambridge.

It furthers the University's mission by disseminating knowledge in the pursuit of
education, learning, and research at the highest international levels of excellence.

www.cambridge.org
Information on this title: www.cambridge.org/9781108499279
DOI: 10.1017/9781108580557

© Phillip Harding 2021

This publication is in copyright. Subject to statutory exception
and to the provisions of relevant collective licensing agreements,
no reproduction of any part may take place without the written
permission of Cambridge University Press.

First published 2021

Printed in the United Kingdom by TJ Books Limited, Padstow Cornwall

A catalogue record for this publication is available from the British Library.

Library of Congress Cataloging-in-Publication Data
Names: Diodorus, Siculus, author. | Harding, Phillip, translator.
Title: Bibliotheke historike / Diodoros of Sicily ; translated with introduction
and notes by Phillip Harding, University of British Columbia.
Other titles: Bibliotheca historica. Book 14-20. English
Description: New York : Cambridge University Press, [2021]- | Includes
bibliographical references and index. | Contents: v. 1. Books 14-15, The Greek
world in the fourth century BC from the end of the Peloponnesian War to
the death of Artaxerxes II (Mnemon)
Identifiers: LCCN 2021012621 (print) | LCCN 2021012622 (ebook) |
ISBN 9781108499279 (v.1 ; hardback) | ISBN 9781108706346 (v.1 ; paperback) |
ISBN 9781108580557 (v.1 ; ebook)
Subjects: LCSH: History, Ancient – Early works to 1800. | BISAC: HISTORY /
Ancient / General
Classification: LCC PA3965.D4 E5 2021 (print) | LCC PA3965.D4 (ebook) |
DDC 938/.04–dc23
LC record available at https://lccn.loc.gov/2021012621
LC ebook record available at https://lccn.loc.gov/2021012622

ISBN 978-1-108-49927-9 Hardback
ISBN 978-1-108-70634-6 Paperback

Cambridge University Press has no responsibility for the persistence or accuracy of
URLs for external or third-party internet websites referred to in this publication
and does not guarantee that any content on such websites is, or will remain,
accurate or appropriate.

To the memory of Angela Harding (1937–2020)
Atque in perpetuum, soror, ave atque vale.

Contents

List of Maps	page viii
Preface	ix
List of Abbreviations	xi
Maps	xiii
Introduction	xxv
Book 14	**1**
Book 15	**139**
Appendix: Modern Chronological Outline	255
Glossary	266
Bibliography	271
Index	278

Maps

1. Attica — *page* xiii
2. Plan of Peiraieus — xiv
3. Sicily — xv
4. Plan of Syracuse under Dionysios I — xvi
5. Persian Empire and March of the Ten Thousand — xvii
6. Plan of Motye — xviii
7. Hellespont and the Black Sea — xix
8. Greece and the Aegean — xx
9. Diagram of Agesilaos' route to Sardis: Xenophon v. Diodoros — xxi
10. Central and Northern Greece and Euboia — xxii
11. Peloponnese — xxiii
12. Italy — xxiv

Preface

This is the first volume of a planned three-volume English translation, with detailed notes, of books 14–20 of Diodoros of Sicily's *Bibliotheke Historike*. This volume covers books 14 and 15, the period from the end of the Peloponnesian War to the death of Artaxerxes II (Mnemon) in 360/59. The second volume will deal with the careers of Philip II of Macedon and Alexander the Great, as narrated in books 16 and 17. The third, books 18–20, will treat the post-Alexandrian period, so-called Hellenistic, down to the end of the fourth century. The choice of these seven books is motivated by the fact that they provide the only complete extant ancient narrative of the fourth century. The only competitor is Xenophon, but his *Hellenika* is deficient in several respects: it does not treat Sicilian affairs, which Diodoros covers extensively, and it ends with the Battle of Mantineia in 362/1. Furthermore, there are many important differences between the accounts of Xenophon and Diodoros even for the period which they both cover.

My plan was to offer an updated translation of the five volumes of the Loeb Classical Library, good though they are. However, since I began work, two other translations have appeared, one by Peter Green of selections of Books 14–16 as an appendix to the Landmark *Xenophon*, the other by Robin Waterfield of Books 16–20 for Oxford University Press. These are both elegant versions, but, in my opinion, make Diodoros into more of a literary star than he is. His style is, in fact, rather monotonous and uninspired. I have tried to make my translation reflect this reality, while, I hope, producing a readable text.

More importantly, the notes in this and the other projected volumes are more detailed than any that exist in English at this time, including the works just referred to above. These notes are designed to help readers compare Diodoros with his peers, namely the other ancient sources for the period, so that they can distinguish where Diodoros is providing new evidence, where he is in conflict with others, and where he is manifestly wrong. These sources include fragmentary historians and documentary inscriptions, which are referred to where appropriate. Not everyone will be interested in following up on these references, but, for those who do, the historians are to be found in the updated version of Jacoby's *Die Fragmente der griechischen Historiker* called Brill's New Jacoby (*BNJ*) and many of the inscriptions are now accessible in Attic Inscriptions Online in both Greek and English. The notes do not attempt to be a full commentary, since I have largely avoided entering into the field of modern scholarly debate. The few references I have added are designed to be helpful in matters such as topography and dating.

A mandatory note is required about names. As usual, when dealing with a Greek author, the preference is to use Greek spelling, and I adhere to this practice except in the case of the most well known names, including Thucydides, Corinth, Cyprus, Syracuse. I have also given the Roman names for the consuls and military tribunes, even though Diodoros writes them in Greek.

In the text I have capitalized the word "king" for the Great King of Persia alone.

Unless otherwise stated, all dates are BC.

The text upon which I have based my translation has been the modern Budé edition by Martine Bonnet and Eric Bennett for Book 14 and Claude Vial for Book 15. I have carefully compared their readings with those of Friedrich Vögel and Kurt Fischer in the Teubner series and with the Loeb editions of C. H. Oldfather and C. L. Sherman. In discussion of matters of text I have used Greek font. Otherwise, Greek terms have been transliterated and have been explained in the Glossary.

I want to thank Michael Sharp and the Syndics of Cambridge University Press for their support of this project and four anonymous readers whose suggestions and corrections have greatly improved this volume. Any errors that remain are mine.

Finally, I acknowledge with gratitude the great work of the whole production team at CUP and especially the careful reading of the text by my eagle-eyed copy-editor, Malcolm Todd. And the record would not be complete without thanking my wife for all the innumerable ways she has on this occasion, as always, assisted my endeavours.

Abbreviations

All Classical authors are cited from standard editions in the Loeb series

Aelian, *VH*	Aelian, *Varia Historia*
APF	J. K. Davies, *Athenian Propertied Families*, Oxford, 1971
Aristotle, *AP*	Aristotle,* *Athenaion Politeia*
Athenaios, *Deip.*	Athenaios, *Deipnosophistai*
BNJ	Brill's New Jacoby, ed. I. Worthington, Leiden, ongoing
Develin, *AO*	R. Develin, *Athenian Officials*, Cambridge, 1989
Dindorf	L. Dindorf, *Diodori Bibliotheca Historica*, 5 vols., Leipzig, 1866–1868
FGrHist	F. Jacoby, *Die Fragmente der griechischen Historiker*, Berlin and Leiden, 1923–
GHI	R. Meiggs and D. M. Lewis, *A Selection of Greek Historical Inscriptions to the End of the Fifth Century BC*, Oxford, 1969, (rev. edn, 1988)
Gomme, *Commentary*	A. W. Gomme, A. Andrewes and K. J. Dover, *A Historical Commentary on Thucydides*, 5 vols., Oxford, 1956–1981
Hell. Oxy.	*Hellenika Oxyrhynkhia*
IG	*Inscriptiones Graecae*, Berlin, 1873–
Livy	Livy, *Ab Urbe Condita*
O&R	R. Osborne and P. J. Rhodes, *Greek Historical Inscriptions, 478–404 BC*, Oxford, 2017
Pausanias	Pausanias, *Hellados Periegesis*
Pliny, *NH*	Pliny, *Naturalis Historia*
Plut. *Ages.*	Plutarch, *Lives, Agesilaos*
Plut. *Alex.*	Plutarch, *Lives, Alexander*
Plut. *Alk.*	Plutarch, *Lives, Alkibiades*
Plut. *Artax.*	Plutarch, *Lives, Artaxerxes*
Plut. *Cam.*	Plutarch, *Lives, Camillus*
Plut. *Dem.*	Plutarch, *Lives, Demosthenes*
Plut. *Lyk.*	Plutarch, *Lives, Lykourgos*

Plut. *Lys.*	Plutarch, *Lives, Lysander*
Plut. *Pelop.*	Plutarch, *Lives, Pelopidas*
Plut. *Per.*	Plutarch, *Lives, Perikles*
Plut. *Tim.*	Plutarch, *Lives, Timoleon*
R&O	P. J. Rhodes and R. Osborne, *Greek Historical Inscriptions, 404–323 BC,* Oxford, 2003
Rhodes, *Commentary*	P. J. Rhodes, *A Commentary on the Aristotelian Athenaion Politeia,* Oxford, 1981, rev. edn, 1993
SEG	*Supplementum Epigraphicum Graecum*
SIG	W. Dittenberger, *Sylloge Inscriptionum Graecarum*³, Leipzig, 1915–1924
Strabo	Strabo, *Geographika*
Stylianou, *Commentary*	P. J. Stylianou, *A Historical Commentary on Diodorus Siculus, Book 15,* Oxford, 1998
TDGR1	C. W. Fornara (ed.), *Translated Documents of Greece and Rome,* Vol. 1, Cambridge, 1983
TDGR2	P. Harding (ed.), *Translated Documents of Greece and Rome,* Vol. 2, Cambridge, 1985
Walbank, *Commentary*	F. W. Walbank, *A Historical Commentary on Polybius,* 2 vols., Oxford, 1957–1967
Wesseling	P. Wesseling, *Diodori Siculi Bibliothecae historicae libri qui supersunt e recensione Petri Wesselingii cum interpretatione latina L. Rhodomani atque annotationibus variorum integris indicibusque locupletissimis,* Biponti, 1793–1807
Xen. *Ages.*	Xenophon, *Agesilaos*
Xen. *Anab.*	Xenophon, *Anabasis*
Xen. *Hell.*	Xenophon, *Hellenika*

*NB: Despite the concerns raised by some scholars related to the authorship of this work, I continue to believe that it was by Aristotle, as did the ancient commentators.

Map 1 Attica

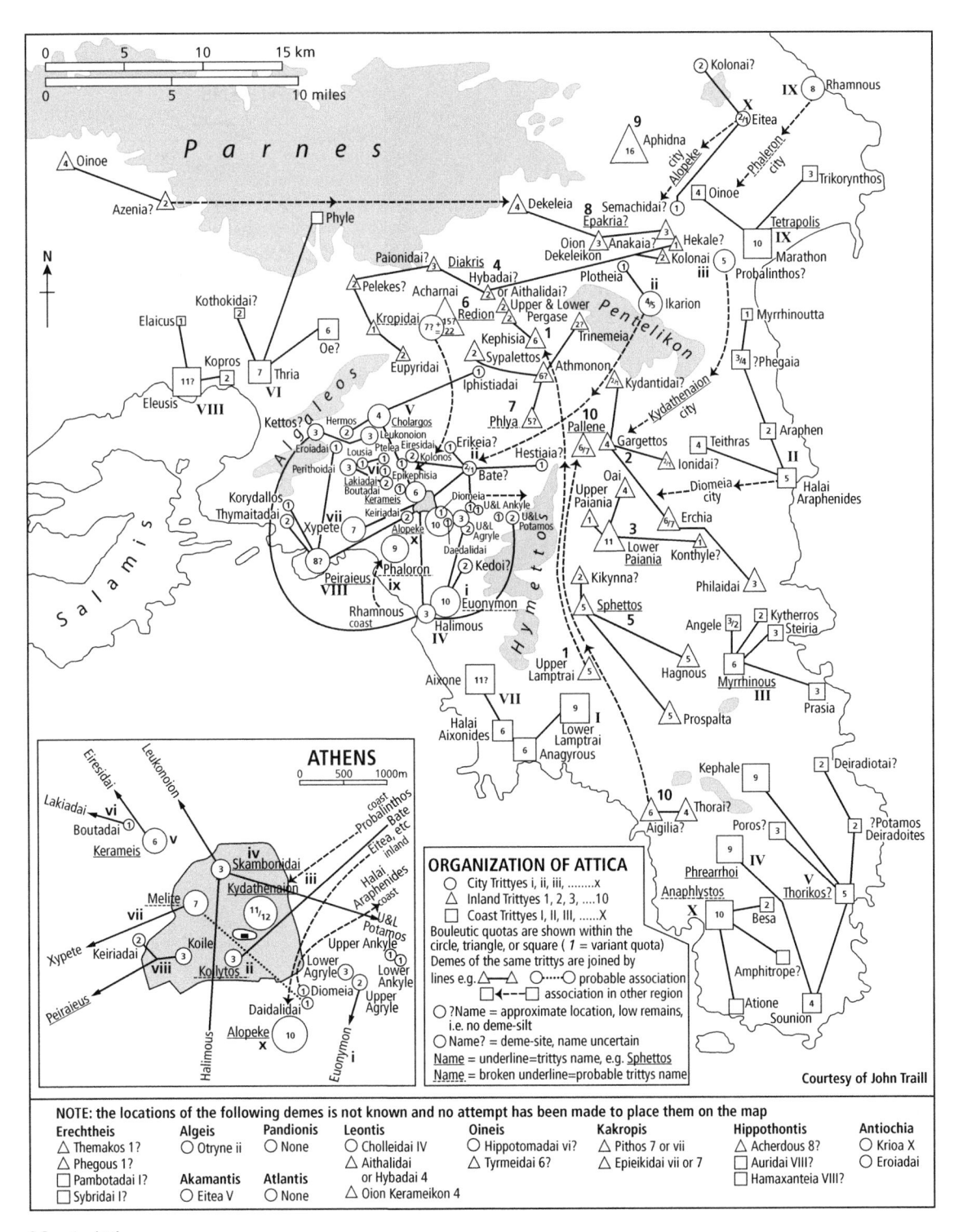

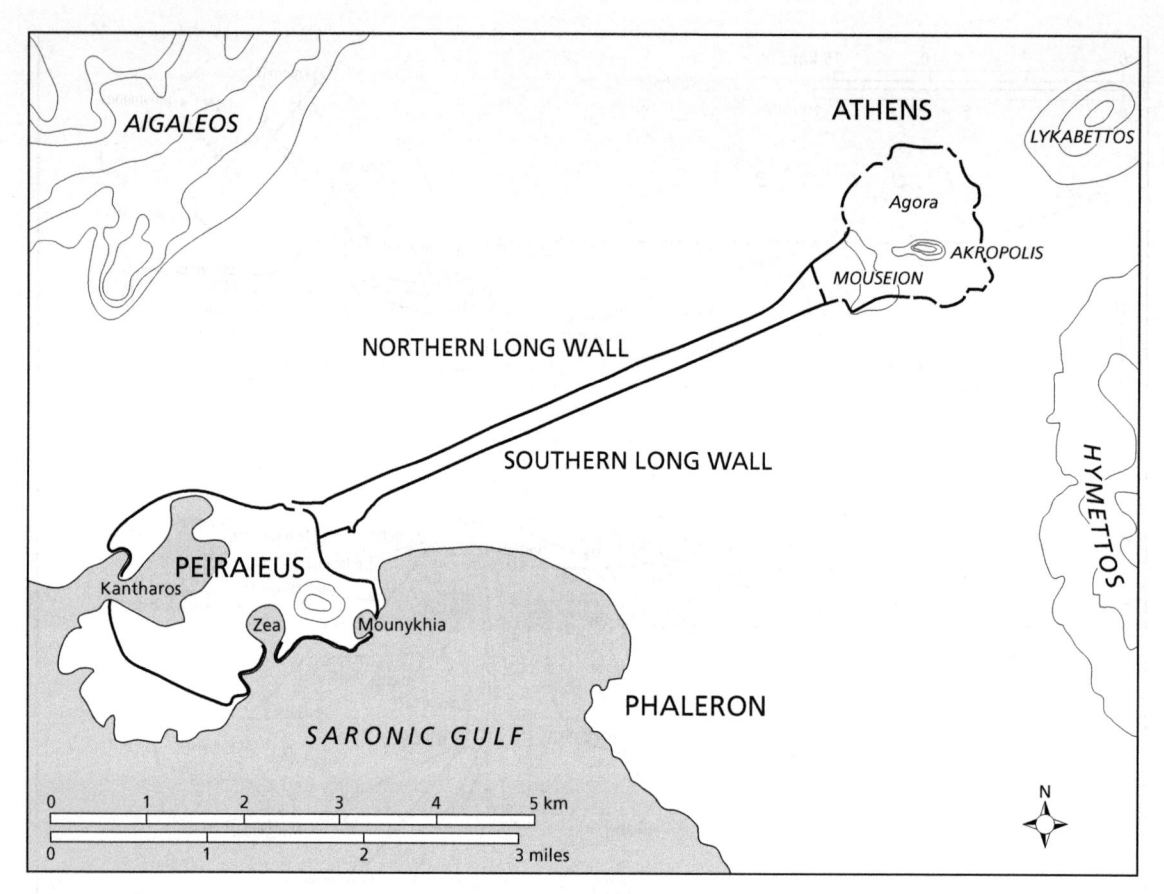

Map 2 Plan of Peiraieus

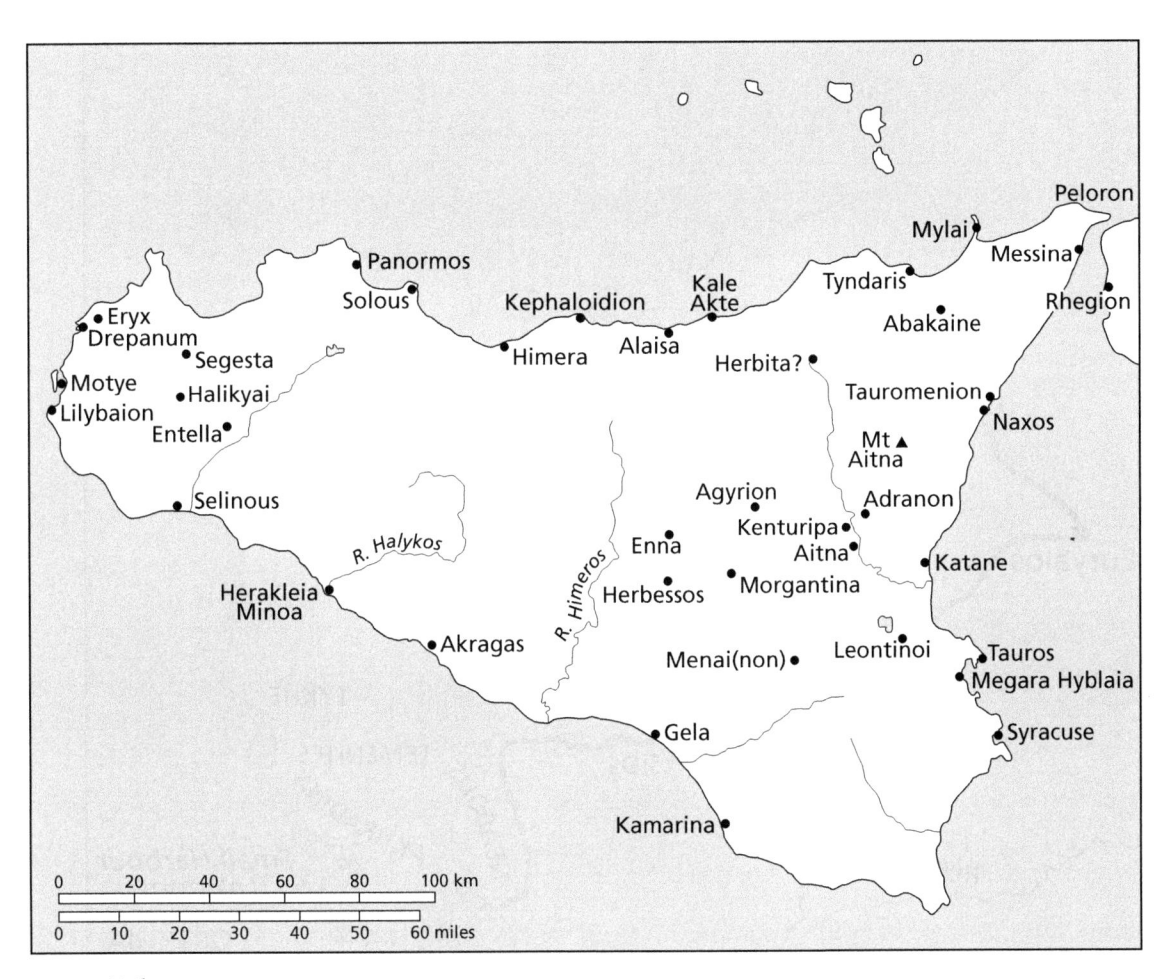

Map 3 Sicily

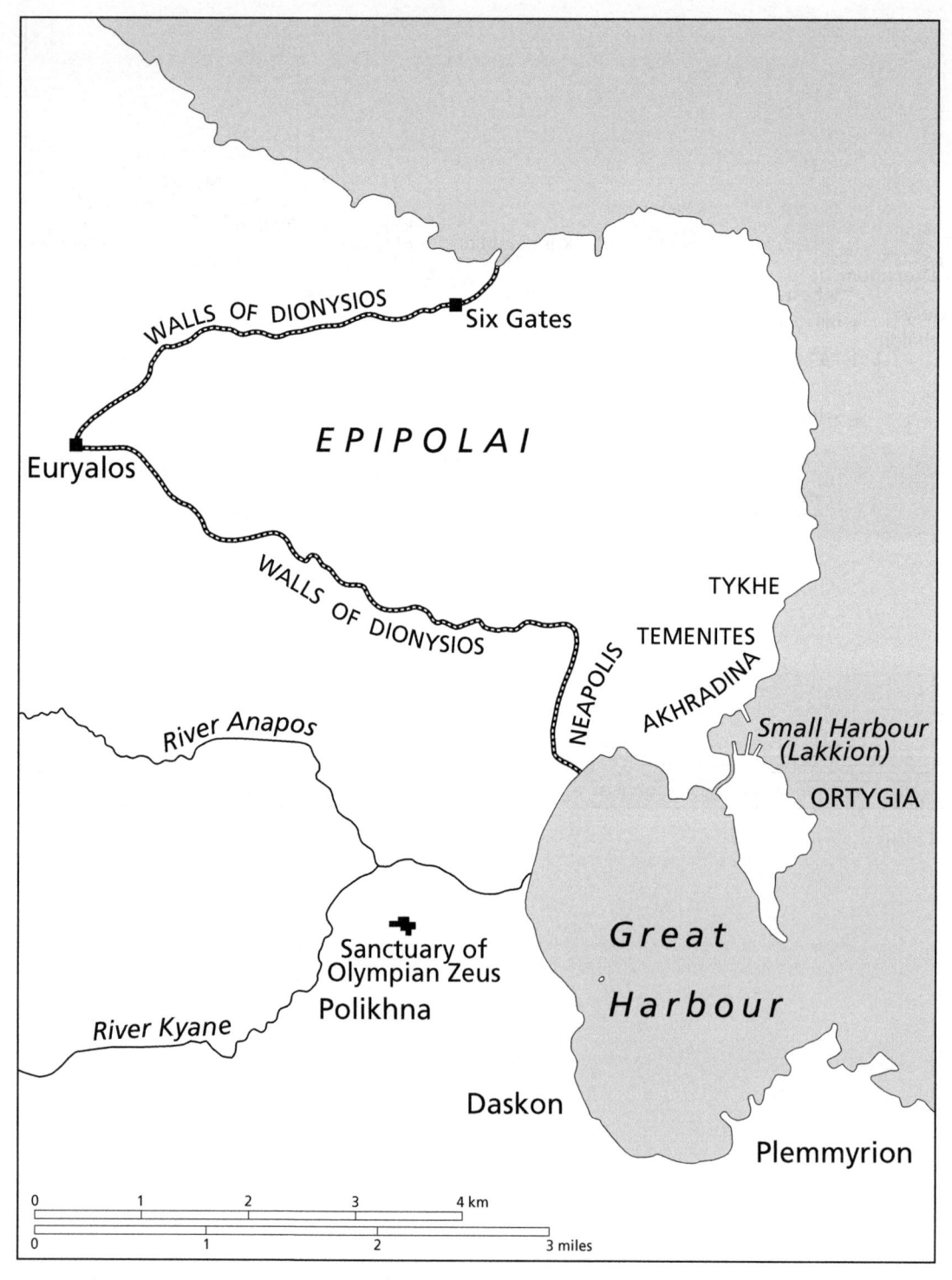

Map 4 Plan of Syracuse under Dionysios I

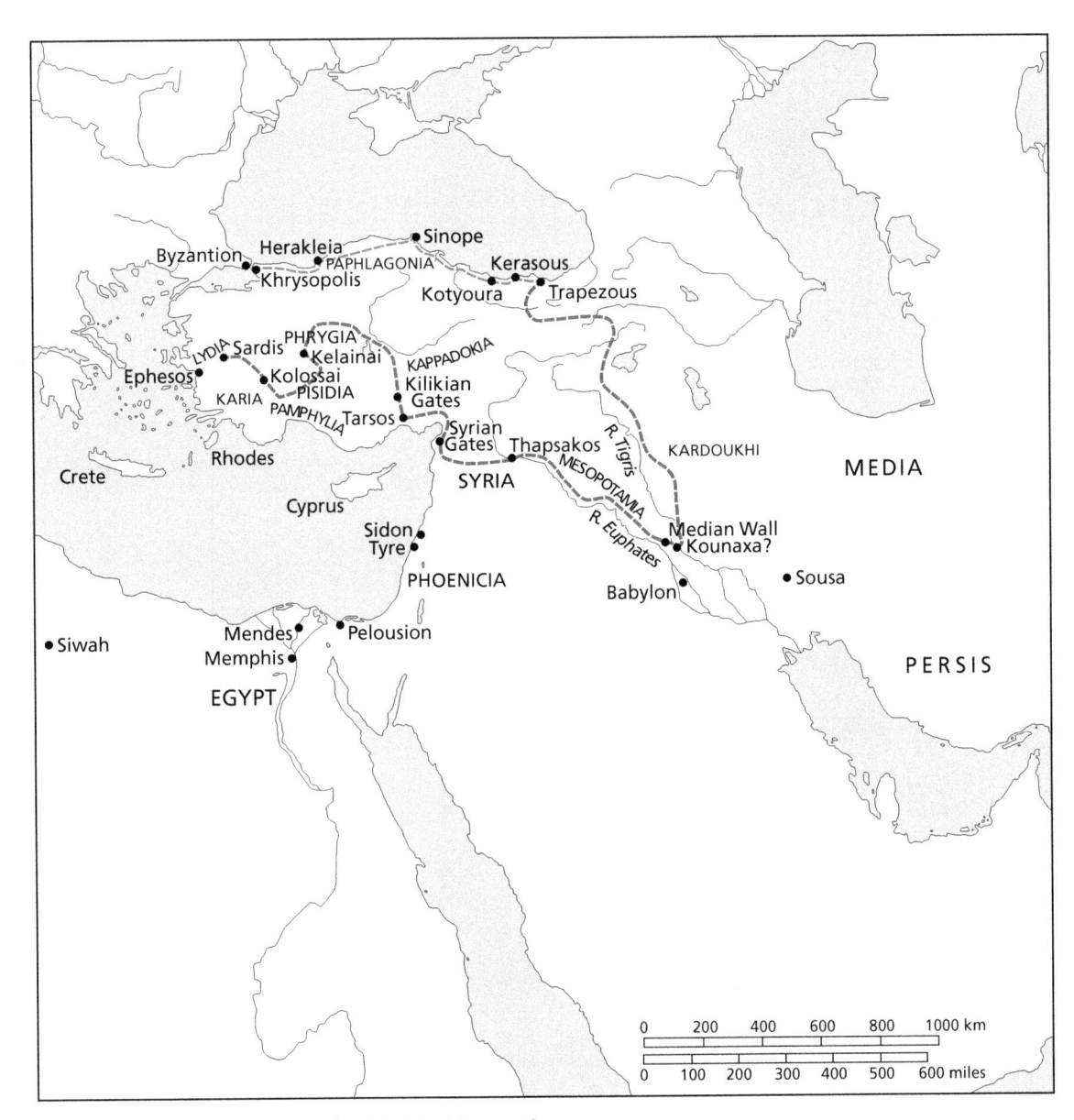

Map 5 Persian Empire and March of the Ten Thousand

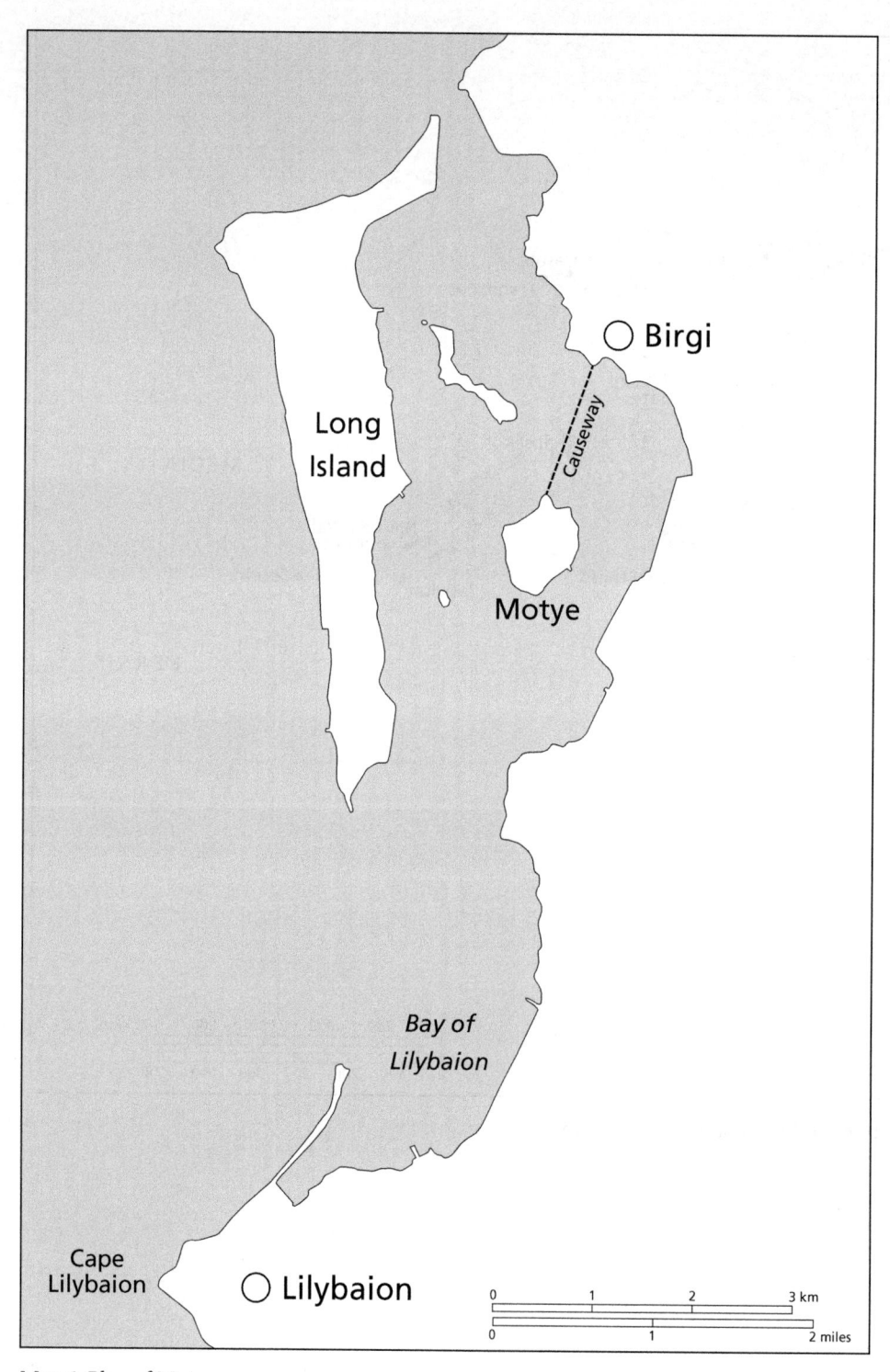

Map 6 Plan of Motye

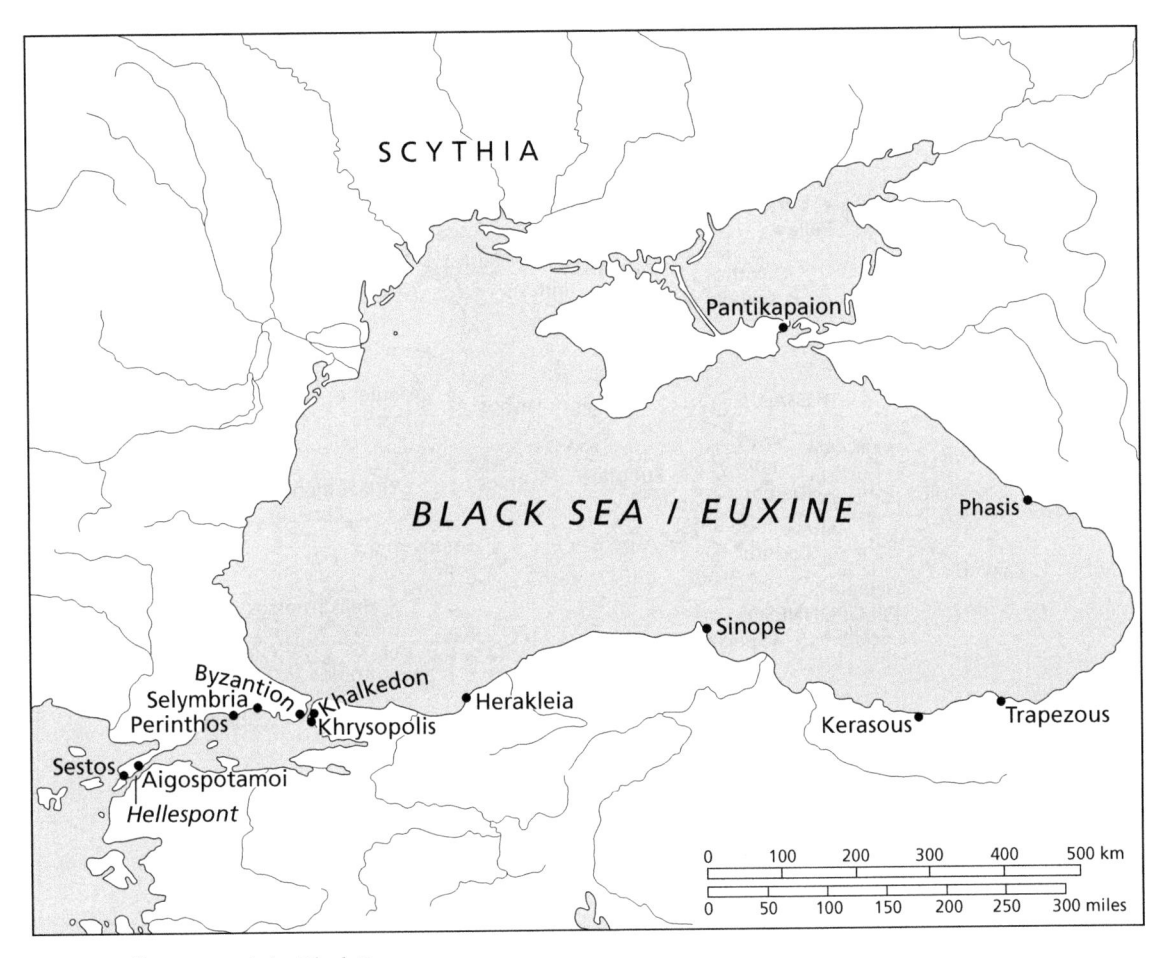

Map 7 Hellespont and the Black Sea

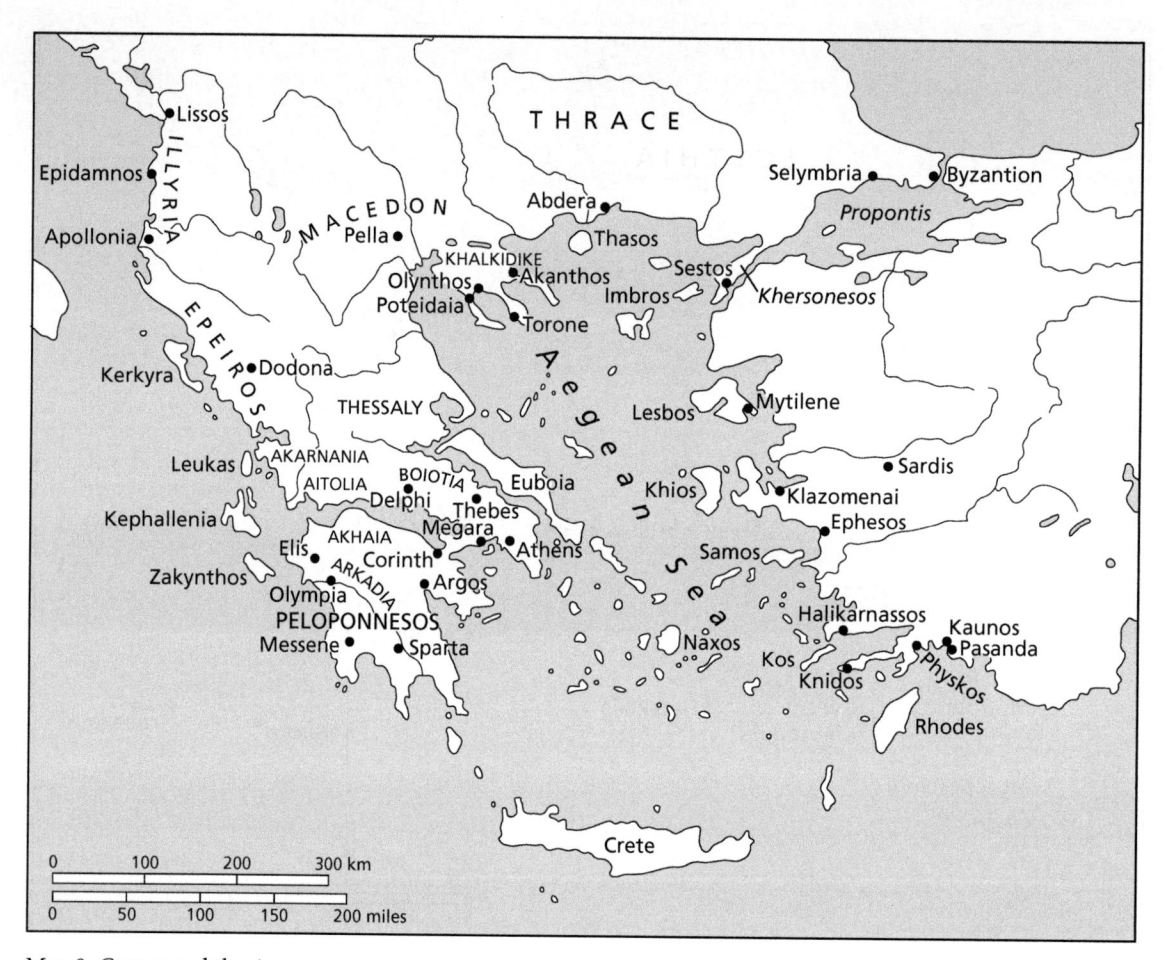

Map 8 Greece and the Aegean

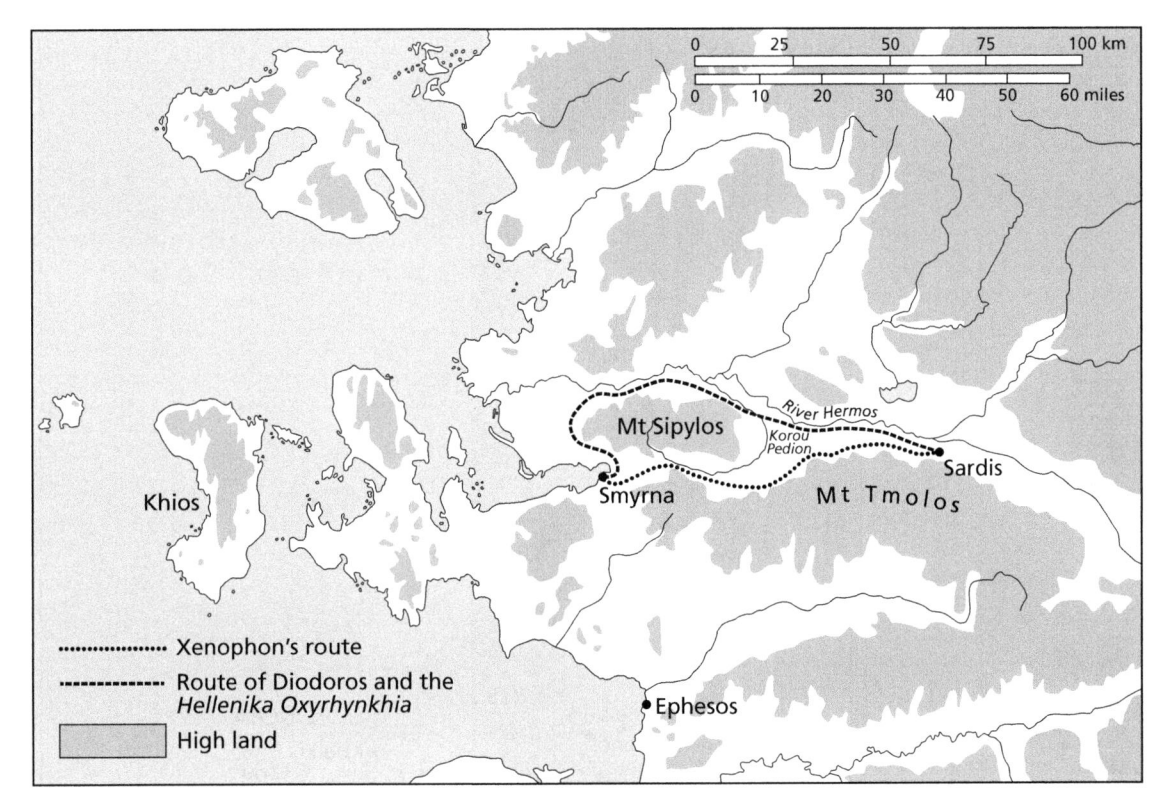

Map 9 Diagram of Agesilaos' route to Sardis: Xenophon v. Diodoros

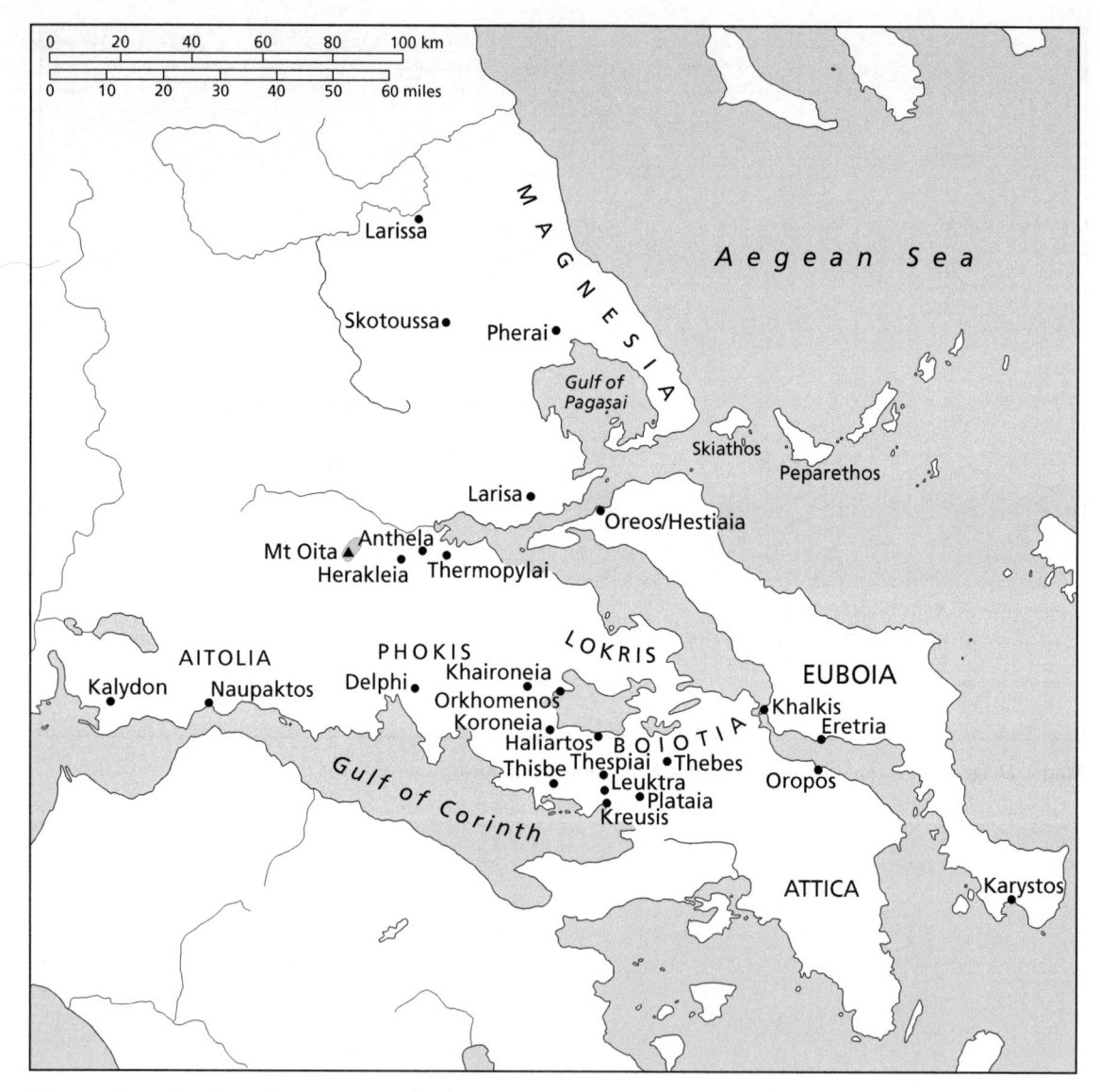

Map 10 Central and Northern Greece and Euboia

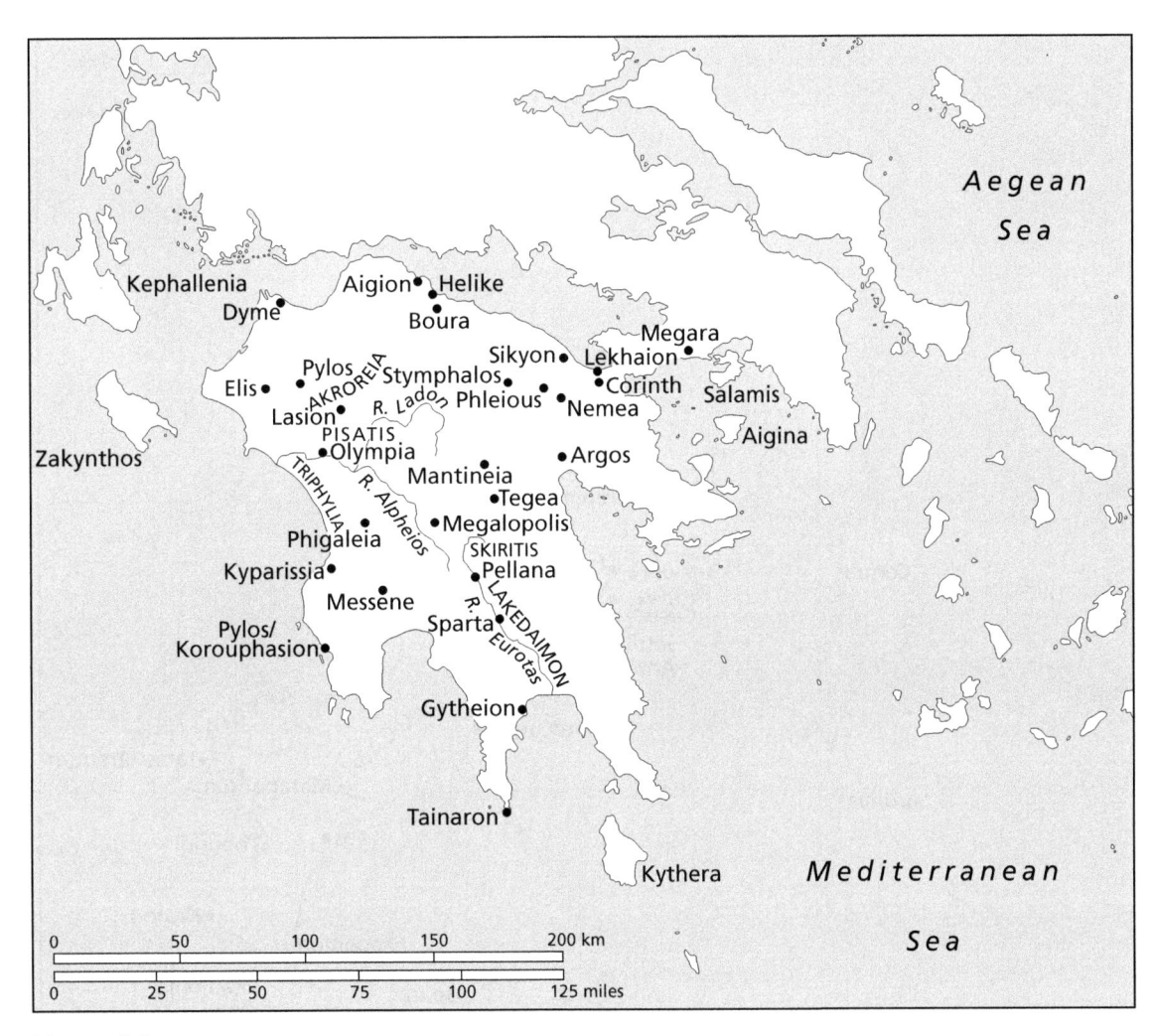

Map 11 Peloponnese

Map 12 Italy

Introduction

Diodoros of Sicily lived and worked in the last century before Christ (*c.*90–*c.*30 or *c.*20). He witnessed the rise of Rome to supremacy, the eclipse of Greek empires in the east, and the unification of the inhabited world (the *oikoumene*) under Roman dominance, especially through the conquests of Pompey the Great and Julius Caesar. At some point in his life Diodoros conceived the ambition of writing a history of the world from its mythical beginnings to his own day. For that purpose he read and studied the works of his great predecessors in historiography, Herodotos, Thucydides, Xenophon, Ephoros, Theopompos, Polybios, Poseidonios and many lesser known authors. Over thirty years of labour he produced an encyclopedic compendium of world history in forty books, which he called the Library (*Bibliotheke*). Writing in the dying days of Greek historiography, he was uniquely positioned to survey and summarize the continuum of history. Although more than half of this work has been lost in transmission, substantial portions remain, particularly the books that cover the narrative of Greek affairs from 480/79 to 302/1, from Xerxes' invasion of Greece, through Alexander the Great's conquest of the Persian Empire, to the first round in the struggle for his empire. In fact, Diodoros' is the only surviving, connected account of those years. The books translated in this volume, books 14 and 15, form part of that narrative, covering the years from the end of the Peloponnesian War to the aftermath of the Battle of Mantineia in 362/1. These are crucial years in the struggle for supremacy in Greece amongst the Greek states, Sparta, Athens and Thebes, before they were overtaken by the unexpected rise of Macedon.[1]

DIODOROS: THE MAN AND HIS WORK

In the prologue to Book One of the *Bibliotheke* Diodoros himself tells us (1.4.4) that he was a native of Agyrion in Sicily, a small inland town, west of Mt Aitna, whose ruler, Agyris, plays a not insignificant role in Book 14. In the fourth century Agyrion had been a prosperous town, surrounded by acres of fertile land,

---

[1] It is not my intent in this brief Introduction to summarize or review the extensive modern scholarship on Diodoros. The reader will find plenty on that subject in the Bibliography. I restrict references to modern scholarship to places where I feel it might be helpful for understanding the issues. See Preface.

sufficient to accommodate 10,000 colonists from Greece in 339/8 (16.83.3). It also possessed a nearby quarry, from which it exported stone (4.80). But, like most of Sicily, it suffered from the constant warfare that the island experienced between Greeks and Carthaginians, Romans and Carthaginians and, worst of all, from the corruption of Roman provincial administration. During Diodoros' lifetime the depredations of the notorious Gaius Verres pillaged the island's prosperity.[2] Agyrion did not escape. How Diodoros felt about all this he never reveals. Like most Greeks, however, he was likely to have had ambivalent feelings about the new rulers of his world. Nevertheless, Diodoros' family must have retained some wealth, since he never seemed to lack for resources.

Diodoros was proud of his hometown. He locates Agyrion in the mythical past, by recounting how Herakles, the beneficent hero of his early books, visited the town during his tenth labour, was well received, and, in return, set up sacred areas to his nephew and assistant Iolaos and to the three-bodied monster Geryon there. In addition, he says, Herakles created a local lake (4.24). In fact, such was Diodoros' fondness for his home that he may even have returned there to die, if the tombstone from Agyrion, inscribed to "Diodoros, son of Apollonios," (*IG* XIV 588) belongs to him.

The dates of Diodoros' birth and death are not recorded, but the tenth-century Byzantine encyclopedia *Suda* (*s.v.* Diodoros) states that he lived during the time of Julius Caesar, whom he admired (1.4.7),[3] and Augustus.[4] His view of the latter may well have been less positive, since he reports rather negatively that, during his lifetime, Augustus was responsible for the expulsion of the citizens of Tauromenion from their city and their replacement with a Roman *colonia* (16.7.1). This expulsion is thought to have been an act of revenge by Augustus against the Tauromenians for siding with Sextus Pompeius in their conflict for control of the Roman Empire after the death of Julius Caesar. At that time their resistance had created a situation that had endangered Augustus' life (Appian, *Civil Wars*, 5.109–112). Augustus' expulsion of the Tauromenians and settlement of a Roman colony is the latest event mentioned by Diodoros and, consequently, proves that he had not published his *Bibliotheke* by then. Unfortunately, the date is uncertain. The expulsion may have

---

2 Corruption and extortion were endemic problems in the Roman provincial administration of the late Republic. Politicians, who had spent large sums to secure election in Rome, afterwards went out to provinces to recoup their expenses. One of the worst offenders was Gaius Verres, governor of Sicily from 73 to 70. He was successfully prosecuted by Marcus Tullius Cicero in 70 (*In Verrem* 1–2).

3 He also praised Pompey. See R. Westall in Hau, Meeus and Sheridan (2018), 91–127.

4 His actual words were "during the time of Augustus and before."

taken place in or around 36, soon after the event Appian reports, but it could also have been part of a major settlement project in Sicily instituted by Augustus in 21, that is recorded by Dio Cassius (*History of Rome*, 54.7.1).

Therefore, exactly when Diodoros did publish his huge work, and, by extension, when he died, cannot be affirmed with certainty, but the consensus of opinion coalesces around a date between 30 and 20. Support for the upper date can be found in the fact that he fails to mention Rome in a list (1.44.1–4) of the foreign rulers of Egypt, even though Egypt became part of the Roman Empire in 31/0. Furthermore, since he claims to have spent thirty years composing his history (1.4.1), it can be assumed that he began work around or before 60, which date fits with his claim that he was in Egypt researching by 59/8 (1.44.1). In that case, his birthdate should belong before 90, since he would hardly have begun such an ambitious project before he reached the age of maturity.

At 1.4.6 Diodoros announces that his previously unpublished work is now complete and ready to see the light of day, but this claim is open to question on two accounts. On the one hand there are signs of lack of revision in the *Bibliotheke*, for example in the disagreement over the projected end date for the history at 1.4.7 and 1.5.1 (on which see below, p. xxxii). It is also possible that at least part of his work had been published previously. According to the *Chronicle* of Saint Jerome he achieved chronographic fame as an historian (*Diodoros Siculus Graecae scriptor historiae clarus habetur*) already in 49,[5] presumably for the publication of some part of his history. Now, this statement could refer to the illicit circulation of some of his books that he complains of in Book 40, fragment 9: "Because some books (of the history) were stolen and put out in public before they had been revised and received finishing touches, when we were not yet satisfied with the style, we disown those books." On the other hand, it seems unlikely that he would have achieved fame for something that happened against his will. More likely, he did, indeed, present part of his work in public in 49 to test reaction and later revised them for the final publication of the *Bibliotheke* as a whole in or about 30 BC.

TRAVELS

At 1.4.1 Diodoros claims to have experienced great hardship and many dangers as he visited much of Asia and Europe in order to see for himself the most relevant sites, so as to avoid the errors of the run-of-the-mill historians,

---

5 Year of Abraham 1968, J. K. Fotheringham, *Eusebii Pamphili Chronici Canones*, London, 1923, p. 237.

who are ignorant of topography. In this claim, also, he is stretching the truth. He certainly went to Egypt and stayed there for some time. That fact is fully substantiated by his narrative in the early books. By contrast, he demonstrates no similar familiarity with other places in either Asia or Europe, except, that is, with Sicily and with Rome, where he "resided for quite a long time" (1.4.3). It was in Rome that he found the resources for his research most readily available. Unlike other Greek intellectuals, however, for example Polybios, he seems to have had no powerful friends and connections in Rome. Indeed, his lack of sponsorship suggests that, as well as being an outsider, he was a man of independent means, who was able to fund his own project.

UNIVERSAL HISTORY

The project that he took upon himself was to compile or compose a Common or Universal History (*Koine Historia*) for the benefit of common or universal existence (i.e. all humankind) (1.1.1).[6] A Common or Universal History is one that treats the peoples and places of the inhabited world (*Oikoumene*), in contrast to a monograph on a specific topic or place, like Thucydides' *History of the Peloponnesian War* or even Xenophon's *Hellenika* (*History of Greek Affairs*). Diodoros had many models for such an undertaking. Perhaps the earliest was the fifth-century author **Herodotos**,[7] who began his *Histories* by stating that he had two aims, the first of which was to "record the amazing achievements of both Greeks and barbarians." In fulfilling this aim, he covered the known world in space and time by a series of "relevant digressions" on his second purpose, which was to focus on the theme "why they came into conflict."

Following Herodotos, the fourth-century historian **Ephoros of Kyme** (400–330)[8] wrote a Universal History in thirty books (the last written by his son and editor Demophilos), covering the period from the return of the descendants of Herakles (*c*.1104) to the siege of Perinthos by Philip II of Macedon in 340. Ignoring Herodotos, the Hellenistic historian Polybios celebrated Ephoros as "the first and the only man [before himself, that is] who undertook to write a Universal History" (Polybios, *Histories*, 5.32.2), although, in a manner typical of the competitive nature of Greek historians, he had to criticize Ephoros, asserting that, although he gave good accounts of naval engagements, his treatment of land battles, like Leuktra or Mantineia, was "quite imaginary"

---

6 For a useful discussion of the genre as Diodoros conceived it see Sulimani (2011), 21–55.
7 Herodotos was recognized as a Universal historian by Diodoros at 11.37.6.
8 Diodoros credits Ephoros with the writing of a Universal History at 5.1.4, 16.76.5. Ephoros' history has only survived in fragments, which can be found at *FGrHist/BNJ* 70.

(*Histories*, 12.25f.). Ephoros was also the first to divide his work by books and to preface each book with a prologue (*prooimion*), as Diodoros did later. Like Herodotos, and unlike Diodoros, Ephoros wrote by themes (*kata genos*), rather than chronologically. Also, unlike Diodoros, he avoided the mythical period before the Trojan War, but, like Diodoros, he appears to have been uninvolved in the politics of his time and more concerned with issues of morality.

Theopompos of Khios (*c*.380–*c*.320), was a contemporary of Ephoros, but unlike him was active in his island's politics. He was a skilled rhetorician as well as an historian. He wrote a *History of Greek Affairs* (*Hellenika*), which continued Thucydides' history from where it left off to the Battle of Knidos (394), and a *Philippika*, that was centred upon the life and affairs of Philip II of Macedon. This work digressed upon a great number of topics in its fifty-eight books and consequently could pass as a type of Universal History.[9] From the fragments that have survived (*c*.200) it is apparent that he tended to make sharply prejudiced judgements about his subjects.

Timaios of Tauromenion, who lived from about the middle of the fourth century to the middle of the third, was a Sicilian like Diodoros. Timaios was the son of Andromakhos, refounder and ruler of Tauromenion in 358/7 (Diod. 16.7.1). His father had supported Timoleon in his efforts to revive Greek Sicily after Dionysios II. Timaios probably favoured Timoleon also. In or about 316 Timaios was exiled by Agathokles, when he became tyrant of Syracuse and captured Tauromenion. Timaios spent his exile in Athens, where he lived for fifty years. There he wrote his *History of the Greeks in the West* from the mythical accounts of their early settlements to 289, the year of Agathokles' death. Subsequently, he composed a separate monograph on Pyrrhos' war with Rome (282–275), which he may have carried down to the beginning of the First Punic War in 264. At least, the later historian Polybios says (1.5.1; 39.8.4) that his *Histories*, which began at the year 264, picked up where Timaios left off. Since Timaios' works, like so many others, have only survived in fragments,[10] our judgement of their quality is dependent on Polybios' very critical attack upon him throughout Book 12.[11] One aspect of Timaios' work is, however, well known; that is his attempt to create a system of comparative chronology for dating purposes. Even his critic Polybios acknowledges this, when he describes Timaios as the man who "creates a comparison from early times of

---

9 Like Ephoros', Theopompos' works have only survived in fragments, which can be found at *FGrHist/BNJ* 115.
10 *FGrHist/BNJ* 566. See also Baron (2013).
11 But note that Diodoros also criticizes him for his "lengthy censures," for which he acquired the nickname "Epitimaios," the Censurer (5.1.3).

ephors with the kings in Lakedaimon, of archons at Athens and Priestesses of Hera at Argos with the Olympiads" (*Histories* 12.11.1).

Closer to Diodoros' own time, two important Hellenistic historians, **Polybios of Megalopolis** (*c.*200–*c.*118) and **Poseidonios of Apameia** (*c.*135–*c.*51), both composed large-scale histories, but chose as their theme the rise of Rome to world dominance. **Polybios'** background was different from Diodoros'. He was born in Megalopolis, the son of Lykortas, the leading man in the Akhaian League in the Peloponnese, and consequently grew up in a world of political and military affairs. He had already risen to the command of the League's cavalry and was poised to succeed his father at the head of the League, when he was taken in 167 as one of a thousand hostages to Rome. There he became the tutor and friend of Scipio Aemilianus, with whose career he became intimately involved. Polybios was a hostage in Rome for seventeen years and while there he began his most important work, the *Histories*, in which he intended to trace the rise of Rome to world domination in the fifty-three years from 220 to 167.[12] At some point he expanded his plan to take his narrative down to 146, the infamous year when Rome wiped two great cities, Carthage and Corinth, from the face of the earth. His plan was that his forty-volume work would explain Rome and the phenomenal expansion of its power over the whole *oikoumene* to his fellow Greeks. Like Thucydides, to whom he is often compared, Polybios was a witness to the events he wrote about and this informed his approach to the writing of history. He had no respect for historians who were inexperienced in politics or warfare, or who had not visited the relevant sites. Only those who had that experience were qualified, in his view, to write about them and analyse their causes and effects. Unfortunately, we have only the first five of his forty books completely intact. There are, however, large fragments from the other books. The text and translation take up six Loeb volumes and there is a detailed commentary by F. W. Walbank.

Poseidonios was born in Apameia on the Orontes, but lived and worked for most of his life on Rhodes, where he was active in civic affairs. He also ran a school of philosophy there. Before he settled in Rhodes he had studied in Athens with the Stoic philosopher, Panaitios. He was reputedly the most learned man of his time (Strabo, 16.2.10 C753) and wrote on a vast range of topics, based upon extensive travels to most parts of the inhabited world. Philosopher, geographer, ethnographer, astronomer, he also wrote a huge fifty-two-book history of Rome, picking up where Polybios had left off and continuing to *c.*80. Thus, like Polybios, his work was more a monograph temporally,

---

12 By way of background he sketched in the years 264–220.

while a Universal History geographically. Given his Stoic background and his knowledge of and interest in the peoples of the world, it is not surprising that he emphasized the theme of the unity of mankind in the cosmos. Also, unlike Polybios, he appears to have elaborated less on the rise of Rome than its decline due to luxury.[13]

One final model deserves notice. That is the genre of **Local History**, the history of a single community, best represented by the *Atthis*, the local history of Athens.[14] The authors of this genre follow the same structural approach as the *Bibliotheke*, beginning with the mythical origins of their people, passing on to the unstructured period of monarchic and aristocratic rule, then concluding with the later recorded years, which they organize chronologically by magistrates down to their own day. Like Diodoros they treat the mythical origins of their community as paradigms for later history and institutions. That this model was also in Diodoros' mind is shown by two revealing references (at 1.1.3 and 1.3.6). In the first, he likens the work of Universal historians to Divine Providence, in that the latter orders all elements of the Universe into a coherent unit, while Universal historians "write down the common affairs of the *Oikoumene* as if they belonged to a single city." In the second, he refers to the immense labour of recording the affairs of the entire world "as though they were the affairs of a single city." Thus, Diodoros might well have considered Universal History as Local History writ large.

All these above-mentioned compositions were potential models for Diodoros and were certainly sources that he consulted for his narrative, but none attempts the huge scope of his undertaking: to trace the history of the inhabited world from its mythical beginnings to his own time, structured chronologically by archons, consuls and Olympiads. In that respect, his claim to originality at Book 1.3–4 is fully justified. There, after confessing that he was motivated to join the ranks of historians because they were held in the highest esteem, he goes on to say that when he reviewed the works of his predecessors, he found them lacking for one reason or another and resolved to undertake the great task of composing his history of the world from its mythical beginnings to his own day, organized according to the most accurate chronology. Thus, he lays claim to the superior value of his particular approach to Universal History.

---

13 All the fragments of Poseidonios' works are accessible in L. Edelstein and I. G. Kidd (eds.), *Posidonius: Fragments*, 3 vols. Cambridge and New York, 1989–1999. The 124 specifically historical fragments can be found at *FGrHist/BNJ* 87.

14 See Harding (2007; 2008), Thomas (2019).

PLAN

Diodoros lays out the plan for his history at 1.4.6–5.1:

The first six of our books contain the actions and the mythical accounts from before the Trojan War, three setting forth the ancient accounts of the barbarians, the next three almost exclusively those of the Greeks. In the following eleven books we have written down the history of the world to the time of Alexander. In the next twenty-three books we have laid out the remaining events down to the beginning of the Roman war against the Celts. In the course of that war, the man in command, namely Gaius Julius Caesar, overcame the most numerous and warlike Celtic peoples and advanced Roman supremacy to the Britannic Isles, for which achievements he was deified. The initial engagements in that war were carried out in the first year of the 180th Olympiad, when Herodes was archon at Athens [60/59]. Regarding the blocks of time encompassed in this work, we have not delimited in a precise manner those that precede the Trojan War, due to our inability to find a reliable chronological table for them; from the Trojan War[15] to the Return of the Herakleidai, following Apollodoros the Athenian,[16] we allocate eighty years;[17] from that point to the first Olympiad (we allocate) 328 years,[18] basing our calculation of the dates upon the reigns of the kings in Lakedaimon; from the first Olympiad to the beginning of the Celtic War, which we have made the terminal point of our history, 730 years.[19] Thus, our whole forty-book long work encompasses 1,138 years, excluding the period of time that encompassed the events that preceded the Trojan War [1184–46].

The *Bibliotheke* has suffered the fate of so many ancient texts. The last time a complete text of Diodoros was seen was in Constantinople just before it was

---

15 The accepted date for the end of the War, calculated by the Alexandrian scholar Eratosthenes of Kyrene, was 1184.
16 Apollodoros of Athens was a second-century BC scholar, who, amongst other works, wrote a well-respected *Khronika* (Chronicle) of Greece, from 1184, the end of the Trojan War, to 119, in verse. His work is preserved only in fragments, but clearly, for the historical period, his chronology was based on a list of Athenian archons. The fragments can be found at *FGrHist/BNJ* 244.
17 The return of the descendants of Herakles to the Peloponnese was traditionally dated to the year 1104.
18 776/5.
19 I.e. 46. Readers will notice a discrepancy between the date given for the beginning of the Celtic War at 1.4.7 and that given here and reinforced by the calculation in the next sentence. One popular solution is to assume that Diodoros originally intended to include Caesar's campaigns in Gaul and Britain and carry his history to the *end* of the Celtic War, but later, for some reason, changed his mind and decided to end at year 60. However, in this passage he clearly associates the year 46 with the *beginning* of the Celtic War, which rather undermines this solution. As for why he might have changed his end date, suggestions include tiredness, old age, or, possibly, reluctance to get involved in narrating the Civil War.

captured by the Turks.[20] Less than half of it has survived. We have only fifteen of the forty books intact: the first five books, which contain his opening statement about his purpose in writing and five-sixths of his discourse on the myths and pre-history of the known world, and Books 11–20, which cover the history of Greece, Asia, Macedon, Egypt, Sicily and, to a lesser extent, Rome, in an annual chronology based upon Athenian archons, Roman consuls and Olympiads, from 480, the year of Xerxes' invasion of Europe, down to 302/1, the eve of the Battle of Ipsos. Of the rest we have only fragments.

DIODOROS' VIEW OF HISTORY

Who better to ask about their view of history or their purpose in writing than the historian himself? Diodoros reveals his view in his prologue to Book 1 (1.1.1–1.2.8). The function of history is education, he says, and of Universal History is universal education. By treating all peoples as a united whole, it serves all peoples. One can learn from experience, but that is the hard way. In words highly reminiscent of Polybios' comments on the reversal of Fortune experienced by the Roman consul Regulus in Africa (*Histories* 1.35.7–10), Diodoros maintains that, whilst experience is a path to understanding, it is full of pain and hardship, but the reader of his history can learn the same lessons painlessly. The young can become as wise as the old, and the old can become even wiser. Universal historians, he claims, are servants of Divine Providence, which orders the Universe. In this way he aligns himself with Stoic teaching about the unity of mankind.

Clearly, for Diodoros, education is about morality, not fact. So, he passes on to develop the well-worn theme of praise (*epainos*) and blame (*psogos*). He alleges that, by praising the examples of good behaviour and by censuring the bad, history teaches valuable lessons, both to those who aspire to public office and those who are already leaders. History encourages virtuous men to greater deeds and is a witness to the evil deeds of bad men, and in this way is a "benefactor" (*euergetes*) to all mankind. It is the proclaimer of the truth and the mother-city of philosophy (i.e. the primary discipline), since it alone confers immortality upon its subjects. He chooses to highlight the example of Herakles, who laboured and suffered in his life as he strove to be a benefactor to humans. For that, he, and heroes like him, gained the immortality

---

20 Constantine Lascaris, *De scriptoribus Graecis Patria Siculis*, 9: *Ego autem omnes eius libros vidi in bibliotheca imperatoris C[onstantino]politani*. For a very thorough treatment of the history of transmission of Diodoros' text see F. Chamoux, P. Bertrac and Y. Vernière, *Diodore de Sicile: Bibliothèque, Livre I* (Paris, 1993), LXXVIII–CXLII.

of history. So, by preserving the memory of the past, history educates. It can also create memory for the future, as he threatens frequently in his prologues, not least to Book 14. The Thirty Tyrants and Dionysios I will be made into immortal exempla of evil by his writing, and the Lakedaimonians will serve as a reminder of the fate of those who hold supreme power but fail to treat their subjects with respectful moderation (*epieikeia*).[21] On the other hand, examples of history's immortalizing power through praise are the eulogies of Pelopidas and Epameinondas in Book 15.

Memory is the key to Diodoros' belief in the continuity (*to sunekhes*) of history. As he states at the beginning of chapter 9 of Book 1, he will attempt to describe "the events that have been handed down to memory from all over the inhabited world." He begins many books with the statement that, now that he has completed the assignment he set himself for the preceding book, he will proceed to the continuation of his narrative. This is not just a simple transitional sentence. It reflects a basic element in his historiography, namely that a history that contains a connected narrative of events "surpasses all others to the same extent as the whole is more useful than the part and continuity than discontinuity" (1.3.8).[22] This continuity is reinforced by the idea that there are themes that recur, and pervade his work. These themes are usually set out in his prologues, which are crucial to an understanding of Diodoros' purpose in writing.

Besides the laboured theme of the educational utility of history, the prologues contain several ideas that are present throughout the extant portions of Diodoros' work, not least in the two books translated here. One is the Stoic notion of the Divine Spirit that pervades and unifies the Universe. It appears on many occasions in Books 14 and 15, often in conjunction with *Tykhe* (Chance or Fortune), but more as a vengeful force that punishes those who offend against the Divine or whose ambition exceeds due proportion. A case in point is the punishment of the Carthaginian leader, Himilkon, described at 14.76.

Another major element of Diodoros' world-view is euergetism or benefaction. History is a benefactor of humans, much as Herakles, Osiris and other heroes and illustrious men have benefitted society over time.[23] Some of those mythical heroes had attained immortality as gods as a memorial for their deeds. In the real world the concept of generosity in pursuit of ambition had

---

21 The fate of the Lakedaimonians has been taken to be a warning to the new super-power, Rome, and could well reflect a Sicilian Greek view of Roman power, given the rapaciousness of a governor such as Verres.
22 Cf. the prologue to Book 16.
23 Sulimani (2011), 64–72.

a long history in Greece. It had achieved a new significance in the Hellenistic period. As the city-states fell under the control of autocrats near the end of the fourth century, the democratic economic system of obligatory public services (liturgies) imposed upon the elite, which was essentially taxation of the very wealthy, was replaced by the encouragement of voluntary donations by benefactors (*euergetai*). These men were rewarded with worldly immortality in the form of lengthy honorary decrees and statues. Only the Hellenistic kings actually declared themselves gods, some of whom explicitly associated their divinity with benefaction by adopting the title *Euergetes*, e.g. Ptolemy III Euergetes of Egypt (246–221). This system was adopted by Rome and became standard. Julius Caesar was the first to be given the title *divus* "for his [beneficent] accomplishments of subduing warlike peoples and extending the Roman Empire to the British Islands" (Diod. 1.4.7). Diodoros elevates this feature of Hellenistic administration into a historiographical principle.

Given the significance of his prologues for Diodoros' historiography and the unity of his work,[24] it is perhaps disappointing to find that the ideas that they contain from the prologue to Book 1 onward reflect ideas that were current in Hellenistic historiography and are, therefore, not particularly original. Some take him to task for this and accuse him of deriving his prologues from his predecessors.[25] This has been an invitation to speculate about their source. Leading candidates are Ephoros, Polybios and Poseidonios.[26] Ephoros is the least likely, since the emphasis on euergetism is a phenomenon that postdated his lifetime. Furthermore, he cannot be the source of the echoes of Stoic philosophy, since he was long dead when Zeno began to expound his ideas in the Stoa Poikile at Athens. Poseidonios is more plausible, given his association with Stoicism, but the most likely is Polybios, who begins his *Histories* with a similar reference to the educational value of History and agrees that "the most effective and sole instructor of the best way to put up bravely with the vicissitudes of Fortune (*Tykhe*), is the memory of the sudden reversals experienced by others" (1.1.2). But, the fact that each of these authors can be advocated with equal intensity by their supporters suggests that no single one is his source. Maybe, they all are in a way. That is what is suggested by the context in which Polybios introduces the above-cited quotation. Such statements are, Polybios says, the stock-in-trade of all historians without exception and have been used so many times that he feels no compulsion to repeat them. In other

---

24 Sacks (1990), 9–22.
25 The most vigorous contemporary proponent of this view is Stylianou, *Commentary*, 1–139.
26 For the supporters of the different candidates see A. Meeus in Hau, Meeus and Sheridan (2018), 150.

words, Diodoros was indeed just writing what every other historian of his day was writing, and there was no need for him to have cribbed these ideas from any of the postulated sources. He was simply in tune with the intellectual climate of his time.

Just as Diodoros' approach to History as an instructor of moral behaviour was standard in an ancient world that had become fixated on issues of morality even before the time of Sokrates, so this approach continued to be the main purpose for writing history into the late Classical period, and was espoused especially by Christian historians. Even in the Renaissance and for several centuries after, what survived of Diodoros' narrative was well respected. Things changed, however, with the emergence of rational enquiry in the nineteenth century, when scholars wanted to read history for an accurate representation of the facts, not simply for moral edification. Then it became important to test the validity of the factual details in the *Bibliotheke* and to seek to find out where Diodoros acquired his information, in other words to identify his sources.

SOURCES

Diodoros' *Bibliotheke Historike* makes easy reading, but it can be a challenging work both in the sense that the information it contains often challenges that provided by some of our most respected writers, like Thucydides and Xenophon, but also because of the challenge we experience in finding out where he acquired this information. While contemporary scholarship accepts Diodoros' claims in the prologue to his first Book and treats the *Bibliotheke* as a unified whole, written by a person who had a clear vision of what he was doing in the context of Hellenistic historiography,[27] the contentious issue of Diodoros' sources and how he used them is still current and is an inescapable subject for anyone who wishes to achieve a well-rounded understanding of Diodoros. It is separate from the question of his purpose in writing or the influence of the intellectual climate in which he worked. Simply put, it is the question whether he read the works he refers to or whether he derived those references from a single source that he was copying slavishly.

In the case of the books translated here, the traditional view, established by Volquardsen,[28] and maintained adamantly by his modern supporters,

---

27 See Rubincam (1987, 1989, 1998); Sacks (1990); Green (2006); Sulimani (2011); Hau, Meeus and Sheridan (2018).
28 Volquardsen (1868).

Stylianou[29] and Parker,[30] is that for his history of Greece in Books 11 through 16 Diodoros copied exclusively from one source, Ephoros, with maybe some input from Timaios. This view is based upon a few undoubted references to these authors and a series of questionable assumptions. To begin with the latter: the first assumption is that we know what Ephoros' history was like. This is based partly upon the surviving fragments of his work, but more upon the tradition that he was a pupil of the rhetorician Isokrates. The classic source for this idea is Cicero (*de Oratore* 2.94), who lists amongst Isokrates' students all the major orators and historians of the fourth century. "Then behold! There arose Isokrates, the *magister rhetorum*, from whose school, as from the Horse of Troy, none but leaders emerged … men like Theopompus, Ephorus, Philistus, Naucrates … and those who turned to the legal profession, as did Demosthenes, Lycurgus, Aeschines, Dinarchus and several others." It is demonstrably impossible that everyone on this list studied with Isokrates and not impossible that none did. After all, when Isokrates lists his favourite pupils at *Antidosis* 93, he names none of those named by Cicero.

The corollary to the assumption that Ephoros studied with Isokrates is that he absorbed and followed his ideas. Unfortunately, it is rather presumptuous, in my opinion, to think that we know what Isokrates' ideas were, or even if he held any definite views. To be sure, Isokrates' writings were responsible for popularizing many of the moralizing themes we find in Diodoros. By Diodoros' day they were pervasive throughout intellectual circles. He did not need to borrow them from Ephoros or anyone else; he imbibed them from his mother's milk. In the matter of real political ideas, however, Isokrates' record is not so clear. His opinion on various issues, like for example the Athenian Empire, changes with the wind. He was after all a sophist, who taught rhetoric, nothing more. Though his compositions are often seen as political pamphlets, there is no evidence that he even tried to influence contemporary affairs, and certainly none that he ever succeeded. I have argued in several places that his works were exercises to demonstrate various rhetorical techniques to his students and that they often contain humorous paradoxes.[31]

It is true, of course, that Diodoros does make several references to Ephoros and some to Timaios, and there are a few established contacts with some fragments of Ephoros. One such reference to both authors occurs at the beginning of Book 5 (5.1.1–4). There, Diodoros credits Timaios for his precise

---

29 Stylianou (1998).
30 Parker at *BNJ* 70.
31 Harding (1974a, 1986, 1988).

chronology and respect for experience, but criticizes him for his excessive habit of censuring individuals. He goes on to praise Ephoros for the structure of his work and his decision to focus each of his books on a single topic. He states that he will follow Ephoros' practice in this regard. He may also have followed him in the use of introductory chapters or prologues that summarized the content of each book (16.76.5), though that was a well established feature of historical writing by Polybios' time.

But adopting Ephoros' structure is one thing, copying his narrative in detail is another. The evidence is not sufficient to justify the common assumption, "if some, therefore all," which has allowed scholars to extrapolate Ephoros' history from the *Bibliotheke*. After all, Diodoros was not afraid to criticize Ephoros, as is most apparent in the discussion of the source and flooding of the Nile in Book 1 (1.37.1–39.13). After ridiculing Ephoros' theories, he concludes, "However, one would not search for total accuracy in Ephoros, considering that he makes light of the truth in many instances." The idea that Diodoros restricted himself to one author exclusively is obviously at odds with Diodoros himself, who cites numerous authors, whose works he claims to know. Most of them were good, or, at least, the best available. If we accept his claim, his choice shows that he had good judgement. It also shows that he had read widely and was a diligent scholar. This is the conflict between Diodoros and his critics. How can it be resolved?

To begin with, we have to recognize that he was not a "mere copyist." Not only is that charge refuted by the evidence that he composed his material in his own style and vocabulary,[32] this is probably not the way he worked. We are, after all, dealing with scrolls, not books. It was not as easy to find one's way back and forth to relevant passages in a scroll as it is with a book. Ancient scholars read and memorized. Just as we saw in the case of the prologue to Book 1, Diodoros read, absorbed and digested a body of material and then produced his own version in his own words, probably dictating them orally to a slave. This, at any rate, is my view of the way he worked. It explains, though it does not excuse, his manifold faults: the omissions, the compressions, the abridgements and mistaken names. It can, however, acquit him of the charge of being "a mindless *Dummkopf*,"[33] who could not even copy what was in front of him. A possible example of his method may be found in chapters 75 and 76 of Book 15, which are just notes, waiting to be presented in a more stylish form from his recollection of what he had read. We can, perhaps, support

32 Palm (1955).
33 Green (2006), x.

this interpretation from an investigation of three other sources that have been recognized in Books 14 and 15: Ktesias of Knidos, the *Hellenika Oxyrhynkhia* and Philistos.

Ktesias of Knidos

Ktesias of Knidos was a Greek doctor, who served in the court of Artaxerxes II (Mnemon) from 404–398/7. He wrote a History of Persia (*Persika*) in twenty-three books and also a work on India (*Indika*). His works were full of anecdote and exaggeration, but he was a source for Diodoros.[34] Diodoros knew Ktesias' *Persika* and cites it for the account of Ninos and Semiramis in Book 2.1–20. Later, at 14.46.6, he reports the conclusion of the *Persika* in 398. Undoubtedly, he had read this work. At one point (14.20.2–3) we can see him reworking Ktesias for his own purpose. Diodoros gives a totally different version of Syennesis' encounter with Kyros from Xenophon's (see n. 153 on the translation). In his version, Syennesis is duplicitous and pretends to support Kyros, while colluding with Artaxerxes. The only other source to refer to the double-dealing of Syennesis is Ktesias, fragment 16, as reported by Photios, summarizing the nineteenth book of the *Persika*: "How Syennesis, king of the Kilikians, was an ally with both Kyros and Artoxerxes."[35] We do not, of course, know how Ktesias embellished this story, but Diodoros' version contains elements of Diodoran morality. Syennesis was a "cunning rogue," who was "preparing himself against the unpredictability of Fortune (*Tykhe*)."

Hellenika Oxyrhynkhia

This is the name given to a work that has been preserved in possibly eleven papyrus fragments from Oxyrhynkhos in Egypt. It is a history of Greece (*Hellenika*) that manifestly continued from where Thucydides left off. Where it ended is not clear.[36] The author is unknown. Various candidates have been advanced. The fragment that is relevant to Book 14 is the London fragment, which contains a detailed narrative of the year 396/5. It has long been accepted that this narrative lies behind much of Diodoros' history from the point where Thucydides left off to, at least, the Battle of Knidos (394) and, maybe, to the King's Peace (387/6). In reference to Book 14, this explains the considerable

---

34 The fragments of his works are to be found at *FGrHist* 688 (not yet updated by *BNJ*).
35 Photius, *Bibliotheca*, s.v. Ctesias, *Persica*.
36 The fragments can be found at *FGrHist/BNJ* 66. There is a commentary by I. A. F. Bruce (1967).

difference between Diodoros' account of the Battle of Sardis and Xenophon's, as noted in the translation at nn. 479–492. It probably also explains Diodoros' strange insistence on depicting Theramenes as a staunch democrat at 14.3.7.[37] Now, whilst the identity of the author of the *Hellenika* was either unknown or, at least, attributed to a shadowy historian, like the Athenian Kratippos,[38] who was never mentioned by Diodoros, it was usual to claim Ephoros as the intermediary. Occhipinti (2016), however, has recently argued that Diodoros may have used the *Hellenika Oxyrhynkhia* directly. This possibility, combined with the convincing revival by Billows in his commentary on the *Hellenika Oxyrhynkhia* for the *BNJ* of the old view that Theopompos was the author,[39] puts the situation in a new light. Diodoros is well aware of Theopompos' *Hellenika*, as is evident from 14.84.7, where he records the starting point (Battle of Kynossema) and finishing point (Battle of Knidos) and the number of books (17) in Theopompos' history. The notion that Diodoros took these details from some chronographic source and had not read the work is not convincing. Theopompos was, along with Ephoros and Philistos of Syracuse and Xenophon, one of the most respected post-Thucydidean historians. The revelation that several people in small-town Egypt in the first and second centuries AD were eagerly copying sections of Theopompos' work for personal use makes it most unlikely that a well-read scholar like Diodoros was not familiar with it. In short, if Theopompos was the author of the *Hellenika Oxyrhynkhia*, it is far more credible that Diodoros read that work directly than that he consulted it *via* Ephoros.[40]

Philistos

It should not be a surprise to anyone that, when Diodoros came to write about Dionysios I of Syracuse, he used the *Sikelika* of his fellow-Sicilian Philistos, who was both a respected historian and a member of Dionysios' inner circle (14.8.5 and n. 60). His intimate knowledge of Philistos' work is revealed by several references. At 13.103.3 he writes: "Philistos concluded the first part of his *Sikelika* at this year (406) with the capture of Akragas, having covered a period of more than 800 years in seven books. He then began the second part

---

37 See n. 25 on the translation.
38 An author whose candidacy I once supported (Harding, 1987).
39 A view argued also by Bleckmann (1998), 199–268; (2005), 32–35, 139–143.
40 Furthermore, if Hammond (1938, 144) is correct, Diod. may well have used an excursus on Sicilian affairs in Theopompos' *Philippika* for his account of the last part of Dionysios' rule in Book 15.

where the first ended and wrote four books" on Dionysios I. Later, at 15.89.3, Diodoros records the conclusion of two further books on Dionysios II, that brings Philistos' total output to thirteen books. Finally, at 15.94.4 he notes: "Athanas of Syracuse began his thirteen-book account of the deeds of Dion at this point, but prefaced it with one book covering the unrecorded seven years from the end of Philistos' narrative. By reporting those events in summary fashion, he connected the two histories in a continuous narrative."

Diodoros' intimate knowledge and use of Philistos' history are confirmed by many passages in Books 14 and 15, in which he seems to know Dionysios' plans or intentions, as I indicate in the relevant notes. There are also graphic descriptions of Dionysios' involvement in his building programme (14.18), of his preparations for war against Carthage (14.41–4, with Philistos, *FGrHist/BNJ* 556 F28), of the siege of Motye and of activity at court (15.6–7). Finally, the magnificent burial Dionysios the Younger gave his father, referred to at 15.74.5, was clearly described in extravagant terms by Philistos (F28 and F40a and 40b). Philistos' tendency to dramatize, hinted at by Plutarch (*Pelop.* 34.1), might suggest he was behind the theatrical description of the naval battle in the Great Harbour of Syracuse (14.72.4–74.4), incorporated though it is in Diodoros' own narrative of the *peripeteia* of Himilkon's fortunes for his sacrilege. In sum, it is again far more reasonable to accept that these vivid passages demonstrate Diodoros' own recollection of the original than that they were transmitted *verbatim* from an intermediary source.[41]

Other Sources

None of this, of course, refutes the view that Ephoros, and to a lesser extent, Timaios, were sources for Books 14 and 15. It simply shows that other accounts were mixed in. One such situation is found at Book 14, chapter 11. Diodoros begins by stating that Pharnabazos had arrested Alkibiades and put him to death to please the Lakedaimonians, then continues, "But, since Ephoros has written that he was plotted against for other reasons, I think it is not without use to lay out the way the plot against Alkibiades has been transmitted by the historian." He then proceeds to narrate the death of Alkibiades, as narrated by Ephoros in his seventeenth book. This simultaneously demonstrates both the use of Ephoros and the knowledge of an alternative version.

Furthermore, in one place we might even find evidence for the possibility of original composition by Diodoros. Although he was philosophically opposed

---

41 Caven (1990), 5 also ascribes these passages to Philistos.

to lengthy speeches (20.1.1–4), in chapters 65 to 69 of Book 14 he provides a long speech, delivered by an unknown Syracusan, named Theodoros, at an assembly convened by Dionysios. This speech emphasizes the many military failures of Dionysios in contrast to a naval victory against the Carthaginians that the Syracusans had supposedly just won by themselves. On this basis Theodoros exhorts the Syracusans to depose the tyrant and reclaim their liberty. Following the speech, when the Syracusans were aroused and expected that a Spartan general, who was present, would help them secure their liberty, they were reduced to dumbfounded silence, when the Spartan general curtly announced that he had been sent out by Sparta only to support Dionysios. This unexpected turn of events reminds us that Diodoros does allow that it is admissible to compose speeches in works of history, "when an event turns out contrary to expectation" (20.2.2), as it does here. This speech is set in a narrative context, parts of which may be suspect,[42] that is designed to set up the expectation of regaining freedom that is then dashed by Spartan duplicity. Both the theme of liberty from oppression and the duplicity of the Spartans are Diodoran themes in Book 14.[43] In fact, as Diodoros points out (14.70.3) the Syracusans should have known better than to expect help from Sparta, after their earlier experience with Aristos/Aretes[44] in 405/4, described in similar terms at 14.10.2–3.

Xenophon

Finally, in this review of the Greek sources for these books, we have to come to the questions regarding Xenophon. The modern reader, who is familiar with the many writings of Xenophon, may wonder why Diodoros never refers to Xenophon as a source and even doubt that he had read Xenophon's works, let alone used them as a source. True, at 15.89.3, he records the fact that Xenophon ended his *Hellenika* with the death of Epameinondas. So, he knew of the work, but it is the very briefest of notices compared to those on other authors, even in the same paragraph. Furthermore, there is no reference at all to the *Anabasis*, even though Diodoros gives a potted version of that expedition at 14.19.2–14.31.5. He mentions Xenophon only at the end of the story, when the remaining Greek mercenaries cross over to the Khersonesos to work for Seuthes under his leadership (14.37.1–2).

---

42 As I suggest at n. 413 on the translation.
43 A different interpretation of this speech is given by C. Baron in Hau, Meeus and Sheridan (2018), 491–504.
44 See n. 70 on the translation.

Yet the basic order of progress of Kyros' expedition and, subsequently, of the march of the Ten Thousand to the Black Sea follows that described by Xenophon. Further, as reported in the footnotes, there are places where the two versions agree almost *verbatim*, though elsewhere details differ. But Diodoros also used Ephoros, whom he actually cites at 14.22.2 for the number of Artaxerxes' forces at the Battle of Kounaxa, namely 400,000. Xenophon, by contrast, gives the incredible figure of 1,200,000 infantry, plus 6,000 cavalry and 200 scythe-bearing chariots! (*Anab.* 1.7.11.) But, Ephoros' number agrees with that attributed to Ktesias by Plutarch, *Artax.* 13.3, and Ktesias was almost certainly the source for the sections of the narrative that concern Artaxerxes and the Persians, since we are given information from the Persian side that neither Xenophon nor Ephoros could have known.

Confusion is further increased by the possibility that there was an alternative account of the March of the Ten Thousand by Sophainetos of Stymphalos, one of Xenophon's colleagues (*FGrHist/BNJ* 109), which Ephoros or even Diodoros could have used.[45] But, the existence of that work is attested by only four references in a very late authority (Stephanos of Byzantion) and it can hardly have been as respected as Xenophon's, because no one else refers to it. In fact, the supposed presence of Sophainetos in Diodoros is based upon the slimmest basis imaginable, namely, that one of his four fragments, F2, Stephanos of Byzantion, *s.v. Taokhoi*, reads: "A people within the Pontos. Their territory (is named) likewise. Some people call them Taoi, as Sophainetos says in his *Anabasis*." "Taoi," it is felt, is closer to Diodoros' name "Khaoi" for these people (14.29.1) than Xenophon's "Taokhoi" and, therefore, reveals the use of Sophainetos! Not only is that thesis far-fetched, it is a misinterpretation of the fragment, which does not say that Sophainetos used the name "Taoi," just that he says that "some people" do.

My own feeling here is the same as elsewhere: For his account of Kyros' campaign and its aftermath Diodoros read Xenophon's *Anabasis*, Ephoros' *History* and Ktesias' *Persika*, then compressed and abridged what he had read and cobbled it into his own eclectic version. This may not save his reputation, but we do have to remember that he was writing a history of the world, and this rather minor incident hardly deserved more space than he gave it.

Regarding the allusions to Roman history, scholars have been hard pressed to agree on a source. Although Diodoros claims to be able to read Latin, the likelihood is that he took some of his information from Timaios, but more

---

45 On this possibility see the conflicting opinions of G. L. Cawkwell and P. Stylianou in Lane Fox (2004), pp. 47–67, 68–96.

from a third-century Roman author, Fabius Pictor, who wrote a history of Rome, probably annalistically, in Greek. Diodoros cites this author at 7.5.4.

CHRONOLOGY

As mentioned earlier, Diodoros arranged his account of the historical period annalistically, using Athenian archons and Roman consuls, or in these books mostly military tribunes, as his annual criteria, interspersed with the Olympiads every fourth year. He surely took the names of the eponymous Athenian archons from Apollodoros of Athens, whose work he acknowledged at 1.5.1.[46] Since Apollodoros' *Khronika* ended at 119, he needed a source for the years 119 to 60 and that is usually assumed to have been the first-century BC author Kastor of Rhodes,[47] whose compilation of comparative chronologies concluded conveniently at the year 61/0. By his time Greek scholars had collated numerous lists of different national magistrates or dignitaries, beginning in the fifth century with the work of Hellanikos of Lesbos, who collected the archons of Athens and the Priestesses of Hera at Argos, and Hippias of Elis, who created a list of Olympic victors. In the fourth century Aristotle and his grand-nephew, Kallisthenes of Olynthos, compiled a list of victors at the Pythian games. Later, lists of Macedonian kings, Persian monarchs, Assyrian, Babylonian, Median rulers, amongst others, followed, so that the science of comparative chronology emerged, which attempted to correlate these lists to one another to create a basis for world history. One of the most influential scholars in this field was the Alexandrian polymath Eratosthenes of Kyrene, whose work formed a basis for Apollodoros. As already noted, another person who was interested in this activity was the Sicilian historian Timaios. Some use of his data by Diodoros might, therefore, be expected.

Regarding the names of Roman consuls and military tribunes we are less well informed. The most reliable source for this information is the Roman historian Livy (*c*.64/59 BC–AD 17), but he wrote after Diodoros. Nevertheless, the number of Livy's entries agrees with Diodoros' for the period down to 387/6, after which things go awry, as detailed in the applicable notes. The names are a somewhat different matter. Diodoros sometimes promises six names for the tribunes, but gives only four. Other times he says there were fewer tribunes than the names given by Livy. And the spelling of the names

---

46 See n. 16 in this Introduction.
47 *FGrHist* 250.

is largely Greek, which leads to some serious errors, but suggests the source was not written in Latin. Many of these errors can, however, be attributed to the manuscript tradition, since the names provided by the different manuscripts differ greatly in number and spelling. There was, however, one technical problem that may have confused Diodoros' chronological scheme. While Athenian archons took office in mid-summer and the Olympic festivals were celebrated about the same time of year, the date when Roman consuls took office varied. For most of the period covered here their term of office began at January the first.

Finally, since the reader will find frequent reference to "the Varronian year," a word is necessary about Varronian chronology. Marcus Terentius Varro (116–27) created a list of Roman magistrates that was made authoritative by the emperor Augustus. It was inscribed either on the walls of the Regia in the forum or on Augustus' triumphal arch. This list became the basis of what is now called the *Fasti Capitolini* and is canonical. The problem with this list is that it disagrees with the chronology developed by the Greek scholars by varying amounts. In our case, the difference is three or four years up to 387/6 and varying amounts thereafter. The most notorious result of this discrepancy involves the date of the sack of Rome by the Gauls. On the Varronian chronology it was 390, the date every student of Roman history has fixed in their brain. For the Greeks, probably correctly, it was 387/6, as was corroborated for them by the synchronism of the sack of Rome with the destruction of Rhegion and the King's Peace. While Livy's list of magistrates agrees more or less with the *Fasti*, it is not certain that he followed the Varronian dating.

STYLE

Diodoros is not a stylish writer, nor is he a good storyteller, like Herodotos, nor a penetrating political analyst, like Thucydides, or Polybios. He is a reporter. His vocabulary is rather restricted and repetitive. He has his favourite words, of which ἀξιόλογος ("impressive") is a notorious example.[48] He uses standard phrases, such as "In their term of office," or "At the same time these events were taking place / Contemporaneous with these events." Successful generals, such as Iphikrates (15.44.1), Khabrias (15.29.2), Epameinondas (15.39.2, 15.88.1) and Agesilaos (15.92.2), all "excel/surpass/stand out for courage and knowledge/comprehension of military affairs." Worse still, he has some formulaic scenes, especially when he is describing battles. A battle is usually long and

---

48 See n. 854 on the translation.

hard and evenly balanced. The turning point often involves an act of courage or recklessness by an individual. Some examples are Kyros' loss to Artaxerxes at Kounaxa, occasioned by his recklessness and death (14.23); the defeat of Leptines by Magon in the naval battle near Syracuse, resulting from Leptines' disobeying of Dionysios' advice (14.60); the defeat of Evagoras by Glôs in the naval battle near Kition (15.3) through over-confidence; Pelopidas' heroic victory over Alexander of Pherai at Kynoskephalai that cost him his life through overeagerness (15.80.4); and Epameinondas' crucial intervention at a key point in the battle of Mantineia (15.86.4–87.1) and his death, because he was "driven by passion." Fate brings the combatants together, as Diodoros states explicitly in the case of Kyros and Artaxerxes, but it is the actions of the individuals themselves that cause the result. The emphasis upon the individual is a feature of Diodoros' style and need not be attributed to his sources.

At times, however, he can achieve almost Homeric heights in describing the battle over the body of a fallen leader, as, for example, over the body of Kleombrotos at Leuktra (15.55.5) or Epameinondas at Mantineia (15.87.1). And, nothing can be more overtly dramatized than his narration of the battle in the Great Harbour of Syracuse (14.73–4). Another set piece that is surely Diodoran involves the siege of a city. In Book 14 there are two notable examples: the siege and capture of Motye (48.1–53.3) and the siege and sack of Rhegion (100.1–112.5). The siege of Motye is particularly illustrative, since it is so similar to Alexander's siege of Tyre in Book 17 (40.3–46.5), which comes from a different source. In both, the defenders are at first not overawed by the attack, because of the strength of their position. Both attackers have to build moles and both meet with setbacks, but persevere. The defenders invent ingenious devices to blunt the force of the attack, but eventually are driven to desperation. A stalemate ensues, which is broken by the action of one man, Arkhytos at Motye and Alexander himself at Tyre. The result is the slaughter of the men and the selling of the women and children into slavery. Similar topography leads to similar strategy, but the emphatic conclusion is the pitiful fate of the besieged.

The tale of Rhegion is similar in the conclusion, though it ends a long history of hatred for the city by Dionysios for the seemingly insignificant insult over his marriage request. In this case, the cunning attacker has deprived the citizens of Rhegion of all potential allies and taken away their fleet. They resist desperately, led by their general, Phyton, whose courage at the moment of his abominable murder by Dionysios epitomizes their suffering. Diodoros makes a point of noting that Phyton's behaviour is lauded by all civilized people (112.3–5). In these and other siege situations throughout his history, Diodoros shows a distinct sympathy for the victims of war, especially the innocent civilians.

FORMAT

In his mode of presentation Diodoros suffers a common difficulty faced by all historians, that it is impossible for a writer to narrate simultaneously events that are happening at the same time in different places, a difficulty which he himself recognizes at 20.43.7:

Here one might find fault with history, observing that in life many different actions are completed at the same time, but that those recording these actions are compelled to interrupt their narrative and to apportion pieces of time unnaturally to events that were completed at the same time. The result of this is that, while the experience of the events is true, the written account is deprived of the corresponding ability to imitate the events and falls far short of an accurate representation.

Quite apart from this basic issue, the chronicle format creates special difficulties for an author like Diodoros, who repeatedly emphasizes "the continuity of history." This problem presents itself on many occasions in Books 14 and 15, but nowhere more graphically than in the early chapters of Book 14. For the first eighteen chapters Diodoros sticks to his annalistic approach, providing snippets of information on the Thirty at Athens (14.3–6), Dionysios (14.7–9), Sparta in Greece and in Syracuse (14.10) and the death of Alkibiades in Phrygia (14.11) under 404/3; Klearkhos in Byzantion and Lysander's machinations in 14.12–13 and Dionysios in Sicily in 14.14–16 under 403/2; Oropos and Thebes and Sparta in Elis (14.17) and Dionysios' fortification programme (14.18) under 402/1. Readers will appreciate the extent to which the continuity of narrative of any particular theme is broken up by this annual record. On the other hand, from chapters 19–31 onward Diodoros follows a thematic approach, such as it is believed was used by Ephoros, as he recounts the tale of Kyros' March Upcountry and the subsequent journey of the Ten Thousand. In doing this he not only blurs the chronology by narrating events that covered portions of two years under one, but he also seriously disrupts his accounts of other affairs to the extent that he has to flash back (at 14.32) to 404/3 to resume his narrative of the Thirty at Athens, which he left off twenty-six chapters before. The fact is that neither writing annalistically nor thematically is an answer to the challenge of writing history, but trying to blend the two is worse. The quotation cited above shows that Diodoros was aware of this difficulty.

SUBSTANCE

Diodoros provides us with a considerably different account of the years covered in Books 14 and 15 from that of our other extant version by Xenophon. One of the most obvious differences is dating. Xenophon is cagey, if not confusing, about dates.[49] Diodoros, on the other hand, bases his narrative of the "historical" period on annual magistracies. Quite apart from the period covered by these two books, his references are invaluable for our own attempts to arrive at precise dates for some important events in Greek history, where information is not provided by our other authors. While he may not be as reliable on Roman chronology as he is on Greek, his list of Athenian archons and Olympiads is fundamental.

More substantially, Diodoros provides the only extant account of Sicilian affairs for these years. He is invaluable for any evaluation of the career of Dionysios I of Syracuse and his conflict with Carthage and its various leaders. The same goes for the history of Evagoras of Cyprus' war with Artaxerxes and all affairs concerning Egypt, none of which is treated by Xenophon. Even for Greek affairs, to which Xenophon naturally restricted himself since he was writing a *Hellenika*, there are places where Diodoros provides information Xenophon neglects. A notorious example is the foundation of the Second Athenian Confederacy in 378/7, which is totally ignored by Xenophon. Diodoros, by contrast, gives an abbreviated, but fairly accurate account of the alliances and the charter of the League (15.28.2–4). More egregiously, Xenophon, out of his antipathy towards Thebes, does his best not to name the two great Thebans of the period, Pelopidas and Epameinondas, while Diodoros mentions them and eulogizes them both. Other instances where Diodoros fills in gaps in the information provided by Xenophon can be found in the notes. Even his disagreements with other accounts, not least in the case of the battle of the Allia, should not be dismissed lightly.

What has just been said is not intended to discount the many places, recorded in the notes, where Diodoros confuses chronology, misinterprets or misrepresents issues, misspells names or even kills off someone like Khabrias years too early. Every piece of information provided by Diodoros must be evaluated critically. That is the historian's task. But, it is important to bear in mind that his account does contain valuable material. In the end, readers will reach their own conclusion about Diodoros. Those who come to him holding the prejudice that he is a "mere copyist," and an incompetent one at that, whose every

---

49 See D. H. Thomas in Strassler (2009), 331–339.

word is cribbed from someone else, will find much to support that view. But those who read him with an open mind, will, I hope, find that he has a voice of his own. Then, I think, they will agree that he is who he says he is: a Sicilian Greek of the first century BC writing a history of the known world, based upon extensive and diligent study of numerous sources; that his purpose in writing was for the moral betterment of his readers, so that they might learn from the virtues and vices of others. He praises courage, but criticizes recklessness and over-confidence, including over-indulgence in victory. He believes that those in positions of leadership and power should treat those beneath them with respect and moderation. He feels for the innocent victims of war. He sides with religion over science. His philosophy is basically Stoic, but he can appreciate others. He is intrigued by natural phenomena, such as earthquakes and tsunamis, snowstorms and magic honey, and the effect of non-human causation like Panic. These can involve him in digressions that are disproportionate to his mission. Above all, he wrote history the way the Roman historian Tacitus promised, *sine ira et studio*, "without anger or bias" (*Annals* 1.1).

Book 14

The following events are contained in the fourteenth book of Diodoros' *History*:[1]

404/3

In Athens, the bringing to an end of the democracy and the setting up of the Thirty (**chs. 3–4**)

Illegal actions of the Thirty against their fellow citizens (**chs. 5–6**)

How the tyrant Dionysios constructed a citadel (on Ortygia) and apportioned out the city and its territory among the masses (**ch. 7**)

How contrary to expectation Dionysios regained his tyranny as it was beginning to fall apart (**chs. 8–9**)

How the Lakedaimonians managed affairs throughout Hellas (**ch. 10**)

The death of Alkibiades (**ch. 11**)

403/2

The tyranny of Klearkhos the Lakonian in Byzantion and its overthrow (**ch. 12**)

How Lysander the Lakedaimonian failed in his attempt to overthrow the descendants of Herakles (**ch. 13**)

How Dionysios enslaved the people of Katane and Naxos and transplanted the Leontinians to Syracuse (**chs. 14–15**)

The foundation of Alaisa (Halaesa) in Sicily (**ch. 16**)

402/1

The Lakedaimonians' war against the Eleians (**ch. 17**)

How Dionysios constructed the wall at the Six Gates (**ch. 18**)

---

1 The following list of contents is handed down in our manuscripts, the earliest of which is from the tenth century. Similar lists (*prographai*) exist for most extant books. Whether they originated with Diodoros, as was the case with Polybios (*Histories*, 11.1–2; Walbank, *Commentary*, 2.266), or were the work of either Alexandrian or Byzantine scholars is not easily determined. These lists are quite eclectic and do not constitute a comprehensive list of topics in each book. Missing topics are added in italics. Relevant chapters are indicated in bold. The dates provided are Diodoros'.

401/0

How Kyros made a campaign against his brother and was killed (**chs. 19–31**)

Further crimes of the Thirty; Thrasyboulos brings about their fall and restores democracy at Athens (**chs. 32–33**)

The Eleians surrender to Sparta; the Spartans expel the Messenians from the Peloponnese, some going to Sicily, some dying in Kyrene (**ch. 34**)

400/399

How the Lakedaimonians came to the aid of the Greeks in Asia (**chs. 35–36**)

The foundation of Adranon in Sicily and the death of the philosopher Sokrates (**ch. 37**)

399/8

The construction of the wall for Khersonesos (**ch. 38**)

Pharnabazos persuades the King to appoint Konon as admiral of a fleet to fight the Spartans; Pharnabazos and Tissaphernes lead an army against Ephesos; they are opposed by Derkylidas; a truce is concluded (**ch. 39**)

The people of Rhegion decide to go to war with Dionysios and persuade the Messinans to join them; the Messinans have a change of heart and both conclude peace with Dionysios (**ch. 40**)

Dionysios' preparation for war against the Carthaginians and his manufacturing of weapons, during the course of which he invented the catapult missile (**chs. 41–44**)

398/7

How the war got started between the Carthaginians and Dionysios (**chs. 45–47**)

397/6

How Dionysios took by siege Motye, a conspicuous Carthaginian city (**chs. 48–53**)

396/5

How the people of Egesta set fire to Dionysios' encampment (**ch. 54**)

How the Carthaginians crossed over to Sicily with 300,000 men and began to make war on Dionysios (**ch. 55**)

Dionysios' retreat to Syracuse (**ch. 55**)

Campaign of the Carthaginians to the Strait (of Messina) and their capture of Messina (**chs. 56–58**)

The great naval Battle between the Carthaginians and Dionysios and the Carthaginian victory (**chs. 59–62**)

Pillaging of the temples of Demeter and Kore by the Carthaginians (**ch. 63**)

Punishment by the gods of the temple robbers and destruction of the Carthaginian forces by a plague (**chs. 63, 70–71**)

The naval battle between the Syracusans and the Carthaginians and the victory of the Syracusans (**ch. 64**)

Theodoros' harangue to the people on the subject of freedom (**chs. 65–69**)

Syracusan hopes of liberty dashed by action of Spartan general (**ch. 70**)

How Dionysios outmanoeuvred the 1,000 most insubordinate of his mercenary troops and brought about their massacre (**ch. 72**)

How Dionysios besieged the forts and encampment of the Carthaginians (**ch. 72**)

How Dionysios overwhelmed the Carthaginians by siege and set fire to many of the enemies' ships (**ch. 73**)

Simultaneous defeat of the Carthaginians both by land and by sea (**ch. 74**)

The nighttime deception[2] of the Carthaginians with the collaboration of Dionysios, without the knowledge of the Syracusans, for a bribe of 400[3] *talents* (**ch. 75**)

The misfortunes that befell the Carthaginians as a result of their impiety against the divine (**chs. 76–77**)

The refounding by merger of the cities that had been destroyed throughout Sicily (**ch. 78**)

How Dionysios took some of the cities of the Sikels by siege and brought others into alliance (**ch. 78**)

How he arranged a treaty of friendship with the despots Agyris of Agyrion and Nikodemos[4] of Kenturipa (**ch. 78**)

---

2 All manuscripts read δόλος ("trick," "deception"), and this reading is defended by Bonnet in the Budé, even though it is awkward. Suggested emendations are στόλος ("voyage") by Wesseling and δρασμός ("flight") by Vögel in the Teubner. Vögel's suggestion is adopted by Oldfather in the Loeb.
3 In the narrative of this event in ch. 75 the figure given is always 300.
4 In the text of ch. 78 the name is Damon.

How Agesilaos, king of the Spartiates, crossed over into Asia with an army and ravaged the territory that was under Persian control (**ch. 79**)

Spartan embassy to Egypt; Pharax besieges Konon at Kaunos; Konon is relieved by Pharnabazos and Artaphernes and is welcomed at Rhodes (**ch. 79**)

How Agesilaos was victorious in a battle (*at Sardis*) against the Persians under Pharnabazos'[5] leadership (**ch. 80**)

Concerning the Boiotian War and what was done in it (**ch. 81**)

Defeat and death of Lysander at Haliartos (**ch. 81**)

395/4

How Konon was appointed *strategos* by the Persians (**ch. 81**) and rebuilt the walls of the Athenians (**ch. 85**)

Alliance of Athens, Thebes, Corinth and Argos against Sparta and outbreak of the Corinthian War; allied campaigns in Thessaly and Phokis (**ch. 82**)

Spartan victory against the allies at Nemea; recall of Agesilaos from Asia; defeat of Spartan fleet and death of Peisander at Knidos by Konon and Pharnabazos (**ch. 83**)

Spartan victory at Koroneia; Konon and Pharnabazos liberate many islands from Spartan control and sail to Corinth; death of Aëropos of Macedon; conclusion of Theopompos' Hellenika (**ch. 84**)

394/3

Tiribazos lures Konon to Sardis and arrests him (**ch. 85**)

How the Lakedaimonians were victorious against the Boiotians in the vicinity of Corinth and this war was named "The Corinthian War" (**ch. 86**)

The people of Rhegion, angered that Dionysios is fortifying Messina, settle his opponents at Mylai and attack Messina, but are defeated (**ch. 87**)

How Dionysios, who had stolen his way into Tauromenion at great personal risk, was thrown out (**chs. 87–88**)

Exile of Pausanias, king of Sparta, and death of Pausanias, king of Macedon (**ch. 89**)

393/2

How the Carthaginians were defeated by Dionysios near Bakaine[6] (**ch. 90**)

---

5 In ch. 80 Agesilaos' opponent is Tissaphernes.
6 The name of this place is given as Abakaine in ch. 90 and elsewhere in Diod. and other authors.

Italiots form an alliance against Dionysios; fighting around Corinth and Iphikrates' defeat of a Spartan infantry unit by peltasts (**ch. 91**)

Argives take control of Corinth; Iphikrates is recalled to Athens and replaced by Khabrias; Amyntas of Macedon, driven out by Illyrians, donates territory to Olynthos (**ch. 92**)

Roman capture of Veii by Marcus Furius Camillus; Roman dedication to Delphi hijacked by pirates, but restored by Timasitheos, the general of the Lipari Islands (**ch. 93**)

392/1

Campaign of Thrasyboulos in Hellespont and Lesbos; after defeating the Methymnaians, he sails for Rhodes (**ch. 94**)

The Carthaginian expedition into Sicily and the conclusion of hostilities (**chs. 95–96**)

391/0

Oligarchic revolution at Rhodes; Spartan fleet occupies Samos and Rhodes; Agesilaos ravages the Argolid (**ch. 97**)

Evagoras becomes king of Salamis on Cyprus and wins control of most of the island; Artaxerxes is persuaded by opposing Cypriot states to campaign against Evagoras (**ch. 98**)

390/89

How Thibros[7] the Lakedaimonian general was defeated and killed by the Persians (**ch. 99**)

Thrasyboulos sails to Aspendos, where he is killed (**ch. 99**)

Dionysios, planning to go to war against the Greeks of Italy (Italiots), decides to attack Rhegion first; Italiot league sends ships to Rhegion, which are attacked by Dionysios; a storm wrecks many of Dionysios' ships and he barely survives (**ch. 100**)

The people of Thourioi attack the Leukanians, but suffer a huge defeat; survivors, fleeing to the sea, are rescued by Leptines, Dionysios' brother; Dionysios is not pleased and replaces Leptines by Thearides (**chs. 101–102**)

---

7 Undoubtedly an error. The correct name, Thibron, is in Diod.'s text and throughout the narrative of these events by Xenophon (*Hell.* 4.8.18–19).

389/8

How Dionysios put Rhegion under siege (**chs. 108, 111**)

How the Greeks throughout Italy combined together into one political union and arrayed themselves against Dionysios (**ch. 103**)

The Italiots are defeated at the Battle of the Eleporos River (**ch. 104**)

How Dionysios, after his victory in battle and his capture of 10,000 prisoners, let (the prisoners) go without ransom and conceded to the cities the right to live under their own laws (**ch. 105**)

The capture and razing to the ground of Kaulonia (**ch. 106**)

388/7

Capture of Hipponion and the transfer of their citizens to Syracuse (**ch. 107**)

Dionysios sends Thearides to Olympia with a delegation, including several four-horse chariots, expensive pavilions and professional performers of his poetry; people are at first impressed, but disaster results (**ch. 109**)

387/6

How the Greeks concluded the Peace of Antalkidas with Artaxerxes (**ch. 110**)

The capture of Rhegion and the misfortunes that befell the city (**ch. 112**)

Celtic tribes invade Tyrrhenia; mini-history of Tyrrhenia; Roman ambassador at Clusium kills Celtic chief; Celts demand recompense, granted by Senate, but rejected by popular assembly (**ch. 113**)

Sack of Rome by the Gauls with the exception of the Capitol (**chs. 114–117**)

Introduction: Book 14.1.1–2.4

1.1. It is understandable, I suppose, that all men object to hearing critical statements against themselves. Indeed, even those who are so thoroughly aware of their own wrongdoing that denial is impossible are, nevertheless, very angry when found fault with, and attempt to talk their way out of the accusation. So, it is absolutely necessary for everyone to be careful not to commit any base act, but especially necessary for those who aim for leadership or have experienced some outstanding good luck. 2. For, since the way of life of such men is totally open to view on account of their distinction, it cannot hide its own lack of understanding. So, let no man, who has achieved any prominence, hope that, if he commits great crimes, he will get away forever unpunished. Indeed, even if he escapes the reckoning of punishment during his lifetime, he should expect that the truth will catch up with him later on and will proclaim in an outspokenly frank way [with *parrhesia*] details that have been unspoken for a long time. 3. Consequently, it is a harsh reality for bad men that they leave behind after their own death an undying impression of their whole life for future generations.[8] For, even if it is no matter for us what happens after our death, as some philosophers keep babbling,[9] nevertheless, the life we have lived beforehand is rendered much worse for all time, if it is remembered for evil. Shining examples of this fact can be gathered by the readers of individual parts of this book.

Diodoros introduces the moralizing theme of this book, which is essentially "the evil that men do lives after them"

2.1. For example, amongst the Athenians, thirty men, who seized power unconstitutionally out of their own desire for gain, involved their country in great misfortunes and, although they were quickly thrown out of power, have left behind undying[10] disgrace for themselves. Furthermore, the Lakedaimonians, after acquiring for themselves the undisputed rulership of Greece, were later deprived of it, when they began to behave unjustly towards their allies. For,

---

8 This is the interpretation of Diod.'s meaning here by modern translators, e.g. Oldfather (Loeb), Bonnet (Budé), Green (Landmark), but another less likely meaning has been suggested: "Consequently, it is difficult for base men to leave behind after their own death an immortal (i.e. godlike) impression of their whole life for future generations," although this involves Diodoros in an inconsistent usage of the word *athanaton* (see n. 10), which would be uncharacteristic.

9 Presumably Diod. is referring disparagingly to the views of the philosophers called Atomists, like Demokritos and Epikouros, who deny the immortality of the soul, in contrast to the different conclusion reached by Sokrates in the *Phaidon*.

10 The word here, again, is *athanaton*, which can hardly have a positive meaning.

leaders preserve their periods of supremacy by goodwill and just behaviour, but lose them by criminal acts that incur the hatred of their subjects. 2. A similar example is that of Dionysios, tyrant of the Syracusans. Although he was a ruler most blessed by fortune, his life was subject to constant plots and, through fear, he was compelled to wear an iron breastplate over his clothes, and after his death he left behind his life as the most outstanding example for moral criticism to all succeeding ages. 3. But we plan to make clearer reference to each of these issues at the appropriate point in the narrative. Right now we shall return to the continuation[11] of our history from the place where we left off, digressing only briefly for the following chronological summary. 4. In the preceding books we have recorded the things that happened after the capture of Troy up to the end of the Peloponnesian War and of the Athenian hegemony, encompassing a period of 779 years. In this book we shall carry on our continuous narrative of events, starting with the setting up of the Thirty Tyrants at Athens and leaving off at the sack of Rome by the Gauls, comprising a total of eighteen years.

404/3: Book 14.3.1–11.6

In Athens, the democracy is brought to an end and the government of the Thirty is set up

3.1. In the 708th year after the capture of Troy there was no eponymous archon at Athens[12] on account of the dissolution of their hegemony,[13] while in Rome four military tribunes held the highest magistracy:[14] Gaius Fulvius, Gaius Servilius, Gaius Valerius and Numerius Fabius; this was also the year when the ninety-fourth Olympic Games were celebrated, in which Korkinas[15] of Lamia was the winner.[16] 2. During this time the Athenians, overcome by exhaustion, made a treaty with the Lakedaimonians in accordance with which they had to

---

11 The theme of the continuity of history (*to sunekhes*) is central to Diod.'s purpose in writing. See Introduction.

12 Diod. is not exactly correct here. Pythodoros was the archon eponymous for the year 404/3 (Aristotle, *AP* 35.1; 41.1). Xenophon (*Hell.* 2.3.1) provides the information that the Athenians did not use his name, but called the year a year without an archon (*anarkhia*), but this chronographic passage in Xenophon is considered interpolated. For chronological problems in Xenophon see D. H. Thomas in Strassler (2009), 331–339.

13 This was not, of course, the reason for the *anarkhia*. At best this is a compression of the facts.

14 *Tribuni militum consulare potestate*, originally three but rising to six, were elected in place of consuls in most years from 445/4 to 367/6 as a result of the conflict between the patricians and plebeians over the consulship. Livy (4.57.12) names the tribunes for this year (Varronian 407) as: Lucius Furius Medullinus, Gaius Valerius Potitus, Gnaeus Fabius Vibulanus and Gaius Servilius Ahala. Some of his names agree with Diodoros', some do not.

15 Xenophon (*Hell.* 2.3.1) gives the alternative spelling Krokinas.

16 In the single-length footrace over 600 Greek feet (*stadion*), originally the only athletic competition at the Olympic Games and the standard entry in the Olympic victor lists. For footraces at the Festival Games see Miller (2004), 31–46.

destroy the walls of the city[17] and return to their ancestral constitution.[18] As for the walls, they did indeed take those down,[19] but they did not agree about the form of government. 3. For, those who aimed at oligarchy announced that they would share between themselves the age-old system, under which few men had complete charge of all affairs. On the other hand, the majority, who were keen supporters of democracy, championed the constitution of their fathers, which they claimed was acknowledged to be democracy. 4. After argument over these issues had persisted for several days, the adherents of oligarchy sent an embassy to Lysander, the Spartiate [the officer class in Sparta]. Their hope was that he would assist in the undertaking of their plot. It was based on the reasonable grounds that when, after the conclusion of the [Peloponnesian] War, he had been sent out to administer affairs throughout the cities, the result in most cases had been the establishment of oligarchies.[20] So, they [i.e. the embassy][21] sailed across to Samos, since Lysander happened to be residing there, after only recently capturing the city [of Samos].[22] 5. When they began exhorting him to join them in their endeavour, he assented and, after he had appointed Thorax,[23] the Spartiate, as governor [*harmost*] of Samos, he sailed

---

17 The terms are more fully laid out by Diod. at 13.107.4. They included the destruction of the fortifications of the Peiraieus and the limitation of the size of the Athenian fleet. According to Xenophon (*Hell*. 2.2.15) only ten *stades* (c.2,000 yards or 1,830 metres) of each of the Long Walls were to be torn down. But see Lysias 13, *Against Agoratos*, 14, where it is stated that Theramenes returned with a treaty that required that all the Long Walls be torn down instead of just ten *stades*.
18 The *patrios politeia*, a term much bandied about in the constitutional wrangling that went on in Athens from the time of the Revolution of the Four Hundred (411/0) to the end of the fifth century. See Aristotle, *AP* 29.3.
19 According to both Xenophon (*Hell*. 2.2.23) and Plutarch (*Lys*. 15.5) the walls were pulled down to the accompaniment of *auloi* (a double-reeded wind instrument). Only Plutarch has this happen after the change in the constitution has been forced upon the Athenians by Lysander.
20 Usually councils of ten men, called decarchies (Xen. *Hell*. 2.3.7; 2.4.2). See 14.13.1 and n. 87.
21 According to Xenophon (*Hell*. 2.2.16), the embassy was sent to find out what Lysander's intentions were regarding Athens' capitulation. Although Diod. does not name the leader of this embassy, Xenophon states that it was proposed and led by Theramenes, who purposely delayed his return for three months to increase the suffering in Athens and decrease resistance. This embassy should not be confused with a separate one to Sparta, also led by Theramenes (Xen. *Hell*. 2.2.16; Lysias 12, *Against Eratosthenes*, 68–70; 13, *Against Agoratos*, 9–14; and the author of the so-called Theramenes papyrus, which is now treated as F10 of the *Hellenika Oxyrhynkhia*).
22 The pro-Athenian Samians resisted Lysander longer than the Athenians. For their final capitulation (November 405), see Xen. *Hell*. 2.3.6–7. In recognition of their loyalty the Athenian democracy honoured them with a grant of citizenship. See *IG* II² 1; *TDGR*2, no. 5; O&R, no. 191; R&O, no. 2.
23 Thorax had campaigned with Lysander in the Hellespont and at Aigospotamoi (Xen. *Hell*. 2.1.18–19; 2.1.28), but came to a sticky end later (Plut. *Lys*. 19.7).

Opposition of Theramenes to Lysander and the oligarchs

back to the Peiraieus with 100 ships. There he convened the Assembly and advised the Athenians to choose thirty men to lead the government and manage all business in the city.[24] 6. At that, Theramenes spoke out in opposition and reminded [him] of the terms of the agreement, namely that he had agreed they could use their ancestral constitution, and claiming that it was a terrible thing if they should be deprived of their liberty [*eleutheria*] contrary to the sworn oaths. Lysander replied by blaming the Athenians for breaking the terms of the agreement, in as much as they had taken down the walls later than the agreed upon date. He also levelled the most severe threats against Theramenes, saying that he would have him put to death, if he did not stop his opposition to the Lakedaimonians. 7. For this reason, both Theramenes and the assembled citizens [*ho demos*] were struck dumb with fear and compelled to dissolve the democracy by a show of hands.[25] And so thirty men were chosen to manage the public affairs of the city. They were in name "governors," but in reality "tyrants."

4.1. The People [*ho demos*], observing Theramenes' fairness and thinking that the greed of those set over them would be checked to a certain extent by his noble character, voted him in also as one of the thirty leaders.[26] The first task for the men chosen was to appoint a Council and select the other officials; after that they were to write up laws by which they were going to govern.[27]

---

24 There exist several other accounts of the capitulation of Athens and the tyranny of the Thirty: Xenophon, *Hell.* 2.2.1–23, 2.3.2–3, 2.3.11–2.4.43; Lysias 12, *Against Eratosthenes*, passim, especially 43–46, 62–78; Lysias 13, *Against Agoratos*, passim; Aristotle, *AP* 34.2–41.1; Plut. *Lys.* 14–15; Justin, *Epitoma*, 8–10. These sources disagree on many points, one of which is whether Lysander was the prime mover of the establishment of the Thirty or merely an interested observer. A thorough discussion of the issues can be found in Rhodes, *Commentary*, 415–482. He provides a useful chart comparing the different accounts at 416–419.

25 The sources mentioned above have very different views about Theramenes: Xenophon follows Thucydides in depicting him as traitorous to his oligarchic colleagues; Lysias represents him as a leader amongst the oligarchs; for Aristotle, he was neither of those things, but a leader of a moderate group. Only Diod., or rather his source, presents him as a champion of democracy. For a discussion about the source for Diod.'s unique view, perhaps based upon the *Hellenika Oxyrhynkhia*, see the Introduction. On the tradition regarding Theramenes see Harding (1974b).

26 The Thirty are named by Xenophon (*Hell.* 2.3.2). On their election and affiliation see Krentz (1982), 51–56; Walbank (1982); and Develin, *AO*, 184–185. According to Lysias 12, *Against Eratosthenes*, 76, Theramenes chose ten of the Thirty.

27 Xenophon, in the passage cited above, alleges that the Thirty were elected as *syngrapheis* (commissioners) with a mandate to revise the laws. There is disagreement amongst Xenophon scholars whether he agreed with Diodoros that the Thirty were elected to govern or were simply legal commissioners. See Krentz (1982), 50 and Marincola in Strassler (2009), 53.

2. Now, as for the work of lawmaking, they kept on putting that off, ever offering fair-sounding excuses, but they did appoint a Council and the other officials from their own personal friends. The result was that these were in name magistrates, but in reality servants of the Thirty. In the beginning, they [the Thirty] handed the lowliest members of the population[28] over to trial and had them condemned to death. Up to that point their actions were quite acceptable even to the most respectable citizens. 3. But after that, out of a desire to operate with more violence and illegality, they [the Thirty] asked the Lakedaimonians for a garrison, on the pretext that they were going to institute a constitution that was advantageous [to Sparta]. For, they knew that they would not be able to carry out their murderous designs without the aid of military support from outside, since all [Athenians] could be expected to hold out for their mutual security. 4. After the Lakedaimonians had sent the garrison and Kallibios to be its commander,[29] the Thirty courted him with bribes and all manner of other gratuities. In addition, they made a list of the wealthy men who were suited to their purpose, arrested them on the grounds that they were revolutionaries, put them to death and expropriated their property.[30] 5. But Theramenes began opposing his colleagues in power and was threatening to resist them, by siding with those who were striving to preserve lives. At that, the Thirty convened the Council. There, Kritias, their leader, made a long speech of accusation against Theramenes, saying that he was betraying the very constitution that he himself was a party to. Theramenes replied by defending himself against the charges point-by-point and succeeded in gaining the goodwill of the whole Council.[31] 6. Kritias and his group became afraid that Theramenes might break up the oligarchy, so they surrounded the Council chamber with soldiers with their swords drawn and attempted to arrest Theramenes. 7. But, he anticipated their move and leapt up onto the altar of Hestia of the Council. He cried out that he

The Thirty request and receive a Spartan garrison

---

28 In other sources these are specified as *sykophantai* (informers and prosecutors against those they saw transgressing the laws). See Glossary.
29 Diod. is here in agreement with Xenophon (*Hell*. 2.3.13–14) in bringing the Spartan garrison to Athens before the showdown between Kritias and Theramenes. Aristotle (*AP* 37.2) reverses the two events.
30 Amongst those eliminated by the Thirty at this time were some of the most influential citizens: Strombikhides, the general (Lysias 13, *Against Agoratos*, 13; 30, *Against Nikomakhos*, 14), Leon of Salamis (Xen. *Hell*. 2.3.39; Plato, *Apology*, 32e), Eukrates, brother of Nikias (Lysias 13, *Against Agoratos*, 4–5), Nikeratos, son of Nikias (14.5.5 below; Xen. *Hell*. 2.3.39: Lysias 13, *Against Agoratos*, 6), Antiphon, son of Lysonides (Xen. *Hell*. 2.3.40), Lykourgos, son of Lykomedes, of Boutadai ([Plutarch], *Lives of the Ten Orators* = *Moralia*, 841e) and Autolykos, son of Lykon, of Thorikos (14.5.7 below).
31 Xenophon provides a dramatized version of the speeches of Kritias and Theramenes (*Hell*. 2.3.24–49).

was taking refuge with the gods, not because he believed he would be saved but out of an eagerness to involve his killers in an act of impiety to the gods.

Death of Theramenes at the hands of the Thirty

5.1. The agents [of the Thirty][32] came forward and dragged him off the altar. For his part Theramenes bore this unfortunate turn of events with courage, not surprisingly since he had become very acquainted with philosophy in the company of Sokrates,[33] but the rest of the gathering pitied him in his misfortune. Nevertheless, they did not dare to assist him, since there was a large number of armed men around them. 2. Sokrates and two of his acquaintances ran forward and attempted to obstruct the arresting agents, but Theramenes begged them to do no such thing. He said that he praised them for their friendship and courage, but that it would be the greatest of disasters for him should he be the cause of the death of men to whom he was so closely attached. 3. Sokrates and his followers, realizing that they had no help from others and perceiving the increasing defiance of those in power, stayed quiet. Then, those who had been assigned to the task pulled Theramenes from the altar and dragged him through the middle of the *agora* to his death. 4. The crowd [in the *agora*], although paralyzed with fear by the sight of the weapons of the guard, nevertheless empathized with the grief of the unfortunate victim, weeping simultaneously for his suffering and for their own enslavement. For each and every one of those lowly people, on seeing how contemptuously the manly courage of Theramenes was treated, assumed that in their weakness they would be easily disposed of without any reckoning.[34]

Illegal actions of the Thirty against their fellow citizens

5. Following Theramenes' death[35] the Thirty continued targeting the wealthy. They kept concocting false accusations against them, putting them to death and seizing their estates. They even did

---

32 According to Xenophon (*Hell.* 2.3.54) these were the Eleven police commissioners, for whom see Aristotle, *AP* 52.

33 The involvement of Sokrates in this event is attested by no other source, and explicitly denied by Xenophon's account (*Hell.* 2.3.54–56). Indeed, it is most unlikely that Theramenes had been a student of Sokrates, who was on the other hand very closely associated with Theramenes' opponent, Kritias. Furthermore, earlier in 406 Sokrates had opposed the illegal condemnation *en bloc* of the Arginousai generals that had been instigated by Theramenes (Xen. *Hell.* 1.7.15; Plato, *Apology*, 32b).

34 Diod. ignores the more heroic account of Theramenes' death reported by Xenophon (*Hell.* 2.3.56).

35 Diod.'s chronology for the death of Theramenes is quite different from Xenophon's, for whom the death of Nikeratos could be cited by Theramenes in his speech before he was put to death (*Hell.* 2.3.39). Whilst Aristotle does not specify the victims of the Thirty, he does place their elimination before the death of Theramenes (*AP* 35.4). On the other hand, Aristotle puts Thrasyboulos' seizure of Phyle before the death of Theramenes against the testimony of both Diod. (14.32.1) and Xenophon (*Hell.* 2.4.2). See Rhodes, *Commentary*, 416–419.

away with Nikeratos, son of the Nikias who led the expedition against the Syracusans. Nikeratos was a man who treated everyone with respect and generosity, and who was close to being the first amongst the Athenians in wealth and reputation. 6. So, this man's death resulted in a common grief for every Athenian household, since the recollection of his decent nature brought people to tears. In spite of that, the tyrants did not in the least cease from their lawless behaviour; rather their insanity gained ground in every way. For example, in the case of the resident aliens [*metoikoi*] they slaughtered the sixty[36] richest to gain control of their property. As for the citizens, they were being eliminated on a daily basis.[37] Consequently, almost all those who were well-off financially fled the city. 7. And they [the Thirty] even did away with Autolykos, a man who was not afraid to speak his mind.[38] Overall, their practice was to pick upon the cream of society. To such an extent did they devastate the city that more than half the Athenians fled.[39]

6.1. The Lakedaimonians, who were keeping an eye[40] on the city of Athens because they did not want the Athenians to become powerful ever again, were happy at this and made their attitude crystal clear by voting that Athenian exiles from all over Greece were to be arrested and sent to the Thirty, adding that anyone who obstructed this order was to be liable to a fine of five *talents*.[41]

Reaction of other Greek states to the plight of the Athenian exiles

---

36 Xenophon (*Hell.* 2.3.41) says the Thirty were each to arrest one metic, i.e. a total of thirty, while Lysias (12, *Against Eratosthenes*, 7) gives the number of resident aliens targeted as ten. For metics (*metoikoi*) see Glossary.
37 According to Isokrates (7, *Areopagitikos*, 67) and Aristotle (*AP* 35.3) as many as 1,500 citizens died in this reign of terror. A famously undeserving victim was Leon of Salamis (Xen. *Hell.* 2.3.39). One of those detailed to arrest him was Sokrates, who reportedly refused (Plato, *Apology*, 32c). Supposedly, this was the tipping point for Plato, who then rejected the overtures of his relatives to join the oligarchs (Plato, *Epistle* 7.324f–325a).
38 Autolykos, son of Lykon, was a famous Athenian Olympic victor in the *pankration*. As a result his statue was on show in the *prytaneion* at Athens (Paus. 1.18.3, 9.32.8). He was also featured as an object of affection of Kallias in Xenophon's *Symposion*. Plutarch (*Lys.* 15.7) says that his death was designed to please Kallibios, who had a personal grudge against him, but Pausanias (9.32.8) tells the same story with a different name.
39 Usually considered an exaggeration, because Isokrates (7, *Areopagitikos*, 67) says only that "more than 5,000 were forced to flee to the Peiraieus." But after the nomination of the Three Thousand who were to have citizenship (*AP* 36–37; not mentioned by Diodoros), the remaining Athenians were essentially exiles. Cf. Lysias 12, *Against Eratosthenes*, 96–97.
40 A somewhat unusual usage of the Greek verb *horao*, which simply means to "have sight"/ "see." Not surprisingly, many editors have felt the need to supplement the text to read "seeing the city in a lowly state" (*vel sim.*). Vögel (Teubner) emends *polin* ("city") to *stasin* with the sense "seeing the strife amongst the Athenians."
41 Cf. Plut. *Lys.* 27.5–6.

2. Although this was an outrageous decree, most cities obeyed, because they were thoroughly scared of the heavy hand of the Spartiates, but the Argives, out of hatred for the harshness of the Lakedaimonians, were the first to show pity for the fate of these poor wretches and welcomed the exiles with generosity. 3. The Thebans also voted a decree that anyone who saw an exile being arrested and did not assist him to the utmost of their ability would be liable to a fine.[42] So, that is how affairs at Athens stood.

Dionysios, the tyrant of Syracuse, constructs a citadel (on Ortygia) and apportions out the city and its territory among the masses

7.1. [July 405] In Sicily, Dionysios, tyrant of the Sikels,[43] since he had made peace with the Carthaginians,[44] was taking thought how to secure the future of his tyranny, since he was presuming that the Syracusans, now that the war was over, would have the time to strive to regain their liberty.[45] 2. Perceiving that the island [Ortygia] was the most secure part of the city and also the most capable of being easily defended, he shut this off from the rest of the city with a wall,[46] sparing no expense, since he not only built tall towers into it at frequent intervals, but also in front of it set business establishments and stoas that could accommodate crowds of people. 3. Furthermore, he fortified an acropolis on the island at great cost, against the eventuality that he might need to take refuge unexpectedly, and encompassed within its walls the dockyards beside the little harbour that is called Lakkion.[47] These dockyards could hold sixty triremes and were closed by a gate, through which only one ship at a time could sail in. 4. Then, choosing out the best of the territory [of Syracuse], he parcelled it out as gifts to his friends and to the men he had appointed to positions of command. The rest he allotted to both citizens and foreigners on an equal basis, although he included under the category of citizens the liberated

---

42 Cf. Plut. *Lys.* 27.3.
43 Diod. resumes his narrative of Sicilian affairs from Book 13.114.3. Only here and at 14.18.1 is Dionysios ever given the title "tyrant of the Sikels," on whom see n. 347. His normal description is *turannos* or *dynastes ton Surakousion* ("tyrant of the Syracusans"). His ambition, of course, was to rule all of Sicily, which is reflected in the official Athenian documentary title for him – *archon tes Sikelias* ("ruler of Sicily"), attested in three inscriptions from 394/3 to 368/7 (*TDGR2*, nos. 20 and 52; R&O, nos. 10, 33 and 34).
44 The terms of the treaty of 405 are given by Diod. at 13.114.1. It left the Carthaginians in control of the non-Greek peoples of western Sicily; required that the Greek cities of Selinous, Akragas, Himera, Gela and Kamarina pay tribute to the Carthaginians; and guaranteed the autonomy of the citizens of Leontinoi and Messina, as well as of the native Sikels. It did, however, concede control of Syracuse to Dionysios.
45 The revolt against Dionysios, led by the cavalry, and his ruthless response are described by Diodoros in Book 13, chs. 112 and 113.
46 See Map 4.
47 Today's Porto Piccolo, between Ortygia and Santa Lucia to the north. Cf. Thuc. 7.22.1.

slaves, whom he called New Citizens. 5. He also made presents of houses to the masses, except, that is, of the houses on the Island. Those he gave as gifts to his friends and his hired mercenaries.[48] When he thought he had done a good job arranging matters related to his tyranny, Dionysios began a campaign against the Sikels,[49] partly because he wanted to bring all the autonomous peoples under his control, but the Sikels in particular because of their previous alliance with the Carthaginians. 6. But, while he was moving his forces against the city of Herbessos[50] and was making preparations for its siege, the Syracusans in his army, now that they had regained their weapons, began gathering in conspiratorial groups and reprimanding each other for not joining the cavalry in their attempt to overthrow the tyranny. The man appointed by Dionysios as leader of the soldiers first made threats at one of the rabble-rousers, but, when that man answered back in a spirited manner, he went up to him to hit him. 7. At that, the enraged soldiers slew the officer, whose name was Dorikos. Then, calling upon the citizens to strive for liberty, they sent for the cavalry from Aitna. The cavalry had been living there as their fortress, after they had been exiled [from Syracuse] at the beginning of the tyranny.[51]

Dionysios campaigns against the Sikels

The Syracusans in Dionysios' army mutiny

8.1. Dionysios, panicked by the revolt of the Syracusans, broke off his siege and hastened to Syracuse, eager to secure control of the city. Once he had fled, those who had brought about the revolt chose as generals [*strategoi*] the men who slew the officer and, gathering to their side the cavalry from Aitna, set up camp on the heights called Epipolai,[52] thus precluding the tyrant from escape to the countryside. 2. Following that, they dispatched ambassadors to the citizens of Messina and Rhegion, requesting that they join them in their attempt to regain their liberty by taking action at sea.[53] This request was based upon the fact that at that time these cities were in the habit of keeping not less than eighty triremes manned and ready for action. And the cities did, in fact,

Dionysios despairs of keeping his tyranny and consults his friends for advice

---

48 Redistribution of land was a classic technique of tyrants. So, too, was cancellation of debts, liberation and enfranchisement of slaves and transference of populations. In all likelihood the basis of Plato's description of the tyrant (*Republic* 8.565e–569c) was his knowledge of the career of Dionysios.
49 In open contravention of the terms of the treaty with Carthage, mentioned above (n. 44).
50 See Map 3.
51 As described by Diod. at 13.113.3.
52 The heights that overlook the city to the west, occupied by the Athenians during the Sicilian Expedition (Thuc. 6.96–7). See Map 4. Dionysios himself later fortified these heights extensively, as described by Diod. at 14.18.2–8.
53 These two powerful states, situated strategically on either side of the Strait of Messina, were strongly opposed to Dionysios, out of hostility to tyranny and fear of his growing power.

send these triremes to the Syracusans, because they were eager to take part in the struggle for liberty. 3. Furthermore, they [the rebels] had a herald proclaim a large sum of money to any people who did away with the tyrant and made a promise of a share in the citizenship to any mercenaries who changed sides. In addition, they built siege-engines, with which they hoped to knock down and destroy the walls, kept up a daily assault on the Island and welcomed with open arms mercenaries who defected to them. 4. But Dionysios, since he was shut out from escape to the country and found himself being abandoned by his hired troops, gathered his friends together to take counsel with them about the situation.[54] For, so completely had he lost hope for his tyrannical power that he was not looking for a way to overcome the Syracusans in war, but rather to find what kind of death he had to endure in order to avoid ending his tyranny in complete disgrace. 5. First Heloris, one of his friends[55] or, as some say, his adoptive[56] father, repeated to him the saying that "tyranny makes a noble shroud." Next, Polyxenos, his brother-in-law,[57] gave his opinion that Dionysios should take his swiftest horse and ride off into the realm of the Carthaginians to the Campanians, whom Himilkon[58] had left behind to keep watch over the Carthaginian possessions in Sicily. Finally, Philistos,[59] the man who subsequently wrote his *Histories*,[60] spoke in opposition to Polyxenos, saying that it was not seemly to jump out of a tyranny by riding off on horseback

---

54 Diod. recounts the same story at 20.78.2.
55 "Friends" is a politically charged term that signifies "circle of close advisers."
56 Accepting Wesseling's emendation *poietos* ("adoptive") for the manuscripts' *poietes* ("poet"). But at 20.78.2 Diod. calls Heloris only "the most senior of Dionysios' friends."
57 At 13.96.3 Diod. gives precise details of Dionysios' relationship to Polyxenos. In 406/5 Dionysios married the daughter of the Syracusan leader Hermokrates (named Theste in Plutarch, *Dion*, 21.7), and gave his own sister in marriage to Polyxenos, brother of Hermokrates' wife. Yet, at 20.78.2 Diodoros calls Dionysios' brother-in-law Megakles.
58 Probably, in fact, not Himilkon, but Hannibal, the most recent Carthaginian mentioned by Diod. to have commanded the Campanians (13.62.5).
59 Philistos was a strong supporter of Dionysios I from the beginning (Diod. 13.91.4), who acted as an adviser and military commander under his regime. He was exiled by Dionysios in 387/6 (Diod. 15.7.3) and spent his time in Thourioi writing his history. Sources disagree whether he ever returned during the reign of Dionysios I, but he was certainly in favour with Dionysios II, in whose service he died (Diod. 16.16.3–4; Plutarch, *Dion*, 35.2–6).
60 Philistos, despite his reputation as the "most loyal" (*pistotatos*) of the "friends" of the tyrants, wrote a well-respected *History of Sicily* in thirteen books. Seven covered the period from the mythical beginnings to the capture of Akragas by the Carthaginians in 406/5, four were devoted to the reign of Dionysios I to his death in 368/7 (Diod. 13.103.3). The remaining two were about the career of Dionysios II (Diod. 15.89.3). His *History* was undoubtedly used by Ephoros and was clearly known to Diodoros. See Introduction. The few fragments of his work that survive are in *FGrHist/BNJ* 556.

at high speed. Rather, one should be ejected from it, dragged out by the leg.[61] 6. Dionysios paid attention to Philistos' advice and determined to put up with anything before quitting his position of power willingly. For that reason he sent a delegation to the rebels, requesting that they grant him and his close friends leave to depart from the city. Meanwhile, however, he secretly sent messages to the Campanians, in which he agreed to give them whatever pay they asked in return for their assistance in the siege.

9.1. Once these negotiations had been completed, the Syracusans granted the tyrant leave to sail away with five ships. After that, they became rather casual. They dismissed <the cavalry> as being not useful for a siege, while the majority of the infantry dispersed throughout the countryside, assuming that the tyranny was already finished. 2. But the Campanians, buoyed up by Dionysios' promises, had first of all made their way to Agyrion,[62] where they deposited their baggage with Agyris, the city's tyrant. From there, 1,200 cavalry strong, they set out lightly equipped for Syracuse. 3. They traversed the distance speedily and took the Syracusans by surprise. After killing many, they forced their way through to Dionysios. At the same moment 300 mercenaries sailed in to assist the tyrant, whose hopes perked up as a result. 4. For their part the Syracusans, now that Dionysios' power was once again growing strong, began squabbling amongst themselves, one group arguing for staying and continuing the siege, the other for breaking camp and abandoning the city. 5. Observing this, Dionysios led out his army against them and, falling upon them while they were in disarray, easily routed them in the neighbourhood that is called the New City [*Neapolis*].[63] Only a few were killed, however, because Dionysios rode around giving orders not to kill the fugitives. For the time being the Syracusans were scattered throughout the countryside, but after a short while more than 7,000 of them had gathered together at Aitna with the cavalry. 6. Dionysios gave the fallen Syracusans a decent burial, then sent an embassy to Aitna, asking the exiles to agree to a settlement and come back to live in their native land. He gave them a solemn pledge that he would not bear any grudges. 7. And, in fact, some, who had left children and wives behind, felt compelled to yield to his inducements. The rest, however, when the ambassadors were citing

Contrary to expectation Dionysios regains his tyranny as it is beginning to fall apart

---

61 At 20.78.2 Diod. assigns to Megakles the advice attributed here to Philistos. Cf. Plutarch, *Dion*, 35.6–7, where the same advice is attributed to Philistos, even though he is quoted as explicitly denying giving it.
62 Diod.'s home town.
63 Identified with the area referred to by Thucydides (6.75.1; 7.3.3) as Temenites in Cicero, *Against Verres* II, iv. 4.119. See Map 4.

Dionysios' kindness over the burial of the fallen, replied that he deserved to meet the same favour himself and they prayed to the gods that they should see him experience this fate at the earliest possible moment. 8. Consequently, these men, since there was no way they could bring themselves to trust the tyrant, stayed in Aitna, watching for an opportue time to attack him. For his part Dionysios treated the exiles who returned in a generous manner, wishing in this way to encourage the rest also to come back to their homeland. As for the Campanians, after paying them the agreed upon gifts, Dionysios sent them out of the city, since he was suspicious of their unstable character. 9. They made their way to Entella,[64] where they persuaded the citizens to take them in as fellow-citizens, but then attacked them during the night. They slaughtered the young men, took in marriage the wives of the men they had betrayed and became masters of the city.[65]

Dionysios' Campanian mercenaries capture Entella

Lakedaimonian conduct of affairs throughout Greece after their victory in the Peloponnesian War

10.1. In Greece, the Lakedaimonians, having brought the Peloponnesian War to a successful conclusion, held the uncontested leadership both by land and sea. They appointed Lysander as *navarch*[66] and gave him instructions to journey around the cities and establish in each the magistrates they called "harmosts."[67] For, the Lakedaimonians, being ill-disposed to democracies, wanted the cities to be administered by oligarchies. 2. They also assessed tribute payments for the defeated and, although previously they had not used coined money,[68] from that time on they gathered in more than 1,000 *talents* annually from the tribute.[69] Then, once they had arranged affairs throughout Greece to their liking, they [the Spartans] sent Aristos,[70] one of their illustrious men, to Syracuse

Duplicitous policy of the Spartans in Syracuse

64 See Map 3. The city was still under control of the Campanians in 345/4 (Diod. 16.67.3).
65 Not unusual behaviour for mercenaries, cf. Diod. 21.18.2–3.
66 This is incorrect. Lysander had served as *navarch* in 408/7 (Diod. 13.70.1) and could not hold the same position twice (Diod. 13.100.8; Xen. *Hell.* 2.1.7; Plut. *Lys.* 7.3). The Spartan authorities had found a way around this by appointing him as secretary (*epistoleus*) to Arakos, the *navarch* for 405/4 (Xen. *Hell.* 2.1.7), and presumably this position was either extended or renewed in 404.
67 Here, and at 14.13.1, Diodoros represents Lysander as acting on orders of the Spartan state, unlike the depiction given by Plutarch (*Lys.* 13) that Lysander was laying the foundations for a personal supremacy.
68 A restriction traced by Spartans to the legendary lawgiver Lykourgos (Xen. *Laconian Constitution*, 7.6; Plut. *Lyk*, 17.3–6).
69 A *talent* was the equivalent of 6,000 *drachmas*. This figure is attested only by Diod. and is often considered an exaggeration. That the Spartans imposed tribute on their subjects is suggested also by Aristotle, *AP* 39.2. This tribute is separate, of course, from the huge amount of silver, possibly as much as 1,500 *talents* (Diod. 13.106.8), that Lysander sent back to Sparta as booty.
70 This man is named Aretes by Diod. at 14.70.3.

under the ostensible pretence of putting down the rule of the autocrat, but really out of eagerness to increase the power of the tyranny. For they were hoping that, by helping to establish Dionysios' rule, they would acquire him as a subject ally in return for their generosity.[71] 3. After sailing into Syracuse and after having secret discussions with the tyrant on these matters, Aristos began by arousing the Syracusans with promises that he would restore their liberty. Then, he did away with the Corinthian Nikoteles, who was a leader of the Syracusans,[72] and betrayed those who had put their trust in him. Thus Aristos succeeded in putting the tyrant securely in power. But, through this activity he caused disgrace to fall simultaneously upon himself and his country. 4. After sending the Syracusans out to bring in the harvest, Dionysios broke into their houses and took away their weapons from the whole populace.[73] Following that, he constructed another wall around the citadel, started equipping warships, began gathering a large number of mercenaries and kept making preparations in all remaining respects for the safety of his tyranny, behaving as one would, who had already experienced from their actions that the Syracusans would put up with anything not to be enslaved.

Actions of Dionysios to strengthen his tyranny

11.1. While this was going on, Pharnabazos,[74] one of King Dareios' satraps [provincial governors], arrested Alkibiades, the Athenian, and put him to death, out of a desire to win favour with the Lakedaimonians. But, since Ephoros has written that he was plotted against for other reasons, I think it is not without use to lay out the way the plot against Alkibiades has been transmitted by the historian. 2. For, in his seventeenth book, he says that when Kyros and the Lakedaimonians were secretly making preparations for a combined campaign against Artaxerxes, the brother of Kyros, Alkibiades, who had learned of Kyros' plot from some source, went to Pharnabazos and, after divulging the whole affair in detail, asked him to provide passage for a

Pharnabazos brings about the death of Alkibiades

Ephoros' different account of the death of Alkibiades is narrated

---

71 This was the beginning of a long and mutually beneficial relationship between Dionysios and Sparta that lasted until his death in 368/7.
72 It is not surprising to find a Corinthian active in Syracusan affairs, since the Corinthians had founded the city and always preserved close relations with it.
73 Disarming the people was a standard ploy of tyrants, cf. Aristotle, *Politics*, 5.8.7.1311a. One of the best known examples is that of Peisistratos (Aristotle, *AP* 15.3).
74 Pharnabazos, son of Pharnakes, relative and son-in-law of Artaxerxes II, was governor of Hellespontine Phrygia. His palace was at Daskyleion and his estate there is vividly described by Xenophon (*Hell.* 4.1.15–16). In line with Persian policy, he actively supported the Spartan cause in the last phase of the Peloponnesian War. After 400/399, however, as Sparta alienated Artaxerxes, Pharnabazos turned against Sparta and was supreme commander of the Persian fleet that, under the generalship of Konon of Athens, defeated the Spartan navy at the battle of Knidos in 394.

journey upcountry to Artaxerxes.⁷⁵ [Ephoros says] that Alkibiades wanted to be the first to expose the plot to the King. 3. But, [he goes on to say] that when Pharnabazos heard the story, he took upon himself the role of reporter and sent men loyal to himself to reveal the plot to the King. And, according to Ephoros, since Pharnabazos did not give him an escort to the King, Alkibiades set off to the governor [satrap] of Paphlagonia, intending to make his journey upcountry with his help. So, Pharnabazos, fearful that the King might hear the truth of the matter, sent men in pursuit to assassinate Alkibiades along the road. 4. These men caught up with him in a village⁷⁶ in Phrygia, where he was lodging, and piled a mass of wood around the house during the night. When a great fire burst into flame, Alkibiades tried to protect himself, but he was overcome by the fire and the spears that were thrown at him and so died.⁷⁷ 5. About this same time Demokritos, the philosopher, died at the age of ninety.⁷⁸ Also, it is reported that Lasthenes, the Theban, who had won the Olympic footrace that year, competed on foot against a horse and won, over a course from Koroneia to the city of Thebes. 6. In Italy, the Romans who were serving as a garrison in the Volscian city of Erruca⁷⁹ were attacked by enemy forces, which gained control of the city and massacred the majority of the garrison.

403/2: Book 14.12.1–16.5

The Spartan Klearkhos makes himself tyrant in Byzantion

12.1. At the conclusion of this year's events Eukleides became archon at Athens, while in Rome four military tribunes took over the consular power: [they were] Publius Cornelius, Numerius Fabius, Lucius Valerius.⁸⁰ 2. After these men had assumed office, the Byzantines fell upon hard times, because they were at odds with each other at home politically and also at war with the neighbouring Thracians. Since they were unable by themselves to devise a resolution of their animosity towards each other, they asked the Lakedaimonians

---

75 Cf. Plut. *Alk.* 37.6–8.
76 According to Athenaios, *Deip.* 13.574e, the village was called Melissa.
77 Other accounts of Alkibiades' death exist that are well reviewed by Plut. *Alk.* 39, where it is suggested that his death was ordered by Lysander at the instigation of Kritias and the Thirty.
78 This date for the death of Demokritos is far out of line with our other main source, Diogenes Laertios, *Lives of the Great Philosophers*, 9.41–43, which suggests that he lived until the middle of the fourth century.
79 See Livy, 4.58.3, where the town is named Verrugo.
80 Most manuscripts of Diod. give only three names. Only ms F provides Terentius Maximus as a fourth, although its authority is unknown. Diod.'s names are similar (but lacking the *cognomina*) to those given by Livy at 4.58.6, where the names are Publius Cornelius Cossus, Numerius Fabius Ambustus and Lucius Valerius Potitus. Livy adds a Gnaeus Cornelius Cossus to make up the fourth. On the Varronian chronology this is the year 406.

for a general. And so, the Spartiates sent out Klearkhos to establish order in the city.[81] 3. But, once he had been entrusted with the whole administration, he collected a large force of mercenaries and became no longer a champion, but a tyrant. And his first action was to invite the city magistrates to a sacrificial festival of some sort and put them to death. Next, since there was now no government in the city, he seized thirty renowned Byzantines, put a rope around their necks and strangled them to death. After appropriating the property of all the men he had done away with, he had a list made of the wealthy amongst the remainder and, by casting false accusations against them, brought about the death of some, while others he drove into exile. Once he had gained possession of much money and collected a large force of mercenaries, he secured his control of the city. 4. But, when news of the savage and autocratic nature of his tyranny became public, the Lakedaimonians began by sending ambassadors out to him to persuade him to set aside his tyranny. Since, however, he paid no attention to their requests, they dispatched a military force against him under the generalship of Panthoidas. 5. Once Klearkhos got wind of his approach, he transferred his power-base to Selymbria,[82] a city that was also under his control. For, considering the many wrongs he had committed against the Byzantines, he assumed that not only the Lakedaimonians would be hostile to him, but also the men in the city [i.e. Byzantion]. 6. So, judging on this basis that Selymbria was a safer place for carrying on a war, he transferred his money and his forces there. And, as soon as he learned that the Lakedaimonians were in the vicinity, he went out to oppose them and engaged in battle with Panthoidas and his men near the place called "Passage."[83] 7. After the battle had gone on for a long time, because the Lakedaimonians fought brilliantly, the tyrant's forces were destroyed. At first Klearkhos was fenced in at Selymbria and besieged, but later out of fear he ran away during the night and sailed across to Ionia. There he entered into a close acquaintance with Kyros, the brother of the King, and took over command of his troops.[84] 8. For Kyros, who had been appointed commander of the satrapies along the coast [of the Aegean][85] and was a man full of ambition, was planning to lead an expedition against his brother Artaxerxes. 9. So, perceiving that Klearkhos had a daring and conveniently bold character, Kyros gave him funds and instructed him to

The Spartans react to news of Klearkhos' tyranny

Klearkhos is defeated in battle and flees to Ionia

Klearkhos becomes commander of the army of Kyros, who is planning to campaign against Artaxerxes

---

81 Klearkhos had been governor (*harmost*) of Byzantion already in 409. See Diod. 13.66.5–6.
82 Selymbria was situated between Byzantion and Perinthos. See Map 7.
83 Possibly because it was a narrow strip of land between a lake and the coast.
84 At 14.19.8 we are told, more specifically, that on the campaign he commanded the mercenaries from the Peloponnese, excluding the Akhaians.
85 Cf. Xen. *Anab.* 1.1.2, where he is also "general of all who muster in the plain of Paktolos."

collect together as many mercenary troops as possible,[86] in the belief that in him he would have a suitable accomplice for his bold enterprise.

Lysander plots to become king of Sparta

13.1. When Lysander the Spartiate had organized affairs in all the cities subject to the Lakedaimonians in accordance with the will of the ephors, establishing decarchies[87] in some and oligarchies in others, all eyes in Sparta were upon him. For, by bringing the Peloponnesian War to an end, he had conferred upon his country the uncontested leadership both by land and sea. 2. As a consequence, he became puffed up with pride because of these achievements and conceived the notion of putting an end to the kingship of the Herakleidai[88] and making the selection of the kings from the Spartiates at large. Really, he was hoping that the royal power would very quickly devolve upon himself, on account of the fact that he had accomplished the greatest and most prestigious deeds.[89]

To achieve his aims Lysander attempts to bribe the oracles at Delphi, Dodona and Siwah

3. And, observing that the Lakedaimonians paid a great deal of attention to oracular responses, he attempted to corrupt the prophetess at Delphi with money. For, he thought that, if he could get a response that sided with his own designs, his plan would easily come to a successful conclusion. 4. But, since, after a long time of trying, he failed to persuade the staff of the oracle by promising them bribes, he applied his appeals on the same matter to the priestesses who lived around the oracle at Dodona. He did this through the agency of one Pherekrates,[90] an Apolloniate[91] by birth, who had a close acquaintance with those who worked at the sanctuary. 5. Once again he was unable to achieve anything, so he went off on a journey to Kyrene, ostensibly to fulfill vows to Ammon,[92] but really with the intention of corrupting the oracle.[93] And, he took with him a pile of cash, by which he was hoping to win over the employees of the sanctuary. 6. Moreover, Libys, the king of the people who lived in those parts, had a guest-friend relationship with Lysander through his father. Indeed, it so happened that Lysander's brother was named Libys as a result of the friendship with that king. 7. On that account as well as through

---

86 Xen. *Anab.* 1.1.9 specifies that Klearkhos was given 10,000 Darics and that he used these funds to campaign in the Thracian Chersonese on the European side.
87 Government by a body of ten men.
88 The two royal houses in Sparta, the Agiads and the Eurypontids, both claimed to be descended from Herakles. See Herodotos, 6.51–60.
89 Cf. Plut. *Lys.* 24.5–6, 30.4; Nepos, *Lysander*, 3.5; and Aristotle, *Politics*, 5.1.5.1301b.
90 Named Pherekles by Plutarch (*Lys.* 25.2).
91 Probably, given the location of Dodona in Epeiros, this is Apollonia in Illyria. See Map 8.
92 For this vow see Plut. *Lys.* 20.7.
93 The oracle of Zeus-Ammon at the oasis of Siwah. See Map 5. Plutarch (*Lys.* 20.8) gives an alternative version, that Lysander went to Libya because he longed to travel to foreign places.

the cash he was carrying, he hoped to win them over. However, Lysander not only failed to succeed in his plan, but, in addition, the people in charge of the sanctuary sent back with him a delegation [to Sparta] to charge him with corruption of the oracle. So, when Lysander returned to Lakedaimon, the charge was brought forward, but he made a persuasive speech in defence of himself.[94] 8. In fact, at that time the Lakedaimonians had no knowledge of Lysander's plan to put an end to the Heraklid royal houses. But, some time later, after his death, when they were searching his house for some official documents, they found a speech, a costly composition, which he had prepared for presentation to the masses with a view to persuading them that kings should be chosen from the citizenry at large.[95]

Lysander does not succeed in bribing the oracles and is charged in Sparta, but defends himself persuasively

The Spartans were unaware of Lysander's plan

14.1. After Dionysios, tyrant of the Syracusans, had made peace with the Carthaginians and rid himself of factional disturbances in the city, he moved quickly to bring under his control the neighbouring colonies of Khalkis, namely Naxos, Katane and Leontinoi.[96] 2. He was eager to become master of these cities, because they shared borders with Syracuse and also offered many resources for increasing his power. In fact, however, his first campaign was against Aitna, where he captured the fortress,[97] since the exiles were not a match in battle with a great force such as his. 3. After that, he moved his army towards Leontinoi[98] and pitched camp near the city beside the river Terias. Then, after first arraying his army in battle order, he dispatched a herald to the Leontinians, ordering them to surrender their city, for he thought that he had struck fear into the hearts of the inhabitants. 4. But, the Leontinians paid no attention to his command and made every preparation for a siege. So, for the time being Dionysios gave up on the idea of besieging them, because he did not have any siege-weapons. He did, however, plunder their whole territory. 5. From there he moved his forces against the Sikels, making a pretence of

Dionysios initiates assaults on nearby cities in Sicily, but first overcomes the exiles in Aitna

Dionysios attacks Leontinoi, but is rebuffed

Dionysios induces Aeimnestos to aim for tyranny in Enna

---

94 This whole account of Lysander's attempts to bribe oracles is attributed to Ephoros by Plutarch (*Lys.* 25.2). Plutarch goes on to narrate a far more elaborate scheme (*Lys.* 26).

95 According to Plutarch (*Lys.* 25.1, 30.3–4), the speech was composed by the sophist Kleon of Halikarnassos, whose fee was presumably high, hence costly.

96 For the Greek settlements in Sicily, see Thucydides, 6.3–5. Naxos was the earliest, founded by a group from the Ionian city, Khalkis, in Euboia, one year before Syracuse was settled by colonists from Dorian Corinth. From Naxos settlers moved out later to found Leontinoi and Katane. The traditional antipathy between Dorians and Ionians persisted in Sicily. For these places, see Map 3.

97 Dionysios later, in 396, installed his Campanian mercenaries, to whom he had given the city of Katane in 403 (14.15.3), in this fortress. See below, 14.58.2.

98 Dionysios' attack on Leontinoi was in contravention of the terms negotiated with Carthage, as reported by Diod. at 13.114.1.

entering upon a war against them so that the Katanians and the Naxians would become slacker about guarding their city. 6. And while he was spending time in the vicinity of Enna,[99] he persuaded an Ennaian, Aeimnestos, to make a bid for tyranny, promising that he would help him in the purpose. 7. But, after that man achieved his aim and then did not admit Dionysios into the city, Dionysios fell into a rage and, changing his approach, started encouraging the Ennaians to put an end to the tyranny. They ran together into the *agora* with their weapons and began agitating for their liberty, so the whole city was in a state of confusion. 8. Now, when Dionysios found out about the civil strife, he grabbed some light-armed troops and made a sudden forced entry into the city through a deserted spot. Then, after arresting Aeimnestos, he handed him over to the Ennaians for punishment and left the city without having committed any wrongdoing himself. He behaved this way not so much out of consideration for what was just, but out of a desire to encourage other cities to put their trust in him.[100]

Katane and Naxos are betrayed to Dionysios, who sells the citizens into slavery

15.1. From there [Enna] he moved his forces to Herbita[101] and attempted to take the city by storm, but, having no success, he made peace with the citizens.[102] Next, he led his army against Katane, since Arkesilaos, *strategos* of the Katanians, was promising to betray the city to him. In due course, he was secretly admitted into the city by this man and became master of Katane. Then, he stripped the citizens of their weapons[103] and posted a suitable garrison in the city. 2. Following that, Prokles, leader of the Naxians, won over by the magnitude of Dionysios' promises, surrendered his city to him. And Dionysios, after paying out the bribes to the traitor and releasing his relatives to him as a favour, sold the citizens into slavery, handed over their property to his soldiers to plunder and razed the walls and houses to the ground.[104] 3. And he treated the Katanians in a very similar manner, by selling those he had taken prisoner as booty in Syracuse. Furthermore, he gave the territory of the Naxians as a gift to the neighbouring Sikels and handed over the city of Katane to his Campanians to make their home in.[105] 4. After that, he marched straight against Leontinoi in full force and pitched his camp around the city. Then, he

The people of Leontinoi surrender to Dionysios and move to Syracuse

99 For the location of Enna, on a plateau in the centre of Sicily, see Map 3.
100 Diod. makes a point of emphasizing Dionysios' lack of moral conscience.
101 The location of Herbita is disputed, and is not shown on the Barrington Atlas. It probably lay north of Enna, in the direction of Alaisa.
102 Renewed in 396/5. See 14.78.7.
103 Cf. n. 73.
104 This was the ultimate penalty meted out to opponents in Greek warfare.
105 Cf. n. 97.

sent an embassy to those within and bade them surrender their city and move to Syracuse to become citizens there.[106] And the Leontinians, not expecting to receive any help and taking note of the disasters that had befallen the Naxians and Katanians, fell into a panic, fearing that they would experience the same misfortunes. Consequently, they yielded to circumstance and agreed. They abandoned their city and moved to Syracuse.

16.1. After the *demos* of the Herbitaians had concluded peace with Dionysios, Arkhonides,[107] the leading man in Herbita, conceived the idea of founding a [separate] city. For, he had a large number of mercenaries and an assorted crowd [of followers] that had gathered into the city in haste during the war with Dionysios. Furthermore, many of the destitute Herbitaians were promising him that they would join in the colony. 2. So, gathering up the assembled crowd, he took possession of one of the hills that was situated eight *stades* [1,600 yards or 1,463 metres] from the sea and founded there the city of Alaisa.[108] And, since there were other cities in Sicily called Alaisa,[109] he called this one Alaisa Arkhonidios after himself. 3. But, when in later times the city prospered greatly thanks to its maritime activity and the fact that it had been granted exemption from taxation by the Romans,[110] the Alaisians refused to acknowledge their kinship with the Herbitaians, considering it a disgrace that they be thought to be colonists from a less significant city. 4. Yet, in spite of that, right up to the present there remain on both sides rather many indications of kinship and in particular the fact that they conduct the sacrifices at the temple of Apollo with the same customs. But some say that Alaisa was founded by the Carthaginians at the time when Himilkon made the peace treaty with Dionysios.[111] 5. In Italy a war arose between the Romans and the people of

Arkhonides of Herbita founds Alaisa

The Romans declare war on Veii and capture Anxur

---

106 The policy of incorporating citizens from one community into another (*synoikismos*) was not new, but became even more prevalent amongst the Hellenistic monarchs, for whom Dionysios was in many ways a precursor.
107 Arkhonides was the namesake (maybe also a descendant) of an earlier ruler of Herbita, who joined with Douketios in founding Kale Akte in the 440s (Diod. 12.8.2) and was a powerful friend of Athens (Thuc. 7.1.4).
108 In Latin, Halaesa. The site is on the north coast, about a kilometre and a half inland, midway between Kephaloidion (Cefalu) and Kale Akte.
109 No others are on record.
110 Alaisa appears to have benefitted from the revival in Sicilian prosperity under Timoleon, and the fortifications on its acropolis date from this period. Its coinage from this time suggests it was head of an alliance. It sided with Rome during the First Punic War, for which it was granted the privilege mentioned here. In the first century it was plundered by Verres and never recovered.
111 In 405. See Diod. 13.114.1.

Veii[112] for the following causes. ...[113] Then for the first time the Romans voted to give an annual stipend to their soldiers for travel expenses.[114] They also took by siege the Volscian city, which at that time was called Anxor,[115] but today is named Tarracina.

402/1: Book 14.17.1–18.7
Oropos is annexed by Thebes

17.1 Once the year had come to an end, Mikion[116] became archon at Athens, while in Rome three military tribunes took over the consular power: [they were] Titus Quinctius, Gaius Julius and Aulus Mamilos.[117] These men had only just assumed office when the inhabitants of Oropos, because they were feuding with each other politically, sent some of their citizens into exile. 2. For a while the exiles were attempting to bring about their return by their own devices, but finding that they were unable to bring their plan to fruition, they persuaded the Thebans to send a force to help them. 3. The Thebans marched out against the Oropians and, after taking possession of the city,[118] they moved the citizens and resettled them about seven *stades* [1,400 yards or 1,280 metres] from the sea.[119] For a certain period of time they allowed them to govern themselves under their own constitution, but later they gave them citizenship and annexed their territory to Boiotia.[120] 4. As these events were taking place, the Lakedaimonians began bringing a series of complaints against the Eleians, not least the fact that they had prevented Pausanias,[121] their king, from sacrificing to the

The Lakedaimonians declare war against Elis

---

112 The ms text has Boioi, a Gallic tribe from the Po valley. The emendation to Beioi (Veii) is clearly correct. Cf. Livy, 4.58.1–10. See also 14.43.5.
113 Something is obviously missing from the text here.
114 See Livy, 4.59.11.
115 Anxur in Latin. For the capture and brutal sack see Livy, 4.59.3–10.
116 Actually Mikon. See Develin, *AO*, 201.
117 There were in fact six. Two manuscripts (M and F) give the correct number, but without names. Livy, 4.61.1, names the six military tribunes: T. Quinctius Capitolinus, Q. Quinctius Cincinnatus, C. Julius Julus, A. Manlius, L. Furius Medullinus, M. Aemilius Mamercus. Clearly Diod. has misspelled Manlius. The year is 405 on the Varronian chronology.
118 Oropos was situated on the borderland between Attica and Boiotia in the plain of Tanagra on territory that was disputed by Athens and Thebes throughout the fifth and fourth centuries; eventually, after changing hands several times, it ended up as a member of the Boiotian League in 311. It was valuable for its port, which gave access to Euboia, and for the sanctuary of Amphiaraos.
119 Thus cutting them off from their port and depriving the Athenians of this route to Euboia.
120 The Thebans took advantage of the occupation of Dekeleia by Sparta in the latter part of the Peloponnesian War to assert control of most of Boiotia and even pillage Attica. See *Hell. Oxy.* 17.3.
121 In Xenophon's account of the Eleian War (*Hell.* 3.2.21–31) the Spartan forces are led by Agis, who is the king who had been prevented from sacrificing to Zeus (probably in 414 or 413). Consequently, some emend Pausanias to Agis here, but Diod.'s version is clearly based upon a different source, which may indeed have attributed the campaign to Pausanias. Indeed,

god[122] and had not permitted the Lakedaimonians to compete at the Olympic Games.[123] 5. As a result, after deciding to wage war upon them, they dispatched ten ambassadors, who began by ordering them [the Eleians] to allow their neighbouring cities[124] to be autonomous. Next they demanded the portion of the expenses of the war against the Athenians that was due from them.[125] 6. They did this in order that they should have fair-sounding excuses and convincing causes for starting a war. And, when the Eleians paid no attention, but even countered with the accusation that the Lakedaimonians were enslaving the Greeks, the Lakedaimonians sent out against them Pausanias, one of their two kings, with a force of 4,000 soldiers. 7. He was accompanied by a large contingent of soldiers from almost all of the allies. Only the Boiotians and the Corinthians did not participate in the expedition against Elis out of their great displeasure at the actions of the Lakedaimonians.[126] 8. So Pausanias made his assault upon Elis through Arkadia and immediately captured the fortress of Lasion at the first assault.[127] After that, he led his army through Akroreia and gained the allegiance of four cities, Thraistos, Halion, Epitalion and Opus. 9. From there he pitched his camp near Pylos[128] and quickly took that place also, which was only about seventy *stades* [*c*.8 miles or 12.8 km] from Elis. Next, he advanced against Elis itself and set up camp on the hills across the river.[129] A little while before this the Eleians had acquired from the Aitolians 1,000 elite soldiers as allies. To these they had assigned the area around the gymnasion[130] to protect. 10. So, when Pausanias made his first attempt at a siege of this place,

Invasion of Elis by Pausanias

Pausanias is worsted and retires to Dyme for the winter

the two accounts are thoroughly different and quite irreconcilable. In any case, Xenophon's date for the Eleian War ("at the same time as the campaigns of Derkylidas," i.e. 399 BC) is certainly wrong, or at least inconsistent with his own account, since Agis had died in the summer of 400, and Diodoros' date is probably to be preferred.

122 Olympian Zeus.
123 These were the games of 420 BC. See Thucydides, 5.49–50 for a detailed description of the incident. It is also referred to by Xenophon at *Hell.* 3.2.21.
124 The cities of Pisa, Triphylia and Akroreia, over which Elis had extended its control against the wishes of Sparta.
125 This complaint is not mentioned by Xenophon and is the only indication that Sparta required contributions from its allies for the war against Athens.
126 Cf. Xen. *Hell.* 3.2.25.
127 There is no mention of this in Xenophon's account, in which Agis attacks from Aulon, far to the south of Olympia (*Hell.* 3.2.25).
128 This is not Nestor's Pylos, but another of the same name that is situated at the junction of the Peneios and the Ladon, due east of Elis (cf. Pausanias, 6.22.5 and Strabo, 8.3.C339, who quotes the saying, "There is a Pylos before Pylos and yet another Pylos"). See Map 11.
129 The Peneios.
130 Actually more than one gymnasion. They are described by Pausanias at 6.23.1–7.

contemptuously thinking that the Eleians would never dare to make a sortie, suddenly the Aitolians and a large number of the citizens poured out of the city and caused the Lakedaimonians to panic. They even struck down about thirty of them. 11. For the moment Pausanias broke off his siege, but later, seeing that the capture [of the city of Elis] was hard work, he went away ravaging and laying waste to the countryside, despite the fact that it was sacred territory, and succeeded in amassing a huge amount of booty.[131] 12. But, since by now winter was approaching, after building guard posts around Elis and manning them with sufficient troops, he himself took up winter quarters in Dyme[132] with the remainder of his army.

Dionysios, planning to go to war with Carthage, fortifies Epipolai by constructing the wall at the Six Gates

18.1. In Sicily, Dionysios, tyrant of the Sikels,[133] now that matters related to his rule were proceeding as he planned, was of a mind to make war upon the Carthaginians. But, since he was not yet at an adequate stage in his preparations, he kept this plan secret and applied himself to making the most useful preparations against future dangers. 2. So, being aware that during the Attic War[134] the city had been cut off by a wall from sea to sea,[135] he attempted to take care that, if ever he experienced similar reversals, he should not be excluded from an escape route into the countryside. For, he saw that the area called Epipolai naturally held a commanding position overlooking the city of Syracuse.[136] 3. For that reason he brought together his architects and, following their advice, decided to fortify Epipolai, [starting] at the place where there now exists the wall beside the Six Gates.[137] 4. For, this place faces north, is everywhere precipitous and, because of the rough terrain, is virtually inaccessible from the outside. Furthermore, because he wanted the building of the walls to be done quickly, he gathered the mass of citizens from the countryside and from amongst them he selected up to 60,000 free men, who were suited to the task, and apportioned out the space to be walled amongst them. 5. To supervise each *stade*[138] [of the fortification] he appointed architects and in charge

The wall is built in twenty days, with participation from Dionysios

---

131 Cf. Xen. *Hell.* 3.2.26.
132 A port city on the north coast of the Peloponnese, east of Patras. See Map 11.
133 See ch. 7.1 with n. 43.
134 The Athenian invasion and siege of 415–413.
135 Cf. Thuc. 6.97–104; Diod.13.7.4–6.
136 See Thuc. 6.96.1–2.
137 Modern *Scala Graeca*, on the north coast below the plateau of Epipolai in the direction of Leontinoi. This north wall extended from there westward to the key fort of Euryalos. Later (i.e. before 398/7) Dionysios built a south wall from Euryalos to the Great Harbour that encompassed Neapolis, Akhradina and Temenites.
138 About 600 feet (182.8 metres).

of each *plethron*[139] he set builders, with 200 of the private citizens to assist them as labourers for each *plethron*. Apart from these, a vast number of other men were quarrying unfinished blocks of stone and 6,000 yoke of oxen were supplying [the stones] to the relevant places. 6. The combined activity of the workers, who were all striving to complete the task assigned to them, filled observers with amazement. For, Dionysios was stimulating the enthusiasm of the host of workers by offering large gifts to those who finished first, separate ones for the architects, others for the builders and yet others for the labourers. Moreover, he himself together with his friends kept an eye on the enterprise all the time each and every day, putting in an appearance at every location and always ready to lend a hand to any who were in difficulties. 7. In a word, he set aside the dignity of his office and behaved like an ordinary man and, applying himself to the heaviest of tasks, he endured the same hardship as the rest. In this way, a great competition was generated and some even extended their day's labours into part of the night. Such was the magnitude of the eagerness that had overtaken the mass of workers. 8. Consequently, contrary to expectation, the wall was finished in twenty days. In length the construction covered thirty *stades*[140] and its height was commensurate. As a result, when the strength of its position was combined with the wall, it became unassailable by force. For, it was equipped at frequent intervals with high towers, which were constructed of blocks of stone four feet long that were fitted together with care.[141]

19.1. Once this year had come to an end, Exainetos[143] became archon at Athens, while in Rome six military tribunes took over the consular power: [they were] Publius Cornelius, Caeso Fabius, Spurius Nautius, Gaius Valerius, Manius Sergius.[144] 2. About this time, Kyros, the man in charge of the coastal satrapies, was intending to fulfill his long-held plan to lead an expedition against

---

139 About 100 feet (30.5 metres).
140 About 18,000 feet; almost 3½ miles (*c.*5.5 km).
141 Diod.'s literary description of the building of the fortifications is corroborated by the documentary accounts of the building of similar walls at Athens from about the same time. Cf. *IG* II² 1656–1664.
142 This long digression (19.1–31.5) on Kyros' campaign, which begins in the spring of 401 and ends in the autumn of 400, creates problems for Diod.'s chronological system, which has already been led off track by Sicilian and Spartan activities. He finds himself having to flashback to the Thirty Tyrants in Athens in 404/3 at 14.32.
143 The name was actually Xenainetos. For the numerous references see Develin, *AO*, 202.
144 Diod. names only five. The full six with their *cognomina* are given by Livy, 4.61.4. They were: Gaius Valerius Potitus, Manius Sergius Fidenas, Publius Cornelius Maluginensis, Caeso Fabius Ambustus, Spurius Nautilus Rutulus and Gnaeus Cornelius Cossus. The last named was the one missed by Diodoros. The year is 404 on the Varronian chronology.

401/0: Book 14.19.1–34.7[142]

Kyros, younger son of Dareios, plans to challenge his brother, Artaxerxes, for the throne of Persia

his brother Artaxerxes.¹⁴⁵ For, he was a young man full of ambition, with a zeal for the contests of war that was not beyond his reach. 3. However, when a sufficient number of mercenaries had been gathered and his preparations for the campaign had been completed, he did not reveal the truth to his men, but announced rather that he was leading his army into Kilikia against some tyrants, who were in revolt against the King. 4. He also dispatched ambassadors to the Lakedaimonians to refresh their memory of his good services to them during the war against the Athenians and to encourage them to join him as allies. And, the Lakedaimonians, thinking that the war would benefit themselves, decided to assist Kyros. Straight away, they sent out representatives to their *navarch*, whose name was Samos, telling him to do whatever Kyros asked.¹⁴⁶ 5. Samos had twenty-five triremes. Sailing with these to Kyros' naval commander at Ephesos, he made himself available to join him in every action. In addition [the Lakedaimonians] sent out 800 infantry soldiers, putting Kheirisophos in charge. The commander of the foreign fleet [i.e. Kyros'] was Tamôs, who had fifty expensively equipped triremes. After the Lakedaimonian ships had sailed in, the fleets put to sea, making course for Kilikia.¹⁴⁷ 6. Kyros gathered his troops, both the levy from Asia and 13,000 mercenaries, at Sardis. Next, he established men to govern his satrapies; for Lydia and Phrygia [he chose] his own Persian relatives, but for Ionia and Aiolis and the bordering territories, Tamôs, a trusted friend of his, who was a native of Memphis. Then he advanced with his army in the direction of Kilikia and Pisidia, giving out the story that some of the inhabitants of those regions were in revolt.¹⁴⁸ 7. The soldiers he had from Asia were 70,000 in total,¹⁴⁹ of whom 3,000 were cavalry. From the Peloponnese and the rest of Greece [he had] 13,000 mercenaries. 8. Commanding the men from the Peloponnese, with the exception of the Akhaians, was Klearkhos the Lakedaimonian; Proxenos, the Theban, was commander of the men from Boiotia, while Sokrates, the Akhaian, led the Akhaians and Menon from Larissa the men from Thessaly.¹⁵⁰ 9. Persians held the lesser commands over the foreigners,

The Lakedaimonians decide to assist Kyros

Kyros advances into Kilikia and Pisidia

Enumeration of the forces with Kyros

---

145 Cf. 12.8 and n. 85. According to Xen. *Anab.* 1.1.3, he had been accused of treason to Artaxerxes by Tissaphernes and, consequently, arrested by Artaxerxes and was under threat of death. The intercession of his mother, Parysatis, had saved him.

146 Closely parallel to the account in Xen. *Hell.* 3.1.1, except that Samos is called Samios.

147 According to Xenophon, *Anab.* 1.4.2, when the fleets reached Issos in Kilikia, the Peloponnesian ships numbered 35 (not 25) and their *navarch* was named Pythagoras (not Samos or Samios), while Tamôs had only 25 triremes (not 50).

148 Xenophon, *Anab.* 1.2.1, gives only the Pisidians as Kyros' pretext.

149 At *Anab.* 1.7.10 the number of Kyros' non-Greek troops is 100,000.

150 The raising of the various contingents of mercenaries in different parts of Greece and their eventual arrival at Sardis are described by Xenophon at *Anab.* 1.1.6–1.2.3. Xenophon names

while Kyros himself was commander-in-chief of the whole army. Kyros had revealed to his generals that the expedition was against his brother, but he kept this fact hidden from the rank and file[151] out of concern that they might desert because of the magnitude of the undertaking. For that reason, with an eye to the future, even during the march he was very solicitous of his soldiers, presenting himself as one of them and making sure they had plenty of food.

Kyros reveals his plans to his generals

20.1. After he [Kyros] had traversed Lydia and Phrygia as well as the regions neighbouring Kilikia [so, mss: others emend to Kappadokia], he arrived at the borders of Kilikia and the pass at the Kilikian Gates. This pass, which stretches for 20 *stades* [4,000 yards or 3,658 metres], is narrow and steep, being bordered on both sides by exceedingly large and inaccessible mountains. Furthermore, walls stretch down from the mountains on each side as far as the road, across which gates have been constructed. 2. Leading his army through these, he came out into a plain that was second to none in Asia for beauty.[152] Once through the pass he made his way to Tarsos, the largest city in Kilikia, and quickly took control of it. When Syennesis, who was the ruler of Kilikia, heard how great the invading force was, he was thrown into great confusion, since he was not a match for it militarily. 3. But, when Kyros sent for him and guaranteed his safety, he made his way to him and, on learning what the war was really about, he agreed to be his ally against Artaxerxes. In addition, he sent one of his sons along with Kyros and gave him an adequate force of Kilikians for the campaign. However, because he was a cunning rogue and one who prepared himself against the unpredictability of Fortune [*Tykhe*], he secretly sent his other son to the King to inform him about the forces that were being massed against him and to explain that he [Syennesis] was joining in Kyros' alliance under constraint, but, continuing in his goodwill [i.e. to the King], he would, if the opportunity arose, desert him [Kyros] and join the King's forces.[153] 4. Kyros let his army rest in Tarsos for twenty days. But later, as he was in the process of breaking camp, the rank and file began to suspect that the expedition was directed against Artaxerxes. And, as

Kyros passes through the Kilikian Gates to Tarsos

The duplicity of Syennesis

The troops, suspecting the real purpose of the expedition, threaten to mutiny

three commanders more than Diod., namely, Xenias of Arkadia, Sophainetos of Stymphalos and Pasion of Megara. Also, in his account, Menon and his men did not join at Sardis, but at Kolossai in Phrygia (*Anab*. 1.2.6).
151 From the Greek mercenaries as well (Xen. *Anab*. 1.3.1–21).
152 Cf. Xen. *Anab*. 1.2.21–22. Xenophon fails to mention the fortifications, but waxes more eloquent about the beauty of the plain.
153 Xenophon and Diod. have very different accounts of the behaviour of Syennesis. Xenophon (*Anab*. 1.2.12, 21–27) makes no mention of his duplicity, but describes at length the involvement of his wife Epyaxa as a go-between. Further, in Xenophon Syennesis gives Kyros money, not troops, and nothing is said about the sons.

each man reckoned up the length of the marches and the great number of hostile peoples through whose territory he would have to travel, he became thoroughly distressed. For the rumour was spread that the march to Baktria would take an army four months and that a force of more than 400,000 had been amassed for the King. 5. For these reasons they became very fearful and most anxious. Growing angry at their commanders, they attempted to put them to death, on the grounds that they had betrayed them. But, when Kyros pleaded with them all and assured them that he was making his campaign against a certain satrap[154] of Syria, and not against Artaxerxes, the soldiers were persuaded and, after receiving an increase in pay, they returned to their original state of goodwill.[155]

Kyros wins them over by lying about his plans

Kyros arrives at Issos, where he is joined by the Spartan fleet and infantry

21.1. After Kyros had traversed Kilikia, he reached the city of Issos, which was situated on the coast at the furthest point of Kilikia. At about the same time the Lakedaimonians' fleet sailed in there. They disembarked[156] and, once in the presence of Kyros, they reported the goodwill of the Spartans towards him. Also, they brought ashore the 800 infantry that were with Kheirisophos and handed them over to him.[157] 2. The pretence was that the friends of Kyros had sent these men as mercenaries, although in truth everything was being done in accordance with the ephors' directive. But the Lakedaimonians were not yet openly entering the conflict, rather they were keeping their plan secret, watching the way the war turned out. Kyros broke camp and set off in the direction of Syria with his army.[158] He ordered his naval commanders to sail along beside him with the whole fleet. 3. When he arrived at the place called "The Gates,"[159] he was overjoyed to find it unguarded, for he was very worried that someone might have occupied it before him. The place is by nature narrow and precipitous and easily capable of being defended by a few men. 4. For there are mountains situated close to each other, one of which is rugged with impressive crags, while the other, called Libanos,[160] rises up straight from the road. It is the

Kyros passes through the Syrian Gates unopposed and reaches Thapsakos

---

154 Called Abrokomas at Xen. *Anab.* 1.3.20.
155 This incident takes up the whole of ch. 3 of Book 1 of Xenophon's *Anabasis*. Xenophon's account differs greatly from Diodoros'. He does not give the credit for averting the mutiny to Kyros, but to Klearkhos, who delivers a lengthy and deliberately misleading speech.
156 For the collective noun "fleet" to be followed by a plural verb is not unusual, especially for Diodoros.
157 Xenophon (*Anab.* 1.4.3) states that Kheirisophos continued to command the Spartan troops.
158 He marched south down the coast towards Myriandos (Xen. *Anab.* 1.4.6).
159 The Syrian Gates, over the Amanos range. Cf. Xen. *Anab.* 1.4.4–5 and see Map 5.
160 All manuscripts of Diod. read Libanos here, which is clearly a mistake for Amanos. It is not, however, a copyist's error, since Diodoros, or his source, correctly identified Mt Libanos as stretching the whole length of Phoenicia.

biggest mountain in those parts and stretches the whole length of Phoenicia. The passage between the mountains, which is about three *stades* [600 yards or *c*.550 metres] long, is entirely fortified and equipped with gates that hem it into a narrow defile. 5. Then, after passing through these Gates unscathed, Kyros sent off the remainder of his fleet to return to Ephesos, since it was no longer of use to him, now that he was about to make his way inland. And, after travelling for twenty days, he reached the city of Thapsakos, which was situated on the banks of the river Euphrates. 6. He spent five days there and, after ingratiating himself with his army by way of an abundance of supplies and booty from foraging, he summoned an Assembly and revealed the true intention of his campaign. And, when the soldiers responded with hostility to his speech, Kyros pleaded with them all not to abandon him. He promised them great rewards, in particular saying that, when he reached Babylon, he would give each man five *minas* [500 *drachmas*] of silver. And so the soldiers, buoyed up by expectations, were persuaded to follow him. 7. Then Kyros, after he had brought his army across the Euphrates, hastened straight along the route without halting and rested his army only when he had reached the borders of Babylonia.[161]

At Thapsakos Kyros reveals his true purpose to the army. The soldiers are angry, but he placates them by promises and advances to Babylonia

22.1. King Artaxerxes had learned a long time before from Pharnabazos that Kyros was secretly massing an army against him,[162] and now, when he was informed of his march inland, he summoned his forces from all points [in his empire] to come to Ekbatana in Media. 2. But, since the contingents from the Indians and some other peoples were too late arriving, because those regions were far distant, he set off to confront Kyros with the troops he had already gathered. According to Ephoros he had a total force, including the cavalry, of no fewer than 400,000 men.[163] 3. When he reached the Plain of Babylon, he [Artaxerxes] pitched his camp alongside the Euphrates, planning to leave his baggage behind in it. For, he was informed that the enemy was not far off and he was worried about their reckless boldness. 4. For that reason he had a trench dug that was sixty feet in width and ten feet deep[164] and also arranged

Artaxerxes, warned by Pharnabazos of Kyros' attack, leads his army to Babylon

Artaxerxes arrives in the plain of Babylon, makes camp, and advances to battle

161 This is a very abbreviated version of the detailed narrative in Xen. *Anab.* 1.4.4–1.6.11.
162 See 14.11.3.
163 The same figure is given above at 14.20.4 and is in agreement with the number attributed to Ktesias by Plutarch (*Artax.* 13.3). Ktesias was probably Ephoros' source. Other figures circulated. For example, Plutarch has a different number of 900,000 at *Artax.* 7.3 and Xenophon provides the amazing number of 1,200,000 infantry, plus 6,000 cavalry and 200 scythe-bearing chariots (*Anab.* 1.7.11).
164 According to Xenophon (*Anab.* 1.7.15–16) the trench stretched 12 parasangs (360 *stades*, *c*.41 miles or 66 km) across the plain from the wall of Media towards the Euphrates, but was 20 feet short of the riverbank when Kyros arrived, enabling his army to get through.

Kyros and Artaxerxes array their troops for battle

his accompanying baggage-carts in a circle [around the camp], like a fortification wall. Then, after leaving his baggage and a crowd of non-combatants behind in the camp and posting an adequate guard for it, in person at the head of his battle-ready army he advanced to meet the enemy, who were already near at hand. 5. When Kyros saw the King's army approaching, he immediately organized his own forces into battle order. The right wing, which stretched along beside the Euphrates, was held by the Lakedaimonian infantry and some of the mercenaries. Klearkhos, the Lakedaimonian, was in overall command.[165] He had the assistance of more than 1,000 cavalry, who had been levied from Paphlagonia. The men from Phrygia and Lydia held the left wing, in addition to whom there were about 1,000 cavalry under the command of Arrhidaios.[166] 6. Kyros himself had taken up position in the centre of his battle-line with the best troops from the Persians and the other barbarians, about 10,000 in number. Stationed in front of him were the 1,000[167] best-equipped cavalry, armed with Greek breastplates and daggers. 7. Artaxerxes stationed a large number of scythe-bearing chariots in front of his whole battle-line.[168] He put the Persian generals in command of the wings, while he was positioned in the centre with no fewer than 50,000 of his elite troops.

The Battle of Kounaxa[169]

23.1. When the armies were about three *stades* [600 yards or *c*.550 metres] from each other, the Greeks, having raised the paian,[170] began their advance, proceeding at first at a leisurely pace, but, once they got within missile range, they broke into a very energetic run.[171] It was Klearkhos the Lakedaimonian who had ordered them to do this. For, it was his opinion that not running over a long distance was going to keep the combatants fresh in body for the

---

  Different figures are given for the width and depth of the trench by Xenophon (*Anab.* 1.7.14), 30 feet wide, 18 feet deep, and Plutarch (*Artax.* 7.1), 60 feet wide, 60 feet deep.
165 Diod. fails to mention that before the battle Kyros asked Klearkhos to attack the centre of Artaxerxes' line, but Klearkhos declined (Xen. *Anab.* 1.8.13). This was the cause for a lengthy criticism of Klearkhos in Plut. *Artax.* 8.3–7.
166 Diod. follows the details of Xenophon's account (*Anab.* 1.8.4–7), except that Xenophon has Ariaios (correctly) for Arrhidaios.
167 Stated to be 600 in Xen. *Anab.* 1.8.6 and 1.8.25.
168 The scythe-bearing chariots are mentioned also by Xenophon, *Anab.* 1.8.10 and Plutarch, *Artax.* 7.6, but were useless in the battle (*Anab.* 1.8.20).
169 The name of the place where the battle took place is given only by Plutarch, *Artax.* 8.2. The battle itself is described with detailed embellishment by Xenophon, *Anab.* 1.8.17–29, 1.10.1–16. On the battle see Briant (2002), 627–630 and, in a more dramatized form, Waterfield (2006), 1–19.
170 The "Io Paian" was the standard shout for Greek hoplites as they prepared to charge.
171 As they had done at Marathon in 490. Cf. Herodotos, 6.112.

conflict, while advancing at the double when at close quarters would cause the missiles of the bows and other artillery to fly over their heads. 2. Indeed, when Kyros' troops drew close to the King's army, such a mass of missiles was discharged against them as one would expect to be produced by an army composed of 400,000 men. Despite that, the javelin-contest was extremely short and after that for the remainder of the battle they engaged in hand-to-hand combat. 3. The Lakedaimonians and the mercenaries right away at the first encounter struck panic into the opposing barbarians both with the splendor of their armour and by their skillful techniques. 4. For, most of the barbarian contingents were lightly armed and protected by small shields, in addition to which they were inexperienced in the dangers of war. The Greeks, on the other hand, due to the length of the Peloponnesian War, because they had been continuously in battle, were greatly superior in experience. Consequently, they immediately put their opponents to flight, and in the pursuit they killed many of the barbarians. 5. Now, it chanced[172] that both of the men competing for the throne were stationed in the centre of the line. And so, when they realized that this was the case, they charged at each other, eager to settle the conflict by themselves. For, Chance [*Tykhe*], so it seems, had brought the brothers' rivalry for the leadership to the point of single combat, as though in imitation of that ancient example of rashness involving Eteokles and Polyneikes, celebrated in tragedy.[173] 6. Kyros was the first to act and threw his spear from a distance. He struck the King and brought him to the ground. But, the men around him quickly snatched him up and carried him out of the battle.[174] And Tissaphernes, a Persian, taking over the King's command, shouted encouragement to the rank and file and carried on fighting bravely himself. Making up for the setback caused by what had happened to the King and presenting himself everywhere with his elite troops, he slew many of those arrayed against him, so that his presence was outstanding even from far away.[175] 7. Kyros, elated at the success of his companions, forced his way into the midst of the enemy. And, at first, fighting with unstinting daring, he slew many, but later, over-rashly

On the right the Greeks are victorious

In the centre Kyros and Artaxerxes engage in single combat

Kyros wounds Artaxerxes, who is carried off the field

Kyros, over-confident, drives forward, but is slain

---

172 Actually, they were stationed in the centre following established Persian custom; see Xen. *Anab*. 1.8.22.
173 Most famously in Aeschylus' *Seven Against Thebes*.
174 Accounts of the duel between Kyros and Artaxerxes and the death of Kyros differ. See Xen. *Anab*. 1.8.26–29 and Plut. *Artax*. 9.4–11.6. Plutarch cites Xenophon, Ktesias and Deinon. Xenophon himself was not on site and could only be reporting hearsay. Ktesias was present, and his version is the most detailed. It is mentioned by both Xenophon and Deinon and was surely known to Ephoros. Whether Diod. based his account on Ephoros alone, or consulted Ktesias directly, is in question, but see the Introduction under Sources.
175 This extensive eulogy of Tissaphernes is unique to Diodoros.

exposing himself to danger, he was struck a mortal blow by a common Persian soldier[176] and fell to his death. After his removal, the King's men plucked up their courage for battle and, finally, by virtue of their number and their daring they wore down their opponents.

Kyros' troops on the left are defeated

24.1. On the other wing Arrhidaios, one of Kyros' satraps, who had been appointed to that command, at first withstood vigorously the onslaught of the barbarians, but later, as he was being encircled by their greatly extended battle-line and after he had learned of Kyros' death, fled with his own men to one of the staging-posts he had used before, which provided a viable means of escape.

The Greeks cease their pursuit

2. And Klearkhos, seeing that the centre and the other units of the alliance were in flight, put a stop to the pursuit and, recalling his soldiers, set their ranks in order. For, he was afraid that, if the whole enemy army attacked the Greeks, they might be surrounded and slaughtered to the last man.

The King's troops pillage Kyros' camp, then attack the Greeks, but are repelled

3. The forces arrayed with the King, after putting their opponents to flight, fell first to pillaging Kyros' baggage-train, and then, since night had already fallen, turned *en masse* against the Greeks. But, as these withstood the attack bravely, the barbarians held their ground only briefly and soon turned to flight, overcome by the courage and skill [of the Greeks]. 4. And, Klearkhos' men, after slaying a large number of the barbarians, since it was already night, returned and set up a trophy. Then, sometime around the second watch,[177] they reached the camp unharmed.

Casualties of the battle

5. Such was the conclusion of the battle. Of the King's men more than 15,000 were killed,[178] of whom most were slain by the Lakedaimonians and the mercenaries, who served with Klearkhos. 6. On the other side, about 3,000 of Kyros' soldiers fell, but none of the Greeks, they say, was killed, although a few were wounded.

Arrhidaios urges Klearkhos to join him and plan escape

7. When night was over, Arrhidaios, the man who had fled to the staging-post, sent men to Klearkhos, encouraging him to bring his soldiers over to him and to try together to make an escape to places on the coast. For, since Kyros was now dead and the King's forces had the upper hand, a huge concern weighed upon those who had dared to join a campaign aimed at removing Artaxerxes from his throne.

The King demands submission from the Greeks

25.1. So Klearkhos summoned the generals and the other commanders and began a discussion about their circumstances. While they were engaged in

---

176 Named Mithridates by Ktesias (Plut. *Artax.* 11.3), although in his version the final blow was struck by an anonymous Kaunian (*Artax.* 11.6) or, according to Deinon, a Karian (*Artax.* 10.3).
177 Between 10 p.m. and midnight.
178 Plutarch (*Artax.* 13.3) cites Ktesias as saying that the number of dead on the Persian side was reported to be 9,000, but that he (Ktesias) personally reckoned the figure was 20,000.

this, ambassadors from the King arrived, the headman of whom was a Greek, by name Phalynos, a Zakynthian.[179] Once introduced into the Assembly, they made a speech, saying: "King Artaxerxes says: Since I am victorious and have killed Kyros, surrender your weapons and come to my doors [i.e. palace], to find out in what way you may win me over and achieve some good result."[180] 2. After these men had delivered their message, each of the generals gave a reply, similar in vein to the one Leonidas gave at the time when he was guarding the pass at Thermopylai and Xerxes sent messengers ordering him to hand over his weapons. 3. For, at that time Leonidas told them to take [this message] back to the King: "We believe that, even if we become the King's friends, we would be better allies if we were armed, but if we have to go to war against him, we shall make a better contest of it with them in our hands."[181] 4. After Klearkhos had given a rather similar response to the demands, Proxenos, the Theban, said: "Now that we have lost just about everything else, all we have left is our courage and our weapons. So, we believe that, if we keep hold of our weapons, our courage also will be of use to us, but, if we hand our weapons over, not even our courage will help us." Consequently, he instructed them to say to the King, that, "If he is planning to do us any harm, with our weapons we shall fight him for the common good."[182] 5. Sophilos, one of the commanders, is also reported to have said that he was amazed at the King's words. "For," he said, " if he thinks he is stronger than the Greeks, let him come with his army and take our weapons from us, but if he prefers to use persuasion, let him state what worthy favour he will give us in return for them." 6. Next Sokrates, the Akhaian, spoke, saying: "The King is certainly dealing with us in a very surprising manner. For, the things that he wants to take from us he demands right away, while he bids us agree to ask him later what he will give in return. In short, if in ignorance of who are the true victors he bids us do what he orders like defeated men, let him come with his whole army and learn to whom the victory belongs, but if in full knowledge that we are the victors he is playing false, how will we trust him

The Greek generals reject the King's demand

---

179 An expert on military tactics. See Xen. *Anab*. 2.1.7.
180 Virtually word for word for Xen. *Anab*. 2.1.8.
181 A slightly abbreviated version of the response attributed to Leonidas at 11.5.5, although not recorded by Herodotos. A different response ("Come and take them") is attributed to Leonidas by Plutarch, *Moralia*, 225D.
182 "Over the good things that are common" is the reading of all manuscripts and preserved by Bonnet, but has occasioned serious doubts. Vögel in the Teubner assumes a *lacuna* after "fight him" and Oldfather in the Loeb reads "over the good things that are his" on the basis of *Anab*. 2.1.12.

The Greeks join the troops at the staging-post, where together they plan their escape to the coast

about his future promises?"[183] 7. Such, then, were the kinds of replies that the messengers carried away with them when they departed. But Klearkhos and his men moved off to the staging-post, to which the remainder of the army that had survived had retreated. When all the army was gathered there, they began to take counsel together about the route they should take for their way back to the coast. 8. In their deliberation, they made a decision not to return by the same way they had come. For, much of it was desert, in which they did not think they would be able to get supplies, especially when they were being pursued by an enemy force. So, resolving to travel via Paphlagonia, they set out for Paphlagonia with the army, making their way in a leisurely fashion, as one would when collecting supplies at the same time.

The King pursues the Greeks, but ends up agreeing to a truce

26.1. The King was by now recovered from his wound and, when he learned that his enemy was marching off, thinking this meant they were running away, he set out after them with his army at full speed. 2. He caught up with them, because they were travelling slowly, but, since it was already nighttime, pitched his camp close by. At daybreak, however, when the Greeks drew up their forces in battle formation, he sent messengers and negotiated a temporary truce for three days.[184] 3. During this period both sides came to an agreement on the following terms: the King would guarantee them safe passage, give them guides to lead them to the coast and supply them with a market as they travelled; for their part, the mercenaries under Klearkhos and all those with Arrhidaios would traverse the King's territory without doing any damage.[185] 4. Following this agreement, the Greeks went about their journey, while the King led his army back to Babylon. There, he handed out appropriate honours to each of those who had demonstrated bravery in the battle,[186] but deemed Tissaphernes

They negotiate an agreement to let the Greeks and allies retreat to the coast provided they do no harm en route

The King rewards Tissaphernes

---

183 Xenophon's account of this incident is at *Anab.* 2.1.10–23. It is far more detailed and different in many ways. For example, in Xenophon Klearkhos absents himself for most of the time and only returns at the end to bandy words with Phalynos. Also, Proxenos is given the speech that Diod. assigns to Sophilos, who is not even mentioned by Xenophon, and the speech Diod. attributes to Proxenos is given in Xenophon by Theopompos, or maybe even Xenophon himself (the mss differ). Furthermore, Xenophon does not mention any speech by Sokrates the Akhaian. Not all of these differences can be put down to carelessness on Diodoros' part; some of them suggest that he had an alternative source.

184 Cf. Xen. *Anab.* 2.3.2–9, where the purpose of the truce was for the Greeks to be provided with provisions. They were taken to a market, where they stayed for three days.

185 The same terms are reported by Xenophon, *Anab.* 2.3.26–29, but Xenophon also details the preceding negotiations that were conducted between Klearkhos and Tissaphernes (*Anab.* 2.3.17–25). Diod. omits the intervening period.

186 The handing out of rewards and punishments by the King is described in detail by Plutarch (*Artax.* 14). Plutarch's account does not mention Tissaphernes.

to have been the most courageous of all. Consequently, he showered him with numerous gifts and, moreover, gave him his daughter in marriage[187] and for the future continued treating him as his most loyal friend. In addition, he put him in charge of the coastal satrapies that Kyros had commanded.[188] 5. Now, Tissaphernes, observing that the King was angry at the Greeks, promised him that he would eliminate them all, provided that the King gave him the [necessary] forces and patched up his differences with Arrhidaios, since he was confident that that was the man who would betray the Greeks during the march.[189] The King was pleased to hear what he said and allowed him to select as many of the best troops from the whole army as he chose. 6. […] to/for/with the other generals in particular[190] to come to hear what he had to say face-to-face. Consequently almost all the generals[191] and about twenty of the unit commanders went together with Klearkhos to meet Tissaphernes. Also, about 200 of the rank and file, who wanted to go to market, tagged along. 7. Tissaphernes invited the generals into his tent, while the unit commanders waited outside by the doors. After a little while, when a red flag had been raised from his tent, Tissaphernes had the generals inside arrested, while men who had been delegated to the task fell upon the unit commanders and killed them. Yet others did away with the soldiers who had come for the market. Only one[192] of those managed to flee to his own camp and reveal the disaster.[193]

Tissaphernes is appointed to pursue the Greeks

Tissaphernes invites the Greek generals to a meeting, where they are arrested

27.1. When the soldiers learned what had happened, for the time being they panicked and all rushed to arms in great disarray, since they were leaderless. But later, since no one came to bother them, they chose new generals for themselves and gave the overall command to one amongst these, namely Kheirisophos the

After initial panic the Greeks choose new generals and proceed

187 This is incorrect. Tissaphernes is not recorded as having married a daughter of the King. It was Orontes, satrap of Armenia, who married Artaxerxes' daughter, Rhodogune, at this time (Xen. *Anab.* 2.4.8; Plut. *Artax.* 27.7).
188 Cf. Xen. *Hell.* 3.1.3.
189 Diod. does not mention Arrhidaios again, even though he did in fact betray the Greeks (*Anab.* 2.6.35–40).
190 There is a textual difficulty here. Two manuscripts indicate a gap in the text (*lacuna*), maybe as long as a line. Suggested restorations are "When Tissaphernes caught up with the Greeks he sent word for Klearkhos *and* for …" (Oldfather) or "Tissaphernes then proposed to Klearkhos *and* to …" (Bonnet, followed by Green). The sense is probably on the right lines, but the grammar is not. The Greek particle (γε) is never a connective ("and"). It emphasizes or limits, hence my translation "in particular." It also tends to position itself near the beginning of a sentence or phrase.
191 According to Xenophon, *Anab.* 2.5.31, the generals were five: Proxenos, Menon, Agias, Klearkhos and Sokrates. He gives his personal appraisal of each in *Anab.* 2.6.1–30.
192 Nikarkhos, an Arkadian (*Anab.* 2.5.33).
193 For a detailed account of this whole incident see Xen. *Anab.* 2.5.2–27.

Tissaphernes sends the generals to the King and sets off in pursuit of the Greeks

Lakedaimonian.¹⁹⁴ 2. These generals organized the army for the march in the manner that they thought best and led them on into Paphlagonia. As for Tissaphernes, he put the generals in bonds and sent them off to Artaxerxes, who had them all put to death, with the single exception of Menon. He let him go, since he alone seemed ready to betray the Greeks on account of his disputes with the allies.¹⁹⁵ 3. Tissaphernes followed the Greeks very closely with his army, but he did not dare to confront them in face-to-face combat, from fear of the reckless boldness of desperate men. So, although he harassed them when the terrain was suitable, he was not able to inflict any serious damage. He continued following them with little effect until he reached the territory of the people called Kardoukhoi.

The Greeks take seven days to traverse the territory of the Kardoukhoi, suffering losses

4. Then, Tissaphernes, because he was no longer able to be effective, moved off with his army in the direction of Ionia. The Greeks spent seven days traversing the mountainous territory of the Kardoukhoi, during which they suffered much hardship at the hands of the locals, who were both brave fighters and familiar with the terrain. 5. They were an independent people, who were enemies of the King and spent time practising their military skills.¹⁹⁶ They devoted their greatest effort in training how to throw the biggest possible stones with slings and to handle huge arrows. By means of these weapons they kept on wounding the Greeks from high ground, killing many and inflicting serious injury on not a few. 6. For, their missiles were more than two cubits¹⁹⁷ long and pierced through shields and breastplates, so that no armour was strong enough to withstand their force. Indeed, it is reported that the arrows they used were so long that the Greeks would throw back the discharged missiles, using them as javelins by fitting thongs to them.¹⁹⁸ 7. So, after traversing with difficulty the aforementioned territory, they reached the river Kentrites,¹⁹⁹ crossing which they entered Armenia. The satrap [governor] of Armenia was Tiribazos. They concluded a truce with him²⁰⁰ and so passed through the territory on friendly terms.²⁰¹

---

194 Diod. ignores Xenophon's dramatic emergence on the scene at *Anab.* 3.1.4 and his subsequent leadership role.
195 This was not just the King's view, but was held by Menon's Greek colleagues (*Anab.* 2.5.28; 2.6.21–29). That he was a guest-friend (*xenos*) of the King is confirmed by Plato, *Menon*, 78D, a dialogue in which he is the central character. Despite this relationship, the King tortured him to death a year later (*Anab.* 2.5.29).
196 Cf. Xen. *Anab.* 3.5.16.
197 About 3 feet or 91 cm.
198 Cf. Xen. *Anab.* 4.2.27–28.
199 A tributary of the Tigris that separated the territory of the Kardoukhoi from Armenia.
200 Cf. *Anab.* 4.4.6.
201 Not entirely, since Tiribazos played them false (*Anab.* 4.4.18–22).

28.1. As they were making their way through the mountains of Armenia, they were caught by a snowstorm, in which the whole army was at risk of perishing. There came a disturbance in the air, after which the snow began to fall from the sky, at first only little by little, so that it did not in any way impede the travellers in their progress, but later, when the wind got up, it fell ever more rapidly and covered the ground, so that it was no longer possible to see the road or even distinguish the particular characteristics of the terrain. 2. As a result, dismay and fear overcame the soldiers, since they were unwilling to turn back into certain destruction,[203] but unable to go forward because of the massive snowfall. As the storm increased in intensity, a huge wind came up accompanied by much hail, so that with the gusts blowing in their faces the whole army was forced to come to a halt. For, since they were unable to endure the hardship of the march, each man was forced to stop wherever he happened to be. 3. And so, lacking basic supplies, they all stuck it out without shelter through that day and night, suffering greatly. For, because of the mass of the continuously falling snow, all their weapons were covered and their bodies were frozen stiff by the frost in the air. And their overwhelming sufferings prevented them from getting any sleep all night long. Some found succour in lighting fires, but others, whose bodies were overtaken by the frost, gave up all hope of rescue, since almost all their extremities were dying of frostbite. 4. And so, when night had passed, most of the beasts of burden were found to have perished and many of the men were dead also, while not a few were unable to move their limbs because of the frost, although they were still conscious. Some even lost the sight in their eyes on account of the cold and the glare from the snow. 5. Indeed, all of them would eventually have died, had they not moved a little forward and found some villages that were loaded with supplies. These villages had underground passages dug out for the beasts of burden, and other [passages] for the people [which they accessed] by ladders....[204] <And in> the houses the cattle were nourished by fodder, and there was a great abundance of the necessities of life for the people.

In Armenia the Greeks are caught in a snowstorm and many die[202]

They finally take refuge in some well-provided villages

---

202 The following chapter is an abbreviated version of Xenophon's account in *Anab.* 4.4.7–4.6.3, although with a greater emphasis on the weather, especially its demoralizing effects, and ignoring the interaction between the Greeks and the villagers.
203 Because they were being followed by Tiribazos' army, which Diod. fails to mention.
204 Something seems to have fallen out of the text here, but the sense can be re-created from *Anab.* 4.5.25, upon which this passage is based.

After eight days in these villages the Greeks march to the river Phasis

The Greeks march on to Gymnasia

The ruler of Gymnasia gives them guides to lead them towards the sea

The Greeks give thanks to the gods and raise cairns as a memorial

After a ceremonial exchange of spears the Greeks march peacefully through the land of the Makrones

29.1. After staying in the villages for eight days, they moved on and reached the river Phasis.[205] There they spent a full four days before proceeding on through the territory of the Khaoi[206] and the Phasians. When the locals attacked them, they defeated them in battle and killed many.[207] After that, they seized their properties that were loaded with goods and lived in them for fifteen days. 2. Moving on from there, in seven days they passed through the territory named after the Khaldaians[208] and arrived at the river called Harpagos,[209] which was four *plethra* wide. Travelling on from there through the lands of the Skytini, they marched along a road that crossed a plain, where for three days they revived themselves, well provided with all they needed. Moving on again after that, on the fourth day they arrived at a large city, called Gymnasia.[210] 3. There, the ruler of that region made a truce with them and arranged for guides to lead the way to the sea. Reaching Mt Khenion[211] in fifteen days,[212] the men at the front of the march caught sight of the sea and, when they did so, they were overjoyed and created such a noise that those in the rear assumed that there was an enemy attack and ran to their weapons. 4. But, when they all got up to the place from which it was possible to see the sea, they raised their hands and gave thanks to the gods, in the belief that they had already reached safety. After gathering together a mass of stones into one place and forming great cairns out of them, they dedicated some spoils that they had taken from the barbarians, because they wished to leave behind an undying memorial of their march.[213] And they made a gift of a silver bowl and a Persian robe[214] to the guide, who then took his leave, after showing them the way to the Makrones. 5. When the Greeks entered the territory of the Makrones, they concluded a

205 This is not the river Phasis (modern Rioni) that flows into the Black Sea at Poti (ancient Phasis) in Georgia (ancient Kolkhis), but the upper reaches of the Araxes (Aras), which rises at Erzurum in Turkey and flows eastward into the Caspian.
206 Cf. Xen. *Anab.* 4.6.5, where they are called Taokhoi. Diod.'s spelling Khaoi is closer to the Taoi attributed to Sophainetos by Stephanos of Byzantion (*s.v.* Taoi). See Introduction under Sources.
207 Rather a bland, formulaic (cf. below at 29.6) representation of the vivid description by Xenophon, *Anab.* 4.7.1–14.
208 Xenophon, *Anab.* 4.7.15, names them Khalybes and calls them the "bravest people the Greeks encountered."
209 Called the Harpasos by Xenophon, *Anab.* 4.7.18.
210 Gymnias in Xen. *Anab.* 4.7.19.
211 Thekhes in Xen. *Anab.* 4.7.21.
212 On the fifth day, according to Xen. *Anab.* 4.7.21.
213 This famous scene is memorably described by Xenophon at *Anab.* 4.7.21–24. A potential cairn has recently been identified on the top of Deveboynu Tepe. For a personal account and a picture see Waterfield (2006), 151–153.
214 Plus a horse and ten Darics, according to Xenophon, *Anab.* 4.7.27.

truce and, as a pledge of good faith, they received from them a spear of barbarian type, while they themselves gave a Greek one in return. The barbarians said that this practice had been handed down to them from their ancestors as the strongest assurance of good faith.[215] Then, when they had passed across their borders, they arrived in the territory of the Kolkhians.[216] 6. There the people of the region gathered in force against them, but the Greeks defeated them in battle and killed many. After taking possession of a hill as a stronghold, they began plundering the land. Then, bringing their booty onto this hill, they revived themselves with an abundance of supplies.

Attacked by the Kolkhians, the Greeks defeat them, kill many and plunder their land

30.1. In this region there were to be found very many beehives which produced a much valued type of honey. Those who tasted it encountered a strange experience. The ones who partook lost consciousness, fell to the ground and behaved as though they were dead. 2. Since many ate [the honey] on account of the sweetness of its taste, the number of those who fell to the ground soon resembled a defeat in battle. Indeed, for the whole of that day the army was in a state of dismay, scared by the unexpected occurrence and the number of those who had experienced this misfortune. But, about the same hour of the next day they all revived and stood up, regaining their mental faculties little by little; their physical state was like that of men who had recovered from drinking a drug.[218] 3. They spent three days reviving themselves and then marched on to Trapezous,[219] a Greek city, a colony of the Sinopeans, that was situated in the land of the Kolkhians. There they stayed for thirty days, enjoying the splendid hospitality of the local inhabitants. They made sacrifice to Herakles

Many Greek soldiers are overcome by the effects of miel fou[217]

After recovering, the Greeks march on to Trapezous

---

215 The practice of exchanging armour or weapons as a token of good faith was not unknown to the Greeks, as exemplified by the exchanges in the *Iliad* between Diomedes and Glaukos (*Iliad*, 6.230-233) and Hektor and Ajax (*Iliad*, 7.303-305).
216 The Kolkhoi were a people who lived just south of Trapezous and are not to be confused with the people of Kolkhis at the eastern end of the Black Sea. See n. 221.
217 *Miel fou* or *Deli Bal* is honey produced from the pollen of the *rhododendron ponticum* or *luteum*. Its potency is the result of a type of neurotoxin (called grayanotoxin) in its nectar. It is particularly associated with the region of Turkey south of Trapezous, from where it was later exported to Europe in the eighteenth century to add potency to beer. This is the first recorded case of its effects, which became famous (Pliny, *NH*, 21.77) and are now well documented.
218 Although Diod. manages to compress the seven books of Xenophon's *Anabasis* into thirteen chapters, he devotes as much space to this incident as does Xenophon (*Anab.* 4.8.20-21). Here, as in ch. 28, his interest is caught by the demoralizing effect of the natural world upon humans.
219 Trapezous and Sinope were both settled by Milesians in the seventh century BC. Much later, after the sack of Constantinople by the Fourth Crusade in AD 1204, Trapezous was taken over by the Komnenoi and became the breakaway kingdom of Trebizond, until it was overcome by Mehmet II in 1261. Today it is the Turkish city of Trabzon.

Kheirisophos is sent to Byzantion for ships

and to Zeus the Saviour[220] and held an athletic contest, on the very spot where people say the Argo sailed in with Jason and his companions.[221] 4. From there they sent Kheirisophos, their commander, off to Byzantion in search of transport boats and triremes, because he said that he was a friend of Anaxibios, the [Spartan] *navarch* in Byzantion.[222] Him they sent off in a swift cutter, while they got two little oared boats[223] from the Trapezountines, which they used to plunder the neighbouring barbarians both by land and by sea. 5. Then, they waited for Kheirisophos for thirty days, but since he kept on delaying and food supplies for the men were becoming scarce, they moved on from Trapezous and within three days arrived at Kerasous,[224] a Greek city that was a colony of the Sinopeans. After spending a few days[225] there, they [went on and] reached the tribe of the Mossynoikians. 6. When the barbarians formed up against them, they overcame them in battle and killed many.[226] And, when the Mossynoikians fled for refuge to a place in which they lived, where they had towers made of wood that were seven storeys high,[227] the Greeks made successive assaults [upon it] and took it by force. This place was the metropolis of their other strongholds, and their king lived there on the highest spot. 7. It is their ancestral custom for the king to stay in it all his life and to issue edicts to his subjects from there.[228] The soldiers said that this was the most barbarous tribe they had passed through; that they have sexual intercourse with their women in full view of everyone; that the children of the wealthiest are raised on boiled nuts and that all of them from childhood on are tattooed with designs on their back and chest.[229] So they travelled through this territory in eight days and through the next, which was called Tibarene, in three.

The Greeks move on overland and are attacked by the Mossynoikians

After defeating the Mossynoikians, they attack their stronghold

The barbarous habits of the Mossynoikians

220 Fulfilling a vow made at the beginning of the retreat. Cf. *Anab.* 3.2.9.
221 Diod. seems here to be confusing the Kolkhoi near Trapezous with Kolkhis at the eastern end of the Black Sea, where Jason and the Argonauts were traditionally believed to have landed. Cf. n. 216.
222 Cf. *Anab.* 5.1.4, where Kheirisophos proposes the idea.
223 Cf. *Anab.* 5.1.15–16, where the boats are specified as (1), a fifty-oared ship that was allocated to the Lakonian Dexippos, who promptly sailed away, and (2) a thirty-oared vessel allocated to Polykrates, an Athenian, which brought in much plunder.
224 See Map 7.
225 Ten, according to Xenophon, *Anab.* 5.3.2.
226 Another formulaic expression, ignoring the detailed account in *Anab.* 5.4.1–26, where one group of Mossynoikians sides with the Greeks against the dominant faction.
227 These towers were called *mossynes*, after which the people were named.
228 This goes beyond Xenophon's statement (*Anab.* 5.4.26) that the king refused to leave his tower when the stronghold was captured and was consequently burned to death.
229 An abbreviated version of *Anab.* 5.4.27–34. Diodoros highlights only three of the many unusual customs of the Mossynoikians, which Xenophon describes as "the most different from Greek customs."

31.1. From there they reached the Greek city of Kotyôra, a colony of Sinope. They stayed there for fifty days,[230] plundering the neighbouring Paphlagonians and the other barbarians.[231] Then, the people of Herakleia and Sinope sent them transport boats, by which they and their equipment were carried across [to Sinope]. 2. Sinope was a Milesian colony, situated on Paphlagonian territory, and held in the highest repute in that region. In fact, it was there that in our time[232] Mithridates,[233] the man who made war against the Romans, had his biggest palaces. 3. At Sinope there also arrived Kheirisophos, the man who had been sent off in search of triremes. He had been unsuccessful. Despite that, the Sinopeans gave them friendly hospitality and sent them on by sea to Herakleia,[234] which was a Megarian colony. The whole fleet dropped anchor off the Akherousian peninsula, the place where Herakles, according to tradition, brought up Kerberos from Hades.[235] 4. From there, as they marched through Bithynia,[236] they encountered dangers, since the natives dogged their footsteps along the whole route. So, it was with difficulty that the remaining 8,300 survivors[237] of the 10,000 made their way to safety at Khrysopolis[238] in Khalkedonia. 5. From there on, some easily made their way safely home to their native lands, while the remainder collected in the Khersonesos and plundered the

At Kotyôra the Greeks acquire transport ships

Sinope, colony of Miletos, was the base for Mithridates

Kheirisophos returns without ships; the Sinopeans transport them to Herakleia

The Greeks finally reach Khrysopolis on the Bosporos

---

230 Forty-five days according to Xenophon (*Anab.* 5.5.5).
231 This is hardly an accurate representation of the difficult relations described by Xenophon at *Anab.* 5.5.6-24. The Kotyôrans denied the Greeks a market. In return the Greeks plundered their land, which led to the intervention of Sinope and some lengthy negotiations.
232 An indication that Diodoros was alive some time during the reign of Mithridates.
233 Mithridates VI was born in Sinope about 135 BC. He was ruler of the kingdom of Pontos in one form or another from the death of his father, Mithridates V, in 120 until his defeat by Lucullus and Pompey in 66, and died in Pantikapaion in 63. He made Sinope his capital. His expansive ambition round the Black Sea, in Greece and in Asia Minor brought him into conflict with Rome, against whom he fought three wars (89-66).
234 No doubt eager to be rid of such a large, unruly force.
235 The Akherousian peninsula (modern Cape Baba) is north of Herakleia. There is a huge cave there, around which grew up the story of Herakles and Kerberos referred to here. Cf. *Anab.* 6.2.2 and Apollonios of Rhodes, *Argonautika*, 2.734-736.
236 Diod. fails to mention that the Greeks broke into three groups, only one of which, led by Kheirisophos, went overland all the way to Kalpe Harbour, where the three sections reunited. Cf *Anab.* 6.2.16-6.3.26.
237 This number is certainly too high and is contradicted by Diod. himself at 14.37.1. When the soldiers were reviewed at Kerasous, there were already only 8,600 (*Anab.* 5.3.3). At Herakleia Xenophon (*Anab.* 6.2.16) details the number in each of the three groups when they separated, and the total was only 7,400. And the Greeks suffered numerous losses between there and Khrysopolis, e.g. 500 alone in a skirmish with Pharnabazos and some Bithynians (*Anab.* 6.4.24).
238 Khrysopolis was on the Asian side of the Bosporos, just above Khalkedon and opposite Byzantion. Their arrival belongs in the autumn of 400.

neighbouring territory of the Thracians.²³⁹ Such, then, was the conclusion of Kyros' campaign against Artaxerxes.

404/3–401/0: *Return to the tyranny at Athens*²⁴⁰
In Athens the Thirty Tyrants put many to death. In response Thrasyboulos seizes Phyle

The Thirty mount an abortive attack on Phyle

The Thirty move the disenfranchised Athenians to the Peiraieus. They also kill the males of Eleusis and Salamis

32.1. The Thirty Tyrants, who held power in Athens, were continuously exiling or killing people day by day. And the Thebans, because they were angered at what was happening, welcomed the exiles warmly. So, Thrasyboulos, the Steirian as he was called,²⁴¹ an Athenian who had been driven into exile by the Thirty, with the secret assistance of the Thebans seized a place in Attica called Phyle.²⁴² This was a very strong fort that was only 100 *stades*²⁴³ from Athens, so that it provided them with many opportunities for attack. 2. When the Thirty Tyrants learned of this event, their first response was to lead out their forces against them, so as to put the place under siege. But, while they were encamped near Phyle, a large snowfall occurred. 3. And, when some began to attempt to move their tents, the majority assumed they were running away and that some hostile army was at hand. So, a confusion that is commonly called Panic descended upon the army and they moved camp to another location.²⁴⁴ 4. And the Thirty, seeing that those citizens in Athens who were not included in the constitution of the Three Thousand²⁴⁵ were being roused up to bring about the end of their rule, transferred them to the Peiraieus and kept the city under strict control by means of mercenaries. They also brought the charge of siding with the exiles against the men of Eleusis and Salamis and put them all

---

239 Under the command of Xenophon. Their number was 5,000 according to Diod. (14.37.1) or 6,000 according to Xenophon (*Anab*. 7.7.23).

240 Having followed the theme of Kyros' campaign to its conclusion, Diodoros decides to pick up his account of Athenian affairs where he left off in 404/3 at ch. 6. This is an example of the difficulty of trying to blend a source that wrote by theme (*kata genos*) with a chronological structure.

241 All Athenians were known by their patronymic (father's name) and their demotic (deme name). So, Thrasyboulos was "son of Lykos, of the deme Steiria." He was wealthy enough to be a trierarch in 411/0 and 406/5, but the source of his wealth is unknown. Nevertheless, his democratic credentials were impeccable.

242 The fort at Phyle was located in the Parnes range on the border between Attica and Boiotia. See Map 1. Diod. follows Xenophon in putting the seizure of Phyle after the murder of Theramenes, in disagreement with Aristotle. Cf. n. 35.

243 11⅓ miles or 18.24 km.

244 Panic is named after the god Pan. For this incident, cf. Xen. *Hell*. 2.4.2–3, although the psychological reference to Panic is lacking. It probably reflects Diodoros' own interest in natural or non-human causation. See Introduction.

245 The Three Thousand were those registered to vote by the Thirty (Xen. *Hell*. 2.3.18; Aristotle, *AP* 36). All others were excluded from the franchise and liable to summary execution by the Thirty (*AP* 37.1). Xenophon (*Hell*. 2.4.1) says all except the Three Thousand were forbidden to enter the city and, driven from their estates, they fled to the Peiraieus, from where they were also expelled.

to death.²⁴⁶ 5. While this was going on, many of those who were in exile rushed to join Thrasyboulos' party.²⁴⁷ <So, the Thirty sent an embassy to him>, on the face of it to hold discussions about some prisoners, but secretly to advise him to dissolve his band of exiles and to join with themselves in ruling the city, elected to the position held by Theramenes. They also bade him take advantage of the ability [which they were offering] to restore to their homeland any ten exiles he should choose. 6. For his part, Thrasyboulos replied that he preferred his present exile to rule with the Thirty and said that he would not put an end to the war unless all the citizens were allowed to return home and unless the People regained their ancestral constitution.²⁴⁸ So, the Thirty, seeing that many were defecting from their side out of hatred and that the number of exiles was growing bigger every day, sent ambassadors to Sparta to ask for assistance,²⁴⁹ while they themselves gathered as many men as they could and set up camp in the open air near the place called Akharnai.²⁵⁰

As many join Thrasyboulos at Phyle, the Thirty try to get him to join them

Thrasyboulos rejects this advance, so the Thirty march out against him and camp near Akharnai

33.1. Thrasyboulos left behind an adequate garrison for the fort and led out his army of exiles, which numbered 1,200. By making a surprise nighttime attack on the enemy's encampment and killing many, he struck fear into the rest by this unexpected action and forced them to flee back to Athens.²⁵¹ 2. Immediately after the battle Thrasyboulos set out for the Peiraieus and took possession of Mounykhia, an uninhabited hill that was a strong position.²⁵² Then, the tyrants went down to the Peiraieus in full force and attacked Mounykhia with Kritias in charge. The battle was hard-fought and went on for a long time,²⁵³ because the tyrants were superior in numbers, while the exiles had

Thrasyboulos defeats the Thirty in battle at Akharnai

Thrasyboulos captures Mounykhia hill. The Thirty attack, but are defeated

246 Xenophon narrates this incident at *Hell.* 2.4.8–10 without mentioning the Salaminians. Eleusis was to be a place of refuge for the oligarchs in case of defeat. In fact, that is what it became under the terms of the Reconciliation Agreement (*AP* 39). Aristotle does not mention the execution of the Eleusinians and tacitly denies it by reference to the process whereby emigrating exiles had to negotiate purchase of houses with Eleusinian citizens (*AP* 39.3). The Agreement or Settlement is discussed by Krentz (1982), 102–108.
247 According to Xenophon (*Hell.* 2.4.2), the original group that seized Phyle was seventy strong. These men were singled out for special honours after the restoration of Democracy. See *SEG* LXII, no. 50; *TDGR2*, no. 7. Gradually the number had increased to about 700, according to Xenophon (*Hell.* 2.4.5) or 1,200 in Diod. (14.33.1).
248 No other source mentions this offer by the Thirty or Thrasyboulos' rejection.
249 Cf. Aristotle, *AP* 37.2, where, however, it is made the occasion for sending the Spartan garrison under Kallibios, although that had been in Athens since the beginning of the tyranny according to Diod. (14.4.4) and Xenophon (*Hell.* 2.3.14).
250 Spring 403. For the location of Akharnai, see Map 1.
251 Cf. Xen. *Hell.* 2.4.5–7.
252 For the strategic location of the hill of Mounykhia see Map 2.
253 A formulaic description of a battle in Diodoros.

Thrasyboulos captures the Peiraieus

The men in the city depose the Thirty and replace them with the Ten

Pausanias, king of Sparta, negotiates a reconciliation

the advantage in the strength of their location. 3. In the end, after Kritias had fallen, the men on the side of the Thirty panicked and ran back down to more level terrain, where the exiles did not dare to march down against them.[254] After that, since many were defecting to the side of the exiles, Thrasyboulos and his men made a sudden attack upon the enemy and, by defeating them in battle, gained control of the Peiraieus.[255] 4. Right away, many of the people in the city, being eager to get rid of the tyranny, poured into the Peiraieus. In addition, all the exiles who had been scattered amongst the cities, hearing of the successes of Thrasyboulos' faction, came to the Peiraieus and from that time on the exiles' forces were far superior in number. 5. The men in the city put an end to the rule of the Thirty and sent them out of the city. They then appointed ten men with full authority to bring an end to the war in a most amicable manner, if they could. But these men, once they had assumed power, ignored these instructions, and, showing themselves to be tyrants, sent for forty ships and 1,000 soldiers from Lakedaimon, under the command of Lysander.[256] 6. But, Pausanias, king of the Lakedaimonians, because he was jealous of Lysander and because he perceived that Sparta was in bad repute amongst the Greeks,[257] marched out with a large force and, once arrived at Athens, reconciled the men in the city with the exiles.[258] In this way the Athenians recovered their homeland and for the future governed themselves by their own laws. And they allowed those who were concerned that they might suffer some harm as a result of their succession of wrongdoings to go away and live in Eleusis.[259]

---

254 This important battle for the Peiraieus is described in more detail by Xenophon at *Hell.* 2.4.10–23. See also Aristotle, *AP* 38.1. Those involved on the democratic side in this battle and a subsequent one against Pausanias were honoured in a large decree in the archonship of Xenainetos (401/0). See R&O, no. 4.

255 This second engagement is not mentioned by Xenophon and is unnecessary.

256 Cf. Lysias 12, *Against Eratosthenes*, 58 and Aristotle, *AP* 38.1, although Aristotle goes on uniquely to claim that this board of Ten was deposed and replaced by another of the same number (*AP* 38.3). Xenophon, on the other hand, states that it was the Thirty in Eleusis and the Three Thousand who sent to Sparta for help and that it was Lysander who supported the request. The Spartans also loaned the oligarchs some money (*AP* 38.1), specified as 100 talents by Xenophon (*Hell.* 2.4.28), Lysias (12, *Against Eratosthenes,* 59), Plutarch (*Lys.* 21.4) and Isokrates (7, *Areopagitikos,* 68).

257 Cf. Xen. *Hell.* 2.4.29–30. The disapproving Greek states were Corinth and Thebes.

258 This version, rather casually, like the account in *AP* 38.4, neglects to mention the battle that was fought between Pausanias and the men in the Peiraieus (*Hell.* 2.4.30–38).

259 The Reconciliation took place in the archonship of Eukleides (403/2), probably early in his term in Boedromion. Part of the terms of the Reconciliation Agreement are given by Aristotle, *AP* 39.1–6. See also Xen. *Hell.* 2.4.38. The holdouts in Eleusis were later overcome and re-integrated into the citizen-body according to Xenophon, *Hell.* 2.4.43, and Aristotle, *AP* 40.4, who provides the date (archonship of Xenainetos, 401/0).

34.1. The Eleians, fearing the greater strength of the Lakedaimonians, brought an end to their war against them, on the condition that they surrender their triremes to the Lakedaimonians and allow their neighbouring cities to live by their own laws.[261] 2. And the Lakedaimonians, now that they had brought their wars to an end and were uninvolved, made a campaign against the Messenians, some of whom lived in a fortress on Kephallenia, while others inhabited Naupaktos amongst the Western Lokrians, a gift of the Athenians.[262] Driving them out from these places, they gave back the fortresses, one to the people who lived in Kephallenia, the other to the Lokrians. 3. The Messenians were driven out from everywhere because of the ages-old hatred of the Spartiates. Taking their weapons, they quit Greece. Some sailed to Sicily and became mercenary troops for Dionysios,[263] but about 3,000 sailed to Kyrene[264] and aligned themselves with the exiles there. 4. For, at that time the Kyrenaians were in a state of tumult, since Ariston and some others had seized the city. Only recently 500 of the most powerful Kyrenaians had been eliminated, while the most respected men that remained had been exiled. 5. In spite of that, the exiles, adding the Messenians to their number, went to battle against those who had seized the city. While many of the Kyrenaians fell on both sides, the Messenians perished almost to a man. 6. After the engagement the Kyrenaians sent ambassadors to each other and brought about a reconciliation. Right then and there they swore oaths not to bear grudges for the past and settled down together in the city. 7. About the same time the Romans added settlers to the place called Velitrae.[265]

Sparta overcomes Elis and expels the Messenians from Kephallenia and Naupaktos[260]

Some of the Messenians go to Sicily, some to Kyrene where they die in the civil war

The Romans add settlers to Velitrae

35.1. Once this year had come to an end, Lakhes became archon at Athens, while in Rome military tribunes administered the consular power: [they were] Manius Claudius, Marcus Quinctius, Lucius Julius, Marcus Furius and Lucius

400/399: Book 14.35.1–37.7

---

260 Diod. is picking up his narrative of the Eleian War, which he left off at 17.12. He has now returned to the year 401/0 (archonship of Xenainetos).
261 The terms are confirmed by Xenophon (*Hell*. 3.2.30–31) and Pausanias, 3.8.5, except that neither mentions the triremes. Confusingly, Xenophon dates the conclusion of the Eleian War to 398/7, while Pausanias puts it in the fifth century, during the Dekeleian War.
262 This gift was made after the capitulation of the Messenian Helots on Ithome during the Pentekontaetia. See Thucydides, 1.103.3; Diod. 11.84.7–8 and Pausanias, 4.24.7–25.1.
263 See 14.78.5–6.
264 Pausanias, 4.26.2.
265 Velitrae was a Volscian town in the Alban hills south of Rome. It was first captured and colonized in 494, but subsequently lost, probably in the 480s. It was re-settled in 401, as referred to here, but continued to fight Rome during the Volscian Wars of the fourth century. It was recaptured by Camillus in 367 (Plut. *Cam*. 42.1).

Artaxerxes sends Pharnabazos to Ionia to take over Kyros' satrapies

Valerius.²⁶⁶ And the ninety-fifth Olympic Games took place, in which Minos, an Athenian, won the footrace. 2. At this time Artaxerxes, King of Asia, having defeated Kyros in battle, dispatched Pharnabazos²⁶⁷ to take over control of all the coastal satrapies. As a result those satraps and cities that had fought on the side of Kyros were very worried that they would pay a penalty for their crimes against the king. 3. Now, the other satraps sent ambassadors to Tissaphernes, courted his favour and aligned their policy with his as far as they could, but Tamôs, who was the most powerful of them and was in charge of Ionia,²⁶⁸ put his possessions and all his sons onto triremes, except one called Glôs,²⁶⁹ who was sometime later to become commander of the royal forces. 4. So, Tamôs, wary of Tissaphernes, put to sea with his fleet towards Egypt, and fled for refuge to Psammetikhos, king of the Egyptians, who was a descendant of *the* Psammetikhos.²⁷⁰ On account of an act of kindness he had performed for the king in the past, Tamôs assumed that he would find him like a sort of harbour from the perils he faced from the King. 5. But Psammetikhos, disregarding the act of kindness and the holy obligation owed to suppliants, slew the man who was his suppliant and friend along with his children, just so that he could take possession of his belongings and his fleet.²⁷¹ 6. When the Greek cities throughout Asia learned that Tissaphernes was about to descend upon them, they were very worried for themselves and sent ambassadors to the Lakedaimonians, begging them not to turn a blind eye to their being destroyed by the barbarians.²⁷² The Lakedaimonians promised that they would help and sent ambassadors to Tissaphernes to tell him not to make hostile moves against the Greek cities.²⁷³ 7. But Tissaphernes, arriving with his army at the first city,

Tamôs, satrap of Ionia, flees to Psammetikhos in Egypt, who kills him

The Greek cities in Asia, fearing Tissaphernes, request help from Sparta

Tissaphernes attacks Kyme

---

266 Cf. Livy, 5.1.2, who says that this year (Varronian chronology 403) the number of tribunes was increased to eight, though his number is questioned. The names given by Livy are: Manius Aemilius Mamercus, Lucius Valerius Potitus, Appius Claudius Crassus, Marcus Quinctilius Varus, Lucius Julius Julus, Marcus Postimius, Marcus Furius Camillus, Marcus Postumius Albinus.

267 This is a careless error on Diod.'s part, present in all manuscripts. As is clear from the subsequent narrative and especially 35.6, Diodoros knew that it was Tissaphernes who was appointed governor of all the coastal satrapies. Cf. Xen. *Hell.* 3.1.3.

268 See 19.6.

269 Glôs had originally been on the side of Kyros but defected after Kounaxa (*Anab.* 2.4.24).

270 Psamtik (Psammetikhos) I (664–610) was the founder of the Twenty-sixth (Saite) Dynasty in Egypt. See Herodotos, 2.151–154.

271 Diod. expresses moral repulsion at Psammetikhos' behaviour. But the name may be wrong. Unless Psammetikhos was a rival, the legitimate ruler of Egypt at this time was Amyrtaios II (404–399).

272 Cf. Xen. *Hell.* 3.1.3.

273 This embassy is not mentioned by Xenophon.

Kyme, laid waste to the whole territory and took many prisoners. After that he bottled the Kymeans up under siege. When, however, winter was approaching and he had not been able to take the city, he gave the prisoners back for a large ransom and broke off the siege.[274]

36.1. The Lakedaimonians appointed Thibron as commander of the war against the King. They gave him a force of 1,000 citizens and told him to levy from the allies any soldiers that seemed to him serviceable.[275] 2. Thibron travelled to Corinth, from where he summoned troops from the allies. He then sailed to Ephesos with no more than 5,000 men. And, after enrolling about 2,000 more from the cities loyal to him and other ones, he marched out with a force that numbered 7,000 in total.[276] Advancing about 120 *stades* [13½ miles or 21.7 km], he came to Magnesia, which was under the control of Tissaphernes. After capturing this at the first assault, he moved on swiftly to Tralles in Ionia and attempted to take the city by siege. But he was unable to succeed because of its strong position, so he returned to Magnesia. 3. This city was unwalled and for this reason Thibron was afraid that Tissaphernes would gain possession of it once he departed, so he relocated it to a nearby hill, called Thorax.[277] Thibron then made incursions into the territory of his enemy and acquired a wealth of booty of all kinds for his soldiers. But when Tissaphernes showed up with a strong cavalry force, out of an abundance of caution he retreated to Ephesos.

37.1. About the same time, some of those men who had campaigned with Kyros and had arrived safely back in Greece dispersed to their own homelands, but the majority, almost 5,000 in number, because they were accustomed to the soldier's life, chose Xenophon as their general.[278] 2. And Xenophon, taking charge of the army, set off to fight the Thracians who live around

Thibron is sent to Asia by the Spartans and sails to Ephesos

Thibron attacks Magnesia and captures it, but fails to take Tralles. He retires to Magnesia, which he relocates

When Tissaphernes comes up with many cavalry, Thibron retreats to Ephesos

5,000 of the Greeks who campaigned with Kyros had been fighting in Thrace under the command of Xenophon. On Thibron's request they join him

---

274 Tissaphernes' assault upon and siege of Kyme are not mentioned by Xenophon. It is likely that Diod. got this information from Ephoros, whose home town was Kyme.
275 See Xenophon, *Hell.* 3.1.4, who specifies that Thibron had the title "harmost." He also describes the 1,000 troops from Sparta as *neodamodeis* (liberated helots) and adds that Thibron asked for 300 cavalry from Athens. Given the involvement of the cavalry with the oligarchs, the restored democrats were glad to send them, "thinking that for them to live and die in foreign parts would be good for the democracy."
276 See Xenophon, *Hell.* 3.1.5, who, however, does not specify the eventual total.
277 None of this is mentioned by Xenophon, who, by contrast, maintains that Thibron accomplished nothing, before he was joined by the remnants of the Ten Thousand (*Hell.* 3.1.5).
278 A rather over-compressed repetition of 14.31.4–5. The Greek forces separated at Khrysopolis. This is Diod.'s first mention of Xenophon, whom he has studiously ignored throughout the narrative of Kyros' campaigns.

Salmydessos.²⁷⁹ This city is situated on the left side of the Pontos and, because it sticks out a long way, causes many shipwrecks.²⁸⁰ 3. Moreover, the Thracians were in the habit of lying in ambush around these spots and making prisoners of the shipwrecked merchants. But Xenophon, with his assembled army, attacked their territory, defeated them in battle and set fire to most of their villages.²⁸¹ 4. Later, however, when Thibron sent for them with offers of pay, they went over to his side and joined the Lakedaimonians in making war upon the Persians.²⁸² 5. While this was going on, in Sicily, Dionysios founded a city right below the hill of Aitna and named it Adranon after a certain well-known temple.²⁸³ 6. And in Macedon, Arkhelaos,²⁸⁴ the king, was unintentionally struck with a spear by his beloved, Krateros,²⁸⁵ on a hunting expedition and quit this life, after being king for seven years. His son Orestes succeeded to the throne, but Aëropos, who was his guardian, did away with him and ruled as monarch for six years.²⁸⁶ 7. In Athens, Sokrates, the philosopher, was brought to trial by Anytos and Meletos²⁸⁷ on the charge of impiety and corruption of the young, was condemned to death, and ended his life by drinking hemlock. But, since the accusation was unjust, the People repented, seeing that a man of such

Other events of the year: Foundation of Adranon; death of Arkhelaos; condemnation and death of Sokrates

---

279 Actually, Xenophon, who had quit the expedition, had been persuaded to go to Perinthos by Anaxibios, *navarch* at Byzantion, to take charge of the mercenaries and ship them over into Asia to get them out of his territory (*Anab.* 7.2.8–9). Prevented from finding ships to do this, he accepted an offer from Seuthes, king of the Odrysians, and led the men north into the Thracian Khersonesos (*Anab.* 7.2.12–7.3.6). The attack upon Salmydessos was the last action the Greeks performed with Seuthes.

280 Cf. Xen. *Anab.* 7.5.12–13.

281 A stock description in Diod. Xenophon does not mention burning villages (*Anab.* 7.5.14).

282 Cf. *Hell.* 3.1.6. See also *Anab.* 7.6.1–7.8.24, which records the first contact up to the final juncture, via the protracted negotiations with Seuthes about pay for the soldiers and Xenophon's own lengthy speeches in self-defence. Diod. sensibly cut those out.

283 Adranon was situated at the foot of Aitna, to the south-west. Adranos was an ancient Sicilian god of fire, who was greatly revered throughout Sicily (Plut. *Tim.* 12.2) and in some traditions believed to be the father of the Palici, on whom see Diod. 11.88.6–89.8.

284 Arkhelaos I (413–399) was an illegitimate son of Perdikkas II (452–413). If Plato is correct (*Gorgias*, 471c–d), his rise to power was brought about through murder. He was, however, an effective king (Thuc. 2.100.2). He probably moved the capital from Aigai to Pella, which he made into a cultural centre. He was honoured by the Athenians in 407/6 for help with timber (see *IG* I³ 117; O&R, no. 188; *TDGR*1, no. 161).

285 The name is probably incorrect. He is called Krateuas by Aelian (*VH*, 5.8.9) and Krataias in Aristotle (*Politics*, 5.8.11.1311b), who gives a complex narrative of slighted love and makes it clear that Arkhelaos was assassinated. His death marked the beginning of a period of instability in Macedon, as descendants of the sons of Alexander I (479–452) competed for control of the throne.

286 Diod. records the death of Aëropos from illness in 385/4 at 14.84.6.

287 The prosecutors of Sokrates were three in number: Meletos for the poets, Anytos for the politicians and Lykon for the orators (Plato, *Apol.* 23e).

quality had been done away with. For that reason they became angry with his accusers and finally put them to death without trial.[288]

38.1. Once the year had come to an end, Aristokrates assumed the archonship at Athens, while in Rome six military tribunes took over the consular power: [they were] Gaius Servilius, Lucius Verginius, Quintus Sulpicius, Aulus Mutilius, Manius Sergius.[289] 2. After these men had assumed office, the Lakedaimonians, on learning that Thibron was doing a bad job of managing the war [in Asia],[290] sent out Derkylidas as general for Asia. He took over control of the army and began to campaign against the cities in the Troad. 3. And, indeed, he captured Hamaxitos, Kolonai and Arisbe[291] at the first assault, and after them Ilion, Kebrynia and all the other cities throughout the Troad, taking some by trickery, gaining possession of others by force.[292] Then, he concluded an eight-month truce with Pharnabazos[293] and directed his campaign against the Thracians, who at that time lived in Bithynia. After devastating their territory he led his troops away into winter quarters. 4. When civil discord broke out in Herakleia in Trakhis,[294] the Lakedaimonians sent out Herippidas to put affairs in order. On arrival in Herakleia, he convened an Assembly of the people, surrounded them with men at arms, arrested those responsible [for the discord] and had them put to death. They were about 500 in number. 5. And when the people who lived around Oita[295] revolted, he made war on them. After subjecting them to great suffering, he forced them to leave their land.[296] Most of

399/8: Book 14.38.1–43.5

The Spartans replace Thibron with Derkylidas, who campaigns in the Troad and Bithynia

Herippidas deals forcibly with civil discord in Herakleia in Trakhis

Herippidas makes war on the people around Mt Oita

---

288 This is probably wishful thinking on Diod.'s part. According to our main source for this outcome, Diogenes Laertios, *Lives of the Great Philosophers*, 2.43, 6.9, the Athenians did, indeed, put Meletos to death, but exiled the others. No one records the end of Lykon, but Anytos, a prominent democrat (see Davies, *APF*, no. 1324), was still active in the Athenian Assembly as late as 396 (*Hell. Oxy.* 6.2); sometime later he went, or was sent, to Herakleia on the Euxine and may have died there.

289 Although the text says six, most mss of Diod. name only five (with much variety). See Livy, 5.8.1 and the *Fasti Capitolini* (under the Varronian year 402) for the correct list: Gaius Servilius Ahala, Quintus Servilius, Lucius Verginius, Quintus Sulpicius, Aulus Manlius, Manius Sergius.

290 See Xen. *Hell.* 3.1.8. Thibron was accused of plundering by Sparta's allies, put on trial when he returned home, and executed.

291 Xenophon (*Hell.* 3.1.16) calls the third city Larisa. Arisbe is too far to the north and east to be correct.

292 An abbreviated account of Xen. *Hell.* 3.1.16–28.

293 Xen. *Hell.* 3.2.1, where, however, the time limit of eight months is not mentioned.

294 Herakleia in Trakhis was a refoundation of the former Trakhinian town of Trakhis by the Spartans in 426 (Thuc. 3.92). See Map 10.

295 Mt Oita is about 12 km west of Trakhis. The Oitaians and the Trakhinians were on hostile terms. See Map 10.

296 Neither the discord in Herakleia nor the revolt of the Oitaians is recorded by Xenophon.

Derkylidas crosses to the Khersonesos and builds a wall to keep the Thracians out

them fled to Thessaly with their wives and children. Five years later they were brought back to Oitaia.²⁹⁷ 6. At the same time as these events the Thracians invaded the Khersonesos²⁹⁸ with a vast horde and, after ravaging the whole territory, kept the cities there under siege. So, the inhabitants of the Khersonesos, worn down by the war, sent a request to Derkylidas, the Lakedaimonian, to come over from Asia. 7. And, he brought his army over and drove the Thracians out of the territory. Then, he built a wall across the Khersonesos from sea to sea. By doing this, he prevented future invasions by the Thracians and garnered for himself a shower of gifts, after which he transported his army back to Asia.²⁹⁹

Pharnabazos persuades Artaxerxes to build a fleet and put Konon in charge

Pharnabazos orders the building of 100 triremes and appoints Konon as admiral

Konon sails to Kilikia with forty ships

Derkylidas prepares for battle against Pharnabazos and Tissaphernes but agrees to a truce

39.1. After he had concluded the truce with the Lakedaimonians, Pharnabazos travelled upcountry to the King and persuaded him to equip a fleet of ships and put Konon, the Athenian, in charge. For Konon was well versed in military conflict, and especially familiar with the [present] enemy. Although he was very much a man of war, he was at leisure in Cyprus at the court of king Evagoras.³⁰⁰ After getting the King's approval, Pharnabazos took 500 *talents* of silver and got ready to build a fleet. 2. So, he sailed across to Cyprus and gave orders to the kings there to make ready 100 triremes. Then, after having a conversation with Konon about the admiralship, he appointed him commander at sea, hinting at great things he might hope for from the King. 3. And Konon accepted the command, both because he hoped to regain the supremacy for his country, if the Lakedaimonians should be defeated in war, and at the same time to acquire great distinction for himself. 4. But, since the whole fleet was not yet finished, Konon took the forty ships that were ready and sailed across to Kilikia and there began to make preparations for the war.³⁰¹ Meanwhile

---

297 All mss read "to Boiotia" here. The emendation "to Oitaia," adopted by Bonnet, was suggested by Vögel, even though he actually adopted Dindorf's emendation "by the Boiotians," which was also accepted by Oldfather.

298 What is now the Gallipoli Peninsula.

299 See Xenophon, *Hell.* 3.2.10, who specifies that the wall was 37 *stades* (c.4¼ miles or 6.8 km) long. It was not the first wall. Miltiades had built a wall from Kardia to Paktya in the sixth century (Herod. 6.36.2) and Perikles built a wall across the neck of the isthmus in 447 (Plut. *Per.* 19.1).

300 For the family history of Konon, son of Timotheos, of Anaphlystos, see Davies, *APF*, no. 13,700. Konon had escaped to Cyprus after the battle of Aigospotamoi and taken refuge with his family friend, Evagoras, king of Salamis (Diod. 13.106.6; Xen. *Hell.* 2.1.29).

301 Diod. acquired this information about Konon's movements from a source other than Xenophon, who makes no mention of Konon between the battles of Aigospotamoi (405) and Knidos (394). His account contains many similarities with that of the late-fourth, early-third century Atthidographer Philokhoros (*FGrHist/BNJ* 328 FF144–146), as reported by Didymos, *On Demosthenes*, col. 7.28–51, although Philokhoros dates the beginning of Konon's activities two years later (397/6) in the archonship of Souniades of Akharnai. See *TDGR2*, no. 11A.

Pharnabazos and Tissaphernes levied soldiers from their respective satrapies and marched out, making their way towards Ephesos, because that was where the enemy had their army. 5. And the force that came with them was composed of 20,000 infantry and 10,000 cavalry. On hearing of the approach of the Persians, Derkylidas, the Lakedaimonian commander, led out his army also, although he had in total no more than 7,000 men. 6. But when the armies were close to each other, they concluded a truce and defined a period of time for Pharnabazos to consult the King about the terms of a treaty, in case he should be willing to make an end to the war, and for Derkylidas similarly to inform the Spartiates. So, on these conditions, the commanders disbanded their forces.[302]

40.1. The citizens of Rhegion [in Italy], who were colonists of the Khalkidians [in Euboia],[303] were watching with distress the growth of Dionysios' power. For, he had sold their relatives, the Naxians and Katanians, into slavery. Since they shared the same origin as those unfortunate people, the event caused them extraordinary concern, out of fear that they might suffer the same sad fate. 2. So, they resolved to go to war with the tyrant quickly, before he became overwhelmingly strong. In addition, those who had been exiled from Syracuse by Dionysios had been given considerable commitments for war by the Rhegian people.[304] For, at that time, most of them were living in Rhegion and were continually lobbying for war, giving assurances that all Syracusans were swayed by the opportunity of the moment.[305] 3. Finally, the Rhegians appointed generals and sent them out, accompanied by a force of 6,000 infantry, 600 cavalry and 50 triremes. These men sailed across the Strait [of Messina] and talked the Messinan generals into joining the war, claiming that it was a disgrace to stand by and watch their neighbouring Greek cities being utterly destroyed by the tyrant. 4. Persuaded by the Rhegians' argument, the generals led out their army, without getting the approval of the People. They had 4,000 infantry, 400 cavalry and 30 triremes. But when the aforementioned forces

The people of Rhegion and Messina prepare to make war upon Dionysios, but then make peace with him

---

302 Cf. the account in Xen. *Hell.* 3.2.12–20, which gives different movements for Derkylidas, does not have the troop figures for the Persians, but does provide the terms that were proposed by both sides.
303 Rhegion was on the toe of Italy across the Strait from Messina (originally Zankle). For the history of Greek settlement in Sicily see Thucydides, 6.3–6. The different settlers brought with them the traditional difference between Ionians and Dorians, which was exacerbated by the conflict between Dorian Sparta and Ionian Athens in the Peloponnesian War.
304 I translate with reservation Bonnet's speculative restoration of this very corrupt passage.
305 A rather cryptic expression, signifying that they had no loyalty to any side, but followed the winner.

had advanced to the borders of Messina, a dispute arose amongst the soldiers, generated by a speech by Laomedon of Messina. 5. His advice was not to start a war against Dionysios, if he had done them no wrong. The soldiers from Messina were immediately persuaded by this argument, since the People had not made a declaration of war, and, deserting their generals, returned home. 6. And the Rhegians also, since they were not a match in battle [against Dionysios] by themselves, when they saw that the Messinans were dissolving their army, quickly turned back to Rhegion. Now, initially, Dionysios had led out his troops to the borders of Syracuse in anticipation of the enemy's attack, but, when he heard of their retreat, he took his army back to Syracuse. 7. And, when the Rhegians and the Messinans sent ambassadors to negotiate for peace, he judged that it was to his advantage to put an end to his hostility with these cities and agreed to peace terms.

Dionysios decides it is in his interest to go to war with Carthage

41.1. Perceiving that some of the Greeks were defecting to the realm of the Carthaginians and taking with them their cities and possessions, Dionysios began to think that, so long as his peace with the Carthaginians was in place, many of the peoples under his control would wish to become part of the Carthaginians' sphere of influence, but that, if war broke out, all those who had been enslaved by the Carthaginians would defect to his side. Furthermore, he heard that a large number of the Carthaginians in Libya had perished, overcome by a plague.

Realizing that this will be a major conflict, Dionysios feels it necessary to make adequate preparations[306]

2. So, for these reasons he thought that this was a golden opportunity for him to undertake the war, but decided that he ought first to get prepared. For, he assumed that this would be a major and lengthy conflict, as was bound to be the case for one about to go to war with the greatest power in Europe. 3. Consequently, he immediately began gathering skilled craftsmen, some by order from the cities under his control, and attracting others from Italy and Greece, and even from the realm of the Carthaginians, with high wages. For, his intention was to get ready a huge number of weapons and missiles of all kinds. In addition, he planned to build quadriremes and quinqueremes,[307]

---

306 From this point to the end of chapter 43 is an extensive description of Dionysios' preparations, his *modus operandi*, the enthusiastic reaction of the Syracusans and the amazement of all who observed. It reads like an enlarged and more detailed version of the account of the building of the wall on Epipolai in chapter 18. The laudatory tone of both passages is in conflict with Diodoros' stated assessment of Dionysios in chapter 2.2, that his life served "as the most outstanding example for moral criticism to all succeeding ages." The tone must, therefore, derive from his source, usually believed to be Timaios, but more likely Philistos. See Introduction under Sources.

307 These were ships with four or five men at the oars. For Dionysios' involvement with the invention of either, both or neither, see n. 311.

even though no ship of the quinquereme-type had as yet been built in those times. 4. Once he had assembled a great number of skilled craftsmen, he divided them into groups according to their particular craft and put the most distinguished citizens in charge, offering great rewards as inducement to those who were fabricating the weapons. And, he also distributed a template of each kind of weapon [to the workmen], because his mercenaries had been collected from many peoples. 5. For, he was eager that each member of his army should be equipped with the weapons he was used to, in the belief that as a result of this his army would cause great fear and that in battle all his combatants would achieve the best results by using their customary armaments. 6. And, since the Syracusans were very enthusiastic about Dionysios' plan, the result was that there was much competition over the preparation of the weapons. For, not only was every spot in the vestibules and rear rooms of the temples, in the gymnasia and in the stoas of the *agora* full of men working, but, quite apart from the public spaces, a huge supply of weapons was being fabricated in the most illustrious private homes.

42.1. And, in fact, it was at this time that the catapult was invented in Syracuse,[308] as could happen when the best craftsmen from all over the world were gathered together into one place.[309] For, the lavish pay and the numerous prizes that were offered to those who were judged best elicited a zealous response. And apart from these inducements Dionysios made the rounds of his workers on a daily basis, chatting with them in friendly terms and rewarding the most enthusiastic with gifts, even inviting them to share his dinner table. 2. And so, because the craftsmen brought unsurpassable competitiveness to their task, they invented many missiles and siege-weapons that were unusual and capable of providing great service. He also began to construct quadriremes and quinqueremes,[310] being the first to devise the construction of these types of

With Dionysios' enthusiastic support and supervision his workmen invent many new weapons, including the catapult

---

308 From Diodoros' description of the siege of Motye in 397/6 (14.48–53) it is clear that Dionysios' forces had many different types of siege artillery at their disposal, types that had not previously been used by the Greeks, especially the arrow-firing catapult. There is no doubt that his works led to a transformation in Greek siegecraft, from which the Macedonians in particular benefitted. The question is whether these weapons were invented at this time, as Diodoros claims, or copied from Phoenician models, since the peoples of the Near East had for centuries been more skilled in siegecraft than the Greeks. The latter is the more likely. There is also disagreement whether the invention was some type of large crossbow or a torsion catapult. In this case the former is more likely, since the torsion catapult first appears in the mid-fourth century. See Marsden (1969).
309 Note that this clause indicates only the potentiality.
310 Since it is beyond question that the trireme ("three-rowed") used three banks of oars, the terms quadrireme ("four-rowed") and quinquereme ("five-rowed") should denote four and

ships.³¹¹ 3. It was because Dionysios had heard that the trireme had first been built in Corinth,³¹² that he was eager for his city, which was a colony of the Corinthians, to increase the size of the ships it constructed. 4. After he had secured the right to export wood from Italy,³¹³ he sent half of his lumbermen to the mountain near Aitna, which in those days was full of valuable stands of fir and pine, while the other half was sent to Italy, where he had prepared yoke of oxen for transportation to the seashore and ships and crew to carry the cut logs swiftly to Syracuse.³¹⁴ 5. And, when Dionysios had collected enough timber, he began simultaneously to construct more than 200 new ships and to refit the 110 existing ones. He also initiated the building of 160 lavish shipsheds in a circle around what is now called the harbour,³¹⁵ most of which could house two ships, and he saw to the maintenance of the 150 that existed already.

Dionysios' preparations continue

43.1. Not surprisingly, the phenomenon of so many sheds and ships being constructed in one place caused much amazement to the onlookers. For, whenever a person directed his eyes towards the energetic shipbuilding, he thought that every man in Sicily was engaged in that activity, but when, in turn, he came upon the labours of those who were making weapons or artillery, he thought that the whole attention of the workers was focused on these things alone. 2. What is more, despite the exceptional energy devoted to these activities, they

---

five banks of oars, but that is not workable. The most plausible hypothesis is that there were either two or three banks of oars, with two men to each oar in a quadrireme, and two to each oar on the two top levels and one to the oar on the bottom level in a quinquereme. See Casson (1971), Morrison and Williams (1968) and Morrison and Coates (1996).

311 Diod. is the only source for this attribution. Pliny, *NH*, 7.207 attributes the invention of the quadrireme to the Carthaginians. Given that Dionysios culled craftsmen from Carthaginian territory (41.3), it is possible that his men built some of these, although the first documented reference to them is in the Athenian naval inventory of 330/29 (*IG* II² 1627.275–278). As for quinqueremes, the evidence is even less positive. They are first attested in the Athenian naval inventory of 325/4 (*IG* II² 1629.811).

312 See Thuc. 1.13.2, who, more precisely, attributes the first trireme to be built in Greece to Corinth.

313 The forests of southern Italy were rich in timber. States and individuals could own the trees, so Dionysios would have had to negotiate permission to log the wood.

314 The ancient system of using oxen to cart the wood to water (either a river or the sea) and then raft the logs into booms to float to a place where they could be milled into planks is little different from that in use in the early days of the modern lumber industry before the introduction of large trucks and mechanized equipment.

315 A name seems to be called for here, although none is provided by any manuscript. Oldfather adopts Wesseling's suggestion μεγάλου ("great"). Another suggestion is Lakkion, the name for the small harbour (14.7.3). There were similar sheds at Zea in Athens, that also housed two triremes.

fabricated 140,000 shields and almost the same number of daggers and helmets. In addition, they also made ready more than 14,000 breastplates, in a great variety of styles and crafted with exquisite skill. 3. He planned to distribute these to his cavalry, the men in charge of units of the infantry and those of his mercenaries, who were going to form his bodyguard. And all sorts of catapults were fabricated, as well as a vast number of other missiles. 4. When the warships were ready, half of them were manned by citizen officers at prow and stern and, in addition, citizen rowers, while for the other half Dionysios hired mercenaries. Then, when he had completed his naval and armament preparation, he began to turn his attention to assembling his troops. For, he had decided it was not to his advantage to hire these much in advance so as not to incur great expense. 5. Astydamas, the writer of tragedies,[316] produced a play for the first time. He lived [or was aged] sixty years. While the Romans were besieging the [town of] Veii,[317] a sally was made from the city and some of the Romans were cut down by the [people of] Veii, while others were put to flight disgracefully.

Astydamas produces his first tragedy and the Romans are defeated by the Veiians

44.1. Once the year had come to an end, Ithykles assumed the archonship at Athens, while in Rome five military tribunes were appointed in place of the consuls: [they were] Lucius Julius, Marcus Furius, Marcus Aemilius, Gaius Cornelius, Caeso Fabius.[318] When Dionysios, the tyrant of the Syracusans, had completed most of the work on his armaments-manufacture and shipbuilding, he turned his attention right away to assembling his troops. 2. Starting with the Syracusans, he enlisted those who were fit to serve into military units, and from the cities that were subject to him he summoned the eligible males. Furthermore, he gathered mercenaries from Greece and especially from the Lakedaimonians. For, the Lakedaimonians, with a view to assisting him in the increase of his power, gave him permission to hire as many mercenaries as he wished from amongst them. On the whole, because he was eager to gather a mercenary army from many nations and because he was offering big pay, he

398/7: Book 14.44.1– 46.6

Dionysios assembles his army

---

316 This must be the older of two fourth-century tragic dramatists of the same name, father and son. Both were descendants of Morsimos, son of Aeschylus' nephew, Philokles. The son, whose first victory was recorded in 373/2 (*Marmor Parium*, ep. 71), was more famous than the father.

317 All manuscripts read Boii here, when it should be Veii. This is the same mistake as at 14.16.5. For the event see Livy, 5.7.1–3, under the Varronian year 403.

318 The number five is incorrect, but the names are correct (except that Aemilius Mamercus' *praenomen* was Manius). Some manuscripts have the correct number six, but with the wrong names. See Livy, 5.10.1 (and the *Fasti Capitolini* under the Varronian year 401): Lucius Valerius Potitus, Marcus Furius Camillus, Manius Aemilius Mamercus, Gnaeus Cossus, Caeso Fabius Ambustus, Lucius Julius Julus.

Dionysios tries to improve relations with the people of Rhegion and Messina

found willing respondents. 3. As he was on the verge of starting up a great conflict, Dionysios began making friendly overtures to the cities in the island, trying to elicit their goodwill. And seeing that the people of Rhegion and Messina, who lived by the Strait, had a competent military force ready for action, he was concerned that, if ever the Carthaginians crossed over into Sicily, they might be quick to join them. For, these cities carried no small effect on the balance of power for whichever side they allied with in the war. 4. Since he was very concerned about this, Dionysios gave the Messinans a large piece of territory on their border, aiming to get them on his side by this generosity. And, to the people of Rhegion he sent ambassadors inviting them to make a marriage alliance by giving him a daughter of one of their citizens to live with. Further, he promised to acquire for them a large area of bordering territory and said that he would increase the power of the city as far as he had the power to do. 5. For, since his wife, the daughter of Hermokrates,[319] had been killed during the revolt of the cavalry,[320] he was eager to have children in the belief that the securest protection for his rule lay in the goodwill of his offspring. Despite that, when an Assembly was held in Rhegion on this matter, after many speeches had been made, the People decided not to accept the marriage alliance.[321] 6. After failing in this approach, Dionysios sent ambassadors to the people of Lokroi.[322] They voted in favour of the marriage alliance and Dionysios took as his wife Doris,[323] the daughter of Xenetos, who was the most respected citizen at that time. 7. A few days before the marriage he sent a quinquereme to Lokroi, the first one that had been built, decorated with gold and silver fittings. He had the maiden transported to Syracuse on this ship and led her up to the acropolis. 8. He also sought the hand in marriage of Aristomakhe,[324] a woman

He offers the people of Rhegion a marriage alliance, but is rejected

Dionysios marries Doris of Lokroi and Aristomakhe of Syracuse

---

319 Hermokrates, son of Hermon, was not only Dionysios' father-in-law but also, in many ways, his model. Described by Thucydides as a man of intelligence, military experience and courage (6.72.1), he inspired the resistance to the Athenian Invasion of 415–413. Neither a democrat nor an oligarch, he was an active proponent of Sicilian unity. Banished by his democratic opponents after the Athenian victory at Kyzikos, he attempted to regain his position in Syracuse by force and was killed in the process. One of his supporters who survived his death was Dionysios (Diod. 13.63 and 13.75).

320 Abused by the cavalry, she committed suicide (Diod. 13.112.4; Plut. *Dion*, 3.1).

321 Supposedly, they added the insult that the only girl they were willing to give him was the daughter of their public executioner (14.107.3; Strabo, 6.1.6 C258). Dionysios avenged this insult cruelly some years later (Diod. 14.106.1–112.5).

322 Epizephyrian Lokroi, on the coast of Bruttium in Calabria, was a traditional enemy of Rhegion (Thuc. 4.1.2–3; 24.2–3).

323 The mother of Dionysios II (Diod. 16.6.2).

324 A Syracusan woman, daughter of Hipparinos (Diod. 16.6.2) and sister of Dion (Plut. *Dion*, 3.3; 4.1).

who was the most illustrious amongst the citizens. He sent a chariot drawn by four white horses for her and conveyed her to his own home.

45.1. After celebrating his wedding to both women on the same day one after the other,[325] he held public feasts for his soldiers and most of the citizens. For, he now began to set aside the harsh character of his tyranny and, changing to reasonable ways, he ruled his subjects in a more humane fashion, neither condemning them to death, nor sending them into exile, as he was used to. 2. He allowed a few days to pass after his weddings and then convened an Assembly[326] in which he exhorted the Syracusans to make war upon the Carthaginians, declaring that they were the worst enemy of the Greeks in general and were at every opportunity plotting against the Sicilians in particular.[327] 3. And, he pointed out that for the moment they remained inactive on account of the plague that had befallen them, which had killed most of the inhabitants of Libya, but that, once they had regained their strength, they would not leave the Sicilians alone, against whom they had been plotting from time immemorial. So, he said, it was a better choice now to make war on them when they were weak, than to fight it out with them sometime later when they were strong. 4. At the same time he pointed out that it was a disgrace to neglect the Greek cities that had been enslaved by barbarians, cities which would be all the more ready to share in the struggle, in as much as they desired to gain their liberty. Furthermore, he put forward many other arguments in support of this proposal, after which he soon had the Syracusans agreeing with him. 5. For, they were just as eager as he for the war to take place. Their first reason was their hatred of the Carthaginians and the fact that they were the cause of their being forced to take orders from the tyrant. Secondly, they were hoping that Dionysios would treat them more humanely, if he was afraid not only of the enemy, but also of an attack by those he had enslaved. But their greatest hope

Dionysios celebrates his two weddings lavishly

Dionysios gains Syracusan approval for a war against Carthage

---

325 See also Plut. *Dion*, 3.4. Polygamy was practised by tyrants of the Archaic period and the habit was renewed by later rulers in the Hellenistic period.

326 Dionysios was attempting to preserve the appearance of democratic procedure. In his speech he employed an appeal to the theme of "Freeing Greek cities" that was a common feature of Greek propaganda from the Peloponnesian War to Alexander's campaign, and even used by the Roman, Titus Flamininus.

327 Throughout this translation, the term "Sicilians" (Greek, *Sikeliotai*) denotes the Greeks of Sicily, as opposed to the native Sikels or Sikans. The first Carthaginian invasion, in 480, which led to Gelon's victory at the battle of Himera, was the sad result of Greek city-state rivalry (Herod. 7.165–168). Himera was the focus of Carthaginian vengeance in 409 (Diod. 13.54–62). The failure of Syracusan generals in this conflict led to Dionysios' rise to power (Diod.13.91–96).

was that, once in possession of their weapons, if ever Chance should provide an opportunity, they would regain their liberty.

Dionysios allows the Syracusans and other Sicilians to plunder Carthaginian possessions and abuse Carthaginian citizens in Sicily

46.1. Following the Assembly, with Dionysios' permission, the Syracusans plundered the possessions of the Phoenicians. For, a great number of Carthaginians lived in Syracuse and owned luxurious properties, and many of their traders had ships in the harbour loaded with cargo.[328] Everything was pillaged by the Syracusans. 2. In like manner, the rest of the Sicilians also expelled their resident Phoenicians and seized their property. For, although they hated the tyranny of Dionysios, they nevertheless were pleased to take part in the war on the Carthaginians, because of the brutality of that people.[329] 3. Indeed, for these very reasons, once Dionysios began to wage war openly, even the Greek cities that were living under the rule of the Carthaginians made clear their hatred of the Phoenicians. For, not only did they plunder their properties, but they also seized their persons and inflicted upon their bodies every kind of abuse and indignity, inspired by the recollection of the things they themselves had suffered during their captivity.

The Carthaginians learn not to abuse their subjects

4. To such great lengths did they go in their vengeance upon the Phoenicians both at that time and later that the Carthaginians were taught never again to treat abusively those who fell under their power. For, learning from experience, they began to understand that Fortune is impartial in warfare and that both sides are compelled to experience in defeat the very same things they themselves would inflict upon the unfortunate losers.

Dionysios plans to declare war on Carthage

5. Now, when Dionysios had completed his preparations for war, he was planning to send ambassadors to Carthage to deliver the following message: "The Syracusans declare war upon the Carthaginians, unless they set free the Greek cities that they have enslaved." Well, that was what Dionysios was up to.

In this year Ktesias ends his History of Persia and three composers of Dithyrambs reach their prime

6. With this year Ktesias,[330] the author of the *History of the Persians*, brought his work to a conclusion, a work which he began from the time of Ninos and Semiramis.[331] Also in this year the most famous composers of dithyrambs[332]

---

328 A clear indication of an active trading relationship between Greeks and Phoenicians.
329 For another statement of Carthaginian brutality by Diodoros, see his description of the sack of Selinous in 409 (13.57.1–6). But Greeks could be just as brutal, as we will see. Similarly, the lesson learned by the Carthaginians about what happens to powers that abuse their subjects (below), a key theme for Diod. in this book, is one experienced by the Athenians after their defeat at Aigospotamoi (Xen. *Hell*. 2.2.3).
330 For Diodoros' use of Ktesias see the Introduction under Sources.
331 Two mythical rulers of Assyria, founders respectively of Nineveh and Babylon. See Diod. 2.1–20, whose account is, on his own admission, derived from Ktesias. For Semiramis see also Herod. 1.184.
332 Dithyrambs were choral songs originally in honour of Dionysos. Later they evolved into any kind of heroic narrative. In Athens they were composed for competitions of boys' and mens'

reached their prime. They were: Philoxenos of Kythera,[333] Timotheos of Miletos,[334] Telestes of Selinous[335] and Polyeidos,[336] who was also skilled in painting and music.

47.1. Once the year had come to an end, Lysiades[337] assumed the archonship at Athens, while in Rome six military tribunes managed the consulship: [they were] Popilius Mallius, Publius Mannius, Spurius Furius and Lucius Publius.[338] When Dionysios, the tyrant of the Syracusans, had effected all his preparations for war according to his original plan, he sent a herald to Carthage, entrusting him with a letter for the Council of Elders. 2. In it was written the message that the Syracusans had resolved to go to war against the Carthaginians, unless they withdraw their forces from the Greek cities. So, the herald, according to his instructions, sailed to Libya and delivered the letter to the Council. After the letter had been read out in the Council and later before the People, the thought of war aroused considerable anxiety amongst the Carthaginians, since the plague had killed very many of them and they were unprepared in all respects. 3. Despite that, they decided to wait and see what the Syracusans were

397/6: Book 14.47.1–53.6

Dionysios declares war on Carthage

---

choirs from the ten tribes held at the major festivals. The origin and meaning of the name are disputed. See Pickard-Cambridge (1962).

333 Philoxenos of Kythera (435/4–380/79) was one of the most prolific and innovative composers of dithyrambs in the late fifth and early fourth century. He spent some time at Dionysios' court, where his frank appraisal of the tyrant's verses got him into some trouble (Diod. 15.6.2-5). His notorious work, the *Loves of Galatea and Kyklops*, was parodied by Aristophanes in *Ploutos*, 290ff., and played by Antigeneides at the court of Philip of Macedon shortly before Philip lost his eye at Methone in 354 (Didymos, *On Demosthenes*, 12.59–60), but served as a model for Theokritos (Idyll XI). His dithyrambs were read by Alexander the Great (Plut. *Alex*. 8.3).

334 Despite the fact that all mss of Diod. give his ethnic as *Philesios*, Timotheos was from Miletos. Born about 450, he lived until 360. He was also known as an innovator in his style of dithyramb, combining different musical modes and metrics. His music and language are said to have influenced Euripides. A large fragment of his *Persians*, with a prologue by Euripides, has survived on a fourth-century papyrus. For the fragments of his works see Hordern (2002).

335 According to the *Marmor Parium*, ep. 79, Telestes won a victory at Athens in 402/1. He ended his life in Sikyon, where he was honoured with a monument by the tyrant Aristrates (Pliny, *NH*, 35.109). He probably left Selinous when it was sacked by the Carthaginians in 409.

336 We know little of Polyeidos, except that he wrote an *Iphigeneia* and was for some reason dubbed "the sophist" by Aristotle (*Poetics* 1455a6 and 1455b8).

337 An error. The correct name is Souniades of Akharnai. See Develin, *AO*, 205 and n. 301 above.

338 Despite saying the tribunes were six, Diod. gives only four names. Six is the correct number, confirmed by the *Fasti Capitolini* (under the Varronian year 400) and Livy, 5.12.9–10, who gives the following names: Publius Licinius Calvus, Publius Manlius, Lucius Titinius, Publius Maelius, Lucius Furius Medullinus and Lucius Publilius Volscus. Not all Livy's names agree with those on the *Fasti*.

Dionysios advances across Sicily towards Eryx and Motye, gathering troops as he goes

planning, and meanwhile sent out members of the Council with large sums of money to enlist mercenary troops from Europe. 4. Dionysios, with the Syracusans and his mercenaries and his allies as well, marched out from Syracuse in the direction of Mt Eryx. For, not far from this hill was the city of Motye, a colony of the Carthaginians, which they used as the main base for their attacks on Sicily.[339] His hope was that, if he became master of this city, he would have a great advantage over his enemy. 5. Along the way from time to time he picked up contingents from the Greek cities, all of which he equipped with arms. They joined him on his campaign enthusiastically, both out of hatred for the heavy hand of Phoenician dominion and out of a desire that one day they would gain their independence. 6. The first contingent he picked up was from Kamarina; next the men from Gela and Akragas. After these he summoned the Himeraians, who lived on the other coast of Sicily.[340] Finally, after adding the contingent from Selinous as he passed by, he arrived in the vicinity of Motye with his whole army. 7. He had 80,000 infantry, many more than 3,000 cavalry and only a few less than 200 warships. In addition, he was accompanied by no fewer than 500 freighters, loaded with a large number of siege-engines and all other necessary provisions.

Dionysios arrives at Motye with all his forces

The people of Eryx join Dionysios, but the Motyans prepare for a siege

48.1. Since such was the magnitude of Dionysios' expedition, the people of Eryx[341] decided to join his side, both because they were frightened by the size of his army and out of hatred of the Carthaginians. The inhabitants of Motye, by contrast, because they were expecting to receive help from the Carthaginians, did not panic at the sight of Dionysios' army, but began making preparations for a siege. For, they were not unaware that the Syracusans would try to sack Motye first, because it was the city most loyal to the Carthaginians. 2. This city was situated on an island that was six *stades*[342] off the coast of Sicily.[343] It had been adorned extravagantly by the artistry of its many beautiful houses thanks to the prosperity of its inhabitants. It was joined to the coast of Sicily

Description of Motye

---

339 Motye was an eighth-century Phoenician trading settlement that by this time was subject to Carthage, along with Panormos and Solous.
340 His progress was along the southern part of Sicily, liberating the Greek cities that had been taken by the Carthaginians in the campaign of 406. The only contingent from the northern part was from Himera.
341 Eryx, like Egesta (Segesta), was a city of the Elymoi, who were believed to be Trojan refugees. See Thuc. 6.2, although Diodoros (4.23.1–3) has a different version. Nevertheless, excavation shows that it had a significant Phoenician presence. Eryx is situated on a rocky mountain (modern Mt San Giuliano). See Map 3.
342 About 1 km or ⅗ of a mile.
343 See Map 3.

by a narrow, man-made road,[344] which the Motyans breached at this time, to prevent the enemy having access to them by this route. 3. Dionysios, after surveying the terrain with his master-craftsmen, initiated the construction of a causeway towards Motye,[345] drew up his warships on dry land beside the entrance to the harbour and had the freighters drop anchor along the beach. 4. Then, leaving behind Leptines,[346] the commander of his fleet, as supervisor of the construction project, he marched out with his infantry against the cities that were allied to the Carthaginians. All the Sikan[347] communities, being wary of the size of his army, went over to the Syracusans, and only five of the other cities remained loyal to their friendship with the Carthaginians. These were Halikyai, Solous, Egesta, Panormos and Entella.[348] 5. So, Dionysios plundered the territory of Solous, and Panormos, and Halikyai as well, and cut down their trees, but he invaded the territory of Egesta and Entella with a large army and launched repeated attacks against them, since he was eager to gain possession of them by force. That was how Dionysios' affairs stood.

Dionysios begins preparations for the siege and campaigns against Carthaginian allies in the vicinity

49.1. Himilkon, the Carthaginian commander-in-chief [*strategos*],[349] was personally involved in the business of gathering an army and making other preparations, but he dispatched the commander of his fleet [*navarch*] with ten triremes with orders to sail with all speed secretly to Syracuse, to sail into the harbour under cover of night and destroy the ships that had been left behind there. 2. He took this action in the belief that it would cause a diversion and force Dionysios to send part of his fleet back to help the Syracusans. The naval commander assigned to the task promptly carried out his orders and sailed by night into the harbour[350] at Syracuse, without anyone knowing what was happening. Making a surprise attack, he rammed the ships that were anchored there. After sinking almost all of them, he returned to Carthage. 3. But Dionysios, after laying waste all the territory subject to the Carthaginians and

Himilkon, the Carthaginian general, sends ten triremes to attack the Syracusan harbour by night

Undeterred, Dionysios returns to the siege of Motye

344 This causeway was about 2km long and ran from the north gate to the necropolis at Birgi.
345 Although Diod. represents Dionysios as building a new causeway, it is most likely that he used the remains of the Motyan causeway, which are still visible, although he may have widened it.
346 Dionysios' brother.
347 For the distinction between Sikans and Sikels and their relationship, see Thuc. 6.2. The Sikans were the earlier inhabitants of the island, but had been driven to the south and west by the Sikels.
348 For the location of these places see Map 3.
349 I have used this translation to distinguish Himilkon's superior authority as *strategos* from the commander of the navy (*navarch*) mentioned below. But inconsistently Diod. uses the term *navarch* to describe Himilkon at the beginning of ch. 50.
350 Presumably the so-called Great Harbour.

shutting his enemies up within their walls, led his whole army back to Motye. For, his hope was that, once this place had been taken by assault, the others would quickly surrender themselves. So, he kept up the work filling in the passage between the island and the coast, by immediately increasing the number of men involved in the construction many times over. At the same time as the causeway progressed, he advanced his siege-engines little by little towards the walls.

Himilkon plans a surprise attack upon Dionysios' fleet at Motye

50.1 Meanwhile, when Himilkon, the commander of the Carthaginian navy [*navarch*], heard that Dionysios had drawn up his warships onto dry land, he immediately manned his 100 best triremes. His assumption was that, if he appeared unexpectedly,[351] he would easily gain control of the ships that were drawn up on land in the harbour, thus becoming master of the sea. And he thought that, once that was accomplished, he would both lift the siege of Motye and transfer the war to the city of Syracuse. 2. So, sailing out with 100 ships, he put into shore at the territory of Selinous during the night and, after rounding the promontory at Lilybaion,[352] he arrived at Motye at daybreak. His appearance took his opponents by surprise and, because Dionysios' men could not come to their assistance, he stove in some of the ships that were at anchor and burnt others.[353] 3. Then, he sailed into the harbour and drew up his fleet for an attack upon the ships that had been dragged up onto the shore by his enemy. Dionysios massed his army at the mouth of the harbour but, observing that the enemy were guarding the passage out of the harbour, he was afraid to launch his ships into the harbour For, because the mouth of the harbour was narrow, he realized that he was going to have to risk fighting with a few ships against many times their number. 4. So, taking advantage of the large number of his soldiers, he easily dragged his vessels over the land into the sea outside the harbour and thus saved his ships.[354] And, when Himilkon began

Initially Himilkon's surprise attack is successful, but he is eventually thwarted by Dionysios' catapults and sails away

---

351 As many have noted, Diod., or his source, lays emphasis upon the Carthaginian use of stealth and surprise both here, in the attack on Syracuse (above), and later in the capture of Messina (14.57.1–4).

352 For the location of Lilybaion at the end of the lagoon, see Map 3. After Dionysios' destruction of Motye, the Carthaginians moved their base of operations in Sicily to Lilybaion, where they built a strong fortress. During the First Punic War (264–241) the Romans besieged Lilybaion but failed to capture it. It was lost to Carthage under the terms that ended that war.

353 These were the freighters.

354 Diod.'s description is so sketchy that it is difficult to agree on the topography of this battle. The location of the promontory is particularly controversial, although it is most usually considered to be the narrow, 550-metre spit at the northern tip of the long island that closes off the lagoon on the west, despite the fact that Polyainos (*Strategemata*, 5.2.6) says that eighty triremes were dragged over a distance of 20 *stades* (c.2½ miles or 4 km). See Map 6.

attacking the first [of Dionysios'] ships, he was restrained by the mass of missiles. For Dionysios had put on board his ships a large number of archers and sling-throwers, while the Syracusans on the shore killed many of the enemy with catapults firing sharp-pointed missiles. Indeed, this weapon caused great panic, because it had just been invented at that time. As a result Himilkon was unable to be victorious in his attack and sailed away to Libya, deeming it disadvantageous to fight a naval battle, since the enemy fleet outnumbered his two to one.

51.1. Thanks to the abundance of his workforce Dionysios completed the causeway and then brought a great variety of siege-engines up to the walls. With the rams he kept battering the towers and with the catapults he was driving the defenders off the ramparts. He also brought wheeled towers up to the walls, six levels high, which he had had made to equal the height of the houses. 2. Nevertheless, the inhabitants of Motye, now that they were face-to-face with the danger, were not overawed by Dionysios' forces, even though they were without allies at the time. Surpassing their besiegers in their zeal for glory, to begin with they suspended men in baskets from yard-arms that were affixed to the top of very large beams, then these men from their elevated positions threw down flaming torches and pieces of hemp burning with pitch upon the enemies' siege-engines. 3. The fire swiftly enveloped the wood, but the Sicilians quickly rushed to the rescue and put it out and by repeated attacks with their rams broke down a portion of the wall. Men from both sides ran in crowds to this spot and a vigorous battle ensued. 4. For, the Sicilians [see n. 327], on their part, thinking that they were already masters of the city, stopped at nothing in their efforts to take revenge on the Phoenicians for the wrongs they had committed against them in the past, while the men of the city, with the sufferings of captivity before their eyes and the realization that there was no escape either by land or sea, faced death with courage. 5. And, seeing the protection of their walls eliminated, they barricaded their narrow passageways and used the outermost houses as expensively constructed walls. As a result Dionysios' men found themselves in greater difficulty. 6. For, after penetrating the walls and thinking they were already in possession of the city, they kept being wounded from above by the defenders from their elevated positions in the houses. Despite that, they brought wooden towers that they had equipped with gangways

Dionysios completes the causeway and attacks Motye with his siege-engines[355]

The Motyans resist bravely

The walls are breached but the Motyans fight in the streets and from the rooftops

---

[355] Dionysios' siege techniques revolutionized the art of siegecraft in Greece, which had long been inferior to that used in the Near East. A similar siege of an island city was carried out in 332 by Alexander the Great against Tyre in Phoenicia, the mother city of Carthage. See Diod. 17.40–46; Arrian, *Anab.* 2.18–24; Curtius, 4.2–4.

up to the houses. And, since these machines were equal in height to the houses, the result was that from this point on the battle was fought hand-to-hand. For, by means of the gangways that they were throwing onto the houses, the Sicilians kept forcing their way in.

Encouraged by their wives and children the Motyans fight even more desperately

52.1. But the Motyans, recognizing the magnitude of their danger and having their wives and children before their eyes, fought all the more earnestly, out of fear on their account. Indeed, some, whose courage had been aroused by the pleas of their parents, who were crowding around begging them not to allow them to be surrendered to the violent abuse of the enemy, were giving no thought to saving their own lives, while others, hearing the wailing of their wives and infant children, hastened to die a noble death before having to witness the captivity of their children. 2. For, it was not possible to escape from the city, since it was entirely surrounded by the sea, which their enemy controlled. What scared the Phoenicians most and caused them the greatest despair was the cruel way they had treated their Greek captives, since they expected that they would suffer the same treatment. So, all that remained for them was to fight bravely and either win or die. 3. Since such a sense of desperate abandon had possessed the minds of the besieged, the Sicilians found themselves up against a difficult situation. 4. For, since they were fighting from the planks of wood they had suspended against the houses, things were going very badly for them, both because of the narrow passage and the fact that their enemy were prepared to risk their lives without a thought for the consequences, as would be the case with those who had given up on life. As a result, some, who were locked in hand-to-hand combat, died in the exchange of wounds, while others, who were pushed back by the Motyans, perished by falling off the wooden planks onto the ground. 5. In the end, as the siege went on in a similar fashion for days, Dionysios made a practice of always breaking off the siege towards nightfall by calling back his fighters with a trumpet call. Then, after getting the Motyans accustomed to this habit, [one evening] when the fighters on both sides had withdrawn, he sent out Arkhylos of Thourioi with the elite troops. 6. Under cover of darkness this man raised ladders against the collapsed houses, by means of which he climbed up and seized control of an advantageous position and admitted Dionysios' men. 7. Once the Motyans realized what had happened, they immediately ran to help with all speed and, although they were too late, faced the danger nonetheless. As the battle raged and more men climbed up [the ladders], the Sicilians with much effort wore down their opponents by weight of numbers.

The defenders hold off the Greeks for several days

Dionysios breaks into the city by a ruse

53.1. Right away Dionysios' whole army as well, advancing by the causeway, burst into the city, and every quarter was filled with scenes of people being slaughtered. For, the Sicilians, in their eagerness to avenge savagery with savagery, were killing everyone indiscriminately one after the other, sparing neither child, nor woman, nor the aged.[356] 2. But, Dionysios, because he wanted to sell the citizens into slavery to collect the booty, at first tried to restrain his soldiers from killing the prisoners. But, when no one paid any attention to him and he realized that the assault of the Sicilians could not be checked, he posted heralds around the city to shout out to the Motyans to take refuge in the sacred places that were revered by the Greeks. 3. Once this happened, the soldiers gave up killing and turned their attention instead to looting the properties. They carried off as plunder a huge amount of silver, much gold, expensive clothes and a mass of other luxurious articles. And Dionysios allowed his soldiers to plunder the city, because he wanted to rouse their enthusiasm for facing upcoming dangers. 4. After finishing with this, he rewarded Arkhylos, the first man to get up on the wall, with a gift of 100 *minas*[357] and honoured each of the other men, who had behaved with bravery, according to his merits; he also sold the Motyans who had been left behind, as booty. Daimenes and some other Greek allies of the Carthaginians, whom he had captured, he had crucified.[358] 5. Next, he posted guards over the city and appointed Biton, the Syracusan, as their garrison-commander. The majority of the guards were Sikels. <He dispatched>[359] Leptines, his naval commander, with 120 ships to guard against any force crossing over from Carthage and also delegated to him the task of besieging Egesta and Entella, as it had been his intention to sack these towns from the very beginning. Then, since the summer was on the way out, he marched back to Syracuse with his army. 6. In Athens, Sophokles, son of Sophokles, put on his first tragedy and achieved twelve victories.[360]

Mass slaughter takes place

Dionysios eventually stops the carnage and the soldiers turn to looting

Dionysios rewards Arkhylos and others, sells the Motyans for booty and crucifies Greek traitors; then he returns to Syracuse

54.1. Once the year had come to an end, Phormion assumed the archonship at Athens, while in Rome there were six military tribunes in place of the consuls: [they were] Gnaeus Genucius, Lucius Atilius, Marcus Pomponius, Gaius

396/5: Book 14.54.1–81.6

---

356 See Diod. 13.57.2 for an identical description of the Carthaginian slaughter of the inhabitants of Selinous.
357 A huge sum. One hundred *minas* (10,000 *drachmas*) was the equivalent of 10,000 days' pay for the average worker or soldier.
358 Business is business. Just as there were Carthaginians living and trading in Syracuse (above, 14.46.1), so it is no surprise that there were Greeks doing the same in Motye. Dionysios treated them as traitors.
359 Something is missing in the text, and a verb like this has to be supplied.
360 I.e. in his lifetime. Actually, he was the son of Ariston and grandson of the famous Sophokles.

Dionysios continues his campaign against Carthaginian possessions in Sicily

Duilius, Marcus Veturius and Valerius Publilius.³⁶¹ The ninety-sixth Olympic Games were celebrated, <in> which Eupolis of Elis was the victor.³⁶² 2. When these men had assumed office, Dionysios, the tyrant of the Syracusans, led his whole army out of Syracuse and invaded the realm of the Carthaginians.³⁶³ As he was devastating the countryside, the people of Halikyai, out of fear, sent ambassadors to him and made an alliance. The Egestaians, by contrast, made a surprise night attack upon their besiegers and, by setting fire to the tents in the camp, generated mass confusion amongst the soldiers. 3. As the flames spread far and wide and the fire got out of control, a few of the soldiers, who came running to the rescue, died, and most of the horses were incinerated along with the tents. 4. Yet, Dionysios continued to devastate the countryside unopposed, and Leptines, his naval commander, spent his time around Motye

The Carthaginians prepare a huge force for a counter-attack

on the watch for a landing by the enemy. But, the Carthaginians, after learning how large Dionysios' force was, decided to prepare a force far greater than his. 5. Consequently, after investing Himilkon with royal authority in accordance with the law,³⁶⁴ they assembled forces from all over Libya and yet more from Iberia, summoning some from their allies, hiring others as mercenaries. In the end they assembled more than 300,000 infantry and 4,000 cavalry excluding the chariots, of which there were 400. They had 400 warships and more than 600 transports for carrying food and siege-weapons and the rest of their manpower.³⁶⁵ [These are the figures] according to Ephoros.³⁶⁶ 6. However, Timaios says that the forces that crossed over from Libya numbered no more

---

361 For these names compare Livy, 5.13.3. They are almost identical, except that Duilius' *praenomen* is Gnaeus and Publilius' is Volero. The year is 399 by the Varronian chronology.

362 The victory was in the footrace (*stadion*), as usual. Pausanias (8.45.4) names the victor Eupolemos of Elis. He had a statue by Daidalos of Sikyon, even though there was a dispute over his victory (Paus. 6.3.7).

363 As defined by the treaty of 405 (13.114.1).

364 Himilkon, who has been described above as *strategos* (14.49.1) and *navarch* (14.50.1) is now made *basileus kata nomon*. That, in the fifth and fourth centuries, the Carthaginians had constitutionally elected (or selected) kings is affirmed by several sources: Herodotos, 7.166–167; Aristotle, *Politics*, 2.8.5.1273a; Polybios, 6.51. Their role appears to be mainly religious and military, as distinct from the other powerful officials, the two *suffetes* (judges), though the two are sometimes equated (e.g. by Oldfather in the Loeb). See, in general, Markoe (2000). Different here is the implication that Himilkon became *strategos* (leader of the military) before being appointed to the kingship, which seems to conflict with the statements at 13.43.5 and 15.15.2, where kingship comes first. Whilst the circumstances in this case are not at all impossible, it has led to the suggestion that the text be amended to read "after appointing Himilkon, <the> king in accordance with the law, <as *strategos*>" (Parker at *BNJ* 70 F204).

365 As can be seen from 55.3, each transport carried 100 soldiers.

366 *FGrHist/BNJ* 70 F204.

than 100,000. He also states that, in addition to these, another 30,000 were levied in Sicily.³⁶⁷

55.1. Himilkon gave all his helmsmen a sealed document with orders only to open it when they were out at sea. Then, they were to do whatever was written there. He devised this plan to prevent any spies from reporting to Dionysios the planned landing place. And their written instructions were to make their landing at Panormos.³⁶⁸ 2. So, when the wind blew fair, all the ships cast off their stern-cables. The transports sailed out into the open sea, but the triremes hugged the shore [of Sicily] on their way to Lilybaion. Sailing with a favourable wind, the first transports were soon visible from Sicily, and Dionysios dispatched Leptines with thirty triremes under orders to ram and destroy all that he caught. 3. And he sailed out quickly, engaged right away with the leading ships and sank some along with their crews. But the rest, since they were fully manned and had the wind in their sails, easily escaped. Nevertheless, he did sink fifty ships and the 5,000 soldiers on board, along with 200 chariots. 4. Himilkon sailed into harbour at Panormos and, after disembarking his troops, led them against the enemy. He ordered his warships to sail along the coast beside him. He, himself, in his advance, captured Eryx³⁶⁹ through treachery, and then pitched camp near Motye. And, since Dionysios was at that time with his army at Egesta, Himilkon took Motye by siege. 5. Although the Sicilians were eager to contest the issue, Dionysios determined that it was more to his advantage to resume the war in other places for two simultaneous reasons: he was separated a long way from the cities allied to him and his supply-chain was deficient. 6. So, resolved to withdraw, he tried to persuade the Sikans to leave their cities behind for the time being and campaign with him. In return, he promised to give them better land, equal in area, and said that after the conclusion of the war he would restore any who wished to their ancestral homes. 7. Only a few of the Sikans, because they were afraid that, by refusing, their property would be looted by the soldiers, agreed to the terms offered by

Himilkon gives secret orders for his ships to sail to Panormos

Dionysios sends Leptines to attack the Carthaginian transports

Himilkon disembarks his army, advances to Motye, and takes it by siege

Dionysios withdraws; he tries to persuade the Sikans to abandon their homes and join him

Few of the Sikans agree and Dionysios returns to Syracuse

---

367 *FGrHist/BNJ* 556 F108. Timaios' figures are more credible and Diodoros seems to follow them, at least to the extent that the figures he gives for Himilkon's total naval complement at 56.1 and 59.7 are more in line with Timaios' troop numbers than Ephoros' (cf. n. 363). Here, as elsewhere, is evidence that Diodoros consulted more than one source and used his judgement about whom to follow. But see n. 402.

368 Modern Palermo. Panormos ("harbour for all") is the Greek name for the city that was adopted by the Romans. It was originally named *Ziz* by the Phoenicians, who founded it in c.734. It became part of the Carthaginian sphere of influence and remained loyal to Carthage until it was taken over by the Romans after the Second Punic War.

369 See n. 341.

Dionysios.³⁷⁰ Like the majority of the Sikans, the Halikyaians³⁷¹ also defected. Moreover, they sent ambassadors to the Carthaginian camp and made an alliance. Dionysios set off for Syracuse, devastating the countryside through which he led his army.

Himilkon prepares to lead his army along the north coast to Messina

56.1. Now that affairs were going the way he wanted, Himilkon began making preparations to lead his army against Messina,³⁷² since he was eager to get control of it because of its advantageous location. For it had a well-equipped harbour, capable of accommodating his whole fleet of more than 600 ships. Also, Himilkon hoped that, by taking possession of the area around the Strait, he could bar any help [coming to Dionysios] from Italy and hold off any fleets from the Peloponnese.³⁷³

Himilkon concludes friendship with Himera and Kephaloidion, captures Lipara and approaches Messina

2. With the intention of accomplishing this plan, he concluded friendly relations with the people of Himera³⁷⁴ and the inhabitants of the fort at Kephaloidion³⁷⁵ and took control of the city of Lipara,³⁷⁶ exacting thirty *talents* from the island's inhabitants. Then he set out for Messina with his whole army, while his ships sailed along the coast beside him. 3. He completed the journey quickly and set up camp in the Peloris,³⁷⁷ 100 *stades*³⁷⁸ from Messina.

The Messinans are divided in opinion as to how to react to the danger

When the inhabitants of the city learned of the enemy's presence, there was a difference of opinion amongst them about how to deal with the war. 4. For some of them, on hearing the size of the enemy forces and reflecting that they were devoid of allies – that, furthermore, even their own cavalry were

---

370 This is a backhanded way of saying that most of the Sikans refused his offer. The Sikans had usually sided with the Carthaginians.

371 Diod. here appears to distinguish the Halikyaians from the Sikans, possibly supporting the theory that they were Elymian. But, like the Sikans, in the past they had sided with the Carthaginians.

372 Although a faction of the Messinans had been willing to join the Rhegians in a war against Dionysios in 399, the rank and file was opposed (14.40) and the city had made peace then. Later in 398, Dionysios secured their alliance (14.44.3–4) by a gift of territory.

373 Control of the Strait of Messina had been a key element of Carthaginian strategy in Sicily since the beginning of the fifth century. Himilkon's subsequent action (14.58.4) is consequently anomalous.

374 Himera, the site of the great victory by Sicilian Greeks over the Carthaginians in 480 (Diod. 11.20–22; Herodotos, 7.167), had been razed to the ground by Hannibal in 409 in revenge (Diod. 13.62.3–4). Diod. (11.49.4) says it was still deserted in his day. Probably the city that is named here, and elsewhere, as Himera was the nearby town of Therma Himerensis, founded by the Carthaginians in 407 (Diod. 13.79.8; Cicero, *Against Verres* II, 35) as a home for the survivors.

375 Modern Cephalu. For location see Map 3.

376 Lipara (modern Lipari) is the largest of the Aeolian Islands. See Map 12.

377 This term denotes the extent of Cape Peloron (Capo Peloro), the farthest north-east point of Sicily. See Map 12.

378 About 11⅓ miles or 18.25 km.

away in Syracuse[379] – despaired of coming out of the siege alive. What made them most disheartened was the decrepit state of their fortifications and the fact that the crisis offered them no leisure for making repairs. Consequently, they sent their children, their wives and their most valuable possessions out of the city to neighbouring communities. 5. But some of the Messinans, hearing that they had a very old oracle that stated that "the Carthaginians would have to be carriers of water in the city," interpreted this saying as favourable to themselves, thinking it meant that the Carthaginians would serve as slaves in Messina. 6. Consequently, aroused as they were in spirit, they even made many others eager to face danger for the sake of liberty. Rapidly enlisting the bravest of the young men, they sent them to the Peloris to prevent the enemy from entering Messinan territory.

The Messinan soldiers march out to resist Himilkon at his landing place at Cape Peloron

57.1. While the Messinans were occupied in this, Himilkon, seeing that they were marching out to fight at his landing place, dispatched 200 of his ships to attack the city. For he was hoping, quite reasonably, that, while their soldiers were trying to prevent his attack by land, the men on his ships would have no difficulty getting control of Messina, as it lacked defenders. 2. A north wind blew up, with the result that the ships made their way rapidly under full sail into the harbour and the Messinans, who had gone out on guard on the Peloris, got back after the arrival of the ships, even though they rushed at full speed. 3. As a consequence, the Carthaginians put Messina under siege and gained control of the city, by forcing their way in through the decrepit fortifications. 4. Some of the Messinans were killed fighting bravely, others fled to the nearby cities, but the bulk of the people set off through the surrounding mountains and scattered to the territory's forts. 5. Of those that remained, some were taken prisoner by the enemy, others, who had been cornered into the area beside the harbour, threw themselves into the sea in the hope of swimming across the intervening Strait. There were more than 200 of these, of whom most were carried away to their death by the current, but fifty did make their way safely to Italy. 6. After bringing his whole army into the city, Himilkon began by attempting to destroy the neighbouring forts, but these were strong and the men who had fled there resisted bravely, so he returned to the city, having failed to capture them.[380] After that he gave his army a rest, while he was making preparations for the march to Syracuse.

Himilkon makes a surprise naval attack on Messina and captures the city

The Messinans suffer various fates

Himilkon prepares to march to Syracuse

---

379 Presumably one of the conditions of their alliance with Dionysios.
380 Here, as elsewhere on this campaign, Himilkon seems to lack effective siege equipment, despite what we are told at 54.5.

The Sikels defect to Himilkon

Dionysios makes counter-preparations

58.1. The Sikels, who had a long-standing hatred of Dionysios, grasped the opportunity to revolt at this time, and went over to the Carthaginians as a group, with the exception of the citizens of Assoros. But, in Syracuse, Dionysios liberated the slaves and used them to man sixty ships.[381] He also sent for over 1,000 mercenaries from the Lakedaimonians[382] and made a tour of the territory's forts, strengthened their fortifications and stocked them with food supplies. However, he gave particular care to the fortifications of the acropoleis in Leontinoi and filled them with food supplies from the countryside. 2. He also persuaded the Campanians who inhabited Katane[383] to move to the place that is now called Aitna, because the fort there was exceedingly strong. After that, he led his whole army forward 160 *stades*[384] from Syracuse and made camp near the place called Tauros ["Bull"].[385] At that time he had 30,000 infantry and more than 3,000 cavalry. In addition, he had 180 warships, of which only a few were triremes.[386] 3. After he had utterly destroyed the walls of Messina, Himilkon ordered his soldiers to raze the houses to the ground, leaving behind neither a tile, nor a piece of wood, nor anything else, but to burn some things and smash others. Thanks to the huge manpower at his disposal, the work was swiftly accomplished, so that no one could tell that the city had once been occupied. 4. For, observing that the place was far removed from the cities that were allied to him, but yet was one of the most strategic locations in Sicily, his preference was for one of two options, either to keep the place entirely uninhabited or to make its refounding difficult and time-consuming.[387]

Dionysios marches out to battle

Himilkon utterly destroys Messina

Himilkon advances to the site of the future Tauromenion

59.1. After thus demonstrating his hatred for the Greeks through the tragic misfortune of the Messinans, Himilkon dispatched Magon,[388] his naval commander, with orders to sail with the fleet along the coast to a hill called Tauros ["Bull"].[389] This hill was in the possession of a large number of leaderless

---

381 Slaves were not often used as rowers by the Greeks. Hence the need for Dionysios to liberate them first.
382 The Spartans had been allies of Syracuse since the time of the Athenian Expedition of 415 and had transferred their support to Dionysios. See 44.2.
383 Given to them by Dionysios in 403 (14.15.3).
384 About 18 miles or 29 km.
385 A promontory north of Syracuse at the top of the Bay of Megara. See Map 3.
386 Presumably the rest were quadriremes or quinqueremes.
387 This contradicts the view attributed to him at 56.1. Actually, Messina was repopulated by Dionysios soon after (78.4–5).
388 From his name Magon was clearly of the same family as Himilkon, the family (Magonids) that had dominated Carthaginian affairs since the early fifth century. Whether he is the same man who was general in 393 (90.2–4) and/or was king in 383 (15.15.2) is not agreed.
389 A rather confusing coincidence. This was not the Tauros promontory, mentioned in 58.2.

Sikels. 2. These were the people to whom Dionysios had previously given the territory of the Naxians. But, at this time, induced by Himilkon's promises, they had taken possession of the hill. Since it was a strong position, they encircled it with a wall and made their home there both then and after the war and they named their city Tauromenion,[390] because those who gathered there had "remained" [*menein*].[391] 3. After resting his army, Himilkon resumed his march and advanced so energetically that he reached the previously mentioned location in the territory of Naxos at the same time as Magon sailed to shore. But a fiery eruption had recently poured from Aitna[392] and reached as far as the seashore, so that it was no longer possible to lead the army along the coast with the ships sailing alongside. For, the area beside the shore had been consumed by lava, as it is called, and it was necessary for the army to make a detour around Mount Aitna. 4. Consequently, he instructed Magon to sail down the coast and put in at Katane, while he set off swiftly through the interior and hurried to join the fleet on the beach at Katane. For, he was concerned that, with his forces divided, the Sicilians might engage Magon's men in a naval battle. And that is exactly what came to pass. 5. For, Dionysios, knowing that Magon's journey by sea was a short one, while the way for the infantry was long and difficult, hastened to Katane with the intention of engaging Magon at sea before Himilkon and his men arrived. 6. His hope was that, by drawing up his infantry along the shore, he would inspire courage in his own men and the enemy would be more frightened. But, his most important consideration was that, in the event of a defeat, his damaged ships would be able to flee to the infantry camp for refuge. 7. After forming this plan, he sent out Leptines with the whole fleet, ordering him to engage the enemy in close formation and telling him not to break his line to avoid being endangered by the great number of the enemy's ships.[393] For, including the transports and the other oared boats equipped with bronze beaks, Magon had no fewer than 500 ships.

Himilkon, forced to turn inland by an eruption of Aitna, is separated from his fleet

Dionysios hastens to Katane and orders Leptines to attack Magon's fleet

---

390 Modern Taormina.
391 This is a typical example of the kind of etymology favoured by the Greeks. Diod. repeats the story at 16.7.1, but in a different context, attributing the foundation and naming of the settlement to Andromakhos, father of the historian Timaios, in 358/7. An alternative account can be found in Strabo (6.2.3 C268), who follows Ephoros in claiming that Tauromenion was an early foundation of the Zankleans from Megara Hyblaia.
392 This must be the fourth eruption known to the Greeks, since according to Thucydides (3.116.1–2) the eruption which he recorded in 425 was the third. For a poetic description of an eruption, see Pindar, *Pythian* I, 21–28, and for something more prosaic, see Strabo, 6.2.3 C269.
393 Leptines had only 180 warships (58.2).

The Carthaginians at first head for the shore, but change their mind and prepare to fight at sea

Leptines opens the attack with thirty ships; initially successful, his forces are eventually overwhelmed

The Carthaginians win a great victory over Dionysios' fleet

60.1. But, when the Carthaginians saw that the beach was covered with infantrymen and that the Greek ships were bearing down upon them, they were greatly alarmed and attempted to sail to shore. But, after a while they came to the realization that they would be taking a risk in fighting against the ships and the land forces at the same time, and they quickly changed their mind. So, having decided to fight a naval engagement, they drew up their ships and awaited the enemy's attack. 2. Leptines advanced with his thirty best ships far ahead of the rest and engaged in battle courageously, but unwisely.[394] For, falling right away upon the leading Carthaginian ships, at first he sank not a few of the triremes ranged against him, but when Magon crowded around the thirty with his ships in close formation, then the Carthaginians had the advantage in numbers, even though Leptines and his men excelled in courage. 3. So, as the battle grew more intense and the helmsmen conducted the contest broadside to broadside, the conflict became similar to a battle on land. For, they were not driving into the enemy's ships with their rams from a distance, but, since the ships were bound together, they fought it out hand-to-hand. Some men fell into the sea, as they were trying to jump onto their opponents' ships, while others, who had made the leap successfully, were engaged in conflict onboard the enemy's ships. 4. In the end, Leptines was forced back and compelled to flee out to open water. When the rest of his fleet made a disorganized attack, they were worsted by the Carthaginians. For, the defeat suffered by the [Sicilian] commander increased the courage of the Carthaginians, but threw the Sicilians into a state of dismay like no other. 5. Such was the conclusion of the battle and the Carthaginians, pursuing with increased zeal the ships that were fleeing them in disarray, destroyed more than 100 of them. Also, stationing their smaller boats along the seashore, they killed those sailors who were trying to swim across to the soldiers on the land. 6. Since many were perishing at no great distance from the land, because Dionysios' men were completely incapable of coming to their assistance, the whole area was littered with corpses and pieces of wreckage. The number of Carthaginians who perished in the battle was not insignificant, but the Sicilians lost more than 100 ships and over 20,000 men. 7. After the battle the Phoenicians moored their triremes off Katane, took the ships they had captured in tow, brought them to port and

---

394 The account of this naval engagement is artfully designed to lay the blame for the defeat upon Leptines. Advised by Dionysios "not to break his line," he raced ahead of the fleet with thirty ships and engaged "unwisely." Although his men "excelled in courage," his rash action led them into a trap, in which they were surrounded. His flight left the rest of the fleet in disarray and dispirited without a commander. Neither Diod. nor his main sources (Ephoros and Timaios) had any motive for this bias, which surely derives from Dionysios' supporter, Philistos.

repaired them. As a result the magnitude of their superiority was made not only a matter of talk, but visibly manifest for the Carthaginians.

61.1. The Sicilians began to make their way towards Syracuse, but on realizing that they would for sure be enclosed and involved in a laborious siege, they urged Dionysios to confront Himilkon and his men over the recent victory. For, they said, the barbarians would quickly be thrown into a panic by the surprise of his appearance and the defeat he had suffered would be reversed. 2. At first, Dionysios was persuaded by their urgings and was prepared to lead his army against Himilkon, but when some of his friends[395] advised him that he was running a risk of losing the city, if Magon led his whole fleet against Syracuse, he quickly changed his mind. For, he was well aware that Messina had fallen under the control of the barbarians in a similar fashion. And so, deeming it unsafe to leave the city bereft of defenders, he led his army back to Syracuse. 3. Most of the Sicilians were angry at his unwillingness to confront the enemy and deserted Dionysios, going away, some to their own lands, others to the forts nearby. 4. Himilkon arrived at the beach at Katane in two days. There, since a strong wind was blowing up, he had all his ships drawn up on land. Then, giving his troops a few days' rest, he sent ambassadors to the Campanians who occupied Aitna,[396] urging them to defect from Dionysios. 5. He promised to make them a gift of a large tract of land and to give them a share of the booty from the war. He informed them that the Campanians, who lived at Entella,[397] were well disposed towards the Carthaginians and were their allies against the Syracusans. Furthermore, he made it clear that in general the Greek race was hostile to all other peoples. 6. However, since the Campanians had given hostages to Dionysios and sent their bravest soldiers to Syracuse,[398] they felt compelled to stick to their alliance with Dionysios, even though they really wanted to change sides over to the Carthaginians.

The Sicilians are angry when Dionysios refuses to engage Himilkon and chooses to retire to Syracuse

Himilkon tries to persuade the Campanians in Aitna to join him, but fails

62.1. Following this Dionysios, because he was scared of the Carthaginians, sent out his brother-in-law, Polyxenos,[399] as ambassador to the Greeks in Italy, to the Lakedaimonians and, in addition, to the Corinthians, entreating them

Dionysios in a panic sends out appeals for help and troops

---

395   His close advisers. For these, see 8.5 and n. 54. See also 13.111.1.
396   They had only just moved there from Katane (58.2).
397   Entella, an Elymian town, had been violently taken over by Dionysios' dismissed Campanian mercenaries in 404 (14.9.8–9). It had been loyal to Carthage in 397 and besieged (presumably unsuccessfully) by Dionysios for that reason (14.48.4–5). For its location, see Map 3.
398   Standard procedure for Dionysios. Compare the situation of the Messinans at 56.4.
399   For Polyxenos' marriage to Theste, Dionysios' sister, see 8.5 and n. 57. He is mentioned along with Dionysios and his brothers in an Athenian honorary decree of 393 (*TDGR*2, no. 20;

Himilkon moves his fleet into the Great Harbour at Syracuse and brings his army up to the city

to give assistance and not to allow the Greek cities in Sicily to be totally wiped out. He also dispatched recruiters of mercenaries with large sums of money, instructing them to gather as many soldiers as possible, sparing no expense.[400] 2. Himilkon, after decorating his ships with the spoils taken from his enemies, sailed down into the Great Harbour of Syracuse and aroused great consternation amongst the people in the city. For 250 warships sailed in, plying their oars in unison and adorned lavishly with the spoils of war, and after that came the transports … .[401] As a result, it turned out that the Syracusan harbour, large though it was, was chock-full of ships and almost entirely blanketed in sails. 3. No sooner had the ships dropped anchor, than the land army marched up from the opposite side. According to some accounts it was composed of 300,000 infantry and 3,000 cavalry.[402] So, then, Himilkon, the commander of the force, took up his quarters in the temple of Zeus,[403] while the rest of his host encamped nearby, about twelve *stades*[404] from the city. 4. Following this, Himilkon led out his whole army and marshalled his forces before the walls, attempting to provoke the Syracusans to battle. He also had 100 of his best ships attack the harbours to instill fear into the people in the city and to force them to concede that they were inferior even at sea. 5. But, when no one dared come out against him, for the time being he led his army back to camp. But, after that, he spent thirty days going around the countryside, cutting down trees and creating devastation everywhere, his dual purpose being to satiate his soldiers with every kind of booty and at the same time to generate a mood of despair amongst the inhabitants of the city.

Himilkon's offer of battle is declined; he spends the next 30 days plundering

Himilkon captures Akhradina and despoils the sanctuary of Demeter and Kore

63.1. He also took possession of the suburb of Akhradina[405] and looted the temples of Demeter and Kore.[406] For that act of impiety against divinity he

      R&O, no.10). In 387 he was in charge of twenty ships sent by Dionysios to Antalkidas in the Hellespont (Xen. *Hell.* 5.1.26). He was one of the "friends," but like most of them he ended up in exile (Plut. *Dion*, 21.7–8).
400 It is a puzzling question where Dionysios' money came from, but see n. 421.
401 The next two lines are impossibly corrupt and have resisted all attempts at emendation.
402 These are Ephoros' figures. Strangely Diodoros elects to cite them here. See n. 367.
403 The Temple of Olympian Zeus was a sixth-century peripteral Doric temple, with a double row of six columns along the front and seventeen along the sides. It was situated in Polikhna. For its location, see Map 4.
404 About 1⅓ miles or 2 km.
405 For the location of Akhradina and its strategic position, see Map 4.
406 The mystery cult of Demeter and Kore (Persephone), the Twin Goddesses, was celebrated throughout the Greek world, not least in Sicily. Their most famous sanctuary was at Eleusis in Attica.

soon suffered fitting punishment. For, affairs rapidly began to turn out less well for him day by day and, whenever Dionysios got up the courage to make sallies, the Syracusans gained the upper hand. 2. Also strange disturbances occurred in the camp at night and men ran together under arms, as if the enemy were attacking the palisade. On top of this there arose a plague, which was the cause of all their troubles. But we shall speak about that a little later, in order not to let our account get ahead of events. 3. Now Himilkon, in the process of throwing a wall around his encampment, destroyed almost all the tombs in the vicinity, amongst which were the exquisitely constructed ones of Gelon and his wife Demarete.[407] He also built three forts along the coast, one at Plemmyrion,[408] another at the middle of the harbour and the third by the temple of Zeus. Into these he brought wine and grain and all other kinds of supplies, in the belief that the siege was going to last a long time. 4. Furthermore he dispatched merchant ships to Sardinia[409] and Libya to bring back grain and other food supplies. Meanwhile Polyxenos, brother-in-law of Dionysios, arrived back from Italy and the Peloponnese,[410] bringing with him thirty warships from their allies, under the command of Pharakidas[411] the Lakedaimonian.

Polyxenos arrives with assistance from Italy and the Peloponnese

64.1. Later, Dionysios and Leptines <sailed out>[412] with some warships to obtain food supplies. The Syracusans, left by themselves, happened to see a grain ship approaching and sailed out to attack it with five ships. They overpowered it and brought it back to the city. 2. When the Carthaginians launched forty ships against them, the Syracusans responded by manning all their ships. A naval battle ensued in which the Syracusans captured the enemy's flagship

While Dionysios and Leptines are out getting supplies, the Syracusans win a naval engagement against the Carthaginians

---

407 It is not surprising that Himilkon would want to destroy anything to do with Gelon, the victor of the battle of Himera against the Carthaginians in 480. For Gelon's death and burial, see Diod. 11.38.2-4. It appears his burial was not as inexpensive as he wanted.
408 For the location of Plemmyrion, see Map 4.
409 The Phoenicians had had settlements in Sardinia since the ninth century BC, of which Carthage had assumed control in the sixth.
410 He had completed his mission in just over thirty days. On the return journey the Spartan ships captured nine or ten Carthaginian ships, which they used as a cover to enable them to pass the main Carthaginian fleet and get into the Great Harbour, according to Polyainos, *Strategemata*, 2.11 and Frontinus, *Strategemata*, 1.4.12.
411 We know the names of the Spartan *navarchs* for the years 399/8–394/3 and none of them have this name. Even though Diod. repeats the error in chs. 70 and 72, and Polyainos also uses the same name in the passage referred to above, it is clearly a mistake for the well-known *navarch* from this time – Pharax – on whom see more below at 79.4-6. Diod.'s date (396/5) is, however, incorrect, since Pharax was *navarch* for 398/7 and the *navarch* for 396/5 was either Pollis or Kheirikrates.
412 Some such verb needs to be supplied.

The Syracusans begin to talk of removing Dionysios

and destroyed twenty-four of the rest. The remainder fled to their anchorage pursued by the Syracusans, who proceeded to challenge the Carthaginians to battle. 3. The Carthaginians, for their part, were unnerved by the unexpected turn of events and made no move, and the Syracusans took the captured ships in tow and brought them back to the city.[413] Buoyed up by their success and reckoning that Dionysios had been beaten by the Carthaginians many times, while they had been victorious without him, the Syracusans were puffed up with pride. 4. Crowding together, they began talking amongst themselves, saying that they were allowing themselves to be enslaved by Dionysios, even when they had this opportunity of putting an end to him. For, up to now they had been unarmed,[414] but at this time, thanks to the war, they possessed weapons.

Dionysios returns, convenes an assembly and promises to bring the war to a speedy conclusion, but is challenged by Theodoros

5. However, as such talk was going on, Dionysios sailed into harbour. Convening an Assembly, he applauded the Syracusans and exhorted them to take heart, promising that he would bring the war to a speedy conclusion. But, as he was already on the point of dissolving the assembly, a Syracusan named Theodoros, a highly respected member of the cavalry with a reputation as a man of action, stood up and boldly made the following speech about liberty.

Theodoros makes a long speech denouncing the tyranny of Dionysios and inciting the Syracusans to remove him[415]

65.1. "Even if Dionysios has told some lies, there is truth in his final statement, namely that 'he will bring the war to a speedy conclusion.' But he would not be able to achieve that by being in charge himself, for he has often been defeated, but by giving back to the citizens [of Syracuse] their inherited liberty. 2. For, as it is now, none of us is eager to expose himself to danger, in a situation where victory is nothing short of defeat. For, if we are defeated, we will have to obey the orders of the Carthaginians, while, if we are victorious, we will have to endure Dionysios as a harsher ruler than they [would be]. You see, if,

---

413 While most scholars accept the historicity of this incident, there are some troubling elements to the narrative. (1) Is it likely that Dionysios would himself go in search of food supplies? (2) If he did, is it likely that he left no one of his "friends" in charge? (3) Were the Syracusans really in a position to take such an independent initiative? (4) Would the Carthaginian fleet with its numerical superiority really have cowered in harbour, as described? The narrative provides the material for Theodoros' speech that follows, with which it is intricately linked. Both lead to the unexpected reaction of the Spartan *navarch* in ch. 70.

414 See above at 14.10.4. It is unlikely, however, that Dionysios had not given weapons back to the Syracusans, given his need for warriors.

415 There is much debate over Diodoros' source for this speech, some favouring Timaios, some Ephoros, some, improbably, Philistos. Others attribute it to a rhetorical exercise. The possibility that Diodoros composed it himself has also been suggested, in favour of which is his own statement (20.1–2) about the situations when it is admissible to compose speeches in works of history, one of which is "when an event turns out contrary to expectation," as it does here. See n. 413, and Introduction under Sources.

indeed, the Carthaginians win the war, they would exact a defined amount of tribute, but they would not prevent us from governing our city by our ancestral laws,[416] whereas, this man, who has despoiled our sacred places and stripped the riches from private citizens, while robbing the owners of their lives, pays servants to accomplish the enslavement of their masters. Indeed, the terrible misfortunes that befall those cities that are captured in war, he inflicts on us in peace time, all the while promising that he will bring an end to the war with the Carthaginians. 3. For, my fellow citizens, it is just as necessary for us to put an end to the tyranny within our walls, as it is to bring an end to the Phoenician war. In truth, the acropolis that is guarded by armed slaves has been made into a fortress against the city and the horde of hired mercenaries has been assembled for the purpose of enslaving Syracusans. Furthermore, he controls the city not like a judge administering justice on an equal basis, but like an absolute monarch, deeming it right to make all decisions for his own profit. And, while right now the enemy is in possession of a part of our territory, Dionysios has uprooted all the land and given it out as gifts to those who increase his tyrannical power. 4. For how long, then, will we put up with sufferings that brave men would rather die than experience? Although we endure extreme dangers courageously in combatting the Carthaginians, we do not even dare to speak out frankly [with *parrhesia*], in fighting for the liberty of our country against a harsh tyrant. We face up to so many tens of thousands of the enemy, but shiver in our boots before a single ruler, who does not even possess the courage of a decent slave.

66.1. "For, surely, no one would dream of comparing Dionysios with our ancestor Gelon.[417] For, Gelon, by his own courage, in conjunction with the Syracusans and the rest of the Sicilians, liberated the whole of Sicily, while Dionysios, having inherited cities that were free, has put the rest of them in the hands of the enemy and has himself deprived his own city of its liberty. 2. And, while Gelon fought many battles in defence of Sicily and brought it about that his allies in the cities did not even have to see the faces of the enemy, Dionysios ran away from Motye across the whole extent of the island and

---

416 As can be seen from the terms of the treaty of 405 (13.114.1).
417 Gelon, tyrant of Syracuse from 485 to 478, was revered by the Syracusans for his great victory over the Carthaginians at Himera in 480. Even when the Syracusans were so short of funds that they were forced to auction off their public statues in 342, those of Gelon were exempt (Plut. *Tim*. 23.8). Nevertheless, he was hardly less ruthless than Dionysios in his opposition to democracy, his deportations of peoples and his suppression of liberty. Further, the victory at Himera did not drive the Carthaginians out of the west of Sicily.

shut himself up inside his walls, full of bravado amongst his fellow citizens, but lacking the courage even to look upon his enemies face-to-face. 3. That was the reason why Gelon, for his courage and his great accomplishments, gained the uncontested leadership not only of the Syracusans, but also of the Sicilians, while Dionysios' campaigning has led to the destruction of his allies and the enslavement of his fellow citizens. Surely he deserves to be hated by everyone! For, he is not only unworthy of leadership, but rather deserves to die ten thousand deaths. 4. Thanks to him, Gela and Kamarina have been destroyed, Messina has been wiped out, and 20,000 of our allies have perished in a battle at sea. In a nutshell, we have been corralled into one city, while all the Greek cities in Sicily have been done away with. For, in addition to these other disasters, he has sold the citizens of Naxos and Katane into slavery, and has utterly destroyed cities that were our allies and cities that were helpful to us. 5. Indeed, he has been involved against the Carthaginians in battle on two occasions and has been defeated in each. But, when he was entrusted by his fellow-citizens with supreme command only once, he immediately stripped them of their liberty, putting to death those who spoke out frankly [with *parrhesia*] in defence of the laws, sending into exile those who were prominent for their possessions, supplying their wives as bedmates for slaves and men of mixed race and putting barbarian mercenaries in control of the citizens' weapons. Those were the actions, by Zeus and all the gods, of an office boy in the archives, a desperado!

67.1. "What has happened to the Syracusan love of liberty? What has happened to the great deeds of our ancestors? I shall not mention the 300,000 Carthaginians[418] wiped out at Himera. I pass over the tyrants they deposed after Gelon.[419] But only yesterday or the day before, when the Athenians made an expedition against Syracuse with incredible forces, our fathers left not even one man alive to report the disaster.[420] 2. When we have such examples of courage from our fathers, are we going to obey Dionysios' orders, especially when we are in possession of our weapons? Some divine providence has brought us together with our allies under arms for the purpose of regaining our liberty, and it is possible today, if we behave courageously and with one mind, to be rid of his heavy oppression. 3. For, up to now, perhaps, when we have been deprived of our weapons, when we were <devoid> of allies and watched over by a host of

---

418 An exaggerated figure. Modern estimates are closer to 30,000.
419 Actually, the Syracusans experienced the tyranny of Hieron I (478–467), brother of Gelon, and only got rid of their tyrants when they drove out Thrasyboulos, Hieron's brother, in 466/5.
420 Cf. Thucydides, 7.87.6.

mercenaries, we were almost giving in to the force of circumstance, but now that we have our weapons and allies both to help and bear witness to our courage, let us not give way, but let us make clear that it was through circumstance, not lack of courage, that we allowed ourselves to be enslaved. 4. Do we not feel shame at having as our leader in war a man who has despoiled the sacred places throughout our city?[421] Do we not feel shame at putting in charge of such momentous affairs a man, to whom no individual in his right mind would entrust the management of his own private affairs? And, when other people show most respect for their sacred obligations to the gods during wartime, because of the magnitude of the dangers, are we expecting that a man whose name is synonymous with impiety will bring an end to <the> war?

68.1. "In fact, if one wants to examine the matter precisely, he will find that Dionysios is just as wary of peace as he is of war. For, at present, he thinks that the Syracusans will not attempt to take any action against him, because of their fear of the enemy, but that, once the Carthaginians have been overcome, they will strive to recover their liberty, because they have their weapons and are encouraged by pride in their achievements. 2. Indeed, in my opinion, it was for that reason that during the first war he betrayed Gela and Kamarina and left them uninhabited,[422] and why in the [subsequent] treaty[423] he agreed to surrender the majority of the Greek cities. 3. And [that is why] later in peacetime, after selling the citizens of Naxos and Katane into slavery in contravention of the treaty, he destroyed the one and gave the other to the Campanians from Italy to be their home.[424] 4. Finally, since those who had survived their massacre kept mounting frequent attempts to put an end to his tyranny, [that is why] he announced a war against the Carthaginians once again. For, he is not so much concerned about breaking agreements in contravention of his oaths, as he is afraid of the combination of the remaining legitimate Sicilian governments. For, it is clear that he spends all his wakeful hours plotting their destruction. 5. First of all, when he could have marshalled his troops to oppose the enemy at Panormos, as they were disembarking from their ships and their bodies were in bad shape after the rough crossing, he was unwilling to do so.[425] Next, he allowed a great and strategically located city such as Messina to be razed to

---

421 Perhaps this assault upon the treasuries of the religious sanctuaries of Syracuse was one of the main sources of Dionysios' finances.
422 Cf. 13.111.
423 In 405. For the terms, see 13.114.1.
424 See 14.15.1–3.
425 See 14.55.5.

the ground without raising a finger to help, so that not only as many Sicilians as possible might be killed, but also that the Carthaginians might prevent reinforcements coming from Italy and fleets from the Peloponnese.[426] 6. Finally, he engaged in battle off the beach at Katane, although he could have held the battle close to the city in order to give the defeated the opportunity to flee to their own harbours. Even after the naval engagement, when a strong wind blew up and the Carthaginians were forced to haul their fleet onshore, he had a perfect opportunity for victory. 7. For, the enemy's infantry had not yet arrived and the great storm had driven their ships on the beach.[427] If we had attacked at that time on land with our whole army, the enemy would have been forced to choose between being easily captured, as they disembarked, or being forced out into the waves and strewing the beach with pieces of wreckage.[428]

69.1. "But, I think there is no need to make any further accusations against Dionysios amongst Syracusans. For, if men who have suffered unendurably through his very actions are not aroused to anger, will they be any the more incited by words to take vengeance on him, especially when they have seen that he is the lowest born of citizens, the harshest of tyrants and the most ignoble of all generals? 2. As many times as we have gone to battle under his leadership, all those times we have been defeated. But, just now, by ourselves with a few ships we defeated the whole complement of the enemy in a naval battle.[429] So, it is necessary for us to look for another leader, to prevent us from having the gods as our enemy in the war, because we have as our general the man who despoils their temples. 3. For, clearly, divinity works against those who have chosen for their leader the most impious of men. For, how is the fact that all our forces are defeated when he is present, while without him even a small part is sufficient to beat the Carthaginians, not a sure sign to everyone of the manifest presence of the gods? 4. So, citizens, if he willingly lays aside his rule, let us allow him to quit the city with his possessions, but, if he is not willing, the present opportunity is the best we have to regain our liberty. We are all here together, we have our weapons and we have allies with us, not only the Greeks from Italy, but also those from the Peloponnese. 5. According to our laws, the leadership must be given either to the citizens, or to the Corinthians, because they inhabit our founding city, or to the Spartans, as the dominant power in Greece."

---

426 That was Himilkon's stated intent at 14.56.1, contradicted by his action at 14.58.4. Cf. n. 387.
427 This is not quite the way it is narrated at 14.61.4.
428 See 14.61.1–2.
429 Cf. n. 413.

70.1. With such words as these Theodoros raised the spirits of the Syracusans to great heights and they kept their gaze fixed upon their allies. When Pharakidas, the Spartan *navarch*[430] in command of the allies, approached the speaker's stone [*bema*], everyone was anticipating that he would become the instigator of their liberty. 2. But, because he was well disposed to matters related to the tyrant, he said that he had been sent by the Lakedaimonians to help the Syracusans and Dionysios in their battle with the Carthaginians, but not to put down Dionysios' rule. Because his negative response was contrary to all expectation, the mercenaries ran and gathered around Dionysios, while the Syracusans stayed still out of fear, although they heaped curses upon the Spartans. 3. For, indeed, previously Aretes the Lakedaimonian, who was meant to be assisting them in their desire for liberty, had betrayed them,[431] and, on this occasion also, Pharakidas was standing in the way of the Syracusans' desires. As for Dionysios, for the time being he was full of trepidation and dissolved the Assembly meeting, but later he ingratiated himself with the populace with kindly words and honoured some with gifts and invited others to public banquets. 4. After the Carthaginian capture of the suburb [Akhradina] and their pillaging of the sanctuary of Demeter and Kore, their army was struck by a plague. And disaster[432] was aided and abetted by the fact that tens of thousands were crowded into the same space and that this was the most active time of year for disease. Added to this, that summer had experienced exceptional spells of hot weather.[433] 5. Furthermore, it is likely that the place itself was responsible for the extreme extent of the disaster. For, on a previous occasion, when the Athenians occupied the same encampment, many of them died of the plague, because the location was enclosed and marshy.[434] 6. To begin with, before the sun had risen, their bodies were seized by fits of shivering caused by the cold breezes that came off the waters. But, by midday the heat was stifling, as would be the case when so many men were crowded into a narrow space.

The Syracusans' hopes are dashed by the Spartan navarch's response and Dionysios regains control

The Carthaginians are struck by a plague

---

430 See above, n. 411.
431 See 14.10.2, where he is named Aristos. As noted in n. 71, the Spartans maintained their support for Dionysios throughout his tyranny and he, in turn, was careful not to offend them (cf. 14.78.5).
432 Throughout this account of the plague and the subsequent disgrace and suicide of Himilkon, Diod. emphasizes the element of divine retribution for wrongdoing against gods and men. This is consistent with one of the unifying themes of his history, as exemplified by the introduction to this Book (14.1–2).
433 For the summer of the year 396/5 (Varronian year 399) Livy records excessive heat and a plague in Rome (5.13.4).
434 Cf. Thucydides, 7.47 and Diod. 13.12.1.

First to suffer were the Libyans. Description of the symptoms[435]

71.1. The plague first attacked the Libyans.[436] Initially, as many amongst them were dying, they buried the dead, but later, because of the mass of corpses and because those who were tending the sick were being carried off by the disease, no one dared to approach the afflicted. As a result, once this medical treatment had been withdrawn, the disaster was irremediable. 2. The first symptom of the disease was catarrh, caused by the foul stench of the unburied corpses and the putrid exhalations from the marshes. This was followed by swellings in the throat. Shortly after this came bouts of fever, aches in the sinews along the back and sensations of heaviness in the limbs. Then, dysentery ensued and blisters over the whole visible surface of the body. 3. This was the extent of the suffering for most people, but some fell into a state of madness and lost all memory. Quite out of their minds, they wandered around the camp, striking anyone they met. On the whole, it turned out that even the assistance of doctors was ineffectual, both because of the enormity of the suffering and the swiftness of death. For, on the fifth or more often the sixth day they passed away, after enduring terrible torture, so that everyone considered those who had died in the war to be the lucky ones. 4. Indeed, those who attended upon the afflicted all caught the disease. The result was a terrible fate for the sick in that no one was willing to assist the poor souls. It was not only those who were entirely unrelated, who abandoned each other, but even brothers were forced to reject brothers, and friends friends, out of fear for themselves.

Dionysios goes on the attack by land and sea[437]

72.1. When Dionysios heard about the disaster that had befallen the Carthaginians, he had eighty warships manned and gave orders to the naval commanders, Pharakidas and Leptines, to make an assault upon the enemy's ships at daybreak. For his part, under cover of a moonless night, he led his army

---

435 Descriptions of plagues were frequent in ancient literature from Homer (*Iliad*, 1.43–52) on, but for historians the archetype was Thucydides' description of the Athenian plague (2.47–53), recounted by Diod. at 12.58.1–7. Diod., or his source (probably Philistos), is writing within this genre. Other famous examples include Galen's analysis (*Methodus Medendi*, 5.12) of the Antonine plague that struck the Roman world between AD 165 and 180 and Procopius' account (*De Bellis*, 2.23.1) of the Justinianic plague of AD 541–542. Poetic versions include Lucretius, *De Rerum Natura*, 6.1138–1251; Vergil, *Georgics*, 3.478–497 and Ovid, *Metamorphoses*, 7.523–613.

436 Probably it originated with them, since there had been a plague in Libya already; see 14.41.1 and 45.3. The nature of the disease is still debated, but smallpox and some sort of viral hemorrhagic fever, like Ebola, are still prime suspects, although the Justinianic plague might have been caused by a first manifestation of the bubonic plague.

437 The whole subsequent, highly dramatized, account of the battles by sea and land has the air of first-hand witness and surely derives from Philistos.

on a circular route up to the sanctuary of Kyane,[438] and reached the enemy's camp at dawn, undetected. 2. From there, he sent ahead the cavalry and 1,000 of his hired infantry against the part of the Carthaginian camp that faced the interior. These mercenaries were the most disloyal to Dionysios amongst all his hired troops and were the source of frequent quarrels and riots. 3. For that reason, Dionysios had given orders to the cavalry to turn tail and abandon the mercenaries, whenever they encountered the enemy. They carried out his command, and the mercenaries were all slaughtered.[439] Meanwhile Dionysios undertook the siege of the camp and the forts simultaneously. While the barbarians were in a state of confusion at this unexpected event and were rallying assistance in a disorderly fashion, Dionysios took by force the fortress called Polikhna, and from the other quarter the cavalry, with the help of some of the triremes that sailed up in support, took by storm the area beside Daskon. 4. Then right away the whole fleet went on the attack and, when the army raised the paian over the capture of the forts, the barbarians were thrown into a deep state of fear. For, at first, they had all run together to oppose the infantry, in an attempt to ward off those who were besieging the camp, but, when they perceived the naval assault, they rushed back again to help at the harbour. However, overtaken by the speed of events, their own haste was ineffectual. 5. Furthermore, as they were going on board deck and manning their triremes, the opposing ships, driven on by their rowers, had <no> difficulty ramming them broadside. In fact, with one well-timed strike they would sink the crippled ships. But, it was the blows that broke the fastened timbers by repeated rammings that struck terrible fear into the fighters. 6. As the mightiest ships were being shattered in all directions, the sound of rending by the rams created an incredible din, while the beach that flanked the battle was full of corpses.

First, he betrays and eliminates a disloyal force of mercenaries, then captures Polikhna

A naval battle ensues

73.1. In their ambition for victory the Syracusans competed with each other very enthusiastically to be the first to leap onto the enemy ships. They poured around the barbarians, who were panic stricken at the gravity of their situation, and slaughtered them. 2. Nor, yet, were the infantry any the less enthusiastic in their attack upon the harbour, amongst whom chanced to be Dionysios himself, riding on horseback in the vicinity of Daskon. There they found forty pentekonters[440] drawn up on shore and right next to them some merchant ships and triremes at anchor, and they set fire to them. 3. As the fire

The Syracusans vie with each other to board the enemy ships and the infantry attack the harbour, where they set fire to some Carthaginian ships

438 South-east of Polikhna.
439 Dionysios appears to have had some trouble keeping the loyalty of his mercenaries. Cf. 14.78.1–3.
440 A fifty-oared warship that was the predecessor of the trireme.

raged aloft and spread over a large area, the ships were engulfed in flame. None of the merchants or ships' captains was able to come to the rescue, because of the intensity of the fire. And, when a great wind blew up, the fire was carried from the boats that were drawn up on shore onto the merchant ships at anchor. 4. As the crews were jumping overboard out of fear of being suffocated and the anchor ropes were being burnt through, the ships began to crash together due to the rough water. Some ships were destroyed by being crushed by each other, some by being thrown around by the wind, but most were consumed by the fire. 5. Thereupon, as the flames were borne up through the sails of the merchant ships and set fire to the yard-arms, the spectacle turned out to be like a scene from the theatre for the people in the city, and the annihilation of the barbarians seemed very similar to the fate of people being struck by a thunderbolt for impiety.

The Syracusans plunder the Carthaginian ships

74.1. And then, elated by their good fortune, the oldest boys and the aged men, those who, although past their prime, were not totally worn down by old age, manned small boats and sailed *en masse* in no particular order out to the ships in the harbour. They plundered the ships that had already been destroyed by the fire, selecting from the serviceable material anything that could be saved. As for the undamaged ships, they attached ropes to them and brought them back to the city. 2. So, not even those who were exempt from involvement in war by virtue of their age were able to restrain themselves, but out of an excess of joy their spirited ambition won out over their age. And, as the news of the victory raced through the city, women and children left their homes with their servants in tow and rushed to the city walls, so that the whole place was packed with spectators. 3. Some of them raised their hands to the heavens and were giving thanks to the gods, while others were saying that the barbarians had been overtaken by divine punishment for their despoiling of the temples. 4. Observed from a distance, the scene resembled a battle of the gods with so many ships on fire and the flames racing up on high through the sails; with the Greeks signalling each sign of victory with wild shouts and the barbarians kicking up a great fuss of distressed screams from their fear of disaster. 5. Nevertheless, at that time, as night approached, the battle broke off, but Dionysios continued his offensive against the barbarians, pitching his camp near the temple of Zeus.

Women and children rush to the walls to witness the victory

After their defeat the Carthaginians ask Dionysios to allow them to sail home and for a price he agrees, without telling the Syracusans

75.1. Defeated simultaneously on land and sea, the Carthaginians sent a secret embassy to Dionysios, behind the backs of the Syracusans, asking him to allow their remaining forces to be transported back to Libya and promising to give him the 300 *talents* they had in the camp. 2. Dionysios responded that it was not possible for them all to escape, but agreed to let just the Carthaginian citizens depart secretly by sea during the night. [He made this agreement secretly], because he knew that neither the Syracusans nor the allies would entrust him to conclude terms with the enemy on these matters. 3. Dionysios' action was prompted by his desire that the Carthaginian forces not be totally destroyed, so that the Syracusans might never have the leisure to strive for liberty on account of their fear of the Carthaginians.[441] So, after agreeing with the Carthaginians that they take flight on the fourth day under cover of darkness, Dionysios led his army back into the city. 4. Himilkon had the 300 *talents* carried up to the acropolis by night and handed over to the tyrant's appointees on the Island.[442] Then, when the agreed time arrived, during the night he manned forty triremes with citizen crews and set out to escape, abandoning the whole of the rest of his army. 5. He had already sailed across the harbour, when some of the Corinthians caught sight of his flight and swiftly reported the news to Dionysios. As he was taking his time summoning his soldiers to arms and bringing together the captains, the Corinthians did not wait for him, but swiftly put to sea against the Carthaginians and, competing with each other in rowing, they caught up with the last of the Phoenician ships and sank them, by smashing with their rams. 6. Later, Dionysios led out his army, but before the Syracusans arrived the Sikel allies of the Carthaginians made their escape through the interior and almost all of them reached their homelands safely. 7. Then, Dionysios, after posting guards at intervals along the roads, led his army against the enemy encampment while it was still night. The barbarians were disheartened at being abandoned by their general and the Carthaginians, as well as by the Sikels, and fled in panic. 8. Some were caught as they fell in with the guards stationed on the roads, but the majority threw away their weapons and came forward with hands outstretched, supplicating for their lives to be

Himilkon pays the agreed price and prepares his escape

The Corinthians catch and sink some of his ships

Dionysios captures the Carthaginian camp

---

441 Some commentators deny the authenticity of this agreement between Dionysios and Himilkon, arguing that it was more in Dionysios' interest for the Carthaginians to be completely destroyed and that, if so, he would capture the 300 *talents* anyway. Also, they point out that Himilkon still commanded Plemmyrion and so could exit the Great Harbour without Dionysios' help. See Stroheker (1958), 79, n. 101; Meister (1967), 95; Bennett in the Budé, *ad loc*. But, as is shown by the success of the Corinthian attack (14.75.5), it was not so easy for Himilkon to escape, and the calculation attributed to Dionysios is quite rational, although devious, and may come from the intimate knowledge of Diodoros' source (Philistos). Dionysios achieved the defeat of the Carthaginian forces and the acquisition of 300 *talents* without risking further loss of men, especially given that his mercenaries were mutinous.

442 Ortygia, which Dionysios had turned into his personal fortress (14.7.1–5).

spared. Only the Iberians kept together as a group under arms and sent a herald to negotiate an alliance. 9. Dionysios made a treaty with them and enrolled the Iberians amongst his mercenaries,[443] but he took captive the rest of the host and handed over the remaining baggage to his soldiers to plunder.

Chance (Tyche) reveals its power over the affairs of the Carthaginians

76.1. So, in this way Chance brought about a swift reversal of fortune for the Carthaginians and demonstrated to all mankind that those whose ambition exceeds due proportion soon give proof of their own weakness. 2. For, those who were in control of almost all the cities in Sicily except Syracuse, and were expecting that they would capture that, were suddenly compelled to worry about their own land; those who overturned the tombs of the Syracusans looked upon 150,000[444] [of their own men] piled up unburied due to the plague; those who set fire to the territory of the Syracusans, in return, suddenly saw their own fleet go up in flames; those who sailed arrogantly into the harbour with their full force and paraded their good fortune before the Syracusans did not imagine that they would run away secretly by night and leave behind their allies, surrendering them to the enemy. 3. And the general himself, he who had taken the temple of Zeus for his quarters and treated the wealth plundered from the temples as his own revenue, fled home to Carthage shamefully with only a few men, so that, while he escaped intact from his acts of impiety by not paying the debt of death owed to nature, he would have a life of notorious disgrace in his homeland, reviled by everyone. 4. Indeed, he reached such a depth of misfortune that he went around the city's temples in the meanest attire, denouncing himself for impiety and paying fitting penalty to the divinity for his crimes against the gods. In the end he condemned himself to death and killed himself by starvation, bequeathing to his fellow citizens a profound fear of the Divine.[445] For, Chance [*Tyche*] soon came down upon them in other matters related to the war also.

Himilkon returns to Carthage in disgrace and commits suicide

On the news of the Carthaginian defeat their allies in Libya revolt and march against Carthage

77.1. When the news of the disaster was heralded abroad throughout Libya, their allies, who had for a long time hated the burdensome rule of the Carthaginians, were then enflamed all the more in their hatred because of the

---

443 Iberian mercenaries were still in the service of Dionysios in 369/8, when he sent them to help the Spartans against the Thebans (Diod. 15.70.1; Xen. *Hell.* 7.1.20–22).

444 A gross exaggeration, considering Timaios' figure of 100,000 for the whole Carthaginian force (14.54.6).

445 See n. 432. The disgrace and death of Himilkon are also recorded by Justin (*Epitoma* 2.7–11; 3.1–12). It was a significant blow to the dominance of the Magonids, the family that had wielded virtually monarchic power in Carthage since about 550 BC, and began their steady decline. An aristocratic oligarchy followed.

betrayal of their soldiers at Syracuse. 2. And so, driven by their hatred and at the same time despising the Carthaginians on account of their misfortune, they made an attempt to achieve their liberty.⁴⁴⁶ After sending ambassadors back and forth between them, they amassed an army and, moving forward, pitched camp in the open. 3. And, as not only freemen but also slaves quickly rushed to join them, in a short time they had collected a force of 200,000 men. Seizing control of Tynes,⁴⁴⁷ a city situated no great distance from Carthage, they made it their base of operations and, since they had the upper hand in the fighting, they constrained the Phoenicians within their walls. 4. At first the Carthaginians, since the gods were clearly hostile to them, gathered in small groups in a very agitated state and kept beseeching the divine to cease its anger. But, later, a profound fear of the divine and dread took possession of the whole city, as each person imagined in their mind the enslavement of the city. And so, they passed a resolution to placate by all possible means the gods, against whom sacrilege had been committed. 5. Not having previously admitted either Kore or Demeter amongst their sacrifices, they appointed their most outstanding citizens to be their priests and, after setting up their images with all appropriate ceremony, they made sacrifice to them according to Greek custom. Furthermore, they selected the most respected from amongst the Greeks that resided with them and put them in charge of the service to the goddesses.⁴⁴⁸ After that, they equipped their ships for action and carefully made all other preparations for war. 6. The members of the revolt were a motley group, who lacked competent leaders, but their biggest problem was that they had insufficient supplies for their large number. The Carthaginians, on the other hand, were supplied by sea from Sardinia. In addition, the rebels were at odds with each other over the command, and some, who had been bribed by the Carthaginians, deserted the common enterprise. So, because of the shortage of supplies and the treachery of some of their members, they dispersed to their homelands and delivered the Carthaginians from their greatest fear. Such was the state of affairs in Libya.

Amassing a large force, they seize Tynes and besiege Carthage

The Carthaginians attempt to placate the gods and prepare for war

The people in revolt, lacking leadership and provisions, eventually disperse

78.1. When Dionysios perceived that his mercenaries were very disaffected, fearing that they might put an end to his rule, he began by having Aristoteles,

Dionysios, fearing a revolt by his mercenaries, arrests their leader and offers the territory of Leontinoi to the rest

---

446 The Carthaginians experienced a far more challenging revolt in Libya in 241–238, described in detail by Polybios (1.65–88).
447 Modern Tunis.
448 As stated, Diod. likes to emphasize the notion of divine vengeance and the need to placate the offended divinities. The cult of the Greek goddesses seems, indeed, to have been introduced at this time, but it never became as popular as that of the local goddess, Tanit.

their leader, arrested. 2. Next, when a crowd of them came running together with their weapons and were angrily demanding their pay, he told them that he was sending Aristoteles to Lakedaimon to undergo trial amongst his own citizens, and to the mercenaries, who numbered about 10,000, he offered the city and territory of the Leontinians in place of their pay. 3. They were happy to accept [this offer] because of the excellence of the land. They divided the territory into plots and took up residence in Leontinoi. As for Dionysios, he recruited other mercenaries and entrusted the safety of his rule to them and his household of liberated slaves. 4. After the disaster that had befallen the Carthaginians, the survivors from the cities in Sicily, whose citizens had been sold into slavery, regrouped and restored their circumstances, by taking back their own lands. 5. And Dionysios settled in Messina 1,000 Lokrians,[449] 4,000 Medmaians[450] and 600 Messenians from the Peloponnese, fugitives from Zakynthos[451] and Naupaktos. But, when he perceived that the Lakedaimonians were offended that the Messenians, who had been expelled by themselves, were being settled in a significant city, he removed them from Messina[452] and, after granting them a little land on the coast, detached some of the territory of Abakaine and included the part he had detached within their boundaries. 6. The Messenians gave the name Tyndaris[453] to the city and, by living together in harmony <and> enrolling many into the citizen body, their number soon grew to more than 5,000. 7. After this, Dionysios made numerous campaigns[454] into the territory of the Sikels capturing Menainon[455] and Morgantinon[456] and concluding treaties with Agyris, tyrant of the Agyrinaians, with Damon,[457] the ruler of Kenturipa, and also with the Herbitaians

After the defeat of the Carthaginians, enslaved Sicilians regain their cities and Dionysios resettles Messina

Dionysios campaigns against the Sikels

---

449 This was a strategic move by Dionysios, exploiting the hostility between the Lokrians and the citizens of Rhegion, with whom he was not on friendly terms (cf. 14.40 and 14.44.3–7).
450 All manuscripts read Medimnaians, but there is no known place with this name. All editors adopt the emendation to Medmaians, from Medma in Bruttium, a city founded by the Lokrians.
451 At 14.34.2 the fugitives were expelled from Kephallenia not Zakynthos.
452 See n. 431.
453 For the location of Tyndaris, see Map 3. Its Greek, Roman and Byzantine remains are extensive.
454 Clearly these campaigns extended beyond the year 396/5, probably well into 394.
455 Menainon is an emendation by the eighteenth-century scholar Wesseling for the unintelligible reading of the mss. It was originally an indigenous settlement, called Menai, that was refounded as Menainon by the Sikel leader Douketios in 459 (Diod. 11.78.5). According to Diod., Douketios was a native of the city, which he later moved down to the plain (11.88.6).
456 Situated in south-central Sicily, Morgantina (as it is best known) had a long history of settlement from the Bronze Age onwards. It became a Greek/Sikel city in the fifth century BC.
457 Called Nikodemos in the summary and in one manuscript.

and the Assorinoi. By means of treachery he took Kephaloidion, Solous and Enna. In addition, he made peace with the citizens of Herbessos.[458] Such was the state of affairs in Sicily.

79.1. In Greece,[459] the Lakedaimonians, foreseeing that the war against the Persians was a major one,[460] put Agesilaos,[461] one of their two kings, in charge.[462] And Agesilaos, after raising a levy of 6,000 men[463] and constituting a council of thirty of his most distinguished citizens,[464] brought his army over from Euboia[465] to Ephesos. 2. After enlisting 4,000 soldiers there, he led his army of 10,000 infantry and 400 cavalry forward into open country. And the crowd of people that accompanied them, selling supplies and hoping for plunder, was no less than the above. 3. On his way through the plain of Kaÿster he devastated the territory that was under Persian control until he reached Kyme.[466] Making his base there, he spent the majority of the summer plundering Phrygia and its environs.[467] Then in the autumn,

Agesilaos is put in charge of the campaign against Persia and sails from Euboia to Ephesos

Agesilaos spends the summer devastating Phrygia before returning to Ephesos in autumn

---

458 For the location of these places, see Map 3.
459 Diod. resumes his account of Greek affairs from chapter 39.
460 From information provided by a Syracusan called Herodas (Xen. *Hell*. 3.4.1).
461 Agesilaos II, son of Arkhidamos II and half-brother of Agis II of the Eurypontid line, succeeded in 400 to the throne in place of Agis' son, Latykhidas, who was deemed to be illegitimate (see Plut. *Lys*. 22.3). Although physically disabled in one of his legs, Agesilaos campaigned extensively and played a leading role in Greek affairs until his death in 360.
462 According to Xenophon (*Hell*. 3.4.2), Lysander instigated this choice and accompanied Agesilaos to Asia. See also Plut. *Ages*. 6.1–3.
463 Xenophon (*Hell*. 3.4.2) states that the 6,000 were allied troops and adds 2,000 liberated Helots to the total force.
464 These would be Spartiates of the officer rank.
465 The mss' readings are either *Asia* or *Europe*. The first is not credible, the second too broad. Vögel's emendation, *Aulis*, has merit, because Agesilaos wanted to imitate Agamemnon by sacrificing there before going to Asia (cf. Xen. *Hell*. 3.4.3; Plut. *Ages*. 6.4–6), and it is accepted by Oldfather, but Bennett (Budé) prefers Knoepfler's suggestion, *Euboia*, since it was from Geraistos at the tip of Euboia that Agesilaos' force actually set out for Ephesos (Xen. *Hell*. 3.4.4).
466 It is common to use this mention of Kyme as evidence that Ephoros was Diod.'s source here, since Ephoros was notorious for inserting his hometown into the narrative, wherever possible. On the other hand, Kyme was surely, in fact, Agesilaos' base of operations in Phrygia (cf. Xen. *Hell*. 3.4.27).
467 Diod. has compressed events considerably. He neglects to mention that Agesilaos and Tissaphernes initially agreed to a truce so that Tissaphernes could convey Agesilaos' demand "that the Greek cities be free" to the King. He also fails to report the falling out between Agesilaos and Lysander. All this is narrated by Xenophon at *Hell*. 3.4.5–10. See also Plut. *Lys*. 23.1–9; *Ages*. 7.1–9.5.

The Spartans seek an alliance with Egypt

Pharax, the Spartan navarch, blockades Konon in Kaunos, but is forced to retreat to Rhodes

The Rhodians revolt from Sparta and welcome Konon to the city

when he had satisfied his army's desire for booty, he made his way back to Ephesos.[468] 4. While this was happening, the Lakedaimonians sent ambassadors to Nephereus,[469] the king of Egypt, to seek an alliance, but instead of the manpower [requested] he made a gift to the Spartiates of equipment for 100 triremes and 500,000 measures of grain.[470] And Pharax,[471] the Lakedaimonian *navarch*, set out from Rhodes with 120 ships and sailed down to Sasanda[472] in Karia, a fortified place that was 150 *stades*[473] from Kaunos.[474] 5. Making his base there, he initiated a siege of Kaunos and a blockade of Konon, the commander of the King's fleet, who was stationed there with forty ships. But when Artaphernes and Pharnabazos came to the assistance of the Kaunians with a large force, Pharax broke off his siege and retired to Rhodes with his whole fleet. 6. After that, Konon gathered eighty triremes and set sail for the Khersonesos,[475] but the Rhodians, after expelling the Lakedaimonian fleet, revolted from the Lakedaimonians and welcomed Konon and his whole fleet into their city.[476] 7. And, the Lakedaimonians, who were transporting the gift of grain from Egypt, being ignorant of the revolt of the Rhodians, sailed to the island with confidence. The Rhodians and Konon, the Persians' *navarch*, brought their ships into harbour and filled the city's granaries with grain. 8. Konon was joined by ninety additional triremes, ten from Kilikia and eighty from Phoenicia, under the leadership of the king of the Sidonians.[477]

---

468 See Xen. *Hell*. 3.4.12–15.
469 Called Nepherites by Manethon, *Aigyptiaka*, Fr. 73a. Nephereus/Nepherites was the founder of the Twenty-ninth (Mendesian) Dynasty. He ruled for six years, from 400/399 to 395/4.
470 This information is perhaps referred to by Justin, *Epitoma*, 6.2, although he calls the king Hercynio. The report (14.79.7) of the capture of the grain by the Rhodians is not found in any other extant source.
471 See n. 411.
472 No place of this name is known. Probably the reference is to Pasanda, which is located south of Kaunos.
473 About 17 miles or 27 km.
474 For the location of Kaunos, see Map 8.
475 The peninsula of Knidos. The movements of Konon at this time are ignored by Xenophon, but are narrated in the *Hellenika Oxyrhynkhia* (*Hell. Oxy.* 9.2–3; 15.1–3) and by the Atthidographer Philokhoros (*FGrHist/BNJ* 328 FF144–146), as preserved in a fragmentary state by Didymos in his *Commentary on Demosthenes*, col. 7.28ff., for which see Harding (2006), 67, 177–182.
476 Diod. fails to report the role played by Konon in the overthrow of the Diagoreans and the revolt of Rhodes from Sparta that is narrated in *Hell. Oxy.* 15.1–3 and referred to by Pausanias (6.7.6), citing the Atthidographer Androtion (*FGrHist/BNJ* 324 F46). See Harding (1994), 71–72, 166–168.
477 This precise detail is found in *Hell. Oxy.* 9.2.

80.1. After that, Agesilaos led his army out into the Plain of Kaÿster and the area around Mount Sipylos,[479] and destroyed the homes of the locals. But Tissaphernes amassed a force of 10,000 cavalry and 50,000 infantry[480] and followed the Lakedaimonians,[481] picking off any soldiers who became separated from the line of march, as they were foraging.[482] So, Agesilaos arranged his troops into a square and hugged the foothills beside Mount Sipylos, watching for an opportune occasion for an assault upon the enemy. 2. As he advanced through the countryside as far as Sardis, Agesilaos destroyed the fruit trees, and also the pleasure garden of Tissaphernes, which had been designed with lavish artistry with plants and other effects for luxury and for the enjoyment of the good life in peacetime.[483] After that, he turned back, but, when he reached the midpoint between Sardis and Thybarnai, he dispatched Xenokles, the Spartiate, with 1,400 men by night to a heavily wooded location, to lie in ambush for the barbarians.[484] 3. At daybreak, he resumed his march with the army. When he had passed by the point of ambush and as the barbarians were harassing the men in his rearguard, attacking in a disorderly fashion, he suddenly and unexpectedly turned upon the Persians. A violent conflict ensued. But, when the signal for those in the ambush was raised, they sang the paian and fell upon the enemy. The Persians, seeing that they were caught between two forces, panicked and fled immediately. 4. Agesilaos' men pursued them for a distance,

The Battle at Sardis:[478] *Agesilaos advances into the Plain of Kaÿster and ravages the land, closely followed by Tissaphernes with a huge army*

Agesilaos sets an ambush and defeats Tissaphernes

---

478 Diodoros' account of the battle of Sardis is clearly derived directly or indirectly from the *Hell. Oxy.* 11.4–6. It disagrees in many details with Xenophon's (*Hell.* 3.4.22–24), to which it is usually preferred. Even though Xenophon was supposedly present, his account is superficial and lacks the detail provided by the Oxyrhynkhos Historian. See *TDGR*2, no.13; Bruce (1967), 77–88; *FGrHist/BNJ* 66 F7.
479 This suggests that Agesilaos followed a different route from that implied by Xenophon (*Hell.* 3.4.20–22), who states that the king marched by the shortest route from Ephesos directly to the territory of Sardis and arrived at the river Paktolos after three days. This would have taken him by the main road, along the river Kaÿster and over Mt Tmolos. Diodoros and the Oxyrhynkhos Historian's route takes him further north, towards Smyrna, then past Mt Sipylos (perhaps through the Karabel Pass) to the river Hermos and thence to Sardis. See Map 9.
480 The figures at *Hell. Oxy.* 11.3 are not fully preserved, but appear to be less than Diod.'s.
481 According to Xenophon (*Hell.* 3.4.21), Tissaphernes thought Agesilaos was going to attack Karia, so he moved his infantry there and stationed his cavalry in the Maiander plain. Indeed, in Xenophon's account (*Hell.* 3.4.23) there was no Persian infantry at the battle. Xenophon is followed by Plutarch, *Ages.* 10.1–3.
482 According to Xenophon (*Hell.* 3.4.21), Agesilaos marched for three days without meeting any enemy.
483 This detail is not found in the account of the Oxyrhynkhos Historian.
484 Xenophon (*Hell.* 3.4.20) names Xenokles as one of the thirty Spartiates who replaced the original thirty at the end of the campaigning season, and states that he was one of two men put in charge of the cavalry, but neither he nor Plutarch (*Ages.* 10.1–3) makes any mention of this ambush.

Tissaphernes retires to Sardis and Agesilaos to Ephesos

Artaxerxes replaces Tissaphernes with Tithraustes

Tithraustes has Tissaphernes beheaded and makes a truce with Agesilaos

The Boiotian War breaks out between Phokis and Boiotia. Sparta allies with Phokis and sends first Lysander, then king Pausanias[493]

killing over 6,000[485] and gathering a great number of captives. They also plundered the camp, that was loaded with much wealth. 5. Tissaphernes retired from the battle and withdrew to Sardis,[486] thoroughly shaken by the boldness of the Lakedaimonians, while Agesilaos, who was planning an incursion into the satrapies beyond, after failing to get favourable omens,[487] led his army back to the coast. 6. When Artaxerxes, the King of Asia, learned of the defeat, he was angry with Tissaphernes, because he was also afraid of war against the Greeks. For, he held Tissaphernes responsible for the conflict.[488] In addition, he was being petitioned by his mother, Parysatis, to grant her vengeance against Tissaphernes, since she had a quarrel to settle with him for his slandering of her son, Kyros, at the time of his campaign against his brother.[489] 7. So, after appointing Tithraustes to the command, he gave him orders to arrest Tissaphernes, and sent letters to the cities and the satrapies that they should all obey his instructions. 8. When Tithraustes arrived at Kolossai[490] in Phrygia, he caught Tissaphernes in his bath, thanks to the connivance of the satrap Ariaios.[491] He had his head cut off and sent to the King. Then, he persuaded Agesilaos to enter into negotiations and concluded a six-month truce.[492]

81.1. [spring 395]. While matters in Asia were being carried on as described, the Phokians, who were at war with the Boiotians over some

---

485 The number in *Hell. Oxy.* 11.6 is 600.
486 Xenophon states that Tissaphernes was not at the battle, but in Sardis all the time (*Hell.* 3.4.25).
487 This is a compressed version of *Hell. Oxy.* 12.1–4, which names Phrygia Megale as the satrapy Agesilaos was planning to invade and the Maiander River as the place where he sacrificed. Consulting omens before battle or commencing a campaign was standard practice for Greek generals, but it was particularly characteristic of the Spartans. Xenophon mentions none of this.
488 Cf. Xen. *Hell.* 3.4.25.
489 Parysatis, wife of Darius II, was mother of (amongst others) both Arsaces (= Artaxerxes II) and Kyros, the latter of whom she favoured. Cf. Plut. *Artax.* 23.1 and see n. 145.
490 See Map 5.
491 Xenophon, *Hell.* 3.4.25 (followed by Plutarch, *Ages.* 10.4) records the beheading of Tissaphernes, but lacks the details reported here. They are certainly derived from the Oxyrhynkhos Historian (in the fragmentary chapter 13), who is followed closely by Polyainos, *Strategemata* 7.16.1.
492 Cf. Xen. *Hell.* 3.4.25–26. The truce was supposedly to enable Agesilaos to consult the ephors over the King's demands: that he leave Asia; that the Greek cities there should be self-governing, but pay the King their traditional tribute.
493 The events, described briefly in paragraphs 1–3 of this chapter, are narrated at greater length by Xenophon (*Hell.* 3.5.1–25), the Oxyrhynkhos Historian (*Hell. Oxy.* 16.1; 18.1–5), Pausanias (3.5.3–7; 3.9.8–13) and Plutarch (*Lys.* 28.1–6).

disputes,[494] persuaded the Lakedaimonians to become their ally against the Boiotians. And, to begin with, the Lakedaimonians sent Lysander out to them with a few soldiers. After he arrived in Phokis, Lysander collected an army, but later king Pausanias was also sent with a force of 6,000 soldiers. 2. The Boiotians persuaded the Athenians to join them in the conflict,[495] but for the time being they marched out by themselves and found Haliartos[496] under siege by Lysander and the Phokians. A battle ensued, in which Lysander and many of the Lakedaimonians and their allies were killed. The whole Boiotian *phalanx* quickly turned back from the pursuit, but 200 Thebans took themselves rather rashly into rugged terrain and were slaughtered.[497] 3. Well, this war was called the Boiotian War.[498] When Pausanias, the Lakedaimonian king, learned of the defeat, he made a truce with the Boiotians[499] and led his army back to the Peloponnese.[500] 4. Konon, admiral of the Persians, put two Athenians, Hieronymos and Nikophemos,[501] in charge of the fleet, while he set sail along

The Spartans are defeated at Haliartos and Lysander dies

Konon visits Artaxerxes in Babylon

494 The dispute was a long-standing one between the Lokrians (Xenophon, probably correctly, names the Opuntian or Eastern Lokrians, the Oxyrhynkhos Historian and Pausanias specify the Ozolian or Western Lokrians) and the Phokians over a piece of land around Mt Parnassos. Most authors, except Plutarch (*Lys.* 27.1–4), agree that it was a faction amongst the Thebans, led by Androkleidas and Ismenias, who secretly stirred up this particular incident, hoping to precipitate a conflict with Sparta, but, while Xenophon says they instigated the Lokrians, their allies, to initiate the quarrel, the Oxyrhynkhos Historian says they persuaded the Phokians, ally of Sparta, to do so. In this instance, the details in Xenophon are more credible. The story is complex and Diod. was perhaps wise to skip over it, but his compression leaves the misleading impression that the Spartans were the aggressors.

495 The alliance between Boiotia and Athens is extant as *IG* II² 14 and recorded by the Atthidographer Philokhoros (*FGrHist/BNJ* 328 F148). Compare Xen. *Hell.* 3.5.7–16; Andokides, 3, *On the Peace*, 25; Lysias 16, *For Mantitheos*, 13; and Pausanias, 3.5.4. Also extant is an alliance between Athens and the Lokrians (*IG* II² 15), probably from the same date (late summer 395). See *TDGR2*, nos.14 and 16.

496 Haliartos was in Boiotia, near the south shore of Lake Copais, about 20 km west of Thebes. It existed from the Bronze Age down to 171 BC, when it was razed to the ground by the Romans and never refounded. From 447 to 386 and from 371 to 338 it was a member of the Boiotian League.

497 According to Xenophon (*Hell.* 3.5.17–21) and Plutarch (*Lys.* 28.1–6), the plan was for Pausanias to attack Boiotia from the south, while Lysander and the Phokians moved down from the north, but Pausanias was late and Lysander did not wait. Only Plutarch gives the number of Theban dead as 300.

498 Although it was just a prelude to the subsequent Corinthian War (395–386).

499 The truce was for the purpose of recovering the bodies of the dead Spartans, including Lysander's, but the Thebans demanded in return that the Spartans leave Boiotia (Xen. *Hell.* 3.5.22–24).

500 King Pausanias was later prosecuted for his part in this action, tried and exiled. See 14.89.1 and cf. Xen. *Hell.* 3.5.25 and Plut. *Lys.* 30.1.

501 Nikophemos is an emendation for Nikodemos, which is the reading of all mss. The emendation is based upon the name in *Hell. Oxy.* 15.1, Xen. *Hell.* 4.8.8 and Lysias 19, *For the Estate of Aristophanes*, 7.

the coast to Kilikia with the aim of having an audience with the King. From Kilikia he travelled inland to Thapsakos in Syria and sailed up the Euphrates river to Babylon. 5. There he gained audience with the King and promised that he would defeat the Lakedaimonians at sea, if only the King equipped him with money and supplies in accordance with his specific stipulations. 6. Artaxerxes greeted him warmly and honoured him with rich gifts, then appointed a treasurer to orchestrate the payment of whatever sum of money Konon asked for.[502] He also granted him the liberty to choose any Persian he wished to be his joint-commander for the war. And Konon chose the satrap Pharnabazos,[503] then went back down to the coast, after arranging matters to his satisfaction.[504]

395/4: Book 14.82.1–84.7

The Boiotians, Athenians, Corinthians and Argives form an alliance against the Lakedaimonians

82.1 [mid-summer 395]. Once this year had come to an end, Diophantos[505] assumed the archonship at Athens, while in Rome six military tribunes managed the consulship: [they were] Lucius Valerius, Marcus Furius, Quintus Servilius, Quintus Sulpicius.[506] After these men had assumed office, the Boiotians and Athenians, together with the Corinthians and Argives, concluded an alliance with each other.[507] 2. For, since the Lakedaimonians were hated by their allies for their heavy-handed rule, they thought it would be easy to bring an end to their hegemony, if the most powerful cities were of like mind.

---

502 According to *Hell. Oxy.* 19.2, the Great King was a notoriously bad paymaster. Diod.'s statement that Konon actually had audience with Artaxerxes is denied by the Oxyrhynkhos Historian (*Hell. Oxy.* 19.1–3), who more plausibly has Konon meet Tithraustes and Pharnabazos. Tithraustes advances him 220 *talents* and transmits his request to Artaxerxes. See also, Nepos, *Conon*, 3.2–4 and Justin, *Epitoma*, 6.2.12–13, both of whom say his request was delivered by letter.

503 This is a direct contradiction of what Diod. himself wrote at 14.39.1–3.

504 Diod. fails to mention the serious mutiny amongst the Cypriot troops that Konon faced when he returned to Kaunos. The lengthy, but rather fragmentary, chapter 20 of the *Hellenika Oxyrhynkhia* describes this mutiny and the forceful way he dealt with it.

505 Diophantos of Sphettos (Develin, *AO*, 207) was a prominent Athenian politician, active down to the 350s, when he was associated with the distributions of the Theoric Fund, on which see *TDGR2*, no. 75C.

506 Livy (5.14.5) gives the six names in full: Lucius Valerius Potitus, Marcus Valerius Maximus, Marcus Furius Camillus, Lucius Furius Medullinus, Quintus Servilius Fidenas and Quintus Sulpicius Camerinus. This is the Varronian year 398.

507 This coalition was an extension of the alliance between Athens and Thebes referred to above (n. 495). Diod. makes no mention of the involvement of a Rhodian, called Timokrates, and the 50 *talents* of Persian money he brought, which other sources claim prompted the outbreak of the Corinthian War. See Xen. *Hell.* 3.5.1–2; Pausanias, 3.9.8; Plutarch, *Lys.* 27.1, *Ages.* 15.6, *Artax.* 20.3–4. But see contra, *Hell. Oxy.* 7.1–5, where other reasons are given for the cities' hostility to Sparta. Over and above this point, our sources disagree on such major issues as who sent Timokrates (Pharnabazos or Tithraustes), when (397/6, 396/5 or summer 395), and who took his bribes (Xenophon denies that any Athenians accepted money).

First, after establishing a joint council at Corinth, they sent delegates there to deliberate and jointly took care of the preparations for the war. Next, they sent ambassadors around the cities and caused many allies to revolt from the Lakedaimonians. 3. For, right away, the whole of Euboia came over to their side. So, too, did the Leukadians, as well as the Akarnanians and the Ambrakiots and the Khalkidians-by-Thrace. 4. They tried to persuade the inhabitants of the Peloponnese also to revolt from the Lakedaimonians, but none obeyed. For, Sparta, lying along their flank, was like a kind of acropolis and guardpost for the whole Peloponnese. 5. But when Medios, the ruler of Larissa[508] in Thessaly, who was at war with Lykophron, tyrant of Pherai,[509] asked them to send him help, the council sent him 2,000 soldiers. 6. After the allied force arrived, Medios captured Pharsalos,[510] which was being defended by a Lakedaimonian garrison, and sold the inhabitants as booty. Next, the Boiotians and the Argives, after taking leave of Medios, took by storm Herakleia in Trakhis. Having been admitted within the walls during the night by some individuals, they slaughtered the Lakedaimonians they captured, whilst they allowed others from the Peloponnese to depart with their belongings. 7. They called back to the city the Trakhinians who had been exiled from their homeland by the Lakedaimonians[511] and gave it to them to live in. These people were the most ancient inhabitants of that territory. Then, Ismenias, the Boiotian leader,[512] after leaving the Argives behind in the city as a garrison, persuaded the Ainianians and the Athamanians to defect from their alliance with the Lakedaimonians. From these and their allies he gathered troops, numbering a little less than 6,000, with whom he launched a campaign against the Phokians.[513] 8. As he was pitching camp against Naryx in Lokris, a place where rumour

Many other states join the alliance, but none from the Peloponnese

The allies help Medios capture Pharsalos and, by themselves, take Herakleia in Trakhis

The Boiotians and allies invade Phokis and a battle takes place at Naryx, which the Boiotians win

---

508 Larissa was the home base of the Aleuadai, the aristocratic clan that had long dominated in Thessaly, maybe through the position of *Tagos* (chief commander of Thessalian forces).
509 Pherai, on the gulf of Pagasai, became the base of a family that challenged the dominance of the Aleuadai. Already in 404 Lykophron had defeated them in battle (Xen. *Hell.* 2.3.4), and later his successor, Jason, was elected to the position of *Tagos* in 375 (Xen. *Hell.* 6.1.18) or 371 (Diod. 15.60.1–2). The challenge to their dominance from the tyrants of Pherai led the Aleuadai to seek help from outside Thessaly, eventually giving Philip II of Macedon his opening to take control there.
510 Pharsalos and Herakleia in Trakhis were Spartan bases of influence in central Greece.
511 Cf. 14.38.4–5.
512 Ismenias was one of the leaders of the anti-Spartan faction in Thebes, Leontiades of the pro-Spartans (*Hell. Oxy.* 17.1). At this point Ismenias was dominant, but later, in 382, Leontiades helped the Spartan Phoibidas seize control of Thebes, and Ismenias was tried and put to death (Xen. *Hell.* 5.2.25–36).
513 Xenophon makes no mention of this Boiotian invasion of Phokis. It is a reasonable guess that Diod. acquired this information from a lost section of the *Hellenika Oxyrhynkhia*.

has it Ajax was born, the full levy of the Phokians came out under arms to oppose him, under the leadership of the Lakonian, Alkisthenes. 9. A fierce battle ensued and lasted for a long time, but the Boiotians emerged victorious. They pursued the fugitives until nightfall, killing just short of 1,000, but they lost about 500 of their own men in the battle. 10. After the engagement both sides dismissed their troops to their own home states. But the members of the alliance, after convening the council in Corinth, since affairs were progressing as they expected, began assembling soldiers from all the [member] states at Corinth, more than 15,000 infantry and about 500 cavalry.[514]

Both sides dismiss their troops, but the allies begin assembling their forces at Corinth

The Lakedaimonians recall Agesilaos from Asia and prepare for battle

83.1. Once the Lakedaimonians realized that the most powerful cities in Greece were combined in opposition against them, they voted to summon Agesilaos and his army back from Asia,[515] and in the meantime they levied from their own people and from their allies a force of 23,000 infantry and 500 cavalry and marched out to oppose their enemies. 2. An engagement occurred beside the river Nemea[516] that lasted until nightfall. Sections of each army gained the upper hand, but the losses amongst the Lakedaimonians and their allies were 1,100, whilst those of the Boiotians and their allies were about 2,800.[517] 3. After Agesilaos had brought his army over from Asia to Europe, at first he was opposed by some Thracians[518] with a large force. He defeated the barbarians in a battle and killed the majority of them. Following that, he made his way through

A battle ensues near the river Nemea

Agesilaos leads his army back to Greece

514 There are serious problems with the troop numbers here and at 14.83.1. In contrast to Diod.'s overall total for the allied force given here, Xenophon (*Hell.* 4.2.17) gives a list of the allied contingents at the battle of the Nemea River that comes to a total of 24,000 infantry and 1,550 cavalry. On the other hand, Xenophon's figure for the Peloponnesian force is 13,500 infantry and 600 cavalry (*Hell.* 4.2.16) as opposed to Diod.'s 23,000 infantry and 500 cavalry. Since Xenophon omits from his list of Peloponnesian troops the contingents from Tegea, Mantineia and Akhaia, the total on the Spartan side was probably close to Diod.'s figure, but no easy explanation can be found for Diod.'s low numbers for the allies.

515 For accounts of what Agesilaos had been up to in Asia during the remainder of the campaigning season of 395 since the battle of Sardis, see Xen. *Hell.* 4.1.1–41; Plut. *Ages.* 10–15; *Hell. Oxy.* 21–22.

516 A more detailed account of the battle is provided by Xenophon (*Hell.* 4.2.18–23). The river Nemea flows north into the Corinthian gulf, cutting the plain between Sikyon and Corinth virtually in half. The battle took place on the Corinthian side and was regularly referred to by the Athenians as "the battle in Corinth" (Dem. *Against Leptines*, 52; *IG* II² 5221 and 5222; cf. *TDGR2*, no. 19). For a discussion of the topography of the battle see Pritchett (1969), 73–84.

517 The heaviest losses were amongst the Athenian hoplites (Xen. *Hell.* 4.2.21). In fact, both Ephoros (*FGrHist/BNJ* 70 F209) and Androtion (*FGrHist/BNJ* 324 F47) called it a "crushing" defeat. The infantry casualties were honoured, along with those who died at Koroneia, with a public monument, *IG* II² 5221. The cavalry casualties were recorded separately, *IG* II² 5222 and 6217. See *TDGR2*, no. 19; R&O, no. 7.

518 According to Plutarch (*Ages.* 16.1), they were the Trallians.

Macedon, traversing the very same route travelled by Xerxes, when he led his campaign against the Greeks.[519] 4. So, Agesilaos, after he had travelled through Macedon and Thessaly and made his way through the Pass at Thermopylai, continued his journey <…>.[520] Now, Konon and Pharnabazos, commanders of the King's fleet, were lying in wait at Loryma on the Khersonesos[521] with more than ninety triremes. 5. When they learned that the enemy's navy was stationed at Knidos, they began to make preparations for a naval battle. But Peisander,[522] the Lakedaimonian *navarch*, sailed out from Knidos with eighty-five triremes and put in to harbour at Physkos[523] on the Khersonesos. 6. From there he sallied forth and encountered the King's fleet. On engagement, he got the better of the vanguard, but when the Persians came to their assistance with their triremes in massed formation, then all his allies fled to the shore. But he turned his own ship to face them, considering it a disgrace unworthy of Sparta to turn in flight ignobly. 7. He fought brilliantly and slew many of the enemy, but in the end he was killed, fighting in a manner worthy of his country. Konon's men pursued the Lakedaimonians as far as the shore and gained possession of fifty triremes. As for the crews, most of them jumped overboard and escaped overland, but about 500 were taken prisoner. The remaining triremes got away safely to Knidos.[524]

Konon and Pharnabazos prepare for battle with the Spartan fleet

Peisander, the Spartan navarch, engages Konon and Pharnabazos near Knidos

519 According to Polyainos (*Strategemata*, 2.1.17), Aëropos, king of Macedon, attempted to hinder Agesilaos' transit, but was outwitted by a ruse.
520 A gap in the text (*lacuna*) is suspected here. A phrase such as "through Phokis" is a possible restoration. For a fuller account of Agesilaos' journey from the Hellespont to Boiotia see Xen. *Hell.* 4.3.1–9 and Plut. *Ages.* 16.
521 *Khersonesos* is the Greek for peninsula. The best-known places thus referred to are the Thracian Chersonese (Gallipoli) and the Tauric Chersonese (Crimea). Loryma was situated on the tip of the peninsula that extends southward at right angles to the Knidian Chersonese. It was ideally located between Rhodes and Knidos to watch the movements of the Peloponnesian fleet.
522 Peisander was the brother of Agesilaos' wife, Kleora, and, so, the king's brother-in-law. It was a mistaken act of nepotism for Agesilaos to appoint this inexperienced (Xen. *Hell.* 3.4.29) individual to this exceptional position, replacing the official *navarch*, Kheirikrates (*Hell. Oxy.* 19.1).
523 The best-known and only identifiable place of this name was situated midway between Kaunos and Loryma, at the south end of the road north to Ephesos (Strabo, 14.2.4 C652, 14.2.6 C653). This description of Peisander's movements is echoed by Philokhoros (*FGrHist/BNJ* 328 FF144–145), as found in Didymos' *Commentary on Demosthenes* (Harding, 2006, 67, 181–182). It presents an unlikely tactical situation, in that Peisander appears to have sailed right past Konon's position at Loryma without either side noticing the other. The problem might be resolved if we translate the verb (καταφέρω) as "was carried down towards" rather than the usual "put in to harbour," since then the battle could have occurred as he was passing. But it is clear from the following sentence that Diod. thought that Peisander reached Physkos.
524 Xenophon's brief account of the battle of Knidos (*Hell.* 4.3.10–14) adds only the detail that it took place during an eclipse, which enables us to fix the event to 14 August 394. This means that both the battles of Knidos and Koroneia took place in the archonship of Euboulides (394/3) and Diod. has compressed the chronology.

Agesilaos defeats the allies at Koroneia but is wounded

84.1. When Agesilaos, who had received some additional troops from the Peloponnese, arrived with his army in Boiotia, the Boiotians and their allies immediately went out to oppose him at Koroneia.[525] In the ensuing battle,[526] the Thebans put their opponents to flight and pursued them as far as their camp, but the rest [of the allied army], after holding out for a short while, were forced to flee by Agesilaos and his troops. 2. Consequently, the Lakedaimonians determined that they had won the battle.[527] They set up a trophy and gave the corpses back to the enemy under a truce. More than 600 of the Boiotians and their allies were killed, but of the Lakedaimonians and those who fought on their side, just 350.[528] Agesilaos, who had suffered many wounds, was carried to Delphi, where he received treatment for his body.[529]

Pharnabazos and Konon put an end to Spartan naval supremacy

3. After the naval battle [off Knidos], Pharnabazos and Konon set sail with their whole fleet against the allies of the Lakedaimonians.[530] And, first of all, they brought about the defection of the Koans, then the Nisyrians and the Telians.[531] Next, the Khians expelled the [Spartan] garrison and joined Konon. In a similar fashion the Mytilenians and Ephesians and Erythraians[532] changed allegiance. 4. Such being the state of affairs, a sense of urgency infected the cities, some of whom expelled their Lakedaimonian garrisons and strove to maintain their independence, while others attached themselves to Konon's side. And, indeed, it was from this moment that the Lakedaimonians lost their mastery at sea. But Konon,[533] after deciding to sail with the whole fleet to Attica, set out.[534] On the way he gained

Konon and Pharnabazos sail to Corinth via the Cyclades and Kythera

---

525 Koroneia is located between the foothills of Mt Helikon and Lake Kopais, on a significant route through Boiotia. See Map 10. For a discussion of the topography of the battle see Pritchett (1969), 85–95.

526 Xenophon, who was surely present at the battle, gives a more detailed account (*Hell.* 4.3.16–20; *Ages.* 2.6–12). Cf. Plut. *Ages.*18.

527 In fact, the Theban contingent was undefeated (Plut. *Ages.* 18.4) and the Spartans were forced to give up their plan of returning to the Peloponnese via Boiotia.

528 Neither Xenophon nor Plutarch provides a casualty figure.

529 Both Xenophon and Plutarch agree that Agesilaos was wounded (Xen. *Hell.* 4.3.20; Plut. *Ages.* 18.3), but neither states that he went to Delphi to recuperate, although Plutarch acknowledges he was at Delphi, but to celebrate the Pythian Games.

530 According to Xenophon (*Hell.* 4.8.1–6), after Knidos, Pharnabazos and Konon sailed to Ephesos. From there Pharnabazos went overland to the Hellespont, while Konon sailed up the coast and joined him at Sestos. They spent the autumn of 394 campaigning against Derkylidas, trying unsuccessfully to wrest Sestos and Abydos from Spartan control.

531 This is an emendation for the mss' "Teians." The island of Teos lies much too far to the north to be pertinent and Telos, close to Kos, fits better.

532 They did so with some alacrity and enthusiasm to judge from the honours and statues voted to Konon by several states, including Erythrai, Ephesos and Samos. See Pausanias, 6.3.16. Cf. *SIG* 126; *TDGR2*, no. 12D.

533 Diod. (or his source) treats Konon as the prime mover, while Xenophon consistently and surely correctly gives the credit to Pharnabazos.

534 Xenophon (*Hell.* 4.8.7) dates this to the spring of 393.

the allegiance of the islands of the Cyclades and then sailed against the island of Kythera. 5. Gaining possession of that island immediately on the first assault, he sent the Kytherians over to Lakonia under a truce, and then sailed on towards Corinth, after leaving an adequate garrison in the city.[535] Once they had put into harbour there, they held talks with the delegates of the council on any topic they wanted, concluded an alliance with them and left them some funds.[536] Then, they sailed away in the direction of Asia.[537] 6. About the same time Aëropos, king of the Macedonians, died of a sickness, after reigning for six years.[538] Pausanias, his son, succeeded to the throne and ruled for one year.[539] 7. And Theopompos the Khian brought the twelve books of his History of Greek affairs [*Hellenika*] to an end with this year and with the naval battle off Knidos.[540] This historian had begun his work with the naval battle at Kynossema at the place where Thucydides left off.[541] His history covered a period of seventeen years.

Meeting with the allies, they conclude an alliance, leave funds and sail back towards Asia

Aëropos, king of Macedon dies; Theopompos ends his Hellenika *with the battle of Knidos*

85.1. Once this year had come to an end, Euboulides[542] assumed the archonship at Athens, while in Rome six military tribunes managed the consulship: [they were] Lucius Sergius, Aulus Postumius, Publius Cornelius, Quintus Manlius.[543]

394/3: Book 14.85.1–89.2

Konon sails to Peiraieus and helps rebuild the fortifications

535 Cf. Xenophon (*Hell.* 4.8.7–8), who again attributes the decisions to Pharnabazos. He also names Nikophemos as the commander of the garrison.
536 Xenophon (*Hell.* 4.4.8) says that Pharnabazos left the allies all the money he had and encouraged them to continue the war and show the King that they could be trusted.
537 Only Pharnabazos sailed back to Asia. He left Konon in Greece with the bulk of the fleet (Xen. *Hell.* 4.8.9).
538 Cf. 13.37.6. Aëropos was a son of Perdikkas II, one of the sons of Alexander I (479–452). Regarding the date of his death there is disagreement, but it is not unlikely that it belonged in the next year, 394/3, since he was still alive in July 394, when he attempted to hinder Agesilaos' advance through Macedon. See Hammond and Griffith (1979), 167–172.
539 See 14.89.2. Both there and here Diod. (or his source) ignores an Amyntas, whose name appears in the chronographic lists between Aëropos and Pausanias. Presuming his existence, he might have been a son of Menelaus, another of the sons of Alexander I. In any case, his rule must have been very short.
540 Since the battle of Knidos certainly took place in the archonship of Euboulides (394/3), Theopompos ended his history in that year, not 395/4, as Diod. states.
541 Thucydides recounts the battle of Kynossema at 8.104–106, and continues his narrative for three more chapters.
542 Euboulides was the son of Epikleides from the deme Eleusis (see Develin, *AO*, 208). Two years after his archonship, in 392/1, Euboulides was one of several Athenian delegates to a peace conference at Sparta. They agreed to the terms put forward by the Spartans (essentially those described in n. 549) and for that were exiled by the Athenians. Another member of the delegation was the orator, Andokides, who made a vigorous speech in defence of the negotiations (*On the Peace*). Neither Xenophon nor Diod. makes any mention of this conference, but it is recorded by the Atthidographer Philokhoros (*FGrHist* 328 F149a). See *TDGR*2, no. 23 and Didymos, *On Demosthenes*, col. 7.11–28 (Harding, 2006, 67, 168–177).
543 Again Diod. gives less than the full number of names and one (Quintus Manlius) is incorrect. Livy, 5.16.1, gives the full list: Lucius Julius Julus, Lucius Furius Medullinus, Lucius

2. About this time, Konon, who was the commander of the King's fleet, sailed into the Peiraieus[544] with eighty triremes and promised his fellow citizens that he would rebuild the city's circuit of walls.[545] For, the fortifications of the Peiraieus and the Long Walls had been destroyed in accordance with their treaty with the Lakedaimonians at the time of their defeat in the Peloponnesian War.[546] 3. So, Konon hired a large number of craftsmen, put the mass of his rowers at their service, and quickly got the majority of the wall rebuilt. Indeed, the Thebans too sent 500 craftsmen and stone-cutters,[547] and some of the other cities also lent support. 4. But Tiribazos, the man who was in command of the infantry forces in Asia, grew envious of Konon's successes.[548] On the pretext that Konon was using the King's resources to win the cities over to Athens, he lured him to Sardis,[549] where he had him arrested, shackled and imprisoned.[550]

Tiribazos lures Konon to Asia, arrests and imprisons him

    Sergius Fidenas, Aulus Postumius Regillensis, Publius Cornelius Maluginensis and Aulus Manlius. Livy's list agrees with the *Fasti Capitolini* (under the Varronian year 397).
544 Almost immediately after the Battle of Knidos Konon was voted extravagant honours, and a bronze statue for him was set up in the agora in front of the stoa of Zeus Eleutherios. Also honoured in a similar way and at the same time was Evagoras, king of Salamis in Cyprus, who may even have visited Athens at this time (*IG* II² 20; R&O, no. 11). Later a statue of Konon's son, Timotheos, was added to the group (Demosthenes 20, *Against Leptines*, 68–74; Pausanias, 1.3.2, 1.24.3; Isokrates 9, *Evagoras*, 52–57; *IG* II² 3774).
545 Actually, Konon arrived in the spring of 393, more than halfway through the archonship of Euboulides. The inscriptional evidence (*IG* II² 1656) shows that the Athenians had already started rebuilding their fortifications by the last month of Diophantos' archonship, before the battle of Knidos and long before Konon's return. See *TDGR2*, no. 17. Nevertheless, Konon's arrival and the presence of his crews facilitated the rebuilding process, although even then it took until 391 to complete (*IG* II² 1657–1664).
546 Diod. 13.107.4; Xen. *Hell.* 2.2.23; Plut. *Lys.* 15.4.
547 *IG* II² 1657 from the archonship of Euboulides records that the contractor for the transportation of stones was Demosthenes of Boiotia (see *TDGR2*, no. 17).
548 Diod. is again compressing here. Konon's trip to Asia was in the next archon year (393/2). Diod. fails to mention that, while in Athens, Konon initiated an attempted rapprochement with Dionysios of Syracuse, sending ambassadors to try to arrange a marriage alliance between him and Evagoras (Lysias 19, *On the Estate of Aristophanes*, 19–20).
549 A similar account is given by Nepos (*Conon*, 5). But, according to Xenophon, Konon had gone to Sardis as part of a delegation from the allies to counter Sparta's diplomacy, not "lured" by Tiribazos. Xenophon's more fulsome account (*Hell.* 4.8.12–16) states that it was the Spartans, through the agency of their ambassador Antalkidas, who persuaded Tiribazos that Athens was taking advantage of the King and won him to their side by offering to give up any claim to the Greek cities in Asia and agreeing to leave the islands and other cities in Greece to be free and autonomous. These were the terms (except for giving Lemnos, Imbros and Skyros to Athens) that were on the table at the conference in Sparta in 392/1 (n. 542) and are, of course, the very terms of the Great King's Peace of 387/6, negotiated by Antalkidas.
550 Konon's fate is unknown. Nepos (*Conon*, 5) states that some say he was sent up to Artaxerxes and put to death, but also cites Deinon of Kolophon (*FGrHist* 690, not yet updated by *BNJ*) for the view that he escaped. Since Tiribazos was immediately replaced by Strouthas,

86.1. In Corinth, some passionate activists formed groups[551] and, taking advantage of the fact that there were contests taking place in the theatre,[552] initiated a massacre and stirred up political strife throughout the city.[553] And when the Argives provided active support for their daring action, they slaughtered 120 of their fellow citizens and drove 500 into exile. 2. The Lakedaimonians started making preparations to restore the exiles and began collecting an army, whereupon the Athenians and the Boiotians came to the aid of the killers, their purpose being to gain control of the city for themselves. 3. And the exiles, along with the Lakedaimonians and their allies, made a night attack upon Lekhaion[554] and the docks and took them by storm.[555] Next day, men from the city made a counter-attack, under the leadership of Iphikrates. A battle took place, in which the Lakedaimonians were victorious, killing many. 4. After that, the Boiotians and Athenians, along with the Argives and Corinthians, advanced in full force towards Lekhaion and put it under siege. At first, they succeeded in forcing their way into the area inside the outer defences, but then the Lakedaimonians and the exiles fought back brilliantly and the Boiotians and all with them were expelled, and they retired to the city, having lost about 1,000 of their men.[556] 5. Immediately after this, when the Isthmian Games were about to begin, there arose a dispute over their organization. There was much contention, but the Lakedaimonians prevailed and appointed the exiles to organize the festival.[557] 6. Since the worst encounters of the war took place

Political strife breaks out in Corinth. Argos, Boiotia and Athens support one side, Sparta the other

The exiles seize Lekhaion, the port of Corinth

The allies attack Lekhaion in full force, but are repulsed by the Lakedaimonians

Dispute arises over the supervision of the Isthmian Games

The Corinthian War lasted eight years

a pro-Athenian satrap (Xen. *Hell.* 4.8.17), it is not unlikely that he was allowed to get away. Lysias 19, *On the Estate of Aristophanes*, 39, suggests that he died in Cyprus.

551 Those in favour of Corinth joining the Argives, Athenians and Boiotians against Sparta. "Passionate activists" reflects the difficult reading of all mss. Oldfather has "men who favoured a democracy," following the emended text of Vögel-Fischer.
552 The festival of Artemis Eukleia (Xen. *Hell.* 4.4.2).
553 According to Xenophon (*Hell.* 4.4.2–4), the massacre was planned by the allies out of fear that conservative Corinthians were leaning towards returning to their alliance with Sparta.
554 Lekhaion was one of the two ports of Corinth, joined to the city by long walls. The other was Kenkhreai.
555 The gate was opened to them by two Corinthians, Pasimelos and Alkimenes (Xen. *Hell.* 4.4.8).
556 Cf. Xenophon (*Hell.* 4.4.9–12), whose account is quite different.
557 The Isthmian Games were held at the Isthmus and were in honour of Poseidon. They took place two years apart, on the year after an Olympic Festival and on the year before the next. 394/3 was not an Isthmian year. The festival in question took place either in 393/2 or, more likely, in 391/0. According to Xenophon (*Hell.* 4.5.1–2) the Argives, perhaps because of their *isopoliy* with Corinth (see n. 580), were in the process of celebrating the Games when Agesilaos approached. They abandoned the site, and Agesilaos made sure that the Corinthian exiles organized the Games, but after he left the Argives returned and celebrated a second festival.

almost exclusively in Corinthian territory, this war has been named the Corinthian War. It lasted eight years.[558]

In Sicily, the people of Rhegion lay siege to Messina

87.1. In Sicily, the people of Rhegion accused Dionysios of preparing to attack them by fortifying Messina[559] and responded initially by welcoming into their city the men who had been exiled by Dionysios and those who were working against him. Next, after settling the remnants of the population of Naxos and Katane[560] in Mylai,[561] they got ready an army, put Heloris[562] in charge, and sent him out to besiege Messina. 2. When he made a reckless assault upon the acropolis, the Messinans, who were in the city, combined with Dionysios' mercenaries and went out to oppose him. A battle ensued, in which the Messinans were victorious, killing more than 500. 3. Right after this, the Messinans attacked Mylai and captured the city, but allowed the Naxians, who were living there, to depart under a truce. So, these dispersed amongst the Sikels and the other Greek cities, each settling in a different place. 4. Dionysios, now that the area around the Strait was well-disposed to him, decided to mount a campaign against Rhegion, but to his annoyance the Sikels, who held Tauromenion, stood in his way.[563] 5. Consequently, judging that it was to his advantage to attack them first, he led his forces out against them. Making his camp on the side facing Naxos, he stuck doggedly to his siege throughout the winter, convinced that the Sikels would abandon the heights, because they had not inhabited them for a long time.

A battle takes place, which is won by the Messinans

The Messinans capture Mylai

Dionysios, on his way to attack Rhegion, is impeded by the Sikels

He attacks the Sikels, who resist stubbornly

88.1. But the Sikels had a long-held ancestral tradition that that part of the island had been in their possession when the Greeks first landed, founded Naxos and drove the Sikels, who were living there at the time, out of the place. So, declaring that they had reclaimed ancestral territory and that they were within their rights in avenging the crimes that the Greeks had committed against their forefathers, they got ready to hold on to the heights. 2. As both sides

Dionysios mounts a surprise attack, but is repelled and barely escapes

---

558 395/4–387/6. Diod.'s account, especially of the action around Corinth and Lekhaion, but also of the movements of Konon, is confused and confusing, because he compresses the chronology.
559 See 14.78.5 and n. 449.
560 See 14.15.1–3, 40.1.
561 Mylai (modern Milazzo) had been founded by the colonists at Zankle (later Messina) in the late eighth century to secure the agricultural land their own site lacked. How or when it came under the control of Rhegion is not known.
562 For Heloris, one of Dionysios' "friends," see 14.8.5 and n. 56. Like so many others he ended up in exile (14.103.5), but we are not told the reason.
563 Cf. 14.59.1–2 and nn. 390–391.

were surpassing each other in rivalry, the winter solstice occurred and the area around the acropolis was covered in snow as a result of the ongoing winter storms. Then, Dionysios, finding that the Sikels kept a rather casual guard over the acropolis, because of its strong position and the extreme height of its fortification, set off towards the highest parts during a moonless and stormy night. 3. After suffering many hardships because of the rough and craggy terrain and the depth of the snow, he succeeded in capturing one acropolis, although his face was blistered and his eyes damaged by the cold. Next, he launched a surprise attack on the other position and led his army into the city.[564] But, when the Sikels came to the rescue *en masse*, Dionysios' men were expelled and Dionysios himself, struck on the corslet in his flight, fell head over heels and was almost captured alive. 4. Since the Sikels were attacking from higher ground, more than 600 of Dionysios' men were killed and most abandoned their armour.[565] Dionysios himself only managed to keep his corslet. 5. In the wake of this reverse the Akragantines and the Messinans banished the supporters of Dionysios, embraced their liberty and renounced their alliance with the tyrant.

89.1. Pausanias, the Lakedaimonian king, was put on trial by his fellow citizens and exiled after a reign of fourteen years.[566] Agesipolis, his son, succeeded to the throne and ruled for the same length of time as his father. 2. Also, Pausanias, the king of the Macedonians, died, murdered treacherously by Amyntas, after ruling one year. Amyntas seized the throne and ruled for twenty-four years.[567]

Pausanias, the Spartan king, is exiled and Pausanias, the Macedonian king, is assassinated

90.1. Once this year had come to an end, Demostratos[568] assumed the archonship at Athens, while in Rome six military tribunes managed the consulship: [they were] Lucius Titinius, 2. Publius Licinius, Publius Melaeus, Quintus Mallius, Gnaeus Genucius, Lucius Atilius.[569] After these men had assumed

393/2: Book 14.90.1–93.5

Magon, Carthaginian commander in Sicily, attacks Messina, but is defeated by Dionysios

564 The topography is difficult to recreate.
565 An indication that they were in flight.
566 See 14.81.3 with n. 500. Pausanias took refuge in Tegea, where he died of disease (Xen. *Hell.* 3.5.25).
567 Amyntas III (393–369) was the son of Arrhidaios, and grandson of Amyntas, another of the sons of Alexander I. He was also father of Philip II.
568 Demostratos was from the deme Kerameis. His patronymic is unrecorded. See Develin, *AO*, 210.
569 In this case Diod.'s list agrees with the *Fasti Capitolini* (under the Varronian year 396), with the exception that the spelling of Melaeus should be Maelius and Mallius should be Manlius. According to Livy (5.18.2) the six men elected were the same as in 397/6 (see 14.47.1), except that the elder Publius Licinius stood down in favour of his son (Livy, 5.18.3–6). But, Diod.'s list does not agree with the list he gives at 47.1, nor does Livy's with those he gives at 5.12.10.

Dionysios mounts an attack on Rhegion, but fails and returns to Syracuse

office, Magon,[570] the Carthaginian commander, was busy in Sicily, trying to restore Carthaginian affairs after the disastrous defeat they had suffered.[571] 3. So, he dealt generously with the cities subject to the Carthaginians and embraced those against whom Dionysios was waging war. He also made treaties of alliance with most of the Sikels, and, after collecting an army, marched upon Messina. After laying waste to the territory and amassing a great deal of booty, he moved on and pitched camp close to Abakaine,[572] an allied city. 4. When Dionysios approached with his army, both sides lined up for battle. A vigorous engagement ensued, from which Dionysios' side emerged victorious. For their part, the Carthaginians, after losing more than 800 men, fled into the city, while Dionysios returned to Syracuse for the time being. But, a few days later, he manned 100 triremes and launched a campaign against the people of Rhegion. 5. Appearing at the city unexpectedly during the night, he set fire to the gates and raised his siege-ladders against the walls. At first, the few Rhegians who came to the rescue were trying to put out the flames, but later, when the general Heloris[573] arrived and advised them to adopt the opposite strategy, they managed to save the city. 6. For, since they were very few in number, even if they were successful in putting the fire out, they would not have been strong enough to prevent Dionysios entering the city. But, after gathering firewood and timber from nearby houses, they created a greater conflagration that gave time for the citizen body to gather with their weapons and come to the rescue. 7. Since his plan had failed, Dionysios went around the territory burning and cutting down trees. Later, he concluded a one-year truce and then sailed off to Syracuse.[574]

The Greeks in Italy form an alliance against Dionysios and the Lucanians

91.1. When the Greeks who dwelt in Italy perceived that Dionysios' ambition stretched as far as their territory, they joined in alliance and set up a joint council. They hoped that by doing so they would easily ward Dionysios off and stand up to the neighbouring Lucanians, who were at war with them at that time.[575] 2. The exiles who held Lekhaion in Corinthia were let into the city by

The exiles from Lekhaion attack the walls of Corinth but are driven off

570 See 14.59.1 and n. 388.
571 As described at 14.54.4–77.6.
572 Abakaine/Abakainon was a Sikel city, inland from the coast, about 13 km south of Tyndaris. Part of its territory had been expropriated by Dionysios and given to Tyndaris at the time of its foundation. Cf. 14.78.5.
573 See 14.87.1.
574 While unsuccessful on this occasion, Dionysios ultimately concluded his long-standing feud with Rhegion (see 14.40.1, 44.4–5, 87.1, 87.4) in 390–387 (14.100.1–112.5).
575 Diodoros' suggestion that the Italiot League was founded at this time is probably incorrect. Polybios (2.39.1–7) dates the original initiative from Kroton, Sybaris and Kaulonia earlier in the fifth century. The other states in Magna Graecia, including Thourioi, Hipponion, Elea,

some accomplices during the night and attempted to seize the walls, but when Iphikrates and his men came to the rescue, 300 of them were lost and they fled back to the port.[576] A few days later, as a contingent[577] of the Lakedaimonian army was passing through Corinthian territory, Iphikrates and some of the allies in Corinth fell upon them and killed almost all.[578] 3. And, Iphikrates invaded Phleiasia with his peltasts, engaged in battle with men from the city, and killed more than 300 of them. Later, when he advanced against Sikyon, the Sikyonians lined up for battle in front of their walls, but, after losing about 500 men, they took refuge in the city.[579]

Iphikrates destroys a mora of the Spartan army

92.1. Subsequent to these events, the Argives marched in full force under arms into Corinth, seized the acropolis, took the city for themselves and turned Corinthian territory into Argive.[580] 2. Iphikrates, the Athenian, was also keen on occupying the territory, considering it an ideal place for dominating Greece, but, when the *demos* refused permission,[581] he resigned his command. In his place the Athenians sent out Khabrias[582] to Corinth as their general. 3. In Macedon, Amyntas, father of Philip, was expelled from Pella[583] by the invading Illyrians.[584] Giving up hope for his throne, he made a gift of some neighbouring territory to the Olynthians.[585] For that time he lost his kingdom, but a

The Argives seize control of Corinth

Amyntas is driven out of Pella by the Illyrians, but restored by the Thessalians

Taras (Tarentum) and Rhegion, had clearly joined by this time. As Polybios makes clear, the constitution of the League was modelled upon that of the fifth-century Akhaian League. See Walbank, *Commentary*, 1.225–226.

576 The only possible reference to this event in Xenophon is at *Hell.* 4.5.19.
577 The name for this unit of one-sixth of the Spartan army was a *mora*, although Diod. does not use that term here, as he does later at 97.5. See Glossary.
578 This famous victory, which demonstrated the effectiveness of light-armed troops against hoplites, is described in detail by Xenophon (*Hell.* 4.5.11–18).
579 Cf. Xen. *Hell.* 4.4.15–16, where Iphikrates' invasion of Phleious took place before his defeat of the Spartan *mora*.
580 Argos had been eager to establish a state of *isopolity* (shared citizenship) with Corinth for some time. It is possible that this had already happened at the time of the events described in 14.86.
581 Not wishing to be in conflict with their ally Argos.
582 Khabrias, son of Ktesippos, of Aixone, was one of the best fourth-century Athenian generals, along with Iphikrates, son of Timotheos, of Rhamnous; Timotheos, son of Konon, of Anaphlystos; and Khares, son of Theokhares, of Angele. See Davies, *APF*, nos. 15086, 7737, 13700, 15292.
583 "Pella" is the suggestion of Eric Bennett in the Budé in place of the mss' ΠΟΛΕΩΣ ("city"). Situated in lower Macedon, it was built into the capital city of the Macedonian kingdom by Arkhelaos I (413–399).
584 Under the leadership of their ambitious king, Bardylis.
585 Olynthos, situated at the top of the peninsula of Pallene in Khalkidike, was the largest and most powerful city in the region and since 432 had been the leader of a league of neighbouring states. It was in competition with Athens for control of the timber trade from Macedon.

little later he was restored by the Thessalians, regained his throne and ruled for twenty-four years.[586] 4. But, some say that after the expulsion of Amyntas Argaios was king of the Macedonians for two years,[587] and it was after that that Amyntas regained his kingdom.

Satyros, king of the Bosporos, dies

The Romans capture Veii and enslave the population

Marcus Furius celebrates a triumph

93.1. About the same time Satyros, son of Spartokos, king of the Bosporos died, after a reign of forty-four years.[588] His son, Leukon, succeeded to the rule and reigned for forty years.[589] 2. In Italy, the Romans, who were in the eleventh year of the siege of Veii,[590] appointed Marcus Furius[591] as commander with absolute authority [*dictator*] and Publius Cornelius[592] as cavalry commander [*magister equitum*]. These men restored discipline amongst the troops and forced Veii to surrender by digging a tunnel.[593] They reduced the city to slavery, by selling the people and the other booty for profit. 3. The *dictator* celebrated a triumph,[594] while the people of Rome took a tithe of the proceeds of the booty and had a

586 At 15.19.2–3 Diod. describes in almost identical language another occasion, in 383/2, when Amyntas was forced to flee his kingdom and entrust some territory to Olynthos, except that then it was the Spartans who helped him back to power. There is disagreement whether there were really two such occasions or just one, and, if so, which. We have a fragmentary inscription from Olynthos, announcing a defensive alliance between Amyntas and the Khalkidians, and, on the reverse, granting trading rights for timber, pitch and other commodities from Macedon to the Khalkidians. See *TDGR*2, no. 21; R&O, no. 12. See Hammond and Griffith (1979), 172–180.

587 Argaios is a shadowy character. Some think he was a puppet of the Illyrians in 393–391, others that he was put up by the Olynthians in 385–383. Cf. Hammond and Griffith (1979), 172 and Bennett in the Budé, p. 206, n. 8.

588 Satyros ruled from 433 and actually died in 389. This Bosporan kingdom, based upon the city of Pantikapaion in the Crimea, was rich and powerful, and very long-lasting. Founded by Spartokos in the early 430s, the last member of the dynasty, Pairisades V, died in 109.

589 Leukon was very successful. The Athenians, especially in the fourth century, maintained close personal and trading ties with the kingdom, upon which it depended for most of its grain. See, for example, Isokrates 17, *Trapezikos*, 57; Demosthenes 20, *Against Leptines*, 29f. and *IG* II² 212 (*TDGR*2, no. 82) and, in general, Moreno (2007).

590 Making allowance for the difference in the Varronian dating system, Diodoros and Livy (5.19–22) agree on the date of the fall of Veii. The suspected disagreement over the length of the siege (Livy, 5.22.8 says it took ten years, Diod. here says in the eleventh year) may just be a matter of the difference between systems of reckoning.

591 Marcus Furius Camillus (Livy, 5.19.2), whose fame earned him a biography by Plutarch. He had already been a military tribune in 400/399, 398/7 and 395/4 and his father, Lucius Furius Medullinus, had also been military tribune several times.

592 Publius Cornelius Scipio (Livy, 5.19.2; Plut. *Cam.* 5.1). The *gens Cornelia* was one of the most influential patrician families in republican Rome.

593 By digging a tunnel under the walls, the Romans were able to introduce soldiers into the temple of Juno on the citadel of Veii without the defenders' knowledge. See Livy, 5.21.10; Plut. *Cam.* 5.3–5.

594 Described with obvious embellishment by Livy (5.23.1–7).

golden mixing bowl [*krater*] made for dedication at Delphi.⁵⁹⁵ 4. The ambassadors,⁵⁹⁶ who were transporting it, encountered some pirates from the Lipari Islands, were all taken prisoner and were brought to Lipara.⁵⁹⁷ But, when Timasitheos,⁵⁹⁸ the Liparan general, found out what had happened, he liberated the ambassadors and, after returning the golden bowl, set them back on their way to Delphi. After dedicating it in the treasury of the Massaliots,⁵⁹⁹ the ambassadors returned to Rome. 5. As a consequence, when the people of Rome learned of the honourable behaviour of Timasitheos, they right away at that time honoured him with the gift of public hospitality,⁶⁰⁰ and 137 years later,⁶⁰¹ when they took Lipara away from the Carthaginians, they absolved his descendants of property taxes and made them free men.

94.1. Once this year had come to an end, Philokles⁶⁰² became archon at Athens, while in Rome six military tribunes took over the consulship: [they were] Publius Cornelius,⁶⁰³ Caeso Fabius, Lucius Furius, Quintus Servilius, Marcus Valerius.⁶⁰⁴ In this year the ninety-seventh Olympic Games were celebrated, in which Terires⁶⁰⁵ was the victor. 2. At this time⁶⁰⁶ the Athenians elected

392/1: Book 14.94.1–96.5

Thrasyboulos sails to Thrace and Ionia, where he renews some former alliances

---

595 A *donum amplum* ("generous gift") had been requested at the end of the oracular response given to the delegates by the Pythia, as reported by Livy (5.16.8–11). Exacting this amount from the rank and file of the citizens met with considerable opposition (Livy, 5.23.8–25.10), but eventually led to the donation of their jewellery by the women of Rome. Cf. Plut. *Cam.* 7.4–8.4. The base of the golden bowl, but not the bowl itself, survived the sacrilegious act of the Phokians under Onomarkhos, who melted the Delphic treasures during the Third Sacred War (356–346).
596 According to Livy (5.28.2), they were: Lucius Valerius, Lucius Sergius and Aulus Manlius.
597 The inhabitants of the Lipari Islands were very effective at naval combat. They were also punctilious about making the appropriate donation to Delphi. See Diod. 5.9.4–5; Pausanias, 10.16.7.
598 The story of the intervention of Timasitheos and the recognition it received is frequently told, not only here, but by Livy (5.28.3–5) and Plutarch (*Cam.* 8.6–8).
599 Massalia (Marseilles) had close links with Rome and Delphi. See Justin, *Epitoma*, 43.8.5.
600 *Hospitium*, a formal guest–host relationship between a state and an individual.
601 Rome annexed the Lipari Islands in 252. That would be 146 years later by the Varronian calendar and 141 (not 137) years by Diodoros'.
602 Philokles was from the deme Anaphlystos. See Develin, *AO*, 212.
603 The mss read Publius "and" Cornelius, which is a confusion of the fact that there were two Publii Cornelii (Cossus and Scipio).
604 Livy (5.24.1) gives the full list with complete names: Publius Cornelius Cossus, Publius Cornelius Scipio, Marcus Valerius Maximus, Caeso Fabius Ambustus, Lucius Furius Medullinus and Quintus Servilius. This is the Varronian year 395.
605 The name of the victor in the *stadion* for 392 is otherwise unrecorded. This is not a familiar Greek personal name.
606 Much disagreement exists about the date of Thrasyboulos' expedition amongst modern scholars, dating it variously to 391/0, 390/89 and 389/8 (see *TDGR*2, no. 25, n. 1). This

Thrasyboulos[607] as general [*strategos*] and sent him out on campaign with forty triremes. He sailed to Ionia and exacted funds from allied states.[608] Moving on, he spent time around the Khersonesos,[609] where he secured the alliance of Medokos[610] and Seuthes,[611] the kings of the Thracians. 3. After a while he sailed from the Hellespont to Lesbos and dropped anchor at the beach off Eresos. There a strong windstorm arose and he lost twenty-three triremes. Surviving that, with his remaining ships he approached the cities in Lesbos, in an attempt to win back their allegiance. For, all had defected [from Athens] except Mytilene. 4. Arriving first at Methymna, he engaged in battle with the city's soldiers, whose commander was the Spartiate, Therimakhos.[612] Fighting brilliantly, he killed both Therimakhos himself and many Methymnaians, and shut the rest up within their walls. He ravaged the territory of Methymna and

> disagreement results from confusion in our sources. Xenophon (*Hell.* 4.8.25–31) plausibly narrates the whole of his campaign from the Hellespont to Aspendos in one stretch, while Diod. breaks it up into two pieces over several years (here and at 99.4–5) and re-arranges the countermoves of Sparta in a different order from Xenophon's.
> 607 See 14.32.1ff. and n. 241. Although he had brought about the fall of the Thirty and restored the democracy in 403, Thrasyboulos' influence had been challenged immediately afterwards by his colleague Arkhinos of Koile, who successfully indicted Thrasyboulos' proposal to grant citizenship to all who had joined in the restoration, including metics and slaves (Aristotle, *AP* 40.2). Subsequently, Thrasyboulos had supported Athens' participation in the coalition against Sparta and may have been a general at the battles of Nemea (Lysias 16, *For Mantitheus*, 15) and Koroneia. These defeats, and Konon's victory at Knidos, paved the way for Konon's ascendancy in Athenian politics and Thrasyboulos' eclipse (Aristophanes, *Ekklesiazousai*, 202–203). Konon's death, however, made it possible for Thrasyboulos to return to prominence. Although both followed the same policy of reviving Athenian imperial power, their rivalry was the result of personal animosity. See Strauss (1986), 107–109.
> 608 For the states that Thrasyboulos "liberated" see Xen. *Hell.* 4.8.25–31. *IG* II² 24 and 28 show that he re-introduced the 5 percent tax on imports and exports by sea, which the Athenians had substituted for tribute in 413 (Thuc. 7.28.4), at both Thasos and Klazomenai. Probably he did the same elsewhere. Furthermore, after restoring the democrats to power in Byzantion, he renewed the Athenian duty of 10 percent on goods passing in and out of the Black Sea.
> 609 This is the Thracian Chersonese, modern Gallipoli peninsula.
> 610 Medokos (Amedokos in Xen. *Hell.* 4.8.26) was king (410–390) of the Odrysian Thracians, who had dominated Thrace since the reign of Sitalkes (431–424), on whom see Thucydides, 2.95–101.
> 611 Seuthes II was in control of the coastal region of Thrace. He was a kinsman of Medokos, but had recently turned against him (Xen. *Hell.* 4.8.26; Aristotle, *Politics*, 5.10.24.1312a). His devious ways are described by Xenophon (*Anab.* 7.2.18–7.7.57). Xenophon (*Hell.* 4.8.26) agrees with Diod. that Thrasyboulos reconciled the two kings and brought them into alliance with Athens. *IG* II² 21 and 22 are two fragmentary inscriptions that appear to substantiate this achievement.
> 612 Therimakhos was, in fact, the governor (*harmost*) of Methymna (Xen. *Hell.* 4.8.29).

gained the surrender of Eresos and Antissa. After that, he gathered ships from the Khians and Mytilenians and sailed for Rhodes.[613]

95.1. After slowly pulling themselves together following the disastrous defeat at Syracuse,[614] the Carthaginians resolved to resume their operations in Sicily. Having decided to go to war, they crossed over with only a small number of warships, but with an army that they had collected from Libya, Sardinia and even from the barbarians in Italy.[615] They took meticulous care to arm all these men with the equipment they were used to. The soldiers, no less than 80,000 in number, were transported to Sicily, under the command of Magon. 2. And, indeed, on his advance through Sicily Magon caused most cities to defect from Dionysios. He pitched camp in the territory of Agyrion beside the river Khrysas, close to the road that leads to Morgantina.[616] For, he halted his advance there, since he was unable to secure the alliance of the Agyrinaians and had learned that the enemy forces had set out from Syracuse. 3. Once Dionysios learned that the Carthaginians were advancing through the interior of the island, he hastily raised an army composed of the available Syracusans and of mercenaries, totalling no less than 20,000, and set out. 4. When he got close to the enemy, he sent an embassy to Agyris, the tyrant of the Agyrinaians. This man was the second most powerful tyrant in Sicily after Dionysios, since he controlled almost all the neighbouring forts and ruled over the city of Agyrion, which was very populous at that time with no less than 20,000 citizens. 5. In addition, a great sum of money was deposited on the acropolis for the benefit of this crowd of people that had been assembled in the city, money that Agyris had collected by murdering the wealthiest citizens. 6. But, Dionysios entered the city with only a small retinue and persuaded Agyris to become his ally wholeheartedly,[617] promising to make him a gift of a large tract of neighbouring territory, if the war turned out well. 7. To begin with, Agyris made

The Carthaginians mount a new assault on Sicily under Magon

Magon advances to Agyrion, where he halts

Dionysios hastily raises a force of 20,000 and goes out to Agyrion, whose tyrant he persuades to join him

---

613 Eresos and Antissa remained loyal to Athens and joined the Second Athenian League/Confederacy in 377/6 (*IG* II² 43.116–117). Diodoros' account of Thrasyboulos' campaign on Lesbos agrees essentially with Xenophon's (*Hell.* 4.8.28–30), but adds some details that must come from another source: (1) Xenophon does not mention the windstorm at Eresos and the loss of twenty-three triremes; (2) Xenophon does not describe Thrasyboulos as "fighting brilliantly" against Therimakhos; (3) Xenophon does not name Eresos and Antissa as the cities that surrendered to him.
614 This appears to refer back to the defeat of Himilkon's expedition (14.54.4–77.6) and overlooks Magon's intervening campaign, which ended in the defeat at Abakaine/Abakainon (see 14.90), not Syracuse.
615 Probably from their allies, the Etruscans.
616 See Map 3 for the topography.
617 Dionysios already had a treaty of some kind with Agyris (see 14.78.7).

generous donations of food and all other necessities to Dionysios' whole army, then he led out his full force, joined Dionysios' campaign and fought with him together against the Carthaginians throughout the war.

Magon finds himself in difficulties

The Carthaginians sue for peace. Terms are agreed upon and Magon returns home

96.1. Magon was at a considerable disadvantage, because he was encamped on hostile territory and increasingly lacking in needed supplies. Because Agyris' men were naturally familiar with the lie of the land, they had the advantage in ambushes and kept cutting off food supplies from their enemies. 2. But, when the Syracusans were demanding that the issue be decided by a battle as quickly as possible, Dionysios disagreed, saying that there was no need to take risks, since the barbarians would be destroyed by time and starvation. This response angered the Syracusans so much that they deserted Dionysios. 3. Out of concern at this, Dionysios at first summoned the slaves with a view to setting them free, but later, when the Carthaginians sent ambassadors to discuss peace, he agreed, had the slaves sent back to their owners, and concluded a peace treaty with the Carthaginians. 4. The terms of the treaty were in most respects similar to the previous terms,[618] except that the Sikels had to be subject to Dionysios and that he was to take possession of Tauromenion. Once the treaty had been concluded, Magon sailed away and Dionysios took possession of Tauromenion. He expelled most of the Sikels who lived there, selected the most loyal amongst his own mercenaries and settled them there. 5. That was the state of affairs in Sicily. In Italy, the Romans pillaged the city of Faliscus,[619] belonging to the Faliscan people.

391/0: Book 14.97.1–98.5

Factional strife arises in Rhodes

97.1. Once this year had come to an end, Nikoteles became archon at Athens, while in Rome three military tribunes administered the consular power: [they were] Marcus Furius,[620] Gaius Aemilius.[621] After these men had assumed office, those in Rhodes who favoured a pro-Spartan policy rose up against the *demos* and expelled the pro-Athenian party from the city. 2. The pro-Athenians

618 I.e. the terms agreed upon in 405 (Diod. 13.114.1). Although Dionysios had strengthened his position by gaining control of the Sikels in the east, the Carthaginians had reasserted their authority in the west of the island, which was thus *de facto* divided into two spheres of influence. This agreement lasted for almost ten years, until Dionysios started a new war in 383 (15.15.1).
619 Diodoros means Falerii, the largest city of the Faliscans. It was taken by Camillus in 391 as described by Livy (5.26–27) under the Varronian year 394.
620 I.e. Camillus.
621 Diod. names only two of the three. In fact, there were the usual six according to Livy (5.26) and the *Fasti Capitolini* (under the Varronian year 394). In addition to these two, they were Lucius Furius Medullinus, Lucius Valerius Publicola, Spurius Postumius and Publius Cornelius (unspecified whether Maluginensis, Cossus or Scipio).

rushed together under arms in an attempt to regain control of affairs, but the allies of the Lakedaimonians gained the upper hand, killed many and made a proclamation of banishment upon the fugitives. Right after that they sent ambassadors to Lakedaimon to request help, out of a concern that some citizens might revolt. 3. The Lakedaimonians sent them seven triremes[622] and three men to take charge of affairs: Eudokimos and Philodokos and Diphilas.[623] These men travelled first to Samos and brought about the defection of the city from Athens, then, they sailed on to Rhodes and took charge of affairs there. 4. Since things were going their way, the Lakedaimonians decided to regain dominance at sea and, after assembling a fleet, little by little they began once again to assert their mastery over their allies. So, they descended upon Samos and Knidos and Rhodes, and everywhere they went they requisitioned ships and the elite marines. In this way they fitted out twenty-seven triremes lavishly.[624] 5. And, Agesilaos, king of the Lakedaimonians, when he learned that the Argives were busy at Corinth, led out the full Lakedaimonian levy minus one unit [*mora*]. He traversed the whole Argolid, pillaging the properties. Then, after cutting the trees in the countryside, he went back to Sparta.[625]

The Spartans send help in the hope of regaining naval supremacy

Agesilaos invades the Argolid

98.1. In Cyprus,[626] Evagoras of Salamis,[627] a man of very noble birth, since he was descended from the founders of the city,[628] had been driven into exile in the past as a result of some political unrest, but had subsequently returned

The growing power of Evagoras in Cyprus arouses the hostility of Artaxerxes

---

622 Eight, according to Xenophon (*Hell.* 4.8.20).
623 Eudokimos is named Ekdikos and Diphilas is Diphridas in Xenophon's account (*Hell.* 4.8.22f.). Furthermore, Philodokos is not mentioned by Xenophon, which corroborates the idea that Diod. is following another source (see n. 613). In any case, as mentioned above (n. 606), although there is similarity in the presentation of the overall course of events, Xenophon and Diodoros disagree on the order in which they happened. For Xenophon, the political strife on Rhodes and the dispatch of help from Sparta took place before Thrasyboulos' mission and were, in fact, what prompted it. In addition, Diod. fails to mention that Teleutias, half-brother of Agesilaos, replaced Ekdikos (Xen. *Hell.* 4.8.23).
624 Xenophon (*Hell.* 4.8.23–24) confirms the number of triremes, but gives more details about its composition and names Teleutias as commander (*navarch*).
625 Xenophon (*Hell.* 4.4.19) describes an invasion of the Argolid by Agesilaos in 391.
626 The history of Cyprus in the late fifth and fourth century is not dissimilar from that of Sicily. In both, there was a long-standing involvement and competition between Phoenician and Greek cultures, a dynast who attempted to gain control of the whole island, and the inevitable rivalry between city-states. The difference was that Cyprus was nominally part of the Persian Empire.
627 Evagoras was born about 435 and ruled Salamis from 411 until 374/3, when he was murdered along with his son, Pnytagoras. He was a friend of Konon and a loyal ally to Athens, where he was given honorary citizenship.
628 According to Isokrates (9, *Evagoras*, 18–19), he was descended from the Homeric hero Teukros, brother of Aias, from the island of Salamis, off the coast of Athens.

with a small following.⁶²⁹ He drove out the current ruler of the city, Abdemon of Tyre,⁶³⁰ who was a friend of the King of Persia, and made himself master of the city, which was the largest and most powerful of the cities in Cyprus. That was his first move, but soon, after he had amassed great wealth and had mobilized an army, he made an attempt at bringing the whole island under his rule.⁶³¹ 2. Amongst the cities, there were those that he overcame by force and others that he won over by persuasion, so that he soon gained the leadership of them all, with the exception of Amathous, Soloi and Kition.⁶³² These were fighting a war of resistance and sent an embassy to Artaxerxes, King of the Persians, to ask for help. They accused Evagoras of having killed Agyris,⁶³³ a king, who was an ally of the Persians, and committed themselves to join the King in gaining control of the island. 3. And the King, because at one and the same time he had no wish to see Evagoras carve out greater power and because he appreciated that Cyprus was strategically located and had a large naval force, by means of which he could ward off attacks upon Asia, decided to make an alliance and sent the ambassadors home. Then, he dispatched letters to the cities on the coast and the governors [satraps] in charge of the cities to build triremes and get ready whatever was useful for the fleet with all speed. He also ordered Hekatomnôs,⁶³⁴ the ruler of Karia, to make war upon Evagoras.

629 No more than fifty, according to Isokrates (9, *Evagoras*, 28).
630 Theopompos (*FGrHist/BNJ* 115 F103) says he was from Kition.
631 The author of Lysias 6, *Against Andokides*, 28, refers to Evagoras as being already "king of Cyprus," when Andokides fled to his court in 411/0, although, given the lack of precision in that speech, it is not unlikely he was anachronistically referring to the state of affairs in 400/399, when the speech was delivered. Even then, it is an exaggeration, since at least the three powerful states mentioned below were still resisting him in 391/0.
632 These are three of the other major Greco-Phoenician kingdoms on Cyprus. Kition, in particular, had a strong connection to Phoenicia. All major editions read *Kitieis* for the third name, surely correctly, even though two mss have *Kitreis*. More problematic is the text of Ephoros, fragment 76, which is clearly the basis for Diod. at this point. This fragment of Ephoros' history is quoted by Stephanos of Byzantion (*Ethnika*, s.v. 'Ὠτιεῖς), where it gives 'Ὠτιεῖς as the third name. This has been shown to be an error on Stephanos' part, but the inclusion of the word "still" before "fighting a war of resistance" in the Ephoros fragment suggests that Ephoros' account dated the beginning of Evagoras' expansion in Cyprus before 391/0. (Reid, 1974; *FGrHist/BNJ* 70 F76). Diod.'s annalistic account breaks up Ephoros' thematic model and spreads it over many years, here and at 14.110.5, 15.2.1–4.2 and 15.8.1–9.2.
633 No king of this name is known.
634 Hekatomnôs of Mylasa was appointed satrap of Karia by Artaxerxes II sometime in the 390s. He was the founder of the Hekatomnid dynasty, which he ruled from Mylasa until 377. His son and successor, Mausolos (377–353), moved the capital to Halikarnassos. According to Theopompos (*FGrHist/BNJ* 115 F103), Autophradates, satrap of Lydia, was in charge of this operation, while Hekatomnôs was commander of the fleet.

4. And, [the King] himself[635] travels through the cities of the upper satrapies and crosses over to Cyprus with a large force. 5. That was the state of affairs in Asia. In Italy, the Romans, after making peace with the Faliscans, went to war for the fourth time against the Aequi.[636] They also sent settlers to Sutrium, but were expelled from Verrugo by their enemies.

Affairs in Italy

99.1. Once this year had come to an end, Demostratos became archon at Athens, while in Rome Lucius Lucretius and Servilius assumed power as consuls.[637] At this time, Artaxerxes sent Strouthas, as general, down to the coast with an army to wage war against the Lakedaimonians. When the Spartiates learned of his presence, they sent out Thibron to Asia as their general. He captured a place called Ionda and a high hill, named Kornissos, forty *stades* away from Ephesos.[639] 2. Well, Thibron advanced into the King's territory with an army of 8,000 soldiers, including those he had collected in Asia, and pillaged it, but Strouthas pitched his camp not far from the Lakedaimonians. He had a large force of barbarian cavalry, plus 5,000 hoplites and more than 20,000 light-armed troops. 3. Eventually, when Thibron had gone on a sortie with a detachment of his army and had acquired a great amount of booty, Strouthas went on the attack. In the ensuing battle he slew Thibron and killed most of his soldiers. He took some prisoner and

390/89: Book 14.99.1–102.4

Artaxerxes sends Strouthas to Ionia to fight the Spartans[638]

A battle ensues in which Thibron and most of his men are killed

635 Here I choose to follow the reading of all mss (αὐτός, "he himself"), referring to the King. All editors follow Dindorf in emending to οὗτος ("this man"), referring to Hekatomnôs. Whilst there is no evidence that Artaxerxes ever went to Cyprus, it is equally unclear why Hekatomnôs should have travelled through the upper (eastern) satrapies on his way from Karia to Cyprus. Furthermore, if this operation really happened at this time, there is no record of its accomplishing anything.
636 Cf. Livy, 5.28.5–13.
637 Livy gives the names of the consuls of this year (Varronian 393) in full at 5.29. They were Lucius Lucretius Flavus and Servius Sulpicius Camerinus. It appears from the *Fasti Capitolini* that they were replacements (*suffecti*) for the true consuls, Lucius Valerius Potitus and Servius Cornelius Maluginensis, who abdicated on account of having been improperly elected (*vitio facti*). As Livy observes this was the first time consuls had been elected since 409.
638 The following account of Thibron's campaign against Strouthas and his defeat parallels that by Xenophon (*Hell.* 4.8.17–19), but is not in line with his arrangement of events; see nn. 606, 613 and 623. The appointment of Strouthas, who followed a pro-Athenian policy, in place of Tiribazos indicates where Artaxerxes' favour inclined at this point.
639 Neither site is known. One ms (M) has Koressos for Kornissos. Koressos is the name of a hill near Ephesos, but it is neither high, nor 40 *stades* (*c.*4½ miles or 7 km) away. A case has been made for the mountain Solmissos, south of Ephesos. Ionda may be a mistake for Isinda, which was a tribute-paying member of Athens' fifth-century empire somewhere in the region, although even the Barrington Atlas is not bold enough to situate it. Perhaps it was on or near the site of Pygela.

Thrasyboulos sails to Aspendos and is killed in battle with the Aspendians

only a few escaped to safety at the fort of Knidinion.⁶⁴⁰ 4. Thrasyboulos, the Athenian general, travelled with his fleet from Lesbos to Aspendos and moored his triremes at the river Eurymedon.⁶⁴¹ Although he had received money from the Aspendians, some of his soldiers pillaged their territory. After nightfall, the Aspendians, who were angered by this wrongdoing, attacked the Athenians and killed both Thrasyboulos and some of his men.⁶⁴²

The Athenian captains sail away from Aspendos to Rhodes

The captains of the Athenian triremes [*trierarchs*] were terrified. They hastily manned their ships and sailed away to Rhodes. 5. But, since the city had revolted [from Athens], they joined the exiles, who were in possession of a fort, in fighting against the men in the city. When the Athenians learned of the death of their general, Thrasyboulos, they sent Agyrios⁶⁴³ out as general. Such was the state of affairs in Asia.

In Sicily, Dionysios mounts an expedition against Rhegion

100.1. In Sicily, the Syracusan tyrant Dionysios was eager to add control of the Greeks in Italy [Italiots] to his dominance on the island, but he put off his overall assault upon them to another time, deciding instead that it was to his advantage to attack first the city of Rhegion, because it was the front line of defence for Italy. So, he set out from Syracuse with his army. 2. His force was composed of 20,000 infantry, 1,000 cavalry and 120 warships. He disembarked his troops on the borders of Lokrian territory and proceeded to advance from there overland, cutting down the trees and destroying by fire the territory of the Rhegians. The fleet sailed along the coast towards the other part of the sea

---

640 No such fort is mentioned in Xenophon's account. This detail must come from another source.

641 Eurymedon was well known to Athenians as the site of Kimon's famous double victory against the Persians (Thuc. 1.100.1), for which I accept the date 469.

642 Cf. Xen. *Hell.* 4.8.30–31, who comments that Thrasyboulos was "reputed to be a good man" (ἀνὴρ ἀγαθός).

643 Cf. Xen. *Hell.* 4.8.31. The name is usually spelled Agyrrhios. Agyrrhios of Kollytos was a leading Athenian democratic politician, uncle of the more famous Kallistratos of Aphidna (Sealey, 1956), with a particular interest in financial affairs. He was active from at least 405, when he was involved in the reduction of pay for poets alluded to by Aristophanes (*Frogs*, 367–368). After the restoration of the democracy in 403/2, he introduced a payment of one *obol* for attendance at the Assembly, which he subsequently increased to 3 *obols* in 393/2 (Aristotle, *AP* 41.3). He was secretary of the *Boule* in 403/2 (*IG* II² 1, 41–42) and part of a group that purchased the rights to collect the 2 percent import taxes (*pentekoste*) in 402/1 (Andokides 1, *On the Mysteries*, 133–135). At some time he was found guilty of misappropriating public funds and kept in prison for several years until he paid them back (Demosthenes 24, *Against Timokrates*, 135). Nevertheless, in 374/3 he resurfaced to introduce a recently discovered law regulating the tax on the grain from Lemnos, Imbros and Skyros (*SEG* XLVIII, no. 96; R&O, no. 26). See, in general, Davies, *APF*, 8157, II.

and he pitched camp with his entire force at the Strait.[644] 3. When the Italiots learned of Dionysios' crossing to attack Rhegion, they sent sixty ships from Kroton, eager to hand them over speedily to the Rhegians. While these ships were sailing on the high sea, Dionysios sailed against them with fifty ships. They fled to land, but he kept pressing upon them with undiminished vigour and, by attaching ropes, was trying to drag away those ships that had anchored by the shore. 4. Since the sixty triremes were in danger of being captured, the Rhegians came to the rescue with their full levy and kept Dionysios at bay by the great volleys of missiles they discharged from the shore. But, when a strong gale blew up, the Rhegians pulled the ships on shore. Dionysios, however, suffered violently at the hands of the storm. He lost seven ships and along with them no less than 1,500 men. 5. Since these sailors and their ships were cast on shore in Rhegian territory, the Rhegians took many of them prisoner. But, Dionysios, on board a quinquereme,[645] barely escaped sinking many times and eventually with difficulty reached safety at the harbour in Messina about midnight. Since, moreover, winter was already setting in,[646] Dionysios concluded an alliance with the Lucanians[647] and then led his forces back to Syracuse.

101.1. Later [spring 389], when the Lucanians invaded Thourian[648] territory, the Thourians appealed to their allies to come out quickly with their weapons to oppose them. For, the Greek cities in Italy had the following clauses in their

The Italiots send sixty triremes to help Rhegion, but Dionysios intercepts them

A storm disrupts Dionysios' attack

Dionysios takes his forces back to Syracuse

The Lucanians attack Thourioi

---

644 Diod.'s description of Dionysios' movements, especially of the fleet, is opaque. The best reconstruction is that he landed on the south coast of Italy next to the border of Lokroi Epizephyrioi, his ally. Then, he must have travelled overland, through the mountains, to descend on the coast north of Rhegion. The fleet sailed around the toe ("towards the other part of the sea") to meet him at the Strait opposite Messina.
645 For Dionysios' putative invention of the quinquereme, see n. 311.
646 If the winter season, which brought an end to campaigning, was setting in so soon after Dionysios' expedition, he was either expecting a swift victory, or he made a serious error of judgement.
647 Typically Dionysios was exploiting existing hostilities to advance his own agenda. The Italian Greeks' fear of the Lucanians was long-standing and largely responsible for the formation of the Italiot League. See 14.91.1 and n. 575.
648 Thourioi was a fifth-century foundation that essentially replaced the old city of Sybaris. In its final iteration (444/3), after the expulsion of the obnoxious Sybarites, it was a mixed colony (often called Panhellenic by modern scholars) of settlers from the Peloponnese, Boiotia, Euboia, the Islands and Athens, although the leadership was Athenian, probably an initiative of Perikles (Plut. *Per.* 11.5). For the most detailed narrative of its foundation, see Diod. 12.9.1–11.3 (cf. Strabo, 6.1.13 C263). However, Diod.'s attribution of its laws to the seventh-century lawgiver, Kharondas of Katane (12.11.4–19.3), is clearly mistaken. According to Diogenes Laertios (*Lives of the Great Philosophers* 9.8.50), it was Protagoras of Abdera who created its constitution. For the location of Thourioi, see Map 12.

The Thourians advance into Lucania incautiously and are trapped

treaties, namely that they would all come to the aid of whichever territory was pillaged by the Lucanians and, also, that the generals of any city that did not provide an army of assistance should be put to death. 2. So, after the Thourians sent out messengers to the cities regarding the presence of their enemy, all states began making preparations to mobilize. But, the Thourians started out over-eagerly and did not wait for the bulk of their allies. With an infantry force more than 14,000 strong and almost 1,000 cavalry they set out against the Lucanians. 3. When the Lucanians heard of their enemy's approach, they retired to their own territory. And, the Thourians enthusiastically invaded Lucania. Initially, they captured a fort and acquired an abundance of booty, but, in so doing, they took the bait, as it were, for their own destruction. For, priding themselves on their success and in their eagerness to put the prosperous city of Laos[649] under siege, they advanced incautiously along a narrow route, flanked by precipitous cliffs. 4. Once they had arrived in a plain that was hemmed in by high, steep hills, the Lucanians in full force cut them off from any way of return to their homeland. For, their unexpected appearance in clear view on the crest of the hills struck fear into the hearts of the Greeks, because of the size of their army and the difficulty of the terrain. For, at that time, the Lucanians had 30,000 infantry and no less than 4,000 cavalry.

The Thourians are cut to pieces

Leptines rescues fleeing Thourians and persuades the Lucanians to make peace with the Italiots

Leptines is praised by the Italiots, but Dionysios is not pleased and appoints Thearides in his place

102.1. Now that the Greeks were caught in such an unexpected predicament, the barbarians came down onto the plain. In the ensuing battle the Italiots were overwhelmed by the vast size of the Lucanian forces. More than 10,000 of them were killed, since the Lucanians had given orders not to take any prisoners. Of the remainder, some fled to a hill close to the sea, others, who saw warships sailing towards them which they thought belonged to the Rhegians, rushed in a body into the sea and swam across to the triremes. 2. But, the approaching fleet belonged to the tyrant Dionysios and was under the command of his brother, Leptines, who had been sent to help the Lucanians.[650] However, Leptines received the swimmers humanely, disembarked them on dry land and persuaded the Lucanians to accept a *mina* of silver[651] for each of the captives, who numbered more than 1,000. 3. Leptines stood surety for the money, brought about

649 Laos was a Greek settlement from Sybaris. The date of its foundation is unknown, but it had to be before 510, when Sybaris was destroyed by Kroton. The attack by the Thourians was either an example of Greek inter-state antipathy or an indication that Laos was under Lucanian control, as was the opinion of Strabo, who records this defeat at 6.1.4–7 C253. For the location of Laos, see Map 12.
650 Not surprisingly, since Dionysios was their ally (14.100.5). Possibly, the Lucanian attack upon Thourioi was part of a concerted plan.
651 A *mina* was the equivalent of 100 *drachmas*, or 100 days' pay.

a reconciliation between the Italiots and the Lucanians and persuaded them to make peace. He won great praise from the Italiots by settling the war in this manner, one that was profitable to himself, but not beneficial to Dionysios. For Dionysios was hoping that, if the Italiots were at war with the Lucanians, he could intervene and easily take charge of affairs in Italy, but [he realized] that, if they put an end to such a great conflict, it would be difficult for him to succeed. For that reason, he relieved Leptines of his position as *navarch* and appointed his other brother, Thearides, as commander of the fleet.[652] 4. Some time after these events the Romans divided up the territory of Veii into allotments, giving each recipient four *plethra*, or, as some say, twenty-eight.[653] They prosecuted their war against the Aequi[654] and took the city of Liphlos[655] by storm. When the people of Velitrae revolted, they entered into a war with them. Satricum also revolted from the Romans,[656] who sent out a colony to Circeii.

The Romans redistribute the territory of Veii and continue their wars against the Aequi and others

103.1. Once this year had come to an end, Antipatros became archon at Athens, while in Rome Lucius Valerius and Aulos Mallios managed the consular magistracy.[657] At this time Dionysios, dynast of the Syracusans, unveiled his

389/8: Book 14.103.1–106.4

Dionysios mounts a new assault upon Italy and besieges Kaulonia

652 Thearides was the younger brother, Leptines having commanded the fleet up to this time. Both had been named along with Polyxenos, the tyrant's brother-in-law, in 393 in an Athenian decree honouring Dionysios (see n. 399). Thearides later married Dionysios' daughter Arete. It is an interesting question where this insight into Dionysios' mind originated. Did the action of replacing Leptines suggest the motivation? If so, was the deduction Diod.'s or his source's? Or, was Diod.'s source acquainted with Dionysios' plans? If so, that would surely have been Philistos. But, note that both Philistos and Leptines were exiled by Dionysios shortly after this, in 386, and both took refuge in Thourioi (Diod. 15.7.3–4).

653 The *plethron* is a linear measurement of 100 Greek feet. When used as a measure of area, it was 100 x 100 feet (0.09 of a hectare, 0.22 of an acre) or the area that could be ploughed in one day. In that sense it is often used as an equivalent for the Roman *jugerum*, even though that area was over twice as large (28,000 Roman feet, 0.25 of a hectare or 0.6 of an acre). In his account of the distribution (5.30.7) Livy gives the figure of 7 *jugera* allotted to all freeborn members of a family. Thus a family of four would receive 28 *iugera* (*c*.17 acres or 7 hectares). Somewhere in these figures might lie Diod.'s confusion.

654 The Aequi were an Italic people who lived on the Apennines, east of Latium. They fought many battles against the Romans in the fifth and early fourth century.

655 No such town is known.

656 For Velitrae see n. 265. Satricum was a Volscian town in the coastal plain of Latium. For the location of these and Circeii, see Map 12.

657 Both Livy (5.31.2) and the *Fasti Capitolini* (under the Varronian date 392) identify the two consuls as Lucius Valerius Potitus and Marcus Manlius, who was later called Capitolinus. At 14.116.6 Diod., indeed, names the hero of the repulse of the Gauls from the Capitol as Marcus Manlius. It is usual to assume that he is mistaken in calling the consul Aulos Mallios here, and that the consul and hero are one and the same, but it is not necessarily the case. There were many Manlii Capitolini and the *cognomen* came from their residence on the Capitol rather than any act of heroism.

intention to mount a campaign against Italy and set out from Syracuse with a very large force. 2. It consisted of over 20,000 infantry, about 3,000 cavalry, 40 warships and, in addition, no less than 300 supply vessels. After four days he reached Messina. There, he let his army rest in the city, but he dispatched Thearides, his brother, to the Lipari Islands with thirty ships, since he had been informed that ten of the Rhegians' ships were in those parts. 3. Thearides sailed out and caught the Rhegian squadron of ten ships in a location that was to his advantage. He captured the ships with all their crew and promptly returned to Dionysios at Messina. Dionysios threw the prisoners in chains and handed them over to the Messinans to guard. Then, he brought his army over to Kaulonia,[658] pitched his camp around the city, set up his siege-engines and began to mount a series of assaults. 4. When the Greeks in Italy learned that Dionysios' forces were on their way across the Strait that separated them, they too began to assemble their armies. And, since the city of Kroton was by far the most heavily populated and was home to the largest number of Syracusan exiles, they [the Italian Greeks] put the leadership of the war in their hands. 5. After gathering forces from all quarters, the Krotoniates chose Heloris[659] of Syracuse as general. This man had been exiled by Dionysios and had a reputation for practicality and boldness. Also, he was assumed to be most reliable for prosecuting the war against the tyrant on account of his hatred. Once all the allies had reached Kroton, Heloris arranged them to his liking and set out for Kaulonia with the whole force.[660] 6. For, his thinking was that his simple appearance would put an end to the siege, but that in any case he would be fighting against opponents that were exhausted by their daily assaults. His total force consisted of about 25,000 infantry and approximately 2,000 cavalry.

The Italiots mobilize their forces in response

The Krotoniates choose Heloris the Syracusan as commander and set out to relieve the siege of Kaulonia

The Italiots camp near the Eleporos River and Dionysios leads his army against them

104.1. The Italiots had completed most of their journey and had pitched their camp near the Eleporos river,[661] when Dionysios moved his troops from the city and advanced to meet them. Now, Heloris was out at the front of the army with 500 elite soldiers, while Dionysios happened to have made camp forty *stades*[662] from the enemy. When Dionysios learned from his scouts that the enemy was nearby, he roused his army at first light and led them forward.

658 For the location of Kaulonia, on the toe of Italy 40 km above Lokroi, see Map 12.
659 Heloris, formerly one of Dionysios' close advisers (14.8.5 and n. 56), had been exiled for reasons unknown and was last mentioned as commander of the Rhegian forces (14.87.1 and 90.5).
660 He presumably marched southward along the coastal plain.
661 The Eleporos (Elleporos in Polybios, 1.6.2) river is usually identified with today's Galliparo, near modern Marina di Badolato.
662 About 4½ miles or 7.2 km.

2. At daybreak, Dionysios encountered the small force with Heloris and surprised them with his attack. Since the soldiers with him were battle-ready, he gave his opponents no chance whatsoever to recover. 3. Heloris found himself in a desperate situation, nevertheless he withstood his attackers with the men he had and dispatched some of his friends to the camp, ordering them to hurry the main force along. They promptly carried out his orders. As soon as the Italiots learned that their general and his men were in danger, they ran to the rescue. But, Dionysios with his troops in close order surrounded Heloris and those with him and slaughtered almost all of them, despite their courageous resistance. 4. And, as the Italiots in their eagerness to help were arriving in scattered groups, the Sicilians easily got the better of them, since they kept to their ordered ranks. Despite that, for some time the Italian Greeks stood up to the danger, even though they saw many of their comrades being killed. But, when they learned of the death of their general, since they were also seriously hindered by stumbling into each other in the confusion, the Italiots finally lost heart and turned in flight.

Dionysios catches Heloris unawares

The Italiots rush to the rescue. A battle ensues, in which the Italiots are routed

105.1. In the rout across the plain many were slaughtered, but the bulk of the army took refuge on a hill, one that was strong enough to withstand a siege, but was lacking in a water-supply and easily possible for the enemy to keep under surveillance. Dionysios set up camp all around the hill and kept his men awake under arms throughout that day and the following night, paying personal attention to the guard-posts. The next day the men, who had taken refuge there, experienced hardship on account of the heat and the lack of water. 2. They sent a herald to Dionysios and entreated him to take ransom, but, immoderate in his success, he ordered them to lay down their arms and put themselves in the hands of their conqueror. This was a harsh order, so they continued their resistance for some time, but when they became overwhelmed by their bodily needs, they surrendered themselves at the eighth hour,[663] physically exhausted. 3. As the prisoners descended from the hill, Dionysios counted them, by beating on the ground with a stick. They numbered more than 10,000. They were all suspicious of his savagery, but quite the contrary, he revealed himself the most generous of men. 4. For, he allowed the captives to go free without ransom and, after concluding peace with most of the cities,[664] he allowed them to be independent. On these accounts he was praised by those who had

Many are killed; the remainder take refuge on a hill, but are eventually reduced to surrender

Contrary to expectation Dionysios releases the captives and makes peace with the cities

663 Late afternoon.
664 Not all, of course, since he still had designs on Kaulonia and Rhegion and Hipponion. Dionysios' "generosity" was a calculated ploy to break the cohesion of the Italiot League, and in that it was successful.

experienced his generosity and he was honoured with golden crowns. Indeed, it seemed that this was just about the finest thing he had done[665] in his life.

Dionysios prepares to attack Rhegion. The citizens sue for peace

106.1. Dionysios moved with his army against Rhegion and made preparations for a siege, because of the insult he felt over the marriage issue.[666] As a result the Rhegians were seized with a great anxiety, since they were devoid of allies and did not have a comparable military force. Furthermore, they knew that, when the city fell, neither pity nor prayers would avail them. 2. For that reason they decided to send ambassadors to beseech him to treat them moderately and to beg him not to plan any inhumane action against them. 3. Dionysios demanded a payment of 300 *talents*, took possession of their whole fleet of seventy warships and required that they give 100 hostages. When they had satisfied all his demands, he moved his forces against Kaulonia. He transferred all its inhabitants to Syracuse and granted them citizenship with the concession that they be free from taxation for five years. As for the city, he razed that to the ground and gave the territory of the Kaulonians as a gift to the Lokrians.

Dionysios withdraws from Rhegion and returns to Kaulonia. He destroys the city and gives the land to the Lokrians, his ally

The Romans celebrate the capture of Liphoecua

4. After the Romans captured the city of Liphoecua[667] from the people of the Aequi, they held a great athletic festival in honour of Zeus in fulfillment of the vows of the consuls.[668]

388/7: Book 14.107.1– 109.7

107.1. Once this year had come to an end, Pyrgion became archon at Athens, while in Rome four military tribunes took over the consular magistracy: [they were] Lucius Lucretius, Servius Sulpicius, Gaius Aemilius and Gaius Rufus,[669] and the ninety-eighth Olympiad was celebrated, in which Sosippos from Athens was the victor.[670] 2. Once these men had assumed their office,

Dionysios razes the city of Hipponion and gives the land to the Lokrians

---

665 I translate the reading in the Budé text, with reservation. Both the Budé and Teubner editors, following a suggestion by Dindorf, change the tense of the verb from future (most mss) or present (one ms) to past. Only Oldfather in the Loeb retains the future tense and translates "this would probably be the finest act of his life." Either way, this is not likely to be a judgement made by Diod., but by his source, which, in this case, was probably Philistos once again.

666 See 14.44.5 and n. 321, and 14.107.3.

667 Another unidentified city. It may be the same as the Liphlos mentioned above at 102.4.

668 These games were promised by Camillus after the fall of Veii (Livy, 5.19.6) and carried out by the consuls of 389 (Livy, 5.31.2).

669 At 5.31.9 Livy reports that the consul, Lucius Valerius Potitus, supervised the election of six military tribunes for this year (Varronian 391) and they took office on 1 July (5.32.1). Their names were Lucius Lucretius, Servius Sulpicius, Marcus Aemilius, Lucius Furius Medullinus, Furius Agrippa and Gaius Aemilius. Some variant names are given by the *Fasti Capitolini*, but neither mentions Gaius Rufus.

670 In the *stadion*.

Dionysios, dynast of the Syracusans, marched with his army against Hipponion,[671] transferred its inhabitants to Syracuse and, after razing the city to the ground, allotted its territory <to the Lokrians>. 3. Indeed, he was continually eager to treat the Lokrians well because of their agreement to his marriage, whereas he was keen to take revenge on the Rhegians for their decision about the marriage union. For, it is reported that at the time when he sent an embassy to them to ask them to agree to his marrying a daughter of one of their citizens, the Rhegians replied in public that the only girl they would agree to his marrying was the daughter of the public executioner.[672] 4. Angered at this and believing that he had been grossly insulted, he was intent on taking revenge on them. Indeed, even when he had made peace with them the year before, it was not because he was aiming at friendship, but because he wanted to get possession of their fleet of seventy triremes. For, he determined that, once the city was cut off from help by sea, he would easily take it by siege. 5. For that reason, he was dallying in Italy, searching for a plausible excuse for breaking the treaty, one that would not seem to detract from his own reputation.[673]

108.1. He, therefore, led his forces to the Strait and began to make preparations for a crossing.[674] But first he asked the Rhegians to provide a food-market, promising that he would promptly send back from Syracuse whatever they had given. His motive for doing this was so that he might seem to be in the right in sacking the city, if they did not provide the food, whereas, if they did, he thought that they would exhaust their supplies and so he would swiftly gain possession of the city through starvation, simply by taking up position nearby. 2. The Rhegians, suspecting none of this, at first orchestrated the supply of provisions splendidly for several days, but when he kept dallying longer, sometimes claiming sickness, on others putting forth other excuses, they came to suspect his intent and no longer provided provisions for his army.

Dionysios prepares to cross back to Sicily and requests food supplies from the Rhegians

The Rhegians comply, but soon realize they are being tricked and stop. Dionysios, feigning anger, attacks Rhegion

---

671 Hipponion (later Roman Vibo Valentia) was located on the opposite coast of the toe from Kaulonia, facing the Tyrrhenian Sea and overlooking the Sinus Vibonensis. It was a colony of Lokroi, probably dating from the seventh century. It had revolted from Lokroi in 422 along with Medma, which was also a colony of Lokroi (Thuc. 5.5.3; Strabo, 6.1.5 C256). Its soldiers had fought on the side of the Italiots at the battle of Eleporos. By razing both Kaulonia and Hipponion and moving their people to Syracuse, Dionysios had cut Rhegion off from help from the north.
672 See 14.44.4–5 and n. 321.
673 Diod. had no way on his own of knowing what Dionysios was thinking. This passage must come from a source close to the tyrant, namely Philistos. The same applies to the insights into the thoughts and intentions of Dionysios in the following chapter.
674 I.e. back to Sicily.

The Rhegians choose Phyton as their general and resist valiantly. Dionysios is seriously wounded

3. Dionysios, feigning anger at this, gave the Rhegians back their hostages, encircled the city with his army and commenced making daily attacks upon it. He had a great number of incredibly large siege-engines made, being eager to take the city by storm by battering the walls down. 4. The Rhegians, after choosing Phyton[675] as their general and arming all the adult males, were careful to post sentries and at every opportune moment sallied out and set fire to the enemy's siege-engines. 5. Indeed, these men frequently fought splendidly before their walls on behalf of their country and, in doing so, aroused the anger of their opponents. Although many of their own men fell, a substantial number of the Sicilians died also. 6. Indeed, even Dionysios himself happened to be struck in his groin by a spear. He almost died and only with difficulty recovered from the wound. As the siege dragged on because of the superhuman energy the Rhegians brought to the defence of their liberty, nevertheless Dionysios kept his forces to their daily assaults and did not abandon his original purpose.

Dionysios competes at the Olympic Games in chariot racing and poetry. His entries were at first successful, but ended in disgrace

109.1. Since the Olympic Games were getting close, Dionysios sent to the contest several four-horse chariots that were far superior to others in speed, and pavilions for the festival that were stitched with gold and decorated with expensive multi-coloured hangings. He also sent his best rhapsodes, so that they might make him noteworthy by performing his poems at the festival. For, Dionysios was a passionate aficionado of poetry.[676] 2. He sent his brother, Thearides, along as supervisor. When Thearides arrived at the festival, he was the focus of attention because of the beauty of the pavilions and the great number of four-horse chariots. And, when the rhapsodes set themselves to the task of performing Dionysios' poems, at first a crowd ran up, attracted by the beautiful sound of the actors, and everyone was full of admiration. But later, realizing on reflection the poor quality of his creations, they began to ridicule Dionysios and reached such a point in their condemnation that some people dared to rip apart his pavilions. 3. Moreover, the orator Lysias, who was at that time visiting Olympia, made a speech exhorting the assembled crowd not to admit a delegation from the most impious tyranny to the Sacred Games. In

---

675 A very different story about Phyton is provided by the second/third-century AD sophist, Philostratos, in his *Life of Apollonios* (7.2.2). In his account, Phyton was a philosopher who was living at Dionysios' court, after having been exiled from Rhegion, but was caught passing on information to the Rhegians about Dionysios' plans against them. For this, he was fixed alive to a siege-engine, which was rolled up to the walls. Dionysios calculated that the Rhegians would not shoot at one of their own, but Phyton shouted out to them to do so.

676 Rhapsodes were professional performers of poetry (usually epic) for entertainment. They were there as entertainers, not as competitors in the Olympics. On Dionysios' mania for poetry, see 15.6.1–5.

fact, that was when he delivered the speech he had composed, entitled *Olympiakos*.⁶⁷⁷ 4. As the festival approached conclusion, Chance caused some of his chariots to drive off-course, while others collided with each other and crashed. Similarly, in the case of the ship that was transporting the delegation back from the Games, as it was on its way to Sicily, Chance forced it onto the coast of Italy at Taras by a storm. 5. It is for that reason that it is said that the sailors, who made it to safety at Syracuse, spread the news abroad in the city that the poor quality of his poems had brought disaster not only on the rhapsodes, but, along with them, on the four-horse chariots and their ship. 6. When Dionysios learned of the ridiculing of his poems, because his flatterers told him that all men envy those who are producing beautiful works, but end up admiring them, he did not desist from his zeal for poetry.⁶⁷⁸ 7. The Romans engaged in battle against the Volsinii⁶⁷⁹ at Gourasion and slaughtered many of their opponents.

The Romans defeat the Volsinii at Gourasion

110.1. After the completion of these events the year passed on. Theodotos became archon for the Athenians and in Rome six military tribunes held the consular authority: [they were] Quintus Caeso Sulpicius, Aenus Caeso Fabius, Quintus Servilius, Publius Cornelius.⁶⁸⁰ 2. Once these men had assumed their office, the Lakedaimonians, because they were in difficulties from their wars against both the Greeks and the Persians, sent their *navarch* Antalkidas off to Artaxerxes to negotiate a peace.⁶⁸¹ 3. When he had explained as best he

387/6: Book 14.110.1–117.9

Antalkidas negotiates the Peace of Antalkidas (also known as The Great King's Peace) with Artaxerxes. The Corinthian War ends

---

677 The small fragment of the *Olympiakos*, preserved by Dionysios of Halikarnassos (*On the Ancient Orators: Lysias*, 29–31), is speech 33 in the Lysianic corpus. Although the exhortation Diod. refers to is not in the preserved fragment, the statements in the portion we have are, in my mind, consistent with the historical situation at the Olympics of 388 before the conclusion of the Great King's Peace (Diod.'s date), although many prefer 384 (the 99th Olympiad).
678 At 15.7.2–4 Diodoros repeats this incident, but depicts Dionysios' reaction as so deranged that he exiles both Philistos and Leptines in his anger at his defeat.
679 Volsinii was a major Etruscan city, north of Veii, on the *Lacus Volsiniensis*. The Romans were continuing their expansion into Etruria, while still fighting to control Latium. See Livy, 5.31.5–6 and 32. Gourasion is otherwise unknown.
680 Livy (5.36.11) places the election after the incident at Clusium (below). He gives the following names: Quintus Sulpicius Longus, Quintus Servilius, Publius Servilius Maluginensis and the three sons of Marcus Fabius (Ambustus), who were supposedly responsible for angering the Gauls and bringing about the sack of Rome; one was named Caeso, another Gnaius, and the name of the third can be inferred from the narrative to be Quintus. Livy's Publius Servilius should probably be corrected to Publius Cornelius, as in Diod., since the *cognomen* Maluginensis belonged to the Cornelii, not the Servilii. This is the Varronian year 390.
681 Antalkidas was in a strong position. As described above (14.85.4, n. 549), his influence with the King was aided by the satrap Tiribazos. In any case, it is not surprising that

could the point of his mission, the King declared that he would make peace on the following terms: that the Greek cities in Asia should be subject to the King; that all the other Greeks were to be free and governed by their own laws; and that he would make war upon those who rejected these terms and did not accept the agreement through the agency of those who agreed to it.[682] 4. Now the Lakedaimonians accepted these terms and made no protest,[683] but the Athenians and the Thebans and some of the other states were very distressed at the adandonment of the cities in Asia. But, since they were not capable of carrying on the war by themselves, they had no choice but to acquiesce and accept the peace.[684] 5. And the King, now that his dispute with the Greeks had been resolved, began preparing his forces for a war against Cyprus.[685] For, during the time that Artaxerxes had been distracted by his war against the Greeks,

Artaxerxes prepares to make war on Evagoras on Cyprus

> Artaxerxes was cooling towards the Athenians, given their renewed aggressiveness in the Aegean. Furthermore, Athens' friendship and alliance with the rulers of two rebellious parts of the Persian Empire, Evagoras in Cyprus (see n. 544) and Akoris in Egypt, were not likely to have endeared the Athenians to the King. Also, in the autumn of 388, with the aid of the twenty triremes sent by Dionysios under Polyxenos (14.62.1 and n. 399), Antalkidas had gained control of the Hellespont and cut off Athens' grain supply from the Bosporan kingdom in the Crimea (Xen. *Hell*. 5.1.28; Cf. n. 589). This, coupled with Teleutias' daring raid on the Peiraieus (Xen. *Hell*. 5.1.21-24), dampened Athens' ardour for the war (Xen. *Hell*. 5.1.29).

682 The Peace was concluded in the spring of 386. For a more detailed version of the King's Peace (also called the Peace of Antalkidas) see Xen. *Hell*. 5.1.31. Other useful references are in Plutarch (*Ages*. 23.1-3; *Artax*. 21.4-22.2).

683 A rather naïve statement, since the Spartans had negotiated these terms. Under Agesilaos' leadership, they assumed the role of enforcer of the Peace and thereby reasserted their supremacy in mainland Greece.

684 This summary statement conceals much. Only the Athenians had any interest in the Greek cities in Asia, because they claimed to be their metropolis. They kept this protest on the books for propaganda purposes (see e.g. Demosthenes 23, *Against Aristokrates*, 140), although it would fall to Alexander the Great to take up the cause of the Greek cities and finally "liberate" them. The Athenians were ready to agree to the terms of the King's Peace, because their specific concern – the acknowledgement of their ownership of Lemnos, Imbros and Skyros – was conceded, although they did have to abandon their association with Klazomenai, which they had honoured only months before (see *IG* II² 28; R&O, no. 18). The Thebans had particular reasons for opposition, because the "autonomy for all cities" clause challenged the existence of their Boiotian League. They yielded to this condition only on the threat of military intervention from Sparta by Agesilaos. So, also, Argos was compelled reluctantly to remove its garrison from Corinth and relinquish its plan for *isopolity* with that city, under pressure from Sparta. See Xen. *Hell*. 5.1.32-36.

685 One of the noteworthy omissions by Diod. from his version of the King's Peace is the provision "among the islands, Klazomenai and Cyprus should belong to me" (i.e. Artaxerxes). Thus, Athens was prevented from helping Evagoras. The Persian King was already thinking of reclaiming Cyprus.

Evagoras had gained control of almost the whole island and had amassed powerful military forces.[686]

111.1. Dionysios' siege of Rhegion was now entering its eleventh month[687] and, since he had cut them off from relief on every side, the people in the city were experiencing a terrible shortage of basic necessities. For, the report is that a *medimnos*[688] of grain at that time cost five *minas*[689] in Rhegion. 2. Worn down by lack of food, at first the people ate up the horses and the yoke-animals, next they boiled the hides and fed themselves on that, finally they went out of the city and ate the grass beside the walls, like so many grazing animals. So, the demand of nature forced men to change their normal way of living and seek safety in the diet of creatures that lack reason. 3. But when Dionysios learned what was going on, so far from pitying people who were compelled to endure inhuman sufferings, quite the opposite, he brought in teams of yoke-animals and cleared the grass from the area so that all vegetation disappeared. 4. As a result, overcome by their excessive suffering, the Rhegians surrendered their city to the tyrant, giving him total power over themselves.[690] Throughout the city Dionysios found piles of corpses of people who had died from lack of food. As for the living that he captured, they were physically emaciated and had the appearance of corpses. The number of prisoners he collected was more than 6,000. The majority of these he sent away to Syracuse with orders that those who produced a *mina* of silver be ransomed, but that those who could not pay be sold as slaves.[691]

112.1. When Dionysios captured Phyton, the Rhegian general, he proceeded to have his son drowned in the sea. As for Phyton himself, he first had him tied

Dionysios' siege of Rhegion enters its eleventh month and the people are reduced to dire straits

The Rhegians surrender unconditionally to Dionysios

Dionysios inflicts inhumane acts of vengeance upon Phyton and his family

---

686 See 14.98. The three cities on Cyprus that were opposing Evagoras – Soloi, Amathous and Kition – were probably under his control by now, possibly through the assistance of a squadron of ten triremes from Athens, under the command of Khabrias (Xen. *Hell.* 5.1.10) and Akoris, king of Egypt (Theopompos, *FGrHist/BNJ* 115 F103).
687 Spring 386.
688 A *medimnos* was the equivalent of about 52 litres of dry goods.
689 A *mina* was worth 100 *drachmas*. Thus a *medimnos* in Rhegion was costing 500 *drachmas*, which was 100 times the average cost for a *medimnos* of grain at this time.
690 Diod. makes no comment about the fate of the physical city. Given Dionysios' treatment of Kaulonia and Hipponion (above), one might suspect that Strabo is correct in stating that he destroyed the city (Strabo, 6.1.6 C258), although it has been doubted. Other sources narrate that Dionysios built a palace at Rhegion and decorated the garden with plane trees (Theophrastos, *Historia Plantarum*, 4.5.6; Pliny, *Naturalis Historia*, 12.7).
691 According to ps.-Aristotle, *Oikonomika*, 2.2.20.1349b, in a long section on the devious tricks used by Dionysios to cheat people of their money, the ransom figure was three *minas* and, after it was paid, he sold them into slavery anyway.

to the top of his tallest siege-machine, as if he were exacting punishment in some tragic drama. He also sent one of his servants to tell him that Dionysios had drowned his son the previous day, to whom Phyton replied, "He has been more fortunate than his father by one day." 2. Next, Dionysios had him paraded around the city, being whipped and subjected to every manner of indignity. All the time he was accompanied by a herald, proclaiming that Dionysios was punishing this man in this extraordinary fashion, because he had persuaded his city to choose the path of war. 3. But Phyton, who had proved himself to be a competent general during the siege and was an object of admiration during the rest of his life, endured this ultimate punishment manfully. He maintained a calm state of mind and shouted out that it was because he had not been willing to betray his city to Dionysios that he was enduring this punishment, one that the divine spirit would all too soon visit upon Dionysios himself. The result was that his courage began to be pitied by Dionysios' soldiers, some of whom were already raising a fuss. 4. Dionysios became concerned that some of his soldiers might be so bold as to snatch Phyton out of his hands, so he put an end to the punishment and had the poor wretch drowned at sea along with his relatives. 5. In sum, Phyton experienced monstrous punishment in a way that was unworthy of his virtue. At that time many Greeks mourned his fate and thereafter poets composed lamentations over his pitiful downfall.[692]

The Celts cross the Alps and invade the Transpadane region. The Senones attack Clusium

113.1. At precisely the time when Dionysios was besieging Rhegion,[693] the Celts,[694] who inhabited the region beyond the Alps, poured through the

692 Thus, implicitly, Dionysios' actions are criticized by the whole Greek (i.e. civilized) world. The entire account of the siege and capture of Rhegion and the dishonourable treatment of Phyton and his family is designed to substantiate the evaluation of Dionysios at the beginning of this book (14.2.2) that "he left behind his life as the most outstanding example for moral criticism to all succeeding ages."

693 This synchronism between Dionysios' capture of Rhegion, the King's Peace and the Gallic sack of Rome is common to all Greek historians and those derived from them. It is first extant in Polybios (1.6.1), who writes, "So, it was the nineteenth year after the battle of Aigospotamoi [405] and the sixteenth before the battle of Leuktra [371], the year in which the Spartans ratified the so-called peace of Antalkidas with the King, that in which also Dionysios the Elder, after defeating the Italiots in the battle at the river Elleporos, was besieging Rhegion, and that in which the Gauls, after taking Rome itself by assault, occupied the whole city except the Capitol." This synchronism is assumed to have originated with Timaios, who may himself have derived it from Philistos. It clashes, of course, with the traditional and usually accepted date for the Gallic sack, which was the Varronian (and Livian) date 390.

694 As we know from Caesar (*Bellum Gallicum*, 1.1), Gaul was composed of three peoples, only one of which were the Celts. They were located in the central area of Gaul between the Garonne and the Marne. Most authors, however, made no distinction between the names Gaul and Celt. Diod. (5.32.1) knew of a difference, but his was not the same as Caesar's.

passes⁶⁹⁵ in great force and took possession of the territory that lay between the Apennine mountains and the Alps,⁶⁹⁶ expelling the resident Tyrrhenians.⁶⁹⁷ 2. Regarding these Tyrrhenians, some say that they were colonists from the twelve cities in Tyrrhenia,⁶⁹⁸ but others say that, before the time of the Trojan War, Pelasgians⁶⁹⁹ settled in this region, fleeing the flood that occurred in the time of Deukalion.⁷⁰⁰ 3. Now, when the Celts divided up the territory amongst their tribes, the tribe called the Senones happened to get the region situated furthest from the mountains along the coast.⁷⁰¹ But since this region was arid, they were discontented and hastened to move on. They armed their young men and sent them out to find a land for them to settle in. Well, these young men, numbering about 30,000, invaded Tyrrhenia and ravaged the territory of the people of Clusium.⁷⁰² 4. At this very time the Roman people sent

A Roman ambassador, sent to Clusium, slays a Celtic chieftain

695   Livy's description of their passage is at 5.34.8. It is confusing, since the pass he names appears to be through the Julian Alps, which would take them to the north-east of Italy near Trieste, but the route he traces goes *via* the south-west, north of Marseilles, through the territory of the Taurini to the river Ticinus.

696   Gallic tribes had penetrated beyond the Alps before this, as Livy writes (5.33.2–35.3), although he dates their first penetration almost 100 years too early, in the time of Tarquinius Priscus (616–579).

697   Tyrrhenoi and Tyrsenoi were Greek names for the Etruscans, who dominated most of Italy from the Alps to Campania from the eighth to the fifth century. The Greeks came in contact with them as early as the mid-eighth century, when they first began sending colonies to Italy. The origin of the Etruscans, their language and rich culture are still not fully understood. They are sometimes linked to the Teresh, one of the so-called Sea Peoples, who invaded the eastern Mediterranean at the end of the Bronze Age. Livy gives an account of Etruscan power before the rise of Rome at 5.33.7–11.

698   The Etruscan Confederation was composed of twelve cities. Most commonly listed (in their Roman spelling) are: Arretium, Caere, Clusium, Cortona, Perusia, Populonia, Tarquinii, Veii, Vetulonia, Volaterrae, Volsinii, Vulci.

699   From the earliest writers onwards the Pelasgians are a ubiquitous element in Greek speculation about the peoples who preceded them. The theories run the gamut, from claims that they were barbarians to ideas that they were Greeks, from the belief that they were pre-Greek inhabitants of Greece to the view that they were invaders. Standard references are to Herodotos, 1.56–58 and Thucydides, 1.3, but for this text it is the Atthidographer Hellanikos (*FGrHist/BNJ* 4 F4) who is particularly relevant. He states that the Pelasgians moved to Italy and eventually settled in Tyrsenia, thus generating a tendency to equate the Etruscans with Pelasgians. The most thorough ancient treatment of this idea in the context of the history and migrations of the Pelasgians is by Dionysios of Halikarnassos (*Roman Antiquities*, 1.17–30), but see also Strabo, 6.2.4 C221.

700   Deukalion, son of Prometheus, was a sort of Greek Noah, who survived a great flood. His time was a "watershed moment" in Greek mythical history.

701   The Senones settled on the Adriatic between Ariminum and Ancona in what came to be known as the *Ager Gallicus*.

702   Clusium is in the heart of Etruria, south-west of Lake Trasimene. The Celts had crossed the Apennines and penetrated deep inland. See Map 12.

The Senate agrees to surrender the ambassador. This decision is overturned by the Assembly

ambassadors to Tyrrhenia to spy on the army of the Celts.[703] When the ambassadors arrived at Clusium and saw that a battle had started, they showed more bravery than wisdom and joined in battle with the Clusians against their besiegers. 5. And, one of the two ambassadors succeeded in slaying one of the more renowned enemy chieftains. After the Celts learned what had happened, they sent ambassadors to Rome to demand that the ambassador be handed over for starting an unjust war. 6. At first the Senate tried to persuade the Celtic ambassadors to accept a monetary compensation in return for the wrongs committed, but, when they did not accept, the Senate voted to hand over the man accused.[704] But the father of the man who was about to be handed over was one of the military tribunes with consular power.[705] He appealed the decision to the popular Assembly and, since he was a man of influence over the populace, he persuaded them to render the Senate's decision null and void.[706] 7. Up to this time the populace had obeyed the Senate in all matters, but this occasion marked the beginning of their overturning of the Senate's decisions.

Angered by the Assembly's decision the Celts march on Rome. The Romans march to meet the enemy

114.1. When the Celtic ambassadors arrived back at their own camp, they reported the Romans' reply. At the news the Celts grew exceedingly angry and, after picking up an additional force from one of the related tribes, set off at speed towards Rome itself, over 70,000 strong.[707] When the military

703 Livy, whose whole account of the Gallic attack, from 5.32 onwards, is cast as a moral tale of impending disaster, in which the Romans ignore the ominous warning of Caedicius and exile Camillus ("the only man who could have saved Rome"), and now (5.36.6) depicts the ambassadors as behaving "more like Gauls than Romans and contrary to the law of nations" (*ius gentium*). His account differs from Diod.'s not only in tone, but on specific points of detail: (1) The ambassadors were sent to Clusium because the Clusians had requested help from Rome, not as spies; (2) The number of ambassadors is three, not two, and they are identified as the three sons of Marcus Fabius Ambustus; (3) Fighting started only after an exchange of words between the ambassadors and the Gauls; (4) The ambassador who killed the Gaul is identified as Quintus Fabius. Livy's version is followed closely by Plutarch (*Cam.* 17–18), even in naming the Gallic leader Brennus (Livy, 5.38.3), perhaps anachronistically, since that was the name of the leader of the Gallic invasion of Greece in 280. Dionysios of Halikarnassos (*Roman Antiquities*, 13.12) also identifies the killer of the Gallic chief as Quintus Fabius, but appears to think there were only two ambassadors. Diod.'s less embellished version may be more reliable (cf. Polybios, 2.18.2–3).
704 According to Livy (5.36.9–11), the Senate recognized that right was on the side of the Gauls, but declined to make a decision about such important men and referred the matter to the popular Assembly (*provocatio ad populum*).
705 He was Marcus Fabius Ambustus.
706 In fact, in Livy's account (5.36.11), the three Fabii were promptly elected military tribunes, which incensed the Celts.
707 This is the only figure given for the strength of the Gallic forces. It is considered a gross exaggeration by modern historians, whose estimates range from a low of 12,000 to a high of more than 30,000.

tribunes at Rome heard of the approach of the Celts, acting on their own authority they called all the men of fighting age to arms. 2. They set out in full force, crossed over the Tiber[708] and led the army along the side of the river for eighty *stades*.[709] When it was reported that the Galatians were approaching,[710] they drew up the army for battle. 3. Now, the Romans arrayed their bravest 24,000[711] men between the river and the hills and placed their weakest men on the tops of the hills. The Celts, by contrast, extended their line of battle considerably and, either by chance or prescience, stationed their very best troops on the hills. 4. No sooner had the trumpets on both sides given the signal than the armies engaged in battle with much noise. The elite Celtic troops had no difficulty driving their opponents, the weakest of the Romans, from the hills. 5. Consequently, as these fled in a body towards the Romans on the plain, those ranks were thrown into confusion and, as the Celts pressed on, they fled in panic. Most of them set off rushing along the riverbank. In the confusion they kept getting in each other's way, and the Celts were not slow to slaughter those in the rear repeatedly. As a result the whole plain was covered in dead bodies. 6. The bravest of those who fled to the river were trying to swim across with their weapons, putting the same value on their suits of armour as on their lives. But, since the current was strong, some were carried under by the weight of the armaments and died, while some with great perseverance did barely make it to safety, after being swept along for a considerable distance. 7. Since the enemy were continuing to attack and were killing many along the side of the river, the majority of those who remained cast away their armour and began to swim across the Tiber.

The battle at the Allia follows, in which the Romans are defeated

The flight of the Romans is impeded by the swift current of the Tiber

708 Diod., or probably his source, is the only authority that has the Romans cross the Tiber and therefore situates the battle on the right (western) bank of the river. Rome is situated on the left or eastern side, since the river flows from the Apennines to the sea. Most modern historians think he made a mistake (e.g. Ogilvie, 1965, 717–719), but his version is definitely self-consistent and too detailed to be a simple confusion. See n. 713.
709 That is 9 miles or 15 km. Livy (5.37.7) says they had barely reached the eleventh milestone (about 88 *stades*) from Rome (probably on the *Via Salaria*) when they met the Gallic force. Plutarch (*Cam.* 18.7) gives the figure of 90 *stades*. All figures would place the battle north of Fidenae, "where the Allia descends in a deep gully from the hills of Crustumerium and joins the Tiber" (Livy, 5.37.7).
710 Plutarch is the only source to claim that the Romans pitched camp before the battle (*Cam.* 18.7).
711 Diod.'s figure for the strength of the Roman army is usually considered inflated (Ogilvie, 1965, 717), although Plutarch (*Cam.* 18.5) assigns the Romans not less than 40,000, and the possibility should not be discounted that the Romans had allied soldiers with them, as Polybios states (2.18.2; Walbank, *Commentary*, 1.185).

The Celts continue to slaughter the Romans as they are trying to swim across the river

Most of the Roman survivors take refuge in Veii, but a few reach Rome with news of the defeat

Great despair results and some flee, but the magistrates gather the citizens and stores of food and money on the Capitoline

The Celts hesitate to attack the city for three days, but then break down the gates and pillage the city

115.1. Although the Celts had slain many men along the river bank, they did not, nevertheless, slacken their enthusiasm, but began throwing spears at the men who were trying to swim across. And, since a mass of missiles was being discharged into crowds of men in the river, the result was that the throwers did not fail to hit their mark. In the event, those who were hit with mortal blows died a swift death, but those who were wounded, fainting from loss of blood and from fighting the speed of the current, were swept away. 2. Such was the disaster that befell the Romans. Of those who survived, the majority occupied the city of Veii that had only recently been razed to the ground by themselves.[712] They fortified the place as best they could and welcomed with open arms other survivors from the rout. But a few of those, who had swum across the river without their weapons, fled to Rome and announced the news that everyone had perished.[713] When the news of such great misfortune was announced to those who had been left behind in the city, they all fell into a deep despair.[714] 3. For they understood that resistance was impossible, now that all their young men had perished, and that it was far too dangerous to flee with their wives and children with the enemy nearby. In actual fact, many private individuals did flee to nearby cities with their whole households, but the magistrates of the city roused the spirits of the masses and ordered them to bring up onto the Capitoline with all speed supplies of food and all other necessities. 4. When that was accomplished, both the acropolis and the Capitoline were packed with supplies for nourishment as well as gold and silver and very expensive clothing, as would be the case when the goods from the whole city were gathered into one place. So, the Romans were engaged in carrying up the most valuable of their possessions and in fortifying the aforementioned place, taking advantage of a three-day lull in activity.[715] 5. For, the

---

712 See 14.93.2.
713 Livy's account of the battle (5.38) has many elements in common with Diod's. For example, that the weakest Roman soldiers were posted on the hill that was attacked by the best Gallic forces; that the Roman legions on the plain fled in panic and tried to swim across the Tiber; that most survivors went to Veii; that only a few reached Rome to announce the defeat. But, Livy's version, which located the battle on the left bank of the Tiber, fails to explain why the Romans would need to swim across the river to Veii instead of retreating back to Rome the way they had come. In this regard, Diod.'s version is the more logical.
714 The battle of the Allia took place on 18 July (Livy, 6.1.11; Tacitus, *Histories*, 2.91), 387, or 390 (Varronian). The day was memorialized as a *dies nefastus* in the Roman religious calendar along with the slaughter of the Fabii at the battle of Cremera, which happened on the same day in the year 477. See also Plutarch (*Cam.* 19.1–3).
715 Livy's more dramatic description (5.39.4–5.40.10) includes some extra details, such as: (1) the decision of the elder senators to stay in their homes and die there; (2) that most of the *plebs* fled via the Janiculum to the countryside; and (3) that Caere gave refuge to the priests and priestesses with their sacred cult objects.

Celts spent the first day cutting off the heads of the dead, in keeping with their ancestral custom.[716] For the next two days they camped beside the city. As they observed the deserted walls and heard the commotion that was being made by the people carrying up their most valuable possessions onto the acropolis, they suspected that the Romans were setting a trap for them. 6. But, on the fourth day,[717] when they realized the true situation, they broke down the gates[718] and pillaged the city, with the exception of a few households on the Palatine.[719] Next, they began making daily assaults upon the fortified positions. Although they inflicted no serious damage on their opponents, they suffered many losses themselves. Nevertheless, they did not slacken their enthusiasm, but kept hoping that, even if they could not win by assault, they would at least wear down [the defenders] in time, when they ran out of necessary supplies entirely.[720]

The Celts attack the fortified positions

116.1. While the Romans were in the midst of such confusion, the neighbouring Tyrrhenians made a plundering incursion into Roman territory with a strong force. They captured many prisoners and acquired not a small amount of booty. But the Romans who had fled to Veii fell upon the Tyrrhenians in a surprise attack. They put them to flight, took back the booty and captured their camp.[721] 2. Acquiring also a great supply of weapons, they both distributed them to those who were weaponless and armed the men whom they had gathered from the surrounding area. For, their intention was to extricate the people who had taken refuge on the Capitoline from the siege.[722] 3. But, as they were at a loss how to make this known to the besieged, because the Celts surrounded them with a large army, a certain Cominius Pontius undertook to

The Tyrrhenians attack Roman territory, but are defeated by the men from Veii, who then plan to raise the siege of Rome

Cominius Pontius climbs the Capitol by a trackless route and announces the plan

---

716 This was a known custom amongst the Celts. See Diod. 5.29.4; Strabo, 4.4.5 C198; Livy, 10.26, 23.24.
717 Both Polybios (2.18.2) and Plutarch (*Cam.* 22.1) agree with Diodoros that the Celts entered Rome three days after the battle. Livy (5.39.8, 41.4) has them enter the city on the day after the battle and Tacitus (*Annals*, 15.41.3–4) dates the burning of the city by the Gauls to 19 July 390 BC, i.e. the day after the battle.
718 Both Livy (5.39.2) and Plutarch (*Cam.* 22.1) state that the gates were left open. They also specify that the Gauls entered by the Colline Gate.
719 Diodoros, or his source, fails to mention the tragic slaughter of the aged senators following the pulling of Marcus Papirius' beard, described by Livy (5.41.7–10).
720 The siege went on for probably seven months (Polybios, 2.22.5; Plut. *Cam.* 28.2, 30.1). Diodoros makes no mention of the fact that the Celts also suffered from sickness and shortage of supplies (Livy, 5.48.1–3; Plut. *Cam.* 28.1–2).
721 Cf. Livy, 5.45.4–8.
722 A quite different account, favouring Camillus, is presented by Livy (5.43.6–45.3), followed by Plutarch (*Cam.* 23.1–6). From his exile at Ardea, Camillus led a force of young men to make a surprise nighttime attack on the camp of some inebriated Celtic scavengers. On the basis of his success there, the men in Veii requested that he become their leader, provided the Senate appointed him *dictator*.

bring encouragement to the people on the Capitol.[723] 4. So, he set out alone, swam across the river during the night and made his way unnoticed to a rocky part of the Capitol that was hard to climb. Pulling himself up by this route with difficulty, he gave the news to the men on the Capitol about the force that had been assembled at Veii and said that they were waiting for an opportunity to attack the Celts. He then descended by the way he had climbed up, dived into the Tiber and returned to Veii. 5. But the Celts noticed the tracks of the man who had just ascended, and made arrangements to ascend by the same cliff during the night. And so, about the middle of the night, when the guards had become slack in their watchfulness because of the strength of the terrain, some of the Celts climbed up along the rock. 6. They did, in fact, escape the notice of the guards, but the sacred geese of Hera, that were being reared there, sensed them climbing up and started honking.[724] When the guards rushed to the spot, the Celts panicked and did not dare to proceed. And a certain Marcus Manlius, a man of distinction, who ran to the scene to help, cut off the hand of the first man to reach the top with his sword, struck him in the chest with his shield, and sent him rolling back down from the cliff. 7. When the second climber suffered a very similar fate, the rest quickly started to flee. But, since the cliff was precipitous, they all fell headlong over the edge and were killed.[725] Consequently, when the Romans sent an embassy to discuss a truce, the Celts were persuaded to accept 1,000 pounds of gold in return for leaving the city and quitting Roman territory.[726] 8. And the Romans, because their houses had been razed and most of their citizens had been killed, gave permission to each and every person to build a house wherever they chose, and they contributed roof-tiles at the city's expense, which are right up to this day called "public." 9. And so, since everyone built his house to his own preference, the result was that the city's streets were narrow and winding. As a result, when the city's population increased, they were unable to straighten the streets.[727] Also, some say that in return for their donation of their gold jewellery for the common

---

723 Actually, Pontius Cominius. Diod.'s explanation for his mission is quite different from Livy's (5.46.8–11), where it is claimed he went to secure the Senate's agreement to Camillus' being appointed *dictator*.

724 There is no tradition that suggests that geese were sacred to Hera (Juno). They were probably kept on the Capitoline for the purpose of augury.

725 Livy recounts this incident at 5.47.1–11.

726 Quite a different account is given by Livy (5.48.4–5.49.7) and followed by Plutarch (*Cam.* 29.1–6), in which Camillus arrives in the nick of time, prevents the payment of gold and defeats the Gauls.

727 See Livy (5.55.3–5) for a similar description of the rebuilding, although in his account it was preceded by a debate over the question whether to stay in Rome or move to Veii.

salvation, the women of the city received the city's permission to have the right to drive around the city in chariots.[728]

117.1. Taking advantage of the Romans' weakened condition following the previously described disaster, the Volscians made war upon them. In response, the military tribunes enlisted soldiers and, leading the army out into the field, pitched camp in the place called Marcius, 200 *stades* distant from Rome. 2. Since the Volsci were opposing the Roman camp with superior force and kept attacking their position, the people in Rome became fearful for the men in the camp and decided to elect Marcus Furius[729] as *dictator* ....[730] 3. These men armed all those of military age and set out during the night. At daybreak they surprised the Volscians as they were in the process of attacking the [Roman] camp. Appearing in their rear, they easily sent them fleeing. And, when those in the camp sallied forth, the Volscians were caught between two forces and were cut down virtually to a man. As a result, people who were previously considered powerful became the weakest of the neighbouring tribes following this disaster. 4. After the battle, when the *dictator* heard that the city of Bola[731] was being besieged by the Aeculani, who are now called the Aequicoli,[732] he led the army there and slaughtered most of the besiegers. From there, he moved to the territory of Sutrium, a Roman colony, which the Tyrrhenians had taken by force. Attacking the Tyrrhenians off-guard, he slew many of them and saved the city for the Sutrians.[733] 5. On their way home from Rome, the Gauls stopped to besiege Veascium,[734] a city that was a Roman ally. The *dictator* attacked them, killed most of them and took possession of all their baggage,

While the Romans are so weakened, the Volsci attack, but are defeated by Camillus

Camillus defeats the Aeculani and the Tyrrhenians

Camillus defeats the Gauls at Veascium and regains the gold and most of the booty taken from Rome

---

728 This may not be accurate, since according to Ovid (*Fasti*, 617f.) the women of Rome had had this right from of old. By contrast, Livy (5.50.7) states that the women who had donated were granted the privilege of having eulogies delivered at their funerals. This may also be false, if Cicero (*De Oratore*, 2.44) is correct in stating that Quintus Lutatius Catulus delivered the first eulogy at a woman's funeral over his mother Popilia (in 102 BC).
729 That is, Camillus. As noted above, in Livy, Camillus had been appointed *dictator* long before this.
730 It is obvious that a name has dropped out here because of the plural form that begins the next sentence. It should be the name of the cavalry commander (*magister equitum*), who was usually appointed at the same time. In this case he was Gaius Servilius Ahala (Livy, 6.2.5–6). It should be noted, however, that in his unhistorical elevation of Camillus as the *dictator* who saved Rome, Livy names a Lucius Valerius as the *magister equitum* (5.48.5).
731 For the location of Bola, see Map 12.
732 Actually, the Aequi.
733 Camillus' victories over the Volsci, the Aequi and the Etruscans are described by Livy at 6.2.1–6.3.10.
734 Otherwise unknown. Plutarch (*Cam.* 29.4) has the Celts retire from Rome in the direction of Gabii.

Camillus may have been denied a triumph, although accounts differ

amongst which was the gold that they took as their price for Rome and almost all the other booty they had pillaged in their capture of the city.[735] 6. Despite his great accomplishments [Camillus] was prevented from celebrating a triumph through the envy of the tribunes. But some say that he did celebrate a triumph for his victory over the Etruscans, riding in a chariot pulled by four white horses, and that on that account two years later the People condemned him to pay a large sum of money as a fine. We shall make mention of that at the appropriate time. 7. The Celts who had gone to Iapygia[736] turned back through Roman territory. But, not long after, they were ambushed by the Kerii [Caeretans] at night and all cut to pieces[737] in the Trausian plain. 8. Kallisthenes,[738] the author of a *Hellenika*, began his history from the peace concluded in this year by the Greeks with Artaxerxes, the King of the Persians. He wrote ten books, encompassing a period of thirty years, and ended his composition at the seizure by Philomelos, the Phokian, of the sanctuary at Delphi. 9. But, now that we have reached the peace that was concluded by the Greeks with Artaxerxes and the danger to Rome caused by the Gauls, we shall end this book as planned at the beginning.

Some Celts were cut to pieces on their way back from Iapygia by the Caeretans

Kallisthenes began his Hellenika at this point

---

735 Naturally, neither Livy nor Plutarch includes this tale, since in their version the gold had never been paid. Another account credits the Caeretans with regaining the gold (Strabo, 5.2.3 C220). But, Polybios (2.22.5) has the Insubres and Boii claim in 231 that their ancestors, who had sacked Rome, had arrived home with their booty intact.

736 That these Celts had made their way down to Iapygia in southern Italy suggests that they had been in contact with Dionysios of Syracuse, who was eager to hire Celtic mercenaries for his own wars.

737 Cf. Strabo, 5.2.3 C220. For the location of Caere, see Map 12.

738 Kallisthenes (*c*.360–327), son of Demotimos of Olynthos, was the grand-nephew, student and eventual colleague of Aristotle, with whom he produced a list of the victors at the Pythian Games, for which they were honoured by the Delphic Amphiktyony sometime between 337 and 327 (*TDGR*2, no. 104; R&O, no. 80). He accompanied Aristotle to Assos, when he left Athens in 348/7, and enjoyed the hospitality of Hermeias of Atarneus, over whose death he wrote a eulogy. Although reputedly a rhetorician, he made his name as an historian. His first work was the *Hellenika*, described by Diodoros. He also wrote a History of the Third Sacred War (356–346), but he is best known for his involvement with Alexander the Great. In 334 he joined Alexander's campaign as its self-elected historian, "not for the sake of his own fame, but to make Alexander's" (Arrian, *Anabasis*, 4.10). His work (*The Deeds of Alexander*), which was probably largely propaganda for the Greeks at home and depicted Alexander as a Homeric hero, is lost, but its influence on later writing on Alexander was not insignificant. In 327 he clashed with Alexander over *proskynesis* (doing obeisance) and subsequently was implicated (rightly or wrongly) in the so-called Conspiracy of the Pages and condemned to death (Arrian, *Anabasis*, 4.13–14; Plut. *Alex.* 55). The manner of his dying is disputed. The fragments of his works are accessible in *BNJ* 124.

Book 15

The following events are contained in the fifteenth book of Diodoros' *History*:[739]

386/5–385/4

How the Persians fought the war against Evagoras in Cyprus and brought it to conclusion (**chs. 2-4, 8-9**)

How the Lakedaimonians, in contravention of principles agreed to by all parties, removed the Mantineians from their fatherland (**chs. 5, 12**)

Concerning the poetic creations of Dionysios, the tyrant (**chs. 6-7**)

The revolt of Glôs from the King and his alliance with Egypt and Sparta (**ch 9**)

Concerning the arrest of Tiribazos and his acquittal (**chs. 8, 10-11**)

Dionysios plans to expand his empire into the Adriatic in order to invade Epeiros and pillage Delphi; his alliance with the Illyrians, who attack the Molossians and defeat them; Spartan aid to Molossia; Dionysios' building programme in Syracuse (**ch. 13**)

384/3

Parian colony on Pharos attacked by Illyrians, but saved by Dionysios' fleet (**ch. 14**)

383/2

Concerning the death of Glôs (**ch. 18**) and the condemnation of Orontes (**ch. 11**)

Foundation of Leuke by Takhôs; competition of Klazomenai and Kyme over Leuke (**ch. 18**)

How Amyntas and the Lakedaimonians made war against the Olynthians (**ch. 19**)

---

739 The following list of contents is handed down in our manuscripts, the earliest of which is from the tenth century. Similar lists (*prographai*) exist for all extant books. Whether they originated with Diodoros, as was the case with Polybios (*Histories*, 11.1–2; Walbank, *Commentary*, 2.266), or were the work of either Alexandrian or Byzantine scholars is not easily determined. These lists are quite eclectic and do not constitute a comprehensive list of topics in each book. In the case of Book 15 they are quite inadequate. Missing topics are added in italics. Relevant chapters are indicated in bold. The dates provided are Diodoros'.

382/1

How the Lakedaimonians seized the Kadmeia; *fighting around Olynthos continues; death of Teleutias* (**chs. 20–21**)

381/0

Fighting around Olynthos continues; King Agesipolis takes charge (**ch. 22**)

380/79

Death of Agesipolis; Polybiadas captures Olynthos; How they [the Lakedaimonians] reduced the Greek cities to slavery contrary to the terms of the Peace (**ch. 23**)

385/4

The settlement on the island of Pharos in the Adriatic (**ch. 13**)

384/3

Dionysios' campaign into Tyrrhenia and the pillaging of the temple (**ch. 14**)

383/2

Campaign of Dionysios against the Carthaginians; both (his) victory and defeat (**chs. 15–17**)

379/8

Carthaginian campaign in Italy and restoration of town of Hipponion (**ch. 24**)

378/7

How the Thebans regained possession of the Kadmeia (**chs. 25–27**)

379/8

How the Carthaginians were exposed to danger on being afflicted by a pestilence (**ch. 24**)

377/6

Foundation of the Second Athenian Confederacy (**ch. 28**)

Akoris of Egypt prepares for war against Persia; Khabrias joins him, but is recalled at the demand of Pharnabazos; Iphikrates sent to help Persia; Sphodrias' failed attack on Athens; Athens goes to war with Sparta (**ch. 29**)

Athenian Confederacy grows; conflict in Euboia over Oreôs (**ch. 30**)

Reorganization of the military contributions of the Peloponnesian League; Agesilaos put in charge (**ch. 31**)

Concerning the Boiotian War and its course of events (**chs. 28, 32–34**)

Khabrias defeats Pollis in naval battle near Naxos; Athens regains supremacy at sea (**ch. 34–35**)

376/5

The Triballians' campaign against Abdera (**ch. 36**)

Timotheos sails to Kephallenia and defeats the Lakedaimonians at Alyzeia (**ch. 36**)

Theban victory over Spartan garrison at Orkhomenos (**ch. 37**)

375/4

Artaxerxes plans war against Egypt; needing Greek mercenaries, he arranges a new Common Peace, which all agree to, except Thebes; Sparta and Athens divide supremacy over Greeks between themselves (**ch. 38**)

Thebans full of confidence; their generals the best in Greece (**ch. 39**)

Political strife (stasis) endemic in the Peloponnese (**ch. 40**)

374/3

Campaign of the Persians against Egypt (**chs. 41–43**)

371/0

How the Thebans, after defeating the Lakedaimonians in the most illustrious Battle at Leuktra, made their own claim to the leadership of the Greeks (**chs. 51–56**)

369/8

The things accomplished by the Thebans in the course of their incursions into the Peloponnese (**chs. 62–65**)

374/3

Concerning Iphikrates' leadership and his military innovations (**ch. 44**)

Zakynthian democratic exiles aided by Timotheos; Sparta sends Aristokrates to help oligarchs (**ch. 45**)

Campaign of the Lakedaimonians against Kerkyra (**chs. 46–47**)

Capture of Plataia by Boiotians and expulsion of Plataians to Athens (**ch. 46**)

Assassination of Evagoras; Romans defeat Praenestini (**ch. 47**)

373/2

Concerning the earthquake and tsunami that occurred around the Peloponnese and the torch that appeared in the sky (**chs. 48–50**)

372/1

Artaxerxes calls for another Common Peace (372/1); all accept, except Thebes; Lakedaimonians determine to invade Boiotia (**ch. 50**)

370/69–369/8

Thebans think of attacking Orkhomenos, but Epameinondas deters them (**ch. 57**)

How a huge slaughter took place amongst the Argives, which was given the name *skytalismos* (cudgelling) (**chs. 57–58**)

Foundation of the Arkadian League; Agesilaos invades and devastates Tegea (**ch. 59**)

Concerning Jason, tyrant of Pherai, and his successors (**chs. 57, 60–61**)

The political unification of Messene by the Thebans (**chs. 66**)

The Arkadians sack Pellene and kill the Spartan garrison (**ch. 67**)

Campaign of the Boiotians into Thessaly (**ch. 67**)

Pelopidas invades Macedon and takes Philip as hostage (**ch. 67**)

Epameinondas' second invasion of the Peloponnese forces its way past massed resistance (**ch. 68**)

The Boiotians attack Corinth, but are driven off by Athenian forces, under Khabrias (**ch. 69**)

Celtic and Iberian mercenaries sent by Dionysios to aid Sparta impress with their swordsmanship, but are sent back; Philiskos is sent by Artaxerxes to arrange another Common Peace, but fails; Euphron makes himself tyrant in Sikyon (**ch. 70**)

368/7

Pelopidas, eager for glory, takes a Boiotian force into Thessaly, but is arrested by Alexander of Pherai; a Theban army, sent to rescue him, gets into trouble and retreats; disaster is averted by the leadership of Epameinondas (**ch. 71**)

Reason why Epameinondas was not a general; the Lakedaimonians win the tearless battle against the Arkadians; foundation of Megalopolis (**ch. 72**)

Dionysios begins another war against Carthage, but it ends inconclusively; he then dies (**ch. 73**)

Account of the manner of death of Dionysios; his son, Dionysios II, assumes power and gives his father an extravagant funeral (**ch. 74**)

367/6

Alexander of Pherai slaughters the people of Skotoussa; Epameinondas invades northern Peloponnese; the Boiotians rescue Pelopidas from Thessaly; the Athenian general, Khares, relieves Phleious from Argive attack (**ch. 75**)

366/5

Athens loses Oropos to Thebes; the people of Kos move to a new city; a new attempt at a Common Peace; list of famous intellectuals of the period (**ch. 76**)

365/4

War breaks out between Elis and Arkadia over Triphylia; Elis is defeated and invaded; Ptolemaios of Aloros assassinated in Macedon by Perdikkas (**ch. 77**)

364/3

Pisatans claim control of Olympia and oust Eleians; Epameinondas urges Boiotians to build a fleet and challenge Athens' naval supremacy (**ch. 78–79**)

Thebans attack and sack Orkhomenos (**ch. 79**)

Thessalians, oppressed by Alexander of Pherai, request help from Thebes; Pelopidas leads the Thebans and wins the battle (of Kynoskephalai), but is killed (**ch. 80**)

Eulogy of Pelopidas; Klearkhos makes himself tyrant of Herakleia in Pontos; Timotheos captures Torone and Poteidaia (**ch. 81**)

363/2

Events leading up to and involving the inconclusive battle of Mantineia (**chs. 82–87**)

Eulogy of Epameinondas after his death in battle (**ch. 88**)

Exhausted by constant warfare, the Greek cities conclude a Common Peace and Alliance, to include Messenia; only the Lakedaimonians are opposed; several histories end at this point (**ch. 89**)

362/1

The satraps of the western provinces, joined by Takhôs of Egypt, revolt from Artaxerxes; betrayal of the revolt by Orontes; success of Datames in Kappadokia and his assassination; treachery of Rheomithres; Takhôs fights on in Egypt with help from Khabrias and Agesilaos; death of Artaxerxes (Mnemon), succeeded by Artaxerxes (Okhos); conflict between Takhôs and Nektanébôs for throne of Egypt; death of Agesilaos in Kyrene (**chs. 90–93**)

Citizens of towns forced into the new foundation of Megalopolis try to return to their original homes; the Thebans send an army under Pammenes to preserve Megalopolis (**ch. 94**)

361/0

Alexander of Pherai's pirates attack the Cyclades, land on Peparethos and capture Athenian triremes; Leosthenes, the defeated Athenian general, goes into exile; Khares, appointed in his place, sails away to Kerkyra (**ch. 95**)

Introduction: Book 15.1.1–6

1.1. Throughout the whole of this work our habit has been to use history's usual frankness (*parrhesia historike*) both to address deserved praise to good men for their virtuous deeds and to judge bad men worthy of fitting censure, whenever they do wrong. In this way we think we shall encourage those whose natures incline towards virtue to undertake the noblest pursuits for the reward of immortality that comes from a good reputation, and deter those of an opposite persuasion from the impulse to wrongdoing by fitting reproofs.[741] 2. So, now that we have come to that period in our history when the Lakedaimonians experienced great misfortune as a result of their surprising defeat at Leuktra and, after that, unexpectedly lost their hegemony over the Greeks through their failure at Mantineia,[742] we think that we should maintain the basic principle of our history and apply the appropriate censure to the Lakedaimonians. 3. For, who would not consider them deserving of condemnation, when they inherited from their ancestors a hegemony that was based upon an excellent foundation and one that had been maintained through the virtue of their ancestors for more than 500 years, while they, the Lakedaimonians of today, looked on as it fell apart through their own bad policy?[743] (Such an opinion is) not at all unreasonable. For, their predecessors acquired such a great reputation through much effort and at huge risk, by treating their subjects in a reasonable and humane fashion. But the succeeding generations treated their allies with harsh violence and, furthermore, got involved in unjust and arrogant wars against the Greeks, and so, not unreasonably, lost their empire through their own bad policies. 4. Indeed, in the midst of their misfortunes, the hatred of those they had wronged found an opportunity to take vengeance

Diodoros introduces the theme of this book, which is praise of good men and blame for the bad[740]

The Lakedaimonians' loss of leadership is an object lesson in wrongdoing

---

740 Anyone who desires an exploration of the issues raised in this book that is more comprehensive than is provided here should consult the commentary by Stylianou listed in the bibliography.

741 For the importance of the themes of praise and blame as part of Diod.'s belief in the educational value of history see the Introduction.

742 Whilst the Theban victory at Leuktra (371) was a surprise, the later defeat of the Spartans at the Battle of Mantineia (362) was hardly unexpected. As for the Spartan loss of hegemony over the Greeks, other factors contributed to that, not least the foundation of the Second Athenian Confederacy in 378/7 and Khabrias' reassertion of Athenian naval supremacy in the Aegean by his victory over the Spartan fleet at Naxos in 376.

743 Diod. is clearly echoing standard fourth-century Athenian views about the failure of Spartan imperialism initiated by Isokrates (see e.g. *Panegyrikos*, 123ff.). Diod.'s specific source here is surely Ephoros, as is evident from the citation of Ephoros frag. 118 by Strabo (8.5.4–6 C365). The 500 years would equate to Ephoros' date for Lykourgos, whose reforms in the early ninth century Ephoros believed began the period of Spartan supremacy.

on their previous oppressors, while those who had survived unconquered from the time of their ancestors felt the kind of contempt that is only reasonable to feel towards those who had obliterated their forefathers' deeds of valour. 5. That is the reason why the Thebans, who had previously for many generations been subject to the greater power of the Lakedaimonians, unexpectedly defeated them at this time and became leaders of the Greeks, while the Lakedaimonians, after being deprived of the leadership, were never able to regain their ancestors' good reputation. 6. But, turning from censuring the Lakedaimonians, a subject we have treated sufficiently, we shall proceed to the continuation of our history [by delimiting the period that belongs to this book].[744] So, the preceding book, which was the fourteenth of our whole history, concluded with the events surrounding the enslavement of the Rhegians and the capture of Rome by the Galatians, which took place in the year preceding the Persian campaign to Cyprus against Evagoras the king. In this book we begin from that war and end at the year before the accession to the throne of Philip, son of Amyntas.

Diod. outlines the contents of this book

386/5: Book 15.2.1–7.4

Artaxerxes mounts a campaign against Evagoras of Cyprus

2.1. In the archonship of Mystikhides at Athens,[745] in place of the consuls the Romans elected three military tribunes, Marcus Furius, and also Gaius and Aemilius.[746] In their term of office Artaxerxes, King of the Persians, launched a campaign against Evagoras, king of Cyprus.[747] After spending a long time[748] making his preparations for the war, he amassed a large force of ships and soldiers. His land force numbered 300,000 including the cavalry, and he equipped a fleet of over 300 triremes. 2. As commanders he appointed his son-in-law,

Orontes and Tiribazos cross to Cyprus

---

744 The text is corrupt. The restoration translated here is based on the formula used elsewhere, particularly in this case at 12.2.2.

745 This marks Diod.'s return to the use of his usual, more chronographic, formula for the Athenian archonship from that used in Book 14. The more literary formula reappears in this book at chs. 14, 23, 57, 76 and 82.

746 Probably, the word "and" has been added and the name should be Gaius Aemilius, as at 14.97.1. For the years 386/5–382/1 Diod. appears to repeat the names from the years 391/0–387/6 (Greek chronology). This increases the gap between the Varronian and Greek chronologies from 3 to 8 years. For the full list of military tribunes see note above at 14.97.1 (391/0).

747 Diod. picks up the narrative of Cypriot affairs that he began in 14.98 and last mentioned at 14.110.5.

748 If we accept Diod.'s first date for the Persian preparation for an attack on Evagoras (391/0), as noted in 14.98.3–4, Artaxerxes had spent six years getting ready for this war. On the other hand, the view expressed at 14.110.5 suggests that it was the settlement of the King's Peace in 387/6 that made it possible for Artaxerxes to start making his preparations for the Cypriot War. This is only part of the confusion surrounding the chronology of the Cypriot War. See further at n. 787.

Orontes,[749] over the land army and, over the fleet, Tiribazos,[750] a man who enjoyed high favour amongst the Persians. These men assumed charge of their forces in Phokaia and Kyme,[751] then proceeded down into Kilikia. Crossing over from there into Cyprus, they prosecuted the war energetically. 3. But Evagoras made an alliance with Akoris, king of the Egyptians,[752] who was an enemy of the Persians, and acquired an appreciable force from him. Also from Hekatomnôs, the ruler of Karia, who was secretly assisting him,[753] he received a large sum of money for the support of his mercenary troops. Following the same approach, he tried to persuade others, who were at variance with the Persians, some secretly, others openly, to join in the war against Persia. 4. He controlled almost all the cities in Cyprus, and Tyre and some others in Phoenicia.[754] He possessed a fleet of ninety triremes, twenty of which were Tyrian, seventy from Cyprus. He had 6,000 of his own soldiers and many more than that from his allies.[755] In addition to these he hired a large force of mercenaries, since he had plenty of cash. Furthermore, the king of the Arabs[756] sent him several soldiers, as did some others who were under suspicion by the King of the Persians.

Evagoras prepares to resist with help from Akoris of Egypt and Hekatomnôs of Karia

3.1. So, because he had all these resources, Evagoras felt confident about entering the war. Initially, he used his pirate ships, of which he had many, to ambush the enemy food-supply vessels, some of which were destroyed at sea, others were blocked from their destination, while some were captured. The result of

Evagoras' pirate ships cut off food-supplies to the island and cause a mutiny in the Persian camp

---

749 The mss give various spellings for the name, but there is no doubt that this is the Orontes, satrap of Armenia, who had married Rhodogune, daughter of Artaxerxes (see n. 187).

750 Tiribazos (again variously spelled in the mss) was the man who had successfully negotiated the King's Peace. His role as the commander of the fleet seems, however, to be complicated by Diod.'s later assignment of that role to Glôs (15.3.3; 15.3.6). Perhaps, Tiribazos had some overall command or, more likely, had himself appointed Glôs, who was his son-in-law (15.9.3), to be his *navarch*.

751 Maybe only Tiribazos needed to go to Phokaia and Kyme to pick up triremes from the Spartan fleet that Antalkidas had used so effectively in the Hellespont in 388/7, and also to enlist Greek mercenaries. Orontes meanwhile probably led the remaining Persian land forces directly to Kilikia.

752 Akoris (or Hakoris) had succeeded Nephereus/Nepherites as king in the Twenty-ninth Dynasty in 394/3, after a struggle. He ruled until 381/0.

753 See above at 14.98.4 and nn. 634 and 635.

754 When and how Evagoras acquired control of Phoenicia, especially the important city of Tyre, is not certain, but it was before the publication of Isokrates' *Panegyrikos* in 380 (see *Panegyrikos*, 161 and *Evagoras*, 62).

755 A more reasonable assessment of Evagoras' land forces than the paltry 3,000 peltasts assigned to him by Isokrates (*Panegyrikos*, 141).

756 This is a universally accepted emendation for the mss' reading "of the barbarians." A king of the Arabs is referred to by Herodotos (3.4.3) and Diod. (13.46.4).

Evagoras attacks the Persian fleet on its way to Kition and is defeated[758]

this was that merchants did not dare to transport grain to Cyprus and the Persian camp was seized by a shortage of food, there being a great many soldiers gathered together onto the island. 2. The shortage led to a riot and, when the Persian mercenaries set upon their commanders and killed some, the camp was thrown into a state of mutinous violence. Indeed, it was with difficulty that the Persian generals and the commander of the naval force, whose name was Glôs,[757] put an end to the mutiny. 3. By sailing with the whole fleet to Kilikia and bringing back from there a large supply of grain, they provided an abundance of sustenance. As for Evagoras, he was receiving all the grain he needed from Akoris, king of Egypt, who also sent him money and other equipment. 4. Evagoras, realizing that his navy was seriously outnumbered, manned sixty more ships and asked Akoris to send him fifty others from Egypt. As a result he possessed in all 200 triremes. By dressing these up for combat with a frightening appearance and by putting them through continuous trials and exercises, he made preparations for a battle at sea. Consequently, when he made a surprise attack with his ships in orderly formation upon the royal fleet as it was sailing to Kition,[759] he had a considerable advantage over the Persians. 5. For, with ships in orderly formation he fell upon ships that were not in battle order and, fighting with men forewarned against men taken by surprise, right away at the first contact he anticipated victory. For, sailing with his ships in tight formation against ships that were scattered and disorganized, he sank some and captured others. 6. Nevertheless, since Glôs, the Persian naval commander, and his other captains resisted valiantly, a tough battle ensued, in which Evagoras at first had the upper hand. But later, when Glôs attacked in full force and fought valiantly, the result was that Evagoras turned in flight and lost a great many triremes.

The Persians assemble their forces at Kition and proceed to besiege Salamis

4.1. After their victory in the naval battle the Persians brought together both their land and sea forces to the city[760] of Kition. From this base they prosecuted a siege of Salamis and began a simultaneous devastation of the city both by

---

757 This is Wesseling's generally accepted emendation for the mss' Γαῶ/Γαώ. Glôs is mentioned twice by Xenophon (*Anab.* 1.4.16; 2.1.3), where the name is spelled Gloûs. He was the son of Tamôs (14.35.23). Both father and son were in the service of Kyros. On his position, see n. 750.

758 Ephoros is probably Diodoros' source for the Battle of Kition. In that regard, it is noteworthy that Ephoros received praise from the usually critical Polybios (12.25f.) for his account of this very battle.

759 Kition was the most Phoenician of the major cities in Cyprus and represented the strongest opposition to Evagoras' expansion. It became the base of Persian operations after the Battle of Kition, and may have been so already (see next note).

760 Two mss read "city" (πόλιν) here, but two read "again" (πάλιν). All major editions prefer the former. If "again to Kition" were correct, it would suggest that the Persians were already stationed at Kition and had sailed out from there.

land and sea. 2. Meanwhile, after the sea battle Tiribazos crossed over to Kilikia and travelled from there to the King. He gave him the news of the victory and returned with 2,000 *talents* to finance the war. As for Evagoras, before the battle at sea he had felt confident about the future, because he had got the better of a portion of the enemy's infantry, which he had encountered on land. But, after losing the sea-battle and now that he was under siege, he became despondent. 3. Nevertheless, deciding to continue the war, he left his son, Pnytagoras,[761] behind as commander of all affairs in Cyprus and himself sailed out with ten triremes from Salamis by night unnoticed by the enemy. Travelling to Egypt, he gained audience with the king and exhorted him to continue the war energetically, bearing in mind that the war against the Persians concerned them both.[762]

Despondent after defeat, Evagoras sails to Egypt to get help

5.1. At the very same time[763] these events were taking place, the Lakedaimonians made the decision to launch a campaign against Mantineia,[764] in total disregard of the existing treaty. The cause for this action is as follows. The Greeks were enjoying the Common Peace[765] established in the time of Antalkidas, under the terms of which all cities got rid of their occupying garrisons and regained their right to self-government by common assent.[766] But the Lakedaimonians, who were by their very nature rulers and fond of war by

The Lakedaimonians aggress against Greek cities contrary to the terms of the King's Peace

---

761 All mss have here the name Pythagoras. The emendation by Wesseling to Pnytagoras is universally accepted. It is supported by an inscription from Argos honouring Nikokreon, son of Pnytagoras, king of Cyprus (Tod, *GHI* 194); by the spelling in Photios' epitome of Book 12 of Theopompos' *Philippika* (*FGrHist/BNJ* 115 F103), by the best manuscript (Γ) of Isokrates' *Evagoras* 62 (although all others have a variant of Protagoras) and by Arrian, 2.20.6 and 2.22.2.

762 Probably Akoris/Hakoris was distracted by his own war against the Persians. Isokrates (4, *Panegyrikos*, 140) refers to a failed Persian invasion of Egypt, led by Abrokomas, Tithraustes and Pharnabazos, that lasted for three years. He places this before the Persian war against Evagoras, although the date is much disputed. The Persians lost control of Egypt (the "jewel in their crown") at the end of the fifth century and made numerous attempts to reconquer it in the fourth. Artaxerxes II (Mnemon) made two attempts – this one against Akoris in the 380s and a later one in 375/4 (see 15.38.1 and 15.41.1–43.6). His son, Artaxerxes III (Okhos), tried three more times in or about 354, 351 and in 343/2, when he was finally successful. See Ruzicka (2012).

763 Summer 385.

764 Mantineia was one of the two major cities in Arkadia. The other was Tegea. They were situated at top and bottom of the plain of Tripolis. See Map 11.

765 The Greek term is *Koine Eirene*. The term was first used by Andokides ("a common peace and freedom for all Greeks," *On the Peace*, 17), describing the failed negotiations at Sparta in 392. Since the terms that were discussed at that time were essentially the same as those of the King's Peace of 387/6, *Koine Eirene* came to be the standard way of referring to that Peace and subsequent ones in 375/4 and 372/1.

766 See Diod. 14.110.3 and Xen. *Hell.* 5.1.31 for the autonomy-clause, although neither mentions the removal of garrisons. That clause is, however, referred to by Isokrates (8, *On the Peace*, 16), "that garrisons leave other people's cities," along with the addition that "each state should possess its own territory." That, too, was probably one of the original terms.

preference, found the peace to be a great impediment. In their desire to regain their former dominance over Greece, they jumped at the chance for any opportunities for change.⁷⁶⁷ 2. So, right away they began stirring up trouble in the cities and instigating civil discord through the agency of their own partisans. Some of the cities actually provided them with plausible pretexts for meddling. For, on regaining their autonomy, they demanded a reckoning from those who had been in charge during the period of Lakedaimonian supremacy. When the examinations became intense, because of the People's recollection of the wrongs done to them, and many were being driven into exile, the Lakedaimonians stepped forward as champions of the losing faction.⁷⁶⁸ 3. They took them under their wing and sent them off on their return with military assistance. In this way they at first gained the subservience of the weaker cities, but later, by going to war against those of greater worth, subjected them also. They had not even kept the terms of the Common Peace for two years. <Observing>⁷⁶⁹ that the city of Mantineia was close to their borders and possessed an abundant supply of stalwart males, the Lakedaimonians became suspicious of the city's growth that resulted from the peace and were in a hurry to humble the ambition of its citizens.⁷⁷⁰ 4. So, initially, they sent ambassadors to Mantineia and ordered them to tear down their walls and to dissolve the whole population back into the five original villages,⁷⁷¹ from which long ago they had come together to form the city. When no one paid them any attention, they dispatched

The Spartans besiege the Mantineians for refusing to tear down their walls and break up the city

---

767 This is the characterization of the Spartans adopted in this book. Actually, they adopted the role of guarantors of the King's Peace, a role which they definitely used to their own advantage.

768 The depiction of Spartan agitation of civil discord, by supporting exiles in their attempt to regain power, is demonstrated in the case of Phleious, referred to briefly by Diod. at 15.19.3, but treated more extensively by Xenophon, *Hell.* 5.2.8f.

769 Some verb is lacking in the text, and the emendation adopted by all editors is based upon a similar sentence at 15.20.1.

770 This is a different motivation for the attack than the one offered by Xenophon, according to whom the Spartans had entered into a thirty years' truce following the Battle of Mantineia in 418/7 (Xen. *Hell.* 5.2.2; cf. Thuc. 5.81.1). Since that truce had clearly expired, it made it easier for the Spartans to pick a fight with Mantineia, best described by Xen. *Hell.* 5.2.2–7. Anyway, the Spartan action was viewed as a flagrant transgression of the autonomy clause in the King's Peace and was frequently cited amongst the crimes committed by Sparta between the King's Peace and the Battle of Leuktra (cf. Isokrates 4, *Panegyrikos*, 126; 8, *On the Peace*, 100; Polybios, 4.27.5–7).

771 Like many Greek cities, Mantineia was the result of the political union (*synoikismos*) of a group of smaller communities that had taken place in the late sixth or early fifth century. Diod.'s number for the constitutient villages of Mantineia is either confirmed by or follows Ephoros (*FGrHist* 70 F79), who gives the number five, as does Strabo (8.3.2 C337). According to Xen. *Hell.* 5.2.7, there were only four.

an army and put the city under siege. 5. The Mantineians sent ambassadors to Athens asking them to come to their assistance, but the Athenians chose not to transgress the terms of the Common Peace.[772] Nevertheless, the Mantineians withstood the siege on their own and vigorously resisted their enemy. So, in this way, affairs in Greece experienced the beginning of new conflicts.

The Mantineians ask Athens for help, but are refused

6.1. In Sicily, Dionysios, the tyrant of the Syracusans, was set free from his wars against the Carthaginians and enjoyed much peaceful leisure. As a consequence, he set himself with great dedication to the writing of poetry and invited to court men who had a reputation in that field. Giving them preferential honours, he spent time in their company and treated them as the overseers and critics of his poems. In return for his generous treatment these men flattered him with their opinions. These flatteries went to his head and he began to boast far more of his verses than of his accomplishments in war. 2. One of those in his company was Philoxenos, the dithyrambic poet, a man who was very well respected for his skill in that particular genre.[773] At an after-dinner drinking party, when the tyrant's admittedly awful poems were read aloud, he was asked for his opinion of the poems. When he replied rather too frankly (*parrhesia*), the tyrant took offence at what he said, criticized him on the grounds that he was defaming his work out of envy, and ordered his servants to take him away to the stone-quarries forthwith. 3. Next day, when his friends asked him to pardon Philoxenos, Dionysios forgave him and once again invited the same people to his after-dinner drinking party. After several drinks, Dionysios was again putting on airs about his poems. He declaimed some verses from amongst those that he thought well composed and asked Philoxenos, "How do these poems appear to you?" Philoxenos made no reply, but summoned Dionysios' servants and told them to take him away to the stone-quarries.[774] 4. Well, on that occasion, because of the wit of the response, Dionysios smiled and tolerated his honesty, since the joke had taken the edge off the criticism. But, a little time later, since his friends and Dionysios himself were simultaneously asking him to stop his inopportune honesty, Philoxenos made a rather paradoxical promise. For, he stated that in his replies he would preserve the truth and at the same time keep Dionysios' favour. Nor did he lie. 5. For, when the tyrant was declaiming some verses on a topic of sorrow and suffering and asked, "How do these poems appear to you?," he replied,

Dionysios devotes his leisure time to writing poetry

Philoxenos, the dithyrambic poet, gives honest appraisals of Dionysios' verses

---

772 The Mantineian appeal to Athens is otherwise unattested, but the response is consistent with Athens' careful observation of the terms of the Peace.
773 On Philoxenos, see 14.46.6 and n. 333.
774 This clever retort was alluded to by Cicero (*Ad Atticum*, 4.6.2).

"Pitiful," preserving both parts of his promise through the ambiguity. For, Dionysios took his "pitiful" to mean sorrowful and full of compassion, which are the elements of good poetry. So, he interpreted them as praise for himself. But the rest of the company, who caught the real intent, understood that the word "pitiful" was directed totally at the unsuccessful nature of the composition.[775]

Dionysios has a similar relationship with the philosopher Plato

7.1. By chance, the philosopher Plato experienced rather similar treatment. For, Dionysios invited this man to Syracuse and at first treated him with the greatest respect, observing that he enjoyed a freedom of speech (*parrhesia*) characteristic of philosophy. But later, stung by some of his comments, he turned against him completely, took him off to the market and sold him as a slave for twenty *minas*. However, the philosophers rallied to his assistance and purchased his freedom. They sent him back to Greece, after expressing the friendly advice that a wise man should associate with tyrants as little as possible, or at least on the most agreeable terms possible.[776]

Dionysios' poems are ridiculed at the Olympic Games

2. Dionysios did not give up his enthusiasm for poetry. He dispatched the most melodious actors to the Olympic Festival to recite his poems to musical accompaniment in front of the assembled crowds. At first these actors wowed the audience with the beauty of their voices, but later, on closer examination, they were ridiculed and greeted with guffaws of laughter.[777]

Dionysios is driven mad with grief on news of the reception of his poems

3. When Dionysios learned of the contemptuous reception of his poems, he overreacted and fell into a deep despair. The intensity of his suffering kept constantly increasing until a kind of madness overtook his mind. Alleging that all his friends were jealous of him, he began to suspect that they were conspiring against him. In the end his frenzied despair reached such a point that he did away with many of his friends on false

775 There are numerous accounts of the exchange between Dionysios and Philoxenos. This is one of the more detailed. Most of the others are just references to Philoxenos' being sent to the quarries, but Athenaios (*Deip.* 1.6e) is quite original in asserting that Philoxenos was sent to the quarries for having an affair with Dionysios' mistress, Galatea. Both Athenaios and Aelian (*VH*, 12.44) claim that Philoxenos wrote his *Kyklops* in the quarries.

776 Plato himself refers to this visit to Syracuse in his *Seventh Letter* (326b), when he was about forty (324a), which is consistent with Diod.'s date. The story of his falling out with Dionysios and his being sold into slavery is reported by both Plutarch (*Dion*, 4–5) and Diogenes Laertios (*Lives of the Great Philosophers*, 3.18–20), although neither says that he was sold at Syracuse. Both agree that he was handed over to the Spartan *navarch*, Pollis, who put him on sale in Aigina. But that version encounters serious chronological problems: one Spartan named Pollis was *navarch* in the 390s (probably 396/5), while another commanded the Spartan fleet at the Battle of Naxos (376/5), but neither fits the date required for Plato's first visit to Syracuse.

777 Diod. has already given a fuller version of the reception of Dionysios' poetry at Olympia at 14.109. Vial, in the Budé, sees this as a doublet, but see *contra* Stylianou, *Commentary*, 177–178.

charges, and not a few of them were sent into exile. Amongst those exiled were Philistos and his own brother Leptines, both men of outstanding courage, who had rendered him many valuable services in his wars. 4. These men fled to Thourioi in Italy, where they were treated with great respect by the Italiots, but subsequently, at Dionysios' request, they patched up their quarrel, returned to Syracuse and were restored to their former favour.[778] Leptines even married Dionysios' daughter.[779] Well, that is what happened in this year.

Both Philistos and Leptines are exiled at this time

8.1. In the archonship of Dexitheos at Athens, the Romans appointed as consuls Lucius Lucretius and Servius Sulpicius.[780] In their time Evagoras, king of the Salaminians, arrived in Cyprus from Egypt.[781] He brought funds from Akoris, the king of Egypt, but less than had been expected.[782] So, finding Salamis under active siege and deserted by its allies, he was forced to negotiate for a treaty. 2. Tiribazos, who had the overall command of the Persian forces, said he would agree to a treaty on conditions: that Evagoras withdraw from all the cities in Cyprus except Salamis, of which alone he was king; that he pay a stipulated annual tribute to the King of the Persians; and that he obey orders as a slave to his master. 3. Evagoras, although he was faced with a harsh choice, agreed to all the terms, except he refused "to obey orders as a slave to his master." Instead, he said he should be subject as a king to a king. When Tiribazos did not agree to this, Orontes, the other commander, jealous of Tiribazos' high reputation, secretly sent a letter to Artaxerxes with accusations against Tiribazos.[783] 4. Orontes was making the following accusations against him: That, although he had the opportunity to capture Salamis, he was failing to take it, but was rather entertaining Evagoras' ambassadors and conversing with him about joint action. That, in a similar fashion, he was in private negotiations for an alliance with the Lakedaimonians, whose friend he was. That he had dispatched some men to the Pythian oracle at Delphi to ask the god's advice about rebellion. Most seriously, that he was gaining the loyalty of the commanders of the army by acts of generosity, winning them over by honours,

385/4: Book 15.8.1– 13.5

Evagoras is forced to negotiate a treaty with Tiribazos

Evagoras balks at the last condition

Orontes makes accusations against Tiribazos, who is arrested, brought to the King and put on trial

---

778 Plutarch, *Dion*. 11.6., states categorically that Philistos did not return to Syracuse until after the death of Dionysios, that he left Thourioi and went to Adria, where he wrote his history. See 14.8.5 and nn. 59 and 60.
779 Leptines, on the other hand, did return and was present at the Battle of Kronion (15.17.1). The daughter he married was probably Dikaiosyne, Dionysios' child by Doris of Lokris.
780 Repetition of the consuls (*suffecti*) for 390/89. See above at 14.99.1 and n. 637.
781 Diod. resumes his account of the Cypriot War that he left off at the end of ch. 4.
782 Akoris was either distracted by his own affairs or had lost confidence in Evagoras.
783 According to Theopompos (*FGrHist/BNJ* 115 F103.9), Evagoras made the complaint to the King in collusion with Orontes.

gifts and promises. 5. After reading the letter and being convinced by the false accusations, the King wrote to Orontes telling him to arrest Tiribazos and send him to him. Orontes did as he was ordered.[784] Tiribazos, when he was taken before the King, asked to be given his day in court. For the time being he was put under guard, but later, since the King was busy with a war against the Kadousians[785] and kept postponing the trial, the court case kept being put off.

Orontes, now in charge in Cyprus, makes a deal with Evagoras

9.1. As for Orontes, now that he had taken over the command of the troops in Cyprus, he found that Evagoras had resumed a bold resistance to the siege[786] and, in addition, his own soldiers were not happy about the arrest of Tiribazos and for that reason were insubordinate and not prosecuting the siege energetically. Alarmed at the unexpected change in the state of affairs, Orontes sent representatives to Evagoras to talk about the treaty and to pressure him to agree to the same peace terms he had concluded with Tiribazos. 2. Well, Evagoras, unexpectedly delivered from the capture of his city, agreed to peace on condition that he was to be king of Salamis, that he was to pay a stipulated annual tribute to the King of the Persians, but that he was to obey orders as a king to a king. So, this was the way the Cypriot War ended. It had lasted for almost ten years, although the greater part of that time had been spent in preparation.[787] There had been only two years in total[788] of continuous warfare. 3. But Glôs,[789] the man who held the command of the fleet and was married to the daughter of Tiribazos, being very afraid that he might be thought to have

Evagoras and Orontes conclude the Cypriot War

Glôs, son-in-law of Tiribazos and commander of the Persian fleet, defects

---

784 The arrest of Tiribazos is actually described by Plutarch (*Moralia*, 168e) and Polyainos (*Strategemata*, 14.1), but their different accounts are quite fanciful.

785 "Kadousians" is an emendation by the Byzantine scholar Stephanos (*Bibliotheke*, s.v. μεταξὺ τῆς Κασπίας), for the mss' "Kalousians." The Kadousians inhabited the west coast of the Caspian Sea (Strabo, 11.7.1 C508). Artaxerxes' campaign against them, in which a prominent and successful role was played by a supposedly incarcerated Tiribazos, is described by Plutarch (*Artax*. 24–25).

786 This contradicts the idea of any collusion between Evagoras and Orontes.

787 The chronology of the Cypriot War is problematic. Since Diodoros records its beginning in 391/0 (14.98.3), he should bring it to an end in 381/0, if, as he says, it lasted ten years, not, as here, in 385/4. Further evidence that the war lasted ten years and did, in fact, end in 381/0 is provided by Isokrates (9, *Evagoras*, 64; 4, *Panegyrikos*, 135, 141) and Theopompos (*FGrHist/BNJ* 115 F103.10), who dates the end of the war to the year when Nektanébôs assumed the throne of Egypt after the death of Akoris in 380. For discussions of the chronology see Stylianou, *Commentary*, 143–154 and Ruzicka (2012), 83–98.

788 This is the usual translation and is adopted by both Oldfather and Vial (Budé), but an alternate possibility "at the end/last" is supported by the use of the same phrase at 15.31.2. The issue is whether the years of continuous fighting were "at the end" (i.e. the last two years) or some other two years.

789 See above nn. 750 and 757.

collaborated with Tiribazos in his undertaking and that he might some day be punished by the King, decided to ensure the safety of his affairs by changing his course of action. Since he was well provided with funds and soldiers and had secured the loyalty of *trierarchs* by acts of kindness, he resolved to revolt from the King. 4. So, his first move was to exchange embassies with Akoris,[790] king of the Egyptians, and to conclude an alliance with him against the King. Also, he communicated in writing with the Lakedaimonians, inciting them against the King. He promised that he would give them a great amount of money. He also made other extravagant promises about working with them to help them regain their ancestral leadership in Greece. 5. Indeed, the Spartiates had been determined for a long time to regain their leadership, and at this time were already stirring up discord in the cities, which as everyone perceived was aimed at enslaving them. In addition to this, since they were in ill repute for seeming to have betrayed the Greek cities in Asia in their settlement with the King, they regretted their actions and were looking for an excuse to make war on the King. So, they were happy to conclude an alliance with Glôs.[791]

He secures the alliance of Akoris, king of Egypt, and the Lakedaimonians

10.1. But Artaxerxes, after he had concluded his war against the Kadousians,[792] went ahead with a trial for Tiribazos. As judges he appointed three of the most respected men amongst the Persians. Now, in those days some other judges, who were deemed to have made unjust decisions, had been flayed alive and their skins had been spread over the chairs of the judiciary.[793] The judges in this case were sitting on these very chairs, with a visible indication of the punishment meted out in the case of an unjust decision right before their eyes. 2. Well, the prosecutors read out Orontes' letter and declared that it was all that was needed by way of accusation. But Tiribazos, in response to the false charge related to his dealing with Evagoras, read out the agreement Orontes had made and cited the clause that Evagoras[794] "would obey as a king to a king." He said that he had agreed to peace on terms that Evagoras "obey the king as a slave to his master." With regard to the charges about the oracle, he said that the god

The trial of Tiribazos takes place

Tiribazos refutes the charges

---

790 This statement raises another problem. If Akoris died in 380 and the Cypriot War ended after the accession of Nektanébôs, then Glôs' revolt and his alliance with Akoris must have taken place before the end of the war. His defection would help explain Orontes' decision to come to terms with Evagoras. It appears that Diod. has misplaced the order of events.
791 No other source records an alliance between Sparta and Glôs, even though the motivation attributed to the Spartans is consistent with Diod.'s overall narrative.
792 See n. 785.
793 For a similar situation see Herodotos 5.25.
794 Parts of this sentence from "agreement" to "Evagoras" are lacking and have been restored.

absolutely did not give prophecies that involved death, and he provided all the Greeks present as witnesses. And, concerning his friendship with the Lakedaimonians, he defended himself by saying that it was not for his personal benefit that he had created this relationship of friendship, but for the King's advantage. He pointed out that it was thanks to this that the Greeks in Asia were won away from the Lakedaimonians and were handed over to the King as tribute-paying subjects.[795] Finally, in the conclusion of his defence he reminded the judges of the previous good deeds he had performed for the King. 3. It is reported that amongst the many other services to the King that he pointed to, Tiribazos emphasized one in particular, his greatest, as a result of which he became an object of admiration and one of the King's closest friends. For, on one hunting expedition, as the King was travelling in his chariot, two lions set upon him, tore apart two of the four horses in the team and began to make their attack upon the King himself. At that critical moment Tiribazos appeared on the scene, killed the lions and extracted the King from the dangerous situation. 4. They say that he both stood out for his courage in warfare and was so successful in counsel that the King never went wrong when he followed his advice. On the basis of such a defence Tiribazos was acquitted of the charges by the unanimous decision of all the judges.

The King restores Tiribazos to his former privileges, and punishes Orontes

11.1. The King called the judges up one by one and asked each one what legal criteria he had applied in acquitting the accused. The first one replied [that he had made his decision] because he saw that, while the accusations were disputed, there was no disagreement about the good deeds. The second said that, even allowing that the charges were true, nevertheless his good deeds outweighed his crime. The third said that he set no value on the good deeds, because of the fact that Tiribazos had received in return honours and rewards from the King many times their value, but that, when the accusations were examined individually, they did not seem to apply to the accused. 2. The King praised the judges on the grounds that they had arrived at just decisions, and honoured Tiribazos with the highest available distinctions.[796] As for Orontes, the King decided that he had fabricated a false accusation and expelled him from the circle of his friends and circumscribed him with extreme disgrace.[797] So, affairs in Asia ended in this way.

795 See n. 750.
796 The trial of Tiribazos is full of uncorroborated anecdote, but it is certain that he returned to favour.
797 We have no information about his fate, but an Orontes appears as satrap of Mysia in 362/1 at 15.90.3.

12.1. In Greece, the Lakedaimonians were continuing to besiege Mantineia. Throughout the summer the Mantineians carried on a valiant resistance against their enemy. Indeed, they were reputed to excel the other Arkadians in courage, which is the reason why the Lakedaimonians had previously been in the habit of stationing them at their side in battle and treating them as the loyalest of their allies.[798] But with the onset of winter, the river that flowed beside[799] Mantineia became heavily swollen from the rains. The Lakedaimonians diverted the flow of the river by means of large dykes, redirected the river into the city and turned all the surrounding area into a marsh. 2. And so, as their houses also were collapsing, the Mantineians in desperation were compelled to surrender their city to the Lakedaimonians, who, after taking possession, inflicted no other harm upon the Mantineians than ordering them to dissolve the city into its ancient villages. And so, the Mantineians were compelled to raze their own hometown and move back into the villages.[800]

The Lakedaimonians capture Mantineia and compel the dissolution of the city

13.1. Meanwhile, in Sicily, Dionysios, the tyrant of the Syracusans, conceived the idea of establishing cities throughout the Adriatic. His plan was to get control for himself of what was called the passage through the Ionian Sea so as to secure a safe transit to Epeiros, and to have his own cities where ships could drop anchor. For, he was eager to make a surprise naval assault in force upon the Epeirot region and to go on from there to plunder the sanctuary at Delphi,[801] since it was replete with riches. 2. To that end he also contracted an alliance with the Illyrians through the agency of Alketas the Molossian,[802] who

Dionysios plans to establish settlements in the Adriatic

Dionysios makes an alliance with the Illyrians

---

798 This is hardly true. Although originally a member of the Peloponnesian League, the Mantineians had sided with Argos, Athens and others against Sparta in the Battle of Mantineia of 418 (Thuc. 5.64–74) and remained disaffected for the rest of the century. Revenge was a major reason for the Spartan attack (Xen. *Hell.* 5.2.1).

799 The river was called Ophis ("Snake"). For the origin of the name see Pausanias, 8.8.5. Both Pausanias (8.8.5 and 8.8.7) and Diod. state that the river flowed beside the city, but the contemporary Xenophon (*Hell.* 5.2.5) says that it flowed through the city and describes Agesipolis' tactic as damming up the outflow so that the water backed up inside the walls. Perhaps, when the city was refounded and refortified in 370 (Xen. *Hell.* 6.5.3ff.), the Mantineians wisely left the river outside the walls, and it was this situation that Pausanias and Diod., or his source, described. But, if Ephoros was Diod.'s source, as is usually assumed, he would be guilty of making a rather serious blunder.

800 The city was reconstituted in 370 after the Battle of Leuktra. See n. 799.

801 It is hardly credible that Dionysios planned to plunder Delphi. This claim most likely owes its origin to the tradition that tyrants, especially Dionysios, were sacrilegious (cf. Cicero, *De Natura Deorum*, 3.34).

802 Alketas was king of the Molossians, the dominant tribe in Epeiros (Map 8), at some time in the early fourth century. His name is present on *IG* II² 43 ("Charter of the Second Athenian League," *TDGR*2, no. 35; R&O, no. 22), probably added in 375/4, by which time he was

at that time was living as an exile in Syracuse. And, since the Illyrians were embroiled in a war, he sent them 2,000 allied troops and 500 complete suits of armour of the Greek type. The Illyrians distributed the suits of armour amongst their bravest soldiers and integrated Dionysios' soldiers with their own. 3. Then, after collecting a huge force, they invaded Epeiros and restored Alketas to the throne of the Molossians. Since they received no response, at first they plundered the territory, but later, when the Molossians drew up against them, a great battle took place, in which the Illyrians were victorious and cut down more than 15,000 Molossians. When the Lakedaimonians learned the details of the disaster that had befallen the Molossians, they sent an army to assist the Molossians, by means of which they put an end to the excessive boldness of the barbarians. 4. While these events were taking place, the Parians sent out a colony to the Adriatic in accordance with an oracle and made a settlement on the island called Pharos[803] with the participation of Dionysios. For, not many years previously, he had dispatched a colony to the Adriatic and had founded the city named Lissos.[804] 5. Using this as his base....[805] With time on his hands Dionysios turned to building projects, constructing shipsheds for 200 triremes and encompassing the city with a wall that was so extensive that the city's fortification surpassed in size those of all Greek cities. He also built large gymnasia beside the Anapos river, temples for the gods and other things that contributed to the size and reputation of the city.

The Parians establish a settlement on Pharos

Dionysios carries out building projects in Syracuse

384/3: Book 15.14.1–14.4

Fighting breaks out between the Parians on Pharos and the locals

14.1. Once this year had come to an end, Diotrephes[806] became archon at Athens, while in Rome Lucius Valerius and Aulos Mallios [Manlius] were appointed consuls,[807] and the ninety-ninth Olympiad was celebrated by the Eleians, in which Dikon[808] from Syracuse won the stadion. In their term of

  obviously aligned with Athens. His son, Neoptolemos, whose daughter Olympias married Philip of Macedon and was the mother of Alexander the Great, is listed with him. His other son, Arybbas, who ruled after the death of Neoptolemos, was expelled by Philip and granted asylum in Athens in 343/2 (*IG* II² 226; R&O, no. 70).
803 The island of Pharos is now the Croatian island of Hvar, situated off the coast, mid-way between Trogir and Dubrovnik. See Map 12.
804 Lissos was situated north of Epidamnos in Illyricum. It is identified with modern Lezhë in Albania. See Map 12.
805 A gap in the text (*lacuna*) of indeterminate length is obvious here, as Diodoros changes in mid-sentence to a totally different topic.
806 The name is misspelled; it should be Dieitrephes. See Develin, *AO*, 219. For the introductory formula, see n. 745.
807 Repetition of the names for 389/8, cited at 14.103.1.
808 Dikon was a celebrated runner from Kaulonia in Italy (Pausanias, 6.3.11). He must have become Syracusan after Dionysios destroyed Kaulonia and transferred the population (14.106.3).

office the Parians, who had established a settlement on Pharos, allowed the previous non-Greek inhabitants to occupy unmolested an exceedingly strong location, while they themselves built a fortified city by the seashore. 2. But, subsequently, the previous non-Greek inhabitants of the island found the presence of the Greeks intolerable and sent for help to the Illyrians, who lived on the opposite shore. More than 10,000 of these descended upon Pharos in a myriad of small boats, plundered the Greeks and killed many of them. But, the man who had been appointed by Dionysios as governor on Issa[809] sailed out with a large number of triremes against the little boats of the Illyrians. After sinking some and capturing others, he slaughtered more than 5,000 barbarians and took about 2,000 prisoner. 3. Dionysios, being short of money, launched a campaign against Tyrrhenia with sixty triremes,[810] giving as his pretext the suppression of pirates, but in reality intending to pillage a holy sanctuary,[811] filled with a great many dedications, that had been consecrated in the port of the Tyrrhenian city of Agylle.[812] The name of the port was Pyrgi. 4. Dionysios sailed in during the night and disembarked his troops. Attacking at daybreak, he succeeded in his plan. For, since there were few guards in the area, he overpowered them and then pillaged the sanctuary, amassing no less than 1,000 *talents*.[813] When the Agyllians came out to the rescue, he defeated them in battle. Then, after taking many prisoners and plundering the territory, he returned to Syracuse. From the sale of the booty he took in not less than 500 *talents*. Flushed with money, Dionysios began recruiting a host of mercenaries of various ethnicities. Once he had assembled a respectable force, it became clear that he was intending to go to war with the Carthaginians. Well, those were the events of that year.

Dionysios, in need of money, pillages a temple at Pyrgi in Tyrrhenia

With his coffers filled, Dionysios hires mercenaries from various sources

15.1. In the archonship at Athens of Phanostratos, in place of the consuls the Romans appointed four military tribunes, Lucius Lucretius, Sentius Sulpicius,

383/2: Book 15.15.1–19.4

---

809 The Budé editor (Claude Vial) is surely correct in reading Issa here against all the manuscripts, which have one form or another of Lisa, Lissa or Lissos. The corruption stems from the proximity of Lissos in the text above at 15.13.4. Lissos was 300 km south of Pharos and help would have been a long time coming. The island of Issa (modern Vis), by contrast, is very close and had been settled by Syracusans.
810 According to Polyainos (*Strategemata*, 5.2.21), he had 100 triremes and some transport vessels.
811 The sanctuary was dedicated to Leukothea, according to ps.-Aristotle (*Oikonomika*, 2.2.20.1349b) and Polyainos (*Strategemata*, 5.2.21). Strabo (5.2.8 C226) attributes it to the goddess of childbirth, Eileithyia. Pillaging of temples is elsewhere in Diod. a harbinger of disaster. Cf. 14.63.1 and Himilkon's subsequent fate.
812 Agylle or Agylla was an early name for Caere, according to Strabo (5.2.3 C220), who provides an anecdotal reason for the name change.
813 Only 500 *talents*, according to Polyainos (above).

Dionysios seeks to make war on Carthage[815]

The Carthaginians raise a large force and make war on Dionysios in Sicily and Italy

Dionysios divides his forces and fights on both fronts

Two major battles take place. In the first Dionysios is victorious

Lucius Aemilius and Lucius Furius.[814] In their term of office Dionysios, the tyrant of the Syracusans, after getting himself ready for a conflict with the Carthaginians, was looking for a plausible pretext for war. So, seeing that the cities that were under Carthaginian control were well disposed to revolt, he welcomed those who wanted to defect, made alliances with them and treated them with respect. 2. The first response of the Carthaginians was to send an embassy to the sovereign and ask for the return of their cities. But he ignored them, and this turned out to be the beginning of the war.[816] The Carthaginians concluded an alliance with the Italiots[817] and together combined in making war upon the tyrant. Also, sensibly foreseeing that the war would be long,[818] they enlisted the fittest citizens as soldiers and used the great amount of money they had amassed in advance to hire huge forces of mercenary troops. Then, after appointing Magon, their king, as commander,[819] they transported many tens of thousands of troops into Sicily and Italy, their intention being to wage war on both fronts. 3. Dionysios also divided his forces. With one part he fought against the Italiots and with the other against the Phoenicians. Now, there were many clashes between contingents of the armies and small engagements were going on all the time,[820] in which nothing worth noting happened, but there were two important and celebrated pitched battles. In the first battle Dionysios, by an amazing show of force, came out victorious at a place called Kabala.[821] He killed more than 10,000 of

---

814 Probably a repetition of the college of 388/7 (14.107.1), but with distinct differences. Cf. n. 669.

815 This is now referred to as the Third Carthaginian War. Diod.'s account is seriously criticized. It is not credible that the war began and ended in the one year, especially since in ch. 24, under the year 379/8, Diod. recounts a Carthaginian campaign in Italy that restored the city of Hipponion, clearly showing that hostilities had not ceased in that theatre. Various theories have been advanced to explain his mistake, the most usual one being that he took an excursus on the war from his source and abbreviated it under the initial year. Assuming that his date for the beginning of the war is correct, its conclusion probably belongs in 376/5 or 375/4. See Stylianou, *Commentary*, 200–202.

816 This is probably all that happened in 383/2.

817 "Italiots" is an emendation by Wesseling for the mss' "those present."

818 I.e. the war was not likely to be concluded in one year. Carthaginian preparations for invasions of Sicily usually took some considerable time, even years. Indeed, it is probable that this invasion took place in 379/8, at the same time as the invasion of Italy, recorded in ch. 24.

819 For the role of kings in the Carthaginian constitution, see n. 364.

820 This is a further indication that the war was not of short duration. Indeed, some obscure references help fill in the gaps, at least of operations in Italy. Aelian (*VH*, 12.61) mentions a large expedition by Dionysios against Thourioi that was averted by the weather, and both Livy (24.3.8) and Dionysios of Halikarnassos (*Roman Antiquities*, 20.7.3) imply that Dionysios succeeded in capturing Kroton.

821 This place has not been identified, but is assumed to be in Sicily.

the barbarians and took no less than 5,000 prisoners. He drove the remaining mass to take refuge on a fortified hill that, however, was totally lacking in water. Another casualty of the conflict was Magon, their king, who died after putting up a splendid resistance. 4. The Phoenicians were devastated at the magnitude of the defeat and immediately sent ambassadors to negotiate terms for disengagement. But Dionysios declared that the only settlement he would make with them was on terms that they withdraw from all the cities in Sicily and pay the whole cost of the war.

The Carthaginians sue for peace, but Dionysios demands harsh terms

16.1. The response was considered to be harsh and arrogant, so the Carthaginians outmanoeuvred Dionysios with their customary trickery.[822] While pretending, therefore, to be satisfied with the terms of the agreement, they claimed that they were not empowered to hand over the cities and asked Dionysios to make a truce for a few days so that they could communicate with their leaders on these matters. 2. The dynast agreed and the truce came into effect.[823] Dionysios, for his part, was overjoyed, thinking that he was going to get possession of the whole of Sicily right away, while the Carthaginians gave their king, Magon, a magnificent funeral and appointed, as general in his place, his son, who, although admittedly a very young man, had a noble spirit and excelled in courage. Magon's son spent the duration of the truce drilling and training his army. Through the practice of hard work, words of encouragement and exercise under arms he created an army that was disciplined and powerful.[824] 3. When the period of truce ended, both sides deployed their forces and eagerly joined in battle. A vigorous engagement ensued at a place called Kronion[825] and the power of the divine, favouring each side turn by turn, reversed the Carthaginian defeat by a victory. For those who had been victorious previously, priding themselves on their previous success, suffered an unexpected reverse, while those who had fallen into despair because of their defeat carried off a great, unexpected success.[826]

The Phoenicians negotiate a truce, while they present the terms to the government at Carthage

A second battle takes place at Kronion and the result is reversed

822 The view that non-Greeks were tricky is expressed by Ephoros (*FGrHist/BNJ* 70 F71), albeit about those in Asia.
823 If this narrative is true, Dionysios was indeed duped. He had the remaining Carthaginian forces surrounded on a waterless hill and had 5,000 prisoners in his hands for bargaining.
824 If the truce was only for a few days, this is obviously incredible.
825 The site of this important battle cannot be determined. Kronion, meaning "the place of Kronos," was the name for many hilltops in Sicily, according to Diod. (3.61.3). Only Polyainos (5.10.5) states that it was the name of a town that sided with Carthage against Dionysios in a conflict. He names the Carthaginian leader Himilkon, which may, indeed, have been the name of Magon's son.
826 This is an unquestionably Diodoran view of *Tykhe*.

The war concludes to Dionysios' disadvantage

17.1. Leptines, a man of outstanding courage, was stationed on one of the two wings. Although he fought heroically and killed many Carthaginians, he died, ending his life gloriously.[827] Once he fell, the Phoenicians were emboldened and, pushing forward, put their opponents to flight. 2. On his side, Dionysios with his elite troops was at first getting the better of his opponents, but when the death of Leptines became known and that the other wing was in flight, Dionysios' men panicked and took to flight. 3. When the flight became general, the Carthaginians pursued more zealously and shouted out to each other not to take any prisoners. As a result, since all who were caught were killed, the whole neighbouring region was covered in corpses. 4. Because the Phoenicians were avenging old wrongs, the slaughter was so great that more than 14,000 Sicilians were found to have been killed. The survivors took refuge in the camp and were saved by the arrival of nightfall. And the Carthaginians, after their great victory, went back to Panormos. 5. Reacting to their success with moderation,[828] the Carthaginians sent an embassy to Dionysios, offering him the opportunity to bring a conclusion to the war. The tyrant was pleased to receive their offer and peace was concluded on condition that both sides possess what they had possessed before.[829] The exception was that the Carthaginians acquired the city of Selinous along with its territory and the lands of the Akragantines as far as the river named Halykos.[830] In addition, Dionysios paid the Carthaginians 1,000 *talents*. Such was the state of affairs in Sicily.

In Asia, Glôs is murdered. His successor founds the city of Leuke

18.1. In Asia, Glôs, the commander of the Persian fleet in Cyprus, who had revolted from the King and had incited the Lakedaimonians and the king of Egypt to make war on the Persians, was treacherously murdered by persons unknown, and died without achieving his objective. After his death, Takhôs,[831] the successor to his endeavours, gathered an army to himself and founded a city on a rocky promontory near the sea. The city, which contained a holy

---

827 Other sources (Aelian, *VH*, 13.45 and Plutarch, *Moralia*, 333b) hint at Dionysios' devious complicity in Leptines' death, but without details or substantiation.
828 An unusual credit to the Carthaginians, especially considering their alleged reputation for trickery (see 15.16.1). It stands in sharp contrast to the reported behaviour of Dionysios at 15.16.2.
829 I.e. what they possessed in 392/1 under the terms that concluded the Second Carthaginian War. See 14.96.4 and n. 618.
830 The river Halykos (usually identified with the modern Platani), which flowed from the hills to the north into the sea at Herakleia Minoa, became the recognized dividing line between the Phoenician and the Greek spheres of influence. See Map 3.
831 Probably a relative.

shrine of Apollo, was called Leuke.[832] 2. Not long afterwards, when Takhôs died, the people of Klazomenai and Kyme got into a dispute over control of the city (Leuke). And, at first, they got ready to settle the dispute by a war, but subsequently, when someone suggested that they ask the god which of the two cities he judged should be in control of Leuke, the Pythia issued the decision that this privilege belonged to the first city to sacrifice at Leuke. They were to set out from their own cities at sunrise on a day they had both mutually agreed upon. 3. When the day had been fixed, the Kymeans assumed that they had an advantage, because their city was situated closer, but the Klazomenians, because they were further away, devised the following path to victory. Choosing colonists by lot from amongst themselves, they founded a city nearby Leuke, and setting out from this city at sunrise, they performed the sacrifice before the Kymeans. 4. After gaining control of Leuke by this clever stratagem, they established an appropriately named festival to be celebrated annually, calling this the festival of the Anticipation.[833] After the conclusion of these events, the revolts in Asia ceased of their own accord.

Klazomenai and Kyme compete over control of Leuke

19.1. After the deaths of Glôs and Takhôs the Lakedaimonians renounced their activities in Asia. As for affairs in Greece, however, they arranged those to their own advantage. Winning over some cities by persuasion and gaining control of others forcibly by assisting the return of exiles, they were blatantly already getting the leadership of Greece into their own hands,[834] contrary to the common treaty that was made in the time of Antalkidas with the assistance of the King of the Persians. 2. In Macedon, Amyntas, the king, was defeated by the Illyrians and abdicated his throne. Furthermore, as a result of his abdication he made a gift to the people of Olynthos of a large area of land on their shared border.[835] At first, the Olynthians enjoyed the revenues from the donated territory, and later, when the king unexpectedly pulled himself together and regained control of his whole kingdom, the Olynthians declined to give the land back, when he asked for it.[836] 3. So, Amyntas raised an army of his own

The Lakedaimonians concentrate their efforts on control of Greece

The Lakedaimonians support Amyntas against Olynthos

---

832 According to Strabo (14.38 C646), Leuke/Leukai was a small town, situated between Smyrna and Phokaia. Diod. places it on the mainland, which is certainly assumed by the anecdote that follows, but the Barrington Atlas (Map 56 D4) locates it on an island in the middle of the Bay of Hermos.
833 This whole story, rather out of place in a Universal History, was no doubt recounted by Ephoros, because it involved his home town of Kyme, even though the triumph went to Klazomenai.
834 Diod. continues his theme of Spartan aggression in Greece from 15.5.1 and 15.9.5.
835 Diod. has already described an almost identical situation at 14.92.3. See n. 586.
836 According to Xenophon (*Hell.* 5.2.13), the Olynthians were even in possession of the city of Pella, capital of the Macedonian kingdom.

The Lakedaimonians also overcome Phleious

The two kings of Sparta, Agesipolis and Agesilaos, disagree over policy

and, after contracting an alliance with the Lakedaimonians, persuaded them to send a general with a respectable force against the Olynthians.[837] The Lakedaimonians made the decision to extend their control over the Thraceward region and levied an army of more than 10,000 soldiers, recruiting them from their own citizens and from their allies.[838] Entrusting the army to Phoibidas,[839] the Spartiate, they gave him orders to fight alongside Amyntas and join him in making war on the Olynthians.[840] They also dispatched another army against Phleious. Defeating them in battle, they forced the people of Phleious to be subject to Lakedaimon.[841] 4. During this period the kings of the Lakedaimonians were at odds with each other over policy. For Agesipolis, a peace-loving and just man, who was, in addition, exceedingly intelligent, claimed that the Lakedaimonians ought to remain true to their oaths and should not transgress the common treaty by enslaving the Greeks. He pointed out that Sparta was in disrepute both for making the Greeks in Asia tributary to the Persians and for taking control of the cities in Greece, although they had sworn oaths in the common treaty that they would not enslave them, but would keep them autonomous.[842] Agesilaos, on the other hand, was by nature a man of action, a warmonger, who aimed at absolute power[843] over the Greeks.

382/1: Book 15.20.1–21.3

20.1. In the archonship at Athens of Euandros, in place of the consuls the Romans appointed six military tribunes, Quintus Sulpicius, Gaius Fabius,

---

837 In his account of the Spartan attack on Olynthos Xenophon makes no mention of an appeal by Amyntas to Sparta; instead he attributes it to a delegation from the Greek cities of Akanthos and Apollonia (*Hell.* 5.2.11–19).

838 Cf. Xen. *Hell.* 5.2.20–22.

839 Xenophon says that a Spartiate, named Eudamidas, was put in charge of an advance force of 2,000 troops, and that it was he who persuaded the ephors to allow his brother, Phoibidas, to call up the remaining troops that had been allotted to him and bring them up to join him later (*Hell.* 5.2.24). Diod., who reverses the order (see 15.20.2), provides the information that the force allotted to Eudamidas was 3,000, thus suggesting that Phoibidas was left behind to collect the remaining 1,000, and that it was with these that he captured the Kadmeia.

840 With his advance force Eudamidas succeeded in winning over Poteidaia (Xen. *Hell.* 5.2.24).

841 This is a very abbreviated and incorrectly dated reference to a conflict that began in spring 381 and ended only in 379 (cf. Xen. *Hell.* 5.2.8–10; 5.3.10–17; 5.3.21–25).

842 No other source attributes these views to Agesipolis, although they might have belonged to his exiled father, Pausanias. There was always rivalry between the two royal houses at Sparta, but if Agesipolis disagreed with Agesilaos over any policy, it was likely the treatment of Phleious (Xen. *Hell.* 5.3.10). Otherwise the two kings seem to have enjoyed a close personal relationship (Xen. *Hell.* 5.3.20; Plut. *Ages.* 20.7–9).

843 "Absolute power" (δυναστεία), proposed by Reiske and adopted by all editors, is an emendation for the mss' "power" (δυνάμεως).

Quintus Servilius, Publius Cornelius.⁸⁴⁴ In their term of office the Lakedaimonians seized the Kadmeia in Thebes. Their reasons for doing so are as follows. Perceiving that Boiotia contained a great number of cities and that its inhabitants were men of outstanding courage, and furthermore that Thebes was held in high regard from of old and was, in short, a kind of acropolis for Boiotia,⁸⁴⁵ they were concerned that, if a suitable opportunity arose, it (Boiotia) might challenge them for the leadership (of Greece).⁸⁴⁶ 2. So, the Spartiates sent out a secret order to their commanders to seize the Kadmeia, if they ever had an opportunity.⁸⁴⁷ Since such were his instructions, Phoibidas the Spartiate, who had been appointed to a command and was leading an army against Olynthos, seized the Kadmeia.⁸⁴⁸ When the Thebans rose in anger and ran up with their weapons, he engaged them in a battle, in which he was victorious, and drove the 300 most illustrious Thebans into exile.⁸⁴⁹ He cowed the remaining citizens into submission and established a strong garrison, and then went away to complete his own assignment.⁸⁵⁰ Since the Lakedaimonians fell into disrepute amongst the Greeks over this action, they fined Phoibidas as a punishment, but did not remove their garrison from Thebes.⁸⁵¹ 3. Well, in this way the Thebans

Acting on orders from Sparta, Phoibidas seizes the Kadmeia in Thebes and puts a garrison there

844 As so often Diod. gives only four names. This is, in fact, a repetition of the college of 387/6, given at 14.110.1. See n. 680.
845 Diod. has used this rather hackneyed metaphor above (14.82.4) about Sparta as the "acropolis" of the Peloponnese, and epigram C on the monument at Delphi (O&R, no. 192), celebrating Lysander's victory at Aigospotamoi, describes Sparta as the "acropolis" of Greece. Conversely, Isokrates (12.197) calls Athens the "acropolis" of Greece.
846 Boiotia had been an ally of Sparta during the Peloponnesian War, largely because it was hostile to Athens. It had benefitted materially by pillaging Attica in the last phase of that war (*Hell. Oxy.* 17.3). Afterwards, however, for a number of reasons it had turned against Sparta in the Corinthian War. Its hostility was only increased by the Spartan enforcement of the autonomy clause in the King's Peace, which compelled the dissolution of the Boiotian League. Sparta's concerns about Thebes were justified.
847 Xenophon (*Hell.* 5.2.25–28), who is generally pro-Spartan, gives a very different account. He makes no mention of orders to Phoibidas from the Spartan authorities, and later (*Hell.* 5.2.32) explicitly denies such authorization. Rather he blames Phoibidas' action on internal Theban politics, in which Leontiades, a pro-Spartan politician, offers to betray the Kadmeia to him.
848 On this day, conveniently, the Kadmeia was occupied only by women, celebrating the Thesmophoria, according to Xenophon (*Hell.* 5.2.29).
849 No such engagement is mentioned by Xenophon, who, rather, tells how Leontiades announces the news to the Theban council and at the same time orders the arrest of his opponent, Ismenias. As a result, Ismenias' supporters, 300 in number, flee to Athens (*Hell.* 5.2.29–31). The Atthidographer Androtion (*FGrHist/BNJ* 324 F50, Harding, 1994, 173–174) says that 400 Thebans fled to Athens.
850 I.e. presumably to join his brother in the Khalkidike.
851 Plutarch (*Pelop.* 6.1) says the fine was 100,000 *drachmas*. Xenophon makes no mention of a fine. He agrees that the Spartans were displeased, but credits Agesilaos for getting him off (*Hell.* 5.2.32). Cf. Plut. *Ages.* 23.3–4.

The Spartans relieve Phoibidas of his appointment and send Eudamidas in his place

lost their autonomy and were compelled to be subject to the Lakedaimonians. As the Olynthians were continuing to carry on their war against Amyntas, the king of the Macedonians, the Lakedaimonians relieved Phoibidas of his command and appointed Eudamidas, his brother, general in his place. They gave him 3,000 hoplites and sent him out to fight the war against the Olynthians.[852]

Eudamidas is outmatched by the Olynthians; the Spartans send out a large force under Teleutias

21.1. Eudamidas invaded the territory of the Olynthians and prosecuted the war against them in collaboration with Amyntas.[853] In response the Olynthians collected an impressive force and repeatedly got the better of the battles, because they outnumbered their opponents. But the Lakedaimonians mobilized an impressive[854] force of their own and put Teleutias in charge of it. Teleutias was the brother of Agesilaos, the king, and was much admired by his fellow citizens for his manly virtue.[855] 2. He marched out from the Peloponnese with his army and, when he arrived in the vicinity of Olynthos,

Teleutias plunders Olynthian territory, but dies in battle

assumed command of Eudamidas'[856] troops. Now that his army was a match for the enemy, Teleutias began by plundering the territory of the Olynthians. He gathered a great haul of booty and shared it out amongst his soldiers. And, when the Olynthians and their allies drew up against him with all their men, he joined in battle. The first engagement was inconclusive, so they disengaged, but later a major battle took place, in which Teleutias himself fell,[857] after fighting brilliantly,[858] and more than 1,200 of the Peloponnesians were killed. 3. After this great Olynthian success, the Lakedaimonians, wishing to

The Lakedaimonians resolve to avenge the defeat

redress the loss which they had suffered, started preparing to send out even stronger forces, while the Olynthians, suspecting that the Spartiates would come with an even bigger army and that the war would go on for a long time, began making impressive stockpiles of grain and acquired additional troops from their allies.

852 See n. 839.
853 Diod. continues to involve Amyntas in the conflict, while he plays no part in Xenophon's account.
854 "Impressive," "noteworthy," "respectable" are all possible translations of one of Diod.'s favourite words – ἀξιόλογος, used here twice within two lines.
855 An appraisal echoed by Xenophon (*Hell.* 5.2.37). Teleutias was actually Agesilaos' half-brother.
856 Most mss have Phoibidas here. Only F correctly has Eudamidas.
857 Diod. has again compressed the narrative. From Xenophon (*Hell.* 5.2.40–43) we learn of a first engagement, probably in late summer of 381, which was somewhat inconclusive, although Teleutias claimed victory. Next spring (380) a second battle took place, in which the Olynthians were the victors and Teleutias was killed (*Hell.* 5.3.1–6).
858 According to Xenophon, Teleutias lost his temper and engaged rashly, for which he earned a moralizing lecture (*Hell.* 5.3.7).

22.1. In the archonship at Athens of Demophilos, in place of the consuls the Romans appointed as tribunes Publius Cornelius, Lucius Verginius, Lucius Papirius, Marcus Furius, Valerius, Aulus Manlius, Lucius Postumius.[859] 2. In their term of office the Lakedaimonians passed a resolution declaring war upon the Olynthians and appointed Agesipolis, their king, as commander, providing him with a force equal to his assignment.[860] When Agesipolis reached the territory of the Olynthians, he assumed charge of the soldiers already in the encampment and continued to make war against the local inhabitants.[861] Indeed, overawed by the king's forces, the Olynthians did not engage in any major battles during this year, but instead kept making brief skirmishes with missiles.

381/0: Book 15.22.1–22.2

King Agesipolis leads a new force to Khalkidike

23.1. Once this year had come to an end, Pytheas[862] became archon at Athens, while in Rome in place of the consuls they appointed six military tribunes, Titus Quinctius, Lucius Servilius, Lucius Julius, Aquilius, Lucius Lucretius, Servius Sulpicius.[863] Also the Eleians celebrated the one hundredth Olympic Games, in which Dionysodoros of Taras won the *stadion*. 2. In their term of office Agesipolis, the king of the Lakedaimonians, fell sick and died, after reigning for fourteen years.[864] His brother, Kleombrotos, who succeeded him, was king for nine years. The Lakedaimonians sent out Polybiadas[865] as general for the war against the Olynthians. 3. He assumed command of the army and, by conducting the war with a combination of energy and skillful strategy, kept pulling off many successes. His successes increased day by day and he was victorious in multiple engagements, until he shut the Olynthians within their walls, under siege. In the end he overawed his opponents and commanded their subjection to the Lakedaimonians.[866] Following the enrolment of the Olynthians in the Spartan alliance, many other cities also hastened to be listed as members of the Lakedaimonian hegemony. The result

380/79: Book 15.23.1–23.5

Agesipolis dies in Khalkidike; Polybiadas reduces the Olynthians to submission

Sparta is at the height of its power

---

859 Cf. Livy, 6.1.8, who has four of the same names. He excludes Marcus Furius and Lucius Papirius, replacing one with Lucius Aemilius and clarifying Diod.'s Valerius as Lucius Valerius Publicola. This is the Varronian year 389.
860 Cf. Xen. *Hell.* 5.3.8–9.
861 Cf. Xen. *Hell.* 5.3.18.
862 See Develin, *AO*, 221.
863 Cf. Livy, 6.4.7, where the full names are provided: Titus Quinctius Cincinnatus, Quintus Servilius Fidenas, Lucius Julius Julus, Lucius Aquilius Corvus, Lucius Servilius Tricipitinus, Servius Sulpicius Rufus. This is the Varronian year 388.
864 Cf. Xen. *Hell.* 5.3.19.
865 Given the Greek practice of naming grandsons after their grandfathers, this Polybiadas could be the son of the notoriously fat Naukleidas, son of Polybiadas, who was ephor in 404/3 (Xen. *Hell.* 2.4.36; Athenaios, *Deip.* 12.550d; Aelian, *VH*, 14.7).
866 Cf. Xen. *Hell.* 5.3.26.

was that at this time the Lakedaimonians reached the peak of their power and were dominant in Greece both on land and on sea.[867] 4. For the Thebans were under the control of a garrison, the Corinthians and the Argives were weakened by the recent wars, and the Athenians were in disrepute amongst the Greeks for their settlements on the land of the people they had made war upon. In contrast, the Lakedaimonians had taken great care to have an abundance of manpower that was well trained for war,[868] and were universally feared because of the strength of their hegemony. 5. So, the most powerful rulers of that time, I mean the King of the Persians and the ruler of Sicily, Dionysios, courted Spartan leadership and were eager to conclude an alliance with them.[869]

379/8: Book 15.24.1–24.3

The Carthaginians invade Italy, but subsequently experience a plague

The Libyan and Sardinian subjects of Carthage revolt, but eventually the Carthaginians regain control

24.1. In the archonship at Athens of Nikon,[870] the Romans appointed six military tribunes in place of the consuls, Lucius Papirius, Gaius Servilius, Lucius Quinctius, Lucius Cornelius, Lucius Valerius, Aulus Manlius.[871] In their term of office the Carthaginians made a campaign into Italy and re-established the city (of Hipponion) for the Hipponiates, who had been expelled from their homeland.[872] They restored all the exiles and took great care of them. 2. But later, the inhabitants of Carthage experienced a plague, which was of such virulence that many Carthaginians perished. They were even at risk of losing their empire. For, the Libyans grew contemptuous of them and revolted, and the inhabitants of Sardinia, thinking they had an opportune occasion for attacking the Carthaginians, also revolted. Together they made common cause against the Carthaginians. 3. At the same time a heaven-sent misery descended upon Carthage. For, inexplicable disturbances, fears and the throes of Panic were ceaselessly occurring throughout the city. Many men kept sallying from their houses with their weapons drawn, thinking that enemies had broken into the city. Fighting against each other as though enemies, some died and others were

---

867 An identical evaluation can be found in Xen. *Hell.* 5.3.27.
868 This statement can apply only to the manpower of the Spartan hegemony as a whole, since the number of true Spartiates was in serious decline.
869 It is an exaggeration to say that the King of Persia courted the Spartans. On the other hand, the close relationship between Sparta and Dionysios is beyond question (see 14.10.2 and n. 71; 14.70.3 and n. 431).
870 See Develin, *AO*, 222.
871 This list differs from Livy's (6.5.7) in several respects: (1) Livy's mss give only five names; (2) of those only two agree with Diodoros, Lucius Papirius and Lucius Valerius (Publicola); (3) otherwise Livy names Lucius Aemilius and Lucius Menenius and Gaius Sergius. This is the Varronian year 387.
872 Cf. 14.107.2.

wounded.⁸⁷³ In the end, they placated the divine with expiatory sacrifices and with difficulty rid themselves of their troubles. Soon afterwards they defeated the Libyans in battle and regained control of the island (of Sardinia).⁸⁷⁴

25.1. In the archonship at Athens of Nausinikos,⁸⁷⁵ the Romans appointed four military tribunes in place of the consuls, Marcus Cornelius and Quintus Servilius, Marcus Furius and Lucius Quinctius.⁸⁷⁶ In their term of office what is called the Boiotian War broke out between the Lakedaimonians and the Boiotians.⁸⁷⁷ The reasons are as follows. The Lakedaimonians were maintaining a garrison on the Kadmeia illegally and had driven many of the leading citizens into exile, but the exiles combined together as a group and, with the active collaboration of the Athenians, made their return to their homeland during the night.⁸⁷⁸ 2. Their first action was to murder the members of the pro-Lakedaimonian faction in their own homes, catching them while they were still sleeping.⁸⁷⁹ Next, by appealing to their fellow citizens to strive for freedom, they gained the support of the whole population of Thebes. When a crowd of armed men quickly convened, they began their attempt to besiege the Kadmeia at daybreak. 3. The Lakedaimonians guarding the acropolis, who

378/7: Book 15.25.1–27.4

Theban exiles return and besiege the Spartan garrison on the Kadmeia; outbreak of the Boiotian War

The garrison requests reinforcements from Sparta, whilst the Thebans ask the Athenians for help

---

873 A similar description of the effects of Panic, this time on the Gauls at Delphi in 279, can be found in Pausanias, 10.23.7–8.
874 At 15.73.1, in 368/7, Diodoros describes another plague in Carthage and a revolt of the Libyans. It is possible that the two events are one and the same, but plagues appear to have been very frequent (cf. 14.71) and the Libyans often revolted (cf. 14.77). Also, at 15.73.1 no mention is made of Sardinia.
875 See Develin, *AO*, 222–224.
876 At 6.6.3 Livy gives the following list of six tribunes: Marcus Furius Camillus, Servius Cornelius Maluginensis, Quintus Servilius Fidenas, Lucius Quinctius Cincinnatus, Lucius Horatius Pulvillus, Publius Valerius. This is the Varronian year 386.
877 Other accounts of the Liberation of the Kadmeia are in Xen. *Hell.* 5.4.2–12; Plut. *Pelop.* 7–13 and *De genio Socratis*, *Moralia*, 594b–598f; Deinarkhos, *Against Demosthenes*, 38–39. Diodoros' chronology is suspect here, as the Liberation of the Kadmeia probably belongs earlier in mid-winter 379/8.
878 According to Xenophon, *Hell.* 5.4.3, only seven men were involved in the murder of the pro-Spartans, while Plutarch, *Pelop.* 8, gives the number as twelve.
879 Diodoros misses the opportunity to tell the dramatic story of the conspirators dressing up as women and murdering the pro-Spartans at a drunken party, and fails to mention that Leontiades was killed separately at home. See Xen. *Hell.* 5.4.3–7; Plut. *Pelop.* 9–11. But, like Xenophon, he fails to accredit Pelopidas with the leadership of the conspiracy. Xenophon's antipathy to Pelopidas and Epameinondas, the leaders of the Theban hegemony, explains his silence, but Diod.'s is less easily dismissed, especially since, in his subsequent eulogy of Pelopidas after his death (15.81), he names him as the organizer of the coup. If he was following only one source (Ephoros), as is vigorously maintained, the discrepancy in his accounts is puzzling.

together with their allies numbered no less than 1,500,[880] sent messengers to Sparta to announce the Theban uprising and to ask for reinforcements to be sent as soon as possible, while they themselves resisted the besiegers from their higher ground, killing many and wounding not a few. 4. And the Thebans, in the expectation that a huge army would come from Greece to help the Lakedaimonians, sent ambassadors to Athens. Reminding them that they had also aided in the restoration of the Athenian *demos* at the time when they were being enslaved by the Thirty Tyrants,[881] they asked the Athenians to come to their aid with their whole army and to help in storming the Kadmeia before the arrival of the Lakedaimonians.

The Athenians vote to send help and Demophon leads an advance Athenian force to Thebes

26.1. After the Athenian *demos* heard the ambassadors, they voted to send right away the largest army they could muster for the liberation of Thebes,[882] at one and the same time repaying their debt of gratitude for services rendered and also hoping to win the Boiotians to their side and gain them as powerful allies against the supremacy of the Lakedaimonians. For the people of Boiotia were reputed to be second to none of the Greeks for the size of their manpower and their courage in war. 2. The result was that Demophon, after being appointed general,[883] immediately called up 5,000 hoplites and 500 cavalry and at dawn on the next day led his army out of the city. He made haste with forced marches, eager to arrive before the Lakedaimonians. None the less, the *demos* kept up its preparations to march into Boiotia with their whole army, should the need arise. 3. By taking short cuts, Demophon showed up at Thebes sooner than expected. Also, many soldiers from the other cities throughout Boiotia came running to help and soon a large army had gathered to assist the Thebans. 4. For, no less than 12,000 hoplites had assembled and more than 2,000 cavalry. Everyone threw themselves into the siege with energy. By dividing their forces into groups, they carried on their assaults by turns, resolutely persisting in the danger on a continuous basis both by day and during the night.

880 Plutarch (*Pelop.* 12.4) also gives this figure, while Xenophon (*Hell.* 5.4.11) says they were "few in number."

881 Thebes had given refuge to Thrasyboulos and his fellow exiles at the time of the rule of the Thirty Tyrants (14.6.3, 14.32.1), but had not sent any military assistance to help their return.

882 Deinarkhos, *Against Demosthenes*, 39 also refers to a resolution passed by the Assembly, and says it was on a motion by Kephalos.

883 Demophon was general in 379/8 (Develin, *AO*, 222). If the liberation took place in mid-winter, then Demophon was already general, having been elected, as was usual, in mid-summer (Aristotle, *AP* 44.4).

27.1. On the exhortation of their leaders, the men on the Kadmeia defended themselves vigorously against their enemies, in the expectation that the Lakedaimonians would arrive shortly with a large army. Indeed, so long as they had sufficient supplies, they endured the dangers and kept killing and wounding many of the besiegers. They were helped in this by the precipitous nature of the acropolis. But as the shortage of necessities increased and the Lakedaimonians (in Sparta) were taking time over their preparations, dissension arose amongst them. 2. For, the Lakedaimonians (in the garrison) thought they ought to resist until death, but their fellow soldiers from the allied cities, who were far more numerous, decided to surrender the Kadmeia. So, even those who were from Sparta itself, because of their small number, were compelled to withdraw from the acropolis. As a result, these men were released on terms and withdrew to the Peloponnese under a truce.[884] 3. The Lakedaimonians made their way to Thebes with an impressive army,[885] but failed to achieve anything by their attack, since they arrived a little too late. They did, however, bring to trial the three commanders of the garrison.[886] Two of them they condemned to death, while they imposed such a huge fine upon the third that his estate was unable to pay. 4. Subsequently, the Athenians returned home.[887] The Thebans began to besiege Thespiai, but they failed to achieve anything by their attack. At the same time as these events, the Romans sent out 500 colonists to Sardinia, exempting them from all taxes.[888]

The Spartan garrison runs out of supplies and surrenders the Kadmeia

The Spartan relief force arrives too late; the commanders of the garrison are punished

The Thebans besiege Thespiai unsuccessfully and the Romans send colonists to Sardinia

28.1. In the archonship at Athens of Kallias,[889] the Romans appointed four military tribunes in place of the consuls, Lucius Papirius, Marcus Poplius, Titus

377/6: Book 15.28.1–35.3

---

884 All accounts agree on the basic fact that the Spartans surrendered and departed under a truce, but Plutarch (*Pelop.* 13.1), like Diod., implies that the siege lasted some time, while Xenophon (*Hell.* 5.4.11) suggests that the capitulation happened quickly.

885 Led by King Kleombrotos, brother of Agesipolis, of the Agiad dynasty (see 15.23.2).

886 Xenophon (*Hell.* 5.4.13) says the Spartans put the *harmost* (governor) to death and mentions no other victims, but Plutarch (*Pelop.* 13.3) agrees with Diod. that three commanders (he mistakenly calls them all *harmosts*) were punished, two, Herippidas and Arkesos, with death, the third, Lysanoridas, with a fine he could not pay.

887 This may be somewhat misleading. From both Xenophon (*Hell.* 5.4.19) and Plutarch (*Pelop.* 14.1) we learn that the Athenians were scared by the presence of the Spartan army, renounced the action of the two generals who had supported the Thebans, and put them on trial, condemning one to death and sending the other into exile. The pro-Athenian tradition represented by Diod. and Deinarkhos avoids mentioning this betrayal of the generals and makes the *demos* complicit in their action (see 15.26.1–2 and n. 882).

888 Likely a response to the revolt of Sardinia from Carthage mentioned above (15.24.2).

889 He was probably called Kalleas. See Develin, *AO*, 237.

The Boiotians prepare for an invasion by Sparta and the Athenians solicit alliances for opposition to Sparta

Cornelius, Quintus Lucius.[890] In their term of office, following the Lakedaimonian set-back at Thebes, the Boiotians combined together confidently in a common alliance[891] and raised an impressive[892] army, in the expectation that the Lakedaimonians would attack Boiotia with a massive force. 2. Also, the Athenians sent out their most noteworthy citizens as ambassadors to the cities that were under the control of the Lakedaimonians, to encourage them to become part of the struggle for universal freedom. For, the Lakedaimonians, because of the great size of the forces available to them, ruled their subject cities with arrogant harshness. That was why many of these subject cities were leaning towards the Athenians. 3. The first states that answered the call to revolt were the Khians[893] and the Byzantines,[894] and they were followed by the Rhodians and the Mytilenians and some of the other island cities. As the movement gathered strength amongst the Greeks, many cities joined the Athenians. The *demos*, elated at the enthusiastic response of the allies, set up a common council [*synhedrion*] for all the allies, and appointed delegates from each state. 4. By mutual agreement it was decided that the common council would hold its meetings in Athens, that every city, big or small, would have equal authority, each having one vote. Furthermore all states were to be autonomous, but the Athenians should have the leadership.[895] The Lakedaimonians, perceiving that there was no way they could stop this general rush to defection, nevertheless tried hard to alleviate the mass disaffection by embassies bearing kind words and even promises of

These alliances form the basis of the Second Athenian Confederacy

The Lakedaimonians also prepare for war

---

890 At 6.11.1 Livy gives the following five names: Aulus Manlius, Publius Cornelius, Titus and Lucius Quinctius Capitolinus and Lucius Papirius Cursor. This is the Varronian year 385.

891 Diod. here seems to refer to the refounding of the Boiotian League that had been dissolved as a result of the King's Peace. Diod.'s suggestion that it was refounded this quickly after the Liberation of the Kadmeia is supported by Plutarch, *Pelop*. 13.1, who calls Pelopidas a Boiotarch. Despite the possibility that the new League (or Federation) was somewhat more democratic than its predecessor, which is described in detail in *Hell. Oxy*. 16.2–4 (*TDGR2*, no. 15), it was more firmly under Theban leadership.

892 On Diod's fondness for the Greek word ἀξιόλογος see n. 854. It also appears (as "noteworthy") in the next sentence.

893 The inscriptional evidence (*IG* II² 34; *TDGR2*, no. 31; R&O, no. 20) proves that Athens had concluded an alliance with Khios many years before, in 384/3, in the archonship of Dieitrephes. This alliance, like all Athenian alliances in this period, is careful to state that it does not transgress the terms of the King's Peace.

894 The alliance between Athens and Byzantion is confirmed by *IG* II² 41 (*TDGR2*, no. 34).

895 This appears to be Diod's reference to the foundation document (Charter or Prospectus) of the Second Athenian Confederacy (*IG* II² 43; *TDGR2*, no. 35; R&O, no. 22), which was voted by the Athenians in the spring of 377, in the archonship of Nausinikos. Its promulgated purpose was "that the Lakedaimonians may allow the Hellenes, free and autonomous, to live in peace." Thus, it was designed to capitalize on hostility to Sparta, while professing to adhere to the terms of the King's Peace. Although Diod. gets the date wrong, his summary is correct in the essential points. Xenophon, on the other hand, totally ignores the new Athenian Confederacy.

benefactions. 5. All the same, they paid great attention to their preparations for war, since they expected that the Boiotian War would be a long and difficult one for them, given that the Athenians and all the other Greek states that belonged to the council of the Confederacy were allies of the Thebans.[896]

29.1. Contemporaneous with these events, Akoris, king of Egypt, who was at odds with the King of Persia, amassed an impressive army of mercenaries. For, by offering extravagant pay to any who applied and by acts of generosity to many, he soon acquired a host of Greeks applying to join his campaign. 2. But, since he did not have a general competent for the task, he sent for Khabrias,[897] the Athenian, a man who stood out for his intelligence and his understanding of strategy, and who had built up for himself a strong reputation for courage. As it happened, Khabrias accepted the appointment as general without getting the approval of the *demos*. Taking charge of the Egyptian forces, he got to work enthusiastically getting them ready for war with the Persians.[898] 3. Pharnabazos, who had been appointed commander of the Persian forces by the King, started preparing huge supplies of material needed for the war. And he also sent ambassadors to Athens, first to make accusations against Khabrias, saying that he was alienating the King's goodwill towards Athens by becoming commander of the Egyptian forces, and second to ask them to send him Iphikrates as a general. 4. The Athenians, eager to gain the King of Persia's favour and to get Pharnabazos on their side, promptly recalled Khabrias from Egypt and sent out Iphikrates[899]

Akoris, king of Egypt, prepares for war against Persia and hires Khabrias

Pharnabazos demands the Athenians recall Khabrias from Egypt and send him Iphikrates

---

896 Judging by the signatories to the Charter (*IG* II² 43; R&O, no. 22), Thebes was a member of the Athenian Confederacy. It was one of the first to join (cf. *IG* II² 40; *TDGR*2, no. 33). Thebes was one of a group of states – the Khians, Mytilenians, Rhodians and Byzantines – that had already concluded alliance with Athens and each other, before the Charter or Prospectus was published. Consequently, all these states headed the list of members, and their names were inscribed with the same lettering as the Charter itself. Those who joined later were inscribed with different letters of various kinds. See Cargill (1981), 14–47.

897 Khabrias, son of Ktesippos, of Aixone, was one of the most successful Athenian generals in the fourth century. Born *c*.420 into a wealthy family, he died fighting bravely in 357 at the battle of Khios (Diod. 16.7.4). See 14.92 and nn. 582 and 742, and Davies, *APF*, no. 15086. Cf. Demosthenes 20, *Against Leptines*, 75–78.

898 Khabrias' presence in Egypt is attested by two place names, the Village of Khabrias beside Lake Mareotis in the west (Strabo, 17.1.22 C803), and the Palisade of Khabrias, between Gerrha and Pelousion in the east (Strabo, 16.2.33 C760). In these places he was probably improving the defence of the entrances to the Nile. See Map 5.

899 Iphikrates, of Rhamnous, was another successful Athenian general in the fourth century. Unlike Khabrias, he came from a poor family and made his way to the generalship through his military career. He was most famous for his understanding of the value of light-armed mercenaries (*peltasts*), whose use later became an integral part of ancient warfare. His career is summarized by Diod. in 15.44. On peltasts see Best (1969).

Sphodrias' aborted attack on the Peiraieus causes war between Athens and Sparta

to campaign alongside the Persians.[900] 5. A state of peace had continued to exist between the Peloponnesians and the Athenians up to this time, as a result of the previously existing treaty between them.[901] But, then, Kleombrotos, king of the Lakedaimonians, without consulting the ephors, talked a Spartiate, Sphodriades,[902] a commander with elevated and rash ambitions, into trying to seize the Peiraieus.[903] 6. So, Sphodriades, with more than 10,000 soldiers, set out one night to make his attempt to capture the Peiraieus. But, the Athenians caught sight of him[904] and his attack failed, so he retired without achieving his objective. He was brought to trial in the council of the Spartiates,[905] but got acquitted contrary to justice, because the kings advocated for him.[906] 7. As a result, the Athenians took great offence at what had taken place. After passing a vote that the Lakedaimonians had broken the peace treaty, they made the decision to go to war against them and chose as generals three of their most illustrious citizens, Timotheos,[907] Khabrias and Kallistratos.[908] They also voted to call out

The Athenians declare the treaty broken and mobilize for war

---

900 Diod.'s chronology is once again inaccurate. Akoris' war against Persia took place in the last half of the 380s and he was dead by 380 (see 15.2–4, 8–9, and n. 787). Furthermore Khabrias was home in Athens in mid-winter 379, where he was a general guarding the road to Boiotia at Eleutherai against Kleombrotos (Xen. *Hell.* 5.4.14).

901 This is presumably a reference to the King's Peace.

902 Diod. misspells this man's name Sphodriades throughout his narrative. His correct name was Sphodrias (Xen. *Hell.* 5.4.15–34; Plut. *Pelop.* 14.2, *Ages.* 24–25).

903 According to Xenophon (*Hell.* 5.4.20), it was the Thebans who bribed Sphodrias to make his attack and his attack that precipitated the foundation of the Athenian Confederacy. Plutarch (*Pelop.* 14.2) repeats this story and adds that it was Pelopidas and his fellow Boiotarch, Gorgidas (Melon in Plutarch, *Ages.* 24.4), who were responsible for the plan. This version seems less convincing than Diod.'s, in which the Athenians began soliciting members immediately after the Liberation of the Kadmeia (see 15.28.2).

904 Xenophon (*Hell.* 5.4.21) says that people, who had seen Sphodrias' army during the night, reported the news at Athens and that this was what prompted the Athenian response.

905 Both Xenophon (*Hell.* 5.4.24) and Plutarch (*Ages.* 24.6) state that Sphodrias did not present himself for trial. The council referred to would be the Gerousia and the Ephors.

906 Xenophon's account (*Hell.* 5.4.25–34) is devoted to the tale of the love affair between Sphodrias' son, Kleonymos, and Arkhidamos, son of Agesilaos, as the motivating force for Agesilaos' willingness, against his better judgement, to yield to his son's appeal and vote for Sphodrias' acquittal. He is followed in this by Plutarch (*Ages.* 25).

907 Timotheos, of Anaphlystos, was the son of Konon, victor of the Battle of Knidos. Like Khabrias, Timotheos came from a wealthy family. He was in his own right a successful military commander, who added many members to the Confederacy. He died in 354. See Davies, *APF*, no. 13,700.

908 Kallistratos, son of Kallikrates, of Aphidna, was the most dominant Athenian politician of this period, particularly known for his financial expertise. He may well have had a hand in the reorganization of Athenian finances that took place in the archonship of Nausinikos, on which see the texts collected in *TDGR2*, no. 39. See Davies, *APF*, no. 8157 and Sealey (1956).

a levy of 20,000 hoplite soldiers and 500 cavalry, and to man 200 warships.[909] In addition, they brought the Thebans into the common council, admitting them on precisely the same terms as all the others.[910] 8. Furthermore, they decreed that the land that had been allotted as *kleroukhies* be restored to its former owners, and passed a law that no Athenian could farm land outside Attica.[911] By this act of generosity they regained the goodwill of the Greeks and made their own leadership more secure.[912]

30.1. Therefore, for the reason just mentioned, many other cities were encouraged to lean towards the Athenians. The first and most enthusiastic to join the alliance were the inhabitants of Euboia,[913] with the exception of Hestiaia.[914] For, Hestiaia had been treated with great generosity by the Lakedaimonians, but had suffered terribly in war at the hands of the Athenians. So, quite reasonably, it maintained an implacable hatred for the Athenians and a very strong loyalty to the Spartans. 2. Despite that, seventy cities[915] joined in alliance with the Athenians and took their place in the common council on terms of equality. And so, it came about that, as Athenian power was continually increasing, while that of the Lakedaimonians was growing weaker, the two cities became equal in strength. And the Athenians, now that affairs were progressing in their favour, sent an army over to Euboia to act as a protection for their allies and to make war on their enemies. 3. Shortly before this time, in Euboia, an individual, called Neogenes, had collected an army with the assistance of Jason

Many states join the Athenian Confederacy

The Athenians send a force under Khabrias over to Euboia to attack Hestiaia

---

909 Cf. Xenophon (*Hell.* 5.4.34), who adds that the Athenians finally put a gate on the Peiraieus fortifications. See also Polybios, 2.62.6, who, however, mentions only 10,000 soldiers and 100 ships. At this time begins the long series of naval records of the Superintendents (*epimeletai*) of the shipyards (*IG* II² 1604–1632). For a sample see *TDGR2*, no. 47.

910 Diod.'s ordering of events is controversial. Unlike Xenophon, he has the Confederacy founded before Sphodrias' attack, then admits the Thebans into alliance afterwards, contrary to the documentary evidence.

911 This is not what the decree says. The wording is: "After Nausinikos' archonship (378/7) it shall not be permitted, either privately or publicly, for any Athenian to possess in the lands of the allies either a house or a plot of land, either by purchase or as the result of a mortgage, or by any means at all." It has no reference to past *kleroukhies*.

912 Almost the same language is used by Isokrates (14, *Plataïkos*, 44).

913 The Euboian cities, Karystos, Khalkis and Eretria, were amongst the next group of five names to be added to the list of members on *IG* II² 43, in smaller letters than the first group. See Map 10.

914 Hestiaia (Oreôs) is located on the far northern tip of Euboia. See Map 10.

915 Both Diod.'s number (70) for the members of the Confederacy and Aiskhines' (2, *On the False Embassy*, 70) even larger number (75) are in conflict with the number of names on *IG* II² 43, which is only 60.

of Pherai,[916] seized the acropolis of Hestiaia and declared himself tyrant over the territory[917] and the city of the Oreitans (i.e. Hestiaia). But, since he ruled in a violently arrogant manner, the Lakedaimonians sent out Theripides[918] to oppose him. 4. Now, to begin with, Theripides tried to negotiate the tyrant's withdrawal from the acropolis, but, since Neogenes paid no attention, he summoned the locals to fight for liberty, put the place under siege and restored liberty to the Oreitans.[919] And, that was the reason why the inhabitants of the territory said to belong to the Hestiaians were well disposed to the Spartiates and maintained their steadfast friendship. 5. Khabrias, commander of the army sent out by the Athenians, laid waste the territory of Hestiaiotis. After fortifying a place called Metropolis, which was situated on a deserted hill, he left a garrison there and then sailed off himself to the Cyclades Islands. There, he won over Peparethos and Skiathos and some other islands that had been subject to the Lakedaimonians.[920]

The Lakedaimonians attempt to regain their allies and reorganize their military

31.1. The Lakedaimonians, perceiving that there was no way they could stop this rush to defection by their allies, ceased from their previous harsh treatment and began to deal with the cities in a kindly way. Through kindly communications and acts of generosity they brought all their allies into a more positive frame of mind. Then, seeing that the threat of war was increasing and that it called for serious attention, they applied themselves ambitiously

916 Jason, tyrant of Pherai in Thessaly (see Map 10), rose to power in the 370s and assumed the position of *Tagos* (supreme leader) of all Thessaly *c*.375 (Xen. *Hell*. 6.1.18–19) or after Leuktra (Diod. 15.60.2). He was a dynamic and ambitious commander, who was suspected of having designs on control of all Greece, but was assassinated in 370. His career and character foreshadow Philip II of Macedon. See Xen. *Hell*. 6.1.4–19, 6.4.20–32; Diod. 15.54.5, 15.56.2, 15.60.1–2, 15.60.5.
917 There is no other report of Neogenes' tyranny.
918 No Spartan of this name is known. Probably the reference is to Herippidas, the man who was later one of the commanders on the Kadmeia (see 15.27.3 and n. 886).
919 The reading of the manuscripts, both here and at 15.30.3, is Oropians, but this makes no sense, since Oropos is not on Euboia. Vial, the Budé editor, argues for an emendation to Orobians, a town mentioned by Strabo (10.1.3 C445) as being in the vicinity of Hestiaia, but most editors (e.g. Vögel in the Teubner and Sherman in the Loeb) accept the emendation to Oreitans, since Oreôs came to be another name for Hestiaia (Strabo, 10.1.3 C445).
920 Diod. is very confused (and confusing) about the movements of Khabrias at this time. It is not credible that he jumped over to Hestiaiotis in northern Thessaly, even if there is a place called Metropolis there. Diod. surely means he ravaged the territory of Hestiaia, and we have to assume that there was a nearby hill, called Metropolis. As for Peparethos and Skiathos, those islands are in the northern Aegean and are not usually considered part of the Cyclades. See Map 10. However, the reference to "some other islands" may include Cycladic islands, since there was a large addition to the membership of the Confederacy following Khabrias' campaign.

to their preparations and, in particular, revised and improved the organization and arrangement of their military and its funding.[921] 2. They divided the cities and the soldiers registered for war into ten divisions. The Lakedaimonians comprised the first division, second and third were the Arkadians, fourth were the Eleians, fifth the Akhaians. The Corinthians and the Megarians supplied the sixth and the Sikyonians, Phleiasians and the other inhabitants of the Akte the seventh. The Akarnanians were the eighth and the Phokians and Lokrians the ninth. The last division was made up by the Olynthians and the allies in Thrace. A hoplite was counted the value of two light-armed soldiers, whilst a cavalryman was considered the equivalent of four hoplites.[922] 3. That was the way they organized their military, and they chose king Agesilaos to lead the campaign.[923] He was celebrated for his courage and understanding of the art of war. Furthermore, he was virtually undefeated prior to this. For, in all his other wars he had done amazingly well and, in particular, when the Lakedaimonians were at war with the Persians. Drawn up against a force many times bigger than his own, he had defeated them, and made inroads into a large part of Asia, conquering the open spaces.[924] Indeed, more than that, if the Spartiates had not summoned him home to face a state crisis, he would have exposed almost the whole Persian kingdom to extreme danger.[925] 4. For, this was a man of action, who combined boldness with great intelligence, and was experienced in dangerous undertakings. For that reason, the Spartiates, perceiving that the magnitude of the war called for an impressive commander at this time also, appointed Agesilaos to the supreme command of the war.

The reorganization of the Spartan military

Agesilaos is appointed commander of Spartan forces

921 The reorganization of the forces of the Peloponnesian League described below is found in no other source. Although Xenophon (*Hell.* 5.2.21) describes a kind of reordering of allied obligations before the campaign against Olynthos in 382, it cannot be the same as here, since the Olynthians and the Thracewards allies, included in this list as the tenth division, were not subject to Sparta in 382.
922 Cf. Xen. *Hell.* 5.2.21, where a hoplite is not valued in relation to light-armed troops, but on a monetary scale, at 3 Aiginetan *obols*, i.e. half an Aiginetan *drachma*. The Aiginetan monetary system was widely used in the Peloponnese. Its *drachma* was larger than the Athenian *drachma*, weighing 6.1 grams of silver to the Athenian 4.3. But, since an Athenian citizen could expect to receive one Athenian *drachma* a day for service in the army or navy, the Peloponnesian soldiers were still underpaid by about one third. Xenophon does, however, preserve the equivalence between a cavalryman and four hoplites.
923 What follows is a mini-eulogy of Agesilaos.
924 A reference to Agesilaos' campaign in Asia and the Battle of Sardis (Diod. 14.79.1–3, 80.1–4, 83.1–3; Xen. *Hell.* 3.4.1–29, 4.2.1–3; Xen. *Ages.* 1.30–32; *Hell. Oxy.* 11.1–6).
925 This inflated view of Agesilaos' prospects in Asia can be found in Xen. *Ages.* 1.36, Plut. *Ages.* 15 and Nepos, *Agesilaos*, 4. But Agesilaos was not Alexander, since he had no skill in assaulting fortified positions such as the Macedonian had.

Agesilaos leads his forces into Boiotia

Agesilaos encamps outside Thespiai; the Athenians join the Thebans; both sides prepare for battle

Agesilaos attacks, is frustrated by enemy tactics and retires

32.1. Agesilaos advanced into Boiotia[926] at the head of an army that totalled more than 18,000 soldiers, of which the Lakedaimonians contributed five *morai*.[927] A *mora* consisted of 500 men.[928] According to the Lakedaimonians, the unit called "the Skiritan" does not line up with the rest of the army, but takes up its own position alongside the king and goes to the assistance of those units that are at any time in difficulties. Composed of elite troops it has great effect upon the outcome of engagements and for the most part is responsible for victory.[929] Agesilaos also had 1,500 cavalry. 2. Accordingly, Agesilaos arrived at Thespiai, a town with a Lakedaimonian garrison. He pitched his camp nearby and gave his soldiers a few days' rest after their strenuous march. When the Athenians learned that the Lakedaimonians had arrived in Boiotia, they immediately sent an assisting force to Thebes that consisted of 5,000 infantry and 200 cavalry. 3. Once the Athenian and Theban forces had combined, the Thebans occupied a hill with an oblong surface[930] that was situated twenty *stades* (4,000 yards or 3,658 metres) from the city. Treating the harsh terrain as their defence, they were ready to resist the enemy's attack there, since they avoided taking the risk on equal terms on the level ground out of their great fear of the reputation of Agesilaos. 4. Agesilaos advanced against the Boiotians with his army in battle formation. Once he was in close quarters with the enemy, his first move was to send his light-armed troops against them to test their fighting spirit. When the Thebans easily repulsed them, fighting from their superior position, he led his full force against them, drawn up for battle

---

[926] There is great confusion between our two main sources regarding Agesilaos' invasions of Boiotia. Both Xenophon (5.4.35–55) and Diod. recount two invasions, separated by the heroic death of Phoibidas. Beyond that there is little similarity. It is even difficult to discern which of Diod.'s invasions corresponds to Xenophon's.

[927] This means that Agesilaos was commanding five out of the six Lakedaimonian units (*morai*) of the total Lakedaimonian levy. For the Spartan military unit *mora*, see 14.91.2, n. 577 and Glossary.

[928] According to Plutarch, *Pelop.* 17.4, this is the number of men in a *mora* given by Ephoros. He cites other figures of 700 per unit (from Kallisthenes) and 900 (from Polybios). No doubt Diod. was following Ephoros here.

[929] The Skiritai were from the Skiritis, a region of Arkadia north of Sparta and south of Tegea and east of the Eurotas. See Map 11. Thucydides (5.67.1) says that they were indeed a separate unit, but that they held the left wing. There is no evidence that they formed the sort of unit around the king that Diod. describes. It may be that he has confused them with the elusive unit, "the so-called 300 *hippeis*" (horsemen), mentioned by Thucydides at 5.72.4 as stationed in the centre with Agis at the Battle of Mantineia in 418/7. Xenophon mentions the Skiritai in his account of the second invasion (*Hell.* 5.4.52–53).

[930] This may be the hill named by Xenophon "the old-woman's breast" (*Hell.* 5.4.50), although it is more usually taken to refer to the hilltop positions held by the Thebans in the second invasion (see 15.34.1).

in a manner designed to strike fear. 5. But, Khabrias, the Athenian general, gave the order to the mercenary soldiers under his command, to await the enemy's attack with an air of contempt and, at the same time, to stand their ground in good order, with their shields resting against their knees and their spears held upright.[931] 6. Since these soldiers obeyed the order promptly to a man, Agesilaos was taken aback at the discipline of his opponents and at their display of contempt. So, he decided not to make an assault on the hilltop and to force the enemy to prove their courage in face of a hand-to-hand conflict. Knowing from experience that men, when under pressure, will dare to fight to the last for victory, he tried inviting them to fight down on the plain. But, since the Thebans were not coming down to fight, he led his *phalanx* of infantrymen away, and sent out the cavalry and light-armed detachments to plunder the territory without fear of opposition. And so, he gained possession of a large amount of booty.

33.1. The Spartiate advisers in Agesilaos' entourage and his unit commanders expressed surprise that, despite his reputation as a man of action and even though he had a larger and more powerful army, Agesilaos had not fought it out with the enemy. His reply to them was that on this occasion the Lakedaimonians had won a victory without exposing themselves to danger, since the Boiotians had not dared to come to the rescue of their territory, when it was being plundered. If, however, after the enemy themselves had conceded defeat, he had forced them to confront the terror of battle, perhaps, given the unpredictability of Chance (*Tykhe*), the Lakedaimonians could even have risked suffering an upset.[932] 2. Well, at that time, it seemed that with this answer he had given a balanced estimate of the possible outcome, but later, as a result of subsequent events, it seemed that his response was less the utterance of a man than a prophecy from the gods. For, when the Lakedaimonians did campaign against the Thebans with a huge army and put them in a situation where they had to fight for their liberty, they suffered a major disaster. 3. For, in the first place, when they were defeated at Leuktra, they lost many of their citizens, amongst whom was their king, Kleombrotos. Later, when they fought a battle at Mantineia, they suffered a complete upset and lost their position of leadership, to their surprise. For Chance is good at unexpectedly tripping up those who think too highly of themselves and at teaching them not to nurture

Agesilaos responds to the criticism of his decision

His words later taken to be prophetic

---

931 Xenophon, who does not involve Khabrias at all in the first invasion, fails even to mention this ruse in the second, when he does acknowledge Khabrias' presence only to claim that other mercenaries criticized him for not joining in the battle (*Hell.* 5.4.54).

932 None of this is in Xenophon's account.

Khabrias is celebrated for his stratagem

excessive hopes.[933] At any rate, because he was sensible enough to be satisfied with his initial success, Agesilaos kept his army free from harm. 4. Afterwards, Agesilaos returned to the Peloponnese with his army. But the Thebans, who had been saved by Khabrias' generalship, were impressed by the man's shrewd tactical ability. And, Khabrias, even though he had achieved many noble accomplishments in war, prided himself especially on this stratagem and ordered that the statues that had been dedicated to him by the *demos* adopt this pose.[934]

The Thebans attack Thespiai unsuccessfully; Phoibidas, Spartan commander, is defeated and dies

5. After the departure of Agesilaos, the Thebans made a campaign against Thespiai. But, although they wiped out the 200 defenders in an advance post, their successive assaults on the city did not achieve any noteworthy success, so they led their army back to Thebes. 6. But Phoibidas, the Lakedaimonian, who commanded a sizeable garrison in Thespiai, launched a sally from the city and made a headlong attack upon the retreating Thebans. In this, he lost more than 500 of his soldiers and he himself, although fighting brilliantly, after suffering many wounds face-on, gave up his life like a hero.[935]

The Spartans again invade Boiotia but are repulsed

34.1. Shortly afterwards [Spring 377], the Lakedaimonians once again campaigned against Thebes with the same force as before. The Thebans, by occupying some different positions that were hard to assault, prevented their enemy from plundering their territory, but they did not dare to line up face-to-face against the whole enemy army on the level ground. 2. When, however, Agesilaos provoked an engagement, the Thebans gradually descended to fight. The result was a hotly contested battle that lasted for a long time. At first, Agesilaos' men had the better of it, but later, when the Thebans sallied forth from their city in full force, at the sight of the mass of attackers Agesilaos gave the signal for the trumpeter to recall his soldiers from the battle. That was the first occasion when the Thebans did not feel themselves inferior

---

933 See the Introduction for the influence of Chance (*Tykhe*) on Greek historiography from the fourth century onwards.

934 See Nepos, *Chabrias*, 1.3; Aristotle, *Rhetoric*, 3.10.7.1411b; Aiskhines, 3, *Against Ktesiphon*, 243. The only statue to Khabrias was in the *agora*. It was voted for his victory at Naxos, according to Aiskhines (3, *Against Ktesiphon*, 243). In it he was depicted as a soldier "at ease," as described here (*SEG* XIX 204 = *Agora* XVIII C148). See Stylianou, *Commentary*, 299–301.

935 Cf. Xen. *Hell.* 5.4.42–45. Xenophon, however, does not liken his death to that of a "hero," an expression with particular significance in Greek mythology and to Diod.'s emphasis on the beneficent function of heroes in his introductory books. Diod. uses the analogy often in cases where it signifies more than that a person died bravely. For example, he uses the same analogy to compare the death of Amazons to heroes (2.45.6, 2.46.5), and in this book singles out Iskholaos and Pelopidas for such praise. See nn. 1144 and 1269.

to the Lakedaimonians. They set up a trophy and from that time on faced the Spartan army boldly.[936] 3. Well, such was the conclusion of the infantry battles on land. In naval affairs, about the same time, a great battle took place in the waters between Naxos and Paros. It happened for the following reasons. When Pollis,[937] the Lakedaimonian *navarch*, learned that a large quantity of grain was being shipped to the Athenians in freighters, he lay in ambush, awaiting the passage of the grain convoy, planning to attack the freighters.[938] Now, when the Athenian *demos* was informed about this, they dispatched a fleet to guard the grain convoy, and had it conducted safely through to the Peiraieus.[939] 4. Next, Khabrias, the Athenian naval commander, sailed with his whole fleet to Naxos and put the town under siege. Bringing his siege-engines to bear upon the walls, he shattered them, and tried energetically to take the city by assault. In the meantime, Pollis, the Lakedaimonian *navarch*, sailed up to assist the Naxians.[940] A spirit of ambitious rivalry arose, and the two sides came together for battle. Putting their ships into battle formation, they set sail against each other. 5. Pollis had sixty-five triremes[941] and Khabrias had eighty-three. As the ships were sailing closer to each other, it was Pollis, in command of his right wing, who was the first to attack the opposing triremes on the Athenian left, whose commander was the Athenian Kedon. Fighting brilliantly, he both killed Kedon himself and sank his ship. In a similar fashion, he engaged the other ships as well and, smashing them with his rams, destroyed some and put others to flight. Now, when Khabrias saw what was happening, he dispatched a squadron of the ships he commanded to assist the beleaguered wing, and staved off the defeat of his men. He himself, with the strongest part of the fleet, fought nobly and destroyed many triremes and captured not a few others.[942]

Khabrias wins a naval battle against the Spartan commander, Pollis, near Naxos

936 Xenophon (*Hell.* 5.4.53) allows only that the Thebans set up a trophy for the retreat of the Skiritai.
937 Clearly not the same Pollis who was *navarch* in 396/5, since there was a rule against holding the navarchy twice.
938 According to Xenophon (*Hell.* 5.4.60), it was a strategy adopted by Sparta and her allies to try to starve Athens.
939 Xenophon (*Hell.* 5.4.61), by contrast, maintains that the grain was brought into the Peiraieus only after the battle.
940 Diod.'s account, unlike Xenophon's, provides this undeniable reason why the battle took place near Naxos.
941 Sixty, according to Xenophon (*Hell.* 5.4.61).
942 The Battle of Naxos, which took place on the sixteenth of Boedromion (approximately September), 376 (Plut. *Phokion*, 6.3), together with Timotheos' later victory at Alyzeia in 375 (Xen. *Hell.* 5.4.64–66; Diod. 15.36.5–6), marked Athens' resumption of naval dominance in the Aegean, which ended only with its defeat by Macedon near Amorgos in 322.

Khabrias ceases pursuit to pick up his shipwrecked comrades and bury the dead

35.1. Although he was on the winning side and had forced the whole enemy fleet to turn in flight, Khabrias refrained entirely from pursuing them. He remembered the situation after the battle at Arginousai, when the *demos* had imposed the death penalty on the victorious generals in return for their great service, because they found fault with them for not burying those who had died in the battle.[943] So, since the situation was quite similar, he was careful never to risk suffering a fate at all like that. Consequently, giving up on pursuit, he started picking up those of his fellow citizens who were floating in the water. He saved the ones who were still alive, and gave burial to the dead. If he had not been engaged in this caring deed, he would easily have destroyed the whole enemy fleet. 2. In the naval engagement eighteen Athenian triremes were destroyed, while the Lakedaimonians lost twenty-four,[944] and eight others that were captured with their men on board. Well, after winning an illustrious victory at sea, Khabrias sailed back to the Peiraieus, his ships loaded with booty. There he was greeted by an ecstatic reception from his fellow citizens.[945] For, this was the first victory at sea the Athenians had won since the Peloponnesian War.[946] The naval battle that they fought near Knidos[947] was won not with their own fleet, but by using the King's fleet. 3. Contemporaneous with these events, in Italy at Rome Marcus Manlius made an attempt at a tyranny, was overpowered and killed.[948]

Khabrias is welcomed home ecstatically by the Athenians

376/5: Book 15.36.1–37.3

The Triballi invade southern Thrace and Abdera

36.1. In the archonship at Athens of Kharisandros,[949] the Romans appointed four military tribunes in place of the consuls, Servius Cornelius, Sulpicius, Lucius Papirius, Titus Quinctius,[950] and the Eleians celebrated the one hundred and first Olympiad, in which Damon of Thourioi won the *stadion*.

943 This notorious incident followed the Athenian victory at the Arginousai Islands in 406. See Diod. 13.99–102; Xen. *Hell.* 1.6.26–1.7.34. A major discrepancy between the two accounts is that Diod. states, as he does again here, that the generals were punished for failing to bury the dead, while Xenophon, who was probably present in Athens at the time, says their crime was in not saving the shipwrecked.
944 Pollis lost forty-nine ships, according to Demosthenes (20, *Against Leptines*, 77).
945 Khabrias was loaded with honours: he was granted *ateleia* (freedom from taxation), on which see Demosthenes (20, *Against Leptines*, 75–78), and a statue (see above, n. 934).
946 A sentiment echoed in Plut. *Phokion*, 6.3.
947 See 14.83.4–7.
948 Cf. Livy, 6.15–20.
949 The name is emended, based on documentary evidence, against the mss' reading Khariandros. See Develin, *AO*, 238.
950 See Livy, 6.18.1, who gives six names, as follows: Servius Cornelius Maluginensis, Publius Valerius Potitus, Marcus Furius Camillus, Servius Sulpicius Rufus, Caius Papirius Crassus, Titus Quinctius Cincinnatus. This is Varronian 384.

In their term of office the Triballi[951] in Thrace, under pressure of famine,[952] made a mass invasion into the territory of their neighbours and tried to carry off the produce from other people's land. 2. Numbering more than 30,000, they invaded the part of Thrace next to them and pillaged the territory of the Abderites[953] with impunity. When they were returning with a mass of booty in a disorderly and arrogant fashion, the Abderites took the field against them in full force and, catching them on their way home in scattered groups, they killed more than 2,000. 3. But the barbarians, incensed at what had happened and wanting to exact vengeance from the Abderites, once again invaded their territory. The Abderites, who had won the first encounter, were elated at their victory and, when the neighbouring Thracians sent them some reinforcements, they decided to line up for battle against the barbarians. 4. A vigorous battle ensued, but when their Thracian allies suddenly changed sides, the Abderites found themselves alone. Surrounded by the massive barbarian force, almost all the Abderites who took part in the battle were cut down.[954] At this moment when the Abderites had suffered such a disaster and were about to be put under siege, Khabrias, the Athenian, appeared on the scene with an army.[955] He rescued the Abderites from their dangerous situation and drove the barbarians from their territory. Then, after leaving an impressive garrison behind in the city, he himself was assassinated by some individuals.[956] 5. Timotheos[957] took over the command of the fleet and sailed off to Kephallenia.[958] He gained the allegiance of the cities there, and in the same way persuaded the cities in Akarnania[959] to side with Athens. He

Timotheos replaces Khabrias, campaigns in the west and defeats the Spartans at Alyzeia

---

951 The Triballi were a northern Thracian people, who lived south of the Danube and north of the Balkan mountains, probably in the plain of Kosovo. They were formidable warriors, who worsted even Philip II of Macedon (Justin, *Epitoma*, 9.3.1–3).
952 Strabo (7.3.13 C305) suggests that the Triballi were pressured by other tribes to move, but the narrative is consistent with a plundering raid.
953 For the location of Abdera, see Map 8. It was not a neighbour of the Triballi, who probably accessed it *via* the Nestos valley.
954 An almost identical account is provided by Aineias Taktikos (*How to survive under siege*, 15.9), except that in his account the Abderites were caught in a Triballian ambush.
955 This is after the Battle of Naxos, either in the autumn of 376 or the spring of 375.
956 This is not correct. Khabrias died at the Battle of Khios in 357 (see n. 897).
957 See n. 907. Diod.'s account gives the impression that Timotheos succeeded to Khabrias' position. This is not the case. Both were elected generals (*strategoi*) for this year (see Develin, *AO*, 238–239). Timotheos was given a separate assignment by the *demos* to sail around the Peloponnese and attack Spartan positions in the West. According to Xenophon (*Hell.* 5.4.62), this assignment was requested by the Thebans.
958 A large island in the Ionian Sea. See Map 8..
959 An area in north-west Greece, opposite Kephallenia and Leukas. See Map 8.

acquired Alketas, king of the Molossians,⁹⁶⁰ as a friend of Athens, and, generally speaking, won over most of the cities in that region.⁹⁶¹ Then, he defeated the Lakedaimonians in a naval battle near Leukas.⁹⁶² 6. He accomplished all this quickly and easily, persuading some by his eloquence, and winning victories through courage and strategic ability. The result was that he gained a high reputation both amongst his fellow citizens and the Greeks at large.⁹⁶³ That is the situation regarding Timotheos' affairs.

The Thebans attack Orkhomenos and defeat the Spartan garrison there at Tegyra

37.1. Contemporaneous with these events, the Thebans made an attack upon Orkhomenos with a force of 500 elite troops and achieved a memorable success. For, the Lakedaimonians had many soldiers in a garrison at Orkhomenos, and these lined up for battle against the Thebans. A vigorous battle ensued, in which the Thebans were victorious against a force twice their number.⁹⁶⁴ Nothing like this had ever happened before. Previously it seemed something to be happy about, if a larger army defeated a smaller Spartan force. 2. As a result, the Thebans became flush with confidence and their reputation for courage was spread further abroad. They had clearly established themselves as future contenders for the leadership of Greece.⁹⁶⁵ 3. Amongst historians, Hermeias, the Methymnaian, ended his History of the Sicilians at this year. His composition was ten books long, although some divide it into twelve.⁹⁶⁶

Hermeias of Methymna's history of Sicily ends here

375/4: Book 15.38.1–40.5

Artaxerxes, wanting Greek mercenaries for an invasion of Egypt, initiates a Common Peace

38.1. In the archonship at Athens of Hippodamas,⁹⁶⁷ the Romans appointed four military tribunes in place of the consuls, Lucius Valerius, Lucius Manlius, Servius Sulpicius, Lucretius.⁹⁶⁸ In their term of office, Artaxerxes, King

---

960 See n. 802. This was likely the occasion when Alketas and his son, Neoptolemos, joined the Athenian Confederacy.

961 Timotheos' campaign added many new adherents to the Athenian Confederacy, amongst which was the important island of Kerkyra (Xen. *Hell.* 5.4.64), which Diod. fails to mention.

962 At Alyzeia, according to Xenophon (*Hell.* 5.4.65), against the Spartan fleet under Nikolokhos. Polyainos (*Strategemata*, 3.10.4) says it took place during the festival of Skira (June 375).

963 Timotheos received an extended eulogy from Isokrates (15, *On the Antidosis*, 101–139). He is also praised for his moderation by Xenophon (*Hell.* 5.4.64).

964 I.e. two *morai* of the Spartan army on Diod.'s estimate (see 15.32.1 and n. 927).

965 This campaign is ignored by Xenophon, but fully described by Plutarch, *Pelop.* 16–17, who shares Diod.'s view of the effect this victory had on Theban morale. The battle took place at Tegyra, near Orkhomenos, in the spring of 375. Diod. fails to mention that the Thebans were led by Pelopidas and the core of their force was the Sacred Band of 300 elite troops.

966 On this relatively unknown historian see *FGrHist/BNJ* 558.

967 See Develin, *AO*, 240–243 for the correct genitive, *Hippodamantos*, against Diodoros' *Hippodamou*.

968 Livy, 6.21.1, gives the names of the tribunes as: Lucius Valerius, Aulus Manlius, Servius Sulpicius, Lucius Lucretius, Lucius Aemilius, Marcus Trebonius. This is the Varronian year 383.

of the Persians, resolved to put an end to the conflicts in Greece, because he was planning a war against Egypt[969] and was eager to assemble an impressive army of mercenaries. For, in this way, he was very hopeful that the Greeks, once they had ceased from their domestic conflicts, would be more prone to enlist in foreign service. So, he sent ambassadors to Greece to encourage the cities to agree to a Common Peace (*Koine Eirene*).[970] 2. The Greeks were only too happy to receive his proposal, because they were worn out by their continuous wars. They unanimously agreed to make peace on terms that all cities should live under their own laws (*autonomia*) and be free from foreign garrisons. Also, the Greeks appointed officials for the withdrawal of troops to go to each city and lead out all the garrisons. 3. Only the Thebans were unwilling to accept that the ratification of the treaty should be performed city by city, but wanted the whole of Boiotia to be treated as part of the federation controlled by Thebes.[971] The Athenians objected most vigorously to the Theban position, their argument being presented by the popular leader Kallistratos. Epameinondas argued the case for Thebes in a brilliant speech before the joint council, but when all the other Greeks agreed unanimously to the peace, the Thebans alone were deemed to be excluded. Epameinondas, by his own personal reputation for courage, aroused the spirit of his fellow citizens and emboldened them to oppose the decision of all the other states.[972] 4. For, the Lakedaimonians and the Athenians, who had been in ceaseless competition in the past over the leadership of Greece, now began making concessions to each other, deciding

All the Greek cities, except Thebes, agree

Kallistratos and Epameinondas debate about the peace

The Athenians and the Spartans agree to divide the leadership of Greece

---

969 On Persian attempts to reconquer Egypt see n. 762.
970 The Common Peace of 375/4 (probably summer or autumn 375) was essentially a renewal of the King's Peace of 387/6 (Philokhoros, *FGrHist/BNJ* 328 F151), except that it implicitly recognized the existence of the Second Athenian Confederacy. For a discussion of the chronology of the period 375/4–371/0 see Stylianou, *Commentary*, 349–363.
971 No other source suggests that Thebes refused to sign the Peace of 375/4, although Xenophon (*Hell.* 6.2.2) does indicate growing concern in both Sparta and Athens about the growth of Theban ambition. At this time Thebes was still a member of the Second Athenian Confederacy. The treaty that Thebes actually refused to sign was that of 371/0 (15.50.4; Xen. *Hell.* 16.3.1–20), a refusal that led to the Battle of Leuktra. Diodoros' description of the peace negotiations of 375/4 and 371/0 are so similar that scholars have suspected a doublet. But I feel this is unlikely, since he is correct in most details and especially in associating the negotiations of 375/4 with Artaxerxes' planned invasion of Egypt. Only the view that the Thebans were "deemed to be excluded" on this occasion appears to be wrong.
972 It is possible that Kallistratos and Epameinondas clashed at some meeting during the negotiations in 375/4, maybe in the *synhedrion* of the Athenian Confederacy. A speech by Kallistratos is also reported by Xenophon (*Hell.* 6.3.10–17) at Sparta in 371. Xenophon makes no mention of the presence of Epameinondas on that occasion, but Plutarch (*Ages.* 27.4–28.2) guarantees that he was there and reports the essence of his speech. But, then, his argument was with Agesilaos, not Kallistratos.

that one of them deserved to rule on land, the other by sea.⁹⁷³ As a consequence, they were ill disposed to the leadership being taken over by a third party and kept trying to detach cities in Boiotia from the Theban federation.

The Thebans are ambitious to assume the leadership of Greece by land

39.1. Indeed, the Thebans, who were distinguished for their physical strength and their deeds of valour and who had previously defeated the Lakedaimonians in many battles,⁹⁷⁴ were in high spirits and kept trying to contest the leadership on land. And, they were not deluded in their hopes, both because they possessed the qualities already mentioned and because at that time they had a greater number of excellent military leaders than others. 2. The most illustrious of these were Pelopidas, Gorgidas⁹⁷⁵ and Epameinondas. This last, Epameinondas, far excelled not only his fellow Boiotians, but also all other Greeks, in courage and comprehension of military affairs. For, he had received a well-rounded education in all subjects and was particularly attached to Pythagorean philosophy.⁹⁷⁶ In addition, since he was equipped with superior bodily strength, it is no surprise that he accomplished deeds of the greatest distinction. So, even when he was put in the position of having to fight against the whole combined might of the Lakedaimonians and their allies with only a small force of citizen soldiers, he so outmatched these (previously) unbeaten soldiers that he slew the king of the Spartiates, Kleombrotos, and almost totally annihilated the opposing army.⁹⁷⁷ 3. He accomplished such extraordinary deeds thanks to his shrewd intelligence and the virtue that had been instilled in him by his education. But we shall make a clearer presentation about this a little further on in a separate chapter.⁹⁷⁸ For now we shall return to the continuation of our narrative.

Autonomy leads to political strife in the cities of the Peloponnese

40.1. Following the granting of autonomy to the citizen populations, the cities were thrown into great turmoil and factional strife, especially those in the Peloponnese. For, these cities had been used to oligarchic constitutions, but now

---

973 An idea attributed to Kallistratos by Xenophon (*Hell.* 6.3.13–17). See also Nepos, *Timotheos*, 2.2. This was the same proposal as the one later made in 369 that was changed at the last minute to each side holding supreme command on both land and sea for five days (Xen. *Hell.* 7.1.1–14 and n. 1167 below).

974 This claim is in conflict with the facts (cf. Plut. *Ages.* 27.3) and Diod.'s own words at 15.37.1.

975 A correction for the reading "Gorgias" of the mss that is based upon Plut. *Pelop.* 12.1 and 12.4.

976 See Diod. 10.11.2, where Epameinondas' teacher is named as the Pythagorean philosopher, Lysis of Tarentum. For Epameinondas' education in other disciplines, see Nepos, *Epameinondas*, 2.

977 A reference to the Battle of Leuktra (see 15.51–56).

978 Diod. eulogizes Epameinondas after his death at the Battle of Mantineia in 15.88.

they resorted quite irresponsibly to the liberties that came with democracy.⁹⁷⁹ They drove many of the elite into exile and, after bringing them to trial on fake charges, found them guilty. As a result, they became embroiled in factional strife that resulted in exiles and confiscations of property, especially against those who had been in charge of the states under the rule of the Lakedaimonians. 2. For, since these men had treated their fellow citizens strictly in times past, when the democratic mob gained its freedom, it did not forget its sufferings. First, the exiles from Phialeia⁹⁸⁰ combined together and seized a strong position, called Heraia.⁹⁸¹ Setting out from there, they secretly made their way into the city of Phialeia. Since by chance it was the time of a festival of Dionysos,⁹⁸² they fell upon the spectators in the theatre and slaughtered many of them. Then, after persuading not a few to join in their mad caper, they retired to Sparta. 3. And the exiles from Corinth,⁹⁸³ who were living in large numbers amongst the Argives, made an attempt at a return. They were admitted into the city by some of their relatives and friends, but they were denounced and surrounded. As they were on the point of being arrested, in fear of the abusive treatment that would follow their capture, they slew one another. The Corinthians accused many other citizens of collaborating with the exiles in this enterprise and put some to death, while they exiled others. 4. In Megara, when some tried to bring about a change of constitution, they were overpowered by the popular faction. Many were killed and not a few were expelled. Likewise, some people amongst the Sikyonians attempted to bring about a revolution, but failed and were put to death. 5. In Phleious, the many exiles had seized a strong position within the territory and had hired a large force of mercenaries. The result was a battle against the people of the city in which the exiles were victorious, killing more than 300 Phleiasians. But, some time later, the exiles were betrayed by their guards and the Phleiasians won a battle against the exiles and killed more than 600 of them. They expelled the rest from the land

---

979 In the following narrative Diod. appears to have assembled a collection of examples from different times within the period from the King's Peace to the Battle of Leuktra. The examples are not all in agreement with his thesis. The situation in Phigaleia and Megara clearly involves exiled oligarchs trying to return to power, while in Corinth and Phleious the situation is the reverse. It is perhaps to be doubted that such factional dissension was possible in the states of the Peloponnese subject to Sparta before the defeat of Sparta at Leuktra.

980 The original name of this city was Phigaleia, but the form Phialeia is found in documents from the third century on. This, then, is Diod.'s own usage.

981 A place called Heraia existed on the bank of the river Alpheios, about 20 miles from Phigaleia. This is rather distant for a surprise attack.

982 Most likely in the spring, when festivals of Dionysos usually took place.

983 Clearly democrats, since Argos had a democratic government.

and forced them to take refuge in Argos. Well, such was the sad situation of the cities in the Peloponnese.

374/3: Book 15.41.1–47.8

Artaxerxes mounts a campaign to reconquer Egypt, led by Pharnabazos

41.1. In the archonship at Athens of Sokratides,[984] in place of the consuls the Romans appointed four military tribunes, Quintus Servilius, Cornelius and Spurius Papirius.[985] In their term of office King Artaxerxes mounted a campaign against the Egyptians,[986] who were in a state of revolt from the Persians. The commanders in charge were Pharnabazos, of the barbarian troops, and Iphikrates, the Athenian, of the mercenaries, which numbered 20,000. The King had sent for Iphikrates and appointed him to the command on account of the excellence of his generalship.[987] 2. Since Pharnabazos had already squandered rather many years on his preparations, Iphikrates saw him as a man who was clever at speaking, but a sluggard when it came to acting. So he told him frankly [with *parrhesia*] that he was surprised how sharp he was with words, but slow in actions. And Pharnabazos replied that he was personally master of his words, but that the King was in control of his actions. 3. The Persian forces

The invasion force assembles at Ake

assembled at Ake.[988] The barbarians under Pharnabazos' command numbered 200,000, and the Greek mercenaries led by Iphikrates were 20,000.[989] There were also 300 triremes and 200 triakonters. And the number of transport vessels for food and other supplies was huge. 4. At the beginning of summer[990] the

The assault starts at the beginning of summer

King's commanders set out from their camp with their whole army and advanced against Egypt, accompanied by the fleet. As they approached the Nile, they found that the Egyptians had clearly made themselves ready for the war. 5. The reason was that Pharnabazos was advancing slowly and had given his opponents plenty of time for their preparations. For, as a general rule, Persian

---

984 For Sokratides, see Develin, *AO*, 243.
985 Livy (6.22.1) provides the following six names: Spurius Papirius, Lucius Papirius, Servius Cornelius Maluginensis, Quintus Servilius, Gaius Sulpicius and Lucius Aemilius. This is Varronian 382.
986 Brief mention of this invasion is made by Nepos, *Iphikrates*, 2.4; Plut. *Artax*. 24.1; Pompeius Trogus, *Prologue to Book 10* and Polyainos, *Strategemata*, 3.9.38, 56, 59, but Diod.'s account is by far the most detailed.
987 See 15.29.3.
988 The name is confirmed by Demosthenes (52, *Against Kallippos*, 20) and Polyainos (*Strategemata*, 3.9.56). The reference is to the historically famous city Acre (Akko), although its name has varied considerably over the centuries.
989 Nepos, *Iphikrates*, 2.4, gives the number of mercenaries as 12,000.
990 Probably the early summer (May/June) of 374, although that would actually belong before the beginning of Sokratides' archonship at the end of July. Some prefer the invasion to begin in the early summer of 373, close to the end of Sokratides' archonship, but then it would extend beyond his term.

generals, not being in independent control of the overall campaign, make reference to the King on all matters and await his reply to each question.[991]

42.1. When Nektanébis,[992] king of the Egyptians, found out about the size of the Persian forces, he was not dismayed, putting his confidence chiefly in the natural strength of the country, since Egypt was in all respects hard to access, and secondly in the fact that all points of entry from the land and from the sea had been well blocked by fortifications.[993] 2. For, since the Nile flows out into the Egyptian Sea by seven mouths, a city had been built at each of the mouths. Each city was equipped with massive towers on either side of the channel and a wooden bridge that commanded the access by sea. He built his strongest fortifications at the mouth at Pelousion,[994] because it was situated first on the path of those coming from Syria and seemed for that reason to provide the best point of attack for enemies. 3. He fenced it around with a ditch and walled off the navigable entries at the most suitable places; he turned the land-access routes into marshes by flooding and blocked the sea-approaches with dykes. As a result, it was difficult either for ships to sail in, or for cavalry to get close or for infantry to approach. 4. When Pharnabazos' generals found that the Pelousian mouth was surprisingly strongly fortified and guarded by a host of soldiers, they completely rejected the idea of forcing their way through by that route and resolved to make their landing by some other mouth of the river. So, they sailed out to sea to avoid having their ships seen by the enemy and sailed down to the Mendesian mouth,[995] as it is called, which had a sufficiently extensive beach. There, Pharnabazos and Iphikrates disembarked with 3,000 soldiers and advanced towards the little fortified town at the mouth. 5. The Egyptians rushed to the rescue with 3,000 cavalry and infantry, and a vigorous battle ensued. But, when a large force of reinforcements came from the ships to help the Persians, the Egyptians were surrounded. Many were killed and not a few taken prisoner, while the remainder were chased back to the city. Along with the garrison, Iphikrates' men broke inside the walls and, after taking control of the fortress, they razed it to the ground and enslaved the residents.

Nektanébis, the Egyptian king, is confident in the defences of Egypt

The Persians land at the Mendesian mouth, defeat the Egyptians and capture their fortress

---

991 On the dilatory way the King of Persia supported the campaigns he ordered, especially financially, see *Hell. Oxy.* 19.2.
992 Nektanébis/Nektanébôs assumed the throne of Egypt after the death of Akoris in 380. See n. 787.
993 Not least, ironically, thanks to the strategic advice of Khabrias. See 15.29.2 and n. 898.
994 For the location of Pelousion, see Map 5.
995 Two mouths to the west of Pelousion. See Map 5.

A disagreement arises between Iphikrates and Pharnabazos about how to proceed

43.1. After this a quarrel broke out amongst the generals, which brought about the failure of the invasion.[996] For, when Iphikrates learned from the captives that Memphis, a city of the greatest strategic importance of all the cities in Egypt, was without defenders, he advised that they sail immediately upriver against Memphis[997] before the Egyptian forces arrived. But Pharnabazos and his generals were of the opinion that they should await the arrival of the whole Persian army, because then the attack on Memphis would be less dangerous.

Iphikrates requests permission to attack Memphis but Pharnabazos refuses

2. When Iphikrates requested that the mercenaries that were there be assigned to him and proclaimed that with their help he would capture the city, Pharnabazos became suspicious of his audacious courage, fearing that he might take possession of Egypt on his own. As a consequence, when Pharnabazos refused his permission, Iphikrates issued a solemn protest, saying that if they let this precise moment of opportunity pass, they would bring about the failure of the main objective of the campaign. <The Persian generals>[998] were jealous of him and heaped unjust slanders on him.

Time and the flooding of the Nile wear the Persians down and they decide to abort the mission

3. Meanwhile the Egyptians, given a long respite, sent an adequate defensive force into Memphis, while they turned up in full force at their devastated fortress and fought continuous close engagements with their enemy, enjoying a great advantage thanks to the strength of their position. As their forces kept on growing, they slew large numbers of Persians and acted with confidence towards the enemy. 4. As the fighting over this fortress dragged on and since the Etesian winds[999] had already arrived, the Nile began to flood[1000] and, by covering the whole area with the volume of its water, made Egypt more secure day by day. Since the situation was increasingly working against them, the Persian generals decided to evacuate their army from Egypt.

Accused by Pharnabazos of ruining the invasion, Iphikrates secretly sails off to Athens

5. Now, as they were on their way back to Asia, since Pharnabazos and Iphikrates were not on friendly terms, Iphikrates began to suspect that he might be arrested and suffer punishment in the same way as Konon, the Athenian.[1001] He decided to flee the expedition secretly. So, after securing a boat for

---

996 This information is also found in Plut. *Artax.* 24.1.
997 For the location of Memphis, see Map 5.
998 Something must be missing from the text here, and this is one suggested amendment.
999 The Etesian wind or *meltemi* is a dry wind that blows from the north in the Aegean Sea from mid-July to the end of August. Diod. has slipped here, because he knew better than to associate the flooding of the Nile with the Etesian wind. In his detailed discussion of various explanations of that phenomenon (1.39.7–41.10) he supports the theory of Agatharkhides of Knidos that the cause is heavy rain in the Ethiopian mountains. Nor was the Etesian wind cited as a cause by Ephoros, whose own strange view was ridiculed by Diod. at 1.39.7–13. The idea is attributed to Kallisthenes of Olynthos, grand-nephew of Aristotle and historian of Alexander (*FGrHist/BNJ* 124 F124a–d).
1000 The inundation of the Nile begins about June and continues to September.
1001 See 14.85.4 and n. 550.

himself, he quit during the night without being detected and sailed away to Athens. 6. Pharnabazos sent ambassadors to Athens and accused Iphikrates of being responsible for the failure to conquer Egypt. But the Athenians replied to the Persians that, if they found him guilty of wrongdoing, they would punish him as he deserved. But a short time later they appointed him general in charge of the fleet.

44.1. It is not unfitting to lay out the information that has been recorded about the excellent qualities of Iphikrates.[1002] For it is handed down in the tradition that he possessed a shrewd military mind and brought an exceptional genius to bear on every advantageous idea. So, it is said that, after acquiring a lengthy experience of military affairs in the Persian War, he devised many useful military inventions, devoting particular attention to the details of the soldier's equipment. 2. For example, the Greeks were used to carrying large shields [*aspides*] and for that reason found it hard to manoeuvre. So, he did away with the large shields and produced smaller shields of moderate size [*peltai*], setting his sights accurately on two objectives, both to provide sufficient protection for the body and also to make it possible for those who were carrying the smaller shield to be extremely manoeuvrable because of its light weight. 3. The usefulness of this change was accepted after a trial and those who had previously been called hoplites after their shield then changed their name to peltasts after the *pelte*.[1003] But, his change to the spear and the sword was in the opposite direction. He increased the size of the spears by 50 percent and almost doubled the size of the swords. Usage confirmed the experiment and, as a result of the successful trial, experience made the reputation of the inventiveness of the general. 4. He made shoes for the soldiers that were easy to untie and light of weight, which right up to the present day are called "Iphikratids" after him.[1004] He also made many other useful inventions for campaigning, but it would take

Iphikrates is praised for his contributions to military equipment

---

1002 It is quite unusual to eulogize the career of an individual before his death, but the fact that this chapter attributes Iphikrates' reforms to his experience fighting for Persia, and ends with a summation of the Persian invasion, supports the view that the reforms described here were specific to that campaign and had no wider effect, except, that is, for the shoes.

1003 This notion is not supported by any evidence. The typical Greek infantry soldier in the fourth century remained the hoplite, fighting in the massed formation called the *phalanx*. It is true that later Philip of Macedon created the Macedonian *phalanx* of soldiers who lacked heavy body-armour and used long pikes (*sarissas*), and some have speculated that Iphikrates' changes represented a transitional phase, but there is no evidence of this. Rather than transforming the hoplite, Iphikrates more likely increased the fighting power of the formerly lightly-armed peltasts and probably only for the immediate needs of the Egyptian campaign.

1004 The shoes that Iphikrates invented remained in use until Diod.'s day and well beyond.

a long time to discuss them. So, anyway, the Persian expedition against Egypt, after great preparation, came to an unsuccessful end contrary to expectations.

War breaks out between Sparta and Athens over support for oligarchies and democracies

45.1. Throughout Greece, as cities were in a state of turmoil because of a change in constitution and many uprisings occurred on account of the general anarchy, the Lakedaimonians gave assistance to those which were trying to establish oligarchies, while the Athenians helped the adherents of democracy.[1005] 2. For both these cities observed the treaty for a short time, but soon afterwards, acting in support of their associated cities, they resumed hostilities, no longer giving any thought to the Common Peace that had been agreed upon.[1006]

Conflict first breaks out over Zakynthos

For example, on the island of Zakynthos, those who had been in control of political affairs during the period of Lakedaimonian dominance were subject to the anger and resentment of the *demos* and were all driven into exile…[1007] These men took refuge with Timotheos, the commander of the Athenian navy, joined his fleet and fought on his side. 3. In this way they gained his support and, after he had set them ashore on the island, they took control of a strong position beside the sea and named it Arkadia.[1008] Using this as a base, they made damaging raids upon the residents of the city with Timotheos' help.[1009] 4. The Zakynthians asked for assistance from the Lakedaimonians, whose first response was to send ambassadors to Athens and make accusations against Timotheos.[1010] But, when they saw that the *demos* was inclined in favour of the exiles, they equipped a fleet and, manning twenty-five triremes, sent them out to assist the Zakynthians, entrusting the command to Aristokrates.[1011]

1005 This is a resumption of the point made at 15.40.1, with the addition of the involvement of Athens. Diod. is reverting back in his coverage of Greek affairs to the period after the signing of the Peace of 375/4.
1006 In this case the Peace of 375/4.
1007 A gap in the text of indeterminate length must occur here, since the men who ask for help from Timotheos in the next sentence must be the democrats. The *lacuna* will have narrated the regaining of control by the oligarchs, presumably with Spartan aid.
1008 Cf. Xen. *Hell.* 6.2.2. A democratic faction on "the Nellos" is listed as joining the Athenian Confederacy on the Charter document (*IG* II² 43.131-134). This is no doubt the same group that Timotheos helped, but it is not clear whether "Arkadia" is another name for "the Nellos" or whether the locations are different.
1009 According to Xenophon (*Hell.* 6.2.3), Timotheos' action was construed by the Spartans as "hostile" and fighting began immediately, whereas war did not break out openly until sometime in 373. Timotheos must have returned to Athens after this.
1010 Probably in the autumn of 375.
1011 This expedition probably took place in the spring of 374. Xenophon, our other source for this period, makes no mention of it, nor of Alkidas' subsequent mission (autumn 374 or spring 373) to Kerkyra. Instead, he proceeds directly to Mnasippos' appointment at *Hell.* 6.2.4.

46.1. Contemporaneous with these events, a pro-Lakedaimonian faction from Kerkyra rebelled against the *demos* and called upon the Spartiates to send out a naval force, promising to betray Kerkyra to them. And the Lakedaimonians, aware that Kerkyra was of prime importance to anyone wanting to control the seas, hastened to take possession of that city. 2. So, they immediately dispatched to Kerkyra twenty-two triremes, entrusting the command to Alkidas. So that they might be received as friends by the Kerkyraians and then capture the city with the help of the exiles,[1012] they pretended that this fleet was really on its way to Sicily. 3. But the Kerkyraians, having found out about the Spartan plan, kept a careful guard on the city and sent ambassadors to Athens to ask for help. The Athenians passed a resolution to assist the Kerkyraians and the exiled Zakynthians. They sent out Ktesikles as general in command of the exiles[1013] and began making preparations to dispatch a naval force to Kerkyra. 4. Contemporaneous with these events, in Boiotia, the Plataians, depending on their alliance with the Athenians,[1014] asked them to send soldiers, because they had resolved to put their city in Athenian hands. At this, the Boiotarchs[1015] grew furious with the Plataians and immediately led an impressive army against them, hurrying to reach the city before the arrival of their Athenian allies. 5. When they arrived in the vicinity of the city of Plataia, they made a surprise attack, which caught most of the Plataians out in the countryside. These were seized and carried off by the cavalry. The rest fled to the city, but, bereft of allies, they were compelled to concede to terms that were greatly in favour of their enemy. For they had to agree to leave the city, taking their movable possessions with them, and never to set foot in Boiotia again.[1016]

Factional strife also breaks out on Kerkyra

Plataia, an Athenian ally, is razed to the ground by the Thebans

1012 Xenophon omits all these indications of Spartan aggressive intent.
1013 From Zakynthos, that is. Ktesikles' first objective was Zakynthos. The order of events is different in Xenophon (*Hell.* 6.2.10–11), where Ktesikles is sent out to Kerkyra in response to Mnasippos' invasion, which Diod. describes below in the next chapter.
1014 At this point there is no evidence that the Plataians had an alliance with Athens. True, they had a long-standing relationship with Athens reaching back into the sixth century, when they put their state in Athenian hands as a result of their fear of Theban aggression (Herodotos, 6.108–111). They famously honoured that relationship, by being the only people to fight with Athens at the Battle of Marathon in 490. Later, they suffered the destruction of their city by Thebes and Sparta at the beginning of the Peloponnesian War (Thuc. 2.71–78, 3.20–24, 3.52–68), and the survivors fled to Athens, where they were granted citizenship (see n. 1018). However, after the King's Peace, it was the Spartans, out of hostility to Thebes, who resettled Plataia (Pausanias, 9.1.4), and the Plataians had been their allies since that time.
1015 The elected generals of the Boiotian League. See Glossary.
1016 Most details of this narrative are confirmed by Pausanias (9.1.7–8), except that he describes the terms of surrender as one cloak for a man and two for a woman and dates the event to the archonship of Asteios (373/2). The fate of Plataia is briefly alluded to by Xenophon (*Hell.* 6.3.1), but evoked a major outburst from Isokrates in his *Plataïkos*.

6. Following that, after razing Plataia to the ground, the Thebans plundered Thespiai,[1017] which was disaffected towards them. The Plataians, with their wives and children, fled to Athens, where they were granted full rights of citizenship [*isopolity*] as an act of kindness from the *demos*.[1018] And that was the situation regarding affairs in Boiotia.

The Spartans send Mnasippos to help the oligarchs on Kerkyra

47.1 The Lakedaimonians appointed Mnasippos as general and sent him out to Kerkyra with sixty-five triremes[1019] and 1,500 soldiers.[1020] After landing on the island and picking up the exiles, he sailed into the harbour, where he captured four ships. Three remaining ships fled to shore. These were set on fire by the Kerkyraians to prevent their falling into the hands of the enemy. Mnasippos also won an infantry victory against a group on land, which had occupied a hill,[1021] and on the whole he instilled much fear amongst the Kerkyraians.[1022]

Timotheos is appointed to aid the Kerkyraians, but sails off to Thrace instead. The demos is angry but relents when he arrives with new allies and ships

2. Long before this the Athenians had dispatched Timotheos, the son of Konon, with sixty triremes to bring aid to the Kerkyraians,[1023] but before undertaking this assignment, he had sailed to Thrace.[1024] There he invited many cities into the Athenian alliance and acquired an additional thirty triremes. 3. At that time, because he was late in fulfilling his assignment to aid the Kerkyraians, the Athenian *demos* was initially displeased, and deprived him of his command.[1025] But, when he sailed home along the coast to Athens, bringing a great number of ambassadors from cities ready to become allies and an additional thirty triremes, and moreover with his whole fleet well decked out for war, the People changed their mind and appointed him back again as

---

1017 Another state in Boiotia that resisted Theban aggression.
1018 The Plataians had been granted some form of Athenian citizenship in 427 (Thuc. 3.55.3) and now must have received somewhat the same treatment as had been accorded to the Samians in 405 (*IG* II² 1; *TDGR*1, no. 166; R&O, no. 2). For some restrictions, see Demosthenes 59, *Against Neaira*, 105–106.
1019 Sixty, according to Xenophon (*Hell.* 6.2.3).
1020 This was the number of the mercenaries and excluded the Spartan troops, according to Xenophon (*Hell.* 6.2.5).
1021 None of these details is mentioned by Xenophon, who devotes more space to describing the lushness of the countryside, the luxuriousness of the houses and the great quality of the wine (*Hell.* 6.2.6–8).
1022 Because they were under siege by land and by sea (Xen. *Hell.* 6.2.8).
1023 Following the preparations begun at 15.46.3. Xenophon (*Hell.* 6.2.11) agrees about the number of ships.
1024 Diod. is seriously at fault here. Timotheos did not sail to Thrace at this time. His expedition to Thrace, in which he won over states in the Khalkidike and even Pydna in Macedon was in the 360s (cf. 15.81.6, and Demosthenes 23, *Against Aristokrates*, 149–151). This time he sailed to the islands to hire crew (Xen. *Hell.* 6.2.12).
1025 Cf. Xen. *Hell.* 6.2.13.

general.¹⁰²⁶ 4. The Athenians were getting ready another forty triremes so that their whole fleet was 130. They were also making impressive preparations for supplies of food, missiles and all the other necessities of war. For the time being, however, they chose Ktesikles as general, and sent him out with 500 troops to help the Kerkyraians.¹⁰²⁷ 5. He secretly sailed into Kerkyra without being detected by the besiegers.¹⁰²⁸ Then, finding that the residents were at odds with each other politically and were doing a bad job of conducting the war, he put an end to their disputes and, by giving great attention to the city's affairs, he raised the courage of the besieged. 6. His first action was to make a surprise attack against the besiegers that killed about 200 of them; then, when later a major battle took place, he killed Mnasippos and not a few of his men. Eventually, he earned great praise, by turning the besiegers into the besieged.¹⁰²⁹ 7. When the fighting over Kerkyra was already almost at an end, the Athenian fleet sailed in, under the command of Timotheos and Iphikrates.¹⁰³⁰ Since they arrived too late, they achieved nothing of note, except that they did chance to meet and capture nine Sicilian triremes¹⁰³¹ and their crew, under the command of Kissides and Krinippos,¹⁰³² that had been sent by Dionysios to help the Lakedaimonians.¹⁰³³ The sale of the captured men as booty¹⁰³⁴ netted them more than sixty *talents*, which they used to pay the wages of their troops. 8. Contemporaneous with these events, in Cyprus, the eunuch Nikokles¹⁰³⁵

Ktesikles, Athenian general on Kerkyra, defeats and kills Mnasippos

The Athenian fleet arrives at Kerkyra too late and achieves little, except to capture nine triremes sent by Dionysios

In Cyprus, Evagoras is assassinated by Nikokles. In Italy, the Romans attack Praeneste

1026 This is not the case. Timotheos was prosecuted by Kallistratos and Iphikrates, tried, but acquitted. Nevertheless, he was not reappointed. Instead, he left Athens and went to work for the Great King, while Iphikrates was appointed general in his place (Xen. *Hell*. 6.2.13-14; Demosthenes 49, *Against Timotheos*, 9–11, 25–28).
1027 Either this is a repetition of the information in 15.46.3 or Ktesikles had returned from Zakynthos and was sent out again.
1028 Cf. Xen. *Hell*. 6.2.11, who says they were transported from the mainland by Alketas of Molossia, at the request of Athens.
1029 Xenophon's lengthy description of the battle and the death of Mnasippos (*Hell*. 6.2.15-23) makes no mention of Ktesikles.
1030 Just Iphikrates. Timotheos was not there.
1031 Xenophon (*Hell*. 6.2.33–35) says there were ten ships, but one, captained by Melanippos of Rhodes, escaped.
1032 Xenophon (*Hell*. 6.2.36), mentions only Krinippos, who, he says, committed suicide.
1033 At the request of Sparta (Xen. *Hell*. 6.2.4).
1034 According to Xen. *Hell*. 6.2.36–37, they were not sold but ransomed, while Iphikrates' men earned their wages by working on the land. Possibly, however, Iphikrates made the 60 *talents* by selling expensive dedications that Dionysios was sending on these ships to Olympia and Delphi (Diod. 16.57.2-3).
1035 More confusion here. Nikokles was a son of Evagoras and his successor on the throne. An even more confusing reference to this obscure event is found in Theopompos (*FGrHist/BNJ* 115 F103), who says that a person called Nikokreon plotted against Evagoras, was detected

assassinated Evagoras, the king, and assumed the throne of Salamis. Also, in Italy, the Romans drew up for battle against the people of Praeneste, defeated them and cut to pieces most of their opponents.[1036]

373/2: Book 15.48.1–49.6

An earthquake and tsunami occur in the Gulf of Corinth, destroying the towns of Helike and Boura

48.1. In the archonship at Athens of Asteios,[1037] in place of the consuls the Romans appointed six military tribunes, Marcus Furius, Lucius Furius and also Aulus Postumius, Lucius Lucretius and Marcus Fabius and Lucius Postumius.[1038] In their term of office cities and countryside alike throughout the Peloponnese were hit by massive earthquakes and incredible tidal waves.[1039] Such disasters had never befallen the cities of Greece in times past, and never had whole cities disappeared with all their people. It was as though some divine force had devised the death and destruction of mankind. 2. And the timing of the event increased the magnitude of the disaster. For, the earthquake did not happen during the day, when it was possible for the endangered to help themselves, but the tragedy happened during the night.[1040] The houses collapsed and were destroyed by the magnitude of the quake and the people were unable to find any source of safety in the darkness, because of the unprecedented and surprising nature of the situation. 3. More than half the population disappeared, buried under the fallen debris of their houses. When day broke, some dashed out of their homes in the belief that they had escaped the danger, only to find themselves in an even greater and more unusual peril. For, when the sea rose up to a great height and created a huge wave, the people and their ancestral homeland were all lost, submerged under the water.[1041] This tragedy struck two cities in Akhaia, Helike[1042] and

---

and fled, leaving his daughter behind. A eunuch, Thrasydaios, arranged for both Evagoras and his son, Pnytagoras, to sleep with her and somehow used this to bring about their death. Theopompos' version is somewhat supported by Aristotle, *Politics*, 5.8.10.1311b.

1036 Cf. Livy, 6.27.6–29, who, however, narrates the war under the next year (Varronian 380), giving most of the names of the tribunes that Diod. lists at 50.1.
1037 For Asteios, see Develin, *AO*, 245.
1038 The same names are given by Livy (6.22.5) under the year 381 with the addition of the *cognomina* of the Postumii (Regillensis), of Marcus Fabius (Ambustus) and Marcus Furius (Camillus).
1039 Aristotle, *Meteorologika*, 1.6.343b, Strabo, 8.7.2 C384 and Pausanias, 7.25.4 confirm the date of this disaster as the archonship of Asteios.
1040 This same point is made by Strabo, 8.7.2 C385, citing Herakleides Pontikos.
1041 The tsunami was an aftereffect of the earthquake.
1042 Helike was situated on the coast of the Gulf of Corinth, east of Aigion. It was wiped out by the tsunami (Strabo, 1.3.18 C59) and submerged. Pausanias (7.24.13) claims that one could still see the underwater remains of Helike in his time (late second century AD). See Map 11.

Boura.[1043] Before the earthquake, Helike happened to be the Akhaian city with the highest reputation.[1044] 4. These disasters have been the subject of much speculation. The natural scientists try to trace the causes of such tragedies back to certain inevitable natural circumstances rather than to divine intervention, while those of a pious disposition in religious matters put forward some persuasive reasons for the event, claiming that the disaster was the result of divine anger against the impious.[1045] We, too, will attempt to give a detailed discussion on this topic in another part of my history.[1046]

Different explanations for these phenomena are put forward by scientists and the religious

49.1. In Ionia there were nine cities that used to hold a common meeting, called the Panionia, and to join together to offer extravagant sacrifices of ancient origin to Poseidon in an uninhabited area near the place called Mykale.[1047] But later, because they were unable to hold the Panionia in those parts due to conflicts that had arisen, they changed the venue of the festival to a safe location near Ephesos. They sent a sacred delegation to Pytho (the oracular priestess) in Delphi and received an oracular response, telling them to get copies of the ancient altars,[1048] that belonged to their forefathers, from Helike in Ionia, as it was called then, but is now Akhaia.[1049] 2. So, in accordance with the oracle, the Ionians sent men to Akhaia to get the copies. These presented their case to the federation of the Akhaians[1050] and persuaded them

The destruction of Helike and Boura is punishment for not obeying the Delphic Oracle

---

1043 Boura was situated further east, closer to Aigai. It was also 40 *stades* inland (Strabo, 8.7.5 C386) and in the mountains. It was destroyed by the earthquake (Strabo,1.3.18 C59) and not affected by the tsunami, although see Seneca, *Quaestiones Naturales*, 7.16.2 and Ephoros (*FGrHist* 70 F212). See Map 11.

1044 It was, indeed, probably the oldest city in Akhaia, and the one from which tradition recorded the Ionians took flight from the Peloponnese, after being defeated by the Akhaians (Herodotos, 1.145; Strabo, 8.7.4 C385).

1045 The disagreement between science and religion goes back a long way and is still with us today. Diod. obviously sides with religion, as do Strabo (8.7.2 C385) and Pausanias (7.25.1), both of whom attribute the disaster to the vengeance of Poseidon, the Earth-Shaker. On the side of science is Aristotle (*Meteorologika*, 1.1.343b, 1.7.344b). Plutarch (*Per.* 6) wisely points out that both the scientist and the prophet have their separate functions.

1046 Diod. fulfills this promise at 16.61–64.

1047 Herodotos has a long discourse on the Ionians in Book 1.141.4–148.2. He names twelve (not nine) cities at 1.142.3–4 and describes the sanctuary of Helikian Poseidon at Mykale at 1.148.1–2.

1048 According to Strabo, 8.7.2 C385, they asked for the statue of Poseidon or a model of the temple.

1049 The same observation in Herodotos, 1.146.1.

1050 No specific date for this embassy can be arrived at, but it may not have been too many years before the disaster of 373/2. In any case, the Akhaian federation was already in existence by the beginning of the fourth century, if not before (see n. 575).

to grant their request. But the inhabitants of Helike, because they had an old saying that they would be in danger if ever the Ionians sacrificed on the altar of Poseidon, considered the meaning of the oracle and refused the Ionians' request for the copies, saying that the sanctuary was not the common property of the Akhaians, but belonged to them alone. And the inhabitants of Boura sided with them in this. 3. But, since the Akhaians in their joint decision had granted them permission, the Ionians offered sacrifice on the altar of Poseidon in accordance with the oracle. The people of Helike, however, scattered the Ionians' possessions and seized their delegates, thus committing an act of impiety against the divinity. In response to these acts, they say that Poseidon, in his anger, wreaked havoc on the impious cities by the earthquake and the tsunami.[1051] 4. They say that there exist clear proofs that it was Poseidon's anger towards the cities: first, there is the fact that it is believed that this god has the power over earthquakes and tsunamis; then, because it is an age-old opinion that the Peloponnese was one of Poseidon's residences and the whole territory is considered, as it were, sacred to him; finally, because, in general, all the cities in the Peloponnese honour this god above the other immortals. 5. Furthermore, they say that the Peloponnese has huge caverns under its surface and great accumulations of running water.[1052] In fact, it possesses two rivers that clearly flow underground. One river vanished some time ago, descending into the earth near Pheneos,[1053] where it is stored in caves underground, the other descends into a chasm near Stymphalos and flows for 200 *stades*, hidden under the earth, until it surfaces near the city of Argos.[1054] 6. In addition to these arguments, they point out that no one else, apart from those who committed the sacrilege, suffered from the disaster.[1055] Now, we shall consider sufficient what we have said on the subject of earthquakes and tsunamis.

1051 See n. 1045.
1052 Diod. is describing the phenomenon of the *katavothrai* (sinkholes), which are numerous in the Peloponnese. Some of the most important are located in the plain of Tripoli, between Mantineia and Tegea, and in Corinthia.
1053 This is the river Ladon in Arkadia. According to Pausanias (8.20.1), the water of Lake Pheneos descends into a *katavothra* in the mountains and reappears as a spring that is the source of the Ladon. The Ladon flows into the Alpheios. See Map 11.
1054 The river Stymphalos, arising from Lake Stymphalos, "sinks into a chasm and surfaces in the Argolid as the river Erasinos" (Pausanias, 8.22.3). Cf. Herodotos, 6.76.1 and Strabo, 6.2.9 C275, 8.6.8 C371, 8.8.4 C389.
1055 Aelian, *De Natura Animalium*, 11.19, says that a Spartan squadron of ten ships was in port at Helike at the time and was also destroyed.

50.1. In the archonship at Athens of Alkisthenes,[1056] in place of the consuls the Romans appointed eight military tribunes, Lucius and Publius Valerius, and also Gaius Terentius and Lucius Menenius, and in addition to these Gaius Sulpicius and Titus Papirius and Lucius Aemilius,[1057] and the Eleians celebrated the one hundred and second Olympiad, in which Damon of Thourioi[1058] won the *stadion*. 2. In their term of office, after the Lakedaimonians had maintained their supremacy over Greece for almost 500 years,[1059] a divine omen was sent them, predicting the loss of their domination. For, a large fiery torch was seen in the sky for many nights, which was given the name "burning beam" from its shape. And, a little later the Spartiates were surprisingly defeated in a major battle and unexpectedly lost their position of leadership.[1060] 3. Some of the natural scientists have related the genesis of the torch to natural causes, explaining that such apparitions occur inevitably at defined times and that the Khaldaians in Babylon and other astrologers are successful in making accurate predictions. They say that these astrologers are not surprised when some such event occurs, but rather when it does not, basing their predictions upon the individual circuits of each object as they are completed in perpetual movements over defined courses. Anyway, they say that this torch was so bright and its light so powerful that it cast a shadow on the earth similar to the moon's. 4. During these times Artaxerxes, the King, seeing that Greece was once again in a state of turmoil, sent out ambassadors, encouraging the Greeks to settle their inter-state conflicts and agree to a Common Peace on the same terms as they had made peace before.[1061] All the Greeks were happy to accept his appeal,

372/1: Book 15.50.1–50.6

A comet in the sky predicts the end of Spartan supremacy

Some natural scientists claim they can predict such phenomena

Artaxerxes encourages the Greek cities to make a new Common Peace; all agree, except the Thebans

---

1056 For Alkisthenes see Develin, *AO*, 247.
1057 See n. 1036. Promising eight, Diodoros gives only seven. Some of these agree with the six named by Livy (6.27.2). These are Lucius and Publius Valerius, Lucius Menenius and Publius (rather than Titus) Papirius. Livy also names Gaius Sergius and Servius Cornelius Maluginensis. The *Fasti Capitolini*, which has an entry for this year (Varronian 380), lists nine names that combine those in Livy and in Diod. The Gaius Sulpicius mentioned above was a censor for this year, according to Livy, 6.27.4.
1058 He was also victor in the previous Olympiad in 376. See 15.36.1 and Pausanias, 4.27.9, 6.5.3, 8.27.8.
1059 See 15.1.3 and n. 743. Their supremacy was, of course, over the Peloponnese, not the whole of Greece.
1060 As usual Diod. takes the religious and superstitious approach. Aristotle, by contrast, identifies the "burning beam" as a comet (*Meteorologika*, 1.6, 343b). See also Seneca, *Quaestiones Naturales*, 7.5.3. He cites Kallisthenes for the association of the comet with the earthquake and tsunami.
1061 The Peace is dated to 14 Skirophorion (*c.* mid-June) by Plutarch (*Ages.* 28.5). On the negotiations for the Peace of 372/1 see also Xen. *Hell.* 6.3.1–20 and Plut. *Ages.* 27.4–28.2. As noted, the wording here bears a very strong resemblance to the description of the Peace of

and the cities unanimously concluded a Common Peace, with the exception of the Thebans. For, the Thebans alone, since they were keeping Boiotia united in a federation, were not admitted by the Greeks, because of their unanimous desire to take the oaths and the treaty-libations city by city. So, the Thebans were excluded from the peace treaty, just as previously, and kept Boiotia united in one federation under their control. 5. The Lakedaimonians were enraged at this and resolved to lead a campaign against them with a large army, alleging that they were the enemy of all Greeks. In fact, they were extremely suspicious of the rise of Thebes, out of fear that, as leaders of a united Boiotia, they might put an end to Spartan leadership, if they got the chance.[1062] For the Thebans possessed great strength of body, as a result of spending all their time exercising, and, since they were instinctively warlike, they were second to none amongst the Greeks in acts of courage. 6. Furthermore, they had many generals who were distinguished for their courage, and especially their three greatest, Epameinondas, Gorgidas[1063] and also Pelopidas. The city of Thebes prided itself on the illustrious part its ancestors had played in the days of the Heroes[1064] and had high aspirations. So, the Lakedaimonians spent this year preparing for war and enlisted soldiers from amongst their own citizens and from their allies.

The Lakedaimonians, fearing the rise of Theban confidence, prepare for war

371/0: Book 15.51.1–56.4

51.1. In the archonship at Athens of Phrasikleides,[1065] in place of the consuls the Romans appointed eight military tribunes, Publius Manius, Gaius Erenucius

375/4 in 15.38 and as a result people have accused Diodoros of repeating himself. But see n. 971. In addition to the points made there, note that Diodoros is clearly aware that this was a second negotiation by his reference to the Thebans being "excluded from the peace treaty, just as previously." Diodoros clearly felt that the factors contributing to the making of peace were the same as in 375, with the exception that the King was not motivated by a need for mercenaries to invade Egypt in 372/1. That the King may also, however, have been involved in these peace negotiations is suggested by Dionysios of Halikarnassos, *Lysias*, 12.

1062 Sparta was jealous of her supremacy in Greece and fearful of challengers. In the fifth century this fear had been the "truest cause" of the Peloponnesian War (Thuc. 1.23.6) and the rise of Thebes caused a similar reaction in the fourth. This is a point frequently emphasized by Diod. and the rest of the following paragraph repeats the theme of ch. 39. By contrast, Xenophon (*Hell*. 6.3.1) talks only of Athens' fear of Theban power.

1063 See n. 975.

1064 Thebes plays a significant role in the corpus of Greek myths. The stories are too numerous to recount, but they include the myths of Kadmos, Oidipous, the Seven against Thebes and Antigone, not to mention the fact that Semele was a Theban woman, the seduction of whom by Zeus produced Dionysos. The denial of that god's divinity by Pentheus, king of Thebes, led to his dismemberment by the Bakkhants, led by his mother, Agave. The blind prophet, Teiresias, central to so many stories, was also from Thebes. Finally, the most important hero in Diod.'s early books, Herakles, was born to Alkmene and Zeus at Thebes.

1065 For Phrasikleides see Develin, *AO*, 248.

and Gaius Sesteus [or Sextus], Tiberius Julius, and also Lucius Labinius and Publius Tribonius and Gaius Manlius, and in addition Lucius Anthestius.[1066] In their term of office the Thebans had to undertake the war against the Lakedaimonians on their own, since they had been excluded from the peace treaty. For, no city could fight on their side, because they were all signatories to the Common Peace (*Koine Eirene*). 2. Taking advantage of the isolation of the Thebans, the Lakedaimonians decided to make war upon them and to reduce the city to slavery. Since the Lakedaimonian preparations were out in the open and the Thebans were without allies, everyone expected them to be easily overwhelmed by the Spartiates. 3. So, any Greeks who were well disposed to the Thebans shared their suffering at the impending disaster, while those who were at odds with them were overjoyed at the thought that the Thebans would very soon be enslaved. Finally, once the Lakedaimonians had finished preparing a huge army, they put king Kleombrotos in command of it.[1067] But first, they sent ahead ambassadors to Thebes, ordering them to allow all the cities in Boiotia to govern themselves with their own laws, to repopulate Plataia and Thespiai and to restore the land to its former owners. 4. The Thebans replied that they did not meddle in Lakonian affairs and it was not the Spartans' business to get involved in Boiotia.[1068] Since that was their response, the Lakedaimonians immediately sent Kleombrotos out with the army to attack Thebes. And the allies of the Lakedaimonians were enthusiastic about the war,[1069] in the expectation that there would be neither contest nor battle, but that they would become masters of Boiotia without a struggle.

The Spartans prepare to attack an isolated Thebes

The Spartans deliver an ultimatum to Thebes, but it is rejected

52.1. So, the Lakedaimonians advanced and, when they reached Khaironeia,[1070] they pitched camp to wait for those amongst their allies who were late. In view

The Spartans encamp at Koroneia. The Thebans give Epameinondas command of their forces

---

1066 Livy (6.30.2) has only six tribunes, three patrician, three plebeian. They are: Publius and Gaius Manlius, Lucius Julius, Gaius Sextilius, Marcus Albinius and Lucius Antistius. This year is 379 by the Varronian chronology.
1067 Diod. clearly thought that Kleombrotos was at home in Sparta and led the army from there, but our other sources insist that he was in Phokis and invaded Boiotia from the west, see Xen. *Hell.* 6.4.2–3; Plut. *Ages.* 28.3; Pausanias, 9.13.1.
1068 A somewhat similar version of this exchange, only between Agesilaos and Epameinondas at Sparta, is given by Plut. *Ages.* 28.1.
1069 Other sources (e.g. Plut. *Ages.* 28.5; Pausanias, 9.13.9) claim the Spartan allies were reluctant.
1070 This is the reading of the mss. Wesseling suggested it should be changed to "Koroneia" and his suggestion has been adopted by Vial, Vögel, Sherman in the Loeb, and most analysts of the campaign. A strong case can, however, be made for Khaironeia, since Kleombrotos was approaching from Phokis and we are told below (15.52.7) that Epameinondas reached Koroneia before Kleombrotos.

Bad omens appear for the Thebans as they exit, but Epameinondas dismisses them

of the enemy's presence, the Thebans voted to send their wives and children to Athens for safety,[1071] then they chose Epameinondas as their general and entrusted the management of the war to him, with six Boiotarchs as his assistants. 2. Epameinondas recruited for the battle all the Thebans of military age and those Boiotians who were fit and able. He prepared to lead his army out of Thebes, having no more than 6,000 men in total.[1072] 3. As the soldiers were on their way out of the city, many thought they witnessed omens that were unfavourable for the army. Near the gates Epameinondas and his entourage were met by a blind herald, who was, in the customary fashion, making proclamation about runaway slaves, telling people not to take them out of Thebes nor keep them concealed, but to bring them home and keep them safe.[1073] 4. Well, the older members amongst the herald's audience took this as an omen for the future, but the younger men kept silent, so that they might not be thought to be trying to deter Epameinondas from the campaign out of cowardice. As for Epameinondas, his response to those who were telling him that he ought to pay attention to the omens was: "One omen is best, to fight in defence of the fatherland."[1074] 5. With this blunt statement Epameinondas silenced the superstitious, but then another omen appeared, more unfavourable than the first. For, when the secretary[1075] came forward, holding a spear with a ribbon attached to it, and began announcing the instructions from the generals, a wind blew up, snatched away the ribbon and set it around a pillar that stood on a tomb. In this place some Lakedaimonians and Peloponnesians had been buried, men who had died on campaign with Agesilaos.[1076] 6. Once again, some of the older men, who happened to be there, lodged a protest against his leading

1071 This is quite suspect, although Pausanias, 9.13.6, mentions the idea as a possibility broached by some Boiotarchs before the battle (below at 15.53.3). Although Thebes was still technically a member of the Athenian Confederacy, relations between them had been frosty since the destruction of Plataia in 373 and, through the Peace Treaty of 371, Athens was bound to uphold the autonomy clause.

1072 A reasonable figure. Frontinus, *Strategemata*, 4.2.6, says Epameinondas had only 4,000 troops, of whom 400 were cavalry, but in the same sentence he gives Kleombrotos the incredible figure of 24,000 infantry and 1,600 cavalry, surpassed only by Polyainos' 40,000 (*Strategemata*, 2.3.12). The actual Spartan force was probably closer to the figure given by Plutarch (*Pelop*. 20.1), namely, 10,000 infantry and 1,000 cavalry.

1073 The text here is very corrupt. Amongst the various proposals, this is the one that seems most sensible. In addition, the significance of the omen is elusive. It may be, as Sherman suggests in the Loeb, that Thebans, like slaves, should not leave the city.

1074 Epameinondas is quoting a line from Homer's *Iliad* (12.243), spoken by Hektor. There is irony here, of course, since Hektor's denial of the validity of omens was an act of *hubris* and the first step in his downfall.

1075 Of the Boiotarchs, cf. Xen. *Hell.* 5.4.2; Plut. *Pelop.* 7.4.

1076 See 15.34.2.

out the army, since the gods were clearly opposed. But, without saying a word in answer to them, Epameinondas led the army forward, trusting in his belief that calculation of what was good and mindfulness of what was just were preferable motives than the present omens. 7. Indeed, Epameinondas, who was thoroughly schooled in philosophy and used intelligently the lesson of his education, was at that time criticized by many, but later, on account of his successes, he gained a reputation as a military genius and was the cause of very great benefits for his country. Anyway, he led his army forward right away, seized the pass at Koroneia before his opponents and set up camp.

53.1. When Kleombrotos learned that his enemy had seized the pass before him, he rejected the idea of making his way through by that route. He crossed Phokis and, by travelling along the difficult coastal route, entered Boiotia without resistance. On the way he overcame some forts and captured ten triremes.[1077] 2. After that, he reached the area called Leuktra, where he set up camp and gave his soldiers a rest from their travels. The advancing Boiotian forces were getting close to the enemy. When they reached the summit of some hills, they had their first view of the Lakedaimonians, who were covering the entire plain of Leuktra, and they were stricken with fear at the sight of the vastness of their army. 3. The Boiotarchs held a council and deliberated whether they should stay and fight it out against an army many times their size or retreat and engage in battle on higher ground. The opinions of the commanders were equally divided. For, out of the six Boiotarchs, three thought they should withdraw the army, while three thought they should stay and fight it out. Counted amongst the latter was Epameinondas. As they reached this great, unresolvable impasse, the seventh Boiotarch arrived. Epameinondas had persuaded him to vote on his side and so his opinion prevailed. So, it was in this way that the decision to risk everything on battle won the day.[1078] 4. But Epameinondas, realizing that his soldiers were full of superstitious fear on account of the omens that had occurred, tried to use his own wit and strategic

Kleombrotos decides not to contest the pass, but takes a difficult coastal route via Phokis

The Thebans, though frightened by the size of the Spartan army, decide to fight

Epameinondas devises false omens to allay the fears of his soldiers

---

1077 Other sources help elucidate Kleombrotos' route. Pausanias (9.13.2) says he turned through Phokis to Ambrossos, presumably taking the pass between Parnassos and Helikon. Xenophon (*Hell*. 6.4.3) states he went along an unexpected route by a narrow pass to Thisbe and then to Kreusis (i.e. along the coast), where he captured twelve (not ten) triremes and thence up to the plain of Leuktra. These details would fit well with the reading "Khaironeia" (above at n. 1070). See Map 10. For the topography of the battle see Pritchett (1965), 49–58; Buckler (1980), 46–69.

1078 Pausanias, 9.13.6, provides the names of the Boiotarchs on either side and identifies the man who cast the deciding vote as Brakhylides. Plutarch, *Pelop*. 20.2, by contrast, depicts Pelopidas as the man who broke the tie, even though he admits he was not a Boiotarch at that time.

ability to allay the concerns of the rank and file. So, he persuaded some men who had recently arrived from Thebes to say that the weapons in the temple of Herakles had unexpectedly gone missing and that the story going around Thebes was that the Heroes of old had retrieved them and had set out to help the Boiotians.[1079] He also set up another person to pretend that he had recently come up from the cave of Trophonios[1080] and to say that the god instructed them, when they were victorious at Leuktra, to establish games in honour of Zeus the King, with crowns as prizes. Indeed, it is on this basis that the Boiotians celebrate this festival at Lebadeia.

Other omens and predictions are produced to stiffen the resolve of the Boiotians

54.1. A collaborator in this plan was a Lakedaimonian exile, the Spartiate Leandrias,[1081] who was at that time serving in the Theban army. He was led before the Assembly, where he revealed that there was an old saying amongst the Spartiates, that they would lose their position of leadership at the time when they were defeated at Leuktra by the Thebans. 2. Further, some local soothsayers approached Epameinondas with the message that the Lakedaimonians could not avoid suffering a huge tragedy at the tomb of the daughters of Leuktros and Skedasos. The following was their reason.[1082] 3. Leuktros was the man after whom the plain was named. His daughters and also the girls of a certain Skedasos were raped by some Lakedaimonian ambassadors. The violated girls did not put up with this outrage, but called down curses upon the country that had sent out their violators and then ended their lives by their own hand. 4. Many other stories of a similar nature were told and, when Epameinondas convened an Assembly and delivered his own speech, encouraging the soldiers to battle, they all changed their minds, gave up their superstitious fear and

---

1079 Virtually the same report is given by Xenophon, *Hell.* 6.4.7, although he mentions only Herakles.

1080 Trophonios was a chthonic deity, who prophesied from an underground cave near Lebadeia (modern Livadhia). The oracle was already well enough known to have been consulted by Kroisos before his battle against Kyros the Great in 546 (Herodotos, 1.46.2). The elaborate consultation process is described by Pausanias, 9.39–40.2. See also Plutarch, *De Genio Socratis*, *Moralia*, 590a–592e.

1081 This person is unknown, and the anecdote is not reported elsewhere.

1082 This story is also reported by Xenophon (*Hell.* 6.4.7), without names, and by Pausanias (9.13.3), who gives the names of the girls as Molpia and Hippo, and of the offending Spartans as Phrourarkhidas and Parthenios. He states, however, that the girls were the daughters of Skedasos ("the one who scatters"), and that he committed suicide over their tomb on receiving no satisfaction from Sparta. The same version is given by Plutarch, *Pelop.* 20.3–4, although he adds a strange story that Pelopidas saw the girls in a dream, weeping over their tomb, and that Skedasos urged him to sacrifice a red-haired virgin to them. After much debate about the propriety of such an act, a chestnut filly suddenly appeared, whose sacrifice conveniently met the requirement (*Pelop.* 21.1–22.2). See also Plutarch, *Moralia*, 773c–774d.

became confidently ready for the battle. 5. At that time also an allied force of Thessalians arrived to help the Thebans, comprising 1,500 infantry and 500 cavalry, under the leadership of Jason.[1083] He persuaded the Boiotians and the Lakedaimonians to conclude a truce to guard against the unpredictable nature of Chance (*Tykhe*).[1084] 6. Once the truce was concluded, Kleombrotos was withdrawing his army from Boiotia when he met another large force of Lakedaimonians and their allies, led by Arkhidamos, son of Agesilaos.[1085] For, when the Spartiates saw how prepared the Boiotians were, in an effort to guard against their desperate boldness, they had dispatched this second army, so that by the sheer number of their warriors they might overcome their enemy's daring. 7. After the armies had combined, the Lakedaimonians decided it was disgraceful to be afraid of the Boiotians' courage. So, disregarding the truce, they turned back to Leuktra full of enthusiasm.[1086] Since the Boiotians, too, were ready for battle, both sides deployed their troops.[1087]

Jason, tyrant of Pherai, negotiates an armistice between the opposing sides, but the arrival of a second Spartan army brings about the battle

55.1. On the Lakedaimonian side the descendants of Herakles, namely king Kleombrotos and Arkhidamos, son of Agesilaos,[1088] took up their position as commanders on the wings, while on the Boiotian side Epameinondas deployed his own unusual battle-line and by virtue of his original strategy brought about his celebrated victory. 2. For, he selected the bravest men from his whole army and placed them on one wing, where he also intended to fight. The weakest members he stationed on the other wing, with orders to avoid engagement and to yield to the enemy's attack gradually. And so, by keeping his *phalanx* on a slant, he planned to decide the battle on the wing that had the chosen troops.[1089] 3. When the trumpets on both sides gave the call to battle and the

The Spartans line up in traditional fashion, but Epameinondas adopts a new oblique formation

The massed Theban wing wears down the Spartans opposed to them and finally kills Kleombrotos

1083 For Jason, see n. 916. Diod. is incorrect in claiming that Jason arrived before the battle. See Xen. *Hell.* 6.4.20f.
1084 Jason did help negotiate a truce between the Thebans and Spartans, but after the battle (Xen. *Hell.* 6.4.22–25).
1085 Despite the detailed nature of Diod.'s account, it is contradicted by Xenophon, who states that Arkhidamos and his army were sent out after the news of the defeat had reached Sparta. He met the soldiers returning from Leuktra and led them home (Xen. *Hell.* 6.4.17–18, 26).
1086 None of this is supported by any other source.
1087 Plutarch, *Ages.* 28.5, dates the battle to the fifth of Hekatombaion, which would normally equate to sometime late in June or early in July.
1088 In addition to the notes above, no mention is ever made of Arkhidamos' presence in the battle, even by Diodoros.
1089 This is a description of Epameinondas' tactical innovation that was to be so influential in subsequent battles. By massing his best troops on one wing (the left), according to Xen. *Hell.* 6.4.12, fifty men deep, and by withholding his other troops from combat, he successfully disrupted the enemy line.

armies shouted the paian as they rushed to engage, the Lakedaimonians advanced on both wings with a crescent-shaped formation, while the Boiotians gave way on one wing, but joined in battle with the enemy at the run on the other. 4. When the conflict came to close quarters, at first both sides fought spiritedly and the battle was evenly balanced, but after some time Epameinondas' men gained the advantage through their valour and the dense weight of their *phalanx*, and many Peloponnesians began to perish. For, they could not stand up under the indomitable pressure of the bravery of the elite troops [i.e. the Sacred Band]. Some of those who resisted them were killed, others were wounded in face-to-face combat. 5. As long as Kleombrotos, the Lakedaimonian king, was alive, surrounded by his large bodyguard of shield-bearers who were willing to die for him, the outcome of the battle hung in the balance, but when, after enduring multiple dangers in his unsuccessful attempt to repel his opponents, he died fighting heroically, covered in wounds, then, indeed, as many gathered to fight over his corpse, a huge pile of dead bodies resulted.

The Lakedaimonians resist bravely and secure their king's body, but are eventually routed

56.1. Now that the wing was without a leader, Epameinondas' troops pushed hard against the Lakedaimonians and, at first, forced their opponents back a little off their line, but the Lakedaimonians fought brilliantly about their king and succeeded in gaining possession of his body. They were not, however, strong enough to achieve victory. 2. For, since the elite corps surpassed them in acts of bravery under the powerful effect of Epameinondas' courage and exhortation, after a hard fight the Lakedaimonians were forced to yield. First, in their retreat, they broke their line,[1090] then, in the end, as many were killed and the commander to rally them was dead, a full-scale rout of the army followed.[1091] 3. Epameinondas'

The Thebans win great praise for defeating the previously undefeated Spartans

1090 So the mss, followed by Vial. Others want the Spartans to "maintain" their line (Vögel) or, at least, not break it (Sherman).

1091 The main sources for the Battle of Leuktra, in addition to Diod., are Xen. *Hell.* 6.4.8–15; Plut. *Pelop.* 23 and Pausanias, 9.13.8–14. There are brief references in Nepos (*Pelopidas*) and Deinarkhos and several anecdotes in Polyainos and Frontinus. While they agree on some basic points, i.e. Epameinondas' oblique line, the importance of Kleombrotos' death as a turning point and the great fight over his body, there are major differences: (1) Plutarch stresses the role Pelopidas and the Sacred Band played in the Theban victory. His involvement is briefly mentioned by Nepos, *Pelopidas*, 4.2, and there is a passing reference in Deinarkhos, 1.73. None of the main sources mention his presence, although Diod. was not unaware of his significant contribution (see 15.81.2). Xenophon does not even name Epameinondas. (2) Only Xenophon mentions a cavalry engagement that took place at the beginning of the battle, in which the superior Boiotian cavalry drove the inferior Spartan cavalry back into their own line, causing confusion. (3) Only Xenophon puts the blame for the Spartan defeat on the mistakes of Kleombrotos. See n. 1077. For the epigram celebrating the Theban victory and commemorating the Boiotarch Xenokrates (*IG* VII 2462) see *TDGR2*, no. 46; R&O, no. 30.

men pursued the fugitives, cutting down many of their opponents, and carried off a most illustrious victory. For, in joining battle with the bravest of the Greeks and with few men, unexpectedly getting the better of a force many times their number,[1092] they acquired a great reputation for courage. But their general, Epameinondas, was accorded the greatest praise for defeating the previously unconquered leaders of Greece primarily through his own individual courage and his military acumen.[1093] 4. No fewer than 4,000 Lakedaimonians fell in this battle,[1094] and about 300 Boiotians.[1095] Afterwards, a truce was arranged, allowing for the collecting of corpses and the return of the Lakedaimonians to the Peloponnese. Such was the conclusion of events related to the Battle at Leuktra.[1096]

57.1. Once the year had come to an end, Dysniketos[1097] became archon at Athens; in Rome, in place of the consuls, they appointed four military tribunes, Quintus Servilius and Lucius Furius, and also Gaius Licinius and Publius Coelius.[1098] In their term of office the Thebans campaigned with a large army against Orkhomenos.[1099] Their objective was to reduce the city to slavery, but, on Epameinondas' advice, they changed their mind. He advised them, if they were aiming for the leadership of the Greeks, to preserve by generosity what they had gained by courage. So, they assigned the Orkhomenians to the political status[1100] of the allies. Next, they secured the friendship of the Phokians, Aitolians and the Lokrians, and then made their way back to Boiotia.[1101]

370/69: Book 15.57.1–60.6

The Thebans campaign against Orkhomenos and in central Greece

Jason's campaigns in Lokris and Perrhaibia make other Thessalians suspicious of his power

1092 For the numbers, see n. 1072.
1093 Plutarch, *Pelop.* 23.4, claims that Pelopidas won as much glory as Epameinondas.
1094 An inflated figure. Xen. *Hell.* 6.4.15 gives the more realistic figure of 1,000 Lakedaimonians, of whom 400 were Spartiates. Cf. Plut. *Ages.* 28.5; Pausanias, 9.13.12.
1095 Only 47, according to Pausanias, 9.13.12.
1096 Xen. *Hell.* 6.5.1–3 reports a peace treaty that was negotiated in Athens, following the Battle of Leuktra. The participants appear to have been the members of the Athenian Confederacy and the Peloponnesian League. The Boiotians were surely not present. The treaty was a reaffirmation of the independence and autonomy clause of the King's Peace. No mention of this treaty is made by Diodoros.
1097 For Dysniketos of Phlya see Develin, *AO*, 250.
1098 Livy (6.31.2) gives six names: Spurius Furius, Quintus Servilius, Lucius Menenius, Publius Cloelius, Marcus Horatius and Lucius Geganius. This is the Varronian year 378.
1099 A major town in northern Boiotia (see Map 10), whose oligarchic government was resistant to Theban expansion. The Thebans finally destroyed the city in 364 (15.79.3–6).
1100 I.e. they enrolled Orkhomenos into the Boiotian Confederacy. So, Vial in the Budé, changing the senseless reading "city" (πόλιν), given by most mss, into πολιτείαν. Other editors adopt the reading of mss F, "territory" (χώραν) and translate, "assigning the Orkhomenians to the territory of the allies."
1101 Cf. Xen. *Hell.* 6.5.23, where the members of Thebes' army in their first invasion of Lakonia (370/69) include the Phokians (labelled their subjects) and men from both the Ozolian and Opuntian Lokrians, although Xenophon does not mention the Aitolians.

2. Jason, the tyrant of Pherai, who was growing more powerful day by day, led his forces into Lokris[1102] and, after capturing Herakleia in Trakhis[1103] by treachery, he wiped it out and gave the territory as a gift to the Oitaians and the Malians. Next, he invaded Perrhaibia and acquired the allegiance of some cities by persuasion, while he overpowered others by force. Soon, as his dominance strengthened, the inhabitants of Thessaly began to become suspicious of the increase in his power and his ambition.[1104] 3. Contemporaneous with these events, in the city of Argos there was so great a slaughter, caused by factional strife, as has never been recorded in any other Greek city. This revolution was called cudgelling [*skytalismos*] by the Greeks, getting its name from the way in which this murder was perpetrated.

Factional strife at Argos, called "cudgel-rule," causes great slaughter

Demagogues who incited the massacre end up victims

58.1. Well, this strife arose for the following reasons. The city of Argos had a democratic government and some of the popular leaders roused up the crowd against men who had more wealth and prestige than themselves. These men, objects of the attack, joined together and resolved to put an end to the democracy. 2. Some, who were thought to be part of the conspiracy, were condemned to torture. All except one, out of fear of the punishment that would result from the torture, committed suicide. But one, under torture, confessed and, after getting a pledge of immunity, became an informer and made accusations against thirty of the most distinguished citizens. The People, without making an exact investigation of the facts, put the accused to death and confiscated their property. 3. Many others were under suspicion and the popular leaders fanned the flames by false and slanderous allegations. Many of the wealthiest men were accused and the crowd was driven to such a point of savagery that they condemned them all to death. More than 1,200 of the influential citizens were eliminated.[1105] But the crowd did not even spare the popular leaders themselves. 4. For, because of the terrible tragedy, the popular leaders became afraid that some unpredictable turn of events might befall them, and so ceased their prosecutions. The mob became angry at this, thinking they had been abandoned by the popular leaders, and killed them all. So, these men, as if by

---

1102 For Jason's campaign through Lokris and Perrhaibia on his way home from Leuktra, see Xen. *Hell.* 6.4.27–28. For the location of all the places mentioned here see Map 10.
1103 Herakleia in Trakhis was a colony founded by the Spartans in 426 (Thuc. 3.92–93; Diod. 12.59.3–5). It was situated near the Pass of Thermopylai, which it was intended to control. It had a troubled history (see also Thuc. 5.51.1) in its short existence.
1104 As is evidenced by Polydamas of Pharsalos' speech in Sparta earlier (Xen. *Hell.* 6.1.4–16).
1105 Plutarch, *Moralia*, 814b, who also refers to the cudgelling, gives 1,500 as the number of victims.

some divine vengeance, got their just deserts, and the People ceased their mad conflict and were restored to their previous good sense.[1106]

59.1. About the same time, Lykomedes of Tegea[1107] persuaded the Arkadians to organize as a single confederacy and to hold joint meetings composed of 10,000 men, who had the power to make decisions on war and peace.[1108] 2. But, this created a major incident of factional strife amongst the Arkadians[1109] and they took to settling their differences by force of arms. Many were killed and more than 1,400 fled into exile, some to Sparta, others to Pallantion.[1110] 3. The latter were given back by the Pallantines[1111] and were massacred by the winning party, but those who fled to Sparta[1112] succeeded in persuading the Lakedaimonians to lead an army into Arkadia. 4. Consequently, king Agesilaos invaded the territory of the Tegeans with an army in conjunction with the exiles, because the Tegeans seemed to have been responsible for the civil strife and the flight of the exiles. By ravaging their territory and assaulting the city he inspired fear in the opposition party in Arkadia.[1113]

Lykomedes persuades the Arkadians to form a League

1106 As this story and the one following show all too well, political strife in the Greek city-states, endemic in both the fifth and fourth centuries, was a manifestation of social revolution that resulted from the stress of constant warfare and the class struggle between rich and poor. The exceptional stability of the Athenian democracy in the fourth century was based upon many factors: the reconciliation and the amnesty after the Thirty Tyrants; the Foundation of the Second Confederacy; and the success of its system of wealth distribution in the form of liturgies imposed on the rich.

1107 At 15.62.2 Diod. reveals that Lykomedes was from Mantineia. This fact is confirmed by Xen. *Hell.* 7.1.23 and Pausanias 8.27.2.

1108 Diod. is here giving a very perfunctory reference to the foundation of the Arkadian League or Confederation, probably late in 370. The League had an Assembly of 10,000 men, probably of hoplite rank. This is confirmed not only by literary references (e.g. Xen. *Hell.* 7.1.38; Aiskhines 2, *On the False Embassy*, 79), but also by an inscription (*IG* V (2) 1; *TDGR*2, no. 51; R&O, no. 32) of some time in the 360s. This inscription also provides evidence for a probouleutic council (as in Athens) and a sub-group of fifty officials (*damiorgoi*), who represented ten cities in numbers in proportion to their size. The head of the league was an elected *strategos*.

1109 According to Xen. *Hell*. 6.5.6–10, the factional strife (*stasis*) was restricted to Tegea, where one party, led by Kallibios and Proxenos, was in favour of joining the Arkadian League, another, led by Stasippos, was against.

1110 Pallantion was a small town about 8 km (5 miles) west of Tegea.

1111 Xen. *Hell*. 6.5.9. tells a somewhat different story. It was the anti-League group of Stasippos that fled towards Pallantion and took refuge in the temple of Artemis. They were pelted with tiles from the rooftop and so surrendered. They were led back to Tegea, where they were put to death by the other Tegeans and the Mantineians.

1112 800 members of Stasippos' party, according to Xen. *Hell*. 6.5.10.

1113 A more detailed account of Agesilaos' campaign in Arkadia in the winter of 370/69 is provided by Xen. *Hell*. 6.5.12–21. The campaign was aimed at Mantineia.

Jason of Pherai persuades the Thessalians to claim hegemony over the Greeks under his leadership

But, this year sees the death of Amyntas of Macedon, Agesipolis of Sparta and Jason of Thessaly

Douris of Samos' history

60.1. Contemporaneous with these events, Jason, tyrant of Pherai, by virtue of his excellent command of military matters and by winning over many of his neighbours to alliance, succeeded in persuading the Thessalians to lay claim to hegemony over the Greeks. For, he said it was like a prize of valour ready to be grasped by those who were powerful enough to contest it. 2. Indeed, it so happened that the Lakedaimonians had suffered a great disaster at Leuktra, the Athenians were only aiming at control of the seas, the Thebans were not worthy of the top position and the Argives had been weakened by their murderous class warfare. So, the Thessalians, after first appointing Jason to supreme command,[1114] entrusted him with the conduct of the war. After assuming the leadership, Jason won over to his side some of the neighbouring peoples and concluded an alliance with Amyntas, the Macedonian king.[1115] 3. But, a strange thing happened during this year: three rulers died at almost the same moment. First, Amyntas, son of Arrhidaios,[1116] who was king of the Macedonians, died after a reign of twenty-four years. He left behind three sons, Alexander, Perdikkas and Philip.[1117] His son, Alexander, succeeded to the throne and ruled for one year. 4. Second, Agesipolis, king of the Lakedaimonians, ended his life after ruling for one year.[1118] Kleomenes, his brother, succeeded to the throne and ruled for thirty-four years.[1119] 5. Third, Jason of Pherai, who had been chosen leader of Thessaly and who had a reputation as a fair ruler of his subjects, was assassinated. According to Ephoros' history, he was killed by seven unnamed young conspirators for the sake of honour, but others write that he was killed by his brother, Polydoros.[1120] This very person took over the rule and held it for one year. 6. The historian Douris of Samos began his account of Hellenic affairs from this point.[1121] Well, that is what happened in this year.

1114 This sounds to some like a reference to Jason's being elected *Tagos* of Thessaly, in contrast to the apparent date of 375, suggested by Xen. *Hell.* 6.1.18–19. See n. 916.
1115 For Amyntas III see 14.89.2 and n. 567.
1116 Although the mss here read Tharraleos for Amyntas' father's name, there is no question that it was Arrhidaios (see *IG* II² 102; *TDGR2*, no. 43; cf. *TDGR2*, no. 21, R&O, no. 12).
1117 The future king Philip II, father of Alexander the Great.
1118 This was Agesipolis II, son of Kleombrotos, of the Agiad dynasty.
1119 This would be Kleomenes II (370–309). At 20.29.1 Diodoros corrects himself about the length of his reign and records his death in 309/8, after ruling for more than sixty years.
1120 This is a clear indication that Diodoros was familiar with two sources and was not simply following Ephoros. Ephoros' version (*FGrHist/BNJ* 70 F214) is, however, supported by Xenophon (*Hell.* 6.4.31–32), who provides the additional information that there were two brothers, Polydoros and Polyphron, who both succeeded to the *Tageia*, probably in succession. Both their reigns were short. Diod. is unaware of Polyphron's existence: see 15.61.2 and n. 1124.
1121 For Douris of Samos, see *FGrHist/BNJ* 76. He was a late-fourth-century historian, from a powerful family on Samos. His family went into exile when the Athenians took possession

61.1. In the archonship at Athens of Lysistratos,[1122] civil strife arose amongst the Romans between those who thought they ought to elect consuls and those who wanted to elect tribunes. For a while there was an absence of elected officials [anarchy], but later they decided to elect six military tribunes, Lucius Aemilius, Gaius Verginius, Servius Sulpicius and in addition to these Lucius Quintius, Gaius Cornelius and Gaius Valerius.[1123] 2. In their term of office Polydoros of Pherai, ruler of the Thessalians, was poisoned to death by his nephew, Alexander,[1124] who had challenged him to a drinking contest. Alexander, the nephew,[1125] took over power and ruled for eleven years.[1126] This individual, who had acquired power illegally by force, adhered to this practice in the administration of his reign. In fact, while his predecessors in power used to treat the common folk fairly and were consequently popular, this man was hated for the harsh and violent nature of his rule.[1127] 3. As a result, some of the men of Larissa, who were called Aleuadai[1128] on the basis of their noble lineage, fearing his lawless behaviour, formed a conspiracy to put an end to his rule. They left Larissa and went to Macedon, where they persuaded the king, Alexander, to join them in putting an end to his tyranny.[1129] 4. As they were busy with their plans, Alexander of Pherai, learning of the plot against himself, called up those men who were fit for military service. His intention

369/8: Book 15.61.1–70.3

Polydoros is assassinated by his nephew Alexander, who takes over the rule

---

of Samos in the mid-360s. They went to Sicily. After the death of Alexander, Samos was returned to the Samians, and Douris' father, Kaios, became tyrant, a position to which Douris succeeded. Douris was reputed to be a student of Theophrastos, but that has been questioned. In antiquity, his writing was characterized as sensationalizing. Like his contemporaries, he was certainly moralizing. His major work was a *Makedonika* (History of Macedon). He is not known to have written a History of Greek affairs (*Hellenika*).

1122 For Lysistratos, see Develin, *AO*, 252.
1123 Cf. Livy, 6.32.2, where the names are Lucius Aemilius, Publius Valerius, Gaius Veturius, Servius Sulpicius, Lucius and Gaius Quinctius Cincinnatus. The civil strife referred to was associated with the struggle between the plebeians and patricians that led to the passage of the Licinio-Sextian legislation in 367. See 15.75.1. All the tribunes named here were patrician.
1124 As noted above (n. 1120) Diod., and/or his source, was unaware of the existence of another brother, Polyphron. According to Xen. *Hell.* 6.4.33–35, it was this brother who was killed by Alexander, supposedly in revenge for his own murder of Polydoros.
1125 This is a necessary correction of the mss' reading, "Polydoros, the brother."
1126 I.e. 369/8–358/7.
1127 This judgement of Alexander of Pherai is shared by Xenophon, *Hell.* 6.4.35–37, and Plutarch, *Pelop.* 26.2.
1128 The Aleuadai of Larissa were an aristocratic family which claimed descent from a mythical hero, Aleuas. They had been dominant in Thessalian affairs until their position had been contested by the dynasts of Pherai, beginning with Jason.
1129 Alexander had only recently come to the throne: see 15.60.3. The kings of Macedon and the Thessalian aristocracy, especially the Aleuadai, were traditional allies.

was to undertake a battle inside Macedon, but the king of Macedon, along with the exiles from Larissa, reached Larissa with his army before his enemy. He was secretly introduced within the walls by the Larissaians and took possession of the city, except for the citadel. 5. Later, he took the citadel by siege and, after he had won over the city of Krannon to his side, he made an agreement with the Thessalians that he would give the cities back to them. However, without a thought for his reputation, he put sizeable garrisons into the cities and held on to them himself. As for Alexander of Pherai, he was chased back to Pherai in a state of panic. And that was the situation regarding affairs in Thessaly.

In the Peloponnese a Spartan force under Polytropos is defeated by the Arkadians

62.1. In the Peloponnese,[1130] the Lakedaimonians dispatched their general, Polytropos, to Arkadia with a force of 1,000 citizen hoplites and 500 exiles from Argos and Boiotia.[1131] When he reached Arkadian Orkhomenos, he put a careful guard on that city, since it had a friendly relationship with the Spartiates. 2. Lykomedes of Mantineia, the leader (*strategos*) of the Arkadians, gathered the so-called "chosen ones" (*epilektoi*),[1132] 5,000 in number, and advanced to Orkhomenos.[1133] When the Lakedaimonians led their army out of the city, a vigorous conflict ensued, in which the Lakedaimonian general and 200 of his soldiers were killed. The remainder fled back to the city under close pursuit.[1134]

The Arkadians, although victorious, fear the Spartans and search for allies. Rejected by Athens, they win over the Thebans

3. The Arkadians, although they were the victors, were, nevertheless, nervous of the power of Sparta and did not think that by themselves they would be able to win a war against the Lakedaimonians. So, in combination with the Argives and Eleians, they sent an embassy to Athens, requesting an alliance against the Spartiates, but, when their appeal fell on deaf ears, they sent their embassy over to Thebes and persuaded them to join an alliance against the

---

1130 Diod. fails to report the peace conference held at Athens either late in 371 or early 370 that is described by Xen. *Hell.* 6.5.1-3 (see above n. 1096), and that helps explain subsequent actions, particularly the synoikism and fortification of Mantineia and the movement to create the Arkadian League, led by Mantineia (15.59.1).

1131 According to Xen. *Hell.* 6.5.11, Polytropos was already stationed at Corinth and his force was composed of mercenaries. In fact, Diod. has events in a different order from Xenophon, in whose account Polytropos' defeat by the Mantineians was contemporary with Agesilaos' campaign in Arkadia, narrated in ch. 59.

1132 For Lykomedes see n. 1107. "Epilektoi" is Diodoros' synonym for "eparitoi" ("picked ones"), the usual name for the elite Arkadian force. See Xen. *Hell.* 7.4.22, 33, 36; 7.5.3; Ephoros (*FGrHist/BNJ* 70 F215); Androtion (*FGrHist/BNJ* 324 F51).

1133 This Orkhomenos is in Arkadia and is not to be confused with the more famous city of the same name in Boiotia.

1134 Cf. Xenophon, *Hell.* 6.5.11-14, who adds that the cavalry from Phleious prevented the Mantineians from pursuing the fleeing troops.

Lakedaimonians.¹¹³⁵ 4. Right away the Boiotians led out their army, taking with them their Lokrian and Phokian allies. So, they proceeded to the Peloponnese, under the command of the Boiotarchs, Epameinondas and Pelopidas. For, the other Boiotarchs had willingly yielded the generalship to these men, out of respect for their intelligence and courage. 5. When they arrived in Arkadia, the full levy of the Arkadians, the Eleians, the Argives and all the other allies came to meet them and the assembled force numbered more than 50,000.¹¹³⁷ The commanders held a council meeting, where they made the decision to march against Sparta itself and lay waste to the whole of Lakonia.¹¹³⁸

*The Boiotian army invades the Peloponnese, led by Epameinondas and Pelopidas*¹¹³⁶

63.1. The Lakedaimonians, who had sacrificed many of their young men in the disaster at Leuktra and had lost not a few in other defeats, were, to put it succinctly, restricted to a small number of citizen troops by the blows of Fortune. In addition, some of their allies had defected and others were suffering a shortage of manpower for similar reasons. So, they found themselves at their wit's end. The result was that they were compelled to seek refuge in help from the Athenians, a people over whom in times past they had imposed the Thirty Tyrants, whom they had forbidden to build walls around their city, and whose city they planned to raze to the ground and turn Attica into a sheep-pasturage.¹¹³⁹ 2. But, the fact is that there is nothing more powerful than the

The Lakedaimonians approach Athens for help and receive a positive response

---

1135 Xenophon makes no mention of an Arkadian appeal to Athens, although it is alluded to by Demosthenes (16, *For the Megalopolitans*, 12). However, Xenophon does imply (*Hell.* 6.5.22–23) that the Boiotian army was already on its way to the Peloponnese soon after Agesilaos retired from Arkadia (see 15.59.4). If he is right, the Arkadian appeals for help will have taken place at least at the time of Agesilaos' invasion, if not before.

1136 Plut. *Pelop.* 24.1. states that the invasion took place at the very end of a year (probably 370, Pausanias, 4.27.9), because the Boiotarchs' term of service was due to expire at the winter solstice, a rule that Epameinondas ignored, with Pelopidas' support. Cf. Pausanias, 9.14.5. The campaign also lasted three months, according to Plut. *Ages.* 32.8. For the topography and course of Epameinondas' first invasion see Buckler (1980), 70–90.

1137 At 15.81.2 we are told that Pelopidas commanded 70,000 troops in the Peloponnese. The same number is given by Plut. *Pelop.* 24.2. In his life of *Agesilaos* (31.1), Plutarch more specifically states that the Thebans invaded with a force 40,000 strong, but acquired 30,000 more later.

1138 Diod.'s statement that this was a decision of the Boiotarchs on the spot and not an authorization from the council of the Boiotian Confederacy is supported by Xen. *Hell.* 6.5.23–24, which stresses the pressure applied by the Arkadians upon supposedly rather reluctant Boiotian commanders.

1139 Our sources disagree whether the Spartans imposed the Thirty Tyrants or merely supported them. The building of the walls referred to will be at the time of Themistokles. The final reference must be to the conclusion of the Peloponnesian War, when the Spartans, in contrast to what is said here, resisted the demands of their allies to raze Athens to the ground.

constraint of Fortune, by force of which the Lakedaimonians had to beg help from their worst enemies. Nevertheless, their hopes were not disappointed. The Athenian People, magnanimous and generous as always and not at all cowed by the power of the Thebans, voted to march out in full force to save the Lakedaimonians from slavery.[1140] Right away they appointed Iphikrates general and sent him off that very same day with an army of 12,000 young men. Well, Iphikrates set out rapidly with his army of eager recruits.[1141] 3. The Lakedaimonians, also, now that the enemy was taking up position on the borders of Lakonia, led out their own troops from Sparta in full force and advanced against their opponents. Their numbers were, indeed, considerably reduced, but their hearts were full of courage. 4. Epameinondas and his officers, seeing that the territory of the Lakedaimonians was not easy to penetrate, considered it was not to their advantage to make their assault with so large an army all together, but rather decided to divide the army into four divisions and make their entry at several points.[1142]

The Spartans march out to battle, and Epameinondas prepares his strategy

64.1. The first division, that of the Boiotians, took the straight route towards the town called Sellasia and made the inhabitants defect from the Lakedaimonians. 2. The Argives invaded via the frontier of the Tegeatis, joined in battle with the men guarding the passes, slew the commander of the garrison, a Spartiate called Alexander, and killed up to 200 of the rest, amongst whom were the refugees from Boiotia. 3. The third division, composed of Arkadians, was the one with the greatest number of soldiers. It invaded the area called the Skiritis, which was guarded by a large force led by Iskholas,[1143] a man distinguished for courage and intelligence. This most illustrious soldier accomplished an act of heroism that deserves to be remembered. 4. For, he realized that the huge numerical superiority of the enemy meant that all who engaged them in battle would be killed. In his judgement, quitting his post in the pass would be unworthy of Sparta, but preserving the lives of the soldiers would be useful for his country. To everyone's surprise he found a solution that provided for both options, by emulating the act of courage once performed by king Leonidas at Thermopylai. 5. He chose out the young men and sent them back to Sparta

The Theban forces successfully enter Lakonia by four routes and gather at Sellasia, from where they advance on Sparta

---

1140 This is a very different report from Xenophon (*Hell.* 6.5.33–49), where the appeal to Athens follows the invasion and involves much argumentation. It is usual to prefer Xenophon's order of events; see Buckler (1980), 87–89.

1141 Cf. Xen. *Hell.* 6.5.49, without numbers for the troops.

1142 Xen. *Hell.* 6.5.25 describes only two divisions – the Thebans and the Arkadians – entering respectively via Karyai and Oion. In this case Diod.'s more detailed account is probably more accurate.

1143 Iskholaos in Xen. *Hell.* 6.5.24, 26.

to be of use in her time of ultimate danger, while he and the older men held their position. He slew many of the enemy, but, when he was surrounded by the Arkadians, he died with all his men.[1144] 6. The Eleians, the fourth division, made their way through different low-lying regions and reached Sellasia, which was the place at which they had all been ordered to rendezvous.[1145] Once all the contingents had gathered at Sellasia, they advanced against Sparta itself, all the time pillaging and burning the territory.

65.1. The Lakedaimonians had kept Lakonia safe from depredation for 500 years[1146] and, when they saw it being laid waste at that time, they could not restrain themselves, but, falling into fits of rage, began to rush out of the city. However, the elders talked them out of rushing too far from their native land, out of fear of a chance attack. They persuaded them to stay put and secure the safety of the city. 2. Epameinondas' forces descended from Mt Taygetos[1147] to the river Eurotas and began to cross the river, which was in full flood due to the winter season. When the Lakedaimonians saw that the enemy army was in disarray because of the difficulty of the crossing, they grasped the golden opportunity for an attack. They left behind the women and children, and even the men over sixty, as a guard for the city, drew up the young men for battle, and in full force burst out against their enemy. Their sudden onslaught upon the men crossing the river resulted in great slaughter. 3. But, the Boiotians and Arkadians fought back and began to encircle their opponents with their superior numbers. So, the Spartiates, after slaying many, returned to the city, having given a clear demonstration of their own valour.[1148] 4. After that, Epameinondas and his men began a ferocious assault upon the city with all their forces, but the Spartiates, aided by the natural strength of the location, managed to kill many, as they attacked rashly. And, in the end, just as the besiegers, after

The Lakedaimonians are desperate at seeing Lakonia ravaged

As Epameinondas tries to cross the swollen Eurotas river, he is attacked by a Spartan sally

Epameinondas mounts a ferocious attack upon Sparta, but suffers heavy losses

---

1144 Surprisingly, Xenophon, who normally errs in favour of the Spartans, criticizes Iskholaos' actions and lacks the laudatory comparison to Leonidas (*Hell.* 6.5.26). For the significance of Iskholaos' "act of heroism" see n. 935.
1145 That Sellasia was the gathering spot is confirmed by Xen. *Hell.* 6.5.27.
1146 Stated to be 600 in Plut. *Ages.* 31.2.
1147 Given the approach routes described by both Diod. and Xen., this is not possible. The invading forces were on the opposite side of the river Eurotas. Xenophon (*Hell.* 6.5.27-30) states categorically that the invaders kept the Eurotas on their right until they reached Amyklai, where they then crossed the river.
1148 Xenophon makes no mention of any contest over the river crossing. He does, however, describe an engagement after the crossing in the sanctuary of Poseidon, in which the Spartans were victorious (*Hell.* 6.5.30-31). Plut. *Ages.* 32.2 confirms that the Eurotas was in full flood, but does not mention any fighting. Agesilaos just watched. Cf. Pausanias, 9.14.5. But Polyainos, *Strategemata*, 2.1.27, does describe a contest over the crossing.

applying maximum effort, began at first to imagine that they had taken Sparta by assault, Epameinondas gave the trumpet call for a retreat, because of the number of the attackers who were dead or wounded. Nevertheless, the soldiers, on their own initiative, went up to the city and kept calling the Spartiates out to battle or else bidding them to admit they were lesser men than their enemy. 5. The Spartiates replied that when the right time came they would fight to the finish in a decisive battle. So, Epameinondas and his men withdrew from the city and, after ravaging Lakonia and amassing a quantity of booty that was beyond count, they returned to Arkadia.[1149] 6. Later, the Athenians arrived. They were too late for the action and returned home without accomplishing anything noteworthy,[1150] but 4,000 soldiers from their other allies arrived to help the Lakedaimonians. Added to these were 1,000 recently liberated Helots and 200 of the exiles from Boiotia. Furthermore, they brought in not a few men from neighbouring cities and, in this way, put together an army that was a match for the enemy. Keeping these men all together and training them as a unit, they gained in confidence day by day and got themselves ready for the decisive contest.

The Athenian reinforcements arrive too late and go home, but the Spartans rebuild their army

Epameinondas resettles Messene

66.1. Epameinondas, who was prone by nature to big ideas, especially if they brought him a long-lasting reputation, advised the Arkadians and the other allies to settle Messene, an area left depopulated by the Lakedaimonians for many years and one that was ideal for an attack on Sparta. Gaining unanimous consent, he sought out the surviving Messenians and, after granting citizen rights to anyone else who wanted, he built the city of Messene, providing it with an abundance of inhabitants. By giving these people each a plot of land and by restoring the infrastructure of the territory, he preserved a distinguished Greek city, and won universal acclaim for himself.[1151] 2. Now, since Messene has many times been captured and destroyed,[1152] I think it is not out of place

The history of Messene and the Messenians is reviewed

1149 Neither Xenophon (*Hell.* 6.5.32) nor Plutarch (*Ages.* 32–33) describes this assault upon Sparta itself. In fact, Xenophon specifies that after the engagement in the sanctuary of Poseidon the Thebans marched off down to Helos and Gytheion.

1150 See n. 1140.

1151 The resettlement of Messene was one of Epameinondas' proudest accomplishments, along with the creation of Megalopolis (Pausanias 9.14.5, 9.15.6). The founding itself at the base of Mt Ithome is described in detail by Pausanias, 4.26.3–27 and dated to the archonship of Dysniketos (4.27.9). It is also referred to by Plutarch (*Pelop.* 24.5; *Ages.* 34.1) and numerous other authors. The walls of the city still stand to an impressive height and are an outstanding example of fourth-century fortifications.

1152 Although the Messenians had been persecuted throughout the years and revolted many times, a city called Messene had never existed. Mt Ithome had been their stronghold.

to run briefly over its history from start to finish.[1153] Well, in ancient times up to the era of the Trojan War, it was in the possession of the descendants of Neleus and Nestor,[1154] and after that it belonged to Orestes, son of Agamemnon, and his descendants until the Return of the Herakleidai.[1155] At that time, Kresphontes drew Messenia as his share and he and his descendants ruled it for a time. Later, when the descendants of Kresphontes lost the kingship, the Lakedaimonians became its rulers. 3. Next, after Teleklos,[1156] the Lakedaimonian king, had been killed in battle, the Messenians were defeated in a war by the Lakedaimonians. Tradition has it that this war lasted for twenty years, since the Lakedaimonians had sworn an oath not to return home to Sparta unless they had captured Messene.[1157] It was at that time that the so-called Partheniai[1158] were born and settled the city of Tarentum. Later, when the Messenians were the slaves[1159] of the Lakedaimonians, Aristomenes persuaded them to revolt from the Spartiates and inflicted much harm upon the Spartiates.[1160] That was the time when the poet Tyrtaios was given to the Spartiates by the Athenians to be their leader.[1161] 4. Some say that Aristomenes lived at the time of the

1153 The most complete, if somewhat romanticized, history of Messenia from the Bronze Age to the building of Messene by the Thebans can be found in Book 4 of Pausanias. For all issues concerning the history and traditions of the Messenians see Luraghi (2008).
1154 Kings of Pylos.
1155 The return of the descendants of Herakles was the Greek name for what modern histories used to refer to as the Dorian Invasion. According to tradition, it took place eighty years after the Trojan War (that is, 1104), and involved a taking of control of the Peloponnese from the Akhaians by the descendants of Hyllos, son of Herakles: Temenos, Kresphontes and Aristodemos. They divided up the Peloponnese by casting lots. Temenos won Argos, Kresphontes won Messenia and the sons of Aristodemos, Prokles and Eurysthenes, took Lakonia (Aristodemos having died). Modern archaeological studies have essentially disproven the existence of the Dorian Invasion. See Desborough (1966).
1156 Seventh king of Sparta, of the Agiad line. For the story, see Pausanias, 4.4.2–4.
1157 The beginning of the First Messenian War, which lasted twenty years, is dated variously in our sources from 770 to 735, although either 744–724 or 735–715 fit the evidence best.
1158 I.e. sons of virgins, since no men were meant to be in town, according to their oath. Cf. Strabo, 6.3.3 C279.
1159 The Helots ("captured ones"), as they were called, are rather difficult to categorize. They were clearly enslaved, yet served in a similar capacity to serfs in that they continued to farm their land for their Spartan overlords.
1160 Aristomenes was a cult hero for the Messenians. The reference is to the Second Messenian War, which took place two generations (c.60 years) after the first, according to Tyrtaios in lines referring to the First War, quoted by Pausanias (4.15.2): "The spear-carrying fathers of our fathers fought over it [i.e. Messenia] for nineteen years."
1161 Tyrtaios was a Spartan poet. The tradition that he was an Athenian was probably fourth-century Athenian propaganda. It is cited by the Athenian politician and orator, Lykourgos (*Against Leokrates*, 106). According to Strabo (8.4.10 C362), who sensibly refutes the idea, it was also believed by the historian Kallisthenes and the Atthidographer Philokhoros.

twenty-year war. The last war that the Messenians fought was at the time of a massive earthquake.[1162] When almost the whole of Sparta was shaken to the ground and very few men survived, the remaining Messenians, along with some Helots who had joined the revolt, inhabited Ithome, since Messene had been in ruins for many years. 5. Finally, after meeting with misfortune in all their wars, they were expelled from the land and went to live in Naupaktos, a city that was given to them as a home by the Athenians.[1163] Some of them also were driven out to Kephallenia,[1164] while yet others went to live in Sicily, in a city that was called Messene after themselves.[1165] 6. The conclusion to the history is that the Thebans, at the time under consideration, on the suggestion of Epameinondas, gathered the Messenians from wherever they were, built Messene for them and restored their ancestral territory to them. Such are the many and varied twists and turns of Messene's history.

After building Messene, the Thebans return home

67.1. After completing all the above in eighty-five days,[1166] the Thebans returned to their own land, leaving behind an impressive garrison for Messene. As for the Lakedaimonians, finding themselves unexpectedly rid of their enemy, they sent an embassy to Athens, composed of the most distinguished Spartiates, and concluded terms of agreement regarding the hegemony of Greece, to the effect that the Athenians were to rule the sea and the Lakedaimonians the land. Following that, they created shared commands in both cities.[1167] 2. The Arkadians, after electing Lykomedes as general and putting him in charge of the so-called "chosen men" (*epilektoi*), an elite corps of 5,000 troops, launched a campaign against Pallene[1168] in Lakonia. They took the city

The Arkadians, under Lykomedes, attack and destroy Pallene in Lakonia

---

1162 The Messenian or Helot Revolt and the siege of Ithome took place during the Pentekontaetia in the 460s and 450s and was believed to have lasted for ten years. See Thucydides, 1.101.2–103.3; Diod. 11.63–64, 11.84.7–8; Plutarch, *Kimon*, 16–17.3; Pausanias, 4.24.5–7; Philokhoros, *FGrHist/BNJ* 328 F117. The exact dates when it began and ended are the subject of heated debate, with options ranging from 469/8–460/59 to 465/4–456/5. For a review, see Gomme, *Commentary*, vol. 1, 401–408.
1163 Cf. Thuc. 1.103.3; Diod. 11.84.7.
1164 Later, in 421, at Kranioi in Kephallenia, according to Thuc. 5.35.7.
1165 Cf. Strabo, 6.2.3 C268, who says they went to a place called Zankle and changed its name to Messene, but this was surely earlier in the fifth century. For the fate of the Messenians after the conclusion of the Peloponnesian War see 14.34.2–6. According to Diod. 14.78.5, Dionysios of Syracuse wanted to settle 600 Messenians in Messina, but changed his mind after a protest from Sparta. They were moved to Tyndaris, where they prospered.
1166 Plutarch, *Ages*. 32.8, rounds the figure out to three months.
1167 This is an obscure arrangement, which is better explained by Xen. *Hell*. 7.1.14, where the supreme command by land and sea is to alternate between Athens and Sparta every five days.
1168 The reading of the mss is incorrect. Pallene is the name of a deme in Attica and of one of the peninsulas of Khalkidike. The correct spelling is Pellana (Pausanias, 3.21.2–3). Xenophon's

by assault and slew the Lakedaimonian garrison that had been left there, who numbered more than 300. They enslaved the citizens, laid waste the land and returned to their own land, before help arrived from the Lakedaimonians.[1169] 3. And the Boiotians, when the Thessalians asked them to come to liberate the cities and to put an end to the tyranny of Alexander of Pherai, sent Pelopidas to Thessaly with an army, instructing him to manage affairs in Thessaly to the advantage of the Boiotians. 4. When Pelopidas reached Larissa and found the acropolis held by Alexander of Macedon's garrison, he took possession of the acropolis.[1170] Then, he advanced into Macedon, where he concluded an alliance with Alexander, king of the Macedonians, extracting from him as surety his brother Philip, whom he sent as a hostage to Thebes.[1171] After he had managed affairs in Thessaly in a manner that in his opinion was to the advantage of the Boiotians, he returned to his own land.

Pelopidas campaigns in Thessaly and Macedon, and takes Philip as a hostage to Thebes

68.1. Following upon these events, the Arkadians, Argives and Eleians of common accord resolved to take the field against the Lakedaimonians and sent ambassadors to Thebes, who succeeded in persuading them to join in the war. The Thebans appointed Epameinondas as commander, to be assisted by the other Boiotarchs, and sent him out with a force of 7,000 infantry and 600 cavalry.[1172] When the Athenians learned that the Boiotian army was passing by on its way into the Peloponnese, they sent out an army to oppose them with Khabrias as its general. 2. When Khabrias reached Corinth, he acquired additional soldiers

Epameinondas invades the Peloponnese for a second time

The Athenians send an army under Khabrias to join the Spartans. They take up a fortified position near Corinth

spelling, Pellene (Xen. *Hell.* 7.5.9), is in the Attic dialect and is not to be confused with the Pellene in the northern Peloponnese, between Aigai and Sikyon (n. 1174). Pellana was north-west of Sparta, further up the Eurotas. See Map 11.

1169 There is no other record of this campaign.
1170 Up to this point, Diod. and Plutarch (*Pelop.* 26.1–2) are in such close agreement as to suggest a common source, with the minor exception that Plutarch includes an attempt by Pelopidas to lead Alexander of Pherai to a better way of governing.
1171 Plutarch *Pelop.* 26.3–4, informs us that Alexander was in conflict with Ptolemaios over the kingship and that Pelopidas intervened on the side of Alexander. He also adds that thirty other elite youths were taken as hostages in addition to Philip. Later, at 16.2.2, Diod. tells a different story, that Philip was taken as a hostage from his father Amyntas by the Illyrians, who entrusted him to the Thebans for safekeeping, a strange story that is partially supported by Justin, *Epitoma*, 7.5.1. All accounts agree, however, that he learned military science from Epameinondas.
1172 This, the second Theban invasion of the Peloponnese, is recorded in different terms by Xen. *Hell.* 7.1.15–22. Xenophon does not name Epameinondas or Khabrias, makes no mention of the ditches and palisades, nor does he provide any figures for the forces on either side. In contrast to Diod., however, he depicts the Theban passage into the Peloponnese as being relatively easy, due to the incompetence of the Spartan commander. See Buckler (1980), 90–109.

from Megara, Pellene and also Corinth and ended up with a combined force of 10,000 men. Later, when the Lakedaimonians and their other allies arrived at Corinth, the total assembled force was not less than 20,000. 3. So, they decided to fortify the access routes and prevent the Boiotians from invading the Peloponnese. They closed off the distance from Kenkhreai to Lekhaion[1173] with palisades and deep ditches. Thanks to the many hands involved and the enthusiasm of the men, the work was completed quickly and the whole space was fortified before the arrival of the Boiotians. 4. When Epameinondas arrived with his army, he surveyed the scene and identified the most approachable point of attack to be the place that the Lakedaimonians were guarding. At first, he challenged the enemy to battle, even though they outnumbered him almost three-to-one, but, when no one dared to step forward from their fortified position, but were all ready to defend themselves from behind the palisades, he launched a forceful attack upon the enemy. 5. Along the whole line vigorous assaults were made, but chiefly against the Lakedaimonians, because their sector was easy to access and hard to defend. There was great rivalry between the two sides, but, since Epameinondas had with him the cream of the Theban troops, after a hard fight he forced the Lakedaimonians back. Breaking his way through their defences, he led his army past and advanced into the Peloponnese. In so doing, he accomplished a success that was in no way inferior to any of his previous exploits.

Epameinondas identifies a weak spot and he manages to break through

Epameinondas is checked at Corinth by Khabrias and his Athenian force

69.1. Epameinondas advanced straight against Troizen and Epidauros. He lay waste their territory, but was unable to capture the cities, because they were protected by impressive garrisons. He did, however, scare Sikyon, Phleious and some other cities into joining his side. Then, he led his army to attack Corinth and, when the Corinthians came out to fight him, he defeated them in battle and chased them back inside their walls. The Boiotians were greatly elated at their success and some of them rashly dared to force their way into the city through the gates. At that, the Corinthians fled to their homes, but Khabrias, the Athenian general, put up a smart and courageous resistance and drove the Boiotians out of the city, killing many of them. 2. Passions were aroused. The Boiotians marshalled their whole force and launched a ferocious attack upon Corinth, but Khabrias gathered up his Athenians and led them out of the city. Taking up position on some higher ground, he prepared to resist the enemy's assault. 3. The Boiotians, trusting in their physical strength and in the

---

1173 The two harbours of Corinth. This was neither the first, not the last, attempt to close off entry to the Peloponnese by a wall.

experience gained from a series of wars, expected to overpower the Athenians by force, but Khabrias' men, fighting from the higher ground and receiving copious supplies from the city, killed some of their attackers and wounded others. 4. The Boiotians, after suffering serious losses and failing to achieve any success, made their retreat. Well, in this way Khabrias wore down his opponents and won admiration for his courage and his competence as a general.[1174]

70.1. Now, 2,000 Celtic and Iberian mercenaries sailed to Corinth from Sicily,[1175] sent to fight as allies of the Lakedaimonians by Dionysios the tyrant,[1176] who had paid their wages for five months. The Greeks were keen to try them out and sent them to the front, where they demonstrated their courage in the close conflict of battle, by killing many Boiotians and their allies. Thus, they gained a reputation for outstanding swordsmanship and bravery and, after performing many services for the Lakedaimonians, for which they were honoured, they were sent back to Sicily at the end of the summer. 2. After that, Philiskos sailed across to Greece on orders from Artaxerxes, the King, to encourage the Greeks to cease from their wars and agree to a Common Peace.[1177] Everyone else was only too happy to agree, except for the Thebans, who were excluded for reducing all of Boiotia under one confederacy according to their own design. Since the Common Peace negotiations failed, Philiskos returned to Asia, leaving behind 2,000 crack mercenaries for the Lakedaimonians, their wages already paid. 3. Contemporaneous with these events, Euphron the Sikyonian, a man characterized by an exceptionally senseless audacity, made an

Celtic and Iberian mercenaries from Dionysios of Syracuse help the Spartans

Philiskos is sent by Artaxerxes to negotiate a Common Peace but is unsuccessful

Euphron sets himself up as tyrant of Sikyon

1174 Xenophon's account of the course of the invasion and the return via Corinth (*Hell.* 7.1.18–19) is similar in outline, but different in specifics. He has the Thebans and their allies attack Sikyon and Pellene first, and then Epidauros. He makes no mention of either Phleious or Troizen. Finally, the defence of Corinth is carried out by "some light-armed troops," no mention being made of Khabrias and his Athenian troops.

1175 See Xen. *Hell.* 7.1.20–21. He says that they were transported in twenty triremes. Unlike Diod., he does not give a figure for the size of the whole force, but specifies that there were fifty cavalry, who, in his account, are responsible for all the action.

1176 Dionysios was a consistent ally of Sparta.

1177 See Xen. *Hell.* 7.1.27, where we learn that Philiskos of Abydos was sent by Ariobarzanes, satrap of Hellespontine Phrygia, although no doubt with the approval of Artaxerxes. The meeting was held at Delphi, because it was a neutral site. While Diod. maintains that the exclusion of the Thebans resulted from their subjection of Boiotia, Xenophon specifies that the negotiations fell apart over the Theban defence of the independence of Messene. It is tempting to see a connection between this meeting at Delphi and *IG* II² 103 (R&O, no. 33), an Athenian decree of the last month of 369/8, that honours Dionysios I of Syracuse and two of his sons in the context of a letter he has sent "about the building of the temple *and the peace*" (lines 9–10) – the temple of Apollo having been destroyed by earthquake in 373/2. For a different view of Philiskos see Demosthenes 23, *Against Aristokrates*, 141–142.

attempt at tyranny, with the co-operation of the Argives. Succeeding in his ambition, he drove forty of the wealthiest Sikyonians into exile, sold their property at public auction, and with the huge proceeds hired mercenary troops and so became ruler of the city.[1178]

368/7: Book 15.71.1–74.5

In Macedon, Ptolemaios has Alexander assassinated, while in Thessaly Pelopidas is arrested by Alexander of Pherai

The Thebans send an army to Thessaly, while Alexander receives help from Athens

71.1. In the archonship at Athens of Nausigenes,[1179] in Rome they appointed four military tribunes in place of the consuls, Lucius Papirius, Lucius Menenius, Servius Cornelius, Servius Sulpicius,[1180] and the one hundred and third Olympiad was celebrated by the Eleians, in which Pythostratos of Athens[1181] won the *stadion*. In their term of office, Ptolemaios of Aloros, son of Amyntas, assassinated his brother Alexander and became king of Macedon, which he ruled for three years.[1182] 2. In Boiotia, Pelopidas, whose reputation in matters related to warfare was the equal of Epameinondas', saw that Epameinondas had arranged affairs in the Peloponnese in a manner advantageous to the Boiotians and was eager to be the agent of advancing Boiotian influence outside the Peloponnese.[1183] Taking with him his friend, Ismenias, a man greatly admired for his courage, he went to Thessaly. But, after an encounter with Alexander, tyrant of Pherai, he was unexpectedly arrested along with Ismenias and put under guard.[1184] 3. The Thebans were aroused to anger at this, and quickly dispatched an army of 8,000 infantry and 600 cavalry to Thessaly in

---

1178 Cf. Xen. *Hell*. 7.1.44–46.
1179 For Nausigenes, see Develin, *AO*, 254.
1180 Livy (6.35.10), at 376 on the Varronian dating, gives no magistrates for this and four succeeding years, calling this period a *solitudo magistratuum*, since the two tribunes of the People, Gaius Licinius and Lucius Sextius, did not allow any curule magistrates to be elected. Entries from the *Fasti Capitolini* are missing. Diod. has only one year of anarchy, the last, and dates it to 367/6. See 15.75.1. This difference thus reduces the gap between the Greek and the Varronian chronology to four years.
1181 In Eusebios' *Olympic Victor List* for the 103rd Olympiad, Pythostratos is listed as an Ephesian.
1182 Ptolemaios is not listed as a son of Amyntas at 15.60.3 and cannot, therefore, have been a brother of Alexander. He may well have been the uncle, born of another Amyntas (see 14.84.6 and n. 539) and married to Eurynoe, sister of Alexander (Justin, *Epitoma*, 7.4.5, 7). In that case, he was probably regent, as Plutarch says (*Pelop*. 27.3), for a period of three (not thirty, as in the mss) years. His assassination of Alexander is also reported by Plutarch, *Pelop*. 27.2 and Athenaios, *Deip*. 14.629D. On Ptolemaios see Hammond and Griffith (1979), 181–185.
1183 Plutarch, *Pelop*. 26.1, gives these as Pelopidas' motives before his first campaign in Thessaly.
1184 Diod. has seriously curtailed the narrative. See Plutarch's more fulsome account (*Pelop*. 27.1–6), which recounts Pelopidas' second involvement in Macedon against Ptolemaios before his return to Thessaly and his arrest by Alexander. Pelopidas' arrest is also reported by Pausanias, 9.15.1, Nepos, *Pelopidas*, 5.1 and Polybios, 8.35.7–9, the last of whom is critical of his action.

response.¹¹⁸⁵ Frightened, Alexander sent ambassadors to Athens to negotiate an alliance.¹¹⁸⁶ In response, the *demos* immediately ordered the dispatch of thirty triremes and 1,000 soldiers, under the command of Autokles.¹¹⁸⁷ 4. During the time that Autokles was sailing around Euboia, the Thebans arrived in Thessaly. Now, Alexander had assembled an infantry force and had many times more cavalry than the Boiotians; nevertheless, at first they were of an opinion to decide the war by battle, because they had the Thessalians on their side. But, when they were abandoned by the Thessalians and the Athenians and some other allies joined Alexander, seeing that they were running out of food and drink and other supplies for their men, the Boiotarchs decided to turn back and go home. 5. They broke camp and began making their way over flat open terrain. Alexander followed behind with a large cavalry force and kept attacking their rearguard. Under the continuous rain of spears, some of the Boiotians were killed, others fell wounded. In the end, being prevented from stopping or advancing, they found themselves in a desperate situation, especially since they were short of supplies. 6. They were already giving up hope of reaching safety, when Epameinondas, who was a private soldier at that time, was appointed general by the army.¹¹⁸⁸ Straightaway, choosing the light-armed troops and the cavalry, he took them with him to a position at the rear and with their help pushed back the pursuing enemy and provided complete security to the hoplites at the front. By alternating between retreat and attack in wheeling motions and by employing ingenious tactical manoeuvres, he saved the army. 7. The more he increased his own reputation by his repeated successes, the greater approval he received from the soldiers and the allies. But the Thebans found the Boiotarchs of that campaign guilty and imposed upon them heavy fines.¹¹⁸⁹

The Thessalians desert the Thebans, who retreat with losses

Epameinondas is elected general by the troops and saves the army by his tactics

72.1 In defence of Epameinondas, a suitable explanation should be provided to the question, how it was that a man of his calibre was serving as a private soldier

Epameinondas was a private soldier at the invasion of Thessaly, but his action there led to his reappointment

---

1185 The commanding Boiotarchs were named Kleomenes and Hypatos, according to Pausanias, 9.15.1, who agrees that Epameinondas was a private soldier. Cf. Plutarch, *Pelop.* 28.1, who adds that Epameinondas was at that time out of favour. See also Nepos, *Epameinondas*, 7.1–2.
1186 That there was such an alliance is confirmed obliquely by lines 39–41 of *IG* II² 116, which order the destruction of the *stele* on which it had been inscribed, as a consequence of a new alliance between Athens and the Thessalians against Alexander in 361/0. See *TDGR*2, no. 59; R&O, no. 44.
1187 A speech by Autokles is reported by Xen. *Hell.* 6.3.7–9 at the peace negotiations at Sparta in 371.
1188 The same point is made by Pausanias, 9.15.2.
1189 They were fined 10,000 *drachmas* each (Plutarch, *Pelop.* 29.1).

amongst those sent to invade Thessaly. Well, in the battle near Corinth, after Epameinondas had broken through the Lakedaimonian guard at the trench,[1190] although he was in a position to slaughter many of his opponents, he had been satisfied with his victory and had desisted from further conflict. 2. This generated enough suspicion against him, that he had spared the Lakedaimonians as a personal favour, that those who were envious of his reputation seized the opportunity for making slanderous accusations, which sounded reasonable. So, when they brought the charge of treason against him,[1191] the People were aroused to anger, removed him from his position as Boiotarch and, having reduced him to the ranks of a private citizen, sent him on the campaign with the other troops. But, after the result of his actions had erased the slanders against him, the People then reaffirmed his previous good standing. 3. Somewhat later, a major battle took place between the Lakedaimonians and the Arkadians, in which the Lakedaimonians won a significant victory.[1192] Since their defeat at Leuktra, this was their first success, and quite an unexpected one. For, more than 10,000 Arkadians fell in battle, while the Lakedaimonians lost no one.[1193] In fact, the priestesses at Dodona had predicted to them that this would be a "tearless victory" for the Lakedaimonians.[1194] 4. Following this battle, out of fear of Lakedaimonian incursions, the Arkadians selected a well-situated site where they founded the place called Great City [Megalopolis],[1195] creating it

The Spartans win the "tearless battle" against the Arkadians, who found Megalopolis in response

---

1190 See 15.68.4–5.
1191 This is the only explicit reference to a trial of Epameinondas after the second invasion of the Peloponnese, although the statements by both Pausanias and Plutarch, cited in n. 1185, suggest that he had been demoted for some reason. A better attested trial of both Epameinondas and Pelopidas for exceeding their term of office during the first invasion, not mentioned by Diod., is reported in detail by Plutarch, *Pelop.* 24.1–2, 25.1–2; Pausanias, 9.14.5,7; Nepos, *Epameinondas*, 7.3–8.5, and referred to by several other sources.
1192 This battle is reported by Xenophon (*Hell.* 7.1.28–32), who does not, however, use the name "tearless," and Plutarch (*Ages.* 33.5–8), who does.
1193 That the Spartans, under the leadership of Arkhidamos, son of Agesilaos, suffered not a single loss is the unanimous tradition of our sources, although the number 10,000 for the Arkadian losses is an obvious exaggeration.
1194 The oracle at the sanctuary of Zeus at Dodona was one of the most respected sources of divine revelation for the Greeks. Diod. is the only author to report this prophecy.
1195 The site they chose was in the south-west part of Arkadia, in a valley surrounded by mountains. For a summary history of Megalopolis, see Pausanias, 8.27. He provides the names of the ten *oikistai* (founders) and gives a long list of the villages, almost twice as many as Diod.'s twenty, that were absorbed (synoikized) into the new city. Unlike Diod., he stresses the involvement of Epameinondas (8.27.2). Also, in contrast to Diod., he dates the decision to found the new city to shortly after the Battle of Leuktra in 371, when Phrasikleides was archon at Athens (8.27.8). It is not impossible, however, that it took a few years to organize the synoikism and that the actual building of Megalopolis took place after the "Tearless Battle," as Diod. indicates.

from the combination of twenty villages, whose inhabitants were called Mainalian and Parrhasian Arkadians. And that was the situation regarding affairs amongst the Greeks.

73.1 In Sicily, the tyrant Dionysios decided to mount a campaign against the Carthaginians,[1196] because he was in possession of impressive forces and because he saw that the Carthaginians were not in a good condition to go to war on account of the plague that had befallen them and the revolt of the Libyans.[1197] Not, however, having a convincing reason for the dispute, he pretended that the Phoenicians in their realm[1198] had trespassed on the territory subject to him. 2. So, marshalling a force of 30,000 infantry, 3,000 cavalry, 300 triremes and the ordnance suited to that force, he invaded the territory subject to the Carthaginians. Right away he won over Selinous[1199] and Entella,[1200] then, after laying waste to the whole territory and capturing the city of Eryx,[1201] he began to besiege Lilybaion.[1202] But, he was forced to abandon that siege, because of the strong body of soldiers there. 3. On hearing that the Carthaginian shipsheds had caught fire,[1203] he assumed that their whole fleet had been destroyed and considered it unimportant. So, he dispatched the best 130 of his own triremes to the harbour at Eryx[1204] and sent all the rest back to Syracuse. 4. But, to his surprise, the Carthaginians manned 200 ships and sailed to attack the triremes that were lying at anchor in the harbour at Eryx. Since their attack was completely unexpected,

In Sicily, Dionysios decides to make war on the Carthaginians again

The Carthaginians capture 130 Syracusan triremes at Eryx

1196 This is the Fourth Carthaginian War in modern accounts.
1197 See 15.24.3 and n. 874.
1198 The word translated here and elsewhere as "realm" is *epikrateia*. Diodoros has used it frequently before (at 14.8.5, 14.41.1, 14.41.3, 14.47.5 and 14.54.2). On this occasion it looks as though it is a specific title and some scholars treat it as such regularly, referring to the Carthaginian possessions in Sicily as their Epikraty. See Caven (1990).
1199 The farthest west of the Greek settlements in Sicily, founded from Megara Hyblaia in the late seventh century (see Map 3). Its rivalry with the non-Greek city of Segesta is notorious as a contributing cause for the Athenian Expedition of 415 (Thuc. 6.6–8; Diod. 12.82.3–84.3). It was brutally sacked by the Carthaginians in 409 (Diod. 13.57.1–6) and had passed under Carthaginian control by the treaty that ended the Second Carthaginian War in 383/2 (15.17.5 and n. 830).
1200 See 14.61.5 and n. 397.
1201 See 14.48.1 and n. 341.
1202 See 14.50.2 and n. 352.
1203 A rather opaque report by Justin (*Epitoma*, 20.5.11–12) suggests the possibility of an association of the fire in the shipsheds at Carthage with the opposition to Hanno, the Carthaginian leader, and the treachery of Suniatus, even though no mention is made of this particular event.
1204 The reference is to Drepana/Drepanum (modern Trapani). See Map 3.

they managed to take back with them most of the triremes. After that, since winter had begun, they concluded a truce and separated each to their own cities. 5. Not long after, Dionysios fell sick and died, after holding power for thirty-eight years.[1205] His son, Dionysios, succeeded and ruled as tyrant for twelve years.[1206]

Not long after, Dionysios dies of excessive drinking and is succeeded by his son, Dionysios

74.1. It is not out of character with the investigation that I have undertaken to describe in detail the reasons for his death and the events that happened to this ruler at the end of his life. Well, Dionysios had produced a tragedy at the Lenaian Festival at Athens and won first prize.[1207] One of the members of the chorus, on the assumption that he would be rewarded splendidly should he be the first to report the victory, sailed over to Corinth. There, he found a ship that was sailing out to Sicily, went on board, and with favourable winds reached Syracuse, where he promptly announced the news of the victory to the tyrant.[1208] 2. Dionysios did, indeed, reward the man, and was personally so overjoyed that he made thanksgiving offerings to the gods and put on a celebratory party with food and drink. He feasted his friends splendidly and, at drinking time, applied himself rather enthusiastically to the cup. As a result of the vast amount of liquid he had consumed he fell violently sick.[1209] 3. It had been prophesied by the gods that he would die when he overcame his betters. He thought this prophecy applied to the Carthaginians, considering them to be superior to himself. It was for that reason that in his frequent wars against them he was in the habit of withdrawing at the moment of victory and willingly conceding defeat, just so that he might not appear to be better than

The gods had foretold that he would die when he overcame his betters

---

1205 I.e. from 406/5 to 368/7. Cf. Diod. 13.96.4.
1206 I.e. from 368/7 to 356/5. Cf. Diod. 16.17.2.
1207 The play was called the *Ransom of Hektor*. In our sources, Dionysios is consistently depicted as a frustrated poet (see 14.109, 15.6.1–7.3), much as Hitler was in respect of architecture. Hence, his victory at a celebrated Athenian dramatic festival would have been a coveted achievement. We have no way of knowing whether his work deserved the prize or whether this was a deliberate political act on Athens' part, since she was now looking for rapprochement with the tyrant (see n. 1177). Indeed, it is highly possible that in this very year, the archonship of Nausigenes, Athens concluded an alliance with the tyrant (*IG* II² 105, *TDGR2*, no. 52; R&O, no. 34).
N.B. The verb translated as "produced" involves the use of the technical term *didaskalos* ("trainer"). Dionysios, of course, did not perform that function.
1208 This is an otherwise unattested story.
1209 Two other accounts of his death (Plut. *Dion*, 6.2; Nepos, *Dion*, 2.4–5) make no mention of how Dionysios became ill, but report that he was aided to his death by a drug administered by his doctors. Plutarch explicitly attributes this report to Timaios. Nepos goes even further by laying the responsibility upon his son and successor, Dionysios II.

his superiors.[1210] 4. Yet, despite all his cleverness, he was not, in fact, able to outsmart the Fate that was destined for him, because, although he was a bad poet and had been judged so in Athens, he had won a victory over poets better than himself. So, in a manner consistent with the prophecy his death followed as a consequence of his having overcome his betters.[1211] 5. After the younger Dionysios had taken over the tyranny, the first thing he did was to convene an Assembly of the people, where he exhorted them in a friendly speech to maintain the goodwill towards him that he had inherited from his father.[1212] Then, after giving his father a magnificent funeral[1213] and burying him on the acropolis by the Royal Gates,[1214] he took firm control of the affairs of government.

Dionysios the younger gives his father a magnificent funeral

75.1. In the archonship at Athens of Polyzelos,[1216] in Rome no magistrates were elected as a result of some political strife between factions.[1217] In Greece, Alexander, tyrant of Pherai in Thessaly, brought charges about some matters against the city of the Skotoussians,[1218] summoned the people to an Assembly, surrounded them with his mercenaries and slaughtered them all. Then, after casting the bodies of the dead into the ditch outside the walls, he razed the city to the ground.[1219] 2. The Theban Epameinondas invaded the Peloponnese

367/6: Book 15.75.1–3[1215]
Year of anarchy in Rome; in Thessaly, Alexander of Pherai destroys Skotoussa

Epameinondas campaigns in the northern Peloponnese; the Boiotians liberate Pelopidas

---

1210 But see 14.75.3 and n. 441, where a more calculated reason is given for Dionysios' reluctance to see the Carthaginian threat eliminated from Sicily.
1211 It is tempting to attribute this otherwise unattested story to the malice of Timaios, but it is quite in keeping with Diod.'s own beliefs.
1212 The constitutional basis, if any, for Dionysios' relationship with the Syracusan populace is unclear.
1213 The funeral was clearly described lavishly by Philistos (*FGrHist/BNJ* 556 F28 and F40).
1214 Precisely where these were and why they were called Royal is unknown.
1215 Chs. 75 and 76 are distinctive in being only a series of notices, although 76 is somewhat more detailed. A sign of imprecision is the use of the indefinite "some" three times in ch. 75. On the other hand, a favourite Diodoran word "impressive" (ἀξιόλογος) appears twice in ch. 76, and he uses the more literary form for the archonship formula. The notes may indicate the sort of material Diod. gleaned from his source or, more likely, the notes he took before he wrote up his narrative. In either case they are incomplete, but give an indication of his method.
1216 For Polyzelos, see Develin, *AO*, 256.
1217 Contrary to Livy, Diod. assigns only this one year to the anarchy (*solitudo magistratuum*) at Rome. See 15.71.1 and n. 1180.
1218 The location of Skotoussa, a town in the Pelasgiotis, was about 10 miles (16km) west of Pherai. See Map 10.
1219 The massacre of the inhabitants of Skotoussa is narrated also in Plut. *Pelop.* 29.4 and Pausanias, 6.5.2. Plutarch adds the name of a presently unidentified town called Meliboia to the victims. Pausanias, who dates the incident incorrectly to 371/0, provides the information that the women and children were given to the mercenaries as pay. Neither has the detail of the bodies thrown into the trench.

Khares brings help from Athens to the Phleiasians

with an army and gained the allegiance of the Akhaians and some other cities. He liberated Dyme, Naupaktos and Kalydon from their Akhaian garrisons.[1220] The Boiotians also marched into Thessaly and got Pelopidas back from Alexander, the tyrant of Pherai.[1221] 3. When the Phleiasians were under attack by the Argives, Khares was sent out in command of an army by the Athenians to help them. After he had defeated the Argives in battle twice and made Phleious safe, he returned to Athens.[1222]

366/5: Book 15.76.1–4

The Athenians lose Oropos to the Thebans

76.1. Once this year had come to an end, Kephisodotos[1223] became archon at Athens; in Rome, in place of the consuls, the people appointed four military tribunes, Lucius Furius, Paulus Manlius, Servius Sulpicius, Servius Cornelius.[1224] In their term of office, Themesion,[1225] tyrant of Eretria,[1226] seized Oropos, which was a city belonging to Athens,[1227] but unexpectedly lost possession. For, when the Athenians took the field against him with a far superior

---

1220 For this invasion, cf. Xen. *Hell.* 7.1.41–43, who claims that the result backfired on the Thebans. He also places Euphron's seizure of power in Sikyon after this invasion, contrary to Diod., who treats it as a result of the previous invasion of 369/8 (see 15.70.3). For the locations mentioned see Maps 10 and 11.

1221 It is surprising that Diod. does not mention the involvement of Epameinondas. The rescue of Pelopidas is reported extensively by Plutarch, *Pelop.* 29. In his account Epameinondas was the leader of the expedition and this fact is supported by Nepos, *Pelopidas*, 5.2 and Pausanias, 9.15.1–3. Xenophon, as usual, does not mention Epameinondas' involvement, but does imply that Pelopidas' rescue took place before the campaign in Akhaia (*Hell.* 7.1.33–38).

1222 Xen. *Hell.* 7.2.1–23 is a long excursus on the brave deeds of the Phleiasians. Khares' involvement is described in detail at 7.2.18–23. This is the first recorded action by Khares, who was one of Athens' best, although notorious, generals. See n. 582.

1223 For Kephisodotos see Develin, *AO*, 259. Note the reappearance of the more literary form of the archonship formula (n. 745).

1224 This is now 370 on the Varronian system. For Livy the period of anarchy is over, and at 6.36.3 he gives the following six names for the military tribunes: Lucius Furius, Aulus Manlius, Servius Sulpicius, Servius Cornelius, Publius and Gaius Valerius.

1225 This is the spelling of all mss of Diod., while our other sources give Themison.

1226 This event, without the names of the culprits, is in Xen. *Hell.* 7.4.1. That Themison of Eretria and a certain Theodoros (perhaps an exile from Oropos) were responsible for Athens' loss of this contested property is mentioned by the Athenian orators Aiskhines (3, *Against Ktesiphon*, 85) and Demosthenes (18, *On the Crown*, 99).

1227 Oropos, on the borderland between Attica and Boiotia, was the location of the respected sanctuary of Amphiaraos, the administration of which was of value, and a key port between the mainland and Euboia. It had been an object of contention between Athens and Thebes for many years. Thebes had seized control in 402 (14.17.1–3), but it must have reverted to Athens in the intervening period, probably as a result of the King's Peace. According to Pausanias (1.34.1), it was once again restored to Athenian control by Philip of Macedon, and remained so.

force, the Thebans came to his assistance and took over the city with a commitment to return it, but did not give it back.[1228] 2. Contemporaneous with these events, the people of Kos moved to the city that they now occupy and made it into an impressive foundation.[1229] For, a mass of people flocked to it, its walls were built at great expense and it was equipped with an impressive harbour. From that time onward its public revenues and the wealth of its private citizens were continuously increasing and, to cut a long story short, it grew to rival the major cities of Greece. 3. Contemporaneous with these events, the King of the Persians sent out ambassadors, through whom he persuaded the Greeks to put an end to their wars and to conclude a Common Peace (*Koine Eirene*) with each other.[1230] As a result the so-called Lakonian–Boiotian War was ended, which had been ongoing since the Battle of Leuktra for a period of five years.[1231] 4. In the field of education, there existed during this time some men who deserve to be remembered.[1232] They were: Isokrates, the rhetorician, and those who became his pupils,[1233] and Aristotle, the philosopher, and also

The people of Kos move to a new city

Artaxerxes persuades the Greeks to agree to another Common Peace

Many famous intellectuals lived in this period

1228 According to Demosthenes (21, *Against Meidias*, 64), Khabrias was the Athenian general on this campaign, for which he was brought to trial. Possibly Kallistratos of Aphidna was also involved in this incident, and his powerful rhetoric in his defence is mentioned by Plutarch, *Dem.* 5.1–3.

1229 This move from the original city of Astypalaia to the new site of Kos is reported also by Strabo, 14.2.19 C657, who agrees that the resultant city was impressive.

1230 While Diod. describes the Peace of 366/5 as a Common Peace, initiated by the King of Persia and brought to a successful conclusion, Xenophon, *Hell.* 7.4.6–11, writes of something less ambitious that did not involve the Persians, agreed between only Thebes, Corinth and some northern Peloponnesian states, because Sparta refused to take part, objecting to recognition of the independence of Messene. The situation is further complicated by the fact that earlier in Book 7, before Epameinondas' campaign in Akhaia, Xenophon (*Hell.* 7.1.33–40) refers to an attempt to negotiate a Common Peace by delegations from various states at the court of Artaxerxes, at which Pelopidas was the dominant player (see also Plut. *Pelop.* 30). The gathering at Sousa probably took place in autumn 367 and was followed by a congress of states at Thebes in the spring of 366. According to Xenophon, that initiative failed, because of Spartan objection to the independence of Messene, amongst other things. Diod. implies that it succeeded.

1231 The Lakonian–Boiotian War began with the invasion of Lakonia by Epameinondas and Pelopidas in 369 (15.62–66).

1232 The following list of intellectual luminaries contains two anachronistic references – to Aristotle (384–322) and Anaximenes (380–320), both of whom flourished after the period covered by this book. Some believe that Diod. has botched an excursus on education (*paideia*) by Ephoros, others think that the anachronistic references are interpolations (see Stylianou, *Commentary*, 489–490). But Diod. 12.1.4–5, a Diodoran prologue, contains a similar list of famous men of the Pentekontaetia (the fifty years after the defeat of Xerxes in 480/79) and contains even more egregious anachronisms, by including Plato, Isokrates and Aristotle.

1233 Isokrates, son of Theodoros, of Erkhia (436–338), was one of the most influential of all Greek rhetoricians. He ran a school that was reputed to have educated 1,000 students,

Anaximenes of Lampsakos[1234] and Plato of Athens, and also the last of the Pythagorean philosophers,[1235] and Xenophon, who wrote his histories when he was very old (for, he records the death of Epameinondas, which happened a little after this). And there were both Aristippos and Antisthenes, and, in addition to them, Aiskhines of Sphettos, the Sokratic.[1236]

365/4: Book 15.77.1–77.5

Fighting breaks out between Elis and Arkadia

77.1. In the archonship at Athens of Khion,[1237] in Rome, in place of the consuls, military tribunes were appointed: Quintus Servilius, Gaius Veturius, Aulus Cornelius and, in addition, Marcus Cornelius and Marcus Fabius.[1238] In their term of office, while a state of peace existed throughout Greece,[1239] stirrings of conflict and strange new revolutionary initiatives once again arose in certain cities. For example, the Arkadian exiles, based in Elis, seized a stronghold, called Lasion, in the region named Triphylia.[1240] 2. Over a long period of time the territory of Triphylia had been an object of continuous contention between the Arkadians and the Eleians and, as it changed hands depending on which side was on top, they controlled it turn by turn. Since, at the time under discussion, the Arkadians were in possession of Triphylia, the Eleians used the exiles as their pretext for taking it away from the Arkadians. 3. As a consequence the Arkadians were enraged. They began by sending an embassy to ask for the return of the territory, but, since no one paid them any attention, they summoned assistance from their ally Athens and with it marched against

amongst whom was reputedly Ephoros, one of Diod's sources. As Cicero says (*De Oratore*, 2.94), "from his school, as from the Trojan Horse, none but leaders emerged."

1234 A highly respected rhetorician and historian, who wrote a History of Greece (*Hellenika*) down to the Battle of Mantineia, a History of Philip of Macedon (*Philippika*) and an account of Alexander's campaign, along with speeches and works on rhetoric.

1235 Pythagoras was a sixth-century philosopher, who established his famous school at Kroton in southern Italy, where he promulgated, amongst other things, the thesis of metempsychosis (transmigration of souls). The last of the Pythagoreans are listed by Diogenes Laertios, *Lives of the Great Philosophers*, 8.46.

1236 All three were members of the Sokratic circle (Plato, *Phaidon*, 59b–c). Aristippos from Kyrene (435–356) became the founder of the Cyrenaic School of Philosophy (Diogenes Laertios, *Lives of the Great Philosophers*, 2.65–85); Antisthenes, son of Antisthenes, of Athens (445–365) and Aiskhines, son of Lysanias, of Sphettos (425–350) both wrote Sokratic dialogues (Diogenes Laertios, *Lives of the Great Philosophers*, 2.60–64).

1237 For Khion, see Develin, *AO*, 260–261.

1238 At 6.36.6. Livy lists the following six tribunes: Quintus Servilius, Gaius Veturius, Aulus and Marcus Cornelius, Quintus Quinctius and Marcus Fabius. This is the Varronian year 369.

1239 Diod. continues to insist that a Common Peace had been achieved in 366/5.

1240 Cf. Xenophon, *Hell.* 7.4.12–13, who, however, does not involve any Arkadian exiles in the action.

Lasion.¹²⁴¹ When the Eleians sent reinforcements to the exiles, a battle ensued near Lasion, but, since the Eleians were greatly outnumbered by the Arkadians, they were defeated and lost more than 200 of their soldiers.¹²⁴² 4. That was the beginning of the war, but the dispute between the Arkadians and the Eleians turned out to get much worse. For, right away, the Arkadians, elated at their success, marched into Elis and captured the cities of Margana and Kronion,¹²⁴³ as well as Kyparissia and Koruphasion.¹²⁴⁴ 5. Contemporaneous with these events, in Macedon Ptolemaios of Aloros was assassinated by his brother Perdikkas, after a reign of three years. Perdikkas took over the rule and reigned as king of Macedon for five years.¹²⁴⁵

In Macedon, Ptolemaios is assassinated by his brother Perdikkas

78.1. In the archonship at Athens of Timokrates,¹²⁴⁶ in Rome, in place of the consuls, three military tribunes were appointed: Titus Quinctius, Servius Cornelius and Servius Sulpicius;¹²⁴⁷ and the one hundred and fourth Olympic Festival was celebrated by the Pisatans and the Arkadians, in which Phokides of Athens won the *stadion*.¹²⁴⁸ 2. In their term of office, the Pisatans, by resurrecting the former reputation of their country and by employing some arguments based on ancient myths, tried to claim that the right to celebrate the Olympic Festival belonged to them. And, judging that the present moment was a golden opportunity to assert their right to the Games, they concluded an alliance with the Arkadians, because they were enemies of the Eleians. With them as their

364/3: Book 15.78.1–81.6

The Pisatans celebrate the Olympic Games and repulse the attempt by the Eleians to stop them

1241 Xenophon mentions none of this, although he does concede at *Hell.* 7.4.6 that Athens was bound by alliance to Arkadia.
1242 Cf. Xen. *Hell.* 7.4.13 for this battle.
1243 Xenophon (*Hell.*7.4.12–28) describes three Arkadian campaigns against Elis, which Diodoros appears to have compressed into one, but both locate these events before the 104th Olympiad. Xenophon (*Hell.* 7.4.14) correctly identifies Kronion as the hill of Kronos at Olympia, unlike Diod. Margana, in Pisatis, was soon recaptured by the Eleians (Xen. *Hell.* 7.4.26).
1244 Kyparissia is well south of Elis in Messenia. Koruphasion (Nestor's Pylos) is even farther south. Only Diod. specifies Koruphasion. Xenophon throughout his account uses the name Pylos, which could also refer to the Pylos in Akroreia (see n. 128). Furthermore, according to Xenophon (*Hell.* 7.4.16), it was democratic exiles from Elis who captured Pylos, with the assistance of some Arkadians. He also associates the Eleian recovery of Pylos with their recapture of Margana in Pisatis. While all commentators accept that Diod. and Xenophon are talking about the same place, that is not absolutely clear. See Map 11.
1245 See 15.60.3, 15.71.1 and n. 1182. Perdikkas was not the brother of Ptolemaios, but the nephew.
1246 For Timokrates, see Develin, *AO*, 261–262.
1247 At 6.38.2 Livy lists the following six tribunes: Titus Quinctius, Servius Cornelius, Servius Sulpicius, Spurius Servilius, Lucius Papirius and Lucius Veturius. This is the Varronian year 368.
1248 Phokides' victory in the *stadion* is recorded in Eusebios' *Olympic Victor Lists*, line 303, where it is also noted that the Pisatans held the Games.

Epameinondas persuades the Thebans to challenge Athens for supremacy at sea

assistants, they marched against the Eleians, who were just in the process of holding the Games. 3. The Eleians resisted with all their forces and a vigorous battle ensued, witnessed by the Greeks present at the Festival, who, decked out in their laurel crowns and comfortably out of danger, were applauding the courageous deeds of each side. In the end the Pisatans won and held the Games, but later the Eleians left this Olympiad out of the official record, because they felt it had been celebrated unjustly by force.[1249] 4. Contemporaneous with these events, Epameinondas the Theban, who was held in the highest respect by his fellow citizens, addressed them in an organized Assembly and exhorted them to challenge for supremacy at sea. In the course of his argument, which had been carefully thought out for some time, he tried to demonstrate that this plan was both beneficial and achievable. Amongst the points that he put forward, he laid particular emphasis on the notion that it was easy for those who were dominant on land to acquire supremacy at sea. For, he said, in the war against Xerxes the Athenians manned 200 ships at their own expense, yet were subject to the command of the Lakedaimonians, who provided only ten.[1250] By presenting many other arguments suited to his thesis, he persuaded the Thebans to strive for supremacy at sea.

Epameinondas is sent out to Rhodes, Khios and Byzantion for assistance

79.1. So, there and then, the People voted to start building 100 triremes and an equal number of dockyards,[1251] and to urge the Rhodians, the Khians and the Byzantines to assist them in their project.[1252] Epameinondas himself was

---

1249 For a more detailed account of this incident, which reverses the roles, see Xen. Hell. 7.4.28–35. The celebration of the Olympic Games had been in the hands of Elis from the beginning, but the people of Pisa, who lived close to Olympia, had often contested the right. This was one of three occasions when they succeeded (Pausanias, 8.22.3). The Eleians considered all these occasions "Anolympiads." For the early history of Olympia see Morgan (1990), 26–105.

1250 This is a specious argument, since, despite their overall leadership at Salamis, the Lakedaimonians did not have "supremacy at sea," which is what Epameinondas was supposedly aiming for. Whether that was, in fact, what he intended, some Athenians took the idea seriously. See e.g. Isokrates 5, *To Philip*, 53. We should not, however, give credence to the exaggerated claim made by Aiskhines much later (2, *On the False Embassy*, 105) that Epameinondas told the Boiotian Assembly that "the Propylaia should be moved from the Acropolis at Athens and set at the entrance to the Kadmeia."

1251 Diod. surely meant to write "shipsheds" (νεωσοίκους) rather than "dockyards" (νεώρια). There is no evidence that the Boiotians ever built a fleet *of this size*, and it is doubtful that they had the capability.

1252 No doubt this was the main purpose of Epameinondas' proposal, namely to take advantage of or create disaffection amongst some of the most powerful allies in Athens' Confederacy. Having overcome Sparta, Thebes may have been aiming at supremacy in Greece, by undermining Athens.

sent out with a military force to the above-mentioned states and so scared the Athenian general, Lakhes, who had been sent out with an impressive[1253] fleet to hinder the Thebans, that he forced him to sail off. So, Epameinondas won the states to the Theban side.[1254] 2. Indeed, if this man had lived longer, it is generally agreed that the Thebans would have acquired supremacy at sea in addition to their leadership on land.[1255] But, since a little later he died a heroic death in the Battle at Mantineia, after accomplishing a very illustrious victory for his country, at that very moment Thebes' power died with him.[1256] But, we shall deal with this topic appropriately in more detail a little later.[1257] 3. At that same time, the Thebans resolved to mount a campaign against Orkhomenos. The following are the reasons. Some Theban exiles, who wanted the Theban constitution to change back to aristocracy,[1258] had convinced the 300 members of the Orkhomenian cavalry to join them in their plan. 4. These cavalrymen were in the habit of going to meet their Theban counterparts[1259] on an appointed day for military exercises and they agreed to make their attempt on that day. Along with many other supporters, who had joined the movement, they met at the set time. 5. But, the instigators of the conspiracy got cold feet and, changing their minds, revealed the plot to the Boiotarchs. By their act of public service in betraying their fellow conspirators, they bought themselves immunity from prosecution. The magistrates ordered the arrest of the Orkhomenian cavalry and paraded them in front of the Assembly. There, the People voted

Thebes attacks and destroys Orkhomenos

1253 That word ἀξιόλογος again! How "impressive" Lakhes' fleet was is not clear. He may well have been on guard duty at the Hellespont with the usual squadron of twenty triremes.

1254 Whether Rhodes and Khios defected from Athens at this time or later, in 357 in the Social War, is open to question, but it is quite likely that Byzantion did defect at this time.

1255 The potential for Thebes to wrest naval supremacy from Athens is highly questionable, but the possibility that a Boiotian naval force of any size, operating in the Aegean, could disrupt Athenian trade and grain supplies, as well as causing trouble for the Confederacy, was real. Indeed, the presence of the Boiotian fleet surely led to the defection of the island of Keos (*IG* II² 111; *TDGR*2, no. 55; R&O, no. 39). See, also, the troubled situation for Athens in the next year, described by Apollodoros (Demosthenes 50, *Against Polykles*, 4–7). On Epameinondas' naval programme see Buckler (1980), 160–175.

1256 This point is made repeatedly by multiple sources, but is not entirely true. Under Pammenes and others Thebes tried to remain influential in the 350s.

1257 See ch. 88.

1258 Plutarch, *Pelop.* 25.7, suggests that a man named Menekleidas was the ringleader. For an analysis of internal politics in Thebes at this time see Buckler (1980), 130–150.

1259 Whilst Diod. provides the only detailed account of this event, his narrative is far from coherent. This is not helped by textual issues. The mss' reading "to go out to meet from the Thebans" makes no sense, although it is kept by Vögel. Sherman (Loeb) has "with the Thebans" and Vial (Budé) adopts "from Thebes," but I prefer the suggestion of Dindorf, "to go out to meet those from Thebes."

to put them to death, to reduce the population of Orkhomenos to slavery and to raze the city to the ground. Indeed, from remote antiquity, the Thebans had had a troubled relationship with the Orkhomenians, being forced to pay tribute to the Minyans[1260] in the Age of the Heroes and having to be liberated later by Herakles. 6. So, now, the Thebans thinking they had a golden opportunity and plausible arguments for taking revenge, mounted a campaign against Orkhomenos. After capturing the city, they slaughtered the men and sold the women and children into slavery.[1261]

The Thessalians ask the Boiotians for Pelopidas' support against Alexander of Pherai[1262]

80.1. About the same time, the Thessalians, who had been defeated in the majority of the battles in their war against Alexander, the tyrant of Pherai, and had lost many soldiers, sent an embassy to the Thebans requesting that they would come to their assistance and asking them to send them Pelopidas as their general.[1263] For, they knew that, as a result of his arrest by Alexander, that man was very hostile to the tyrant,[1264] and at the same time was exceptionally courageous and celebrated for his understanding of the art of war. 2. After the joint council of the Boiotians had been convened and the ambassadors had made an address on the object of their mission, the Boiotians agreed to all the Thessalian requests. They assigned approximately 7,000 soldiers to Pelopidas and gave him orders to bring assistance quickly to those in need. Soon, Pelopidas and his army were on their way out, but just then there was an eclipse of the sun.[1265] 3. While the occurrence made many apprehensive, some of the seers proclaimed that the city's sun had been eclipsed by the departure of the soldiers. Indeed, with these words they were predicting the death of Pelopidas, but Pelopidas nonetheless marched out on the campaign, driven by Fate.[1266] 4. When Pelopidas arrived in Thessaly, he found that Alexander had beaten him to possession of the high ground with a force of more than 20,000 troops. He pitched his camp facing his opponents and, after gathering allied troops

An eclipse of the sun predicts disaster, but Pelopidas ignores it

Pelopidas defeats Alexander at Kynoskephalai, but dies

1260 The Minyans were a mythical pre-Greek people, whose most famous city was Orkhomenos in Boiotia. Their legendary history is detailed by Pausanias (9.34.6–37.8).
1261 This massacre is referred to as an outrage by Demosthenes (20, *Against Leptines*, 109) and Pausanias (9.15.3).
1262 The other detailed account of Pelopidas' last campaign is in Plutarch, *Pelop.* 31–32. There is also a brief mention in Nepos, *Pelopidas*, 5.3.
1263 Cf. Plut. *Pelop.* 31.2.
1264 This factor in Pelopidas' motivation is confirmed by Plutarch, *Pelop.* 31.5.
1265 Cf. Plut. *Pelop.* 31.3. It took place on 13 July 364.
1266 Diod. leaves the impression that Pelopidas took his 7,000 soldiers with him, but Plutarch (*Pelop.* 31.4) says he did not want to risk their lives and took only 300 volunteer cavalrymen and some mercenaries.

from the Thessalians, joined battle with the enemy.[1267] 5. Since Alexander had the advantage of his superior positions, in his eagerness to settle the outcome of the battle by his own courage, Pelopidas decided to charge at Alexander himself. The tyrant, supported by his bodyguard of elite troops, resisted,[1268] and a vigorous battle resulted. In that battle, Pelopidas, in a blaze of glory, littered all the ground around him with corpses. He finished the battle as the victor, by putting his opponents to flight, but perished in the process, covered in wounds and sacrificing his life like a hero.[1269] 6. As for Alexander, being on the losing end of a second battle[1270] and totally crushed, he was compelled to agree to return to the Thessalians the cities he had captured, to hand over the Magnetes and the Phthiotian Akhaians[1271] to the Boiotians and, for the future, to become an ally of Boiotia, ruling only Pherai.

Alexander, deflated by defeat, retires to Pherai

81.1. Although the Thebans had won a celebrated victory, they announced to the whole world that it was they who had lost because of the death of Pelopidas. For, after losing such an impressive individual, on balance they judged the victory of less value than the worth of Pelopidas.[1272] He had performed many great services for his country and contributed more than anyone to the increase in Theban power. For, in the case of the assault by the exiles that led to their regaining possession of the Kadmeia, by general agreement everyone assigned to him the principal role in its success. And that felicitous event turned out to be the basis of all their subsequent good fortune. 2. And, Pelopidas was the only Boiotarch present at the Battle of Tegyra,[1273] when he defeated the Lakedaimonians, by far the most powerful amongst the Greeks. That significant victory

The Thebans consider the death of Pelopidas a national tragedy

---

1267 The battle took place at Kynoskephalai, according to Plutarch (*Pelop.* 32.3). For the topography of the battle see Pritchett (1969), 112–119; Buckler (1980), 175–182.
1268 Plutarch, in contrast, says that Alexander did not resist, but fled (*Pelop.* 32.10).
1269 A typical Diodoran passage, involving the gallant death of one commander against extreme odds in conflict with the leader of the opposition. Cf. the death of Epameinondas at Mantineia (15.86.4–87.1) and Kyros at the Battle of Kounaxa (14.23.5–7). More detail is provided by Plutarch (*Pelop.* 32.3–8), who emphasizes the rashness and irresponsibility, generated by anger, of Pelopidas' action.
1270 This obscure reference to a "second battle" is clarified by Plutarch, who says (*Pelop.* 35.2) that, on learning of Pelopidas' death, the Thebans sent out an army of 7,000 infantry and 700 cavalry, led by Malekidas and Diogeiton, which defeated Alexander and forced him to surrender the cities and territories mentioned below.
1271 Alexander's capture of several Thessalian cities and the Magnetes and the Phthiotian Akhaians is confirmed by Plutarch (*Pelop.* 31.2).
1272 Theban grief was outmatched by the outpouring of emotion from the Thessalians, described vividly by Plutarch (*Pelop.* 33), but passed over by Diodoros.
1273 A necessary emendation for the mss' "Tegea."

was the first time that the Thebans erected a trophy over the Lakedaimonians. Then, in the Battle at Leuktra he commanded the Sacred Band, with which he struck the first blow against the Spartiates and initiated the victory. During the campaigns into Lakedaimon, he commanded 70,000 men and erected a trophy at the very gates of Sparta over the Lakedaimonians, who had never before seen their territory ravaged. 3. When he was sent as an ambassador to the King of Persia, in the terms that were jointly agreed upon, he took personal care of the protection of Messene, which the Thebans had rebuilt after 300 years of devastation. Finally, in his conflict with Alexander, whose forces outnumbered his many times over, he was not only brilliantly victorious, but ended his life in a blaze of glory. 4. With respect to his fellow citizens, he treated them so nobly that, from the time of the liberation of Thebes until his death, he was continuously elected Boiotarch every year, an honour that no other citizen was considered worthy of.[1274] So let Pelopidas, who through his own virtue deserves universal accolades, receive from us also the praise of history.[1275] 5. During this same time Klearkhos, a native of Herakleia in the Pontos, made an attempt at tyranny. Having accomplished his aim, he emulated the achievement of Dionysios, the Syracusan tyrant, by ruling brilliantly over the people of Herakleia for twelve years.[1277] 6. Contemporaneous with these events, the Athenian general Timotheos, in command of a land and sea force, captured Torone and Poteidaia by siege and went to the assistance of Kyzikos, which was being besieged.[1278]

Klearkhos becomes tyrant of Herakleia in Pontos; Timotheos captures Torone and Poteidaia and rescues Kyzikos[1276]

1274 Actually, thirteen times (Plut. *Pelop.* 34.7) out of fifteen years.
1275 This eulogistic summary of Pelopidas' career lists many accomplishments that are missing from the appropriate points in Diodoros' previous narrative. See nn. 879, 965, 1091, 1137 and 1230.
1276 The remarks on Klearkhos and Timotheos read like brief notes.
1277 Klearkhos' seizure of power in Herakleia (probably in 364) is narrated by Justin, *Epitoma*, 16.4–5. Called in by the wealthy landowners to help against the demands of the poor for a redistribution of the property, he turned against them and became a leader of the People. By using mercenaries, he turned this position into a tyranny. His method resembles that of Dionysios of Syracuse, whom he clearly admired, even to the point of naming one of his sons Dionysios. Interestingly, he named his other son Timotheos, after the son of Konon. Both Klearkhos and Timotheos had been pupils of Isokrates (Isokrates, *Letter 7, to Timotheos, son of Klearkhos*) and Timotheos had helped Klearkhos gain Athenian citizenship (Demosthenes 20, *Against Leptines*, 84). Indeed, since Timotheos was actively campaigning in the Hellespont at this time (see below and cf. Nepos, *Timotheos*, 1.2), it is possible he helped Klearkhos to power. Whilst Diod. says he ruled "brilliantly," his reputation in other sources was for cruelty and arrogance (Isokrates, *Letter 7*; Memnon, *FGrHist/BNJ* 434 F1; Justin, *Epitoma*, 16.5; Polyainos, *Strategemata*, 30.1–3). He was assassinated in 352 (Diod. 16.36.3; Memnon, *FGrHist/BNJ* 434 F1; Justin, *Epitoma*, 16.5).
1278 Timotheos replaced Iphikrates as Athenian general in the northern Aegean in 366/5, with instructions to campaign against Amphipolis and the Khersonesos (Demosthenes 23,

82.1. Once this year had come to an end, Kharikleides[1279] became archon at Athens; in Rome, Lucius Aemilius Mamercus and Lucius Sextius Laterias were appointed as consuls.[1280] In their term of office, the Arkadians, who had conducted the Olympic Games together with the Pisatans, were now in possession of the sanctuary and the treasures it contained. The Mantineians had already appropriated not a small amount of the dedications for their own personal expenses, and those who had committed this sacrilege were eager to prolong the war against the Eleians, so as not to be held to account in peacetime for what they had spent. 2. But, since the other Arkadians wanted to make peace (i.e. with the Eleians), they stirred up disputes with their fellow countrymen. As a result, two parties emerged, one of which was led by the Tegeans, the other by the Mantineians.[1281] 3. Their quarrel intensified to such an extent that they reached the point of deciding the issue by force of arms. On one side, the Tegeans sent an embassy to the Boiotians and persuaded them to send them assistance. In response, the Boiotians appointed Epameinondas as general in charge of an impressive army and sent him out to help the Tegeans. 4. Then, the Mantineians, in great fear of the Boiotian army and the reputation of Epameinondas, sent ambassadors to the Athenians and Lakedaimonians, the states most hostile to the Boiotians, and persuaded them to fight on their side. Both states quickly dispatched powerful forces, and many violent conflicts resulted throughout the Peloponnese.[1282] 5. For example, the Lakedaimonians immediately invaded the

363/2: Book 15.82.1–89.3

A dispute arises over exploitation of the temple treasures at Olympia

The quarrel between Tegea and Mantineia grows to involve the major states; Epameinondas invades the Peloponnese

---

Against Aristokrates, 149). He failed to capture Amphipolis, but did have success elsewhere. Although assigned to aid the rebel satrap Ariobarzanes, who was being besieged at Adrammyttion in 366, he turned his attention to Samos instead (Demosthenes 15, *On the Freedom of the Rhodians*, 9). He besieged and overpowered the island in 366/5, after a ten-month siege, took Krithote and saved Sestos from the Thracian king Kotys in the Hellespont in 365, then moved to Khalkidike, where he captured Torone and Methone in 364, along with Pydna in Macedon. He also gained control of Poteidaia, probably before his recall in 362. His accomplishments are lauded by his teacher, Isokrates, in speech 15, *On the Antidosis*, 108–113.

1279 For Kharikleides, see Develin, *AO*, 263.
1280 Cf. Livy, 7.1.2. This is the Varronian year 366. The gap between the chronologies has thus shrunk back to three years, because Diod. appears to have missed out Livy's entry (6.42.3) for the military tribunes of the previous year (Varronian 367).
1281 The long-standing rivalry between Tegea and Mantineia, the two major states in Arkadia, guaranteed that the life of the Arkadian League would be short. Ironically, during the Peloponnesian War, Tegea had been oligarchic and loyal to Sparta, while Mantineia was democratic and allied to Argos. At this time the situation was the reverse, Tegea having a democratic government and Mantineia being more conservative. In Xenophon's account of the appropriation of the temple treasures and the disputes that followed (*Hell*. 7.4.33–40), the Tegeans were the guilty party and the Mantineians the ones who objected.
1282 Xenophon (*Hell*. 7.5.1–5) gives a more detailed account of the allies on both sides.

Epameinondas makes a surprise attack upon Sparta, but is outwitted by the Spartan king

neighbouring territory of Arkadia. At that time, Epameinondas and his army were not far distant from Mantineia in their advance, when he was informed by some locals that the Lakedaimonians were out in full force ravaging the territory of Tegea.[1283] 6. Consequently, assuming that there would be no soldiers left to defend Sparta, he conceived an ambitious plan. However, Fortune was working against him.[1284] For, while he set off in haste during the night to attack Sparta, Agis,[1285] king of the Lakedaimonians, suspecting Epameinondas' cunning, made an intelligent guess about what was going to happen and dispatched some Cretan long-distance runners. By means of these he managed to reveal to the people left behind in Sparta, before Epameinondas' arrival, that the Boiotians would soon be coming to Lakedaimon to sack the city and that he would come with his army to the assistance of his country as quickly as he possibly could.[1286] At any rate, he bade the people in Sparta to keep guard over the city and remain calm, for he would appear soon to help.[1287]

83.1. Since the Cretans had carried out their orders promptly, the Lakedaimonians managed, contrary to expectation, to escape the capture of their country. For, if the attack had not been revealed in advance, Epameinondas would have fallen upon Sparta without warning. Now, one could rightly applaud the intellectual ability of both generals, but one has to consider that the strategic acumen of the Lakedaimonian was smarter. 2. To be sure, Epameinondas, by keeping on the move all night and completing the length of the route at top speed, arrived at Sparta at daybreak.[1288] But, since Agesilaos, who had been left

---

1283 Diod. places Epameinondas near Mantineia and the Spartans in Tegean territory, whereas Xenophon (*Hell*. 7.5.6–8) states the opposite: Epameinondas, after a stop in Nemea, goes to Tegea, and his opponents gather at Mantineia. Xenophon's clearly more logical version is followed by Polybios (9.8.2) and Plutarch (*Ages*. 34.3).

1284 A very Diodoran comment, although in this case the same sentiment is expressed by Polybios (9.8.13), and even Xenophon hints at it (*Hell*. 7.5.12).

1285 Diod. (or, his source) has problems with the kings of Sparta. There was no one named Agis at this time. All other sources say that Agesilaos was the leader of the Spartan army in the field. Consequently, he could not have been left behind to protect Sparta, as claimed at 15.83.2. No doubt, that person was Arkhidamos, son of Agesilaos (Xen. *Hell*. 7.5.12-13).

1286 The idea that the Spartan leader guessed Epameinondas' plan is unique to Diod. Other sources say that Agesilaos was informed by a defector: a Cretan (Xen. *Hell*. 7.5.10), a Thespian (Plut. *Ages*. 34.4, citing Kallisthenes), or just someone (Polybios, 9.8.6).

1287 Again, there are two competing versions of events. The whole of Diod.'s narrative to the end of ch. 83 is based upon the premise that the Spartan army had to rush back from Mantineia to save the city (so, also, Polybios, 9.8.6), while Xenophon says Agesilaos had only reached Pellene (Pellana), when he was informed of Epameinondas' movements, and was able to get back to Sparta before the attack (*Hell*. 7.5.9).

1288 At the third hour of the day, according to Polybios (9.8.5), i.e. about 8 or 9 a.m.

behind on guard, had learned a little earlier from the Cretans the details of the plan, he immediately took charge of the defence of the city with great energy. 3. He got the oldest boys and the aged to go up onto the roofs of the houses and instructed them to repel from there any who had forced their way into the city. For his part, he organized the men of fighting age and apportioned them in groups to the difficult approaches outside the city. Then, when he had barricaded all the places that could allow a way through into the city, he waited for the enemy's attack. 4. Epameinondas divided his soldiers into several units and launched his attack from all sides simultaneously, but, when he saw the disposition of the Spartiate troops, he realized right away that his plan had been revealed. Nevertheless, despite the fact that he was attacking at all points separately and that he was at a disadvantage in the rough terrain, he engaged in battle.[1289] 5. With a great deal of give and take he persisted in his bold attempt, until the Lakedaimonian army returned to Sparta. As many other reinforcements came to assist the besieged and since night was taking hold, he put an end to his siege.[1290]

84.1. When Epameinondas learned from some captives that the Mantineians had arrived with their full citizen army to help the Lakedaimonians, for the time being he pulled back a little from the city, pitched camp and gave the order for his men to take their meal. Then, leaving behind some of the cavalrymen with orders to keep the fires burning in the camp until the morning watch, he set off at speed with the army, intending to make a surprise attack on the men left behind in Mantineia.[1291] 2. The next day, after covering a great distance, he burst upon the Mantineians with a sudden and unexpected attack. And yet, he did not achieve his objective, even though he had planned every aspect of his strategy in advance. He encountered a Fortune that was working against him and was deprived of the success he had expected. For, just as he was approaching

Epameinondas turns back and makes a surprise attack on Mantineia, but is thwarted by the arrival of an Athenian force

---

1289 Quite different is Polybios' account (9.8.5), where Epameinondas enters the city unopposed and makes his way as far as the marketplace.
1290 Diod. provides a more detailed account of the attack upon and the defence of Sparta than Xenophon (*Hell.* 7.5.11-13), albeit failing to mention Arkhidamos. Yet, the question remains, who organized the defence of Sparta, Agesilaos or his son?
1291 Xenophon, by contrast, says that Epameinondas sent his cavalry to attack Mantineia, while he rested his troops at Tegea (*Hell.* 7.5.14). This is clearly more credible than the idea that he made a forced march of his infantry from Tegea to Mantineia overnight. In his description of the resultant cavalry engagement (*Hell.* 7.5.15-17), Xenophon praises the courage of the outnumbered Athenian cavalry, remarking that "good men died," which is taken as a stoic epitaph for his own son, Gryllos, whose heroic death probably belongs to this engagement, not the main Battle of Mantineia (see 15.87.1).

the undefended city, there arrived on the opposite side of Mantineia the relief force sent from Athens, 6,000 strong, under the command of Hegelokhos, a man highly esteemed amongst his fellow citizens.[1292] Hegelokhos slipped an adequate defence-force into the city and drew up the rest of his army, ready to contest the issue in battle. 3. Shortly afterwards, both the Lakedaimonians and the Mantineians appeared on the scene, and all involved began to make preparations for a decisive engagement, summoning their allies from all quarters. 4. Now, assisting the Mantineians were the Eleians, the Lakedaimonians, the Athenians and some others. The sum total of their forces was over 20,000 infantry and about 2,000 cavalry. Most of the Arkadians, and their bravest, were fighting on the side of the Tegeans, as were the Akhaians, the Boiotians, the Argives and some other allies from the Peloponnese and beyond. The total of the forces they gathered was more than 30,000 infantry and no fewer than 3,000 cavalry.

Allies arrive for both sides and preparations are made for a decisive battle

Both sides arrange their forces for battle

85.1. After both sides had quickly come down to take up position for the decisive conflict[1293] and drawn up their armies for battle, the prophets in both camps made sacrifice and pronounced that the gods foretold victory each for their own side. 2. Regarding the arrangement of the battle-line, the Mantineians and the other Arkadians held the right wing, with the Lakedaimonians beside them in support. Next to them were the Eleians and Akhaians. The weaker elements of the remaining forces completed the centre, while the Athenians manned the left wing. On the other side, the Thebans lined themselves up on the left wing, with the Arkadians beside them. They left the right wing to the Argives. The rest of their number, the Euboians and the Lokrians and the Sikyonians, along with the Messenians and the Malians and the Ainianians, plus the Thessalians and the remaining allies, made up the centre. Both sides divided their cavalry in two and positioned them on each wing.[1294] 3. That is the way the armies were

The battle begins with cavalry engagements on both wings

1292 Like Diod., Polybios omits the cavalry battle and has Epameinondas march with his army to Mantineia overnight and arrive about midday. They had reached the temple of Poseidon, when the Athenian reinforcements came into sight (9.8.9–11). Ephoros (*FGrHist/BNJ* 70 F85) calls the leader of the Athenian forces Hegesileos, a cousin of the later politician Euboulos (Demosthenes 19, *On the False Embassy*, 290), and names the commander of the Athenian cavalry Kephisodoros (cf. Pausanias, 8.9.10).

1293 The battle took place on the border between Tegean and Mantineian territory, between the hills Mytika and Kapnistra. The date was probably some time in late May or early June, since Xenophon (*Hell*. 7.5.14) says it was time for the grain harvest. For the topography and course of this (and other) battles at Mantineia see Pritchett (1969), 37–72, who has harsh words for Diodoros (Ephoros), and Buckler (1980), 205–219.

1294 Diod. is the only source for the arrangement of troops in the battle-lines. Xenophon fails to provide this information, but he does describe the way Epameinondas packed his *phalanx* on the left (*Hell*. 7.5.22).

arranged for battle. When they were already within range of each other, the trumpets blew the signal for the charge to battle and the armies sent up the war cry, trying to declare victory by the loudness of their shout.[1295] The first engagement involved the cavalry on the wings,[1296] in which all participants tried to surpass their own achievements in their rivalry. 4. For example, after the Athenian cavalry had charged the Theban cavalry,[1297] they were worsted, despite the excellence of their mounts, their own individual courage and their experience in the art of horsemanship (for, in all these respects the Athenian cavalry was second to none). Where they were far inferior to their opponents was in the number and equipment of their light-armed troops,[1298] and in their tactical know-how. They, themselves, had few javelin-throwers, while the Thebans had three times their number of sling-throwers and javelin-throwers, who had been sent to them from areas around Thessaly. 5. The people there strive from childhood onwards to surpass others in this type of fighting and usually made a great difference in the outcome of battles through their expertise in these matters. As a result, the Athenians, because of the wounds inflicted by the light-armed troops, were worn down by their opponents and turned all together in flight. 6. But, by keeping their flight away from the wings, they managed to compensate for their defeat. For, on the one hand, they did not disrupt their own *phalanx* by their retreat, and, at the same time, encountering a group of Euboians and mercenaries, who had been sent out to occupy some nearby hills, they engaged them in battle and killed them all.[1299] 7. The Theban cavalry did not pursue their fleeing opponents, but instead charged the enemy *phalanx* in an ambitious attempt to outflank the infantry. A vigorous battle ensued, and the Athenians, worn down, had turned to flight, when the man in charge of the Eleian cavalry in the rear came to their assistance and, by striking down many of the Boiotians, changed the course of the battle. 8. So, the appearance of the Eleian cavalry on the left wing reversed the defeat suffered by their allies.[1300] On the other wing, the cavalry units clashed violently with each other and for a short time the

---

1295 This glosses over Epameinondas' initial movement, a feint to the west to confuse his enemy into thinking he was not going to fight (Xen. *Hell.* 7.5.21).
1296 Xenophon's account of the battle (*Hell.* 7.5.24–25), although briefer and less detailed than Diod., is essentially in agreement. Epameinondas' tactic was to begin with a cavalry charge.
1297 Given that the Thebans and allies were the aggressors, it is unlikely that the Athenian cavalry charged first. This may be a reflection of the earlier cavalry engagement that is missing from Diod.
1298 Known as *hamippoi*, they were light-armed javelin-throwers that fought alongside cavalry.
1299 Probably the force of cavalry and infantry posted on some hills opposite the Athenians on the right and later eliminated, referred to by Xen. *Hell.* 7.5.24, 25.
1300 This incident is not mentioned by Xenophon.

outcome hung in the balance. But, after a while, the size and quality of the Boiotian and Thessalian cavalry overpowered the men on the Mantineian side, who, after suffering many losses, fled towards their own *phalanx*.

Following the cavalry engagements, the infantry battle begins

86.1. So, such was the way the cavalry engagements turned out for both sides. As for the infantry forces, when they clashed with their enemies at close quarters, the resultant conflicts involved huge numbers and amazing deeds. For, never before in any battle between Greeks had such a large number of troops been involved,[1301] nor did commanders of such impressive reputations or better-prepared soldiers display such acts of courage in conflict. 2. For, when the best prepared infantry troops of that time, the Boiotians and the Lakedaimonians, whose battle-lines faced each other, initiated the clash of arms, they gave no thought for life or limb. They began by striking one another with their spears, but, since most of those were shattered under the hail of blows, they were reduced to fighting with their swords. 3. Locked body-to-body, they inflicted wounds of every description with unflagging spirits. Thanks to the excess of courage on both sides they endured these horrors for a long time, and the battle hung in the balance. For, each man thought little of suffering any harm, but rather aimed at performing some brilliant deed, nobly accepting death for the sake of honour.

As the battle hangs in the balance, Epameinondas decides to intervene

4. As the battle raged violently for a long time without any turning point in the conflict, Epameinondas surmised that victory called for an act of courage on his part and decided to settle the issue through his own intervention. So, he immediately gathered his bravest troops in close formation around himself and charged into the midst of the enemy. At the head of his unit, he was the first to cast his spear, hitting the commander of the Lakedaimonians. 5. Immediately after that, as the rest of his unit came to grips with the foe, he cut his way through the enemy *phalanx*, killing some and striking panic in others. The Lakedaimonians, overwhelmed by fear of Epameinondas' reputation and the powerful impact of the formation around him, retired from the battle. But the Boiotians followed close on their heels, continuously killing those in the rear, until there was a massive pile of corpses.[1302]

1301 This is probably an exaggeration. Although we can rarely trust the battlefield figures provided by our ancient sources, there were possibly more soldiers at the battle at the Nemea River than at Mantineia. But, Diod. finds some support from Xenophon (*Hell.* 7.5.26), who says that "almost the whole of Greece" was involved at Mantineia.

1302 The only reality that can be salvaged from this rhetorical purple passage (86.1–5) is the fact that Epameinondas aimed his *phalanx* specifically at the Spartans ("prow on, like a trireme," Xen. *Hell.* 7.5.23), as he had done at Leuktra. Otherwise, this is a typically formulaic Diodoran description of a battle, on which see the Introduction.

87.1. But, when the Lakedaimonians saw that Epameinondas was attacking too enthusiastically, driven by passion, they focused their attack on him. A thick hail of javelins assailed him, some of which he ducked, others he parried, and yet others he plucked from his body and used them to defend himself from his attackers. But, while thus putting up a heroic struggle for victory, he sustained a fatal wound in his chest.[1303] The spear shaft broke, leaving its iron point in his body. He fell to the ground instantly, deprived of strength by his wound. Fierce competition arose over his body, in which many on both sides were killed, but eventually, with a great effort, thanks to their superior physical strength, the Thebans overpowered the Lakedaimonians. 2. The Lakedaimonians fled. The Boiotians pursued them for a short distance, but then turned back, because they thought it was most essential to take possession of their dead.[1304] So, the trumpeters on both sides sounded the call for the soldiers to return and everyone ceased fighting. Since, however, both sides set up trophies, victory was in dispute. 3. For, the Athenians had defeated the Euboians and their mercenaries in the contest over the hilltop and were in possession of their dead, while the Boiotians, having worsted the Lakedaimonians in a contest of strength and being in possession of the bodies of the fallen, were awarding the victory to themselves. 4. As a result, for some time, neither side sent a delegation to discuss the return of the bodies of the dead, to avoid seeming to concede victory. But, after a while, the Lakedaimonians began the process by sending heralds to request the recovery of their dead. Following that, both sides buried their fallen.[1305] 5. Meanwhile, Epameinondas had been carried back to camp still alive. Doctors were summoned, and, when their prognosis was that, once the spear was pulled from his chest, death would inevitably follow, he chose to end his life with the utmost courage. 6. First, he called for his shield-bearer and asked if he had saved his shield. When he answered in the affirmative and presented it for him to see, Epameinondas asked a second question: which side had won? When the youth revealed that the Boiotians had been victorious, he said, "It is time to die," and ordered them to pull out the spear. His

Epameinondas presses his attack rashly and is struck by a fatal blow

The battle ends inconclusively, with both sides claiming victory

Despite efforts to save his life, Epameinondas dies philosophically

---

1303 According to Plutarch (*Ages.* 35.1), he was killed by a Spartan, named Antikrates. A completely different version is given by Pausanias (8.11.5–6, 9.15.5). He says that a Mantineian or Spartan, named Makhairion, was a candidate, although he clearly favoured the Athenian tradition that it was Gryllos, son of Xenophon, who killed him. That Gryllos fought at the Battle of Mantineia was believed by Ephoros (*FGrHist/BNJ* 70 F85), and both Gryllos and Epameinondas were depicted together in a painting of the battle by Euphranor in the Stoa of Zeus (Pausanias, 1.3.4).
1304 Xenophon, *Hell.* 7.5.25, says that the Thebans ceased their pursuit, because they were devastated by the death of Epameinondas.
1305 Cf. Xen. *Hell.* 7.5.26–27.

friends, gathered around, cried out in protest, and one, with tears in his eyes, exclaimed, "Epameinondas, you are dying childless." "No, by Zeus," he replied, "I leave behind two daughters, my victories at Leuktra and at Mantineia." Then, when the spear-head was withdrawn, he breathed his last quietly.[1306]

Epameinondas' life and achievements are eulogized

88.1. Since it has been our habit at the death of great men to pronounce over them a fitting eulogy, we consider it completely inappropriate to pass by the death of such a great man as Epameinondas without mention. For, in my opinion, he surpassed his contemporaries not only in his comprehension and experience of military affairs, but also in his decency and magnanimity. 2. For, in his generation other men of distinction flourished, such as Pelopidas from Thebes, Timotheos, Konon[1307] and also Khabrias and Iphikrates from Athens, and, additionally, a little earlier, Agesilaos the Spartiate. And there were great men, too, in the previous periods, the critical times of the wars with the Medes and the Persians, namely Solon, Themistokles, Miltiades, also Kimon, Myronides[1308] and Perikles and others from Athens, and in Sicily, there was Gelon, son of Deinomenes, amongst others. 3. Yet, if one compared their qualities with the military skill and the prestige of Epameinondas, he would find that Epameinondas' qualities far exceeded theirs. For, in each of the others one would find that their reputation was based upon a single talent, but in him all talents were combined. Indeed, he far excelled all the others in physical strength and skill in argument, as well as in the brilliance of his mind, his incorruptibility and decency, and, most important of all, in his courage and his comprehension of military affairs.[1309] 4. As a consequence, while he was alive, his country gained hegemony over Greece, but lost it after his death, experiencing a steady decline, until, in the end, thanks to the stupidity of its leaders,

---

1306 Diod. provides the most detailed account of Epameinondas' death. Variants of this narrative of Epameinondas' last moments can be found in Pausanias, 8.11.7, 9.15.5–6, who quotes his epitaph; Nepos, *Epameinondas*, 9.3; Justin, *Epitoma*, 6.8.11–13; and, less useful, Aelian, *VH*, 12.3. Both Justin and Nepos reflect some elements of Diod.'s account. Regarding what Epameinondas considered his legacy, the choice ranges from victories at Leuktra and Mantineia to the foundations of Megalopolis and Messene, and combinations of the above.

1307 Konon is clearly out of place. Maybe, what Diod. wrote, was "Timotheos, son of Konon." On the other hand, Solon, Myronides and Perikles, and possibly even Kimon, are equally out of place in the next list.

1308 Praised by Diod. at 11.81.4–83.4.

1309 This eulogy of Epameinondas departs from Diod.'s usual approach, which is to list the accomplishments of the recipient (cf. e.g. the eulogy of Pelopidas in ch. 81). Here, he concentrates on the character and qualities of Epameinondas, without naming any specific achievement.

it suffered enslavement and destruction.[1310] Well, such was the end of the life of Epameinondas, a man universally celebrated for his excellence.

89.1. After the battle the Greeks, while continuing to disagree over the victory, because they had proved themselves equal in valour, were, nevertheless, exhausted by the continuous fighting and agreed with each other to end the war. They concluded a Common Peace and alliance, including also the Messenians in the alliance. 2. But, the Lakedaimonians, because of their irreconcilable disagreement with the Messenians, chose not to participate in the agreement on their account and were the only Greeks to remain excluded from the treaty.[1311] 3. Amongst the writers of history, Xenophon the Athenian ended his account of Greek affairs (*Hellenika*) at this year with the death of Epameinondas.[1312] Also, Anaximenes of Lampsakos, who wrote "*The First Account of Greek Affairs*," beginning from the birth of the gods and the first generation of humans, ended his work at the Battle of Mantineia and the death of Epameinondas. He encompassed almost all the affairs of Greeks and barbarians in twelve books.[1313] And, Philistos ended his History of Dionysios the younger at this point, covering five years in two books.[1314]

90.1. In the archonship at Athens of Molon,[1315] in Rome, Lucius Genucius and Quintus Servilius were appointed as consuls.[1316] In their term of office, those who lived on the coast of Asia revolted from the Persians, and some of the

The Greeks, weary of war, agree to a Common Peace; only the Spartans refuse

Xenophon, Anaximenes of Lampsakos and Philistos end their histories at this point

362/1: Book 15.90.1–94.4

Some satraps make war on Artaxerxes, as does Takhôs, king of Egypt

---

1310 Thebes' decline was not immediate. See n. 1256. It was destroyed by Alexander the Great in 335.
1311 Diod.'s report of a Common Peace (*Koine Eirene*) in 362/1, after the Battle of Mantineia, from which Sparta excluded itself, is supported by both Polybios (4.33.8–9) and Plutarch (*Ages.* 35.2–4). His other claim, that this was also an alliance (i.e. involving obligations of mutual defence), although disputed, is supported by Polybios and generally accepted. This conclusion is possibly alluded to in a very controversial document (*IG* IV, 556; *TDGR*2, no. 57; R&O, no. 42), which is thought to be a Greek reaction to the Satraps' Revolt.
1312 Xenophon ended with the sad conclusion that "affairs in Greece were even more uncertain and confused after the Battle of Mantineia than before" (*Hell.* 7.5.27), as he handed over the baton to another writer.
1313 Anaximenes of Lampsakos (380–320) was a kind of jack-of-all-trades. After studying with Diogenes the Cynic and the Homeric scholar Zoilos, he spent the rest of his life as a rhetorician, both in practice and as a theorist, tried his hand at epic, but was best known as an historian. He travelled with Alexander and composed a flattering history of his campaigns. The work referred to here is a Universal History, rather like Diod.'s own.
1314 On Philistos, see at 14.8.5 and n. 60 and the Introduction.
1315 For Molon, see Develin, *AO*, 266.
1316 Cf. Livy, 7.1.7. This is now the Varronian year 365.

satraps and generals, rising in rebellion, made war against Artaxerxes.[1317] 2. Like them, Takhôs,[1318] king of Egypt, made the decision to go to war with the Persians. He equipped a navy and assembled an infantry force, hiring many mercenaries from the Greek states and even persuading the Lakedaimonians to become his allies. For, the Lakedaimonians were alienated from Artaxerxes over the fact that the Messenians had been included along with the rest of the Greeks in the Common Peace approved by the King.[1319] In response to such an uprising against Persian rule, the King, in turn, began to make preparation for war. 3. For, at one and the same time, he had to fight against the king of Egypt, the Greek cities in Asia, the Lakedaimonians, and the satraps and generals allied with them – rulers of the coastal territories, who had committed to working together.[1320] Amongst the satraps, the most illustrious were Ariobarzanes,[1321] satrap of Phrygia, who had also taken possession of the kingdom of Mithridates on his death;[1322] Mausolos, ruler of Karia, who possessed many

Artaxerxes is threatened by a huge uprising

1317 Diod.'s account of the so-called "Great Satraps' Revolt" is an excursus (perhaps based upon Ephoros) that combines the events of several years under one year and creates the erroneous impression of a mass revolt against Artaxerxes (Mnemon) in 362. In fact, the western satrapies had been in turmoil for decades, reaching back to the 380s, and probably as an inheritance of Kyros' challenge for the monarchy. The conflict was largely between satraps, rather than against the King. Nevertheless, amongst the numerous conflicting interpretations of the "Revolt," Diodoros' narrative is frequently cited, because it is all we have. On the revolt see Hornblower (1982), 170–182; Weiskopf (1989), *passim*; Stylianou, *Commentary*, 522–543; Briant (2002), 656–675.

1318 Egypt had been out of Persian control since the end of the fifth century: see 15.4.3 and n. 762, 15.38.1 and n. 969. Takhôs (or Teos, as he is called by Manethon) was the second king of the Thirtieth Dynasty. He succeeded his father, Nektanébôs, in 362/1 or 361/0, ruled for two years, and was overthrown by Nektanébôs II in 361/0 or 360/59.

1319 This is probably not a reference to the Common Peace of 362/1, since the King was not involved. It most likely refers back to the Peace of 367/6, negotiated by Pelopidas.

1320 This notion of "combined action/working together" (κοινοπραγία) by the satraps and generals makes it clear that Diod. (and probably Ephoros) believed that this was an organized insurrection.

1321 When Pharnabazos, the long-time satrap of Hellespontine Phrygia (see 14.11.1 and n. 74), was called to Sousa to take charge of the first Persian invasion of Egypt in the 380s and to marry Apame, daughter of Artaxerxes, Ariobarzanes, his relative, was put in charge of the satrapy. Sometime before 367 something caused Ariobarzanes to rebel. Perhaps it was the order from the King that Artabazos, son of Pharnabazos and Apame, reclaim the satrapy, or maybe it was a disagreement over foreign policy. Ariobarzanes' forces were besieged at Assos (or Adrammyttion, across the strait) by Autophradates and Mausolos (Xen. *Ages.* 2.26; Polyainos, *Strategemata*, 7.26). Since Ariobarzanes had received Athenian citizenship and was a friend of Sparta, Athens sent out Timotheos and Sparta sent Agesilaos to help (Xen. *Ages.* 2.26; Demosthenes 15, *On the Freedom of the Rhodians*, 9; Nepos, *Timotheos*, 1.2). The date of their involvement belongs before Timotheos' subjugation of Samos in 366/5. As it was successful, presumably Ariobarzanes' revolt continued.

1322 This reference to the kingdom of Mithridates probably refers to another Ariobarzanes.

fortresses and some impressive cities, of which the cultural centre and metropolis was Halikarnassos with its impressive acropolis, where was located the palace of the kings of Karia.[1323] In addition to these were Orontes, satrap of Mysia,[1324] and Autophradates, of Lydia.[1325] Amongst the peoples[1326] [i.e. in revolt] were the Lykians, the Pisidians, the Pamphylians, the Kilikians, as well as the Syrians, the Phoenicians and almost all the inhabitants of the coastal territories.[1327] 4. As a result of such a massive revolt, the King was deprived of half of his revenues, and the remainder was not enough to pay the cost of the war.

91.1. Those in rebellion against the King chose Orontes as their supreme commander and put him in charge of the whole affair. But, once he had assumed the command and taken possession of the funds for hiring mercenaries – enough to pay for 20,000 soldiers for a year – he betrayed the people who had trusted him. For, on the assumption that he would receive generous gifts from the King and would take over the governorship of the whole coastal territory, if he put the rebels in the hands of the Persians, he first arrested the men who had brought him the money and sent them off to Artaxerxes, then handed over many of the cities and the mercenary soldiers they had hired to the generals

The rebels choose Orontes as their commander-in-chief, but he betrays them

1323 Mausolos was, of course, not a satrap, although he may have thought of himself as one. On the Hekatomnids of Halikarnassos, see 14.98.3 and n. 634. His father was associated with Autophradates in the war against Evagoras in 390 that achieved nothing (Theopompos, *FGrHist/BNJ* 115 F103), and Mausolos himself had partnered with Autophradates in the siege of Ariobarzanes at Assos/Adrammyttion, from which he was "persuaded" to withdraw his fleet (Xen. *Ages.* 2.26). He was active in the Aegean with a fleet of, at least, 100 ships, promoting defections from the Athenian Confederacy. He was definitely playing his own game. See, in general, Hornblower (1982).

1324 Orontes is another controversial figure. Originally satrap of Armenia (Xen. *Anab.* 3.5.17), he had been a supporter of Artaxerxes against Kyros and was married to Rhodogune, one of the King's daughters. He was an assistant to Tissaphernes in the pursuit of the 10,000. For his subsequent involvement in a campaign against Evagoras with Tiribazos, his betrayal of his colleague and resultant disgrace, see 15.2.2 and n. 749, 15.8.3–11.2. Somehow, by now, he was satrap of Mysia (despite Trogus, *Epitoma, Prologue* 10). His duplicity at this time, which probably belongs soon after the insurrection began, should come as no surprise.

1325 Autophradates is perhaps a surprising rebel. Appointed satrap of Lydia in 392/1, he had served the King loyally since then, joining with Hekatomnôs of Karia in command of a campaign against Evagoras of Cyprus (n. 1323), leading an army against Datames of Kappadokia *c.*370 (see below), besieging Ariobarzanes at Assos in 366 (n. 1323). But the view that he fled that siege "in terror out of fear of Agesilaos" (Xen. *Ages.* 2.26) is perhaps deceptive. Sometime between then and 362 he had imprisoned Artabazos, son of Pharnabazos and Apame (Demosthenes 23, *Against Aristokrates*, 154), which suggests that he was already disaffected.

1326 An emendation for the impossible reading "Ionians" of the mss.

1327 For these territories, see Map 5.

A similar attempt at betrayal of Datames, satrap of Kappadokia, fails[1328]

sent out by the King. 2. There was also, similarly, treachery[1329] in Kappadokia, although it took a unique and unexpected form. When Artabazos,[1330] the King's general, invaded Kappadokia with a large army, Datames, the territory's satrap, marched out to oppose him. He had assembled a strong cavalry contingent and had 20,000 hired infantry soldiers fighting on his side. 3. But Datames' father-in-law, commander of the cavalry, wanting to store up favour with the King and at the same time looking out for his own security, defected during the night and rode off with his cavalry to the enemy, having made an agreement with Artabazos about the betrayal the previous day. 4. Datames summoned his mercenaries and, after promising them rewards, set out after the traitors. He caught up with them, when they were already in contact with the enemy. Attacking both Artabazos' men and the cavalry simultaneously, he killed any who came out to fight. 5. Artabazos, who did not at first understand the state of affairs, assumed that the man who had betrayed Datames was double-crossing him and ordered his own troops to kill the approaching cavalry. So, Mithrobarzanes found himself in a dire situation, caught between those who were attacking a traitor and those who were punishing a double-crosser. Since his situation did not allow time for consideration, Mithrobarzanes resorted to force. He fought against both sides and caused great carnage. Finally, after more than 10,000 had been killed, Datames put the remainder to flight. When he had slaughtered many of those, he had his trumpeter summon his soldiers back from pursuit. 6. Some of the surviving cavalry went back to Datames and asked for pardon, but the rest made no move, since they had nowhere to turn. In the end, this group, about 500 in number, was surrounded by Datames

---

1328 This is a digression from the narrative of the Satraps' Revolt. It should probably be dated to 359/8. Most details about the life and death of Datames come from Nepos' *Life of Datames*. Recognized as one of the most successful generals in Persia, he was delegated to share the command of an invasion of Egypt with Pharnabazos and Tithraustes (Nepos, *Datames*, 3). This must be the invasion of 374/3, which failed badly (chs. 41–44). When Pharnabazos was recalled, the overall command fell to Datames. Hearing from a friend that jealous courtiers were scheming against him, he had given up the post and retired to Kappadokia (Nepos, *Datames*, 5).

1329 Diod. presents the whole revolt in terms of treachery and betrayal.

1330 Artabazos, son of Pharnabazos and Apame, grandson of Artaxerxes, was the heir to the family estate at Daskyleion. About 367 he tried to reclaim his position from Ariobarzanes, but was rebuffed, despite the assistance he received from two notorious Greeks, Mentor and Memnon of Rhodes, to whose sister he was married. As noted above (n. 1325), he had been held captive by Autophradates, but now (359/8) was, according to Diod., the King's general against Datames of Kappadokia (Nepos, *Datames*, 7–8 and Frontinus, *Strategemata*, 2.7.9 make Autophradates his opponent). Artabazos' subsequent career, especially the time he spent with his wife and twenty-one children at Pella in Macedon as a guest of Philip II, will be followed in the next volume.

and speared to death.[1331] 7. So, Datames, who even before was admired for his leadership, was all the more celebrated for his courage and comprehension of military matters after this. But, when King Artaxerxes learned of Datames' successful generalship, he was eager to do away with him and conspired to have him assassinated.[1332]

Datames is assassinated on orders of Artaxerxes

92.1. Contemporaneous with these events,[1333] Rheomithres, who had been sent by the rebels to Egypt to visit Takhôs, the king, sailed back to a place called Leukai[1334] in Asia, bringing with him the 500 *talents* of silver and the fifty warships he had been given.[1335] Then, he invited many of the leaders of the rebellion to that city, arrested them and sent them in chains to Artaxerxes. Although himself one of the rebels, he used these gifts of treachery to reconcile himself with the King. 2. In Egypt, Takhôs, the king, had completed his preparations for war.[1336] He possessed 200 expensively equipped triremes and 10,000 elite mercenaries from Greece. In addition to these, he had 80,000 Egyptian soldiers. He entrusted the command of the mercenary troops to the Spartiate, Agesilaos, who had been sent by the Lakedaimonians with 1,000 hoplites under the terms of their alliance.[1337] Agesilaos was a man of proven capability in commanding an army and much admired for his courage and comprehension of military affairs. 3. Takhôs put the command of his navy in the hands of Khabrias, the Athenian. Khabrias had not been sent out by his city on a public assignment, but had been privately persuaded by the king to

Rheomithres brings money and ships from Egypt, but then betrays his colleagues to Artaxerxes

Takhôs prepares for war with the help of Agesilaos and Khabrias; attacks Phoenicia, is betrayed in Egypt and flees for mercy to the King

---

1331 This story is recounted by Nepos, *Datames*, 6, Frontinus, *Strategemata*, 2.7.9 and Polyainos, *Strategemata*, 7.21.7, with different opponents.

1332 According to Nepos, *Datames*, 10–11, he was assassinated by Mithridates, son of Ariobarzanes. Xenophon (*Kyroupaideia*, 8.8.4) reports that Mithridates killed his own father, Ariobarzanes.

1333 Diod. resumes his account of the collapse of the revolt, which he interrupted for the story of Datames.

1334 Leuke/Leukai was founded by another Takhôs (successor to Glôs in 383/2) on the coast of Asia Minor; see above at 15.18.1 and n. 832.

1335 Apparently leaving his wife and children and the children of his friends as hostages (Xen. *Kyroupaideia*, 8.8.4). Xenophon uses Rheomithres as a clear example of the decline in Persian honour.

1336 Takhôs was, of course, not a satrap and was not party to the revolt. He did, however, find it convenient to take advantage of the situation. He began his war most likely in early 361 or, as some think, in 360, since it would have been difficult for either Agesilaos, who had been in the Peloponnese in May/June 362, or Khabrias, who had been a general at Athens until July 362, to have reached Egypt in time for the campaigning season of 362. On Takhôs' war with Persia see Ruzicka (2012), 134–150.

1337 Cf. n. 1321. Plutarch (*Ages.* 36.6) says Agesilaos hired mercenaries with money from Takhôs and that he was accompanied on the expedition by thirty Spartan advisers.

aid his campaign.[1338] The king himself was the leader of the Egyptian contingent and was the supreme commander of the whole force.[1339] As such, he made the mistake of not accepting the excellent advice of Agesilaos, who counselled him to stay in Egypt and to let his generals manage the war. So, when his army had advanced beyond Egypt and was encamped in Phoenicia, the general who had been left in charge of Egypt defected from the king. He sent messages to his son, Nektanébôs,[1340] urging him to lay claim to the throne, and so kindled a great conflict. 4. For, Nektanébôs, who had been appointed by Takhôs as commander of the troops from Egypt and had been sent from Phoenicia into Syria to besiege the cities there, agreed to take part in his father's plot. He turned the allegiance of his unit commanders by bribes and won the soldiers to his side by promises and so persuaded them to become his supporters. 5. Eventually, once Egypt had fallen under the control of the rebels, Takhôs, in a panic, boldly made his way through Arabia up to the court of the King, where he asked to be forgiven for his past mistakes. And, Artaxerxes not only absolved him of all charges, but actually appointed him general of the war against the Egyptians.[1341]

Artaxerxes Mnemon dies and is succeeded by Artaxerxes Okhos

Takhôs is challenged by Nektanébôs to a battle for the throne of Egypt. He retreats with Agesilaos to a large town, where they are besieged

93.1. A little later, the King of the Persians died after a reign of forty-three years and was succeeded on the throne by Okhos. He adopted the name Artaxerxes and ruled for twenty-three years. For, as a result of the excellence of the reign of Artaxerxes [Mnemon], who was in every respect a man of peace and enjoyed good fortune, they made the Kings who followed him change their name and bade them adopt his title.[1342] 2. King Takhôs rejoined Agesilaos and his men, but Nektanébôs, after collecting an army of more than 100,000 soldiers, came out to oppose him and challenged him to a battle for the crown. Now, Agesilaos, perceiving that the king was scared stiff and lacked

1338 Khabrias was an Athenian general in 363/2, so was not a free agent until July 362. He had some previous experience in Egypt: see 15.29.2 and n. 898.
1339 Cf. Plutarch, *Ages.* 37.1–2, who depicts Agesilaos as being aggrieved at not being commander-in-chief.
1340 Called Takhôs' cousin by Plutarch (*Ages.* 37.3). In fact, his father may have been either an uncle or brother of Takhôs.
1341 A not impossible, but quite unsubstantiated, claim. Takhôs never regained the throne of Egypt.
1342 Diod. interrupts his narrative of Egyptian affairs for this note. It is not correct – Mnemon actually ruled for forty-six years and died in the winter of 359/8. If Mnemon was still alive when the fugitive Takhôs arrived at court, then his war was over before that time; see n. 1318. As for the title "Artaxerxes," it was certainly adopted by his successor, Okhos. The disaffection of so many of Mnemon's satraps and his failure to regain control of Egypt might seem to conflict with this laudatory assessment.

the courage for a fight, exhorted him to take heart. "For," he said, "it is not those with superior numbers who win victory, but those who excel in courage." This made no impression on Takhôs, so Agesilaos was forced to retreat with him to a good-sized city. 3. At first the Egyptians tried besieging them, as they were shut up inside, but, as they lost many men in the fighting around the walls, they began encircling the city with a wall and a ditch. Since the work was being accomplished speedily, thanks to the large number of men involved, and provisions (in the city) had run out, Takhôs gave up hope of safety, but Agesilaos, after a speech of encouragement to his men, made a nighttime attack upon the enemy and, against all odds, managed to get his whole army out safely. 4. The Egyptians followed in pursuit and, because the terrain was open and flat, assumed that the enemy would all be totally wiped out, encircled by their huge force. But Agesilaos seized a position that was protected on each side by a man-made ditch full of river water, and there prepared to await the enemy's attack. 5. After disposing his forces in a manner that suited the terrain and using the channels of the river to strengthen his army's position, he engaged in battle. Since the Egyptian numbers now became of no advantage to them, the Greeks, fighting with superior courage, slew many of the Egyptians and forced the remainder to flee. 6. After that, Takhôs easily regained the throne of Egypt, and Agesilaos, who had single-handedly restored the regime, was honoured with gifts appropriate to his service.[1343] But, on his way home through Kyrene, Agesilaos died.[1344] His body, preserved in honey,[1345] was transported back to Sparta, where he received the honorific burial due to a king. And that was how far the situation regarding affairs in Asia progressed this year.

Agesilaos effects a break-out and puts the Egyptians to flight

Takhôs regains his throne and rewards Agesilaos, who dies on his way home

94.1. In the Peloponnese, the Arkadians abided by their oaths and enjoyed the Common Peace that followed the Battle of Mantineia for only one year before they found themselves at war again.[1346] For, amongst the terms they had sworn to was the stipulation that all parties should return to their own country after

In the Peloponnese conflict breaks out over the settlement of Megalopolis

---

1343 This whole incident is reported with some similar details, but fundamental differences, by Plutarch, *Ages.* 38–40. In his more credible version, Takhôs never returns to Egypt; the conflict is between Nektanébôs and a competitor from Mendes, and it is Nektanébôs, once confirmed on the throne through the assistance of Agesilaos, who gives gifts to the Spartan king.

1344 Agesilaos died in 360/59 or 359/8 at the age of 84, having ruled for forty-one years, at a place called the Harbour of Menelaos (Plut. *Ages.* 40.3). On Agesilaos' career after Mantineia in both Asia and Egypt see Cartledge (1987), 325–330.

1345 His body was preserved in wax, according to Plutarch, because they could not get any honey (*Ages.* 40.3).

1346 I.e. in the summer of 361.

The Megalopolitans are supported by the Thebans, who send Pammenes with 3,000 troops

the battle. In the creation of Megalopolis,[1347] however, the inhabitants of the neighbouring cities had been moved from their homes and they were not happy about being taken away from their homeland. When, as a consequence of the peace treaty, they returned to their former cities, the Megalopolitans used force to make them leave their homeland. 2. The result was a dispute, in which the inhabitants of the smaller cities sought the assistance of the Mantineians and some of the other Arkadians, even of the Eleians and the other states that belonged to the Mantineian alliance.[1348] The Megalopolitans, for their part, called upon the Thebans to act as their allies. The Thebans promptly sent them 3,000 hoplites and 300 cavalry, under the command of Pammenes.[1349] 3. Once he arrived, he attacked the little towns, sacking some and intimidating others, and compelled them to move to Megalopolis. Thus, the issues involved in the political unification [*synoikismos*] of the cities, that had come to such a crisis, found the only possible resolution.

Athanas of Syracuse starts his history of Dion at this point

4. Amongst the writers of history, Athanas of Syracuse began his thirteen-book account of the deeds of Dion at this point, but prefaced it with one book covering the unrecorded seven years from the end of Philistos' narrative. By reporting those events in summary fashion, he connected the two histories in a continuous narrative.[1350]

361/0: Book 15.95.1–95.4

In an attack on Peparethos, Alexander, tyrant of Pherai, defeats the Athenian general, Leosthenes

95.1. In the archonship at Athens of Nikophemos,[1351] the consular power in Rome was shared by Gaius Sulpicius and Gaius Licinius.[1352] In their term of office, Alexander, tyrant of Pherai, sent his pirate ships out into the islands of the Cyclades. He took some by storm and acquired many captives.[1353] On

1347 On the founding of Megalopolis, see 15.72.4 and n. 1195.
1348 Probably a reference to the alliance of Athens and her Confederacy with Arkadia (Mantineian part), Akhaia, Elis and Phleious, concluded in the archonship of Molon (*IG* II² 112; *TDGR*2, no. 56; R&O, no. 41).
1349 Pammenes was the most successful Theban general in the period after the death of Pelopidas and Epameinondas. He had been coached by Epameinondas. His home was where Philip of Macedon spent his sojourn as a hostage at Thebes (Plut. *Pelop.* 26.8). He had been in command of a force of 1,000 Boiotian soldiers that had protected Megalopolis, while it was being built (Pausanias, 8.27.2).
1350 Athanas, or Athanis, of Syracuse (*FGrHist/BNJ* 562) wrote a History of Sicily (*Sikelika*) that seems to have included the career of Timoleon, beginning in 355/4 with the rule of Dion. As this note says, he added one transitional book as a preface, to connect his history to the point where Philistos left off in 362/1.
1351 For Nikophemos, see Develin, *AO*, 267.
1352 Cf. Livy, 7.2.1 and the *Fasti Capitolini* (under the Varronian year 364), who give the full names, Gaius Sulpicius Peticus and Gaius Licinius Stolo.
1353 Demosthenes 50, *Against Polykles*, 4, dates Alexander's capture and enslavement of the Cycladic island of Tenos to the second month of the archonship of Molon, i.e. a full year earlier.

Peparethos, he disembarked his mercenary soldiers and began to besiege the city. 2. When the Athenians came to the assistance of the Peparethians and left Leosthenes behind in command, Alexander attacked the Athenians, who happened to be keeping watch over some of Alexander's soldiers billeted in Panormos. Alexander's men made a surprise attack and Alexander was presented with an unexpected success. For, he not only saved the men who had been dropped off at Panormos from extreme danger, but also captured five triremes from Attica and one from Peparethos, as well as acquiring 600 captives.[1354] 3. In a fit of fury, the Athenians condemned Leosthenes to death on a charge of treachery and confiscated his property.[1355] Then, they chose Khares as general and sent him out with a fleet. His practice was to keep a safe distance from the enemy, while inflicting abuse on the allies. For example, he landed on Kerkyra, an allied city, and stirred up violent political strife there, which resulted in many deaths and arrests.[1356] This brought the Athenian *demos* into great disrepute amongst the allies. So, Khares, by committing other similar acts of lawlessness, accomplished no benefit for his country, just condemnation.[1357] 4. Amongst the writers of history, Dionysodoros and Anaxis of Boiotia, authors of *Hellenika*, brought their narratives to a close at this year.[1358]

The Athenians sentence Leosthenes to death. They appoint Khares in his place. Khares sails to Kerkyra

Dionysodoros and Anaxis of Boiotia end their histories at this point

1354 Piracy was endemic in the ancient Mediterranean. Alexander of Pherai's pirate ships seem to have roamed the seas with impunity. From Tenos in the Cyclades to Peparethos in the Sporades of the northern Aegean, even sailing into the Peiraieus and stealing the money off the bankers' tables, if we are to believe two entries in Polyainos' *Strategemata* (6.2.1 and 6.2.2). Peparethos was a member of the Second Athenian Confederacy and a key post on the transit route for grain from the Black Sea to Athens. It is no surprise that the Athenians were unhappy with their general.

1355 For Leosthenes, see Davies, *APF*, 342–344. He was impeached by *eisangelia* (Hypereides 3, *In defence of Euxenippos*, 1) and went into exile in Macedon (Aiskhines 2, *On the False Embassy*, 21, 124). However, his son, Leosthenes, was the most successful commander of Greek forces against Antipater in the Lamian War (323–322).

1356 The revolt was oligarchic, according to Aineias Taktikos (11.13), who, however, says that Khares was residing on the island with a garrison.

1357 Khares has a bad reputation amongst the sources as a brutal and lawless man. It is hard to verify the validity of this reputation. He certainly served the *demos* well for forty years, being elected to the generalship many times. It is not unlikely that this reputation stemmed from the influential pen of Isokrates, who compared the performance of his favourite pupil, Timotheos, son of Konon, to unnamed men of great physical strength but no morality (e.g. 8, *On the Peace*, 50, 54–56; 15, *Antidosis*, 115, 121, 129). This is usually taken as a reference to Khares, who had collaborated with Aristophon of Azenia in a prosecution of Timotheos, Iphikrates and Menestheos after the battle of Embata in 356, a prosecution that led to the disgrace, exile and eventual death of Timotheos.

1358 This is the only reference to the existence of Anaxis, for whom we have no fragments (see *FGrHist/BNJ* 67). Dionysodoros is little better off with only one fragment (*FGrHist/BNJ* 68). Apparently, they both wrote Histories of Greece down to the Battle of Mantineia.

We, also, now that we have covered the events that preceded the time of king Philip, will conclude this book in accordance with its original plan. In the next book, we shall narrate all the achievements of this king from his accession to the throne up to his death, interweaving any other events that took place in the known portions of the inhabited world.

Appendix
Modern Chronological Outline

Since the Athenian administrative year, which constitutes the basis of most chronological schemes, ran from midsummer to midsummer, dates are frequently given covering two calendar years.

405/4
(July 405) In Sicily, Dionysios makes peace with Carthage, yielding control of most of Sicily, but maintaining his tyranny in Syracuse. He fortifies Ortygia.

(Autumn, 405) In Greece, Athenian fleet defeated and captured by Lysander at Aigospotamoi in the Hellespont. Konon flees to his friend Evagoras on Cyprus. Lysander sails to Athens, on the way liberating the islands in the Aegean, except Samos, and establishing *decarchies* (juntas of ten men friendly to Sparta) and Spartan garrisons and governors (*harmosts*). Lysander besieges Athens by sea, and Agis by land.

(Winter) Negotiations held at Sparta regarding Athenian surrender. Athenian delegation led by Theramenes.

(Spring, 404) Athens surrenders. Long Walls demolished.

(June 404) Thirty Tyrants elected at Athens as commissioners (*syngrapheis*) to revise the laws.

404/3
(Summer, 404) In Sicily, Dionysios attacks Herbessos. Syracusans mutiny. Dionysios despairs of keeping his tyranny, but surprisingly overcomes resistance.

In Asia, death of Alkibiades in Phrygia.

(Autumn, 404) In Greece, Samos surrenders to Lysander. Thirty Tyrants begin to eliminate opponents. Flight of Thrasyboulos and others to Thebes. Spartan garrison, led by Kallibios, established on the acropolis at request of the Thirty. Theramenes put to death. Seizure of Phyle by Thrasyboulos. Oligarchs try, but fail, to expel him.

403
In Greece, Thrasyboulos moves to hill of Mounykhia in Peiraieus. The attack by the Thirty is defeated. Death of Kritias and Kharmides. Thirty retreat to Eleusis and are replaced by the Ten.

In Sicily, Dionysios disarms the Syracusans.

403/2

(Autumn) Spartan army under Pausanias defeats Thrasyboulos in Peiraieus and brings about reconciliation amongst Athenians, except for the Thirty at Eleusis and the Peiraieus Ten. Democracy is restored. Klearkhos sets himself up as tyrant in Byzantion, but is driven out and flees to Kyros in Ionia.

In Sicily, Dionysios campaigns against Syracusan cavalry in Aitna, colonies of Khalkis in Naxos, Katane and Leontinoi and Sikels in Enna and Herbita. He captures Katane and Naxos and enslaves the population, and moves the people of Leontinoi to Syracuse.

402/1

In Greece, Thebes annexes Oropos.
In Sicily, Dionysios fortifies Epipolai.

402–400

In Greece, Spartan war against Elis, ending in surrender of Elis.

401

Oligarchs in Eleusis overcome by democratic forces and Attica is reunited.

401/0

In Asia, Kyros' campaign against his brother, Artaxerxes; his defeat at Kounaxa and the march of the Ten Thousand to the Black Sea.

400

In Greece, Sparta expels the Messenians from Naupaktos and Kephallenia.

400/399

In Greece, death of Agis. Also, death of Sokrates.
In Asia, Tamôs flees to Egypt, where he is killed. Greek cities in Asia request Spartan help against Tissaphernes. Thibron sent to Asia Minor to liberate Greek cities from Persia. Requests 300 cavalry from Athens. Thibron accused of plundering allies.
In Sicily, Dionysios founds Adranon.
In Macedon, Arkhelaos, king of Macedon, dies.

399/8

In Greece, Agesilaos chosen to succeed Agis. Herippidas sent out by Sparta to resolve *stasis* in Herakleia Trakhis.

In Asia, Derkylidas sent out to replace Thibron. Makes truce with Pharnabazos and helps Greeks in Khersonesos against Thracians by building a wall.

In Sicily, Rhegion and Messina ally to oppose Dionysios, but their opposition collapses. Dionysios makes preparations for a war against Carthage.

398/7

In Asia, Athenian embassy to Persia caught and arrested by Spartan *navarch*, Pharax. Pharnabazos persuades Artaxerxes to oppose Sparta, to build a fleet and appoint Konon as commander.

(Winter) In Greece, Herodas reports shipbuilding in Phoenicia. In response, Lysander proposes Agesilaos lead a Spartan campaign to Asia.

In Sicily, Dionysios' marriages and his declaration of war against Carthage. Dionysios' forces march West and besiege Motye. Capture and sack of Motye.

397/6

In Asia, Agesilaos takes his army to Ephesos. Sends Lysander off to Bithynia. Worsted in a cavalry battle with Tissaphernes, Agesilaos retires to Ephesos for the winter.

396/5

In Sicily, Himilkon leads a huge Carthaginian response to Dionysios' sack of Motye. Dionysios retreats to Syracuse. Himilkon attacks and takes Messina. Naval battle between Magon and Leptines won by Magon. Carthaginians in Great Harbour and Syracuse under siege. Himilkon's sacrilege repaid by plague. Defeat and humiliation of Himilkon.

In Greece, Konon engineers the revolt of Rhodes from Sparta. Timokrates of Rhodes brings funds from Persia, which help prompt the Greek states Athens, Thebes, Corinth and Argos to combine against Sparta.

(Spring, 395) In Asia, Agesilaos wins the Battle of Sardis.

(Summer, 395) In Greece, war breaks out between Lokris and Phokis. Thebes and Sparta involved. This is the spark that ignites the Corinthian War. Battle of Haliartos in Boiotia; death of Lysander, disgrace of Pausanias.

395/4

(Winter, 395) In Greece, Agesilaos is called back from Asia by Sparta.

(Spring, 394) Sparta defeats the allies at the Battle of Nemea.

394/3

(Autumn, 394) In Aegean, Konon and Pharnabazos defeat the Spartan fleet at the Battle of Knidos.

In Greece, simultaneously, Agesilaos defeats the allies at the Battle of Koroneia in Boiotia and thence returns to Sparta, while Konon and Pharnabazos "liberate" islands in the Aegean from Sparta.

(Spring, 393) Dionysios, his sons and his brother-in-law receive honours at Athens. Konon and Pharnabazos sail to Kythera and then to Corinth. Pharnabazos returns to Asia. Konon proceeds to Athens and sets his crews to help in the rebuilding of Athens' fortifications, that was already underway. Corinthian War reaches a stalemate around Corinth.

In Sicily, conflict between Dionysios and Rhegion.

393/2

(Winter, 393) In Asia, Antalkidas sent on embassy to Tiribazos.

In Sicily, Dionysios besieges Tauromenion and is worsted; almost captured.

(Spring, 392) Magon attacks Messina, but is defeated by Dionysios at Abakaine. Dionysios attacks Rhegion, but is repulsed. Italiot Greeks form alliance against Dionysios.

In Greece, Argos achieves *isopolity* with Corinth.

Betrayal of Lekhaion, the port of Corinth, to Sparta.

(Summer, 392) In Asia, negotiation of peace terms by Antalkidas and Tiribazos. Tiribazos arrests Konon.

In Italy, Veii surrenders to Rome, ending ten-year war.

392/1

(Winter, 392) In Greece, peace conference held at Sparta about terms worked out between Antalkidas and Tiribazos. Athenian delegates accept terms, but they are rejected by the Assembly. Delegates exiled.

In Asia, Konon escapes to Cyprus and dies there. Tiribazos (pro-Spartan) replaced by Strouthas (pro-Athenian) as satrap of Ionia by Artaxerxes.

In Sicily, Magon makes another attempt to regain Carthaginian control, but is defeated and makes peace, yielding subjection of the Sikels to Dionysios and giving up Tauromenion.

391/0

In Aegean, Rhodian oligarchs take back control of Rhodes. Spartan fleet led by Teleutias in the Aegean.

In Cyprus, the growth of Evagoras' power prompts Artaxerxes to prepare for war. Evagoras revolts and makes alliance with Athens and Akoris of Egypt.

In Greece, Iphikrates defeats a unit (*mora*) of the Spartan army, using peltasts. Thrasyboulos sails to Thrace and the Hellespont with an Athenian fleet and

renews old alliances. Makes alliance with Medokos and Seuthes of Thrace. Sails on to Lesbos.
In Italy, Romans make peace with the Faliscans, embark on the fourth war against the Aequi and send colonists to Sutrium.
In Asia, Thibron killed in battle with Strouthas.

390/89

(Autumn, 390) In Italy, Dionysios plans to attack the Italiot Greeks, but first assaults Rhegion. His fleet hit by a storm, from which he barely escapes. Makes alliance with Lucanians and returns to Syracuse.
(Spring, 389) Thourians invade Lucania and suffer huge defeat.
(Summer, 389) In Asia, death of Thrasyboulos at Aspendos. Spartan Anaxibios defeated and killed in battle with Iphikrates at Hellespont.

389/8

In Italy, Dionysios invades and attacks the Italiots, who are defeated at the Eleporos River. Destruction of Kaulonia. Dionysios prepares to assault Rhegion.
(Spring, 388) In Greece, Agesilaos leads Spartan invasion of the Argolid.
In Asia, Artaxerxes changes course and replaces Strouthas with the pro-Spartan Tiribazos.
(Summer, 388) Antalkidas sent out to meet Tiribazos.
In Greece, Dionysios' embarrassment at the Olympic Games.

388/7

In Italy, Dionysios razes Hipponion to the ground and transfers citizens to Syracuse. Dionysios begins the siege of Rhegion.
(Spring, 387) In Greece, Teleutias makes naval raid on the Peiraieus.
(Summer, 387) In Asia, Antalkidas is successful in naval operations in the Hellespont against Athenian fleet.

387/6

(Autumn, 387) In Asia, peace negotiations at Sardis.
In Sicily, fall of Rhegion and massacre of its citizens by Dionysios.
In Italy, sack of Rome by the Gauls.
(Spring, 386) In Greece, King's Peace concluded at Sparta. It is based upon the principle that all Greek states will be free and autonomous under a common peace that all are bound to defend. Sparta is to be the power that guarantees the peace, but uses its position to further its own ends.

386/5–380

In Asia, Persian war against Evagoras. Tiribazos and Orontes lead Persian invasion of Cyprus. Persia also at war with Egypt. Evagoras' fleet is defeated by Tiribazos. Tiribazos besieges Evagoras and proposes terms for surrender. Orontes' complaints lead to recall of Tiribazos. Trial and acquittal of Tiribazos. Disgrace of Orontes. Capitulation of Evagoras on terms.

386/5

In Greece, Sparta demands that the Mantineians dissolve the synoikism of their five constituent villages. They refuse and are besieged.

In Sicily, Dionysios has intellectual disagreements with Philoxenos and Plato.

385/4

(Winter, 385) In Greece, Mantineia surrenders to Sparta and the city is dissolved into five villages. Sparta supports return of oligarchic exiles to Phleious.

In Sicily, Dionysios embarks on his ambition to expand his empire into the Adriatic.

384/3

(Summer, 384) In Greece, Athens makes an alliance with Khios. Athens also allies with Olynthos.

383/2–379?

In Sicily, Dionysios prepares to start another conflict with Carthage and declares war. After some time, the Carthaginians send a large force under Magon in response. The battle of Kabala is a victory for Dionysios and involves the death of Magon. Sometime later, another battle at Kronion is a major victory for Carthage. Peace is concluded, with the river Halykos dividing the two spheres of influence, and involving Dionysios in paying a large indemnity.

383/2

(Summer and Autumn, 382) In Greece, a Spartan expedition is sent out against Olynthos in response to requests from Akanthos and Apollonia. On the way, the general in charge, Phoibidas, seizes the Kadmeia, the citadel of Thebes. Following Theban protests, he is recalled and tried in Sparta, but acquitted. A Spartan garrison is installed on the Kadmeia. Teleutias takes over command against Olynthos.

In Asia, death of Glôs, replaced by Takhôs. Foundation of Leuke.

In Macedon, Amyntas is driven from his throne and gifts some territory to Olynthos.

382/1

(Spring, 381) In Greece, Teleutias dies at Olynthos. Agesilaos begins siege of Phleious.

(Summer, 381) Agesipolis in command at Olynthos.

380/79

In Greece, Agesipolis dies at Olynthos. Polybiadas takes over.

(Spring, 379) Phleious surrenders to Agesilaos.

(Summer, 379) Fall of Olynthos. Its Khalkidic League is dissolved and its members become part of Peloponnesian League.

379/8

(Autumn, 379) In Greece, liberation of the Kadmeia by Thebans led by Pelopidas.

(Spring, 378) Spartan army led by Kleombrotos invades Boiotia, but retires without achievement. In response, Thebes begins reconstitution of the former Boiotian League.

378/7

(Autumn, 378) In Greece, Sphodrias' abortive nighttime raid on Attica. Athens protests to Sparta. Sphodrias tried, but acquitted, thanks to intervention by Agesilaos. Athens makes alliance with Thebes. Also puts gates on the walls around the Peiraieus and starts a programme of shipbuilding. Athenian alliances with Byzantion, Methymna, Mytilene, Rhodes and Khalkidians on Euboia.

(Spring, 377) Decree of Aristoteles (*IG* II^2 43) outlines the terms of the Second Athenian Confederacy, the stated purpose of which is "that the Lakedaimonians may allow the Hellenes, free and autonomous, to live in peace, holding in security the land that is their own."

(Summer, 377) Khabrias campaigns in Euboia.

377/6

(Spring, 376) In Greece, Kleombrotos disappoints Spartan allies by failing to invade Boiotia.

376/5

(Autumn, 376) In Greece, Khabrias wins the Battle of Naxos and revives Athenian supremacy at sea.

(Summer, 375) Numerically superior army from Sparta defeated in battle at Tegyra by an elite Theban unit (the Sacred Band) under Pelopidas. Khabrias campaigns in Thrace and the Hellespont.

Timotheos sails around the Peloponnese, gains many allies for the Athenian Confederacy in the West and fights naval battle at Alyzeia against Spartan Nikolokhos.

375/4

(Autumn, 375) In Greece, a new Common Peace is concluded by Greek states, weary of war.

(Winter, 375) Political strife (*stasis*) breaks out on Kerkyra between oligarchs and democrats.

374/3

Strife on Kerkyra continues, with Mnasippos from Sparta aiding oligarchs, Ktesikles from Athens the democrats.

In Asia, Iphikrates assists Pharnabazos in Persian attempt to recover control of Egypt. The attempt fails and Pharnabazos blames Iphikrates. Evagoras of Salamis on Cyprus dies.

373/2

(Summer, 373) In Greece, Iphikrates, back in Athens, sent out to Kerkyra. Death of Mnasippos. Peace of 375/4 ended and war resumes. Thebes takes control of Thespiai and Tanagra, attacks, captures and destroys Plataia, old ally of Athens. Alienation of Athens from Thebes. Plataian refugees welcomed at Athens and given Athenian citizenship.

372/1

In Greece, Thebes destroys Thespiai.

(Spring, 371) Thebes invades Phokis. Kleombrotos sent with Spartan army to help Phokians, allies of Sparta. King of Persia urges Greeks to conclude a new Common Peace. States meet at Sparta and agree, except Thebes. Agesilaos orders Kleombrotos to invade Boiotia and enforce the peace.

(Summer, 371) Battle of Leuktra. Pelopidas and Epameinondas defeat Spartans and kill Kleombrotos. Defeat of Spartan army shocks Greece.

Spartan relief force under Arkhidamos, son of Agesilaos, rushed to the Isthmus of Corinth. Jason of Pherai, an ally of Thebes, arrives with reinforcements, but is too late. He, however, helps mediate disengagement of Spartan and Boiotian troops. Spartans return home.

Athenians organize a peace conference at Athens, where all agree to peace, except Thebes, which does not attend.

371/0

In Greece, as a result of Sparta's defeat at Leuktra, states in the Peloponnese dispute Sparta's supremacy. Elis tries to recover the possessions it lost in the Eleian War of 402–400 and Mantineia plans to put back together the city that was dissolved by Agesipolis.

Factional strife erupts between pro- and anti-Spartan groups in Tegea, while Mantineia leads the movement towards the creation of an Arkadian League. In response, Agesilaos leads a force into Arkadia that marauds the land, but retires after achieving nothing else. The Arkadian League in response makes alliances with Elis, Argos and the Boiotian League, led by Thebes.

370/69

In Greece, Thebes campaigns against Orkhomenos. Jason expands his power in Thessaly and may have had greater ambitions in Greece, but is assassinated. Civil strife in Argos.

(Winter, 370) Mantineia and Elis ask the Boiotian League to intervene in Peloponnesian affairs. Epameinondas leads the first Theban invasion of the Peloponnese. He ravages Lakonia, assaults Sparta itself, but is repelled, liberates Messenia and founds Messene.

369/8

In Greece, Athens, afraid of the rise of Thebes, becomes an ally of Sparta. The two states agree to divide the hegemony of Greece in an attempt to exclude Thebes. Khabrias is sent to the Peloponnese to aid in preparations against a second invasion by Theban forces. Nevertheless, Epameinondas breaks through the prepared lines of defence and wins Sikyon and Pellene from their alliance with Sparta. After ravaging the area around Epidauros, he returns via the Isthmus, on the way making an attempt to capture Corinth that is prevented by Khabrias.

From Sicily, Dionysios, long time ally of Sparta, sends Celtic and Iberian mercenaries, at his expense, to help Sparta. After demonstrating their skillful swordsmanship, they return to Sicily.

Pelopidas campaigns in Thessaly and Macedon. Alexander of Macedon surrenders hostages to Thebes, one of whom is Philip, future king of Macedon.

368/7

In Greece, Arkhidamos invades Arkadia and wins the "Tearless Battle."
Arkadians found Megalopolis in response, with Theban assistance.
(Spring, 367) Athens makes an alliance with Dionysios I of Syracuse.
Second campaign of Pelopidas into Thessaly and his arrest by Alexander of Pherai. A Boiotian relief force fails to secure his release.
In Sicily, Dionysios begins a new war to drive the Carthaginians out of the island. His campaign is minimally successful, but ended by his death in the Spring of 367. His son, Dionysios II, succeeds.

367/6

In Greece, slaughter of Skotoussians by Alexander of Pherai. Epameinondas marches into Thessaly and gains the release of Pelopidas. Pelopidas goes to Persia and secures a Persian-backed peace that calls for the recognition of the independence of Messene and the retirement of the Athenian fleet.
(Spring, 366) Congress at Thebes about these peace proposals fails.
Third invasion of the Peloponnese (north) by Epameinondas.

366/5

In Greece, Timotheos, Athenian general, campaigns in Thrace and wins Poteidaia, Torone, Pydna and Methone for the Athenian Confederacy. Ordered by the *demos* to aid Ariobarzanes at Assos, he sails on to Samos and captures it. Later an Athenian *kleroukhy* (settlement) is sent to Samos. Thebes again takes Oropos from Athens.
In Asia, probable outbreak of trouble in the western satrapies of the Persian Empire, called the "Satraps' Revolt," which may have ended in 360.

365/4

In Greece, more trouble in the Peloponnese. Conflict flares between Elis and Arkadia over Triphylia. Arkadians seize control of Olympia and give it to Pisa. Elis allies with Sparta and Akhaia.
Epameinondas persuades the Boiotians to build a fleet and sails into the Aegean. Pelopidas campaigns in Thessaly and defeats Alexander of Pherai at Kynoskephalai, but is killed.

364/3

Breakup of the Arkadian League: Tegea sides with Thebes, while Mantineians favour Elis and Sparta.

363/2

Epameinondas leads his fourth invasion of the Peloponnese to defend his settlement, especially the independence of Messene.

(Autumn, 362) Battle of Mantineia leads to inconclusive result: victory of Thebans over Spartans, but success of Athenians on their wing. The death of Epameinondas following the loss of Pelopidas deprives Thebes of its leadership.

362/1 or 361/0

In Asia, Nektanêbôs I of Egypt succeeded by Takhôs. Assisted by Khabrias and Agesilaos, Takhôs goes to war with Persia.

Treachery of Orontes and Rheomithres enables Artaxerxes to reassert his authority in Asia Minor. Death of Ariobarzanes and Datames.

In Greece, trouble in Arkadia threatens Megalopolis. The Theban general Pammenes defends Megalopolis. Alexander of Pherai attacks Peparethos. Leosthenes, Athenian general, condemned to death, goes into exile in Macedon. Replaced by Khares.

360/59 or 359/8

In Asia, Artaxerxes II (Mnemon) dies and is succeeded by Artaxerxes III (Okhos).

Takhôs defeated and replaced in Egypt by Nektanêbôs II. Death of Agesilaos in Kyrene.

Glossary of Greek and Latin Terms

Ager Gallicus	Territory in northern Italy on the Adriatic coast occupied by the Gallic tribe Senones
Agora	Marketplace and/or civic centre of a Greek city
Anarkhia	Year without an eponymous archon in Athens
Anolympiad	Olympic Festival that was not recognized by Elis
Aspis	The large convex shield carried by a Greek infantryman
Ateleia	Exemption from the performance of obligatory public services (liturgies) extended to a citizen of a Greek city for distinguished behaviour; also granted as an honorary privilege to foreign rulers in return for services rendered
Boiotarch	The military commanders of the Boiotian League with political authority similar to Athenian *strategoi*. Originally seven, they sometimes increased to nine
Cognomen	Additional or associated third name of a Roman. Following the *praenomen* (first name, like Marcus or Gaius) and the *nomen* (clan name, like Scipio or Julius), the *cognomen* distinguished a person further by adding a nickname (like Cicero, "chickpea") or a family name to indicate a branch of a clan (like "Caesar")
Damiorgoi	Members of the probouleutic council of the Arkadian League
Demos	The citizen body of a Greek state
Dictator	Roman elected to supreme command of the state in emergency circumstances and only for the duration of the emergency
Dies nefastus	Unpropitious day in the Roman calendar when no public or judicial business was allowed
Drachma	A monetary unit in Greece, the equivalent of a handful of six *obols*
Eisangelia	An indictment at Athens by publicly informing against a person before the Council or Assembly. It could be used in a number of situations, but most frequently it was used as a form of impeachment against public officials for incompetence, malfeasance or treachery
Eleutheria	Freedom from oppression or outside interference. One of the two expectations of a Greek state. The other was living under its own laws (autonomy)

Epikrateia	"Domain." The term is used to describe the Carthaginian sphere of influence in Sicily
Eparitoi/Epilektoi	Elite hoplite troops of the Arkadian League
Epimeletes	Officials at Athens who supervised physical infrastructure, such as the shipyards in the Peiraieus
Epistoleus	Denotes a secretary or dispatch carrier. The Spartans used the term for a vice-admiral or second-in-command of the navy
Fasti Capitolini	A list of Roman magistrates developed by Marcus Terentius Varro that was inscribed either on the walls of the Regia in the forum or by the Emperor Augustus on his triumphal arch. Its fragments are preserved in the museum on the Capitoline Hill, hence its name
Harmost	A Spartan military governor of subject cities. Their use was particularly prevalent after the end of the Peloponnesian War
Hubris	An act of excessive pride or arrogance that invited punishment by the gods (*nemesis*)
Isopolity	The sharing of equal and reciprocal rights between two cities
Jugerum	A Roman unit of area, traditionally the amount of land that could be ploughed in one day. It measured 28,000 Roman feet (0.25 of a hectare or 0.6 of an acre)
Jus gentium	"The law of nations" was Roman international law, as opposed to the law of an individual state (*jus civile*). It was administered by the *praetor Peregrinus* (minister in charge of foreign affairs) initially to deal with lawsuits between Romans and foreigners. It evolved into a concept of natural law shared by all peoples
Katavothra	Denotes a sink-hole
Koine Eirene	Signifies a Common Peace, which granted peace to all signatories while guaranteeing their individual autonomy. This was a concept that became part of Greek International relations in the fourth century, beginning with the King's Peace of 387/6
Magister equitum	The commander of the Roman cavalry. This post was only filled when there was need for a *dictator,* to whom the *magister equitum* was subordinate
Marmor Parium	The *Marmor Parium* is an inscription from the island of Paros that contains a chronological outline of events from the time of Kekrops, the first king of Athens, to 264/3. Only part of it has survived in two fragments. Its fragments can be found at *FGrHist/BNJ* 239

Metoikoi/Metics	The resident aliens in Athens. Men and women who stayed in Athens more than thirty days, usually for trade and doing business, had to register as metics. They lacked political rights and had to pay a sort of head tax (*metoikion*) of 12 *drachmas* per man and 6 per woman. They had to be sponsored by a citizen, were required to serve in the military and make monetary contributions (*eisphorai*) on occasions. Nevertheless, because of Athens' trading dominance, there were large numbers of such people, who lived mostly in the Peiraieus. Many became very rich
Mina	A monetary unit in Greece, the equivalent of 100 *drachmas*
Mora	The largest unit of the Spartan army, comprising one-sixth of the total. It numbered *c.*500
Navarch	Commander of a fleet; admiral
Neodamodeis	The term means "new men of the people." These were former Helots in Sparta who were manumitted after service as hoplites in special units of the Spartan army. Though liberated, they did not become citizens. Dionysios I copied the practice
Obol	The word originally denotes an iron spit, but came to stand for a monetary unit in Greece. The *obol* was worth one-sixth of a *drachma*
Pankration	*Pankration* was the name for all-in or no-holds-barred wrestling. It was the most brutal sport at the Olympics
Parrhesia	Means freedom of speech or frankness. This quality was believed to be a distinct feature of Athenian democracy. Diodoros elevates it into a principle of historiography
Patrios Politeia	"The constitution of our ancestors." In the political strife between oligarchs and democrats in Athens in the last decades of the fifth century this term was used by both sides to invoke some ancient origin for their version of the constitution
Pelte	Light wicker shield carried by a peltast or light-armed soldier
Phalanx	Main tactical formation of Greek heavy infantry. Soldiers were arrayed several deep in a solid line with overlapping shields
Plethron	A Greek unit of linear measure 100 Greek feet long. As a measurement of area it was 100 square feet (*c.*900 square metres or 1076 square yards), or the amount of land that could be ploughed in a day

Proskynesis	*Proskynesis* denotes the act of performing obeisance to a superior. It was standard practice in the Persian Empire and caused an uproar when Alexander the Great tried to institute the same practice
Provocatio ad Populum	The right of a Roman citizen to appeal a penalty imposed by a magistrate to the popular assembly
Prytaneion	The residence of the *prytaneis* (presidents). It served as a sort of townhall in Athens. Visiting dignitaries and honorees were entertained there
Sarissa	The long pike-like spear of the Macedonian infantryman that was introduced by Philip II of Macedon
Skytalismos	The act of cudgelling people to death with clubs
Spartiate	The elite officer class in Sparta
Stade	A Greek measure of distance that was the equivalent of about 600 feet or 183 metres
Stadion	A single-stade race that was originally the only athletic competition at Olympia. The list of the winners in the *stadion* was the standard record in the Olympic victor lists
Stasis	Political strife or factionalism
Strategos	A military commander or general. The Athenians elected 10 each year, who served on both land and sea. Athenian *strategoi* also had considerable political authority. In other communities it was the title of the single elected leader, as in the Arkadian League
Sykophantai	Literally means "fig-revealer." They were informers against and prosecutors of people they saw transgressing the laws. The Athenian legal system depended upon the ordinary citizens to prosecute crime and encouraged them by giving them a certain share of a fine in cases of successful prosecution, although the punishment for failing to make one's case was heavy. These civic-minded citizens were hated by the elite, who believed they were motivated by financial considerations
Syngrapheis	Commissioners at Athens chosen to review the lawcode
Synhedrion	"Place where people sit together," denotes a council or assembly. The term was specifically applied to the council of the allies of Athens in the Second Athenian Confederacy
Synoikismos	Political unification of several smaller communities into one larger unit
Tagos/Tageia	Supreme commander/supreme command of the communities in Thessaly

Talent	The *talent* was a unit of weight that the Greeks had learned from the civilizations in the Near East. Originally a weight in gold, by the fifth and fourth century it was in silver. It was worth sixty *minas*, thus 6,000 *drachmas*
Tribuni militum	Military tribunes were basically commanders of units of the Roman army. The military tribunes with consular power (*tribuni militum consulare potestate*), originally three but rising to six, were elected in place of consuls in most years from 445/4 to 367/6. They were the result of the conflict between the senate and the leaders of the Plebs (*tribuni plebum*) over the consulship
Trierarch	Captain of a trireme. In Athens these were wealthy citizens who were obliged to undertake the cost and captaining of a warship for a year as a public service (liturgy)
Tykhe	Fortune, Chance or Fate. *Tykhe* became recognized as a guiding force in human affairs throughout the Hellenistic period

Bibliography

Publications on the history and historiography of the period 404–362 are very numerous and increasing day-by-day. The following are some suggestions for further reading both for specialists and the general reader.

Historiography – Diodoros

Ambaglio, D. (1995), *La* Bibliotheca storica *di Diodoro Siculo: problemi e metodo*, Como.
Bigwood, J. M. (1980), "Diodorus and Ctesias," *Phoenix* 34: 195–207.
Burton, A. (1972), *Diodorus Siculus Book I: A Commentary*, Leiden.
Drews, R. (1962), "Diodorus and his Sources," *American Journal of Philology* 83: 383–392.
Hammond, N. G. L. (1937), "The Sources of Diodorus Siculus XVI, Part 1," *Classical Quarterly* 31: 79–91.
Hammond, N. G. L. (1938), "The Sources of Diodorus Siculus XVI, Part 2," *Classical Quarterly* 32: 137–151.
Hau, L. I. (2016), *Moral History from Herodotus to Diodorus*, Edinburgh.
Hau, L. I., A. Meeus and B. Sheridan (eds.) (2018), *Diodoros of Sicily: Historiographical Theory and Practice in the* Bibliotheke, Leuven/Paris/Bristol.
Meister, K. (1967), *Die sizilische Geschichte bei Diodor von den Anfängen bis zum Tod des Agathokles: Quellenuntersuchungen zu Buch iv–xxi*, Munich.
Muntz, C. (2017), *Diodorus Siculus and the World of the Late Roman Republic*, Oxford.
Palm, J. (1955), *Über Sprache und Stil des Diodoros von Sizilien: Ein Beitrag zur Beleuchtung der hellenistischen Prosa*, Lund.
Rathman, M. (2016), *Diodor und seine "Bibliotheke"* (*Klio Beihefte*, Band 27), Berlin and Boston.
Reid (Rubincam), C. I. (1974), "Ephoros Fragment 76 and Diodoros on the Cypriote War," *Phoenix* 28: 123–143.
Rubincam, C. I. (1987), "The Organization and Composition of Diodoros' *Bibliotheke*," *Echos du Monde Classique/Classical Views* 31: 313–328.
Rubincam, C. I. (1989), "Cross-References in the *Bibliotheke Historike* of Diodoros," *Phoenix* 43: 39–61.
Rubincam, C. I. (1998), "Did Diodorus Siculus Take Over Cross-References from his Sources?," *American Journal of Philology* 139: 67–87.
Sacks, K. S. (1990), *Diodorus Siculus and the First Century*, Princeton.

Sacks, K. S. (1994), "Diodorus and his Sources: Conformity and Creativity," in S. Hornblower (ed.), *Greek Historiography*, Oxford: 213–232.

Stylianou, P. J. (1998), *A Historical Commentary on Diodorus Siculus Book 15*, Oxford.

Sulimani, I. (2011), *Diodorus' Mythistory and the Pagan Mission*, Leiden and Boston.

Volquardsen, C. A. (1868), *Untersuchungen über die Quellen der griechischen und sizilischen Geschichte bei Diodor, Buch XI bis XVI*, Kiel.

Historiography – General

Barber, G. L. (1935), *The Historian Ephorus*, Cambridge.

Baron, C. A. (2013), *Timaeus of Tauromenium and Hellenistic Historiography*, Cambridge and New York.

Bleckmann, B. (1998), *Athens Weg in die Niederlage: Die letzen Jahre des Peloponnischen Krieges*, Stuttgart.

Bleckmann, B. (2005), *Fiktion als Geschichte: Neue Studien zum Autor der Hellenika Oxyrhynchia und zur Historiographie des vierten vorchristlichen Jahrhunderts*, Göttingen.

Bruce, I. A. F. (1967), *An Historical Commentary on the "Hellenica Oxyrhynchia"*, Cambridge.

Cawkwell, G. L. (2004), "When, How and Why did Xenophon write the *Anabasis*?," in R. Lane Fox (ed.), *The Long March: Xenophon and the Ten Thousand*, New Haven and London: 47–67.

Clarke, K. (2008), *Making Time for the Past: Local History and the Polis*, Oxford and New York.

Flower, M. A. (1994), *Theopompus of Chios: History and Rhetoric in the Fourth Century BC*, Oxford.

Harding, P. (1974a), "The Purpose of Isokrates' *Archidamos* and *On the Peace*," *California Studies in Classical Antiquity* 6: 137–149.

Harding, P. (1974b), "The Theramenes Myth," *Phoenix* 28: 101–111.

Harding, P. (1986), "An Education to All," *Liverpool Classical Monthly* 11: 134–136.

Harding, P. (1987), "The Authorship of the *Hellenika Oxyrhynchia*," *Ancient History Bulletin* 1: 101–104.

Harding, P. (1988), "Laughing at Isokrates: Humour in the *Areopagitikos*?," *Liverpool Classical Monthly* 13: 18–23.

Harding, P. (2007), "Local History and Atthidography," in J. Marincola (ed.), *A Companion to Greek and Roman Historiography*, Oxford: 180–188.

Harding, P. (2008), *The Story of Athens*, London and New York.

Hornblower, J. (1981), *Hieronymus of Cardia*, Oxford.

Hornblower, S. (ed.) (1994), *Greek Historiography*, Oxford.

Lenfant, D. (2004), *Ctésias de Cnide: La Perse, L'Inde, Autres Fragments*, Paris.

Lenfant, D. (ed.) (2011), *Les Perses vus par les Grecs: Lire les sources classiques sur l'empire achéménide*, Paris.

Llewellyn-Jones, L. and J. Robson (2010), *Ctesias' History of Persia: Tales of the Orient*, London and New York.

Luraghi, N. (2008), *The Ancient Messenians: Constructions of Ethnicity and Memory*, Cambridge.

Momigliano, A. (1977), *Essays in Ancient and Modern Historiography*, Oxford.

Occhipinti, E. (2016), *The* Hellenica Oxyrhynchia *and Historiography: New Research Perspectives* (*Mnemosyne*, Supplement 395), Leiden and Boston.

Pownall, F. (2004), *Lessons from the Past: The Moral Use of History in Fourth-Century Prose*, Ann Arbor.

Reed, K. (1976), *Theopompus of Chios: History and Oratory in the Fourth Century*, Diss. Berkeley.

Shrimpton, G. S. (1991), *Theopompus the Historian*, Montreal, Kingston, London, Buffalo.

Stroheker, K. F. (1952), "Timaios und Philistos," in *Satura: Früchte aus der antiken Welt* (In honour of Otto Weinreich), Baden-Baden: 139–161.

Stronk, J. P. (2010), *Ctesias' Persian History*, Düsseldorf.

Stylianou, P. J. (2004), "One *Anabasis* or Two?," in R. Lane Fox (ed.) *The Long March: Xenophon and the Ten Thousand*, New Haven and London: 68–96.

Thomas, R. (2019), *Polis Histories, Collective Memories, and the Greek World*, Cambridge.

Walbank, F. W. (1972), *Polybius*, Berkeley, Los Angeles and London.

Westlake, H. D. (1969), *Essays on the Greek Historians and Greek History*, Manchester and New York.

History

Ameling, W. (1993), *Karthago: Studien zur Militär, Staat und Gesellschaft*, Munich.

Archibald, Z. H. (1998), *The Odrysian Kingdom of Thrace*, Oxford.

Badian, E. (1975), "The Ghost of Empire: Reflections on Athenian Foreign Policy in the Fourth Century BC," in W. Eder (ed.), *Die athenische Demokratie im 4. Jahrhundert v. Chr.*, Stuttgart: 79–105.

Badian, E. (1991), "The King's Peace," in M. A. Flower and M. Toher (eds.), *Georgica: Greek Studies in Honour of George Cawkwell* (*Bulletin of the Institute of Classical Studies*, Supplement 58), London: 25–48.

Berthold, R. M. (1984), *Rhodes in the Hellenistic Age*, Ithaca and London.

Best, J. G. P. (1969), *Thracian Peltasts and their Influence on Greek Warfare*, Groningen.

Blackman, D. and B. Rankov (2013), *Shipsheds of the Ancient Mediterranean*, Cambridge.

Briant, P. (2002), *From Cyrus to Alexander: A History of the Persian Empire*, trans. P. T. Daniels, Winona Lake.

Buck, R. J. (1998), *Thrasybulus and the Athenian Democracy: The Life of an Athenian Statesman*, Stuttgart.

Buckler, J. (1980), *The Theban Hegemony*, Cambridge, Mass. and London.
Buckler, J. (2003), *Aegean Greece in the Fourth Century BC,* Leiden and Boston.
Buckler, J. and H. Beck (2008), *Central Greece and the Politics of Power in the Fourth Century BC*, Cambridge.
Burnett, A. P. (1962), "Thebes and the Expansion of the Second Athenian Confederacy: *IG* II^2 40 and *IG* II^2 43," *Historia* 11: 1–17.
Burstein, S. (1976), *Outpost of Hellenism: The Emergence of Heraclea on the Black Sea*, Berkeley.
Cargill, J. (1981), *The Second Athenian League*, Berkeley, Los Angeles and London.
Cartledge, P. (1987), *Agesilaos and the Crisis of Sparta*, London.
Casson, L. (1971), *Ships and Seamanship in the Ancient World*, Princeton.
Caven, B. (1990), *Dionysios I: War-Lord of Sicily*, New Haven and London.
Cawkwell, G. L. (1963), "Notes on the Peace of 375/4," *Historia* 12: 84–95.
Cawkwell, G. L. (1972), "Epaminondas and Thebes," *Classical Quarterly* 22: 254–278.
Cawkwell, G. L. (1973), "The Foundation of the Second Athenian Confederacy," *Classical Quarterly* 23: 47–60.
Cawkwell, G. L. (1976), "The Imperialism of Thrasybulus," *Classical Quarterly* 26: 270–277.
Cawkwell, G. L. (1981), "The King's Peace," *Classical Quarterly* 31: 69–83.
Cawkwell, G. L. (1983), "The Decline of Sparta," *Classical Quarterly* 33: 385–400.
Cawkwell, G. L. (2005), *The Greek Wars: The Failure of Persia*, Oxford.
Christesen, P. (2007), *Olympic Victor Lists and Ancient Greek History*, Cambridge.
De Angelis, F. (2016), *Archaic and Classical Greek Sicily*, Oxford.
Desborough, V. R. d'A. (1966), *The Last Mycenaeans and their Successors*, Oxford.
De Ste. Croix, G. E. M. (1981), *The Class Struggle in the Ancient Greek World*, Ithaca.
Domingo Gygax, M. (2016), *Benefaction and Rewards in the Ancient Greek City: The Origins of Euergetism*, Princeton.
Drögemüller, H.-P. (1969), *Syrakus: Zur Topographie und Geschichte einer griechischen Stadt*, Heidelberg.
Drummond, A. (1980), "Consular Tribunes in Livy and Diodorus," *Athenaeum* 58: 57–72.
Dunbabin, T. J. (1948), *The Western Greeks*, Oxford.
Duszyński, W. (2016), "Sparta, Its Fleet, and the Aegean Islands in 387–375 BC," *Electrum* 26: 65–76.
Finley, M. I. (1968), *A History of Sicily*, Vol. 1: *Ancient Sicily to the Arab Conquest*, London.
Flower, M. A. (2012), *Xenophon's* Anabasis *or* The Expedition of Cyrus, Oxford.
Fuks, A. (1966), "Social Revolution in Greece in the Hellenistic Age," *La Parola del Passato* 21: 437–448.
Gabrielsen, V. (1994), *Financing the Athenian Fleet*, Baltimore and London.
Garland, R. (1987), *The Piraeus*, Ithaca.
Garnsey, P. (1988), *Famine and Food Supply in the Graeco-Roman World*, Cambridge.

Gray, V. J. (ed.) (2010), *Xenophon*, Oxford and New York.
Green, P. (2006), *Diodorus Siculus, Books 11–12.37.1: Greek History 480–431, The Alternative Version*, Austin.
Guido, M. (1967), *Sicily: An Archaeological Guide*, London.
Hamilton, C. D. (1979), *Sparta's Bitter Victories*, Ithaca and London.
Hamilton, C. D. (1991), *Agesilaus and the Failure of Spartan Hegemony*, Ithaca and London.
Hammond, N. G. L. and G. T. Griffith (1979), *A History of Macedonia*, Vol. 2: *550–336 BC*, Oxford.
Hansen, M. H. (1975), *Eisangelia* (*Odense University Classical Studies*, 6), Odense.
Harding, P. (1994), *Androtion and the* Atthis, Oxford.
Harding, P. (1995), "Athenian Foreign Policy in the Fourth Century," *Klio* 77: 105–125.
Harding, P. (2006), *Didymos on Demosthenes*, Oxford.
Harding, P. (2015), *Athens Transformed, 404–262 BC*, London and New York.
Heskel, J. (1997), *The North Aegean Wars, 371–360 B.C.* (*Historia*, Einzelschriften 102), Stuttgart.
Hordern, J. H. (2002), *The Fragments of Timotheus of Miletus*, Oxford.
Hornblower, S. (1982), *Mausolus*, Oxford.
Isserlin, B. S. J. and J. du Plat Taylor (1974), *Motya: A Phoenician and Carthaginian City in Sicily*, Leiden.
Körner, C. (2016), "The Cypriot Kings under Assyrian and Persian Rule (Eighth to Fourth Century BC): Centre and Periphery in a Relationship of Suzerainty," *Electrum* 23: 25–49.
Kremmydas, C. (2012), *Commentary on Demosthenes* Against Leptines, Oxford.
Krentz, P. (1982), *The Thirty at Athens*, Ithaca and London.
Lane Fox, R. (ed.) (2004), *The Long March: Xenophon and the Ten Thousand*, New Haven and London.
Larsen, J. A. O. (1955), *Representative Government in Greek and Roman History*, Berkeley and Los Angeles.
Larsen, J. A. O. (1968), *Greek Federal States*, Oxford.
Lazenby, J. (1985), *The Spartan Army*, Warminster.
Lee, J. W. I. (2007), *A Greek Army on the March: Soldiers and Survival in Xenophon's Anabasis*, Cambridge.
Lewis, D. M. (1977), *Sparta and Persia*, Leiden.
Lewis, D. M. and R. S. Stroud (1979), "Athens honours King Evagoras of Salamis," *Hesperia* 48: 180–193.
MacDowell, D. M. (1978), *The Law in Classical Athens*, London.
March, D. A. (1995), "The Kings of Macedon: 399–369 B.C.," *Historia* 44: 257–282.
Markoe, G. E. (2000), *The Phoenicians*, London.
Marsden, E. W. (1969), *Greek and Roman Artillery: Historical Development*, Oxford.
McDougall, J. I. (ed.) (1983), *Lexicon in Diodorum Siculum*, 2 vols., Hildesheim, Zürich, New York.

McKechnie, R. and S. J. Kern (1988), *Hellenica Oxyrhynchia*, Warminster.

Mehl, A. (2016), "The Cypriot Kings: Despots or Democrats or...?: Remarks on Cypriot Kingship Especially in the Time of Persian Suzerainty," *Electrum* 23: 51–64.

Meiggs, R. (1982), *Trees and Timber in the Ancient Mediterranean World*, Oxford.

Miller, S. G. (2004), *Ancient Greek Athletics*, New Haven and London.

Moreno, A. (2007), *Feeding the Democracy: The Athenian Grain Supply in the Fifth and Fourth Centuries BC*, Oxford.

Morgan, C. (1990), *Athletes and Oracles: The Transformation of Olympia and Delphi in The Eighth Century BC*, Cambridge, New York, Port Chester, Melbourne, Sydney.

Morrison, J. S. and J. F. Coates (1996), *Greek and Roman Oared Warships*, Oxford.

Morrison, J. S. and R. T. Williams (1968), *Greek Oared Ships, 900–322 BC*, Cambridge.

Mosshammer, A. (1979), *The Chronicle of Eusebius and Greek Chronographic Tradition*, Lewisburg.

Moysey, R. A. (1985), "Chares and Athenian Foreign Policy," *Classical Journal* 80: 221–227.

Németh, G. (2006), *Kritias und die Dreissig Tyrannen* (*Habes*, Band 43), Stuttgart.

Ogilvie, R. M. (1965), *A Commentary on Livy Books 1–5*, Oxford.

Osborne, M. J. (1973), "Orontes," *Historia* 22: 515–551.

Parke, H. W. (1933), *Greek Mercenary Soldiers*, Oxford.

Parker, V. (2003), "Sparta, Amyntas, and the Olynthians in 383 B.C.: A Comparison of Xenophon and Diodorus," *Rheinisches Museum für Philologie* 146: 113–137.

Pickard-Cambridge, A. W. (1962), *Dithyramb, Tragedy and Comedy*, Oxford.

Pritchett, W. K. (1965), *Studies in Ancient Topography, Part I*, Berkeley and Los Angeles.

Pritchett, W. K. (1969), *Studies in Ancient Greek Topography, Part II (Battlefields)*, Berkeley and Los Angeles.

Rhodes, P. J. (1981), *A Commentary on the Aristotelian* Athenaion Politeia, Oxford.

Roisman, J. (2010), "Classical Macedonia to Perdiccas III," in J. Roisman and I. Worthington (eds.), *A Companion to Ancient Macedonia*, Chichester: 145–165.

Roisman, J. (2017), *The Classical Art of Command: Eight Greek generals who shaped the History of Warfare*, Oxford.

Ruzicka, S. (1992), *Politics of a Persian Dynasty: The Hecatomnids in the Fourth Century B.C.*, Norman.

Ruzicka, S. (2012), *Trouble in the West: Egypt and the Persian Empire 525–332 BC*, Oxford.

Ryder, T. T. B. (1965), *Koine Eirene: General Peace and Local Independence in Ancient Greece*, London, New York and Toronto.

Sanders, L. J. (1987), *Dionysios I of Syracuse and Greek Tyranny*, London, New York, Sydney.

Seager, R. (1967), "Thrasybulus, Conon and Athenian Imperialism, 396–386 B.C.," *Journal of Hellenic Studies* 87: 95–115.

Seager, R. (1974), "The King's Peace and the Balance of Power in Greece, 386–362 B.C.," *Athenaeum* 52: 36–63.

Sealey, R. (1956), "Callistratos of Aphidna and his Contemporaries," *Historia* 5: 178–203.

Sealey, R. (1993), *Demosthenes and His Time: A Study in Defeat*, Oxford.

Sprawski, S. (1999), *Jason of Pherai: A Study on History of Thessaly in Years 431–370 B.C.*, Krakow.

Strassler, R. B. (ed.) (2009), *The Landmark Xenophon's* Hellenika, New York.

Strauss, B. (1986), *Athens after the Peloponnesian War*, Ithaca.

Stroheker, K. F. (1958), *Dionysios I: Gestalt und Geschichte des Tyrannen von Syrakus*, Wiesbaden.

Stroud, R. (1974), "An Athenian Law on Silver Coinage," *Hesperia* 43: 157–188.

Stroud, R. (1998), *The Athenian Grain-Tax Law of 374/3* (*Hesperia*, Supplement 29), Princeton.

Talbert, R. J. A. (ed.) (2000), *Barrington Atlas of the Greek and Roman World*, Princeton and Oxford.

Thompson, W. E. (1985), "Chabrias at Corinth," *Greek, Roman and Byzantine Studies* 26: 51–57.

Traill, J. S. (1975), *The Political Organization of Attica* (*Hesperia*, Supplement 14), Princeton.

Tritle, L. A. (ed.) (1997), *The Greek World in the Fourth Century*, London and New York.

Tuplin, C. (ed.) (2004), *Xenophon and his World*, Stuttgart.

Walbank, F. W. (1957), *A Historical Commentary on Polybius*, Vol. 1: *Commentary on Book I–VI*, Oxford.

Walbank, M. B. (1982), "The Confiscation and Sale by the Poletai in 402/1 of the Property of the Thirty Tyrants," *Hesperia* 51: 74–98.

Waterfield, R. (2006), *Xenophon's Retreat: Greece, Persia and the End of the Golden Age*, Cambridge, Mass.

Weiskopf, M. (1989), *The So-Called "Great Satraps' Revolt", 366–360* (*Historia*, Einzelschriften 63), Wiesbaden.

Westlake, H. D. (1935), *Thessaly in the Fourth Century B.C.*, London.

Westlake, H. D. (1983), "Conon and Rhodes: The Troubled Aftermath of Synoecism," *Greek, Roman and Byzantine Studies* 24: 333–344.

Whitaker, J. I. S. (1921), *Motya: A Phoenician Colony in Sicily*, London.

Whitehead, D. (1977), *The Ideology of the Athenian Metic*, Cambridge.

Woodhead, A. G. (1962), *The Greeks in the West*, London.

Woodhead, A. G. (1970), "The 'Adriatic Empire' of Dionysios I of Syracuse," *Klio* 52: 503–512.

Zahrnt, M. (1971), *Olynth und die Chalkidier: Untersuchungen zur Staatenbildung auf der chalkidikischen Halbinsel im 5. Und 4. Jahrhundert v. Chr.* (*Vestigia*, Band 14), Munich.

Index of People, Places and Things

References in the Notes have been listed after those in the Text.

Abakaine: 14.78.5, 14.90.3, Notes: 572, 614
Abdemon, of Tyre: 14.98.1
Abdera/Abderite(s): 15.36.2–4, Notes: 953, 954
Abrokomas: Notes: 154, 762
Abydos: Note: 530
Acropolis (-eis): 14.7.3, 14.44.7, 14.65.3, 14.75.4, 14.82.4, 14.87.2, 14.88.2–3, 14.92.1, 14.95.5, 14.115.4–5, 15.20.1, 15.25.3, 15.27.1–2, 15.30.3–4, 15.67.4, 15.74.5, 15.90.3, Notes: 110, 845, 1250
Adrammyttion: Notes: 1278, 1321, 1323
Adranon: 14.37.5, Note: 283
Adria: Note: 778
Adriatic Sea: 15.13.1, 15.13.4
Aeculani/Aequicoli: *See* Aequi
Aegean Sea: 14.12.8, Notes: 681, 742, 920, 942, 999, 1255, 1278, 1323, 1354
Aeimnestos: 14.14.6, 14.14.8
Aelian: Notes: 285, 775, 820, 827, 865, 1055, 1306
Aemilius:
    Gaius: 14.97.1, 14.107.1, 15.2.1, Notes: 669, 746, 814
    Lucius: 15.15.1, 15.61.1, Notes: 859, 871, 968, 985, 1123
    Marcus: Notes: 669, 814
Aemilius Mamercus:
    Lucius: 15.82.1
    Manius: Notes: 117, 266, 318
    Marcus: 14.44.1
Aequi: 14.98.5, 14.102.4, 14.106.4, 14.117.4, Notes: 654, 732, 733
Aëropos, king of Macedon: 14.37.6, 14.84.6, Notes: 286, 519, 538, 539
Aeschylus, tragedian: Note: 173

Agamemnon, king of Mykenai: 15.66.2, Note: 465
Agatharkhides, of Knidos: Note: 999
Ager Gallicus: Note: 701
Agesilaos II, king of Sparta: 15.21.1, 15.52.5, 15.54.6, 15.55.1, 15.88.2, Notes: 466, 479, 481, 487, 515, 519, 520, 522, 538, 557, 623, 684, 851, 906, 923–925, 927, 972, 1068, 1148, 1193, 1321, 1325
    accession of: Note: 461
    aims for complete power over Greeks: 15.19.4, Note: 683
    campaigns in Boiotia: 15.32.1–5, 15.34.2, Note: 926
    criticized for withdrawing from Boiotia without battle: 15.33.1, 15.33.3–5
    defeats allied coalition at Koroneia: 14.84.1–2
    defeats Tissaphernes near Sardis: 14.80.3–5
    defends Sparta from Epameinondas: 15.83.2, Notes: 1285–1287, 1290
    dies in Kyrene: 15.93.6, Note: 1344
    invades Argolid: 14.97.5, Note: 625
    invades Arkadia: 15.59.4, Notes: 1113, 1131, 1135
    leads Spartan campaign in Asia: 14.79.1, 14.80.1–2, Note: 465
    negotiates truce with Tithraustes: 14.80.8, Note: 492
    recalled from Asia: 14.83.1, 14.83.3–4
    relationship with Agesipolis: 15.19.4, Note: 842
    relationship with Lysander: Notes: 462, 467
    sent to aid Takhôs in Egypt: 15.92.2–3, 15.93.2–4, Notes: 1336–1337, 1339, 1343
    wounded at Koroneia: 14.84.2, Note: 529

Agesipolis I, son of Pausanias, king of Sparta: 14.89.1, 15.19.4, 15.22.2, 15.23.2, Notes: 799, 842, 885
Agesipolis II, son of Kleombrotos, king of Sparta: 15.60.4, Note: 1118
Agiad(s): Notes: 88, 885, 1118, 1156
Agias, Greek general: Note: 191
Agis II, king of Sparta: 15.82.6, Notes: 121, 127, 461, 929, 1285
Agora: 14.5.3–4, 14.14.7, 14.41.6
Agylle/Agyllian(s), Etruscan city (Caere): 15.14.3–4, Note: 812
Agyrion/Agyrinaian(s): 14.9.2, 14.78.7, 14.95.2, 14.95.4
Agyrios/Agyrrhios, of Kollytos, Athenian politician: 14.99.5, Note: 643
Agyris, king on Cyprus: 14.98.2
Agyris, tyrant of Agyrion: 14.9.2, 14.78.7, 14.95.4–7, 14.96.1, Note: 617
Aigai, Akhaian city: Note: 1043
Aigai, ancestral capital of Macedon: Note: 284
Aigina/Aiginetan(s): Notes: 776, 922
Aigion, Akhaian city: Note: 1042
Aigospotamoi: Notes: 23, 300, 301, 693, 845. *See also* Battles
Aineias Taktikos, strategist: Notes: 954, 1356
Ainiania/Ainianian(s): 14.82.7, 15.85.2
Aiolis: 14.19.6
Aiskhines, Athenian orator: Notes: 915, 1108, 1226, 1250, 1355
Aiskhines, son of Lysanias, of Sphettos, Sokratic: 1576.4, Note: 1236
Aitna: 14.7.7, 14.8.1, 14.9.5–6, 14.9.8, 14.14.2, 14.37.5, 14.42.4, 14.58.2, 14.59.3, 14.61.4, Note: 283
Aitolia/Aitolian(s): 14.17.9, 14.17.10, 15.57.1, Note: 1101
Aixone, Athenian deme: Note: 582
Ajax: 14.82.8, Note: 215
Akanthos, in Thrace: Note: 837
Akarnania/Akarnanian(s): 14.82.3, 15.31.2, 15.36.5
Ake (Acre): 15.41.3

Akhaia/Akhaian(s): 14.19.8, 14.25.5, 15.31.2, 15.48.3, 15.49.1–3, 15.75.2, 15.84.4, 15.85.2, Notes: 84, 183, 514, 575, 1044, 1050, 1155, 1221, 1230, 1348
Akhaia Phthiotis/ Phthiotian Akhaian(s): 15.80.6, Note: 1271
Akharnai, Athenian deme: 14.32.6, Notes: 250, 301, 337
Akherousian, peninsula: 14.31.3, Note: 235
Akhradina, suburb of Syracuse: 14.63.1, 14.70.4, Notes: 137, 405
Akoris, king of Egypt: 15.2.3, 15.3.3–4, 15.8.1, 15.9.4, 15.29.1, Notes: 681, 686, 752, 762, 782, 787, 790, 900, 992
Akragas (Agrigentum)/Akragantines: 14.47.6, 14.88.5, 15.17.5, Notes: 44, 60
Akroreia: 14.17.8, Note: 124
Akte (Peloponnese): 15.31.2
Alaisa (Halaesa)/Alaisian(s): 14.16.2–4, Notes: 101, 110
Albinius, Marcus: Note: 1066
Aleuadai: 15.61.3, Notes: 508, 509, 1128, 1129
Alexander, grandson of Amyntas: 15.60.3
Alexander, Spartan general: 15.64.2
Alexander of Pherai: 15.61.2, 15.61.4–5, 15.67.3, 15.71.2, 15.75.1–2, 15.80.1, 15.80.6, 15.95.1, Notes: 1127, 1170, 1354
Alexander III of Macedon (the Great): Notes: 333, 355, 684, 738, 802, 925, 999, 1117, 1121, 1233, 1310
Alketas, king of the Molossians: 15.13.2–3, 15.36.5, Notes: 802, 960, 1028
Alkibiades: 14.11.1–4, Note: 77
Alkidas, Spartan general: 15.46.2
Alkimenes: Note: 555
Alkisthenes, Athenian archon (372/1): 15.50.1, Note: 1056
Alkisthenes, of Lakonia: 14.82.8
Allia, river: Notes: 709, 714. *See also* Battles
Alpheios, river: Notes: 981, 1053
Alps: 14.113.1, Notes: 695–697

Alyzeia: Notes: 942, 962
Amanos, mountain: Notes: 159, 160
Amathous, city on Cyprus: 14.98.2, Note: 686
Ambrakia/Ambrakiot(s): 14.82.3
Ambrossos: Note: 1077
Ammon: *See* Oracle
Amorgos, island: Note: 942
Amphiaraos, sanctuary of: Notes: 118, 1227
Amphiktyony, Delphic: Note: 738
Amphipolis: Note: 1278
Amyklai: Note: 1147
Amyntas, king of Macedon (393–369): 14.89.2, 14.92.3–4, 15.2.6, 15.19.2–3, 15.20.3, 15.21.1, 15.60.2–3, Notes: 567, 586, 837, 853, 1115, 1116, 1171, 1182
Amyntas, of Macedon: Note: 539
Anaphlystos, Athenian deme: Notes: 300, 582, 602, 907
Anapos, river: 15.13.5
Anarkhia/Anarchy: 15.45.1, 15.61.1, Notes: 12, 13, 1180, 1217, 1224
Anaxibios, Spartan *navarch*: 14.30.4, Note: 279
Anaximenes, of Lampsakos: 15.76.4, 15.89.3, Notes: 1232, 1313
Anaxis, of Boiotia: 15.95.4, Note: 1358
Ancestral:
    constitution (*patrios politeia*): 14.3.2, 14.3.6, 14.32.6, Note: 18
    custom: 14.30.7, 14.115.5
    homeland: 15.48.3
    homes: 14.55.6
    laws: 14.65.2
    leadership: 15.9.4
    territory: 14.88.1, 15.66.6
    tradition: 14.88.1
Ancona: Note: 701
Andokides, Athenian orator: Notes: 495, 542, 631, 643
Androkleidas, Theban politician: Note: 494
Andromakhos, father of Timaios: Note: 391
Androtion, an Atthidographer: Notes: 476, 517, 849, 1132
Angele, Athenian deme: Note: 582

Antalkidas, Spartan *navarch*: 14.110.2, 15.5.1, 15.19.1, Notes: 399, 549, 681, 682, 693, 751
Anthestius, Lucius: 15.51.1
Anticipation, festival of: 15.18.4
Antigeneides: Note: 333
Antikrates, a Spartan: Note: 1303
Antipater, Macedonian regent: Note: 1355
Antipatros, Athenian archon (389/8): 14.103.1
Antiphon, son of Lysonides: Note: 30
Antissa, on Lesbos: 14.94.4, Note: 613
Antisthenes, son of Antisthenes, of Athens: 15.76.4, Note: 1236
Antistius, Lucius: Note: 1066
Anxor/Anxur (Tarracina): 14.16.5, Note: 115
Anytos, prosecutor of Sokrates: 14.37.7, Notes: 287, 288
Apame, daughter of Artaxerxes (Mnemon): Notes: 1321, 1325, 1330
Apennine mountains: 14.113.1, Note: 702
Aphidna, Athenian deme: Note: 643
Apollo: 14.16.4, 15.18.1, Note: 1177
Apollonia/Apolloniate(s), in Illyria: 14.13.4, Note: 91
Apollonia, in Thrace: Note: 837
Aquilius Corvus, Lucius: 15.23.1, Note: 863
Arab/Arabia: 15.2.4, 15.92.5, Note: 756
Arakos, Spartan *navarch*: Note: 66
Archon (archonship), eponymous, at Athens: 14.3.1, 14.12.1, 14.17.1, 14.19.1, 14.35.1, 14.38.1, 14.44.1, 14.47.1, 14.54.1, 14.82.1, 14.85.1, 14.90.1, 14.94.1, 14.97.1, 14.99.1, 14.103.1, 14.107.1, 14.110.1, 15.2.1, 15.8.1, 15.14.1, 15.15.1, 15.20.1, 15.22.1, 15.23.1, 15.24.1, 15.25.1, 15.28.1, 15.36.1, 15.38.1, 15.41.1, 15.48.1, 15.50.1, 15.51.1, 15.57.1, 15.61.1, 15.71.1, 15.75.1, 15.76.1, 15.77.1, 15.78.1, 15.82.1, 15.90.1, 15.95.1, Notes: 12, 254, 259, 260, 301, 524, 540, 542, 545, 547, 548, 745, 893, 895, 908, 911, 990, 1016, 1039, 1151, 1195, 1207, 1215, 1223, 1348, 1353

Ardea: Note: 722
Arete, daughter of Dionysios I: Note: 652
Aretes: 14.70.3. *See also* Aristos
Argaios: 14.92.4, Note: 587
Arginousai, islands: 15.35.1, Notes: 33, 943
Argo/Argonaut(s): 14.30.3, Note: 221
Argolid: 14.97.5, Notes: 625, 1054
Argos/Argives: 14.6.2, 14.82.1, 14.82.6–7, 14.86.1, 14.86.4, 14.92.1, 14.97.5, 15.23.4, 15.40.3, 15.40.5, 15.49.5, 15.57.3, 15.58.1, 15.60.2, 15.62.1, 15.62.3, 15.62.5, 15.64.1, 15.68.1, 15.70.3, 15.75.3, 15.84.4, 15.85.2, Notes: 551, 557, 580, 581, 684, 761, 798, 983, 1155, 1281
Ariaios, Persian satrap: 14.80.8, Note: 166
Ariminum, in Adriatic: Note: 701
Ariobarzanes, satrap of Hellespontine Phrygia: 15.90.3, Notes: 1177, 1278, 1321, 1323, 1325, 1330, 1332
Arisbe: 14.38.3, Note: 291
Aristippos, of Kyrene: 15.76.4, Note: 1235
Aristodemos, son of Hyllos: Note: 1155
Aristokrates, Athenian archon (399/8): 14.38.1
Aristokrates, Spartan general: 15.45.4
Aristomakhe, daughter of Hipparinos, wife of Dionysios I: 14.44.8, Note: 324
Aristomenes, Messenian hero: 15.66.3, 15.66.4, Note: 1159
Ariston, of Kyrene: 14.34.4
Ariston, son of Sophokles: Note: 360
Aristophanes, comedian: Notes: 333, 607, 643
Aristophon, of Azenia, Athenian politician: Note: 1357
Aristos, Spartan ambassador: 14.10.2, 14.10.3, Note: 431
Aristoteles, mercenary leader: 14.78.1, 14.78.2
Aristotle, philosopher: 15.76.4, Notes: 12, 18, 24, 25, 29, 35, 37, 69, 73, 89, 242, 245, 246, 249, 254, 256, 259, 285, 336, 364, 607, 611, 643, 691, 738, 883, 999, 1039, 1045, 1060, 1232

Aristrates, tyrant of Sikyon: Note: 335
Arkadia/Arkadian(s): 14.17.8, 15.12.1, 15.31.2, 15.59.1–4, 15.62.1–3, 15.62.5, 15.64.3, 15.64.5, 15.65.3, 15.65.5, 15.66.1, 15.67.2, 15.68.1, 15.72.3–4, 15.77.1–4, 15.78.1–2, 15.82.1–2, 15.82.5, 15.84.4, 15.85.2, 15.94.1–2, Notes: 150, 192, 764, 929, 1053, 1108, 1109, 1113, 1130–1133, 1135, 1138, 1193, 1195, 1240, 1244, 1281, 1348
Arkadia, a fort on Zakynthos: 15.45.3, Note: 1008
Arkesilaos, of Katane: 14.15.1
Arkhelaos, king of Macedon: 14.37.6, Notes: 284, 285, 583
Arkhidamos II, son of Zeuxidamos, king of Sparta (476–427): Note: 461
Arkhidamos III, son of Agesilaos, king of Sparta (360–338): 15.54.6, 15.55.1, Notes: 906, 1085, 1088, 1193, 1285, 1290
Arkhinos, Athenian politician: Note: 607
Arkhonides, of Herbita: 14.16.1, Note: 107
Arkhylos, of Thourioi: 14.52.5, 14.53.4
Armenia: Notes: 187, 199, 749, 1324
Arretium, Etruscan city: Note: 698
Arrhidaios, of Macedon: Note: 567
Arrhidaios, Persian satrap: 14.22.5, 14.24.1, 14.24.7, 14.26.3, 14.26.5, Notes: 166, 189
Artabazos, son of Pharnabazos and Apame: 15.91.2–5, Notes: 1321, 1325, 1330
Artaphernes, Persian satrap: 14.79.5
Artaxerxes II (Mnemon), King of Persia (404–358): 14.20.3–5, 14.22.1, 14.27.2, 14.31.5, 14.98.2, 14.110.5, 14.117.8–9, 15.2.1, 15.8.2–3, 15.38.1, Notes: 74, 145, 165, 187, 489, 502, 550, 685, 749, 1321, 1324, 1330
  absolves Datames of charges: 15.92.5
  and Antalkidas: 14.110.2, Note: 681
  appoints Hekatomnôs satrap of Karia: Note: 634

Artaxerxes II (Mnemon) (*Cont.*)
   brother of Kyros: 14.11.2, 14.12.8, 14.19.2
   campaign against Kadousians: 15.10.1, Note: 785
   camps by Euphrates: 14.22.3
   dies: 15.93.1
   duel with Kyros: 14.23.6, 14.25.1, Note: 174
   greets Konon warmly: 14.81.6
   holds trial of Tiribazos: 15.10.1
   King of Asia: 14.35.2, 14.80.6
   mounts campaign against Egypt: 15.41.1, Note: 971
   Satraps' Revolt against: 15.90.1–2, 15.91.1, 15.92.1, Note: 1317
   sends ambassadors to Greece about Common Peace: 15.50.4, 15.70.2, 15.76.3, Notes: 1177, 1230
   sends Strouthas to coast: 14.99.1, Note: 638
   starts war against Evagoras: 15.2.1, Note: 748
   uses scythe-bearing chariots: 14.22.7
Artaxerxes III (Okhos), King of Persia (358–338): 15.93.1, Notes: 969, 1342
Artemis: Notes: 552, 1111
Arybbas, king of the Molossians: Note: 802
Asia/Asian(s): 14.19.6–7, 14.20.2, 14.35.2, 14.35.6, 14.38.2, 14.38.6–7, 14.80.6, 14.81.1, 14.83.1, 14.83.3, 14.84.5, 14.85.4, 14.98.3, 14.98.5, 14.99.1–2, 14.99.5, 14.110.3–4, 15.9.5, 15.10.2, 15.11.2, 15.18.1, 15.19.1, 15.19.4, 15.31.3, 15.43.5, 15.70.2, 15.90.1, 15.90.3, 15.92.1, Notes: 82, 224, 233, 238, 279, 462, 465, 492, 515, 537, 548, 549, 684, 822, 924, 925
Aspendos/Aspendian(s): 14.99.4, Note: 606
Aspis/aspides: 15.44.2
Assembly, of the People (*ekklesia*): 14.3.5, 14.21.6, 14.25.1, 14.38.4, 14.44.5, 14.45.2, 14.46.1, 14.64.5, 14.70.3, 14.113.6, 15.54.1, 15.54.4, 15.74.5, 15.75.1, 15.78.4, 15.79.5, Notes: 288, 643, 704, 882, 1108
Assoros/Assorinoi: 14.58.1, 14.78.7
Assos: Notes: 738, 1321, 1323, 1325
Asteios, Athenian archon (373/2): 15.48.1, Notes: 1016, 1037, 1039
Astydamas, tragedian: 14.43.5, Note: 316
Astypalaia, city on Kos: Note: 1229
Ateleia (freedom from taxation): Note: 945
Athamanian(s): 14.82.7
Athanas (Athanis), of Syracuse, historian: 15.94.4
Athenaios, of Naukratis, rhetorician: Notes: 76, 775, 865
Athenian(s): *passim*
Athens: *passim*
Atilius, Lucius: 14.54.1, 14.90.1
Atthidographer(s), author(s) of Athenian local history: Notes: 475, 476, 495, 542, 699, 849
Attica: 14.32.1, 14.84.4, 15.29.8, 15.63.1, 15.95.2, Notes: 118, 120, 242, 250, 406, 846, 1227
Aulis, in Boiotia: Note: 465
Autokles, Athenian general: 15.71.3, 15.71.4, Note: 1187
Autolykos, son of Lykon, of Thorikos: 14.5.7, Notes: 30, 38
Autonomy (*autonomia*)/autonomous: 14.7.5, 14.17.5, 15.5.2, 15.19.4, 15.20.3, 15.28.4, 15.38.2, 15.40.1, Notes: 44, 549, 684, 766, 770, 846, 895, 1071, 1096
Autophradates, Persian satrap of Lydia: 15.90.3, Notes: 634, 1321, 1323, 1325, 1330
Azenia, Athenian deme: Note: 1357

Babylon/Babylonia: 14.21.6–7, 14.22.3, 14.26.4, 14.81.4, Note: 331
Baktria: 14.20.4
Balkan, mountains: Note: 951
Bardylis, king of the Illyrians: Note: 584
Battle of:
   Aigospotamoi: Notes: 300, 301, 693

Allia river: 14.114.1–14.115.1, Notes: 708–710, 713, 714
Arginousai islands: 15.35.1
Cremera: Note: 714
Eleporos: Notes: 671, 693
Embata: Note: 1357
Haliartos: 14.81.1-2
Himera: Notes: 327, 407
Kition: Notes: 758, 759
Knidos: 14.83.6-7, 14.84.3, 14.84.7, Notes: 74, 301, 523, 524, 540, 545, 907
Koroneia: 14.84.1, Notes: 524, 525, 607
Kounaxa: 14.23.1–14.24.5, Note: 1269
Kronion: Note: 779
Kynossema: 14.84.7, Note: 541
Leuktra: 15.56.4, 15.76.3, 15.81.2, Notes: 693, 770, 799, 971, 977, 979, 1091, 1096, 1195
Mantineia (418/7): Notes: 770, 798, 929
Mantineia (362/1): 15.33.3, 15.79.2, 15.89.3, 15.96.1, Notes: 742, 978, 1234, 1291, 1301, 1309, 1311, 1358
Marathon: Notes: 171, 1014
Naxos: Notes: 776, 942, 955
Nemea: 14.83.2, Notes: 514, 516, 607
Sardis: 14.80.1-5, Notes: 478, 486, 515
Tegyra: 15.81.2, Note: 965
Birgi, necropolis: Note: 344
Bithynia/Bithynian(s): 14.31.4, 14.38.3, Note: 237
Biton of Syracuse: 14.53.5
Black Sea: Notes: 205, 216, 221, 233, 608, 1354
Boedromion, Athenian month (approx. September): Notes: 259, 942
Boii, Gallic tribe: Note: 735
Boiotarch(s), Boiotian general(s): 15.46.4, 15.52.1, 15.53.3, 15.62.4, 15.68.1, 15.71.4, 15.71.7, 15.72.2, 15.79.5, 15.81.2, Notes: 891, 903, 1015, 1071, 1075, 1078, 1136, 1138, 1185
Boiotia/Boiotian(s): *passim*
Bola, Italy: 14.117.4, Note: 731
Bosporos/Bosporan: 14.93.1, Notes: 238, 588, 681

Boura, Akhaian city: 15.48.3, 15.49.2, Note: 1043
Boutadai, Athenian deme: Note: 30
Brakhylides, a Boiotarch: Note: 1078
Brennus, Celtic chieftain: Note: 703
Bronze Age: Notes: 697, 1153
Bruttium, Italy: Notes: 322, 450
Byzantion/Byzantine(s): 14.12.2, 14.12.3, 14.12.5, 14.30.4, 15.28.3, 15.79.1, Notes: 81, 82, 206, 238, 279, 608, 632, 785, 894, 896, 1254

Caedicius: Note: 703
Caere/Caeretan(s): 14.117.7, Notes: 698, 735, 812
Calabria: Note: 322
Camillus: *See* Furius Camillus, Marcus
Campania/Campanian(s): 14.8.5-6, 14.9.2, 14.9.8, 14.15.3, 14.58.2, 14.61.4-6, 14.68.3, Notes: 58, 64, 97, 397, 697
Capitol/Capitoline, hill: 14.115.3-4, 14.116.2-4, Notes: 657, 693, 724
Carthage: 14.46.5, 14.47.1, 14.49.1, 14.53.5, 14.76.3, 14.77.3, 15.24.2, 15.24.3, Notes: 49, 98, 339, 352, 355, 368, 397, 409, 445, 825, 874, 888, 1203
Carthaginian(s): *passim*
Caspian, Sea: Note: 785
Catapult: 14.42.1, 14.43.3, 14.50.4, 14.51.1, Note: 308
Celt(s)/Celtic: 14.113.1, 14.113.3-5, 14.114.1, 14.114.3, 14.114.5, 14.115.1, 14.115.5, 14.116.3-7, 14.117.7, 15.70.1, Notes: 694, 702, 706, 716, 717, 720, 734, 736
Chance: *See Tykhe*
Cicero, Roman orator: Notes: 63, 374, 728, 774, 801, 1233
Circeii: 14.102.4, Note: 656
Claudius, Manius: 14.35.1
Claudius Crassus, Appius: Note: 266
Cloelius/Coelius, Publius: 15.57.1, Note: 1098
Clusium/Clusian(s): 14.113.3-4, Notes: 680, 698, 702, 703
Cognomen: Notes: 80, 657, 680

Confederacy/Confederation:
  Akhaian: Notes: 575, 1050
  Arkadian: 15.59.1, Notes: 1108, 1109, 1130, 1281
  Boiotian: 15.70.2, Notes: 118, 496, 684, 846, 891, 1015, 1100, 1138
  Etruscan: Note: 698
  Italiot: Notes: 575, 647, 664
  Olynthian: Note: 585
  Peloponnesian: Notes: 798, 921, 1096
  Second Athenian: Notes: 613, 742, 802, 895, 896, 903, 910, 915, 920, 960, 961, 970–972, 1008, 1071, 1096, 1252, 1255, 1323, 1348, 1354
Conspiracy of the Pages: Note: 738
Constantinople: Note: 219
Consul(s)/Consular power: 14.12.1, 14.17.1, 14.19.1, 14.35.1, 14.38.1, 14.44.1, 14.47.1, 14.54.1, 14.82.1, 14.85.1, 14.90.1, 14.97.1, 14.99.1, 14.103.1, 14.106.4, 14.107.1, 14.110.1, 14.113.1, 15.2.1, 15.8.1, 15.14.1, 15.15.1, 15.20.1, 15.22.1, 15.23.1, 15.24.1, 15.25.1, 15.28.1, 15.36.1, 15.38.1, 15.41.1, 15.48.1, 15.50.1, 15.51.1, 15.57.1, 15.61.1, 15.71.1, 15.76.1, 15.77.1, 15.78.1, 15.82.1, 15.90.1, 15.95.1, Notes: 14, 637, 657, 668, 669, 780
Corinth/Corinthian(s): 14.10.3, 14.17.7, 14.36.1, 14.42.3, 14.62.1, 14.69.5, 14.75.5, 14.82.1–2, 14.82.10, 14.84.5, 14.86.1, 14.86.4, 14.86.6, 14.91.2, 14.92.1–2, 14.97.5, 15.31.2, 15.40.3, 15.68.2, 15.69.1–2, 15.70.1, 15.72.1, 15.74.1, Notes: 72, 96, 257, 441, 498, 507, 516, 551, 553–555, 557, 558, 580, 684, 846, 979, 1042, 1131, 1173, 1174, 1230
Cornelius: 15.41.1
  Aulus: 15.77.1, Note: 1238
  Gaius: 15.61.1
  Lucius: 15.24.1
  Marcus: 15.25.1, 15.77.1, Note: 1238
  Titus: 15.28.1

Cornelius Cossus:
  Gnaeus: 14.44.1, Notes: 80, 144, 318
  Publius: 14.12.1, 14.94.1, Notes: 80, 604, 621(?)
Cornelius Maluginensis:
  Publius: 14.19.1, 14.85.1, 14.110.1, 15.20.1, 15.22.1, Notes: 144, 543, 621(?), 680, 890
  Servius: 15.36.1, 15.71.1, 15.76.1, 15.78.1, Notes: 637, 876, 950, 985, 1057, 1224, 1247
Cornelius Scipio, Publius: 14.93.2, Notes: 592, 604, 621(?)
Cortona: Note: 698
Crete/Cretan(s): 15.82.6, 15.83.1–2, Note: 1286
Crimea: Notes: 588, 681
Crustumerium: Note: 709
Cyclades, islands: 14.84.4, 15.30.5, 15.95.1, Notes: 920, 1354
Cyprus/Cypriot(s): 14.39.1–2, 14.98.1, 14.98.3–4, 14.110.5, 15.1.6, 15.2.1–2, 15.2.4, 15.3.1, 15.4.3, 15.8.1–2, 15.9.1–2, 15.47.8, Notes: 300, 504, 544, 550, 626, 631, 632, 635, 681, 685, 696, 747, 748, 759, 761, 781, 787, 790, 1325

Daidalos, of Sikyon, sculptor: Note: 362
Daimenes: 14.53.4
Damiorgoi: Note: 1108
Damon, of Thourioi, Olympic victor: 15.36.1, 15.50.1
Damon, ruler of Kenturipa: 14.78.7
Danube, river: Note: 951
Dareios II, King of Persia (423–404): 14.11.1
Daric(s): Notes: 86, 214
Daskon: 14.72.3, 14.73.1
Daskyleion, in Phrygia: Note: 1330
Datames, satrap of Kappadokia: 15.91.2–7, Notes: 1325, 1328, 1330, 1333
Decarchy (-ies): 14.13.1, Note: 20
Deinarkhos, orator: Note: 1091
Deinon, of Kolophon, historian: Notes: 174, 176, 550

Dekeleia/Dekeleian, Athenian deme: Notes: 120, 261
Delphi/Delphic: 14.13.3, 14.84.2, 14.93.3–4, 14.117.8, 15.8.4, 15.13.1, 15.49.1, Notes: 529, 595, 597, 598, 738, 801, 845, 873, 1034, 1177
Demarete, wife of Gelon: 14.63.3
Demeter: 14.63.1, 14.70.2, 14.77.5, Note: 406
Democracy (-ies)/Democrats: 14.3.3, 14.3.7, 14.10.1, 15.40.1–2, 15.45.1, 15.58.1, Notes: 22, 25, 241, 247, 254, 275, 288, 319, 326, 417, 551, 607, 608, 643, 891, 983, 1007, 1008, 1106, 1281
Demokritos, philosopher: 14.11.5, Notes: 9, 78
Demophilos, Athenian archon (381/0): 15.22.1
Demophon, Athenian general: 15.26.1, 15.26.3, Note: 883
Demos (ho): 14.3.7, 14.4.1, 14.16.1, 14.92.2, 14.97.1, 15.25.4, 15.26.1, 15.26.3, 15.28.3, 15.29.2, 15.33.4, 15.34.3, 15.35.1, 15.45.2, 15.45.4, 15.46.1, 15.46.6, 15.47.3, 15.71.3, 15.95.3, Notes: 887, 957, 1357
Demosthenes, of Boiotia, contractor: Note: 547
Demosthenes, son of Demosthenes, of Paiania, Athenian orator: Notes: 544, 643, 684, 945, 988, 1018, 1026, 1135, 1226, 1228, 1255, 1261, 1277, 1278, 1292, 1321, 1325, 1353
Demostratos, Athenian archon (390/89): 14.99.1
Demostratos, of Kerameis, Athenian archon (393/2): 14.90.1
Demotic (deme name): Note: 241
Derkylidas, Spartan general: 14.38.2, 14.38.6, 14.39.5–6, Notes: 121, 302, 530
Deukalion, son of Prometheus: 14.113.2, Note: 700
Dexippos, of Lakonia: Note: 223

Dexitheos, Athenian archon (385/4): 15.8.1
Diagoreans: Note: 476
Dictator: 14.93.2–3, 14.117.4–5, Notes: 722, 723, 729, 730
Didymos, Hellenistic scholar: Notes: 301, 333, 475, 523, 542
Dieitrephes/Diotrephes, Athenian archon (384/3): 15.14.1, Notes: 806, 893
Dies nefastus (day when public business was forbidden in Rome): Note: 714
Dikaiosyne, daughter of Dionysios I: Note: 779
Dikon, Olympic victor: 15.14.1, Note: 808
Diogeiton, a Boiotarch: Note: 1270
Diogenes, the Cynic: Note: 1313
Diomedes: Note: 215
Dion, of Syracuse: 15.94.4, Notes: 324, 1350
Dionysios I, tyrant of Syracuse (405–368/7): *passim*
Dionysios II, tyrant of Syracuse (367–357): 15.73.5, 15.74.5, 15.89.3, Notes: 59, 60, 1209
Dionysios, of Halikarnassos: Notes: 677, 699, 703
Dionysodoros, historian: 15.95.4, Note: 1358
Dionysodoros, Olympic victor: 15.23.1
Dionysos: 15.40.2, Notes: 982, 1064
Diophantos, of Sphettos, Athenian archon (395/4): 14.82.1, Notes: 505, 545
Diphilas, Spartan general: 14.97.3, Note: 623
Diphridas, Spartan general: Note: 623
Dithyramb/Dithyrambic: 14.46.6, 15.6.2, Notes: 332–334
Divine, the: 14.76.4, 14.77.4, 15.24.3
  anger: 15.48.4
  disaster: 14.70.4
  force: 15.48.1
  intervention: 15.48.4
  omen: 15.50.2
  power of: 15.16.3
  providence: 14.67.2
  punishment: 14.74.3
  retribution: Note: 432

Divine, the (*Cont.*)
   revelation: Note: 1194
   spirit: 14.112.3
   vengeance: 15.58.4, Note: 448
Dodona, oracle of Zeus: 14.13.4, 15.72.3, Notes: 91, 1194
Dorian(s)/Doric: Notes: 96, 303, 403, 1155
Dorikos: 14.7.7
Doris, daughter of Xenetos, wife of Dionysios I: 14.44.6, Notes: 323, 779
Douketios: Notes: 107, 455
Douris, of Samos, historian: 15.60.6, Note: 1121
Drachma(s): 14.21.6, 14.111.4, Notes: 357, 651, 689, 851, 922, 1189
Drepana/Drepanum (Trapani): Note: 1204
Duilius, Gaius: 14.54.1, Note: 361
Dyme: 14.17.12, 15.75.2
Dysniketos, of Phlya, Athenian archon (370/69): 15.57.1, Notes: 1097, 1151

Egesta/Egestaian(s): 14.48.4, 14.48.5, 14.53.5, 14.54.2, 14.55.4, Notes: 341, 1199
Egypt/Egyptian(s): 14.35.4, 14.79.4, 14.79.7, 15.2.3, 15.3.3–4, 15.4.3, 15.8.1, 15.9.4, 15.18.1, 15.29.1–3, 15.38.1, 15.41.1, 15.41.4, 15.42.1–2, 15.42.5, 15.43.1–4, 15.43.6, 15.90.2–3, 15.92.1–5, 15.93.3–6, Notes: 93, 270, 271, 681, 686, 762, 787, 898, 969, 971, 992, 1003, 1061, 1318, 1321, 1328, 1336, 1338, 1341–1343
Eileithyia: Note: 811
Eisangelia (impeachment): Note: 1355
Ekbatana, in Media: 14.22.1
Ekdikos, Spartan general: Note: 623
Elea: Note: 575
Eleporos, river: 14.104.1, Note: 661
Eleusinian(s): Note: 246
Eleusis, Athenian deme: 14.32.4, 14.33.6, Notes: 246, 256, 259, 406, 542
Eleutherai, town in Attica: Note: 900
Eleutheria: *See* Liberty

Eleven, the, Athenian police magistrates: Note: 32
Elis/Eleian(s): 14.17.4–12, 14.34.1, 14.54.1, 15.14.1, 15.23.1–2, 15.31.2, 15.36.1, 15.50.1, 15.62.3, 15.62.5, 15.64.6, 15.68.1, 15.71.1, 15.77.1–4, 15.77.6, 15.78.2–3, 15.82.1–2, 15.84.4, 15.85.2, 15.85.7, 15.94.2, Notes: 121, 124, 128, 260, 261, 362, 1244, 1249, 1348
Elymoi/Elymian(s): Notes: 341, 371, 397
Embata: Note: 1357
Enna/Ennaian(s): 14.14.6–8, 14.15.1, 14.78.7, Notes: 99, 101
Entella: 14.9.9, 14.48.4–5, 14.53.5, Note: 397
Epameinondas, Theban Boiotarch: 15.71.2, 15.72.1, 15.76.4, Notes: 972, 1068, 1070, 1072, 1093, 1136, 1185, 1286, 1287, 1349
   advises foundation of Messene: 15.66.1, 15.66.6, Note: 1151
   advises generosity towards Orkhomenos: 15.57.1
   and Megalopolis: Note: 1195
   and the battle of Leuktra: 15.52.1–7, 15.53.3–4, 15.54.2, 15.54.4, 15.55.1–4, 15.56.1–3
   and the battle of Mantineia: 15.84.4–5, 15.87.1, Notes: 1294–1296
   argues against Peace of 375/4: 15.38.3
   attacks Mantineia: 15.84.1, Notes: 1283, 1289, 1291, 1292, 1302
   death of: 15.87.5–6, 15.89.3, Notes: 1269, 1303, 1304, 1306
   education of: Note: 976
   eulogy of: 15.88.1–4, Notes: 978, 1309
   invades Peloponnese: 15.62.4, 15.63.4, 15.65.2, 15.65.4–5, 15.68.1, 15.68.4–5, 15.69.1, 15.75.2, Notes: 1172, 1191, 1230
   makes surprise attack on Sparta: 15.82.6, 15.83.1–2, 15.83.4
   one of three most illustrious Thebans: 15.39.2, 15.50.6

persuades Boiotians to build navy: 15.78.4, Notes: 1250, 1252
rescue of Pelopidas: Note: 1221
sails to the Aegean: 15.79.1
saves Theban army from Alexander of Pherai: 15.71.6
sent to help Tegea: 15.82.3–5

Eparitoi ("picked ones")/*Epilektoi* ("chosen ones"): 15.62.2, Note: 1132

Epeiros: 15.13.1, 15.13.3, Notes: 91, 802

Ephesos/Ephesian(s): 14.19.4, 14.21.5, 14.36.2, 14.36.3, 14.39.4, 14.79.1, 14.79.3, 14.84.3, 14.99.1, 15.49.1, Notes: 479, 523, 530, 532, 639, 1181

Ephor(s), Spartan magistrate: 14.13.1, 14.21.2, Note: 492

Ephoros, historian: 14.11.1–3, 14.22.2, 14.54.5, 15.60.5, Notes: 60, 94, 163, 174, 175, 274, 308, 367, 391, 394, 402, 415, 466, 517, 632, 743, 758, 771, 799, 822, 833, 879, 928, 999, 1043, 1120, 1132, 1232, 1233, 1293, 1303, 1317, 1320

Epidamnos: Note: 804

Epidauros: 15.69.1, Note: 1174

Epikouros, philosopher: Note: 9

Epikrateia: Note: 1198

Epimeletes (superintendents): Note: 909

Epipolai: 14.8.1, 14.18.2–3, Notes: 137, 306

Epistoleus (secretary): Note: 66

Epitalion, in Akroreia: 14.17.8

Epyaxa, wife of Syennesis: Note: 153

Erasinos, river: Note: 1054

Erenucius, Gaius: 15.51.1

Eresos, on Lesbos: 14.94.3–4, Note: 613

Eretria, Euboian city: 15.76.1, Notes: 913, 1226

Erruca/Verrugo: 14.11.5, 14.98.5, Note: 79

Erythrai/Erythraian(s): 14.84.3, Note: 532

Eryx: 14.47.4, 14.48.1, 14.55.4, 15.73.2–4, Note: 341

Eteokles: 14.23.5

Etesian winds/*meltemi*: 15.43.4, Note: 999

Ethiopia/Ethiopian(s): Note: 999

Etruria: Notes: 679, 702

Etruscan(s): 14.117.6, Notes: 615, 679, 697–699, 733

Euandros, Athenian archon (382/1): 15.20.1

Euboia/Euboian(s): 14.40.1, 14.79.1, 14.82.3, 15.30.1–3, 15.71.4, 15.85.2, 15.85.6, 15.87.3, Notes: 96, 118, 119, 465, 648, 913, 914, 919, 1227

Euboulides, son of Epikleides, of Eleusis, Athenian archon (394/3): 14.85.1, Notes: 524, 540, 542, 545, 547

Euboulos, Athenian politician: Note: 1292

Eudamidas, Spartan general: 15.20.3, 15.21.1–2, Notes: 839, 840, 856

Eudokimos, Spartan general: 14.97.3, Note: 623

Eukleides, Athenian archon (403/2): 14.12.1, Note: 259

Eukrates, brother of Nikias: Note: 30

Euphranor: Note: 1303

Euphrates, river: 14.21.5, 14.21.7, 14.22.3, 14.22.5, 14.81.4, Note: 164

Euphron, of Sikyon: 15.70.3, Note: 1220

Eupolemos, of Elis, Olympic victor: Note: 362

Eupolis, of Elis, Olympic victor: 14.54.1

Europe/European: 14.41.2, 14.47.3, 14.83.3, Notes: 86, 217, 465

Eurotas, river: 15.65.2, Notes: 929, 1147, 1148

Euryalos, fort on Epipolai: Note: 137

Eurymedon, river: 14.99.4, Note: 641

Eurynoe: Note: 1182

Eurypontids: Note: 88

Eurysthenes, son of Aristodemos: Note: 1155

Evagoras, king of Salamis on Cyprus: 14.39.1, 14.98.1–3, 14.110.5, 15.1.6, 15.2.1, 15.2.3, 15.3.1, 15.3.3–4, 15.3.6, 15.4.2, 15.8.1–4, 15.9.1–2, 15.10.2, 15.47.8, Notes: 300, 544, 548, 627–629, 631, 632, 681, 685, 686, 748, 754, 755, 759, 761, 762, 782, 783, 786, 787, 790, 794, 1035, 1323–1325

Exainetos: *See* Xenainetos

Fabius Ambustus:
  Caeso: 14.19.1, 14.44.1, Notes: 144, 318, 604, 680
  Gaius: 15.20.1, Note: 680
  Marcus: 15.48.1, 15.77.1, Notes: 680, 703, 705, 1038, 1238
  Numerius: 14.3.1, 14.12.1
  Quintus: Notes: 680, 703
Fabius Caeso, Aenus: 14.110.1
Fabius Vibulanus, Gnaius: Note: 14
Factional strife/dissension/disturbance (*stasis*): 14.14.1, 15.40.1, 15.57.3, 15.59.1, 15.75.1, Notes: 979, 1109
Falerii, town of the Faliscans: Note: 619
Faliscus/Faliscan(s): 14.96.5, 14.98.5, Note: 619
Fasti Capitolini: Notes: 289, 338, 543, 569, 621, 637, 657, 669
Fate: 15.74.4, 15.80.3
Fidenae: Note: 709
Fortune: *See Tykhe*
Four Hundred, Revolution of: Note: 18
Frontinus, strategist: Notes: 410, 1072, 1091, 1330, 1331
Fulvius, Gaius: 14.3.1
Furius, Agrippa: Notes: 669, 814
Furius, Spurius: 14.47.1
Furius Camillus, Marcus: 14.35.1, 14.44.1, 14.82.1, 14.93.2, 14.97.1, 14.117.2, 15.2.1, 15.22.1, 15.25.1, 15.48.1, Notes: 265, 266, 318, 506, 591, 619, 620, 668, 703, 712, 723, 726, 729, 730, 733, 859, 876, 950, 1038
Furius Medullinus, Lucius: 15.15.1, 15.48.1, 15.57.1, 15.76.1, Notes: 14, 117, 338, 506, 543, 591, 604, 621, 669, 814, 1224

Galatea: Note: 775
Galatian(s): *See* Gaul(s)
Gallic:
  attack: Note: 703
  chief: Note: 703
  force(s): Notes: 707, 709, 713
  invasion: Note: 703
  leader: Note: 703
  mercenaries: Note: 736
  sack, of Rome: Note: 693
  tribe(s): Notes: 112, 696
Garonne, river: Note: 694
Garrison(s):
  Argive in Corinth: Note: 684
  Akhaian: 15.75.2
  Athenian in Abdera: 15.36.4
  Athenian on Kerkyra: Note: 1356
  Athenian in Metropolis: 15.30.5
  Egyptian at Mende: 15.42.5
  on Kythera: 14.84.5, Note: 535
  Macedonian in Larissa and Krannon: 15.61.5, 15.67.4
  occupying: 15.5.1, 15.38.2, Note: 766
  at Phyle: 14.33.1
  Spartan in Athens: 14.4.3–4, Notes: 29, 249
  Spartan in Orkhomenos: 15.37.1
  Spartan in Pallene: 15.67.2
  Spartan in Tegeatis: 15.64.1
  Spartan in Thebes: 15.20.2, 15.23.4, 15.25.1, 15.27.2–3
  Spartan in Thespiai: 15.32.2, 15.33.6
  Theban in Messene: 15.67.1
  in Troizen and Epidauros: 15.69.1
Gates:
  Colline: Note: 718
  Kilikian: 14.20.1
  Royal: 15.74.5, Note: 1214
  Six: 14.18.3
  Syrian: 14.21.3, 14.21.5, Note: 159
Gaul(s)/Galatian(s): 14.2.4, 14.114.2, 14.117.5, 14.117.9, 15.1.6, Notes: 657, 680, 693, 694, 703, 704, 717, 718, 726, 873
Geganius, Lucius: Note: 1098
Gela: 14.66.4, 14.68.2, Note: 44
Gelon, tyrant of Syracuse (485–478): 14.63.3, 14.66.1–3, 14.67.1, 15.88.2, Notes: 327, 407, 417, 419
Genucius, Gnaeus: 14.54.1, 14.90.1
Genucius, Lucius: 15.90.1

Geraistos, on Euboia: Note: 465
Gerrha, Egypt: Note: 898
Glaukos: Note: 215
Glôs, son of Tamôs: 14.35.3, 15.3.2, 15.3.6, 15.9.3, 15.9.5, 15.18.1, 15.19.1, Notes: 269, 750, 757, 790, 791
Gorgidas, Boiotarch: 15.39.2, 15.50.6, Note: 903
Gourasion: 14.109.7, Note: 679
Great Harbour, of Syracuse: 14.62.2, Notes: 137, 350, 410, 441
Gryllos, son of Xenophon: Notes: 1291, 1303
Gymnasia/Gymnias: 14.29.2, Note: 210
Gytheion: Note: 1149

Haliartos, in Boiotia: 14.81.2, Note: 496
Halikarnassos: 15.90.3, Notes: 95, 634, 677, 699, 703, 1323
Halikyai/Halikyaian(s): 14.48.1, 14.48.5, 14.54.2, 14.55.7, Note: 371
Halion, in Akroreia: 14.17.8
Halykos (Platani), river: 15.17.5, Note: 830
Hamaxitos: 14.38.3
Hannibal, Carthaginian commander: Notes: 58, 374
Hanno, Carthaginian commander: Note: 1203
Harmost(s): 14.3.5, 14.10.1, Notes: 81, 275, 612
Harpagos/Harpasos, river: 14.29.2, Note: 209
Hegelokhos/Hegesileos: 15.84.2, Note: 1292
Hegemony:
    Athenian: 14.2.4, 14.3.1, 15.28.4, 15.29.8
    of Greece/over the Greeks: 14.2.1, 15.1.5, 15.9.4–5, 15.19.1, 15.20.1, 15.23.5, 15.33.3, 15.37.2, 15.38.4, 15.39.1, 15.50.2, 15.50.5, 15.54.1, 15.57.1, 15.67.1, 15.88.4, Note: 742
    Spartan: 14.82.2, 15.1.2–3, 15.23.3–4, Notes: 868
    Theban: Note: 879
Hekatomnôs/Hekatomnid(s), ruler(s) of Karia: 14.98.3, 15.2.3, Notes: 634, 635, 1323, 1325

Hektor: Notes: 215, 1074
Helike, Akhaian city: 15.48.3, 15.49.1–3, Notes: 1042, 1055
Helikon, mountain: Notes: 525, 1077
Hellanikos, an Atthidographer: Note: 699
Hellenika Oxyrhynkhia: Notes: 475, 504, 513
Hellenistic, monarchs: Note: 106
Hellespont/Hellespontine: 14.94.3, Notes: 23, 74, 399, 520, 530, 606, 751, 1177, 1253, 1277, 1278
Heloris, friend of Dionysios I: 14.8.5, 14.87.1, 14.90.5, 14.103.5, 14.104.1–3, Notes: 56, 562, 659
Helos: Note: 1149
Helot(s): 15.65.6, 15.66.4, Notes: 262, 275, 463, 1159, 1162
Hera, sacred geese of: 14.116.6, Note: 724
Heraia: 15.40.2
Herakleia, in Black Sea: 14.31.1, 14.31.3, 15.81.5, Notes: 235, 237, 288, 1277
Herakleia, in Trakhis: 14.38.4, 14.82.6, 15.57.2, Notes: 294, 296, 510, 1103
Herakleia Minoa, in Sicily: Note: 830
Herakles/Herakleidai: 14.13.2, 14.30.3, 14.31.3, 15.53.4, 15.55.1, 15.66.2, 15.79.5, Notes: 88, 235, 1079, 1155
Heraklid royal houses, at Sparta: 14.13.8, Note: 88
Herbessos: 14.7.6, 14.78.7
Herbita/Herbitaian(s): 14.15.1, 14.16.1–2, 14.78.7, Notes: 101, 107
Herippidas, Spartan general: Notes: 886, 918
Hermeias of Atarneus: Note: 738
Hermokrates: 14.44.5, Note: 319
Hermos, river: Note: 479
Herodas, a Syracusan: Note: 460
Herodotos, historian: Notes: 88, 171, 181, 270, 364, 374, 699, 756, 1014, 1044, 1047, 1049
Heroes, Age of: 15.50.6, 15.53.4, 15.79.5
Hestia: 14.4.7
Hestiaia/Hestiaian(s)/Oreôs/Oreitan(s): 15.30.1, 15.30.3–4, Notes: 914, 919, 920

Hestiaiotis, in Thessaly: 15.30.5, Note: 920
Hieron I, tyrant of Syracuse (478–467): Note: 419
Hieronymos, an Athenian: 14.81.4
Himera/Himeraian(s): 14.47.6, 14.56.2, 14.67.1, Notes: 44, 327, 340, 374, 407, 417
Himilkon, Carthaginian general: 14.8.5, 14.16.4, 14.49.1, 14.50.1, 14.50.4, 14.54.5, 14.55.1, 14.55.4, 14.56.1, 14.57.1, 14.57.6, 14.58.3, 14.59.1–3, 14.59.5, 14.61.1–2, 14.61.4, 14.62.2–4, 14.63.3, 14.75.4, Notes: 58, 349, 364, 367, 373, 380, 388, 407, 426, 432, 441, 445, 614
Himilkon, son of Magon: Note: 825
Hippo, daughter of Skedasos: Note: 1082
Hippodamas, Athenian archon (375/4): 15.38.1
Hipponion/Hipponiate(s): 14.107.2, 15.24.1, Notes: 575, 664, 671, 690, 815
History:
  continuity of: 14.2.3, 15.1.6, Note: 11
  educational value of: Note: 741
  frankness of: 15.1.1
  of Dionysios the Younger: 15.89.3
  of Greek Affairs (*Hellenika*): 14.84.7, 14.117.8, 15.89.3, 15.95.4, Notes: 1121, 1234
  of Macedon: Note: 1121
  of Persia/Persian(s): 14.46.6, Note: 334
  of Philip of Macedon (*Philippika*): Note: 1234
  of Sicily/Sicilian(s): 15.37.3, Notes: 60, 1350
  of Third Sacred War: Note: 738
  praise of: 15.81.4
  unifying theme of: Note: 432
  Universal: Notes: 833, 1313
Hoplite(s), Greek infantryman: 14.99.2, 15.20.3, 15.26.2, 15.26.4, 15.29.7, 15.31.2, 15.44.3, 15.62.1, 15.71.6, 15.92.5, 15.94.2, Notes: 170, 517, 578, 922, 1003, 1108

Horatius, Marcus: Note: 1098
Horatius Pulvillus, Lucius: Note: 876
Hubris: Note: 1074
Hyllos, son of Herakles: Note: 1155
Hypatos, a Boiotarch: Note: 1185

Iapygia, in Italy: Note: 736
Iberia/Iberian(s): 14.54.5, 14.75.8, 14.75.9, 15.70.1, Note: 443
Ilion: 14.38.3
Illyria/Illyrian(s): 14.92.3, 15.13.2, 15.13.5, 15.14.2, 15.19.2, Notes: 91, 587, 1171
Imbros, island: Notes: 549, 643, 684
Insubres, Gallic tribe: Note: 735
Ionda/Isinda: 14.99.1, Note: 639
Ionia/Ionian(s): 14.12.7, 14.19.6, 14.27.4, 14.35.3, 14.36.2, 14.94.2, 15.13.1, 15.49.1–3, Notes: 96, 303, 958, 1044, 1047, 1326
Iphikrates, son of Timotheos, of Rhamnous, Athenian general: 14.86.3, 14.91.2–3, 14.92.2, 15.29.3–4, 15.41.1–4, 15.42.5, 15.43.1–2, 15.43.5–6, 15.44.1, 15.47.4, 15.63.2, 15.88.2, Notes: 579, 582, 1002–1004, 1026, 1030, 1034, 1278, 1357
Iskholas/Iskholaos, Spartan general: 15.64.3, Notes: 1143, 1144
Ismenias, Theban politician: 14.82.7, 15.71.2, Notes: 494, 512, 849
Isokrates, son of Theodoros, of Erkhia, Athenian rhetorician: 15.76.4, Notes: 37, 39, 256, 544, 589, 628, 629, 743, 754, 755, 761, 762, 766, 770, 787, 845, 912, 963, 1016, 1232, 1233, 1250, 1277, 1278, 1357
Isopolity (shared citizenship): 15.46.6, Notes: 580, 684
Issa: 15.14.2, Note: 809
Issos, in Kilikia: 14.21.1, Note: 147
Isthmian Games: 14.86.5, Note: 557
Italiot(s): 14.9.3, 14.102.1, 14.102.3, 14.104.1, 14.104.3–4, 15.7.4, 15.15.2–3, Notes: 575, 647, 664, 671, 693, 817

Italy: 14.11.5, 14.16.5, 14.40.1, 14.41.3, 14.42.4, 14.56.1, 14.57.5, 14.62.1, 14.63.4, 14.68.3, 14.68.5, 14.69.4, 14.91.1, 14.93.2, 14.95.1, 14.96.5, 14.98.5, 14.100.1, 14.101.1, 14.102.3, 14.103.1, 14.103.4, 14.107.5, 14.109.6, 15.7.4, 15.15.2, 15.24.1, 15.35.3, 15.47.8, Notes: 303, 313, 644, 649, 656, 658, 695, 697, 699, 702, 731, 736, 737, 808, 815, 818, 820, 1235

Ithome, mountain: 15.66.4, Notes: 262, 1151, 1162

Ithykles, Athenian archon (398/7): 14.44.1

Janiculum: Note: 715

Jason, Argonaut: 14.30.3, Note: 221

Jason, of Pherai: 15.30.3, 15.44.5, 15.57.2, 15.60.1–2, 15.60.5, Notes: 509, 916, 1083, 1084, 1102, 1113, 1128

Jugerum/jugera: Note: 653

Julius, Tiberius: 15.51.1

Julius Caesar, Gaius: Note: 694

Julius Julus, Gaius: 14.17.1, Note: 117

Julius Julus, Lucius: 14.35.1, 14.44.1, 15.23.1, Notes: 266, 318, 543, 863, 1066

Jus gentium (law of nations): Note: 703

Kabala, Sicily: 15.15.3, Note: 821

Kadmeia, acropolis of Thebes: 15.20.1–2, 15.25.1–2, 15.25.4, 15.27.1–2, 15.81.1, Notes: 839, 847, 848, 877, 903, 918, 1250

Kadousian(s): 15.8.5, 15.10.1, Note: 785

Kale Akte: Notes: 107, 108

Kalleas/Kallias, Athenian archon (377/6): 15.28.1

Kallibios, Spartan garrison commander: 14.4.4, Notes: 38, 249

Kallibios, Tegean: Note: 1109

Kallisthenes, son of Demotimos, of Olynthos, historian: 14.117.8, Notes: 738, 928, 999, 1060, 1161, 1286

Kallistratos, of Aphidna, Athenian politician: 15.29.7, 15.38.3, Notes: 643, 908, 972, 973, 1026, 1228

Kalpe Harbour: Note: 236

Kalydon: 15.75.2

Kamarina: 14.47.6, 14.66.4, 14.68.2, Note: 44

Kapnistra, hill: Note: 1293

Kappadokia: 15.91.2, Notes: 1325, 1328, 1330

Karabel Pass: Note: 479

Kardia, on the Thracian Chersonese: Note: 299

Kardoukhoi: 14.27.3, 14.27.4, Note: 199

Karia/Karian(s): 14.79.4, 14.98.3, 15.2.3, 15.90.3, Notes: 176, 481, 634, 635, 1325

Karyai: Note: 1142

Karystos, on Euboia: Note: 913

Katane/Katanian(s): 14.14.1, 14.14.5, 14.15.1, 14.15.3–4, 14.40.1, 14.58.2, 14.59.4–5, 14.60.7, 14.61.4, 14.66.4, 14.68.3, 14.68.6, 14.87.1, Notes: 96, 97, 396

Katavothra/katavothrai: Notes: 1052, 1053

Kaulonia/Kaulonian(s): 14.103.3, 14.103.5, 14.106.3, Notes: 575, 658, 664, 671, 690, 808

Kaunos/Kaunian(s): 14.79.4–5, Notes: 176, 472, 474, 504, 523

Kaÿster, river: 14.79.3, 14.80.1, Note: 479

Kebrynia: 14.38.3

Kedon, Athenian general: 14.35.5

Kenkhreai: 15.68.3

Kentrites, river: 14.27.7

Kenturipa: 14.78.7

Keos, island: Note: 1255

Kephallenia: 14.34.2, 15.36.5, 15.66.5, Notes: 451, 958, 1164

Kephaloidion (Cephalu): 14.56.2, 14.78.7, Note: 108

Kephalos, Athenian politician: Note: 882

Kephisodoros, Athenian general: Note: 1292

Kephisodotos, Athenian archon (366/5): 15.76.1, Note: 1223

INDEX

Kerameis, Athenian deme: Note: 568
Kerasous: 14.30.5, Note: 237
Kerberos: 14.31.3, Note: 235
Kerkyra (Corfu)/Kerkyraian(s): 15.46.1–3, 15.47.1–5, 15.47.7, 15.95.3, Notes: 961, 1011, 1013
Khabrias, son of Ktesippos, of Aixone, Athenian general: 14.92.2, 15.29.2–4, 15.29.7, 15.30.5, 15.32.5, 15.33.4, 15.34.4–5, 15.35.1–2, 15.36.4, 15.68.1–2, 15.69.1–4, 15.88.2, 15.92.3, Notes: 583, 687, 742, 897–900, 907, 920, 931, 945, 956, 957, 993, 1172, 1174, 1228, 1336, 1338
Khaironeia: 15.52.1, Notes: 1070, 1077
Khaldaian(s): 14.29.2
Khaldaians, of Babylon, astrologers: 15.50.2
Khalkedon/Khalkedonian(s): 14.31.4, Note: 238
Khalkidike/Khalkidian(s), in Thrace: 14.82.3, Notes: 585, 586, 850, 1024, 1278
Khalkis/Khalkidian(s), on Euboia: 14.14.1, 14.40.1, Notes: 96, 913
Khalybes: Note: 208
Khaoi/Taoi/Taokhoi: 14.29.1, Note: 206
Khares, son of Theokhares, of Angele, Athenian general: 15.75.3, 15.95.3, Notes: 582, 1222, 1356, 1357
Kharikleides, Athenian archon (363/2): 15.82.1, Note: 1279
Kharisandros, Athenian archon (376/5): 15.36.1, Note: 949
Kheirikrates, Spartan *navarch*: Notes: 411, 522
Kheirisophos, Spartan general: 14.19.5, 14.21.1, 14.27.1, 14.30.4–5, 14.31.3, Notes: 222, 236
Khenion, mountain: 14.29.3
Khersonesos:
  Knidian: 14.79.6, 14.83.4, 14.83.5, Note: 521
  Thracian: 14.31.5, 14.38.6, 14.38.7, 14.94.2, Notes: 86, 279, 1278

Khion, Athenian archon (365/4): 15.77.1, Note: 1237
Khios/Khian(s): 14.84.3, 14.84.7, 14.94.4, 15.28.3, 15.79.1, Notes: 893, 896, 897, 956, 1254
Khrysas, river: 14.95.2
Khrysopolis: 14.31.4, Notes: 237, 238
Kilikia/Kilikian(s): 14.19.3, 14.19.5–6, 14.20.1–3, 14.21.1, 14.39.4, 14.79.8, 14.81.4, 15.2.2, 15.3.3, 15.4.2, 15.90.3, Notes: 147, 751
Kimon, Athenian general: 15.88.2, Note: 641
King, the, of Persia: *passim*
Kissides, Sicilian general: 15.47.7
Kition, Cyprian city: 14.98.2, 15.3.4, 15.4.1, Notes: 630, 632, 686, 758–760
Klazomenai/Klazomenian(s): 15.18.2, 15.18.3, Notes: 608, 684, 685, 833
Klearkhos, tyrant of Byzantion: 14.12.2, 14.12.5, 14.12.7–8, 14.19.8, 14.22.5, 14.23.1, 14.24.2, 14.24.4–5, 14.24.7, 14.25.1, 14.25.4, 14.25.7, 14.26.3, 14.26.6, Notes: 81, 86, 151, 155, 165, 183, 185, 190, 191
Klearkhos, tyrant of Herakleia: 15.81.5, Notes: 1276, 1277
Kleombrotos, king of Sparta: 15.23.2, 15.29.5, 15.33.3, 15.39.2, 15.51.3–4, 15.53.1, 15.54.6, 15.55.1, 15.55.5, Notes: 885, 900, 1067, 1070, 1072, 1077, 1091, 1118
Kleomenes, a Boiotarch: Note: 1185
Kleomenes, king of Sparta: 15.60.4, Note: 1119
Kleon, of Halikarnassos, a sophist: Note: 95
Kleonymos, son of Sphodrias: Note: 906
Kleroukhy/kleroukhies: 15.29.8, Note: 911
Knidinion, a fort: 14.99.1, Note: 640
Knidos: 14.83.5, 14.83.7, 14.84.3, 14.84.7, 14.97.4, 15.35.2, Notes: 74, 301, 330, 475, 521, 524, 530, 540, 545, 607, 907, 999
Koile, Athenian deme: Note: 607
Koine Eirene: See Peace, Common
Kolkhis: Notes: 206, 216, 221

Kolkhoi/Kolkhian(s): 14.29.5, Notes: 216, 221
Kollytos, Athenian deme: Note: 643
Kolonai: 14.38.3
Kolossai, in Phrygia: 14.80.8, Note: 150
Komnenoi: Note: 219
Konon, son of Timotheos, of Anaphlystos, Athenian general: 14.39.1–4, 14.79.5–8, 14.81.4, 14.81.6, 14.83.4, 14.83.7, 14.84.3–4, 14.85.2–4, 15.43.5, 15.47.2, 15.88.2, Notes: 74, 300, 301, 475, 476, 502, 523, 530, 532, 533, 537, 544, 545, 548–550, 558, 582, 607, 627, 907, 1277, 1307, 1357
Kopais, lake: Note: 525
Kore (Persephone), daughter of Demeter: 14.63.1, 14.70.4, 14.77.5, Note: 406
Korkinas/Krokinas, of Lamia, Olympic victor: 14.3.1, Note: 15
Kornissos/Koressos: 14.59.1, Note: 639
Koroneia, in Boiotia: 14.11.5, 14.84.1, 15.52.7, Notes: 517, 524, 525, 607, 1070
Koruphasion, Nestor's Pylos: 15.77.6, Note: 1244
Kos/Koan(s): 14.84.3, 15.76.2, Notes: 531, 1229
Kosovo, plain of: Note: 951
Kotyôra/Kotyôran(s): 14.31.1, Note: 231
Kotys, king of Thrace: Note: 1278
Kounaxa: Notes: 269, 1269
Kranii, on Kephallenia: Note: 1164
Krannon, in Thessaly: 15.61.5
Krataias/Krateuas, lover of Arkhelaos: Note: 285
Krateros, lover of Arkhelaos: 14.37.6
Kresphontes, son of Hyllos: 15.66.2, Note: 1155
Kreusis: Note: 1077
Krinippos, Sicilian general: 15.47.7, Note: 1032
Krithote: Note: 1278
Kritias, leader of the Thirty Tyrants: 14.4.5–6, 14.33.2–3, Notes: 29, 31, 33, 77
Kroisos, king of Lydia: Note: 1080

Kronion:
  battle of: Notes: 779, 825
  hill of Kronos at Olympia: Note: 1243
Kroton/Krotoniate(s): 14.100.3, 14.103.4–5, Notes: 575, 649, 820, 1235
Ktesias, historian: 14.46.6, Notes: 163, 174, 176, 178, 330, 331
Ktesikles, Athenian general: 15.46.3, 15.47.4, Notes: 1013, 1027, 1029
Kyane, sanctuary of: 14.72.1
Kyme/Kymean(s): 14.35.7, 14.79.3, 15.2.2, 15.18.2–3, Notes: 274, 466, 751, 833
Kynoskephalai: Note: 1267
Kynossema: 14.84.7, Note: 541
Kyparissia: 15.77.4, Note: 1244
Kyrene/Kyrenaian(s): 14.13.5, 14.34.3–6, 15.93.6, Note: 1236
Kyros, the great, King of Persia: Note: 1080
Kyros, son of Dareios II: 14.19.4, 14.22.1, 14.22.2, 14.23.2, 14.24.1, 14.24.3, 14.24.6–7, 14.25.1, 14.35.2, 14.37.1, Notes: 148–149, 155, 164–165, 269, 757, 1324
  aided by Lakedaimonians: 14.19.4–6
  and Syennesis: 14.20.3, Note: 153
  brother of Artaxerxes: 14.12.7
  campaign of, against Artaxerxes: 14.11.2, 14.31.5, Notes: 142, 240, 278, 1317
  commander of coastal satrapies: 14.12.8, 14.19.2, 14.26.4
  death of, at Kounaxa: 14.23.7, Note: 1269
  enters Babylon: 14.21.7
  fights Artaxerxes at Kounaxa: 14.22.5–6, 14.23.6–7, Note: 174
  gives money to Klearkhos: 14.12.9
  lies to soldiers about plans: 14.20.5
  passes Kilikian Gates: 14.19.2
  passes Syrian Gates: 14.21.3–5
  plot of, against Artaxerxes: 14.11.2
  reaches Issos: 14.21.1
  reaches Tarsos: 14.20.4
  reaches Thapsakos: 14.21.5
  reveals plan to soldiers: 14.21.6
  son of Parysatis: 14.80.6, Note: 489
  traverses Lydia and Phrygia: 14.20.1

Kythera/Kytherian(s): 14.46.6, 14.84.4–5, Note: 333
Kyzikos: 15.81.6

Labinius, Lucius: 15.51.1
Ladon, river: Notes: 128, 1053
Lakedaimon: 14.13.7, 14.33.5, 14.78.2, 14.97.2, 15.19.3, 15.81.2, 15.82.6
Lakedaimonian(s): *passim*
Lakhes, Athenian archon (400/399): 14.35.1
Lakkion: 14.7.3, Note: 315
Lakonia/Lakonian(s): 14.82.8, 14.84.5, 15.51.4, 15.62.5, 15.63.3, 15.65.1, 15.65.5, 15.67.2, 15.76.3, Notes: 223, 1101, 1155
Lamia/Lamian(s): Note: 1355
Laomedon, of Messina: 14.40.4
Laos: 14.101.3, Note: 649
Larisa, in the Troad: Note: 291
Larissa/Larissaian(s), in Thessaly: 14.19.8, 14.82.5, 15.61.3–4, 15.67.4, Notes: 508, 1128
Lasion, a fortress: 14.17.8, 15.77.1, 15.77.3
Lasthenes of Thebes, a runner: 14.11.5
Latykhidas, son of Agis II: Note: 461
Leadership/Rule, of Greece/over Greeks: *See* Hegemony
League: *See* Confederacy/Confederation
Leandrias, an exiled Spartiate: 15.54.1
Lebadeia (Livadhia): 15.53.4, Note: 1080
Lekhaion, port of Corinth: 14.86.3–4, 14.91.2, 15.68.3, Notes: 554, 558
Lemnos, island: Notes: 549, 643, 684
Lenaia/Lenaian, Athenian dramatic festival: 15.74.1
Leon of Salamis: Notes: 30, 37
Leonidas, king of Sparta: 14.25.2–3, 15.64.4, Notes: 181, 1144
Leontiades, Theban politician: Notes: 512, 847, 849, 879
Leontinoi/Leontinian(s): 14.14.1, 14.14.3–4, 14.15.4, 14.58.1, 14.78.3, Notes: 44, 96, 98, 137
Leosthenes, Athenian general: 15.95.2–3, Note: 1355

Leptines, brother of Dionysios I: 14.48.4, 14.53.5, 14.54.4, 14.55.2, 14.59.7, 14.60.2, 14.60.4, 14.64.1, 14.72.1, 14.102.2–3, 15.7.3–4, 15.17.1–2, Notes: 393, 394, 652, 678, 779, 827
Lesbos, island: 14.94.3, 14.99.4, Note: 613
Leukas/Leukadian(s): 14.82.3, 15.36.5, Note: 959
Leuke/Leukai: 15.18.1–4, 15.92.1, Notes: 832, 1334
Leukon, king of the Bosporos: 14.93.1, Note: 589
Leukothea: Note: 811
Leuktra: 15.1.2, 15.33.3, 15.53.2, 15.53.4, 15.54.1, 15.54.7, 15.56.4, 15.60.1, 15.63.1, 15.72.3, 15.76.3, 15.81.2, 15.87.6, Notes: 693, 742, 770, 800, 916, 971, 977, 979, 1077, 1085, 1091, 1096, 1102, 1195, 1302
Leuktros: 15.54.2, 15.54.3
Libanos, mountain: 14.21.4, Note: 160
Liberty: 14.3.6, 14.7.1, 14.7.7, 14.8.2, 14.10.3, 14.14.7, 14.45.4–6, 14.64.5, 14.65.1, 14.65.4, 14.66.1, 14.66.5, 14.67.1–2, 14.68.1, 14.69.4, 14.70.1, 14.70.3, 14.75.3, 14.77.2, 14.88.5, 14.108.6, 15.30.4, 15.33.2, Note: 417
Libya/Libyan(s); 14.14.1, 14.45.3, 14.47.2, 14.50.4, 14.54.5–6, 14.63.4, 14.71.1, 14.75.1, 14.77.1, 14.77.6, 14.95.1, 15.24.2–3, 15.73.1, Note: 93, 436, 446, 874
Libys:
 brother of Lysander: 14.13.6
 king of Libya: 14.13.6
Licinius, Gaius: 15.57.1, 15.95.1, Notes: 1180, 1352
Licinius, Publius: 14.90.2, Note: 569
Licinius Calvus, Publius: Note: 338
Lilybaion: 14.50.2, 14.55.2, 15.73.2, Note: 352
Lipara/Liparan(s), island: 14.93.4, 14.93.5, Note: 376
Liphlos: 14.102.4, Note: 655

Liphoecua: 14.106.4, Note: 667
Lissos: 15.13.4, Notes: 804, 809
Lokris/Lokrian(s): 14.34.2, 14.78.4,
    14.100.2, 14.106.3, 14.107.2–3,
    15.31.2, 15.57.1–2, 15.62.4, 15.85.2,
    Notes: 449, 450, 494, 495, 1101,
    1102
Lokroi (Epizephyrian): 14.44.6, 14.44.7,
    Notes: 322, 644, 658, 671
Loryma: 14.83.4, Notes: 521, 523
Lucania/Lucanian(s): 14.91.1, 14.100.5,
    14.101.1–4, 14.102.1–3, Notes: 647,
    649, 650
Lucius, Quintus: 15.28.1
Lucretius, Lucius: 14.99.1, 14.107.1, 15.8.1,
    15.15.1, 15.23.1, 15.38.1, 15.48.1,
    Notes: 669, 814, 968
Lucretius Flavus, Lucius: Note: 637
Lutatius Catulus, Quintus, orator: Note: 728
Lydia/Lydian(s): 14.19.6, 14.20.1, 14.22.5,
    15.90.3, Notes: 634, 1325
Lykia/Lykian(s): 15.90.3
Lykomedes:
    father of Lykourgos: Note: 30
    of Arkadia: 15.59.1, 15.62.1, 15.67.2,
        Notes: 1107, 1132
Lykon:
    father of Autolykos: Notes: 30, 38
    prosecutor of Sokrates: Notes: 287, 288
Lykophron, tyrant of Pherai: 14.82.5,
    Note: 509
Lykos, father of Thrasyboulos: Note: 241
Lykourgos:
    Spartan lawgiver: Notes: 68, 743
    son of Lykomedes, of Boutadai:
        Note: 30
Lysander, Spartan *navarch*: 14.3.4, 14.3.6,
    14.10.1, 14.13.1, 14.13.6–8,
    14.33.5–6, 14.81.1, 14.81.2, Notes:
    19, 21–24, 66, 67, 69, 77, 89, 93, 94,
    256, 462, 467, 497, 499
Lysiades: *See* Souniades
Lysias, Athenian orator: 14.109.3, Notes:
    17, 21, 24–26, 36, 39, 256, 495, 501,
    548, 550, 607, 631

Lysis, Pythagorean philosopher: Note: 976
Lysistratos, Athenian archon (369/8):
    15.61.1, Note: 1122
Lysonides, father of Antiphon: Note: 30

Macedon/Macedonian(s): 14.37.5, 14.83.3–4,
    14.84.6, 14.89.2, 14.92.3–4, 15.19.2,
    15.20.3, 15.60.2–3, 15.61.3–4,
    15.67.4, 15.71.1, 15.77.5, Notes: 285,
    308, 333, 509, 519, 538, 583, 585,
    586, 802, 836, 916, 925, 942, 951,
    1003, 1024, 1121, 1129, 1184, 1227,
    1234, 1278, 1310, 1330, 1349, 1354
Maelius, Publius: 14.90.2, Notes: 338, 569
Magister equitum (cavalry commander):
    14.93.2, Note: 730
Magnesia: 14.36.2
Magnetes: 15.80.6, Note: 1271
Magon, Carthaginian general: 14.59.1,
    14.59.3–5, 14.59.7, 14.60.2, 14.61.2,
    14.90.2, 14.95.1–2, 14.96.1, 14.96.4,
    15.15.2–3, 15.16.2, Notes: 388, 445,
    614, 825
Maiander, river: Notes: 481, 487
Mainalia/Mainalian: 15.72.4
Makhairion: Note: 1303
Makrones: 14.29.4, 14.29.5
Malekidas, a Boiotian: Note: 1270
Malian(s): 15.57.2, 15.58.2
Mallius, Popillius: *See* Maelius, Publius
Mallius, Quintus: *See* Manlius, Quintus
Manethon, Egyptian chronographer:
    Notes: 469, 1318
Manlius (Manillos, Mallios), Aulus:
    14.17.1, 14.103.1, 15.14.1, 15.22.1,
    15.24.1, Notes: 117, 289, 543, 596,
    890, 968, 1224
Manlius, Gaius: 15.51.1, Note: 1066
Manlius, Lucius: 15.38.1
Manlius, Paulus: 15.76.1
Manlius, Publius: 15.51.1, Notes: 338,
    1066
Manlius, Quintus: 14.85.1, Note: 569
Manlius Capitolinus, Marcus: 14.116.6,
    15.35.3, Note: 657

Mannius, Publius: *See* Manlius, Publius
Mantineia/Mantineian(s): 15.1.2, 15.5.1, 15.5.3–5, 15.12.1–2, 15.33.3, 15.62.2, 15.79.2, 15.82.1–2, 15.82.4–5, 15.84.1–4, 15.85.1, 15.85.8, 15.87.6, 15.89.3, 15.94.1–2, Notes: 514, 742, 764, 770–772, 798, 799, 929, 978, 1052, 1107, 1111, 1113, 1130, 1131, 1134, 1234, 1269, 1281, 1283, 1287, 1291–1293, 1303, 1306, 1311, 1312, 1348, 1358
Marathon: Note: 171
Mareotis, lake: Note: 898
Margana, in Pisatis: 15.77.4, Notes: 1243, 1244
Marmor Parium (Parian Marble): Notes: 316, 335
Marne, river: Note: 694
Massalia (Marseilles)/Massaliot(s): 14.93.4, Notes: 599, 694
Mausolos, ruler of Karia (377–353): 15.90.3, Notes: 634, 1321, 1323
Media/Medes: 14.22.1, 15.88.2, Note: 164
Medimnos: 14.111.1, Notes: 688, 689
Medios, ruler of Larissa: 14.82.5, 14.82.6
Medma/Medmaian(s): 14.78.5, Notes: 450, 671
Medokos, king in Thrace: 14.94.2, Notes: 610, 611
Megakles, brother-in-law of Dionysios I: Notes: 57, 61
Megalopolis/Megalopolitan(s): 15.72.4, 15.94.1–3, Notes: 1151, 1195, 1306, 1347, 1349
Megara/Megarian(s): 15.31.2, 15.40.4, 15.68.2, Notes: 150, 979
Megara Hyblaia: Notes: 391, 1199
  Bay of: Note: 385
Mehmet II, Turkish conqueror: Note: 219
Melaeus, Publius: *See* Maelius, Publius
Meletos: 14.37.7, Notes: 287, 288
Memnon, of Rhodes: Note: 1330
Memphis: 14.19.6, 15.43.1, 15.43.3, Note: 997
Menai/Menainon: 14.78.7, Note: 455

Mendes/Mendesian(s): 15.42.4, Note: 1343
Menekleidas, Theban exile: Note: 1258
Menelaos, harbour of: Note: 1344
Menenius, Lucius: 15.50.1, 15.71.1, Notes: 871, 1057, 1098
Menestheos, Athenian general: Note: 1357
Menon, of Larissa: 14.19.8, 14.27.2, Notes: 150, 191, 195
Mentor, of Rhodes: Note: 1330
Mercenaries: 14.7.5, 14.8.3, 14.9.3, 14.10.4, 14.12.3, 14.16.1, 14.19.3, 14.19.6–7, 14.21.2, 14.22.5, 14.23.3, 14.24.5, 14.26.3, 14.32.4, 14.41.4, 14.43.3–4, 14.44.2, 14.47.4, 14.54.5, 14.58.1, 14.62.1, 14.65.3, 14.66.5, 14.67.3, 14.70.2, 14.72.2–3, 14.75.9, 14.78.1–3, 14.87.2, 14.95.3, 14.96.4, 15.2.3–4, 15.3.2, 15.14.4, 15.29.1, 15.38.1, 15.40.5, 15.41.1, 15.41.3, 15.43.2, 15.70.1, 15.75.1, 15.85.6, 15.87.3, 15.90.2, 15.91.1, 15.91.4, 15.92.2, Notes: 65, 84, 97, 150, 151, 279, 397, 439, 441, 443, 751, 899, 931, 989, 1020, 1061, 1131, 1219, 1266, 1277, 1337
Messene/Messenian(s): 14.34.2–3, 14.34.5, 14.78.5–6, 15.66.1–6, 15.67.1, 15.81.3, 15.85.2, 15.89.1–2, 15.90.2, Notes: 262, 1151–1153, 1155, 1157, 1160, 1162, 1165, 1177, 1230, 1244, 1306
Messina/Messinan(s): 14.8.2, 14.40.3–5, 14.44.3, 14.56.1–3, 14.56.5, 14.57.1, 14.57.3, 14.58.3, 14.61.1, 14.66.4, 14.68.5, 14.78.5, 14.87.1, 14.90.3, 14.100.5, 14.103.2–3, Notes: 44, 53, 303, 351, 373, 387, 561, 644, 1165
Methone: Notes: 333, 1278
Methymna/Methymnaian(s), on Lesbos: 14.94.4, 15.37.3, Note: 612
Metoikoi/Metics (resident aliens): 14.5.6, Notes: 36, 607
Metropolis:
  of Karia: 15.90.3
  on Euboia: 15.30.5, Note: 920

Miel fou: Note: 217
Mikion/Mikon, Athenian archon (402/1): 14.17.1, Note: 116
Miletos/Milesian(s): 14.31.2, 14.46.6, Notes: 219, 334
Military tribunes: 14.3.1, 14.12.1, 14.17.1, 14.19.1, 14.35.1, 14.38.1, 14.44.1, 14.47.1, 14.54.1, 14.82.1, 14.85.1, 14.90.1, 14.94.1, 14.97.1, 14.107.1, 14.110.1, 14.113.6, 14.114.1, 14.117.1, 15.2.1, 15.15.1, 15.20.1, 15.23.1, 15.24.1, 15.25.1, 15.28.1, 15.36.1, 15.38.1, 15.41.1, 15.48.1, 15.50.1, 15.51.1, 15.57.1, 15.61.1, 15.71.1, 15.76.1, 15.77.1, 15.78.1, Notes: 117, 669, 706, 746
Miltiades, of Athens: 15.88.2, Note: 299
Mina: 14.21.6, 14.53.4, 14.102.2, 14.111.1, 14.111.4, 15.7.1, Notes: 357, 651, 689
Minos, Athenian athlete: 14.35.1
Minyan(s): 15.79.5, Note: 1260
Mithridates:
    Persian soldier: Note: 176
    ruler of Pontos: 14.41.2, 15.90.3, Notes: 232, 233, 1322
    son of Ariobarzanes: Note: 1322
Mithrobarzanes: 15.91.5
Mnasippos, Spartan general: 15.47.1, 15.47.6, Notes: 1011, 1013, 1029
Molon, Athenian archon (362/1): 15.90.1, Notes: 1315, 1348, 1353
Molossia/Molossian(s): 15.13.2-3, 15.36.5, Notes: 802, 1028
Molpia, daughter of Skedasos: Note: 1082
Mora (Spartan infantry unit): 14.97.5, 15.32.1, Notes: 577, 579, 927, 928, 964
Morgantinon/Morgantina: 14.78.7, 14.95.2, Note: 456
Morsimos: Note: 316
Mossynoikian(s): 14.30.5-6, Notes: 226, 227, 229
Motyan(s): 14.48.2, 14.52.1, 14.52.5, 14.52.7, 14.53.2, 14.53.4, Note: 345

Motye: 14.47.4, 14.47.6, 14.48.1, 14.48.3, 14.49.3, 14.50.1-2, 14.51.2, 14.54.4, 14.55.4, 14.66.2, Notes: 308, 339, 352, 358
Mounykhia: 14.33.2, Note: 252
Mutilius, Aulus: 14.38.1
Mykale: 15.49.1, Note: 1047
Mylai: 14.87.1, 14.87.3, Note: 561
Mylasa: Note: 634
Myriandos: Note: 158
Myronides, Athenian general: 15.88.2
Mysia: 15.90.3, Notes: 797, 1324
Mystikhides, Athenian archon (386/5): 15.2.1
Mytika, hill: Note: 1293
Mytilene/Mytilenian(s): 14.84.3, 14.94.3-4, 15.28.3, Note: 896

Naryx, in Lokris: 14.82.8
Naukleidas, Spartan ephor: Note: 865
Naupaktos: 14.34.2, 14.78.5, 15.66.5, 15.75.2, Note: 451
Nausigenes, Athenian archon (368/7): 15.71.1, Note: 1179, 1207
Nausinikos, Athenian archon (378/7): 15.25.1, Notes: 895, 908, 911
Nautilus Rutulus, Spurius: 14.19.1, Note: 144
Navarch: 14.10.1, 14.19.4, 14.30.4, 14.49.1, 14.50.1, 14.70.1, 14.79.4, 14.79.7, 14.83.5, 14.102.3, 14.110.2, 15.34.3-4, Notes: 66, 147, 279, 349, 411, 413, 522, 624, 750, 776, 937
Naxos/Naxian(s), Cycladic island: 15.34.3, 15.34.4, Notes: 742, 776, 939, 941, 954
Naxos/Naxian(s), in Sicily: 14.14.1, 14.14.5, 14.15.2-4, 14.40.1, 14.59.2, 14.59.3, 14.66.4, 14.68.3, 14.87.1, 14.87.3-4, 14.88.1, Note: 96
Neapolis (New City), suburb of Syracuse: 14.9.5, Note: 137
Near East: Notes: 308, 355
Nektanébis/Nektanébôs I, king of Egypt: 15.42.1, Notes: 787, 790, 992, 1318

Nektanébis/Nektanébôs II, king of Egypt: 15.92.3–4, 15.93.2, Notes: 1318, 1343
Neleus: 15.66.2
Nellos, the: Note: 1008
Nemea:
   river: 14.83.2, Notes: 514, 516, 607
   city: Note: 1283
Neodamodeis (liberated helots): Note: 275
Neogenes: 15.30.3, 15.30.4, Note: 917
Neoptolemos, king of the Molossians: Notes: 802, 960
Nephereus/Nepherites, king of Egypt: 14.79.4, Notes: 469, 752
Nepos, historian: Notes: 89, 502, 549, 550, 925, 934, 973, 986, 989, 1091, 1184, 1185, 1191, 1209, 1221, 1262, 1277, 1306, 1321, 1328, 1330–1332
Nestor, king of Pylos: 15.66.2, Note: 128
Nestos, river: Note: 953
New citizens (liberated slaves): 14.7.4
Nikarkhos, an Arkadian: Note: 192
Nikeratos, son of Nikias: 14.5.5, Notes: 30, 35
Nikodemos: Notes: 457, 501
Nikokles:
   a eunuch: 15.47.8
   son of Evagoras: Note: 1035
Nikokreon, king on Cyprus: Notes: 761, 1035
Nikolokhos, Spartan general: Note: 962
Nikon, Athenian archon (379/8): 15.24.1
Nikophemos:
   an Athenian: 14.81.4, Notes: 501, 535
   Athenian archon (361/0): 15.95.1, Note: 1351
Nikoteles:
   Athenian archon (391/0): 14.97.1
   of Corinth: 14.10.3
Nile, river: 15.41.4, 15.42.2, 15.43.4, Notes: 89, 999, 1000
Ninos: 14.46.6, Note: 331
Nisyros/Nisyrian(s): 14.84.3

Obol(s): Notes: 643, 922
Oion: Note: 1142

Oita/Oitaian(s): 14.38.5, 15.57.2, Notes: 295, 297
Oligarch(s)/Oligarchic/Oligarchy: 14.3.3–4, 14.3.6, 14.10.1, 15.40.1, 15.45.1, Notes: 25, 27, 246, 256, 319, 445, 979, 1007, 1099, 1281, 1356
Olympia/Olympiad/Olympic: 14.3.1, 14.17.4, 14.35.1, 14.54.1, 14.94.1, 14.109.1, 14.109.3, 15.7.2, 15.14.1, 15.23.1, 15.78.1–2, 15.82.1, Notes: 127, 677, 777, 1034, 1058, 1181, 1243, 1248, 1249
Olympias, wife of Philip II, of Macedon: Note: 802
Olynthos/Olynthian(s): 14.92.3, 15.19.2–3, 15.20.2–3, 15.21.1–3, 15.22.2, 15.23.2–3, 15.31.2, Notes: 585–587, 738, 836, 837, 857, 921, 999
Onomarkhos, Phokian general: Note: 595
Ophis, river: Note: 799
Opus, in Akroreia: 14.17.8
Oracle: 14.56.5, 15.10.2, 15.13.4, 15.49.2–3, Note: 94
   at Delphi: 14.13.4, 15.8.4
   at Dodona: 14.13.4, Note: 1194
   of Trophonios: Note: 1080
   of Zeus-Ammon, at Siwah: 14.13.5, 14.13.7, Note: 93
Oracular response(s): 14.13.3, 15.49.1, Note: 595
Orestes:
   son of Agamemnon: 15.66.2
   son of Arkhelaos, of Macedon: 14.37.6
Orkhomenos/Orkhomenian(s):
   in Arkadia: 15.62.1, 15.62.2, Note: 1133
   in Boiotia: 15.37.1, 15.57.1, 15.79.3, 15.79.5–6, Notes: 965, 1100, 1260
Orontes, satrap of Armenia/Mysia: 15.2.2, 15.8.3–5, 15.9.1, 15.10.2, 15.11.2, 15.90.3, 15.91.1, Notes: 187, 749, 751, 783, 786, 790, 797, 1324
Oropus/Oropian(s): 14.17.1, 14.17.3, 15.30.4, 15.76.1, Notes: 118, 919, 1226, 1227
Ortygia: 14.7.2, Notes: 47, 442

Oxyrhynkhos historian: Notes: 478, 479, 483, 491, 493, 494, 502. *See also* Hellenika Oxyrhynkhia

Paian: 14.23.1, 14.72.4, 14.80.3, Note: 170
Pairisades, king of the Bosporos: Note: 588
Paktolos, river: Notes: 85, 479
Paktya, on Thracian Chersonese: Note: 299
Palatine, hill: 14.115.6
Palici: Note: 283
Pallantion/Pallantine(s): 15.59.2, 15.59.3, Notes: 1110, 1111
Pallene/Pellana/Pellene:
   in Lakonia: 15.67.2, Notes: 1168, 1287
   peninsula: Note: 585
Pammenes, Theban general: 15.94.2, Note: 1349
Pamphylia/Pamphylian(s): 15.90.3
Panic: 14.32.3, 15.24.3, Notes: 244, 873
Panionia, festival: 15.49.1
Pankration: Note: 38
Panormos (Palermo): 14.48.4–5, 14.55.1, 14.55.4, 14.68.5, 15.17.4, Notes: 339, 368
Panormos, on Peparethos: 15.95.2
Panthoidas, Spartan general: 14.12.4, 14.12.6
Pantikapaion: Notes: 233, 588
Paphlagonia/Paphlagonian(s): 14.11.3, 14.22.5, 14.25.8, 14.27.2, 14.31.1–2
Papirius:
   Lucius: 15.22.1, 15.24.1, 15.28.1, 15.36.1, 15.71.1, Notes: 859, 871, 890, 985, 1247
   Marcus: Note: 719
   Publius: Note: 1057
   Spurius: 15.41.1, Note: 985
   Titus: 15.50.1, Note: 1057
Papirius Crassus, Gaius: Note: 950
Parnassos: Notes: 494, 1077
Parnes, mountain range in Attica: Note: 242
Paros/Parian(s): 15.13.4, 15.14.1, 15.34.3
Parrhasia/Parrhasian(s): 15.72.4

Parrhesia (freedom of speech/frankness): 14.1.2, 14.65.4, 14.66.5, 15.1.1, 15.6.2, 15.7.1, 15.41.2, 15.52.5
Partheniai: 15.66.3
Parthenios, Spartan ambassador: Note: 1082
Parysatis, Persian queen: 14.80.6, Notes: 145, 489
Pasanda, in Karia: Note: 472
Pasimelos, of Corinth: Note: 555
Pasion, of Megara: Note: 150
Patras: Note: 132
Patrios politeia: *See* Ancestral Constitution
Patronymic (father's name): Notes: 241, 568
Pausanias:
   king of Macedon: 14.84.6, 14.89.2, Note: 539
   king of Sparta: 14.17.4, 14.17.6, 14.17.8, 14.17.10, 14.17.11, 14.33.6, 14.81.1, 14.81.3, 14.89.1, Notes: 121, 254, 258, 497, 500, 566
Pausanias, travel-writer: Notes: 38, 128, 130, 261, 264, 362, 476, 493–495, 507, 532, 544, 597, 799, 808, 873, 1014, 1016, 1039, 1042, 1045, 1053, 1054, 1058, 1067, 1069, 1071, 1077, 1078, 1080, 1082, 1091, 1094, 1095, 1107, 1136, 1148, 1151, 1153, 1155, 1160, 1162, 1168, 1184, 1185, 1188, 1191, 1195, 1219, 1221, 1227, 1249, 1260, 1261, 1292, 1303, 1305, 1349
Peace:
   Common (*Koine Eirene*): 15.5.1, 15.5.3, 15.5.5, 15.38.1, 15.45.2, 15.50.4, 15.51.1, 15.70.2, 15.76.3, 15.89.1, 15.90.2, 15.94.1, Notes: 765, 970, 1005, 1006, 1061, 1230, 1239, 1311, 1319
   King's: Notes: 549, 677, 682, 684, 685, 693, 748, 750, 765, 770, 846, 868, 891, 893, 895, 901, 970, 979, 1014, 1096
   of Antalkidas: Notes: 682, 693

Peiraieus: 14.3.5, 14.32.4, 14.33.2–4, 14.85.2, 15.29.5–6, 15.34.3, 15.35.2, Notes: 17, 39, 252, 254, 258, 681, 909, 939, 1354

Peisander, Spartan *navarch*: 14.83.5, Notes: 522, 523

Peisistratos, tyrant of Athens: Note: 73

Pelasgian(s): 14.113.2, Note: 699

Pella, capital of Macedon: 14.92.3, Notes: 284, 583, 836, 1330

Pellene, in Arkadia: 15.68.2, Note: 1174

Pelopidas, Theban Boiotarch: 15.39.1, 15.50.6, 15.62.4, 15.67.3, 15.67.4, 15.71.2, 15.75.2, 15.80.1–5, 15.81.1–2, 15.81.4, 15.88.2, Notes: 879, 891, 903, 1078, 1082, 1091, 1093, 1136, 1137, 1170, 1171, 1183, 1184, 1191, 1221, 1230, 1262, 1264, 1266, 1269, 1270, 1275, 1309, 1319, 1349

Peloponnese/Peloponnesian(s): *passim*

Peloris (Peloron): 14.56.3, 14.56.6, 14.57.2, Note: 377

Pelousion/Pelousian, Egypt: 15.42.2, 15.42.4, Notes: 898, 994, 995

Pelte/Peltai/Peltast(s): 14.91.3, 15.44.2, 15.44.3, Notes: 755, 899, 1003

Peneios, river: Notes: 128, 129

Peninsula:
    Akherousian: Note: 235
    Gallipoli: Notes: 298, 609
    of Knidos: Note: 475
    of Pallene: Note: 585

Pentekontaetia: Notes: 262, 1162, 1232

Peparethos/Peparethian(s): 15.30.5, 15.95.1–2, Notes: 920, 1354

Perdikkas, son of Amyntas: 15.60.3, 15.77.5, Note: 1245

Perdikkas II, king of Macedon (452–413): Notes: 284, 538

Perikles, Athenian politician: 15.88.2, Notes: 299, 648

Perinthos: Notes: 82, 279

Perrhaibia: 15.57.2, Note: 1102

Persia/Persian(s): *passim*

Perusia, in Etruria: Note: 698

Phalanx: 14.81.2, 15.32.6, 15.55.2, 15.55.4, 15.85.6–8, 15.86.5, Notes: 1003, 1294, 1302

Phalynos, a Zakynthian: 14.25.1, Note: 183

Phanostratos, Athenian archon (383/2): 15.15.1

Pharakidas, Spartan *navarch*: 14.63.4, 14.70.1, 14.70.3, 14.72.1

Pharax, Spartan *navarch*: 14.79.4–5, Note: 411

Pharnabazos, son of Pharnakes, Persian satrap: 14.11.1–3, 14.22.1, 14.35.2, 14.38.3, 14.39.1, 14.39.4, 14.39.6, 14.79.5, 14.81.6, 14.83.4, 14.84.3, 15.29.3–4, 15.41.1–3, 15.41.5, 15.42.4, 15.43.1–2, 15.43.5–6, Notes: 74, 237, 502, 507, 530, 533, 535–537, 762, 1321, 1325, 1328, 1330

Pharos, island in Adriatic: 15.13.4, 15.14.1, 15.14.2, Note: 803

Pharsalos: 14.82.6, Notes: 510, 1104

Phasians: 14.29.1

Phasis, river: 14.29.1, Note: 205

Pheneos: 15.49.5, Note: 1053

Pherai, in Thessaly: 14.82.5, 15.30.3, 15.57.2, 15.60.1, 15.60.5, 15.61.2, 15.61.4–5, 15.67.3, 15.71.2, 15.75.1–2, 15.80.1, 15.80.6, 15.95.1, Notes: 509, 916, 1127, 1128, 1170, 1218, 1354

Pherekrates: 14.13.4

Phialeia/Phigaleia: 15.40.2, Notes: 979, 980

Philip II, son of Amyntas, king of Macedon: 14.92.3, 15.1.6, 15.60.3, 15.67.4, 15.95.4, Notes: 333, 509, 802, 916, 951, 1003, 1117, 1171, 1227, 1234, 1250, 1330, 1349

Philiskos, of Abydos: 15.70.2, Note: 1177

Philistos, historian: 14.8.5–6, 15.7.3, 15.89.3, 15.94.4, Notes: 59–61, 306, 308, 394, 415, 435, 437, 441, 652, 665, 673, 678, 693, 778, 1213, 1314, 1350

Philodokos, Spartan general: 14.97.3, Note: 623

Philokhoros, Atthidographer: Notes: 301, 475, 495, 523, 542, 970, 1161, 1162
Philokles, Athenian archon (392/1): 14.94.1, Note: 602
Philokles, nephew of Aeschylus: Note: 316
Philomelos, of Phokis: 14.117.8
Philoxenos, of Kythera: 14.46.6, 15.6.2–4, Notes: 333, 773, 775
Phleious/Phleiasian(s): 14.91.3, 15.19.3, 15.31.2, 15.40.5, 15.69.1, 15.75.3, Notes: 579, 768, 842, 979, 1134, 1174, 1222, 1348
Phoenicia/Phoenician(s): 14.21.4, 14.46.1–4, 14.47.5, 14.51.4, 14.52.2, 14.60.7, 14.65.3, 14.75.5, 14.77.3, 14.79.8, 15.2.4, 15.15.3–4, 15.17.1, 15.17.4, 15.73.1, 15.90.3, 15.92.3–4, Notes: 160, 308, 328, 339, 341, 355, 368, 409, 626, 632, 754, 759, 830
Phoibidas, Spartan general: 15.19.3, 15.20.2–3, 15.33.6, Notes: 512, 839, 847, 856, 926
Phokaia: 15.2.2, Notes: 751, 832
Phokides, of Athens, Olympic victor: 15.78.1, Note: 1248
Phokis/Phokian(s): 14.81.1–2, 14.82.7–8, 14.117.8, 15.31.2, 15.53.1, 15.57.1, 15.62.4, Notes: 494, 497, 513, 520, 595, 1067, 1070, 1077, 1101
Phormion, Athenian archon (396/5): 14.54.1
Phrasikleides, Athenian archon (371/0): 15.51.1, Notes: 1065, 1195
Phrourarkhidas, Spartan ambassador: Note: 1082
Phrygia: 14.11.4, 14.19.6, 14.20.1, 14.22.5, 14.79.3, 14.80.8, 15.90.3, Notes: 74, 150, 466, 487, 1177, 1321
Phyle, Athenian deme: 14.32.1, 14.32.2, Notes: 35, 242, 247
Physkos: 14.83.5, Note: 523
Phyton, Rhegian general: 14.108.4, 14.112.1, 14.112.3–5, Notes: 675, 692
Pisa/Pisatan(s)/Pisatis: 15.78.1–3, 15.82.1, Notes: 124, 1243, 1244, 1248, 1249

Pisidia/Pisidian(s): 14.19.6, 15.90.3, Note: 148
Plague: 14.41.1, 14.45.3, 14.47.2, 14.63.2, 14.70.4–5, 14.71.1, 14.76.2, 15.24.2, 15.73.1, Notes: 432, 433, 435, 436, 874
Plataia/Plataian(s): 15.46.4–6, 15.51.3, Notes: 1014, 1016, 1018, 1071
Plato, philosopher: 15.7.1, 15.76.4, Notes: 33, 37, 48, 195, 284, 287, 776, 1232, 1240
Plebs: Note: 715
Plemmyrion: 14.63.3, Notes: 408, 441
Plethron/Plethra: 14.102.4, Note: 653
Pnytagoras, son of Evagoras: 15.4.3, Notes: 627, 761, 1035
Polikhna, suburb of Syracuse: 14.72.3, Notes: 403, 438
Pollis, Spartan *navarch*: 15.34.3–5, Notes: 411, 776, 937, 944
Polyainos, strategist: Notes: 354, 410, 411, 491, 519, 784, 810, 811, 813, 825, 962, 986, 988, 1072, 1091, 1148, 1277, 1321, 1331, 1354
Polybiadas, Spartan general: 15.23.2, Note: 865
Polybios, historian: Notes: 364, 446, 575, 661, 693, 703, 711, 717, 719, 735, 758, 770, 909, 928, 1184, 1283, 1284, 1286–1289, 1292, 1311
Polydamas, of Pharsalos: Note: 1104
Polydoros, of Pherai: 15.60.5, 15.61.2, Notes: 1120, 1124, 1125
Polyeidos: 14.46.6, Note: 336
Polykrates, of Athens: Note: 223
Polyneikes: 14.23.5
Polyphron, of Pherai: Notes: 1120, 1124
Polytropos, Spartan general: 15.62.1, Note: 1131
Polyxenos, brother-in-law of Dionysios I: 14.8.5, 14.62.1, 14.63.4, Notes: 57, 399
Polyzelos, Athenian archon (367/6): 15.75.1, Note: 1216
Pomponius, Marcus: 14.54.1

Pontius, Cominius: 14.116.3, Note: 723
Pontos: 14.37.2, 15.81.5, Note: 233
Popilia: Note: 728
Poplius, Marcus: 15.28.1
Populonia, Etruria: Note: 698
Poseidon, the Earth-Shaker: 15.49.1–4, Notes: 1046, 1047, 1048, 1148, 1149, 1292
Postimius, Marcus: Note: 266
Postumius:
   Lucius: 15.22.1, 15.48.1, Note: 1038
   Spurius: Note: 621
Postumius Albinus, Marcus: Note: 266
Postumius Regillensis, Aulus: 14.85.1, 15.48.1, Notes: 543, 1038
Poteidaia: 15.81.6. Notes: 840, 1278
Praeneste: 15.47.8
Prokles:
   leader of Naxians: 14.15.2
   son of Aristodemos: Note: 1155
Propylaia: Note: 1250
Proskynesis (obeisance): Note: 738
Proxenos:
   of Tegea: Note: 1109
   of Thebes: 14.19.8, 14.25.4, Notes: 183, 191
Prytaneion (town hall): Note: 38
Psamtik/Psammetikhos I, king of Egypt (664–610): Notes: 270, 271
Psamtik (Psamuthes) VI: ruler of Egypt: 14.35.4–5
Ptolemaios, son of Aloros: 15.71.1, 15.97.5, Notes: 1171, 1182, 1184, 1245
Publilius, Valerius (Volero): 14.54.1, Note: 361
Publilius Volscus, Lucius: Note: 338
Punic War:
   First: Notes: 110, 352
   Second: Note: 368
Pydna: Notes: 1024, 1278
Pylos: 14.17.9, Notes: 128, 1154
Pyrgi, Etruria: 15.14.3
Pyrgion, Athenian archon (388/7): 14.107.1
Pythagoras/Pythagorean(s): 15.39.2, 15.76.4, Notes: 976, 1235

Pythagoras:
   of Cyprus: Note: 761
   Spartan *navarch*: Note: 147
Pytheas, Athenian archon (380/79): 15.23.1
Pytho/Pythia/Pythian: 15.8.4, 15.18.2, 15.49.1, Notes: 529, 595, 738
Pythodoros, Athenian archon (404/3): Note: 12
Pythostratos, Olympic victor: 15.71.1, Note: 1181

Quadrireme: Notes: 307, 311
Quinctilius Varus, Marcus: Note: 266
Quinctius, Marcus: 14.35.1
Quinctius Capitolinus:
   Lucius: Note: 890
   Titus: 14.17.1, Note: 890
Quinctius Cincinnatus:
   Gaius: Note: 1123
   Lucius: 15.24.1, 15.25.1, Notes: 876, 1123
   Quintus: Notes: 117, 1238
   Titus: 15.23.1, 15.36.1, 15.78.1, Notes: 863, 950, 1247
Quinquereme: 14.44.7, 14.100.5, Notes: 307, 311, 645
Quintius, Lucius: 15.61.1

Reconciliation: 14.34.6, 14.102.3, Notes: 246, 259
Revolt:
   against Ariobarzanes: Note: 1321
   against the Carthaginians: 15.15.1
   against Dionysios: Note: 45
   against the King: 15.9.3, 15.18.1, 15.41.1, 15.90.1, 15.90.3–4, Note: 790
   against the Spartans: 15.28.3, 15.66.3, 15.66.4
   Helot: Note: 1162
   in Asia: 15.18.4
   in Libya: 14.77.2, 14.77.6, 15.24.2, 15.73.1, Notes: 446, 874
   of Hipponion: 14.107.2, Note: 671
   of Oeta: 14.38.5, Note: 296
   of Rhodes: 14.79.6, 14.79.7, Note: 476

of Sardinia: 15.24.2, Note: 888
on Kerkyra: Note: 1356
Satrap's: Notes: 1311, 1317, 1328, 1329, 1333, 1336
Rhegion/Rhegian(s): 14.8.2, 14.40.1-2, 14.40.4-7, 14.44.3-5, 14.87.1, 14.87.4, 14.90.4, 14.100.1-5, 14.102.1, 14.103.2-3, 14.105.1, 14.106.1, 14.107.3, 14.108.1-4, 14.108.6, 14.111.1, 14.111.4, 14.112.1, 14.113.1, 15.1.6, Notes: 303, 322, 372, 449, 561, 574, 575, 644, 659, 664, 671, 675, 689, 690, 693
Rheomithres: 15.92.1, Note: 1335
Rhodes/Rhodian(s): 14.79.4-7, 14.94.4, 14.97.1, 14.97.3-4, 14.99.4, 15.28.3, 15.79.1, Notes: 470, 476, 507, 521, 623, 896, 1031, 1254, 1330
Rhodogune, daughter of Artaxerxes: Notes: 187, 749, 1324
Rome/Romans: *passim*
Rufus, Gaius: 14.107.1, Note: 669

Sacred Band, Theban: 15.81.2, Notes: 965, 1091
Salamis, Athenian deme/Salaminian(s): 14.32.4, Notes: 30, 37, 246, 628
Salamis, city on Cyprus: 14.98.1, 15.4.1, 15.4.3, 15.8.1-2, 15.8.4, 15.9.2, 15.47.8, Notes: 300, 544, 627
Salamis, island: Notes: 628, 1250
Salmydessos: 14.37.2, Note: 279
Samos/Samian(s): 14.3.4-5, 14.97.3-4, 15.60.6, Notes: 532, 1018, 1121, 1278, 1321
Samos/Samios, Spartan *navarch*: 14.19.4-5, Notes: 146, 147
Sardinia/Sardinian(s): 14.63.4, 14.77.6, 14.95.1, 15.24.2-3, 15.27.4, Notes: 409, 874, 888
Sardis: 14.19.6, 14.80.2, 14.80.5, 14.85.4, Notes: 150, 478, 479, 486, 515, 549, 924
Sarissa (Macedonian pike): Note: 1003

Sasanda, in Karia: 14.7.4
Satrap/Satrapy(-ies): 14.11.1, 14.11.3, 14.19.1, 14.19.6, 14.20.5, 14.24.1, 14.26.4, 14.27.7, 14.35.2-3, 14.39.4, 14.80.5, 14.80.7-8, 14.81.6, 14.98.3-4, 15.90.1, 15.90.3, 15.91.2, Notes: 187, 267, 487, 550, 634, 635, 681, 749, 797, 1177, 1278, 1317, 1320, 1321, 1323-1325, 1336, 1342
Satricum: 14.102.4, Note: 656
Satyros, son of Spartokos, king of Bosporos: 14.93.1, Note: 588
Sea People: Note: 697
Segesta: *See* Egesta
Selinous: 14.46.6, 14.47.6, 14.50.2, 15.17.5, 15.73.2, Notes: 44, 329, 335, 356
Sellasia: 15.64.1, 15.64.6, Note: 1145
Selymbria: 14.12.5-7, Note: 82
Semiramis: 14.46.6, Note: 331
Senate:
    Carthaginian: 14.47.1-3
    Roman: 14.113.6-7, Notes: 704, 722, 723
Senones, Celtic tribe: 14.113.3, Note: 701
Sergius, Gaius: Note: 1057
Sergius Fidenas:
    Lucius: 14.85.1, Notes: 543, 596
    Manius: 14.19.1, 14.38.1, Notes: 144, 289
Servilius: 14.99.1
    Gaius: 15.24.1
    Spurius: Note: 1247
Servilius Ahala, Gaius: 14.3.1, 14.38.1, Notes: 14, 289, 730
Servilius Fidenas, Quintus: 14.82.1, 14.94.1, 14.110.1, 15.20.1, 15.25.1, 15.41.1, 15.57.1, 15.77.1, 15.90.1, Notes: 289, 506, 604, 680, 863, 876, 985, 1098, 1238
Servilius Maluginensis, Publius: Note: 680
Servilius Tricipitinus, Lucius: 15.23.1, Note: 863
Sesteus, Gaius: 15.51.1
Sestos: Notes: 530, 1278
Seuthes, king of the Odrysian Thracians: 14.94.2, Notes: 279, 282, 611
Sextilius, Gaius: Note: 1066

Sextius Laterias, Lucius: 15.82.1, Note: 1180
Sicilian(s): 14.45.2–3, 14.46.2, 14.51.3–5, 14.52.3, 14.52.7, 14.53.1–2, 14.55.5, 14.59.4, 14.60.4, 14.60.6, 14.61.1, 14.61.3, 14.66.1, 14.66.3, 14.68.4–5, 14.104.4, 15.17.4, 15.37.3, 15.47.7, Notes: 52, 110, 142, 283, 319, 327, 374
Sicily: 14.7.1, 14.8.5, 14.16.2, 14.18.1, 14.34.3, 14.37.5, 14.43.1, 14.44.3, 14.47.4, 14.47.6, 14.48.2, 14.55.2, 14.58.4, 14.62.1, 14.66.1–2, 14.66.4, 14.76.2, 14.78.4, 14.78.7, 14.87.1, 14.90.2, 14.95.1–2, 14.95.4–5, 14.100.1, 14.109.4, 15.6.1, 15.13.1, 15.15.2, 15.15.4, 15.16.2, 15.17.5, 15.23.5, 15.46.2, 15.66.5, 15.70.1, 15.73.1, 15.74.1, 15.88.2, Notes: 43, 60, 96, 283, 303, 327, 340, 352, 373, 406, 417, 456, 626, 674, 818, 821, 825, 1121, 1198, 1199, 1204, 1210, 1350
Sidon/Sidonian(s): 14.79.8
Siege: 14.7.6, 14.8.1, 14.8.6, 14.9.1, 14.9.4, 14.16.4–5, 14.17.10–11, 14.32.2, 14.35.7, 14.36.2, 14.38.6, 14.42.1, 14.48.1, 14.49.3, 14.52.5, 14.55.4, 14.56.4, 14.57.3, 14.61.1, 14.63.3, 14.72.3, 14.79.5, 14.81.2, 14.86.4, 14.87.5, 14.93.2, 14.101.3, 14.103.6, 14.105.1, 14.106.1, 14.107.4, 14.108.6, 14.111.1, 14.112.3, 14.116.2, 15.4.1–2, 15.5.4–5, 15.5.8, 15.9.1, 15.12.1, 15.23.3, 15.25.2, 15.26.4, 15.27.4, 15.30.4, 15.34.4, 15.36.4, 15.61.5, 15.73.2, 15.81.6, Notes: 134, 274, 303, 355, 590, 692, 720, 884, 1022, 1162, 1278, 1323, 1325
Siege-artillery: Note: 308
Siegecraft: Notes: 308, 355
Siege-engines: 14.8.3, 14.47.7, 14.49.3, 14.51.1–2, 14.103.3, 14.108.3–4
Siege-equipment: Note: 380
Siege-ladders: 14.90.5
Siege-machines: 14.112.1
Siege-weapons: 14.14.4, 14.42.2, 14.54.5

Sikan(s): 14.48.4, 14.55.6–7, Notes: 327, 347, 370, 371
Sikel(s): 14.7.1, 14.7.5, 14.14.5, 14.15.3, 14.18.1, 14.53.5, 14.58.1, 14.59.1, 14.75.7, 14.78.7, 14.87.3–5, 14.88.1–4, 14.90.3, 14.96.4, Notes: 44, 327, 347, 618
Sikyon/Sikyonian(s): 14.91.3, 15.31.2, 15.40.4, 15.69.1, 15.70.3, 15.85.2, Notes: 335, 1174, 1220
Sinope/Sinopean(s): 14.30.3, 14.30.5, 14.31.1–3, Notes: 219, 231, 233
Sipylos, mountain: 14.80.1, Note: 479
Skedasos: 15.54.2, 15.54.3, Note: 1082
Skiathos: 15.30.5, Note: 920
Skira, festival: Note: 962
Skiritis/Skiritan(s): 15.32.1, 15.64.3, Notes: 929, 936
Skotoussa/Skotoussian(s): 15.75.1, Notes: 1218, 1219
Skyros, island: Notes: 569, 643, 684
Skytalismos (cudgel-rule): 15.57.3
Skytini: 14.29.2
Smyrna: Notes: 479, 832
Sokrates, Akhaian general: 14.19.8, 14.25.6, Notes: 183, 191
Sokrates, philosopher: 14.5.1–3, 14.37.7, Notes: 9, 33, 37, 287
Sokratides, Athenian archon (374/3): 15.41.1, Notes: 984, 990
Soloi, on Cyprus: 14.98.2, Note: 686
Solon: 15.88.2, Note: 1307
Solous: 14.48.4–5, 14.78.7, Note: 339
Sophainetos, of Stymphalos: Notes: 150, 206
Sophilos, Greek general: 14.25.5, Note: 183
Sophokles, son of Sophokles, tragedian: 14.53.6, Note: 360
Sosippos, of Athens, Olympic victor: 14.107.1, Note: 670
Souniades, of Akharnai, Athenian archon (397/6): 14.47.1, Notes: 301, 337
Sousa, Persian capital: Note: 1230
Sparta/Spartan(s)/Spartiate(s): *passim*
Spartokos, king of Bosporos: 14.93.1, Note: 588

Sphodriades/Sphodrias, Spartan general: 15.29.5–6, Notes: 902–904, 906, 910
Stade(s): 14.16.2, 14.17.3, 14.17.9, 14.18.5, 14.18.8, 14.20.1, 14.21.4, 14.23.1, 14.32.1, 14.36.2, 14.48.2, 14.56.3, 14.58.2, 14.62.3, 14.79.4, 14.99.1, 14.104.1, 14.114.2, 14.117.1, 15.32.3, 15.49.5, Notes: 17, 164, 299, 354, 639, 709, 1043
Stadion (footrace): 15.14.1, 15.23.1, 15.36.1, 15.50.1, 15.71.1, 15.78.1, Notes: 16, 605, 678, 1248
Stasippos, of Tegea: Notes: 1109, 1111, 1112
Stasis: *See* Factional Strife
Steiria, Athenian deme: 14.32.1, Note: 241
Stephanos of Byzantion: Notes: 206, 632, 785
Stoa:
    Poikile, in Athens: Note: 1303
    Royal, in Athens: Note: 544
Strabo, geographer: Notes: 128, 321, 391, 392, 523, 648, 649, 671, 690, 699, 716, 735, 737, 743, 771, 785, 811, 812, 832, 898, 919, 952, 1039, 1040, 1042–1045, 1048, 1054, 1161, 1165, 1229
Strait, of Messina: 14.40.3, 14.44.3, 14.56.1, 14.57.5, 14.87.4, 14.100.2, 14.103.4, 14.108.1, Notes: 53, 303, 373, 644
Strategos/strategoi: 14.15.1, 14.49.1, 14.94.1, 15.62.1, Notes: 349, 364, 957, 1108
Strombikhides, Athenian general: Note: 30
Strouthas, Persian satrap: 14.99.1–3, Notes: 550, 638
Stymphalos: 15.49.5, Note: 1054
Suffetes (judges), at Carthage: Note: 364
Sulpicius: 15.36.1
Sulpicius:
    Gaius: 15.50.1, 15.95.1, Notes: 985, 1057, 1352
    Quintus: 14.38.1, 14.82.1, 15.20.1, Note: 289
    Sentius: 15.15.1
Sulpicius Caeso, Quintus: 14.110.1
Sulpicius Camerinus:
    Quintus: Note: 506
    Servius: Note: 637

Sulpicius Longus, Quintus: Note: 680
Sulpicius Rufus, Servius: 14.107.1, 15.8.1, 15.23.1, 15.38.1, 15.61.1, 15.71.1, 15.76.1, 15.78.1, Notes: 814, 863, 950, 968, 1123, 1224, 1247
Suniatus: Note: 1203
Supremacy: 14.2.3, 14.39.3
    naval/at sea: 15.78.4, 15.79.2, Notes: 742, 1250, 1285
    personal: Note: 67
    Spartan/Lakedaimonian: 15.5.2, 15.26.1, 15.50.2, Notes: 683, 743, 1059
Sutrium/Sutrian(s): 14.98.5, 14.117.4
Sybaris: Notes: 575, 648, 649
Syennesis, king of Kilikia: 14.20.2, 14.20.3, Note: 153
Sykophantai (informers): Note: 28
Syngrapheis (commissioners): Note: 27
Synhedrion (common council): 15.28.3, Note: 972
Synoikismos (political unification): Notes: 106, 771
Syracuse/Syracusan(s): *passim*

Tagos/Tageia (supreme leader/leadership of Thessaly): Notes: 508, 509, 916, 1113, 1120, 1128
Takhôs:
    king of Egypt: 15.90.2, 15.92.1–5, 15.93.2–3, 15.93.6, Notes: 1318, 1334, 1336, 1337, 1340–1343
    relative of Glôs: 15.18.1, 15.18.2, 15.19.1
talent(s): 14.6.1, 14.10.2, 14.39.1, 14.56.2, 14.75.1, 14.75.4, 14.106.3, 15.4.2, 15.14.4, 15.17.5, 15.47.7, 15.92.1, Notes: 69, 256, 441, 502, 507, 813, 1034
Tamôs, of Memphis: 14.19.5–6, 14.35.3–4, Notes: 147, 757
Tanagra: Note: 118
Tanit: Note: 448
Taras (Tarentum): 14.109.4, 15.23.1, 15.66.3, Note: 575
Tarquinii, Etruria: Note: 698

Tarquinius Priscus, Roman king (616–579): Note: 696
Tarsos, in Kilikia: 14.20.1, 14.20.4
Taurini: Note: 695
Tauromenion (Taormina): 14.59.2, 14.87.4, 14.96.4, Notes: 390, 391
Tauros:
  hill: 14.59.1
  promontory: 14.58.2, Notes: 385, 389
Taygetos, mountain: 15.65.2
Tegea/Tegean(s)/Tegeatis: 15.59.1, 15.59.4, 15.64.1, 15.82.2–3, 15.82.5, 15.84.4, Notes: 514, 566, 764, 929, 1052, 1109–1111, 1273, 1281, 1283, 1290, 1293
Tegyra, battle of: 15.81.2, Note: 965
Teleklos, Spartan king: 15.66.3
Telestes, of Selinous: 14.46.6, Note: 335
Teleutias, brother of Agesilaos: 15.21.1, 15.21.2, Notes: 623, 624, 681, 857, 858
Telos/Telian(s): 14.84.3, Note: 531
Temenites, suburb of Syracuse: Notes: 63, 137
Temenos, son of Hyllos: Note: 1155
Ten, board of, at Athens: 14.33.5, Note: 256
Tenos, island: Notes: 1353, 1354
Ten Thousand, the: 15.59.1, Notes: 277, 1108
Teos/Teian(s): Note: 531
Terentius, Gaius: 15.50.1
Teresh: Note: 697
Terias, river: 14.14.3
Terires, Olympic victor: 14.94.1
Teukros, brother of Aias: Note: 628
Thapsakos: 14.21.5, 14.81.4
Thearides, brother of Dionysios I: 14.102.3, 14.103.2–3, 14.109.2, Note: 652
Thebes/Theban(s): *passim*
Thekhes, mountain: Note: 211
Themesion/Themison: 15.76.1, Notes: 1225, 1226
Themistokles, Athenian politician: 15.88.2, Note: 1139
Theodoros:
  of Oropos: Note: 1226
  of Syracuse: 14.64.5, 14.70.1, Note: 413

Theodotos, Athenian archon (387/6): 14.110.1
Theokritos: Note: 333
Theopompos:
  Greek general: Note: 183
  historian: 14.84.7, Notes: 539, 630, 634, 686, 761, 783, 787, 1035, 1323
Theoric Fund: Note: 505
Theramenes, son of Hagnon, of Steiria: 14.3.6–7, 14.4.1, 14.4.5–6, 14.5.1–5, 14.32.5, Notes: 17, 21, 25, 26, 29, 31, 33–35
Therimakhos, Spartan *harmost*: 14.94.4, Note: 612
Theripides: 15.30.3, 15.30.4. *See also* Herippidas
Therma Himerensis: Note: 374
Thermopylai: 14.25.2, 14.83.4, 15.64.4, Note: 1103
Thesmophoria, festival: Note: 848
Thespiai, in Boiotia: 15.27.4, 15.32.2, 15.33.5–6, 15.46.6, 15.51.3, Note: 1286
Thessaly/Thessalian(s): 14.19.8, 14.38.5, 14.82.5, 14.83.4, 14.92.3, 15.54.5, 15.57.2, 15.60.1–2, 15.60.5, 15.61.2, 15.61.5, 15.67.3–4, 15.71.2–4, 15.72.1, 15.75.1–2, 15.80.1–2, 15.80.4, 15.80.6, 15.85.2, 15.85.4, 15.85.8, Notes: 508, 509, 916, 920, 1113, 1128, 1129, 1183, 1184, 1186, 1271, 1272
Thibron, Spartan general: 14.36.1–3, 14.37.4, 14.38.2, 14.99.1–3, Notes: 275, 277, 290, 638
Thirty, the (Tyrants at Athens): 14.2.4, 14.3.7, 14.4.1–5, 14.5.1, 14.5.5, 14.5.7, 14.6.1, 14.32.1–2, 14.32.4–6, 14.33.2, 14.33.5, 15.25.4, 15.63.1, Notes: 24, 26, 27, 30, 35, 36, 142, 245, 248, 256, 881, 1139
Thisbe: Note: 1077
Thorax:
  hill in Asia: 14.36.3
  Spartan *harmost*: 14.3.5, Note: 23
Thorikos, Athenian deme: Note: 30

Thourioi/Thourian(s): 14.52.5, 14.101.1–3, 15.7.4, 15.36.1, 15.50.1, Notes: 575, 648, 649, 650, 778
Thrace/Thracian(s): 14.12.2, 14.31.5, 14.37.2–3, 14.38.3, 14.38.6–7, 14.82.3, 14.83.3, 14.94.2, 15.19.3, 15.31.2, 15.36.1–4, 15.47.2, Notes: 86, 279, 609–611, 951, 1024, 1278
Thraistos, in Akroreia: 14.17.8
Thrasyboulos:
  of Syracuse: Note: 419
  son of Lykon, of Steiria, Athenian politician: 14.32.1, 14.32.5–6, 14.33.1–4, 14.94.2, 14.99.4, 14.99.5, Notes: 35, 241, 248, 606, 607, 608, 611, 613, 623, 642, 881
Thrasydaios, a eunuch: Note: 1035
Three Thousand, the: 14.32.4, Notes: 39, 245, 256
Thucydides, historian: Notes: 25, 63, 96, 123, 262, 294, 303, 319, 392, 420, 434, 435, 541, 610, 699, 928, 1013, 1017, 1161
Thybarnai: 14.80.2
Tibarene: 14.30.7
Tiber, river: 14.114.2, 14.114.7, 14.116.4, Notes: 708, 713
Ticinus, river: Note: 695
Timaios, historian: 14.54.6, Notes: 306, 308, 367, 391, 394, 415, 437, 443, 693, 1209, 1211
Timasitheos, Liparan general: 14.93.4, 14.93.5, Note: 598
Timokrates:
  Athenian archon (364/3): 15.78.1, Note: 1245
  of Rhodes: Note: 507
Timoleon: Notes: 110, 1350
Timotheos:
  father of Iphikrates: Note: 582
  father of Konon: Note: 300
  of Miletos, dithyrambic poet: 14.46.6, Note: 334
  son of Konon, of Anaphlystos, Athenian general: 15.29.7, 15.36.5–6, 15.45.2–4, 15.47.2, 15.47.7, 15.81.6, 15.88.2, Notes: 544, 582, 907, 942, 957, 961, 963, 1007–1009, 1024, 1026, 1030, 1276–1278, 1307, 1321, 1357
Tiribazos, Persian satrap: 14.27.7, 14.85.4, 15.2.2, 15.4.1, 15.8.2–3, 15.8.5, 15.9.1, 15.9.3, 15.10.1–4, 15.11.1–2, Notes: 201, 203, 549, 550, 638, 681, 750, 751, 784, 785, 796, 1324
Tissaphernes, Persian satrap: 14.23.6, 14.26.4–7, 14.27.2–4, 14.35.3–4, 14.35.6–7, 14.36.2–3, 14.39.4, 14.80.1–2, 14.80.5–8, Notes: 145, 175, 185, 186, 187, 190, 267, 274, 467, 481, 486, 491, 1324
Tithraustes, Persian satrap: 14.80.7–8, Notes: 502, 507, 762, 1328
Titinius, Lucius: 14.90.1, Note: 338
Tmolos, mountain: Note: 479
Torone: 15.81.6, Note: 1278
Trabzon/Trebizond: Note: 219
Trakhis/Trakhinian(s): 14.82.5–7, Notes: 294, 295, 510
Trallian(s): Note: 518
Trapezous/Trapezountine(s): 14.30.3–5, Notes: 216, 217, 219, 221
Trasimene, lake: Note: 702
Treaty:
  after Leuktra: Notes: 1071, 1096, 1130
  after Mantineia: 15.94.1
  Athenian with Lakedaimonians, 405/4: 14.3.2, 14.85.2, Note: 17
  Carthaginian with Dionysios, of 405: 14.16.4, 14.68.2–3, Notes: 44, 49, 363, 416
  Carthaginian with Dionysios, of 392/1: 14.96.3, 14.96.4
  Carthaginian with Dionysios, of 383/2: Note: 1199
  Common among Greeks: 15.19.1, 15.19.4. *See also* Peace, Common
  Derkyllidas with the King: 14.39.6
  Dionysios with Agyris: Note: 617
  Dionysios with Iberians: Note: 759
  Dionysios with Rhegians: 14.107.5

Treaty (*Cont.*)
   Evagoras with Orontes: 15.9.1
   Evagoras with Tiribazos: 15.8.1, 15.8.2
   Peloponnesians with Athens: 15.29.5, 15.29.7, 15.45.2
   Rejected by Lakedaimonians: 15.89.2
   Rejected by Thebes: 15.38.3, 15.50.4, 15.51.1, Note: 971
   Spartan with Mantineia: 15.5.1
Trebonius, Marcus: Note: 968
Triballi: 15.36.1, Notes: 951–954
Tribonius, Publius: 15.51.1
Tribuni militum: Note: 14. *See also* Military tribunes
Trierarch(s): 14.99.4, 15.9.3
Trieste: Note: 695
Triphylia: 15.77.1, 15.77.2, Note: 124
Tripolis: Note: 746
Trireme(s): 14.7.3, 14.8.2, 14.19.5, 14.30.4, 14.31.3, 14.34.1, 14.35.3, 14.39.2, 14.40.3–4, 14.49.1, 14.50.1, 14.55.2, 14.58.2, 14.60.2, 14.60.7, 14.72.3, 14.72.5, 14.73.2, 14.75.4, 14.79.4, 14.79.6–7, 14.83.4–7, 14.85.2, 14.90.4, 14.94.2–3, 14.97.3–4, 14.98.3, 14.99.4, 14.100.4, 14.102.1, 14.107.4, 15.2.1, 15.2.4, 15.3.4, 15.3.6, 15.4.3, 15.13.5, 15.14.2–3, 15.34.5, 15.35.2, 15.41.3, 15.45.4, 15.46.2, 15.47.1–4, 15.47.7, 15.53.1, 15.71.3, 15.73.2–4, 15.79.1, 15.92.2, 15.95.2, Notes: 147, 261, 354, 613, 624, 681, 686, 751, 810, 1077, 1177, 1253
Troad: 14.38.2, 14.38.3
Troizen: 15.69.1, Note: 1174
Trophonios: 15.53.4, Note: 1080
Troy/Trojan(s): 14.2.4, 14.3.1, 14.113.2, 15.66.2, Notes: 341, 1155, 1233
Twin Goddesses: *See* Demeter, Kore
Tykhe: 14.20.3, 14.23.5, 14.45.5, 14.46.4, 14.74.1, 14.76.1–2, 14.76.4, 14.109.4, 15.33.1, 15.33.3, 15.54.5, 15.63.1–2, 15.82.6, 15.84.2, Notes: 825, 932
Tyndaris: 14.78.6, Notes: 453, 572, 1165

Tynes (Tunis): 14.77.3, Note: 447
Tyranny: 14.7.1, 14.7.5–7, 14.8.4–5, 14.9.1, 14.10.2, 14.10.4, 14.12.4, 14.14.6–7, 14.33.4, 14.45.1, 14.46.2, 14.65.3, 14.68.4, 14.109.3, 15.35.3, 15.61.3, 15.67.3, 15.70.3, 15.74.5, 15.81.5, Notes: 24, 53, 249, 419, 431, 917, 1277
Tyrant(s): 14.3.7, 14.5.6, 14.8.1, 14.8.3, 14.9.1–3, 14.9.8, 14.10.3, 14.12.3, 14.12.7, 14.19.3, 14.32.1–2, 14.40.2–3, 14.45.5, 14.65.4, 14.67.1, 14.69.1, 14.70.2, 14.75.4, 14.88.5, 14.102.2, 14.103.5, 14.111.4, 15.6.2, 15.6.5, 15.7.1, 15.15.2, 15.17.5, 15.30.3, 15.70.1, 15.73.1, 15.73.5, 15.74.1, 15.76.1, 15.80.5, 15.81.5, 15.95.1, Notes: 48, 60, 73, 333, 335, 419, 509, 652, 673, 801, 1207
   of the Agyrinaians: 14.78.7, 14.95.4
   of Eretria: 15.76.1
   of Pherai: 14.82.5, 15.57.2, 15.60.1, 15.71.2, 15.75.1–2, 15.80.1, 15.95.1, Notes: 509, 916
   of the Sikels: 14.7.1, 14.18.1, Note: 43
   of Syracuse/the Syracusans: 14.2.2, 14.14.1, 14.44.1, 14.47.1, 14.54.2, 14.100.1, 15.6.1, 15.13.1, 15.15.1, 15.81.5, Notes: 43, 417
   See also Thirty, the
Tyre/Tyrian(s): 14.98.1, 15.2.4, Notes: 355, 754
Tyrrhenia/Tyrsenia/Tyrrhenian(s): 14.113.1–4, 14.116.1, 14.117.4, 15.14.3, Notes: 671, 699
Tyrrhenoi/Tyrsenoi: Note: 697
Tyrtaios, lyric poet: 15.66.3, Notes: 1160, 1161

Valerius:
   Gaius: 15.61.1, Note: 1224
   Lucius: 15.24.1, 15.38.1, 15.50.1, Notes: 968, 1057
   Publius: 15.50.1, Notes: 1057, 1123, 1224

Valerius Maximus, Marcus: Notes: 506, 604
Valerius Potitus:
   Gaius: 14.3.1, 14.19.1, Notes: 14, 144
   Lucius: 14.12.1, 14.35.1, 14.82.1, 15.14.1, Notes: 80, 266, 318, 506, 596, 637, 657, 669, 730 (?)
   Publius: Note: 950
Varro/Varronian: Notes: 266, 289, 317, 318, 338, 361, 433, 506, 543, 569, 590, 601, 604, 619, 637, 657, 669, 680, 693
Veascium: 14.117.5, Note: 734
Veii: 14.16.5, 14.43.5, 14.93.2, 14.102.4, 14.115.2, 14.116.1, 14.116.4, Notes: 112, 317, 590, 593, 668, 678, 698, 713, 722, 727
Velitrae: 14.34.7, 14.102.4, Notes: 265, 656
Verginius:
   Gaius: 15.61.1
   Lucius: 14.38.1, 15.22.1, Note: 289
Verres, Roman governor of Sicily: Notes: 63, 110, 374
Verrugo, 14.98.5, Note: 79
Vetulonia, Etruria: Note: 698
Veturius:
   Gaius: 15.77.1, Notes: 1123, 1238
   Lucius: Note: 1247
   Marcus: 14.54.1
Volaterrae, Etruria: Note: 698
Volsci/Volscian(s): 14.11.5, 14.16.5, 14.117.1–3, Notes: 265, 656, 733
Volsinii, Etruria: 14.109.7, Notes: 679, 698
Vulci, Etruria: Note: 698

War(s):
   Attic: 14.18.1
   Boiotian: 14.81.3, 15.25.1, 15.28.5, 15.76.3, Note: 1231
   Carthaginian:
      Second: Notes: 829, 1199
      Third: Note: 815
      Fourth: Note: 1196
   Corinthian: 14.86.6, Notes: 499, 507, 846
   Cypriot: 15.9.2, Notes: 748, 781, 787, 790
   Dekeleian: Note: 261
   Eleian: Notes: 121, 260, 261
   Lamian: Note: 1355
   Messenian:
      First: Note: 1157
      Second: Note: 1160
   Peloponnesian: 14.2.4, 14.3.4, 14.10.1, 14.13.1, 14.85.2, 15.35.2, Notes: 74, 120, 303, 846, 1014, 1139, 1165, 1281
   Persian: 15.44.1, Note: 762
   Phoenician: 14.65.3
   Punic:
      First: Notes: 110, 352
      Second: Note: 368
   Sacred, Third: Notes: 595, 738
   Social: Note: 1254
   Trojan: 14.113.2, 15.66.2, Note: 1155
   Volscian: Note: 265

Xenainetos, Athenian archon (401/0): 14.19.1, Notes: 143, 254, 259, 260
Xenias, of Arkadia: Note: 150
Xenokles, a Spartiate: 14.80.2, Note: 484
Xenophon, historian: 14.37.1–3, 14.76.4, 14.89.3, Notes: *passim*
Xerxes, King of Persia: 14.25.2, 14.83.3, 15.78.4, Note: 1232

Zakynthos/Zakynthian(s): 15.45.2, 15.45.4, 15.46.3, Notes: 1013, 1027
Zankle/Zanklean(s): Notes: 303, 391, 561, 1165
Zeus: 14.65.5, 14.106.4, Note: 1064
   sanctuary of: Note: 1194
   temple of: 14.62.3, 14.63.3, 14.74.5, 14.76.3
Zeus, Olympian: Notes: 121, 122, 403
Zeus, the King: 15.53.4
Zeus Ammon: Note: 93
Zeus Eleutherios: Note: 544
Zeus Soterios: 14.30.3
Ziz: *See* Panormos
Zoilos, scholar: Note: 1313